Access® 97 Programming

Scott Billings, Joe Rhemann, et al.

SAMS
PUBLISHING

201 West 103rd Street
Indianapolis, IN 46290

UNLEASHED

Copyright © 1997 by Sams Publishing

FIRST EDITION

International Standard Book Number: 0-672-31049-X

Library of Congress Catalog Card Number: 96-72075

2000   99   98   97   4   3   2

Interpretation of the printing code: the rightmost double-digit number is the year of the book's printing; the rightmost single-digit, the number of the book's printing. For example, a printing code of 97-1 shows that the first printing of the book occurred in 1997.

Composed in AGaramond and MCPdigital by Macmillan Computer Publishing

Printed in the United States of America

Trademarks

Publisher and President	*Richard K. Swadley*
Publishing Manager	*Rosemarie Graham*
Director of Editorial Services	*Cindy Morrow*
Managing Editor	*Kitty Wilson Jarrett*
Director of Marketing	*Kelli S. Spencer*
Product Marketing Manager	*Wendy Gilbride*
Assistant Marketing Manager	*Rachel Wolfe*

Acquisitions Editor
Steve Straiger

Development Editor
Kristi Asher

Software Development Specialist
John Warriner

Production Editor
Mary Ann Abramson

Copy Editor
Mary Ann Faughnan
Kim Hannel
Kitty Wilson Jarrett

Indexer
Erika Millen

Technical Reviewer
Angie Murdock

Editorial Coordinator
Katie Wise

Technical Edit Coordinator
Lynette Quinn

Resource Coordinator
Deborah Frisby

Editorial Assistants
Carol Ackerman
Andi Richter
Rhonda Tinch-Mize

Cover Designer
Jason Grisham

Cover production
Aren Howell

Book Designer
Gary Adair

Copy Writer
David Reichwein

Production Team Supervisors
Brad Chinn
Charlotte Clapp

Production
Carol Bowers
Jeanne Clark
Cyndi Davis
Lana Dominguez

Contents

Part II Programming the Access 97 Primary Components

4 Access 97 Tables   89

Part V Data Access Programming

15 Microsoft Access Object Model 379

Part VII　Customizing Access 97

Part VIII Security and Multiuser Development

22 Security 607

23 Multiuser Development 637

Acknowledgments

The authors acknowledge the contribution and support of the Sams Publishing team who transformed our raw manuscript into a literary work. Those whose names we know are: Steve Straiger, Rosemarie Graham, Kristi Asher, John Warriner, Mary Ann Abramson, Angela Murdock, Mary Ann Faughnan, and Kim Hannel. We also acknowledge the contributions of other Sams personnel (indexers, formatters, copy editors, page layout technicians, proofreaders, and graphic artists, among others) whose work contributed greatly to this project.

A special "thank you" goes to Steve Straiger, our Acquisitions Editor, for his patience, encouragement, and advice throughout this project.

We also wish to acknowledge the following people for their technical assistance and support in this book project: Valerie Chan and Michele D'Amour with Waggener Edstrom; Tracy Van Hoof with Microsoft Public Relations; Will McKnight, Steven VanRoekel, Dave Waldrop, and Shari Wilkison of Microsoft's Houston Division.

A special acknowledgment goes to our families for their understanding and patience during the writing of this book.

Thank you, we could not have accomplished this without you.

Sams Publishing would like to thank James Bettone and Bryce Ferguson for their assistance with Data Access Objects.

About the Authors

Scott C. Billings

Scott Billings is a Microsoft Certified Solution Developer with a background in database application development and systems integration. His Access technical experience is from several years of database application development in the agricultural, legal, and high technology industries. He is also a licensed attorney and member of the Texas Bar Association, with specialized experience in computer law. Today, in addition to his other responsibilities, Scott serves as the Head of Software Development for the Interactive Exploration Board of Advisors. Scott, his wife Patricia, their daughter Phoebe, and their German shepherds live in Houston, Texas.

Scott can be reached via e-mail at scott@planet-ix.com.

Joe D. Rhemann

Joe Rhemann has been an independent consultant for a number of years in application and system design, project modeling, and programming/analysis on various platforms. He was a systems manager and instructor at a classified U.S. facility in the early 1980s, and a certified database analyst/application developer in the late 1980s. He was a consultant on the first relational OODB application on the market and has been a consultant to organizations such as the University of Texas Imaging Research Center in San Antonio, and the MD Anderson Cancer Research Center in Houston. He is an experienced computer engineer, a member of related professional organizations, and has been a guest lecturer at schools such as Rice University and Mount St. Mary's College. Joe served as a member of the White House Military Office for several years, and as a Presidential Appointee with the U.S. Selective Service System. He is the founder and managing partner of Interactive Exploration, an Information Systems consultancy and software development company in Houston, Texas. Joe, his wife Maureen, and their two Scottish Terriers live in Nassau Bay, Texas.

Joe can be reached at jrhemann@planet-ix.com.

Paul Anderson

Paul Anderson has provided applications of leading edge information technology to major corporations and small businesses for 20 years. An early focus on CASE and RAD methods gave him a valuable perspective on software development. His expertise in database, electronic publishing, and multimedia technologies led to a pioneering project at the Smithsonian

Institute and publication in the *Journal of Data Processing*. Currently, he is working on mission-critical decision management systems for the Year 2000 and a grant program for computer education technology.

Contact Paul Anderson at `pta@daedal.net`.

Teresa Bergman

Teresa Bergman currently works for Standard Aero Ltd. in Winnipeg, Manitoba, Canada as a programmer/analyst using Access versions 2.0, 95, and 97. She also runs a consulting and software design business, TESS Consultants, specializing in creating Access add-ins and agricultural applications designed in Access. Teresa has worked with Access since 1993, when she started her consulting and software design business. Currently, she is involved in the redesign, design, and maintenance of Access applications, training fellow employees in Access, providing technical support (hardware and software—primarily MS Office) and answering software-related questions.

Please visit Teresa's Web site at `http://www.cyberspc.mb.ca/~tbergman/index.html` or e-mail her directly at `tbergman@cyberspc.mb.ca`.

Brad Darragh

Brad Darragh is a Microsoft Certified Solutions Developer specializing in Microsoft Access and Visual Basic. As an analyst for ISM Manitoba, an IBM Global Services company, Brad is part of the Client/Server Solutions team that builds custom software solutions tailored to the customers' needs. With more than 11 years of information technology experience, Brad uses a wealth of knowledge to architect solutions ranging from small, standalone Access/VB applications, to large-scale multiuser applications that front-end SQL Server databases. Developing applications for the financial, agricultural, and government sectors has given Brad a wide range of experience.

Tony Gigliotti

Tony Gigliotti has been the Development Manager at VisualAccess Corporation in Charlotte, North Carolina since 1995. He graduated from Belmont Abbey College, in Belmont, North Carolina with a B.S. degree in Computer Information Systems and has been programming in

Access since its first release. Scott has developed dozens of databases in several industries, such as banking/finance, legal, government, and education. He has given several seminars, such as "Microsoft Access 97 Programming Fundamentals" and "What's New in Microsoft Access 97."

Jude Gigliotti-Mullaney

Jude Gigliotti-Mullaney is the founder and CEO of VisualAccess Corporation. Since 1989, she has been meeting clients' needs in the computer industry. VisualAccess Corporation provides solutions for clients such as Michelin North America, First Union National Bank, NationsBank, and WIX Corporation. Her company founded the first Microsoft Access Users Group in Charlotte, North Carolina in April 1993. She is also a contributing author for *Access 95 Unleashed*, *MS Office 95 Unleashed*, and *Access 97 Unleashed*, all from Sams Publishing, as well as *Inside Microsoft Office Professional* and *The Visual Guide to Microsoft Access 2.0*, both from New Riders Publishing. She continues to provide Access development services to the local community and on a national level.

Keith Roark

Keith L. Roark earned a B.S.B.A. from Appalachian State University while studying Computer Information Systems. He worked as a software engineer developing solutions for the top 50 banks in the country before becoming a developer with the VisualAccess Corporation in Charlotte, North Carolina. He has programmed in Access, Visual Basic, FoxPro, and is currently moving into Visual C++. He credits all success to his faith and the patience and love of his wife Catherine and his son Tiernan.

Dave Thompson

Dave Thompson is an independent developer of Microsoft Access projects. He develops both single-user and multiuser applications, making extensive use of VBA. His focus is real-world applications that provide specific, useful solutions for business clients. Starting in the PC business in 1981, he has found the microcomputer world an exciting place to be, and feels fortunate to have witnessed the growth of this dynamic business.

Tell Us What You Think!

As a reader, you are the most important critic and commentator of our books. We value your opinion and want to know what we're doing right, what we could do better, what areas you'd like to see us publish in, and any other words of wisdom you're willing to pass our way. You can help us make strong books that meet your needs and give you the computer guidance you require.

Do you have access to CompuServe or the World Wide Web? Then check out our CompuServe forum by typing GO SAMS at any prompt. If you prefer the World Wide Web, check out our site at http://www.mcp.com.

> **NOTE**
>
> If you have a technical question about this book, call the technical support line at 317-581-3833.

As the publishing manager of the group that created this book, I welcome your comments. You can fax, e-mail, or write me directly to let me know what you did or didn't like about this book—as well as what we can do to make our books stronger. Here's the information:

Fax: 317-581-4669
E-mail: enterprise_mgr@sams.mcp.com
Mail: Rosemarie Graham
       Sams Publishing
       201 W. 103rd Street
       Indianapolis, IN 46290

Introduction

Access 97 Programming Unleashed is the leader of Access 97 technical publications and is a must-have reference tool for Access professionals looking for a thorough resource on application development.

About Access and Microsoft

Access is the product of Microsoft's early desire to offer a robust and user-friendly database tool for individuals and workgroups.

Microsoft is marketing their database application strategy heavily, with SQL products addressing the upper-middle to high-end market and Visual FoxPro and Access products addressing the lower-middle to low-end market. Access has evolved into the leading integrated database developer's tool for small- to medium-sized applications. Access 95 was rated the #1 personal and small workgroup database tool in the industry in 1995 and 1996. It is only a matter of time before Access and its descendants become the most widely used and supported personal, small business, and small workgroup database applications in the world.

Microsoft Access development and marketing strategies are reflected by product features such as built-in migration and upsizing tools, Jet database engine commonality between their desktop and BackOffice products, ODBC connectivity at all levels, integration of Visual Basic for Applications into their Office 97 suite, and Internet operability. Access 97 and other Microsoft database products comply with very aggressive migration strategies, which promise to attract many users of Oracle, Informix, Sybase, and other competitive products. Microsoft's 97 product line moves several steps closer to seamless migration capabilities.

What You Should Know Before Buying This Book

We recommend that you have the following minimum skills and equipment resources in order to understand and use the material covered in this book:

- Minimum Required skills: Understanding basic database programming technology will allow you to fully grasp the information presented in this book. *Access 97 Programming Unleashed* will provide in-depth analysis of development, implementation, and support topics. Prior technical experience in these areas will be beneficial.

- Minimum required software and hardware: IBM PC-compatible system access is recommended for using and understanding *Access 97 Programming Unleashed*. The system should be capable of running Windows 95 and Access 97. The standard configuration that we recommend is a Pentium 133+ CPU with 16MB RAM minimum, plenty of available hard disk space, and a CD-ROM drive. The operating system should be either Windows 95 or NT 3.51/4.*x* with Access 97 standalone, Office 97 Professional, or Office 97 Developer's Edition (highly recommended). If you are running Windows NT 3.51 or 4.*x*, we recommend that your system have at least 32MB RAM and a Pentium 150+ processor.

Who Should Buy This Book?

Primarily, those who will benefit most from *Access 97 Programming Unleashed* will be application developers, programmer/analysts, secondary and post-secondary faculty, students involved in an application development curriculum, technical support personnel, and technical consultants. *Access 97 Programming Unleashed* will benefit power-users, independent and corporate IT professionals, and technical professionals seeking a definitive reference book for their migration to Access 97 programming and development.

What Is Covered in This Book?

Access 97 Programming Unleashed will address the latest technical aspects of Access 97 as they apply to application development.

In this publication, we will address the following features:

- What's New in Access 97 for Developers
- Access 97 Architecture
- Normalization

- Error Messages
- Migration Issues
- File Format Differences
- Access 97 Application Design Specifics
- Active Data Objects
- Data Access APIs
- OLE
- ODBC
- Jet Database Engine
- Replication
- Visual Basic for Applications
- Code Libraries
- Performance Issues
- Optimization
- Visual SourceSafe
- Internet/Intranet Web Connectivity
- O/S Security Issues Relating to Access 97
- Data Security Tools
- Access 97 Application Design
- Access 97 Software and Hardware Compatibility Issues
- Comprehensive Technical Index

Conclusion

Access 97 Programming Unleashed is a high-end reference tool providing a thorough streamlined breakdown of the technical issues and aspects of programming and developing with the new version. You will gain an in-depth understanding of specific Access 97 capabilities as development tools. This book is organized in such a way as to permit you to easily index areas of interest. You will be able to quickly research issues related to your development cycle.

The Access 97 Programming Environment

PART

I

Overview of Access 97

by Joe Rhemann

IN THIS CHAPTER

CHAPTER 1

Welcome to Access 97 programming.

To gain a complete perspective of Access 97 as a developer's tool, you must look at it as a component of the Office 97 application development environment.

Microsoft Office 97 is the most revolutionary release of Office to date. For the first time since its release in 1990, Microsoft Office is fully integrated and contains major upgrades to Access, as well as each of the other standard Office applications. During the development of Office 97, Microsoft conducted research and usability testing at more than 500 enduser sites and spent three years preparing this product for market. Office 97 also addresses many of the roll-out challenges that businesses face in implementing new applications. Special attention has been given to this problem in an effort to minimize the logistical hurdles involved.

Special enhancements have been made to Office 97 to improve its server-based performance. Currently, Office 97 can run close to 90% of its code from a server. With the enormous growth of workgroups and with collaboration over local and remote networks, connectivity issues were a major priority for the Office development team. Internet and intranet functionality has been thoroughly integrated into Office 97.

With more than 40 million current users of its applications, Office is one of the shining stars in Microsoft's galaxy of products. If you want to develop Access 97 applications for the desktop market, this book is a great resource for you to keep on hand as you reach for your goals.

As you move your development resources to Access 97 and Office 97, *Access 97 Programming Unleashed* will be of great value to you. Use this book as a guide to the developmental changes that will be a part of your migration.

How Access 97 Compares to Competing Desktop Database-Development Packages

To date, Access is the most successful desktop database product in the world.

If you are building integrated, data management–oriented desktop applications, Office 97 with Access is the best choice you could make for your development platform.

Full integration with Office 97 is one of the most important reasons to choose Access 97 as a development tool. Microsoft Office is the most popular office productivity suite in the world. Access has grown to become the dominant desktop database package in the marketplace. Perhaps one of the most sensible decisions that you as a developer can make is to leverage Microsoft's marketing and development success into your own business strategy. Once a workgroup masters Office 97 development, it can settle in for a long development platform life cycle.

NOTE

The following facts may be useful when planning your development strategy, especially when developing sales information for customers when you find your products competing against other non–Access 97 desktop database products:

- 100 million copies of Windows 95 have been sold. Microsoft predicts that the number will grow to more than 160 million by the end of 1997.

- Windows NT sales experienced more than 200% growth in 1996 and will probably exceed 400% growth in 1997. Most of Microsoft's database products have seen similar numbers and may grow more than 500% in 1997.

- Microsoft Access has held the largest market share in desktop database sales for the last few years and will probably continue to do so for the foreseeable future. Access 95 accounted for 94% of all new desktop database programs sold for Windows.

- 75% of all desktop database customers are using Access.

- In the last few years, Microsoft has gone from not even having a server-based database application to now being one of Oracle Corporation's primary competitors for the high-end and mid-range database market.

- Since the introduction of Access 1.0 in December 1992, Access has grown to become the best-selling desktop database application worldwide.

- Microsoft Office will probably capture close to 95% of the desktop productivity suite market in 1997.

What Kind of Developer Are You?

If you are a developer who has experience with tools such as dBASE or Paradox, you are used to working with fairly robust development tools. Stepping up to the plate with Access 97 and Visual Basic for Applications (VBA) will place equivalent or greater development power in your hands. Add the integration that is inherent in the Access 97/Office 97 environment, and you will most likely end up with far greater development capabilities. Your chances for hitting a home run in the software market will be even better.

I'm a Corporate Commando

> **NOTE**
>
> If you are a corporate developer, chances are you are developing database solutions for use on a Windows-based platform running Microsoft Office. This means that you are developing products for a market that will be dominated by Office and Office-compatible products for the foreseeable future.

With this market dominance by Office, most corporate end users are already familiar with the Access user interface. They can jump right in and begin using Access with minimal training. An application developed on a non-Office package will most likely require more extensive training and documentation to implement within a corporate computing environment.

I'm Independent, Hear Me Roar!

Independent developers face similar issues. Statistically, you are most likely selling your solutions to customers who are using Microsoft Office as their desktop suite. They are far more likely to spend money on your product if it is compatible with their existing platform. Let the other guy try to sell them a non-Office solution—succeeding as an independent developer is tough enough without handicapping yourself in the marketplace. Developing with Access makes your job easier when selling your solution to Microsoft users.

To reiterate the last point: Developing with Access makes your job easier when selling your solution to Microsoft customers.

Developer's Overview of Access 97

> **TIP**
>
> Because of the differences that most likely exist between a non-Access environment and an Access-based one, you should consider leaving your existing non-Access applications native and begin developing all your new projects on an Access-based platform.

What Can I Do with Microsoft Access 97?

Pretty much anything goes as far as desktop productivity applications when working with Access.

Access 97, as a component of the Office 97 development system, is a powerful application programmer's tool. The door of possibilities is wide open. As someone once said, "The deed is only limited by the imagination of the doer."

Access was originally created as a desktop database tool. Microsoft wanted a product that would appeal to DOS and Windows users and a database application tool that could be integrated into the Office line of products. Almost any business application intended to work with Windows can be developed within the Office 97 environment.

Access 97 and the Other Office 97 Applications Are Integrated Solutions

As far as look and feel are concerned, the Office 97 graphical user interface (GUI) is consistent among all Office products. This means that less training and support are required once an end user is familiar with any one of the Office 97 products.

Other areas of integration include

- Data Access Objects (DAO). This is how the programmer interfaces with Microsoft Jet, the relational database management engine shared by all Office 97 applications, the Visual Basic and Visual C++ programming environments, and Microsoft Project. Using DAO to do your back-end programming of Jet is identical, regardless of which front-end application is being used. In other words, do it right once and move on. There is no need to reinvent the wheel constantly within your application. For more information on DAO development issues and Access 97, read Chapter 3, "Access 97 Development Issues," which deals with Microsoft Jet 3.5 and other pertinent topics.

- Visual Basic for Applications (VBA). VBA is the common development environment within Microsoft Office, Access, Project, and Microsoft Internet products such as FrontPage in the form of VBScript wizards. VBA allows developers to exercise their programming skills across a wide platform of applications. No other programming language offers the same level of benefit when doing cross-application development. For more information on VBA, see the following sections of this book:

    Chapter 3, "Access 97 Development Issues." This chapter contains valuable information on a number of development issues and topics that pertain to your use of VBA and Access 97.

    Part II, "Programming the Access 97 Primary Components." Each chapter briefly covers topical aspects of VBA as it applies to their subject matter.

    Part III, "Access 97 Wizards and Add-Ins." This section briefly discusses the use of VBA to create and customize Access 97 wizards and add-ins.

    Part IV, "Visual Basic for Applications for Access 97." This section deals primarily with VBA. It provides the in-depth programming reference for VBA and Access 97 and should be the center of your focus with respect to using Visual Basic for Applications and Access 97 as your development platform.

Chapter 15, "Microsoft Access Object Model." This chapter provides an analysis of the Access 97 architecture and has valuable information for the Visual Basic application object developer.

Part VI, "ActiveX Controls." This section provides a study of ActiveX control development.

Chapter 25, "Optimizing Code." This chapter offers advice and tips on ways to improve the efficiency and security of your VBA code.

- Indexed and Sequential Access Method (ISAM). Excel is the leading spreadsheet application in the Windows marketplace. Now data can be shared between applications with ease. The ISAM driver allows read/write access to data in Excel from Access. OLE automation is now available, which allows mutual control between Access and Excel. For more information on database connectivity issues, see Chapter 3 for a brief discussion of ISAM, OLEDB, and SQL external data access issues; and Chapter 16, "Importing and Exporting Data," for an in-depth study of data access.

- AutoCorrect. This is a common dictionary tool within Office that memorizes spelling mistakes and corrections and then corrects automatically in the future. This tool applies universally across all the Office platforms. If you misspell a word in Excel, the correction is applied if you type the same thing in Access. You can include customized dictionaries in your applications to help customers with industry-specific words.

- AutoFormat and Format Painter. These are formatting tools to save you hours of redundant GUI development and your customer hours of redundant reformatting. Now you can copy format styles from one Office object to another. This effectively addresses the old headache of creating an application with a consistent GUI; you can develop the desirable format and apply it automatically to any form or report. Thus you can create a unique GUI template that gives your applications a distinctive look.

Integration to this extent gives you the ability to use Microsoft Access as an extremely powerful development tool. Microsoft has repeatedly declared its intention to further integrate its products for developers and end users alike. Get on the train now while it is still building up a head of steam.

VBA Is Better

VBA offers a common application scripting and development environment that can be used on almost any Windows desktop application. It is a part of the following applications:

- All Microsoft Office 97 primary applications, which includes Access, Excel, PowerPoint, and Word
- Microsoft Project

1

■ Microsoft Internet Explorer 3.0, with modifications performed through Internet Explorer Admin Kit (IEAK) wizards

■ VBA 5.0 licensed applications and products from

Adobe Systems, Inc.

Autodesk, Inc.

Micrografx, Inc.

NetManage, Inc.

Rockwell Software, Inc.

Sagent Technology, Inc.

SAP AG

Visio Corp.

Various other third parties, such as Independent Software Vendors (ISV), continue to participate in Microsoft's VBA licensing program. VBA 5.0 will not be distributed as a standalone product, but instead will be licensed to individual ISVs for incorporation into their own products.

VBA 5.0 will be available for Windows 95 and NT on Intel platforms, and for Windows NT on Alpha RISC, MIPS, and PowerPC platforms. It is also available for Apple's Power Macintosh and PowerPC.

The VB family offers powerful 32-bit tools for developing solutions ranging from HTML active content to distributed client/server applications. VBA 5.0 offers a significant leap ahead for developers using VB. It provides an Integrated Development Environment (IDE) containing many of the tools available in VB 4.0 and, in addition to numerous other enhanced features, now has support for forms and ActiveX controls (formerly called OLE controls).

VBA supports full VB syntax but does not contain some VB components such as a database engine and report-writing capabilities. Visual Basic is a three-tiered application development environment. The first tier is VBScript. VBScript is the subset of VBA that was designed as a Web-ready version of Visual Basic, optimized for Internet programmability and integration into the Internet Explorer 3.0 Web browser. VBScript is fully upwardly compatible with VBA and VB. The second tier is VBA, which is specific to the Office 97 development environment, and the third tier is VB itself.

By far the greatest advantage to VBA is that, once you learn how to use it in one Microsoft application, you can use it in any product that hosts VBA. Most other database application languages only allow you to develop singular applications, and when you want to use another set of tools, you have to learn a new language.

For more information on VBA, consult the Table of Contents or the index, or refer back to the section in this chapter titled "Access 97 and the Other Office 97 Applications Are Integrated Solutions" for a brief listing of some of the chapters in this book that deal with VBA.

So, What About Access 97 and Office 97?

Access 97 and Office 97 are a strong one-two punch. Access is a powerful relational database development tool, and Office 97 is a powerful, integrated, application-development environment. Together they promise to give you the knockout combination needed to overpower your competition.

In addition to the following information, see Chapter 28, "Office 97 Integration," for more in-depth information regarding the Access 97 and Office 97 combination.

Office 97 Integration

One of the most monumental new features of Office 97 is that it is now a fully integrated application-development system. It has become a powerful programming platform upon which a company can implement a successful development strategy. The new enhancements to the Office 97 product line will be a boon to developers and end users alike.

The core of this integration is the way that Office 97 was built on top of a common data manager (Microsoft Jet Database Engine, version 3.5) and a common programming language (VBA, version 5). These two features are the cornerstones of the integrated development environment. They are briefly described in the following sections.

Access 97 Programmability

Access 97 includes greatly improved report performance. Aside from simple data-management forms, Access has the capability to store VBA code directly in forms or reports. Because Access 97 also can develop forms without VBA modules in them, it can load forms in a small memory footprint, thereby gaining a significant speed advantage over traditional coded objects. All newly created forms and reports are "lightweight" by default; VBA code is not added until the user makes some modification that requires it. This allows forms and reports to run as much as 50% faster. In addition to faster code management, Access has a new forms and reports property called `HasModule` that allows the user to switch between the coded and uncoded forms. The Access wizards take advantage of this code-management metaphor to create faster-performing database applications. Wherever it is able to do so, an Access wizard uses lightweight forms and navigational hyperlinks rather than creates a new code module in VBA.

Partial replication of a database that contains only a subset of the records in the original is supported in this version. This allows for the replication of only the data that is needed, instead of the entire database. These replicas can then be synchronized with the original or master database according to a practical schedule. This also allows for data access control between the replicas. When data replication is controlled properly, it can reduce the amount of data transferred across a network and the overall demand on the network system. See also Chapters 3 and 23 for more information on developing applications both in and for a multiuser environment.

Access 97 also includes features for source code control that allow you to integrate it with any control application that supports the standard source code control interface. (Microsoft Visual SourceSafe is an optional application available for VB and the Office 97 Developer's Edition.) This allows you to engage a team of developers on one project while still maintaining source code integrity. Using source code control allows a developer to verify which objects in a project are available for checking out, check out an object to work on it, check it back in when done with it, view a history of changes to the object, compare different versions, revert to a different version, or merge changes between versions of an object. Chapter 3 covers source code control and Access 97.

Access allows you to create custom objects with three types of class modules:

- Basic class modules
- Form modules
- Report modules

These class modules are templates for user-defined objects. A developer can change public procedures that define specific properties and methods for the object. When classes are created, the custom methods and properties can be applied in a standard fashion. Refer to Chapter 9, "Access 97 Modules," for more information on module development.

Access 97 includes Internet and intranet connection capabilities in the form of hyperlink support to remote objects or documents. Hyperlinks are stored as a table field, form, or report and are available through multiple controls. Chapter 27, "Access 97 and the Internet," provides an in-depth study of this subject.

As a developer who is planning on distributing a database application, you have the option of creating a whole new version of your application without any source code. This is done when you tell Access to make an MDE file. Make MDE removes all of the VBA source code from the application and gives it an MDE suffix. This database application can be opened normally, but it restricts users from changing the design or creating new objects. Make MDE also prevents someone from "uncompiling" the application and protects your valuable R&D from prying eyes. Chapter 3 covers the different database formats and file types and offers information pertaining to the benefits of each format.

What's New in Access 97?

Access has a multitude of new features that makes it a powerful database development platform. In addition to the developer enhancements discussed in this chapter, here are a few of the major feature enhancements:

- Improved database wizards: Access 97 has 20 new database types that are available from the new database wizard.

■ Improved import/export wizards: Access 97 has three import/export wizards to help in moving text, spreadsheet, and HTML data easily. When you use the Import command to import data, the appropriate wizard takes you step-by-step through the process and gives you a preview of how your data will look in the new format, based on the choices you make.

■ Table Analyzer Wizard: This wizard automatically identifies relationships in unstructured data and recommends the best way to organize that data in a relational database.

■ Simple Query Wizard: This wizard can decide how to bring information together to answer your questions. It automatically includes all the tables necessary to bring the desired data together.

■ Filter By Selection and Filter By Form: Filter By Selection lets the end user highlight the information he or she is looking for and then limits the view of the data to only the items that match the selection. Filter By Form lets users employ familiar forms to find data in the same manner.

■ Improved form and report wizards: The improved form and report wizards now change their parameters to offer the appropriate choices for creating the desired forms or reports.

Summary

As you can see, Access 97 and Office 97 represent a very powerful development platform in the hands of an inspired programmer. If you are making the move to Access 97, you are entering a dynamic new market.

We are pleased that you have decided to invest in our book, and we hope that you benefit greatly from the information contained herein.

Database Design Basics

by Joe Rhemann

IN THIS CHAPTER

CHAPTER 2

This chapter provides you with an overview of the principles of database design. I have tried to include information that will save you time and effort in your development process. From time to time, you may see Notes and Tips that are based on my own experiences. You may find that my way of developing applications doesn't completely suit your needs, but I still encourage you to apply the basic principles that I put forth. Many of the personal Notes, Tips, and Warnings that I have included have saved me from a lot of headaches, and I hope that they do the same for you.

First, let's look at how to start the application design process. Then we'll examine relational database function and object-oriented development as they apply to Microsoft Access 97 and the Office 97 environment. I'll then discuss some data access issues that affect your application design strategy, and finally, in the last section of this chapter, I will discuss some design fundamentals.

Okay, let's get the ball rolling.

Starting the Application Design Process

The best place to start your design process is on paper. The CD-ROM may have been heralded as the "new papyrus," but I am here to tell you that there is no substitute for the old No. 2 pencil. Sit down with your customer and draft the application with pencil and paper before you proceed further. The importance of this meeting with your clients cannot be overstressed.

Sometimes you can get so immersed in your own little developer's world that you are caught by surprise by the changing seasons. Don't forget to try looking at your customer through his eyes, and remember to speak in layman's terms when you should. The more you understand about his world, the better you can address his needs. The more you address his needs, the better he will like your product. The better he likes your product, the more he will buy.

In any case, meeting with your customer will be a good way of letting him know that you care about his needs. It may even give you a chance to get out and get some fresh air. Remember that part of sitting down with the client is taking a look at the hardware and software systems that he has on hand. If you are going to build a custom application for a client who has minimal legacy platforms, you will have to design your application accordingly. Likewise, if the company has high-end RISC (Reduced Instruction Set Chip) workstations in a powerful client/server environment, you can take advantage of that as well.

2

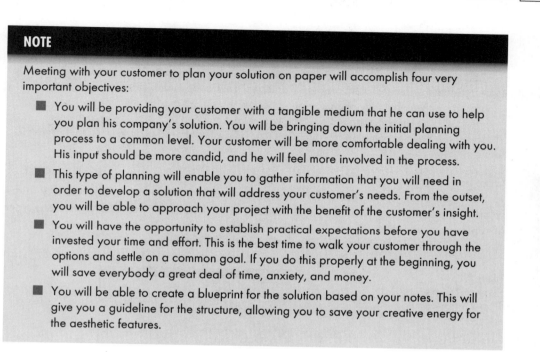

NOTE

Meeting with your customer to plan your solution on paper will accomplish four very important objectives:

■ You will be providing your customer with a tangible medium that he can use to help you plan his company's solution. You will be bringing down the initial planning process to a common level. Your customer will be more comfortable dealing with you. His input should be more candid, and he will feel more involved in the process.

■ This type of planning will enable you to gather information that you will need in order to develop a solution that will address your customer's needs. From the outset, you will be able to approach your project with the benefit of the customer's insight.

■ You will have the opportunity to establish practical expectations before you have invested your time and effort. This is the best time to walk your customer through the options and settle on a common goal. If you do this properly at the beginning, you will save everybody a great deal of time, anxiety, and money.

■ You will be able to create a blueprint for the solution based on your notes. This will give you a guideline for the structure, allowing you to save your creative energy for the aesthetic features.

Keep good notes of your early meetings. If you deliver your product and the customer says the product is not what he asked for, you can refer him back to the original notes. Customers will often inflate their expectations as they wait for you to finish and deliver their solution. If you can show them that what you have produced is exactly what they specified, they should understand that you did your job as expected. This also makes it much easier to deal with a customer if he wants you to make further changes or customizations. Whereas a certain amount of tweaking on a custom application is to be expected, there should be a limit, beyond which your customer knows that he must pay you for your efforts.

Planning the Details

Once you have finished the basic sketch of the solution, as expected by the customer, it is time to begin planning the details. This is also best accomplished with pencil and paper.

Picture an Access application as a container made up of numerous database objects and their components that are tied together to form an application. These basic building blocks are forms, macros, modules, queries, reports, and tables. How well you plan each of these objects on paper will directly influence the quality of your solution.

> **WARNING**
>
> Remember to stick to the form and structure your customer expects to see, and don't complicate the development process. Additional bells and whistles are nice for someone who wants them, but they often confound people who don't ask for them. Keep your application as simple as possible. Once you have a solution that is pleasing to the customer, you have accomplished your mission. It is now time to move on to your next project.

Once you have laid out the framework on paper, examine the possibility of using wizards to generate portions of your application. This is the easiest and quite often the best way to develop an application. The wizard obtains the basic information necessary to develop many types of applications and then creates all your database objects. Figure 2.1 illustrates how to start the Access 97 Database Wizard to create a database application.

FIGURE 2.1.

Using the Database Wizard to create an application.

Customizing an application created with the Database Wizard is a relatively simple process. Access objects can be customized and added easily, building on a properly constructed and successfully compiled framework.

As mentioned in Chapter 1, "Overview of Access 97," Access wizards also create "lightweight" forms and reports by default, unless VBA (Visual Basic for Applications) code needs to be included in the individual object. This makes for an application that can run up to 50% faster. Once you have built your application, additional wizards are available for building individual database objects. Figure 2.2 shows the Access 97 wizard that builds a new individual query for your currently open database.

Figure 2.2.

An example of a wizard that builds a new individual query.

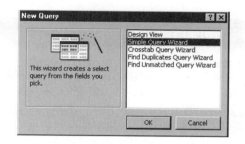

If the Database Wizard does not provide the features you desire, Access still gives you a friendly development environment for building your application. Planning your database objects and components becomes more important to the process and more involved, due to the attention to detail necessary to create an application from scratch.

Once you have created your tables and have properly established component relationships, you can then create forms, reports, and other objects using the standard Access 97 development interface. As shown in Figure 2.3, a developer can manually establish relationships after he has created data tables.

Figure 2.3.

The Access 97 Relationships view showing table relationships.

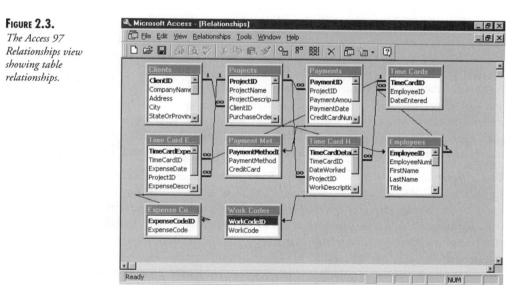

CODELESS DEVELOPMENT IS ON THE HORIZON

Bear in mind that one of Microsoft's goals is apparently to create a codeless development environment that operates through a point-and-click interface. This strategy will increase demand for developers who are superior solution designers instead of just code writers.

Many components, such as ActiveX controls, may still be produced through coding; however, programming language environments such as Microsoft Visual Basic are beginning to develop more automated features with each new release.

Eventually, and quite possibly in the near future, we may see the emergence of codeless programming environments that rely primarily on your ability to plan and design solutions.

Relational Databases Versus the Object-Oriented Programming Environment

It is difficult to present an argument as to whether Access is more of a relational database or an object-oriented programming environment. Access has many capabilities similar to an object-based database, but Access is strictly relational. The data management engine, which is the back-end guts of Access, is Microsoft Jet version 3.5. This is the common data manager that is shared by all the Office 97 applications and Microsoft SQL, and Jet is strictly a relational engine. Although Access itself does not seem to provide common class-development capabilities similar to an object-oriented programming language such as C++, in reality, it does. Until you look at the capabilities of Access from an integrated application developer's perspective, you may not realize this. From this perspective, Access is a tool that can be used to create an object module that can be combined with other Office 97 objects to create or enhance an application.

The programming environment hosted within Access 97 and Office 97 is Visual Basic for Applications (VBA 5.0), the second tier of the three-tiered Visual Basic (VB) programming environment. As a component of the Office 97 development environment, and as an application that hosts VBA, Access provides object-oriented programming capabilities. Keep in mind that one of the most significant improvements to the Visual Basic programming environment occurred when Microsoft introduced VB 4.0, which allowed developers to create common class objects in much the same fashion as in other object-oriented programming languages. The capability to build class objects has also been included in VBA 5.0 and is being enhanced further in the coming release of VB 5.0.

Let's look briefly at Microsoft Access as it compares to Borland Paradox. Access is designed as a fully relational database application within an object-oriented development environment. Access can establish 32,000 separate relationships within a database, create relationships of three types (one-to-one, one-to-many, and many-to-one), is tightly integrated with Office 97, and is based on a container metaphor. For example, in Access you use a container labeled `Tables` in the database to store individual table objects. Figure 2.4 shows the objects within a `Tables` container, demonstrating the object-oriented nature of Access programming. The `Tables` object is a hierarchically higher object that contains numerous smaller objects that are made up of individual pieces of data, controls, and other Access objects. Each object is defined by related objects within its hierarchy.

FIGURE 2.4.

Access objects in a container. As you can see, Access 97 can be described as object-based.

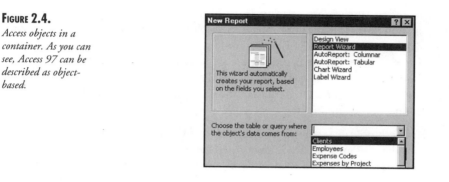

Each of these objects is assigned individual properties, relationships, and so on. Paradox has many similar capabilities and also offers powerful database tools. ObjectPAL, the object-oriented programming environment that has been a part of Paradox for some time, provides object-oriented class-building capability. Paradox can produce high-performance databases, because it is a good development platform based on an excellent engine. However, it does not host VBA, it does not use Microsoft Jet, and it is not integrated with Microsoft Office. Paradox allows you to build good standalone applications, but until Borland licenses VBA 5.0 and Jet from Microsoft, Paradox applications will not fully integrate with Office 97. Not supporting VBA 5.0 and Jet 3.5 would be a major handicap to an application developer who is building solutions for customers that use or interface with Microsoft Office 97. Just for clarification, you can create excellent standalone applications using Office 97 Developer's Edition or Visual Basic that will most likely equal or exceed the power of anything you could build with Paradox.

THE BOTTOM LINE

Your customers might want their solutions integrated with Microsoft Office 97. Microsoft Jet is a relational database engine and is the data manager that is common among each of the Office 97 applications. Visual Basic for Applications, which is the application development language used in Access 97, is shared with all the other Office 97 applications. The bottom line is this: If you are developing desktop database applications for Office 97 users, you should stick with Access 97.

Data Access Issues

External data access is a challenge for the programmer and end user alike. One of the issues that must be attended to is the synchronization of the data source type to the end user's database application. As a developer, you should build external data access capabilities into your applications for a wide range of data types.

You will have to address the various security protocols that are in effect on both ends of the data connection and ensure that the appropriate ISAM (Indexed Sequential Access Method), ODBC (open database activity), or OLE (object linking and embedding) database drivers are registered to the data source. Careful coordination of the various data source types, data access tools, and computing environment variables will enable you to avoid complicated support issues after delivery. You must consider all the variables and carefully confirm the proper interaction of each connection component.

ISAM (a standard desktop data connectivity standard) and ODBC (an SQL data type connection standard) are the two most common data-interchange standards. Keep an eye out for a new standard called OLE DB, which is under development and may soon be released into the general market. An OLE DB driver will probably bridge the gap between the different data sources. It appears that ODBC and ISAM drivers might be replaced, or in some cases enhanced, by OLE DB drivers.

Installable ISAM drivers are included with the Office 97 Value Pack CD-ROM. ISAM and ODBC driver setup for a user data source is easily accomplished through the ODBC Data Source Administrator. The ODBC Data Source Administrator is opened by double-clicking the 32-bit ODBC icon in your Control Panel window, as detailed in the following Tip.

TIP

To install the optional ISAM drivers, insert your Microsoft Office 97 CD-ROM into your system's CD-ROM drive. Click the Start button on the Taskbar, choose Run from the pop-up menu, and then enter the following command string (substitute the drive letter that your Office 97 CD-ROM is in for *X*):

```
X:/Valupack/Dataacc/Dataacc
```

You can also use Windows Explorer to start the Microsoft Data Access Pack Set-Up Wizard. Open the Office 97 CD-ROM, look in the Valupack folder, open the Dataacc folder, and then double-click on the Dataacc icon.

Figure 2.5 shows how to certify ODBC drivers to a data source.

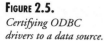

FIGURE 2.5.
*Certifying ODBC
drivers to a data source.*

Figure 2.6 illustrates adding, removing, and configuring ODBC drivers for the appropriate
User Data Source.

FIGURE 2.6.
*Adding, removing, and
configuring ODBC
drivers for the
appropriate User Data
Source.*

Figure 2.7 shows the display of ODBC drivers currently installed on a system.

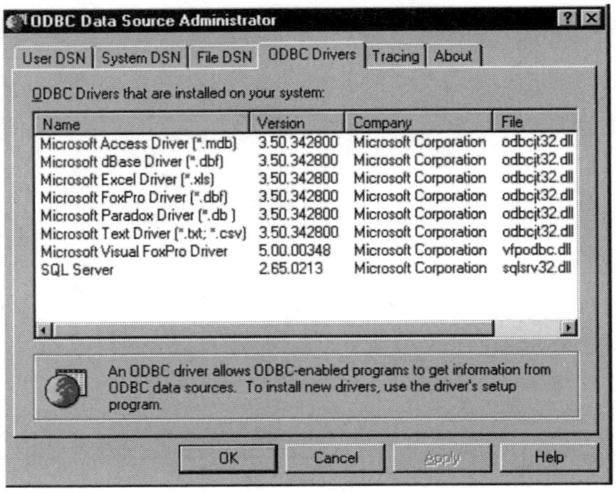

FIGURE 2.7.

In the ODBC Data Source Administrator, this view shows the ODBC drivers that are currently installed on a system.

External data can be retrieved from numerous sources, such as other database tables, spreadsheets, ASCII text files, HTML (Hypertext Markup Language) documents, remote database servers, and LAN/WAN (local area network/wide area network) network data sources, by using the optional ODBC and ISAM drivers that are included with Access 97.

When installing the optional ISAM drivers, the Microsoft Access Setup program creates Registry keys that configure the ISAM drivers. The following is a list of the types of drivers:

- Borland Paradox 3.*x*, 4.*x*, and 5.*x*
- Borland dBASE III, dBASE IV, and dBASE V databases
- Microsoft Excel versions 3, 4, 5, and 8.0 spreadsheets
- Microsoft FoxPro versions 2, 2.5, 2.6, 3.0, and ODBC databases
- Lotus 1-2-3 spreadsheets (WK1,2,3)
- Tab-delimited data within an HTML file
- Tab-delimited and fixed-width tab-formatted text files

Special consideration must be given when attempting to connect to a case-sensitive data source. Microsoft FoxPro and Borland Paradox are, by default, examples of case-sensitive data sources. Access 97, and other applications based on Microsoft Jet, are not case sensitive. If your customer is going to connect to a case-sensitive data source, you will have to build that capability into your Access 97 application.

Remember that objects designed for use with a Microsoft Jet database are not compatible with an external data source that was not designed for a Microsoft Jet database. Please see Chapter 16, "Importing and Exporting Data," and Chapter 17, "ActiveX Controls," for a further discussion of external data access issues.

As mentioned, case-sensitivity issues can cause problems when connecting to external data sources. If the data source is one of the types that is usually case sensitive, you must take the appropriate measures. This applies to ODBC connections to a database server as well. You should synchronize the case-sensitivity settings before attempting to connect. When you access remote data from another server, you must also ensure that your system has permission to connect to the data. Security protocols and permissions must be addressed properly, using Registry settings or DAO (data access objects) when you connect to the data source. Once you have checked to see whether the data source is case sensitive, ensure that your application is set up properly.

One way of setting up your application to do this is to design your queries using the Boolean OR clause to make sure that you receive hits on all the desired data combinations, regardless of the type of case used. When you design your query on multiple data sources, the collating sequence of the database in which the query is stored determines the case-sensitivity setting.

2

DATABASE DESIGN
BASICS

> **TIP**
>
> Case-sensitive data sources will usually not be case sensitive in the following circumstances:
>
> ■ Xbase data sources. When the Windows Registry key `\HKEY_LOCAL_MACHINE\SOFTWARE\Microsoft\Jet\3.5\Engines\Xbase` is configured for `International` instead of `ASCII`, the source will not be case sensitive.
>
> ■ Paradox data sources. When the Windows Registry key `\HKEY_LOCAL_MACHINE\SOFTWARE\Microsoft\Jet\3.5\Engines\Paradox` has the `CollatingSequence` set to `International`, `Norwegian-Danish`, or `Swedish-Finnish`, the data source is not case sensitive. The `CollatingSequence` setting in the Registry must be synchronized with the `CollatingSequence` setting for the data source.

One of the most exciting enhancements to Access 97/Office 97 is the Internet functionality that has been built into the development environment. Now you can retrieve data from and publish data to the Internet with relative ease. Having the ability to add Internet connectivity to your desktop applications opens enormous opportunities, to say the least. Not only can you build great applications for use on your customer's internal desktop environment, but now you can give him worldwide access from his own desk in the blink of an eye. Access database replication and other innovations in the new 97 release will give you the ability to break down the communication barrier for your clients.

Chapter 27, "Access 97 and the Internet," covers Internet functionality in great depth. The chapter provides a thorough breakdown of the developer-oriented issues relating to the Internet, so hold on to your seat!

Design Fundamentals

As mentioned earlier in this chapter, start with your planning phase by meeting with your client and drawing up written plans for the solution.

Plan the advanced details on paper before doing any further development. Work out the appropriate tables and relationships. Then develop your table fields, forms, reports, and queries.

After you have formulated plans for the application components, establish development guidelines for the project. This is where you should establish the boundaries for your development, implementation, and support efforts. Place limitations on the amount of extra features that you will build into the application, and establish deadlines. Remember that the more complicated your solution is, the longer it will take to design, debug, deploy, and support, and the more likely it is that your solution will develop a problem.

Once you have completed these planning phases, you are ready to move on to the actual development of the application. If you can use the Database Wizard, do so (see Figure 2.8). Your development time will be shortened dramatically, and the application can be easily customized.

Figure 2.8 shows how easy it is to use the Access 97 New Report Wizard to create a new database report.

Figure 2.8.

The Access 97 New Report Wizard for creating a new database report.

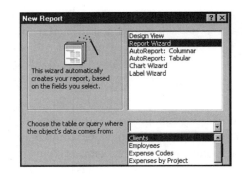

If you do not want to use the Database Wizard, you can follow your development plan and build the application from the ground up. Start with your tables and relationships. Figure 2.9 depicts the process of customizing fields and properties within a table. See Chapter 4, "Access 97 Tables," for more information.

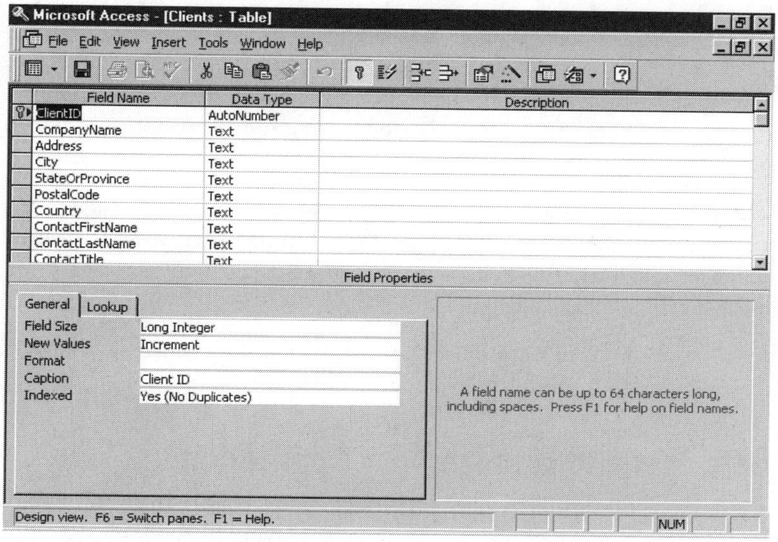

FIGURE 2.9.

Customizing fields and properties within the Clients *table from the* Northwind *database.*

Design Your Database Tables and Assign Relationships

From your planning phase, you should have gathered all the information needed to build your data tables and establish the appropriate relationships.

Tables are the foundation on which your application stands. Slipshod work or poor planning will fundamentally affect your entire application. Place your fields into tables according to their types and the organization of the database. Pay attention to the field properties, and assign the appropriate data formats, field lengths, and so on, as you go. Do not duplicate fields within the same table or between tables.

Take the time to plan and set up your data relationships properly.

Design Your Database Forms and Test Your Table Setup

Using the information from your written plans, create the appropriate forms for your application, and test them thoroughly.

Use creativity in designing the layout and behavior of the forms. Remember that Access 97 applications are event driven, based primarily on form activity. The care and effort that you put into designing the forms will affect your customer the most. Forms and reports can make your application look good. They allow your customer to work with their data. How well you plan and design your forms will make or break your product in the eyes of the customer.

Build the Additional Database Objects as Needed

After testing your forms and tables, it is time to further customize your database application according to your customer's needs. This is where you begin developing queries, reports, macros, modules, help files, and user documentation. Remember to use the wizards as much as possible.

This is an incremental process. Keep track of the changes you make, and always keep a copy of a "good" compile in a safe place. You never know when you might need to go back to a good point to start over. Try to keep incremental backups of your applications in case you discover hidden errors later in the game.

Another option is to use a source code control product such as Microsoft Visual SourceSafe to provide version and multi-developer control.

Beta Test and Finalize Your Application

The beta-testing and finalizing phase gives you a chance to go through some peer review and is indispensable to the development process. Having to acknowledge and correct programming errors that could have been prevented is no fun. This is also the time to finalize your application and compile it into its deliverable form. You have three basic choices with Access 97:

- Supply a full Access 97 MDB database application file that requires that the customer use Access to run the application.
- Strip out the source code and deliver an MDE application file, which also requires that the customer use Access to run the application.
- Use Access 97 for Developers to create a standalone database application using the distributable runtime version of VBA.

Delivery

Present the finished application, along with supporting documentation, to your customer. Be prepared to offer training and initial end-user support for a short period after delivery.

> **WARNING**
>
> Be wary of offering free customization. If you planned properly in the initial stages, you should have included all the requested features. Make sure that your customer understands that he is receiving what he asked you to deliver.
>
> Unless you work for free, you will want to make it clear that additional customization involves a new contract, a new work order, and so on.

Summary

In this chapter I have given you a brief overview of some of the topics important to an application developer. I hope that the Notes and Tips I have included in this chapter will help you avoid learning some of the lessons by trial and error, as I had to do during my own career as a developer.

Now that you have taken a brief look at Access 97 and some aspects of database application development, it is time to study the details. *Access 97 Programming Unleashed* will be useful to you as either a topical reference or an in-depth learning tool. You can refer to the Table of Contents and the index for directions to specific topics, or continue on to Chapter 3, "Access 97 Development Issues."

Access 97 Development Issues

by Joe Rhemann

CHAPTER 3

In this chapter I cover some of the programming environment specifics that you, as an Access developer, should be familiar with.

Conventions and syntax are covered briefly, and then I discuss the Access 97 architecture. It is important to understand how the pieces of Access 97 fit together so that you can guide your development efforts in practical and efficient directions.

I address the enhanced development features of Access 97 that are a part of Office 97 Developer's Edition (ODE). This coverage includes topics such as the Access 97 runtime environment and a suggested ODE development cycle.

For development teams using source code control, I have included a section on Access 97 source code control considerations and Microsoft Visual SourceSafe. Visual SourceSafe is an optional Microsoft product that is available for purchase separately or bundled with Visual Basic 5.0 Enterprise Edition. If you have a multiuser development environment, I highly recommend the Visual SourceSafe product, or some other compatible form of source code control. In addition to the information on source code control in this section, see Chapter 23, "Multiuser Development."

The last brief section in this chapter talks about the date changeover issue, which computer users will face on January 1, 2000.

Conventions

This section covers naming conventions and syntax guidelines for Microsoft Access 97, Office 97 Developer's Edition, Visual Basic, and Visual SourceSafe.

Access Conventions

The following conventions are used for the names of controls, fields, and objects:

- Avoid unexpected results by using the (!) operator instead of the (.) operator when referring to the value of a field, control, or object.
- Do not use spaces in control, field, and object names. This will help prevent VBA application naming conflicts.
- You can use any standard characters, except accent marks, brackets, exclamation marks, and periods.
- The first character of the name must be a character; names cannot begin with leading spaces.
- Values 0 through 30 ASCII control characters cannot be used.
- Names for controls, fields, and objects can be up to 64 characters in length.

By default, Access gives a new project the same name as the name you gave the database file, minus the `.mdb` or `.mde` extension. If you wish to do so, you can use the `ProjectName` property to change the name of your application project. This is done by clicking Options under the Tools menu within Access 97. Select the Advanced tab, and you will see the dialog box shown in Figure 3.1. Enter the name of your project here.

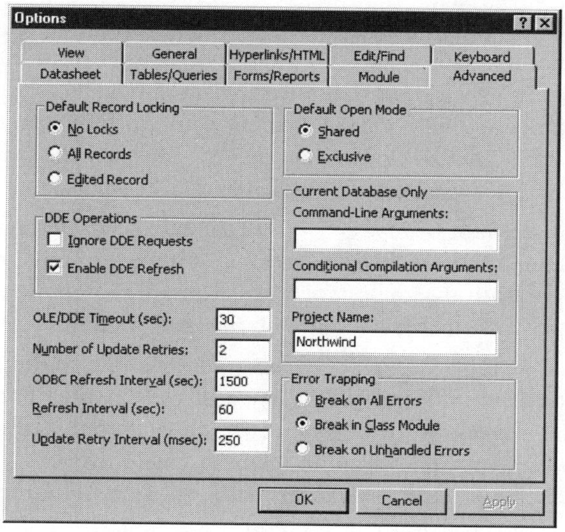

FIGURE 3.1.

Setting the ProjectName *property in the* Northwind *sample database.*

You can also accomplish this within Visual Basic by using the SetOption method as shown below:

```
Application.SetOption "Project Name", "Northwind"
```

The ProjectName property is a string expression that specifies the name of your Access application object. You cannot duplicate the name of an existing Access object; in order to prevent naming conflicts, Access automatically adds an underscore mark to the end of any names that are duplicates.

You must recompile your project after you change the ProjectName property. To do this, close the database, reopen the database, open a module in Design View, and then select Debug | Compile and Save All Modules. Project names can be used as qualified names from other Office 97 applications by using the following syntax:

```
projectname.Application.Forms!formname
```

The following example shows you how to refer to the AuthorID field in a sample Book Collection database on the Authors form from Microsoft Excel. For example, to refer to the LastName field on the Employees form in the Northwind sample database, you set a reference to the Northwind database and then use the following reference:

```
Dim strISBNNumber As String
strISBNNumber = Bookstore.Application.Forms!NonFiction!ISBNNumber
```

Visual Basic Conventions

The following rules apply when you are naming arguments, constants, procedures, and variables in Visual Basic modules:

- Visual Basic is not case-sensitive; however, case is preserved in the name statement.

- Do not use names that have already been assigned to functions, methods, and statements in Visual Basic. Conflicting names must be explicitly identified by preceding the function, method, or statement name with the name of the appropriate library object. If you had a procedure named ISBNDown, you can only invoke a function named ISBNDown by using the syntax VBA.ISBNDown.

- Names cannot be repeated within the same level of scope. You can't declare two arguments named ISBNRegistration within the same procedure. However, you can declare a private argument named ISBNRegistration and a procedure-level variable named ISBNRegistration within the same module.

- Avoid naming conflicts between modules and type libraries. Because there is an existing type library with the name VBA, if you attempt to save the name of a new module as VBA, you will get an error message to this effect. You can't duplicate names between type libraries and modules. Remember this when you set references in your code to an external type library, such as Microsoft Graph.

- Constant, procedure, and variable names can be up to 255 characters long, must begin with a letter, and can include letters, numbers, or underscores (_). However, they can't be VB keywords or include punctuation characters or spaces.

- VB rules must be observed when you name your modules, objects, and procedures.

- You may not use the following characters or symbols in a name: spaces, exclamation points (!), at signs (@), pound signs (#), dollar signs ($), ampersands (&), or periods (.).

- The first character must be a letter.

- Names may not exceed 255 characters.

Modules, Objects, Procedures, and Controls with Similar Names

Avoid conflicts with code that you have written beneath your forms and reports. Do not use Form_ or Report_ when naming a module.

If you are converting an application from an earlier version of Access, prior to conversion the system will display an error message and prompt you to change the names of any modules that do not follow this naming rule.

Although procedures and modules can have similar names, a qualified procedure name, including the module and procedure names, must be used in order to call the procedure from an expression within your application. If a form has a control that has the same name as a procedure you want to call from that form, you must use a qualified procedure call that includes the name of its module. For example, if you want to call a procedure named ScanISBN that is part of a module named NonFiction, which also contains a control named ScanISBN, you must use the qualified name NonFiction.ScanISBN when calling the procedure from a form or form module. However, if there was an existing control named ScanISBN1, there would be a naming conflict. This is because one of the rules pertaining to Access 97 and Visual Basic naming conventions is that names of the same type of component within the same scope (two controls within the NonFiction module, for instance) must have more than one character, space, or symbol difference between their names. If the existing control was named ScanISBN11, there would not be a naming conflict with a new control named ScanISBN.

Modules and Naming Conflicts

Access will display an Expected variables or procedure, not module error message if you try to run a module that has the same name as an existing VB function.

You may encounter compile errors if you attempt to convert your database from an earlier version of Access that has modules with the same name as Access or DAO objects.

Naming Fields with Respect to Expressions, Form and Report Controls, and Methods

Avoid using field names that are the same as a method of the application object when the field will be bound to a control on a form or report, or used in an expression in the ControlSource property. This is easily confirmed by viewing the application object method list as illustrated in Figure 3.2.

FIGURE 3.2.

The method list of an application object.

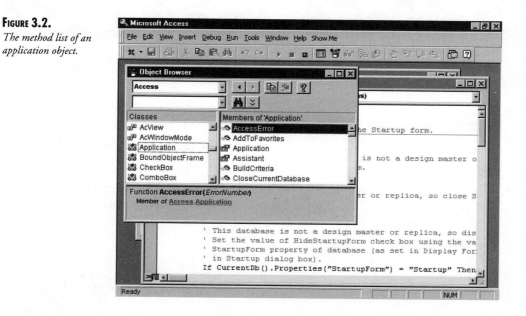

3

ACCESS 97
DEVELOPMENT
ISSUES

Open the application object module in design view and select View | Object Browser from the menu. Select Access from the library box, and then select Application from the Classes window. The methods will be listed in the Members of 'Application' window on the right.

Do not assign any of the following names to a field that will be bound to a control on a form or report or used in an expression in the ControlSource property: AddRef, GetIDsOfNames, GetTypeInfo, GetTypeInfoCount, Invoke, QueryInterFace, or Release.

When you have a field in a table that has the same name as a DAO method on a Recordset object, you must use the (!) syntax to refer to the corresponding field in the Recordset. If you use the dot (.) syntax, Access will display an error message.

If you wanted to refer to a field named AuthorName in a Recordset created from a table called NonFiction within a Book Collection database, you could use the following:

```
Dim dbs As Database, rst As Recordset
Set dbs = CurrentDb
Set rst = dbs.OpenRecordset ("NonFiction")
Debug.Print.rst!AuthorName
```

New Visual Basic Keywords That Cannot Be Used as Identifier Names

VBA 5.0 contains some new VB keywords that you may have been using as identifiers in the past. These new keywords are as follows: AddressOf, Assert, Decimal, DefDec, Enum, Event, Friend, Implements, RaiseEvent, and WithEvents. You will not be able to use these as identifiers with Access 97/VBA 5.

WARNING

If you attempt to convert an older Access application that contains any of these identifiers, you will encounter a compile error. You must rename the old identifiers in order to successfully compile the project for Access 97.

Visual SourceSafe Conventions

Microsoft Visual SourceSafe 5.0 (VSS) has the following naming conventions and limitations:

- VSS supports universal naming convention (UNC) paths; they can be used in any path statement as long as your network operating system (NOS) supports UNC.

- Banyan VINES network users will not be able to use the at symbol (@) in path statements with VSS. The mapped network drive letters must be used in order to work with VSS.

- Total files and objects combined may not exceed 8,191 in a VSS project.
- VSS has a 2GB size ceiling for objects within a project.
- VSS cannot store more than 32,767 versions of an object.
- Names in VSS generally cannot begin or end with spaces or tabs. Any other characters can be used, except for the following:

    Angle brackets (< >)

    Asterisks (*)

    At signs (@)

    Braces ({})

    Brackets ([])

    Carets (^)

    Colons (:) and semicolons (;)

    Commas (,)

    Dollar signs ($)

    Equal signs (=)

    Exclamation points (!)

    Forward slashes (/) and backslashes (\)

    Parentheses (())

    Pipes (|)

    Percent signs (%)

    Question marks (?)

    Single or Double Quotation marks (' ")

    Spaces or Tabs

- File and project labels, and usernames and passwords may be up to 31 characters in length.
- Filenames may be up to 255 characters in length, and can include spaces.
- VSS project paths may be up to 259 characters in length.
- VSS Check Out command comments and VSS search strings may be up to 63 characters in length.
- Other VSS comments may not exceed 4KB in size.

VSS Project Path Syntax

VSS project path syntax and standard Windows directory path syntax are basically the same, except that VSS project paths always start with the dollar sign ($) symbol. VSS identifies the root project directory with the $ symbol. You can also refer to projects according to the following syntax:

Symbol	Description
.	Current project
..	Parent project
...	Parent project's parent
....	Next generational step, and so on
$/	Root project
$/Project	Subproject to the root project
$/Project/File.c	File in the $/Project project
$../File.c	File in the current project's parent project
$Project	Subproject to the current project named Project

Common Syntax in VB and Access 97

Pay close attention to the proper format of syntax within your code. Sloppy code entry will produce unexpected results or errors.

Activate Method Syntax

The following syntax is the proper format for the Activate method syntax:

user code.Activate

In this syntax, **user code** is where you enter your code string. The following subroutine shows how the syntax is used to activate the fourth ISBN menu in the current active object.

```
Sub MakeActive()
Menus(ISBN4).Activate
End Sub
```

MsgBox Function Syntax

This is the proper MsgBox syntax:

MsgBox **"message or prompt"**, **"optional argument1"**, **"optional argument 2"**

You must enter text for the message or prompt. Arguments for functions and methods are specified by their position or name. The following is an example of an argument specified by position where each is one separated by a comma:

MsgBox "The ISBN number has been located.", "ISBN Entry Box"

Name arguments can be specified in any order, as long as you follow the proper syntax. Follow each argument name by a colon and an equal sign, and then enter the argument's value. The following string shows you how to specify an argument by name:

```
MsgBox Title:="ISBN Entry Box", Prompt:="The ISBN number has been located"
```

If your function or method is returning a value, their arguments must be enclosed in parentheses in order to assign a value to a variable. Regardless of whether you are using positional or named arguments, parentheses are not necessary if you don't return values or pass arguments.

The following subroutine is an example of a `MsgBox` function that is returning a value indicating the selected button that is stored in the variable `ISBNCodeStr`. First the variable `ISBNCodeStr` is created to hold a string value, and the `MsgBox` values are assigned. In the following subroutine, the value of the variable is then displayed in a message box. Because the returned value is used, parentheses are required.

```
Dim ISBNCodeStr As String
ISBNCodeStr = MsgBox(Prompt:="The ISBN Number has been
➥ entered correctly.", Title:="ISBN Entry Box", Buttons:="4"
Sub Question()
MsgBox ISBNCodeStr
End Sub
```

Option Compare **Statement Syntax**

The following is the appropriate syntax format for an `Option Compare` statement syntax:

```
Option Compare Binary, Text or Database
```

In an `Option Compare` statement, you must specify either binary, database, or text for the comparison. The following example shows a statement that causes strings to be compared in a sort order within a module:

```
Option Compare Text
```

Dim **Statement Syntax**

The keyword `Dim` and the element `variable` name are the required components of a `Dim` statement. The following statement creates four *variant* variables:

```
Dim VariableName1, VariableName2, VariableName3, VariableName4
```

or

```
Dim ISBNCodeStr, ISBNCodeDef, ISBNRec, ISBNNum
```

If you want to declare a variable as a string, use the following syntax, substituting the desired name of your variable for `VariableName`:

```
Dim VariableName As String
```

> **TIP**
>
> Including the data types in your variable strings saves system memory and makes your code easier to debug.

When you declare several variables in one string statement, include the data types for each variable. Access 97/VBA automatically declares variables without specified data types to be Variant. See the example below for the proper syntax:

```
Dim VariableName1 As Integer, VariableName2 As Text
```

The following string specifies that **VariableName1-3** are specified as Variant types while **VariableName4** is specified as a Text type:

```
Dim VariableName1, VariableName2, VariableName3, VariableName4 As Text
```

`Array` variables are declared by including parentheses. When you create an `array` variable, you provide parameters of the variable's dynamic array. The following statement declares a dynamic array with parameters named **ArrayName1**.

```
Dim ArrayName1()
```

Access Architecture

In this chapter you will learn about the foundation and structure of Access 97. Understanding the way it is put together will help you see how your applications work within the Access framework. Application planning, development, and troubleshooting will be more efficient because you will have a better understanding of what can be done with Access 97.

The Access Framework

The object model diagram for Access 97 is relatively straightforward. Once you have a good grasp of the inner workings of Access 97, you will be much more comfortable using it as a development tool. Figure 3.3 shows the object structure of Access 97; note the relationships between the components within the application structure.

The ovals in Figure 3.3 represent objects and collections, and the boxes represent only objects. DBEngine and CommandBar both have their own complex architectures that are not illustrated in this diagram. MSACC8.OLB is the source for the Access 97 object model; further information may be obtained in the Windows help file ACVBA80.HLP. Both of these files are installed on your hard drive during Access 97/Office 97 setup.

FIGURE 3.3.

An object model diagram of the basic Access 97 architecture.

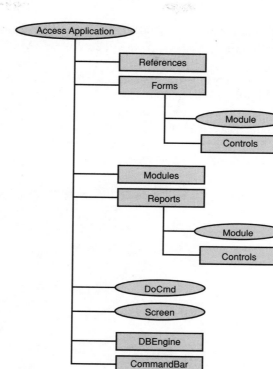

Access 97 is based on a container metaphor, where a database is a collection of objects (forms, reports, queries, modules, add-ins, tables, and macros) usually contained within one file. Access 97 gives you the ability to design two basic types of container files with the suffixes MDB and MDE. See the note below.

THE TWO TYPES OF ACCESS 97 FILES

■ Database files with an .mdb extension. This is the standard file type that holds all of the objects contained in an Access database, including the VBA source code. When you want to give a copy of an Access database to someone, you simply give them a duplicate of the MDB file.

■ Database files with an .mde extension. These are similar to MDB files except that the VBA source code has been stripped out. This is commonly done prior to distribution as a means of locking the application state and protecting the proprietary work of the developer.

Microsoft Office 97 Developer's Edition (ODE) allows you to build an additional type of Access 97 application. Normally Access applications are MDB or MDE container files distributed for use with a copy of Access 97 residing on the end user's machine. The end user must have their own copy of Access 97 before they can use these applications. With ODE you can use the ODE Tools Setup Wizard (see illustration below) to create an Access 97 application that includes a copy of the Access 97 runtime. This creates an application that is capable of running as a standalone product. Access 97 will only run on machines that have Windows 95 or Windows NT 3.51/4.0. Similar restrictions apply to the Access 97 runtime. Figure 3.4 shows the Office 97 Developer's Edition ODE Tools Setup Wizard start screen.

FIGURE 3.4.

The ODE Tools Setup Wizard. Use this wizard if you want to add the Access 97 runtime to any of your applications.

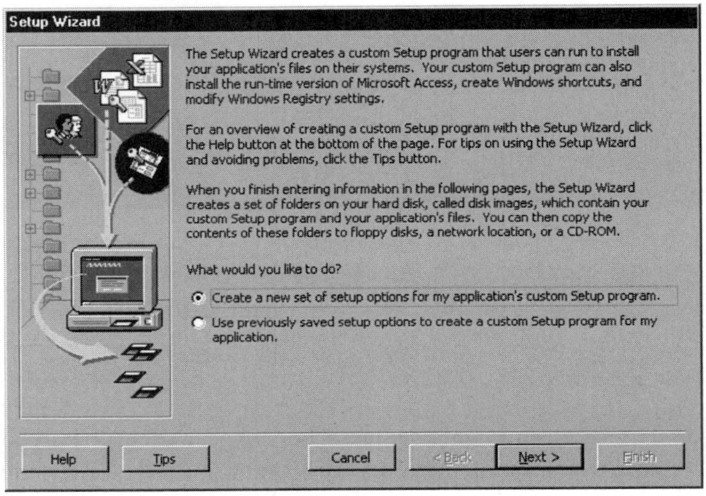

The Anatomy of Tables

The basic foundation of your Access 97 application is its data tables. This is where you store, organize, and work with the data used by your application.

A table is an Access object that is made up of bits and pieces of information organized as a series of fields and records and contained within rows and columns. Imagine a grid on a piece of paper. The vertical columns are the data fields, and the horizontal rows contain the records. In the following illustration, Category ID, Category Name, Description, and so on represent fields within the table. 1, 2, 3, and so on represent the records within the table. As you can see in Figure 3.5, each record contains several fields of data. The grid block where the records and fields intersect represents the specific information for that record's field.

Normalization

Eliminating redundancy within a database by dividing up the data into separate tables is called *normalization.* It is perhaps one of the most overlooked aspects of database design. Essentially, you split up your data fields into a logical table pattern according to the main data topics addressed by the application. Then you use relationships to replicate this data where desired into all of the tables. Relationships are how you draw back together the bits and pieces of your data.

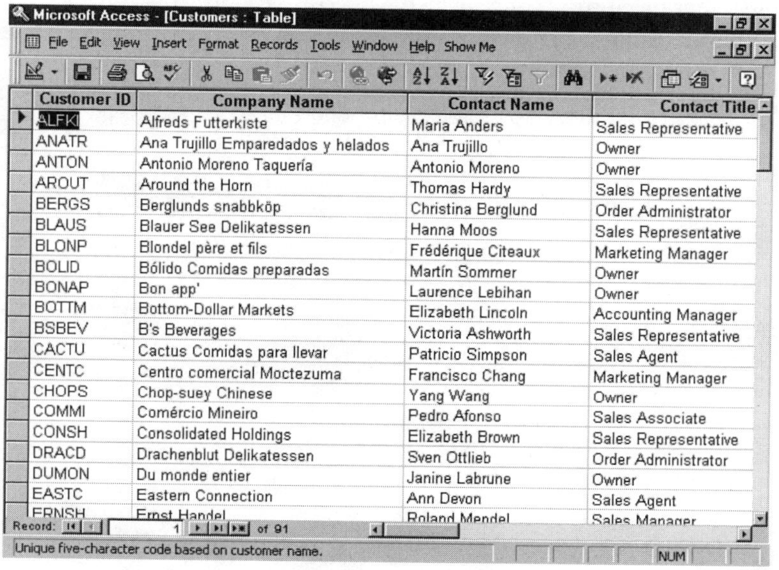

Customer ID	Company Name	Contact Name	Contact Title
ALFKI	Alfreds Futterkiste	Maria Anders	Sales Representative
ANATR	Ana Trujillo Emparedados y helados	Ana Trujillo	Owner
ANTON	Antonio Moreno Taquería	Antonio Moreno	Owner
AROUT	Around the Horn	Thomas Hardy	Sales Representative
BERGS	Berglunds snabbköp	Christina Berglund	Order Administrator
BLAUS	Blauer See Delikatessen	Hanna Moos	Sales Representative
BLONP	Blondel père et fils	Frédérique Citeaux	Marketing Manager
BOLID	Bólido Comidas preparadas	Martín Sommer	Owner
BONAP	Bon app'	Laurence Lebihan	Owner
BOTTM	Bottom-Dollar Markets	Elizabeth Lincoln	Accounting Manager
BSBEV	B's Beverages	Victoria Ashworth	Sales Representative
CACTU	Cactus Comidas para llevar	Patricio Simpson	Sales Agent
CENTC	Centro comercial Moctezuma	Francisco Chang	Marketing Manager
CHOPS	Chop-suey Chinese	Yang Wang	Owner
COMMI	Comércio Mineiro	Pedro Afonso	Sales Associate
CONSH	Consolidated Holdings	Elizabeth Brown	Sales Representative
DRACD	Drachenblut Delikatessen	Sven Ottlieb	Order Administrator
DUMON	Du monde entier	Janine Labrune	Owner
EASTC	Eastern Connection	Ann Devon	Sales Agent
ERNSH	Ernst Handel	Roland Mendel	Sales Manager

FIGURE 3.5.
A data table containing pieces of information organized into records and fields within rows and columns.

TIP

You should design your project around forms, but never forget that tables are the foundation of your database application. When you are drafting your project's blueprint, you should focus primarily on the forms-based interface that will be offered to the end user. From this perspective, you will decide the best way of normalizing your data tables. In a conversation with two Microsoft system engineers in the Houston region, I discussed the importance of normalizing data tables. The engineers' comments reflected my view on this topic as well. Normalize your data tables properly from the outset, or else you or your customers may end up paying far more to manage the database in the long run.

Data tables that have been efficiently separated and logically related can then be considered normalized. This is one area where you can save yourself, the end user, and the product support engineer a lot of headaches.

Eliminating redundancy within a database reduces the likelihood of errors. When an end user has to repeatedly enter redundant data, they are far more likely to make a mistake, and the errors are much more difficult to isolate and correct. Ask any good engineer about taking over the maintenance of a massive database that has not been normalized and they will surely show a lack of enthusiasm.

Normalization is also used by experienced database developers because it requires that the end user enter specific data once, which reduces time and errors at data entry. The Table Analyzer Wizard illustrated in Figure 3.6 is a useful tool for normalizing an Access 97 database.

FIGURE 3.6.

The Table Analyzer Wizard.

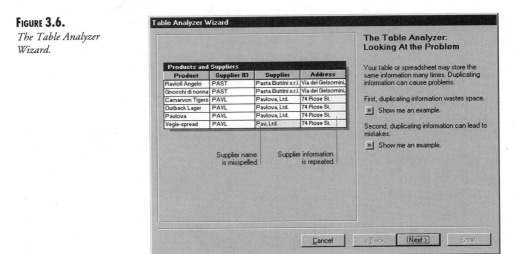

Use of the Table Analyzer Wizard is covered in greater detail in Chapter 19, "Customizing the Access 97 Development Environment."

Establishing Good Relationships

Once you have separated your data into different tables, it is time to set up the relationships. The logical layout of your data tables will dictate the appropriate table-to-table relationships. Previously, I discussed a Bookstore database. Figure 3.7 shows a good example of how to relate tables within a database. In this illustration, there are five separate tables that have been related together in a logical fashion based on the data topics included in the project. The data contained in each of these separate tables is brought back together through relationships and then displayed by forms, queries, and reports.

Once you have established proper and efficient relationships between your data, you can set up forms, reports, and queries to bring in the data as needed from the various tables. Figure 3.8 shows a Books form that uses data from multiple tables. Entering or changing data in a field on this form automatically stores or changes all occurrences of the information in all the related tables.

FIGURE 3.7.

The table relationship display of a sample Book Collection *database.*

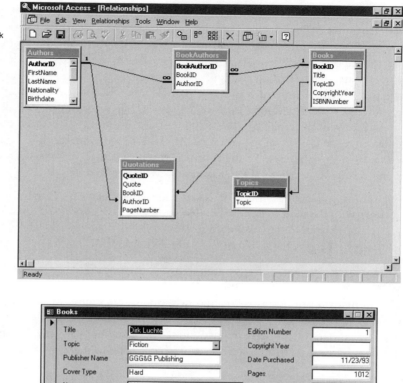

FIGURE 3.8.

The Books *form within the* Book Collection *database.*

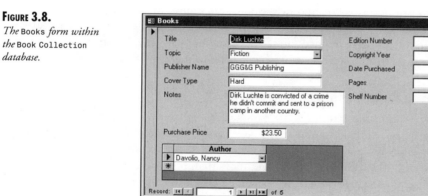

How Do Relationships Work?

In the Book Collection database, the end user needs to work with data that is located within each of five tables. When you establish relationships, you are creating the vehicle through which this can be accomplished. A relationship is usually drawn between tables by matching similar key fields within each table. If you refer back to Figure 3.7, you can see that there are five related tables. The table Authors is related to the tables BookAuthors and Quotations through the shared key field named AuthorID. The field name AuthorID is also the primary key for the Authors table. This will normally be the case with commonly shared fields that have the same name. One of them will be the primary key for one of the tables.

Because `AuthorID` is the primary key for `Authors`, it is considered a foreign key within `BookAuthors` and `Quotations`. Primary keys provide a unique record identifier within their own tables. Microsoft Jet uses primary keys to control common database functions for each record within that table. Foreign keys relate the data in other tables to the specific records in the foreign key's primary table. For example, in Figure 3.7, you can relate the quotations to the authors who originated them. Within each author's record is a field named `AuthorID` that is also the primary key for that table. A unique identifier is added to that record to make it distinct from all the other records in the table. By also including this field in the `Quotations` table, you create the ability to relate individual quotation records back to individual authors by including the field `AuthorID` in their records. To the end user, this means that they can open a form that allows them to enter the author's ID and then retrieve any related quotes.

In Figure 3.7, the table `Authors` is also related to the `Books` table through a one-to-many relationship with the table `BookAuthors`. Because `Books` also has a one-to-many relationship with `BookAuthors`, that means that `Authors` and `Books` share a many-to-many relationship. That brings us to our next topic, the different types of relationships.

One-to-Many Relationships

One-to-many relationships are the most common. An example of a one-to-many relationship in the `Book Collection` database would be the relationship between `Quotations` and `Authors`. Because one author can have many quotes, but one quote will only be attributed to one author, it is appropriate that the `Authors` table shares a one-to-many relationship with `Quotations`.

Many-to-Many Relationships

Many-to-many relationships are the most complex relationships within an Access database. However, they are not difficult to establish. A good example in the `Book Collection` database is the many-to-many relationship between `Authors` and `Books`. Because it is possible to have more than one author working on a book and more than one book associated with each author, you must set up a many-to-many relationship. This is done by creating a junction table, in this case, `BookAuthors`, which has a primary key, `BookAuthorID`, consisting of the two foreign keys, `AuthorID` and `BookID`, from the `Authors` and `Books` tables. Then you draw a one-to-many relationship, from `Authors` and `Books` respectively, over to `BookAuthors`. This junction table transfers that one-to-many relationship through to both tables, in essence creating a many-to-many relationship.

One-to-One Relationships

This is an uncommon type of relationship. Usually data that is directly related in a one-to-one fashion is contained within the same table. However, there are exceptions to most rules. To separate a large table containing many fields of related data into multiple tables, you would want to create a one-to-one relationship. In this case, each record in the original table can only have one matching record in the subset. For instance, if you wanted to create a special subset of a data table and isolate it from use, you would create the subset and then relate it back to its original table with a one-to-one relationship. Let's say you wanted to create a subset of the Books table that only contained information on a specific author's books; you would directly relate the records in that subset back to their original records in the original table. If you wanted to make this a private subset containing additional proprietary information that you did not want other database users to have access to, you would then establish security restrictions for the subset.

Defining the Relationships

Defining relationships takes place within the relationship window. Drag the table that you want to relate to the relationship window and then drag-and-drop the primary key field into the table that you want to relate to. Then you establish the type of relationship between the new table and the existing table, based on the criteria that I have just covered pertaining to one-to-many, many-to-many, and one-to-one relationships, as shown in Figure 3.9. In this case, it would be most appropriate to have a one-to-many relationship from Authors to Authors Contacts.

FIGURE 3.9.

Using the Table Wizard to define a relationship between a new table called Author Contacts *and an existing table named* Authors.

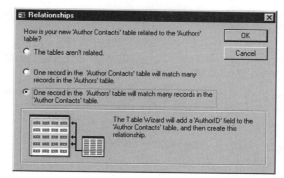

For more information on how to define relationships, see Chapter 4, "Access 97 Tables."

> **NOTE**
>
> If you copy a field to a new table that does not have a key, Access 97 establishes an indeterminate relationship. A default join line is established between the original field and the new field, but referential integrity will not be enforced. As a result, records may not be unique in either table.

To gain a better understanding of the Access 97 relational data environment, take a look at the internal operation of the Microsoft Jet Database Engine, version 3.5. Microsoft Jet is the relational data manager that underpins Access 97, Excel 97, PowerPoint 97, Word 97, other Office 97 applications, and some of the other Microsoft data application environments such as SQL 6.5.

Forms! Forms! Forms!

Forms are the interface through which an end user works with their data. Next to table design, form design is perhaps the most crucial part of your database application. Information stored in a table is entered, analyzed, manipulated, and reviewed through forms and queries. Access 97 uses an event-driven operation model where the back end function is based on the end user's actions within a forms-based interface. Your customer's ability to use the application efficiently will depend mostly on how well you design and implement forms. Templates determine the look and feel of a form and can greatly simplify development. You can create customized templates that incorporate a particular look and feel that uniquely identifies your products. Figure 3.10 shows you an example of a switchboard form.

FIGURE 3.10.

A form as a switchboard in the Northwind *sample database.*

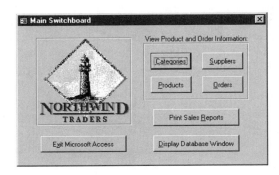

Forms contain navigational links to other objects in the database and are the primary user interface for performing database operations.

Reports

Reports are the output side of an Access 97 application. It is easy to underestimate the challenge faced by report design. A good example is a specialized label-printing system that requires a specific report format in order to print properly on multi-part labels. Special size and alignment considerations come into effect, not to mention the need to set up the form for a specialized printer. Figure 3.11 shows a report generated from data in the Northwind sample database.

Essentially, you use reports to produce printed output from your application. Access 97 allows you to design the appearance of the report. Data generated by a report is extracted from the underlying tables through the use of queries and related procedures.

Queries

Queries are the data analysis tools used to extract specific information from, or cause specific changes to, the data stored in the database. Queries are most easily created using the Query

Wizard, but can be created manually through query design view if desired. The following are common types of queries that can be created using Access.

FIGURE 3.11.

Customer Labels *report for the* Northwind *sample database.*

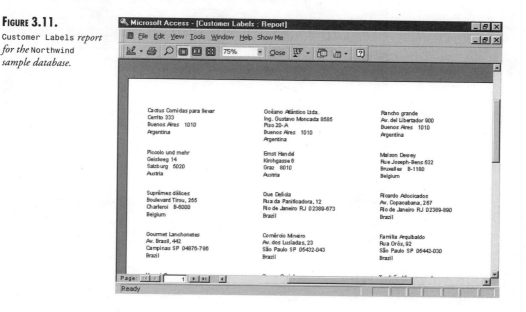

Append Action Queries

An Append query is used to copy records or data from one table to another. The new data is "appended" to the end of the table it is being copied into, or into a specific field based on conditions specified in the query. In the Bookstore example mentioned earlier, you have tables of data for each category of book or publication. If you were to purchase a new collection of books with an existing database, you could use an Append query to add only the information from those tables that are standard in your database. You could also have the Append query add data only to selected fields that already exist within the database.

Crosstab Queries

Crosstab queries are used to extract a display of specific data from a table, based on the intersection of the record and field values that are specified in the query. Then they create a spreadsheet-style document that allows you to derive numeric results based on the extracted data. Figure 3.12 shows a Crosstab query result that has returned the sum of products ordered from each supplier, according to ProductID and Category.

The simplest way of creating a Crosstab query is by use of the Crosstab Query Wizard. Alternatively, instead of creating a Crosstab query within the database, you can use the PivotTable Wizard to display Crosstab data. The information is organized according to x- and y-axis values that can be changed in order to view the data from different parameters.

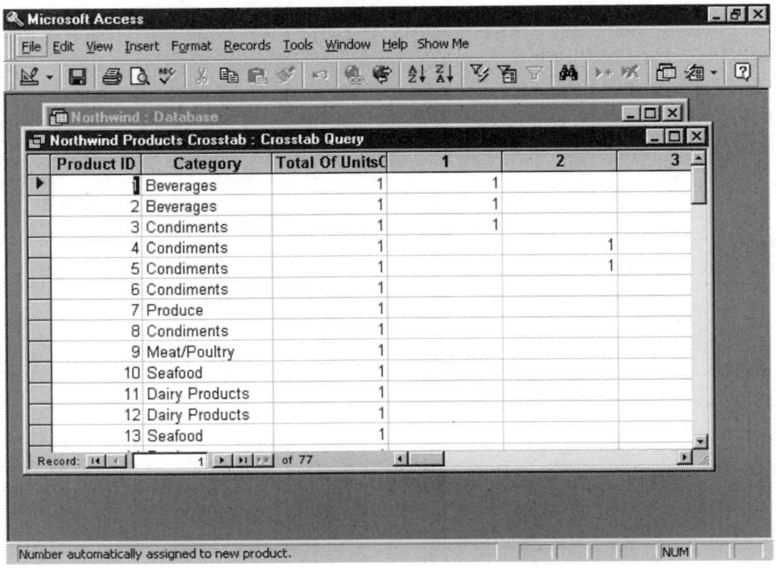

FIGURE 3.12.

A Crosstab query of the Northwind *database* Products *table.*

Product ID	Category	Total Of UnitsC	1	2	3
1	Beverages	1	1		
2	Beverages	1	1		
3	Condiments	1	1		
4	Condiments	1		1	
5	Condiments	1		1	
6	Condiments	1			
7	Produce	1			
8	Condiments	1			
9	Meat/Poultry	1			
10	Seafood	1			
11	Dairy Products	1			
12	Dairy Products	1			
13	Seafood	1			

Record: 1 of 77

Number automatically assigned to new product.

Delete Action Queries

Delete queries are used to remove unwanted records from data tables. In our example of the Bookstore database, the owner might want to remove records for any titles that have gone out of print. Delete queries can only be used for deleting records from a database. You cannot specify selected fields within a record for deletion.

Make-Table Action Queries

A Make-table query is used to create a new table with specific data extracted from one or more existing tables. These queries are especially useful when distributing specific data to other users, analyzing historical data based on dates and times, creating incremental snapshots of your data, and for storing older multi-table data in one archive table for faster search results.

For example, let's say that you purchased all of a museum's books but wanted them to continue to display, manage, and market that portion of your collection along with any books of historical value currently in or added to your collection. You might want to provide the museum curator with that portion of your database that is applicable. You could run a Make-table query to extract only the applicable data from the tables in your main database; the Make-table query would create a new museum book table that you could give to the curator.

If you had separate tables set up for each book category and you wanted to examine book order totals for all categories for the previous year, you could run a Make-table query. The Make-table query would extract the data that was current for the end of the previous year instead of the data that was current as of the date you ran the query.

> **TIP**
>
> If you are designing a large database application, you can increase performance by using a Make-table query. Create a form- or report-specific table that can be assigned as the form or report's data source. Doing this will streamline the event-driven process and speed up operations for the end user.

Forms or reports based on SQL statements and multitable queries run much faster when they are based on one discriminate table created with a Make-table query, instead of one form or report based on multiple tables. Using Make-table queries to bring multitable data into one specalized reference table keeps you from having to run an individual query for each table.

Make-table queries are time- and date-specific as of the date of creation. In order to extract the latest data, you must run a new Make-table query.

Parameter Queries

Parameter queries retrieve information or perform operations based on end user criteria that specifies a range of data. For instance, if you wanted to look up all the books that you purchased between January 1997 and February 1997, this would be a parameter query. Parameter queries are designed so that they prompt the user for values that identify a range of data.

Select Queries

Select queries retrieve information based on specific retrieval criteria established by the programmer creating the query. This is the most prevalent query used in Access databases. Select queries can retrieve data based on any of the standard search criteria and display the results and perform operations on the data. Select queries can be used to calculate values based on the data or group data as desired.

SQL Data Definition Queries

This type of query is a Microsoft Jet–specific tool that uses SQL Data Definition Language (DDL) statements to create indexes and alter, create, or delete tables.

DDL statements will work only with Microsoft Jet format databases. If your end user needs to work with Microsoft SQL Server tables and indexes, they must use a Pass-through query. All other data tables that are supported by Access but were not created in the Microsoft Jet format must use VBA DAO `Create` methods instead.

SQL Pass-Through Queries

Pass-through queries pass commands through to ODBC data sources in command formats that are compatible with the ODBC data source. In a way, a Pass-through query is like a command interpreter between Access 97 and ODBC data sources such as Microsoft SQL Server 6.5. If you are using Access 97 and you wanted to retrieve records from an SQL database, you would use a Pass-through query.

SQL Union Queries

SQL Union queries combine the contents of multiple fields or queries into one result-set field. For instance, if you had three book buyers who supplied you with lists of new collectible book prospects each week, you could combine these lists into one result set, and then run a Make-table query to generate a new table based on the result set.

SQL Subqueries

SQL subqueries are used to generate results, create other subqueries (nested), or define new fields or criteria within a Select or Action query. To create the subquery, an SQL statement is placed in either the field or criteria row of the query design grid. The following illustration shows a Select subquery inside a Select query for the Book Collection database. The subquery will look for any books within the Author query results that will equal AuthorID 4. Figure 3.13 shows a Select subquery inside of a Select query.

FIGURE 3.13.

A select subquery in the Criteria field of a Select query.

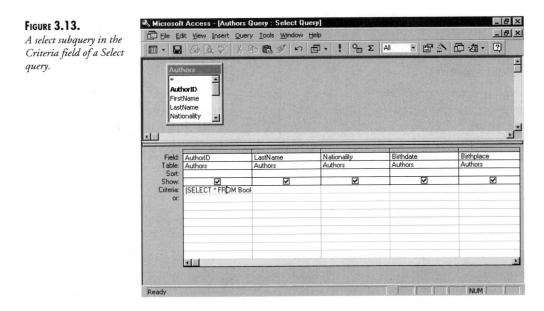

Update Action Queries

Update Action queries make global changes to groups of records in one or more tables. If you sold all the books in your collection that were written by a particular author, you would want to be able to run one operation that would update all of the tables in your database; you would use an Update query.

Macros

Macros are a set of instructions that execute specific actions in a specific order. They are used to automate commonly repeated tasks.

Modules

Modules are containers in which VB code is stored. They are used to automate tasks in a way very similar to macros.

The two types of VB modules used in Access 97 are

- ■ Standard Modules: These modules store VB code that can be run from anywhere in your application. They contain public procedures that can be called from event procedures, expressions, macros, or other standard modules.
- ■ Class Modules: Class modules are used to create specific custom objects.

Form and Report Modules

These are class modules that are built into a form or report. They contain procedures that are specific to the form or report's event properties. When an event occurs within a form or report, the associated module is activated and the desired VB code runs. Sometimes they can contain procedures that are not associated with events.

These modules are specific to forms and reports and cannot be saved or used apart from the object to which they belong. They are a part of the design of the form or report, and therefore always accompany the form or report when they are copied or deleted.

Controls

Controls are objects that are also contained within Access forms and reports. They are the objects that provide the graphic effects, perform actions, and display information.

Access contains a number of built-in and ActiveX controls that can be used in form or report design view.

These controls can be bound to specific fields in underlying queries or tables in order to work with field values in your database. They can also be calculated controls that use expressions as their data source to retrieve information from an underlying form or report table, query, or from other controls. If the control does not have a data source, it is considered to be unbound. Unbound controls usually provide the aesthetic features such as graphics and textures to the form or report.

ActiveX Controls

ActiveX controls are a newer version of the OLE control ideology. ActiveX is the new technology that is enhancing, and in some circumstances replacing, OLE technology.

ActiveX controls are used to add custom features to forms or reports. There are two included ActiveX controls that are a part of Access 97: the Calendar control and the WebBrowser control. The Calendar control is used to display a monthly calendar on forms, and the WebBrowser control makes it easy to display Internet Web pages and other documents inside a form.

TIP

To use the WebBrowser ActiveX control in an Access form, you must have Microsoft Internet Explorer 3.0 or later. IE 3.0+ must be installed prior to adding the ActiveX control to the form.

You can create your own ActiveX controls or purchase them from ISVs (Independent Software Vendors). Office 97 Developer's Edition also includes some additional ActiveX controls.

Form and Report Templates

Templates are used to define the basic characteristics and property values of a form or report. Templates are typically used when you do not want to create the form or report with a wizard.

Access 97 uses Normal as the default template for forms or reports, but you can change this in the Access Options dialog box. Figure 3.14 illustrates this.

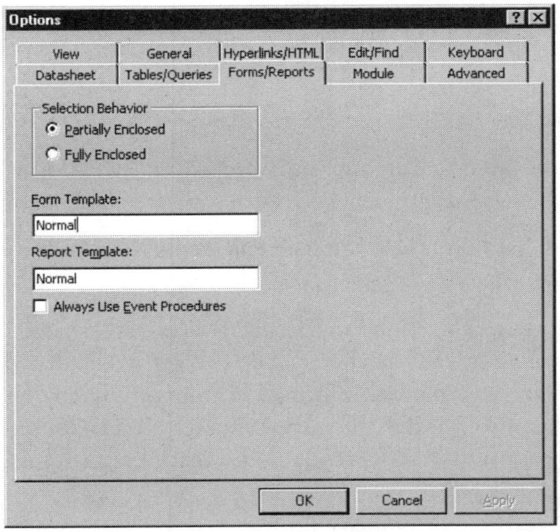

FIGURE 3.14.

Changing the default templates for forms and reports.

When you change the default template, this information is stored in the Windows Registry in the following key and will be used to define all new forms or reports created from that point forward:

```
HKEY_CURRENT_USER\Software\Microsoft\Office\8.0\Access\Settings
```

Form and report templates are easily imported and exported as necessary.

> **TIP**
>
> You can create a template from any form or report. This is an excellent way of giving your application a customized appearance. You can create great forms or reports with customized features that reflect a style that is unique to you and your products, and then designate those forms or reports as your default templates. This is an excellent way of building vendor identity into your products quickly and easily.

Library Databases

Library databases are files used to store routines that are called often in your applications. They have an MDA extension and are made up of a collection of database objects and procedures that can be called from any application, and may be used to distribute application updates to end users.

Library databases can be used by an application after a reference link to the library has been established.

Add-Ins

Add-ins are usually third-party or custom-built enhancements to Access 97. You can create them yourself or obtain them from an ISV. They are related to macros and modules in that they are often used to automate difficult or repetitive tasks. They are also used to add enhanced custom features to an Access application environment.

Add-ins are saved with the `.mda` file extension, just like a library database file, but can also be saved as MDE files with all of the source code stripped out.

There are three basic kinds of Access 97 add-ins:

- Wizards
- Builders
- Menu Add-ins

Wizards

Wizards are interactive tools created to assist Access users with complex tasks. They are a collection of event dialogs built into a user-friendly graphical interface that gather information from the user and then respond to the input by performing specific tasks. Wizards can be used to build almost all components of an Access application. One of the most beneficial features of Access 97 are the included wizards that can be used to build an assortment of Access applications. When you are planning your project, it is a good idea to look at building the core of the project with a database wizard, and then providing additional customization through component wizards wherever possible. Undoubtedly, you will have to use some manual customization to make your applications look just right, but there is no reason to manually reinvent the wheel when you don't have to (especially when you have customers waiting for their applications). Time is money.

Microsoft Access supports control, form, query, report, and table wizards. If you develop any one of these types of wizards, they are available to you just the same as any of the wizards that were included with Access 97.

Builders

Similar to wizards, builders are also information-gathering dialog interfaces used to perform specific tasks. Builders, however, are used mostly to modify or build smaller components of Access objects such as expressions, or to set properties.

Builders can be used to create or customize any property in an Access database. More than one builder can be used on each property, and they are available through the same interface as the builders that were shipped with Access 97. Access 97 supports property and expression builders.

Menu Add-Ins

Menu add-ins are tools that are used to affect wide ranging changes in the Access environment by modifying multiple Access objects or the Access environment. Where builders and wizards are used to create or modify specific objects or properties within Access objects, menu add-ins are used to affect the application in an almost global fashion.

Add-ins are available through Tools | Add-ins in the Access interface. Any time the Tools menu is available to the users, they have access to the application add-ins.

The add-ins shipped with Access 97 are installed during the Access setup phase by telling the setup interface to install all wizards and advanced wizards. Table 3.1 lists the add-ins that Microsoft includes with Access 97.

Table 3.1. Add-ins included with Access 97.

Add-in	Filename	Description
AutoForm	Wzmain80.mde	A form creator that displays the fields and records of a table or query in a particular format.
AutoReport	Wzmain80.mde	A report creator that displays fields and records in tables or queries.
Add-In Manager	Wztool80.mde	Installs and uninstalls add-ins.
Chart Wizard	Wztool80.mde	Adds charts to forms or reports.
Conflict Resolver	Wzcnf80.mde	Resolves synchronization conflicts between replicated databases.
Combo Box Wizard	Wzmain80.mde	A combo box control creator for forms.
Command Button Wizard	Wzmain80.mde	A command button control creator for forms.
Color Builder	Msaccess.exe	Displays a palette for setting the color values for controls and sections in form and report design view. Also used to create color property values for customized colors.
Crosstab Query Wizard	Wzmain80.mde	A Cross-tab query creator.
Database Wizard	Wzmain80.mde	Used to create new Access 97 databases.
Database Splitter Wizard	Wztool80.mde	A client/server tool used to split the database into data and interface portions. Allows clients to be connected to data on the server through the split out interface portion.
Documenter	Wztool80.mde	Creates a report describing the objects in a database.
Export Text Wizard	Wzlib80.mde	Exports data into a text file.
Expression Builder	Utility.mda	Creates expressions for macros, queries, and property sheets.

3

ACCESS 97
DEVELOPMENT
ISSUES

continues

Table 3.1. continued

Add-in	Filename	Description
Field Builder	Wzmain80.mde	Sets new field properties.
Form Wizard	Wzmain80.mde	Creates new forms.
Find Duplicates	Wztool80.mde	Queries records with duplicate field values in tables or queries.
Find Unmatched Query Wizard	Wztool80.mde	Queries for records that have no related records in other tables.
Input Mask Wizard	Wztool80.mde	Creates input masks for fields you choose in tables.
Import HTML Wizard	Wzlib80.mde	Imports HTML-format data into Access tables.
Import Spreadsheet Wizard	Wzlib80.mde	Imports spreadsheet workbooks into a Microsoft Access table.
Import Text Wizard	Wzlib80.mde	Imports a text file into Access tables.
Label Wizard	Wzmain80.mde	Creates mailing labels.
Link HTML Wizard	Wzlib80.mde	Establishes links between Access tables and HTML tables or lists on the Internet/intranet.
Link Spreadsheet Wizard	Wzlib80.mde	Links data on a spreadsheet to an Access table.
Link Text Wizard	Wzlib80.mde	Links text to an Access table.
List Box Wizard	Wzmain80.mde	Creates list box controls on forms.
Lookup Wizard	Wzmain80.mde	Creates lookup values in tables.
Linked Table Manager	Wztool80.mde	Manages table links to other databases.
Macro to Module Converter	Wztool80.mde	Converts macros to VB modules that perform equivalent functions.
Microsoft Word Mail Merge Wizard	Wzmain80.mde	Manages mail merge operations between Word 97 and Access 97.
ODBC Connection String Builder	Wztool80.mde	Creates syntax for a connection to ODBC data sources.
Option Group Wizard	Wztool80.mde	Creates option buttons on forms.

Add-in	Filename	Description
Performance Analyzer	Wztool80.mde	Analyzes the performance of a database and makes suggestions for improvements.
Picture Builder	Wzmain80.mde	Creates bitmaps for forms and reports.
PivotTable Wizard	Wzmain80.mde	Puts Excel PivotTables on Access forms.
Publish to the Web Wizard	Wzmain80.mde	Creates static or dynamic HTML pages from Access applications for use on the Internet/intranet.
Report Wizard	Wzmain80.mde	Creates reports based on tables or queries.
Query Builder	Msaccess.exe	Creates the correct syntax for a query.
Subform/Subreport Field Linker	Msaccess.exe	Links fields in a main form and a subform, or in a main report and a subreport.
Simple Query Wizard	Wzmain80.mde	Creates Select queries from specified fields.
Switchboard Manager	Wzmain80.mde	Creates and manages switchboard forms.
Subform/Subreport Wizard	Wztool80.mde	Creates new subforms or subreports on forms or reports.
Table Analyzer Wizard	Wztool80.mde	Splits large tables with redundant data in smaller, related tables for improved performance.
Table Wizard	Wzmain80.mde	Creates new tables.
User-Level Security Wizard	Wztool80.mde	Creates an encrypted database from an existing database that has user access controls.
Web Publishing Wizard	Wpwiz.exe	Used to publish Access and other Office 97 documents to an Internet/intranet server. This is not the same as the Publish to Web Wizard, but can be used in conjunction with it.

3

ACCESS 97 DEVELOPMENT ISSUES

Workgroup Information Files

At startup, Access looks at workgroup information files in order to recognize users and their configurations within the workgroup. When your workgroup uses user-level security, the workgroup information file contains the user IDs and passwords and the workgroups to which each user belongs.

User-level security is the default security method at Access startup, which means that Access 97 always requires the workgroup information file. This is a required file for Access 97 start-up even when user-level security is not implemented during normal operation. Microsoft built start-up user-level security into Access 97 as a security measure to prevent a startup security backdoor for hackers.

When Access 97 is installed, a file named `System.mdw` is installed in the `Windows/System/` directory. This is the default workgroup information file that is used by Access until you specify a new file using `Wrkgadm.exe`, which is located in `Windows/System/` in Windows 95 or `Windows/System32/` in Windows NT. This default file will log on users with the default admin-level settings. Using an updated workgroup information file and user-level security, you can force all Access 97 users to log on under specific accounts and passwords.

> **WARNING**
>
> Always make backup copies of `System.mdw`. If the workgroup information file becomes corrupted, the backup copy must be installed. Access 97 will not start up or run without it.

In Access 97, all user preferences that are set up in Tools | Options are stored in the following Registry key:

`HKEY_CURRENT_USERSoftware\Microsoft\Office\8.0\Access\Settings`

Previous versions of Access stored these preference settings in the workgroup information file. Running Workgroup Administrator specifies the workgroup information file in the Registry as the setting for the `SystemDB` value in the following key:

`HKEY_LOCAL_MACHINE\SOFTWARE\Microsoft\Office\8.0\Access\Jet\3.5\Engines`

If you want to override the Registry setting temporarily, you can use the `/wrkgrp` command line switch to temporarily specify a new workgroup information file for that session only.

Access and Jet 3.5

The three basic components of Access 97 are the Access 97 application, Visual Basic for Applications version 5.0, and the Microsoft Jet Database Engine version 3.5. Together they form a sophisticated relational database management system (RDBMS). Access provides the application interface for the end user, VBA provides the application program code for performing functions, and Jet provides the relational data management system for working with data sets and managing data connectivity.

The following Dynamic Link Library (DLL) files define Jet:

- Microsoft Jet DLL (`Msjet35.dll`): This is the primary library component of Jet. This library file contains all of the instructions for managing native MDB data.
- Data Access Objects DLL (`Dao350.dll`): This library file provides a Data Access Objects (DAO) development interface for Jet.
- Installable ISAM DLLs: Jet allows access to a number of external indexed sequential access method (ISAM) data sources through installable library files called installable ISAMs. The following ISAM data sources are supported:

ISAM format	Supported by DLL
Xbase (dBASE and FoxPro)	Msxbse35.dll
Paradox	Mspdox35.dll
Lotus	Msltus35.dll
Microsoft Excel	Msexcl35.dll
Microsoft Exchange/Outlook	Msexch35.dll
Text and HTML	Mstext35.dll

Linked Tables

Access 97 gives you the ability to link to tables that exist external to your database. External data tables created in Access, or any of the compatible ISAM or ODBC data sources, can be linked to your project and act like native tables. Linked tables can be used in the same manner as your native tables.

Direct Table Opening

Access 97 generally does not allow you to access an external data source's tables directly. However, VB does give you the ability to use DAO routines to accomplish this.

ODBC Connectivity

ODBC data sources are generally server-specific data sources that can be accessed through Microsoft Jet's connectivity features. Access 97 can open external tables belonging to an ODBC data source through linking, opening, or SQL Pass-through queries. As long as an ODBC driver has been certified to the user's system, he is able to access data from these data sources in much the same fashion as with other ISAM data sources.

Splitting Access Applications

Access 97 allows you to split your application into its database components and its interface components. With this feature you can design applications where the data tables reside safely on a server, while front-end interfaces with links back to the main tables are distributed to each client user.

In a client/server environment, this method reduces network traffic and provides certain security and maintenance advantages over distributing client resident database applications. Global changes are much easier to implement because backing up the database is simpler, and the user is physically separated from the data source. Changes to the user interface can be distributed without making changes to the data source; as new forms, macros, modules, queries, and reports are created, they can be distributed independently of the data.

In environments where the end users may not have standardized to one version of Access, maintaining separate data tables can provide an avenue for users with different versions to access the same data. New front ends based on features in the latest versions of Access can be built into the front-end applications independently of the data source back end.

Customizing Access 97

Access applications can be customized for different user environments, depending on whether the end user environment is individual or multiuser. Access 97 can be customized through Options under the Tools menu, Customize under Toolbars in the View menu, and through Access 97 add-in builders, menu add-ins, and wizards.

User Options

When you make a change in the Options window under the Tools menu, the changes are automatically recorded in the Windows Registry and are active at Access startup.

When multiple users access an Access 97 database over a network, each user will still maintain their own customized preferences. The Windows 95 or NT 4.0 System Policy Editor can be used to establish a standard Access 97 options setup throughout an organization.

The System Policy Editor is available on your Windows 95 system disk. It is used to edit system policies to standardize the appearance and capabilities of Windows 95 for single or multiuser environments. The Windows 95 Resource Kit includes sample system policies and templates in the `admin\reskit\samples\policies` folder. To install the System Policy Editor or support for group policies on your local hard disk, use Add/Remove Programs in Control Panel and select the Windows Setup tab. Select the Have Disk button and install the System Policy Editor from the `admin\apptools\poledit` directory on your Windows 95 system disk. Figure 3.15 shows the Microsoft Windows System Policy Editor.

For additional information on the use of the Windows System Policy Editor, consult your copy of the Windows 95 Resource Kit.

FIGURE 3.15.
The System Policy Editor.

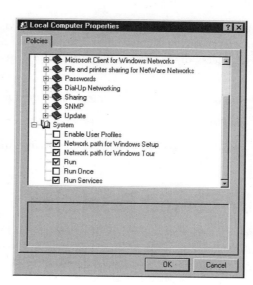

Customizing the Access 97 User Interface with Menus and Toolbars

Access 97 allows you to customize menus and toolbars through the normal point and click interface or through the VB `CommandBar` object. Access 97 and Office 97 give you quite a bit of versatility in customizing the user interface. Now menus and toolbars are basically the same and can be customized the same way. Previous versions of Access allowed the user to customize the particular buttons that appeared on menus and toolbars. Access 97 allows you to customize existing menus and toolbars, or build new ones that contain command buttons and other menus.

These custom menus and toolbars are contained within the database file and are available to anybody who uses the database.

If you wish to import a new menu and toolbar style into your application, you can do so globally; however, individual menus and toolbars cannot be imported selectively. Access 97 also does not allow you to overwrite a menu or toolbar that already exists with an imported one of the same name.

WARNING

If you wish to import a new menu or toolbar style to replace a current one of the same name, you must first remove the unwanted menu or toolbar before you can successfully import the new one.

3
ACCESS 97
DEVELOPMENT
ISSUES

Custom menus and toolbars can be imported by using the Get External Data command under the File menu. Select the Access database file that you want to import from, and click Options in the Import Objects dialog box. Then select the Menus and Toolbars checkbox and click OK.

Customizations to built-in menus and toolbars are stored in the Registry key:

```
HKEY_CURRENT_USER\Software\Microsoft\Office\8.0\Access\Settings\CommandBars
```

These Registry set customizations of built-in menus and toolbars cannot be copied to other users.

Access 97 Conflict Resolution

Through the data management features of Microsoft Jet, Access is able to track and resolve conflicts based on concurrent use of shared databases. The most common conflict is one that occurs when two or more users of a shared database try to change data in the same record.

Conflicts During Replication

This type of error is complicated by replication where you may have several associated copies of a database being edited at the same time. Resolving this kind of conflict is made possible through Microsoft Jet's method of managing changes in the design master database by tracking the globally unique identifiers (GUID) that are associated with each row of data that is copied into replicated databases. When a row of data changes, an incremental counter is applied that tracks these changes across the total distributed database environment. When the same row of data is changed in more than one database at the same time, Access 97 chooses the database that has the highest incremental change count for that particular row. If no database has a higher count for the row, Access randomly accepts the changes from one of the databases. Because there is no way of logically knowing which of the data entry choices are correct, the choice is random. When one row change is accepted over another, the user whose information was rejected receives a message that his data was not accepted and that he must resubmit his change.

Locking Conflicts

Locking conflicts occur when one or more users try to edit the same record in a shared database. Records locking is the method of controlling concurrent read/write access to individual records.

Conflicts can be avoided by setting the locking parameters in the Options dialog box under the Tools menu. Access 97 allows you to have three levels of locking in effect:

- No Locks. This allows concurrent access to records, but does provide an instantaneous lock when the edited changes are being saved.

- All Records. This locks the entire data page on which you are working. Other users cannot have read/write access to this table while you have it locked.

- Edited Record. This provides row-level locking on only the rows that are being edited. Users can edit any rows on the data page except for the one in which you are working.

Office 97 Developer's Edition

A special version of Office 97 has been released specifically for desktop application developers wanting to create Office 97–compatible applications. This is the Office 97 Developer's Edition (ODE). ODE is particularly useful for developers and IS managers.

ODE allows the developer to distribute a royalty-free runtime version of Microsoft Access 97 and Microsoft Graph. Essentially, this means that you as a developer now have a tool for building a completely standalone Access-based application that can be distributed as a turnkey solution. The end user does not need to have Office 97 or Access 97 in order to run the application.

ODE Developer's Tools contains a special Setup Wizard that is used to package your application with a complete setup utility. This allows you to create a distributable version of your application, complete with an automated and professional-looking setup utility built in. This wizard is an extremely useful tool. Once you have finished building your application and it is ready for distribution, you use the Setup Wizard to build a packaged product. Figure 3.16 illustrates the ODE Setup Wizard.

FIGURE 3.16.

The ODE Setup Wizard.

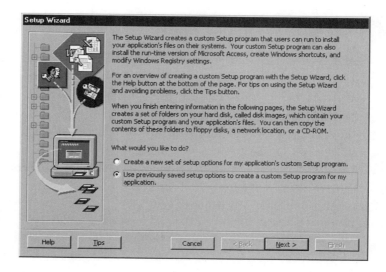

Setup Wizard

The Setup Wizard creates a custom Setup program that users can run to install your application's files on their systems. Your custom Setup program can also install the run-time version of Microsoft Access, create Windows shortcuts, and modify Windows Registry settings.

For an overview of creating a custom Setup program with the Setup Wizard, click the Help button at the bottom of the page. For tips on using the Setup Wizard and avoiding problems, click the Tips button.

When you finish entering information in the following pages, the Setup Wizard creates a set of folders on your hard disk, called disk images, which contain your custom Setup program and your application's files. You can then copy the contents of these folders to floppy disks, a network location, or a CD-ROM.

What would you like to do?

- Create a new set of setup options for my application's custom Setup program.
- Use previously saved setup options to create a custom Setup program for my application.

| Help | Tips | | Cancel | < Back | Next > | Finish |

3

ACCESS 97
DEVELOPMENT
ISSUES

Microsoft Access Source Code Control is another featured component of ODE. This allows you to use source code control to manage your Access 97 development projects. Products such as Microsoft Visual SourceSafe can be integrated in the Access development environment, allowing you to manage and track changes to your projects.

Additional ActiveX controls are included with ODE, such as the `Common Dialog` control and the `ProgressBar` control. Other valuable reference materials are also included with the ODE Developer's Tools CD-ROM.

The Microsoft Replication Manager and Synchronizer is a distributable tool that is used to create and manage replicated database systems. The Win32 API Declarations File and Viewer is included to allow you to view and copy API declarations for use in your applications.

A special tool called the Microsoft Help Workshop is also included, and provides a graphical wizard, such as the interface, that you can use to create help files for use with your applications.

The Access Development Cycle with ODE

Creating an Access 97 application with the ODE tools is not very different from creating one with the standard version of Access 97 and Office 97. The major differences are the special considerations that come into effect when you are using source code control, the Access runtime, and the time- and effort-saving features of the automated ODE tools. Essentially, you use the full version of Access 97 to develop the application, build the help file, and make other enhancements through the ODE platform; you package it with the Access runtime with the Setup Wizard. Voilà.

We have described the basic ODE-oriented development cycle below:

1. Create, test, debug, and secure your standard application with the full-release version of Access 97. As always, give special attention to the design of your forms and tables. Forms become even more important when you use the Access 97 runtime.

2. Use the ODE tools to create help files and other documentation for your application.

3. Debug your application in the runtime environment. Start up your application with the Access `/runtime` command-line switch. You must have ODE tools installed in order to use the Access runtime switch.

4. Use the ODE Setup Wizard to create your application's custom setup program and distribution disk images.

5. Perform a final test and debug of your application by installing it on a test-bed platform that does not have Access 97 installed. The Access 97 runtime requires the same hardware and software parameters as the standard version of Access 97 or Office 97.

6. Burn your program disks, print the user documentation, pack it all in a box, and ship it out.

Forms and the Access 97 Runtime

As with any Access application, you should orient your development strategy around the forms that will be used in the database application. As we have mentioned before, although your tables are the foundation upon which your project is built, they are not the primary user interface. If you know how your forms will be laid out and how the end user will work with the data, you can tailor the makeup of the underlying forms and queries to satisfy your customer's needs.

> **TIP**
>
> Remember that you can develop form and report templates that uniquely identify and set your product apart from the competition. Take the time and effort to build an attractive and functional user interface.

Error Handling and the Access 97 Runtime

When a VB and macro runtime error is not handled, Access 97 responds by closing down the application. No error messages are displayed, the application just shuts down. This would be a major aggravation if you did not know what was going on. If you include error-handling code in your runtime application, not only do you have a more robust product, but you will prevent this shutdown response.

> **TIP**
>
> Macros do not allow you to build in error-handling code, so if you build a buggy macro, your application will continue to shut down every time it has an error until you rewrite the macro. This is one reason why you should try to stick with VB modules instead of macros. You should also try to avoid using End statements in your runtime applications. End statements close your runtime application without producing a trappable error.

Testing Your Runtime Application

With ODE installed, you can test and debug your runtime application by using the Access 97 startup command-line switch /runtime. This disables the features of the Access 97 full release that are not a part of the runtime environment, allowing you to simulate your application's behavior.

Your application will exhibit the runtime characteristics, therefore allowing you to debug problems before releasing the product from the development phase. If you need to test your runtime application on an end user's machine, you can do so by copying Mso97rt.dll to their

3

ACCESS 97
DEVELOPMENT
ISSUES

`\Program Files\Common Files\Microsoft Shared\VBA\` directory. Because you can't display the database window in runtime mode, you must have a startup form in your application that tells the Access 97 runtime how to startup and which objects to make available.

> **WARNING**
>
> Using the runtime simulation does not secure your application. You still need to run it in the full-release version to secure the design. If you do not do so, any user could turn off the command-line switch and access your applications design from full release Access 97.

What's the Difference?

The following list describes the Access 97 features that are not the same in the full version as they are in the runtime version. The Access 97 features listed are either disabled or have been modified in the runtime version:

- You must incorporate VB error handling into your runtime application. As we explained previously, unhandled errors will shut down the application without warning.
- Custom toolbars are supported, but built-in toolbars are not.
- Certain keystroke commands are disabled.
- Some commands, menus, and windows are disabled.
- If you use DDE, the runtime can respond to either Access 97 or the `AppDDEName` setting in the user profile as a valid DDE application.
- Advanced Filter, Database, Design View, Macro, and Module windows are unavailable.
- The only help files available with the runtime version are those that you create and provide with your application.

Features and Items That Are Inaccessible in the Access 97 Runtime Environment

The following list describes Access 97 full-version features that have been disabled in the runtime version. When you are planning and developing your application for runtime use, you must take these issues into account or you will spend a great deal of time trying to debug problems that you could have prevented from the outset.

Keys

The following keys and keystrokes are disabled in the runtime environment:

Keystroke	Function
Ctrl+Break	Halts event processes
Shift	Bypasses system startup procedures and executes `AutoExec` macros
Alt+F1 (F11)	Opens Database window
Alt+F2 (F12)	Opens Save dialog box
Shift+F12 (Alt+Shift+F2)	Saves database objects
Ctrl+G	Opens Debug window
Ctrl+N	Opens a new database project
Ctrl+Enter (Alt+D)	Opens objects in Design View
Ctrl+F11	Switches between built-in and custom toolbar mode

The Ctrl+Break keystroke and the Shift key behave normally as long as they are not being used to halt macros and code executions, to prevent the execution of `AutoExec` macros, or to bypass startup procedures. Bear in mind that all keys will behave normally if an end user runs your application in the full-release version of Access 97. If you wish to prevent this as well, you must create the `AllowBypassKey` and `AllowSpecialKeys` properties using the `CreateProperty` method, append them to the application object's property collection, and then disable them by setting their properties values to `False`. You can also disable the `AllowSpecialKeys` property in the Advanced features portion of the Startup dialog box under the Tools menu. Figure 3.17 illustrates this.

FIGURE 3.17.

Setting the `AllowSpecialKeys` *property for the application in the Startup options dialog box.*

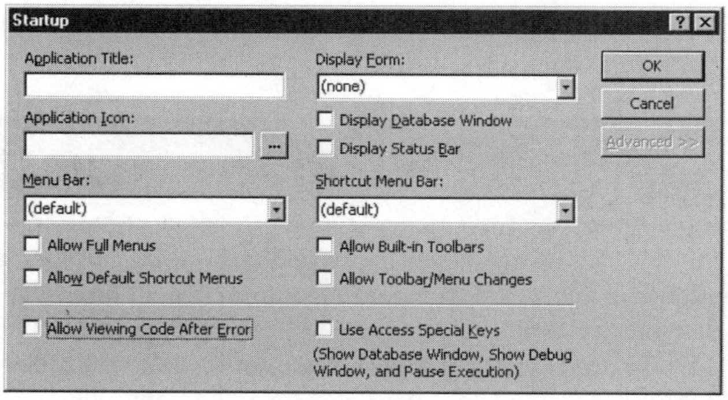

Because macros do not allow you to trap errors in the runtime environment, you would not be able to prevent an end user from using one of these keystroke combinations to interrupt a macro query operation. Instead, use VB for query operations; you can build error handling into the application to trap the end user's attempts to interrupt the query process.

Menus

When you are designing your runtime application, you should try to use custom menus that are a part of the forms around which your application was designed. This prevents the end user from making undesirable changes to the runtime environment.

Normally all Format, Tools, and View menus are removed from all the windows, and some specific command buttons are removed from the Edit, Insert, and Records menus in Data Sheet views of Form View, Print Preview, Queries, and Tables.

Toolbars

Built-in toolbars are not supported by the Access 97 runtime environment. The only toolbars that can be included with a runtime application are custom toolbars that you create and store in the application.

When you create a custom toolbar, it is stored in the current database. It will automatically be available to your application.

In order to tell the runtime environment to display your custom toolbars properly, you will have to customize your forms or reports with the `Toolbar`, `Menubar`, and `ShortCutMenuBar` properties. To make sure that your toolbars are displayed at the appropriate times, use the `ShowToolBar` method in the `Activate` and `Deactivate` event procedures in your forms and reports.

Views

Design Views and Advanced Filter Views are camouflaged the same way that the Access 97 runtime conceals hidden windows.

WARNING

The end user can still make design changes to forms or reports, but they won't be able to see the results of their changes. It is best to remove the function keys that could lead to confusion and accidental changes to the application. You might want to disable the dialog box that asks the user whether they want to save changes to the design of an object before closing it. To do this, turn off system messages by using the `DoCmd` object method `SetWarnings`, or by using the `Quit` method of the application object on the objects `OnClose` property with the option argument set to `acExit`.

Windows

As mentioned previously, the Database, Design View, Filter, Macro, and Module windows are not available in the Access 97 runtime. Though they are still present in the runtime, they are concealed from the user.

In essence, Access 97 runtime camouflages the windows so that they are hidden in the application backgrounds default colors. Even though the menu may be present, the windows functionality cannot be accessed unless you use the RunCommand method. This is one reason for using the Quit method to shut down your application, thereby ensuring that an empty database window doesn't appear after the user has closed the database but not the runtime application environment.

The Runtime Key

When the custom setup program that you supply with your application installs the Access 97 runtime on the user's machine, it makes a change to the licensing section of the Registry. When the end user starts the application, Access 97 checks the licensing section of the Registry to determine which mode it should start up in. A licensing key must exist in the Registry, or the runtime application will not start.

Customizing the Access Runtime

Access 97 initialization settings are stored in the Windows Registry. In order to customize settings for the runtime environment, you must make the following changes to the Registry:

1. Create a user profile. This is done through the Setup Wizard or by modifying the Registry keys directly.
2. Create a key called Runtime Options under your user profile.

Under the Runtime Options key, you can create other keys that specify the following settings for the runtime application:

Key	Description
AppHelpFile	Establishes the default help file.
Icon	Uses the specified icon in the title bar and when the application is minimized.
StartupScreen	Displays the specified bitmap file at application startup.
TitleBar	Displays the specified title in the title bar of your application's main window.

You can customize the title bar and application icon by changing the Registry key settings. If you want to have a customized splash screen, just copy the desired bitmap file into the database directory and add the bitmap name to the command line for starting your application.

3

ACCESS 97
DEVELOPMENT
ISSUES

Securing the Access 97 Runtime Application Against Full Release Users

As we mentioned previously , if you want to secure your runtime application against full re-lease Access 97 users, you must do so in full release Access 97.

The following practices will also help you keep your application's internal structure and com-ponents secure from prying eyes and will keep someone from making unwanted changes to your code:

- Use the /runtime switch on all command line settings used to start the application.
- Use the Security Wizard to encrypt and secure your database.
- Create a unique new workgroup information file. Do not use the default file that was provided when Access 97 was installed.
- Use custom menus and toolbars in your runtime application.
- Do not use toolbar buttons or menu commands that will open Design View, Macro, or Module windows.
- Create the AllowBypassKey and disable it by setting its property to False. This disables the Shift key and keeps a user from bypassing the startup sequence.
- Disable any startup, special key, or error-handling properties that could allow access to the Database, Design View, or Debugging Editor windows, or allow menu or toolbar changes.
- If your database contains VB code, strip the code out by creating an MDE file. This compiles all of the modules and removes any editable source code. This prevents the user or hacker from viewing your VB source code. This operation also compacts the destination MDE file, which adds a further measure of security, because compressed data is far more difficult to hack than standard uncompressed data.

The Microsoft Access Version Number and Environment

In your development process you may want to determine which mode you are running in at any particular time. This will allow you to know which features of your application should be running and which ones should not. When testing and building, you may need to verify your Access environment prior to performing certain operations.

The VB SysCmd function is used to do this. It can check to see which version of Access you are currently running. If you wanted to create and run a GetVersion routine to determine your version of Access, you could use the following code:

```
Function GetVersion() As String
GetVersion = SysCmd (acSysCmdAccessVer)
End Function
```

Runtime Data Maintenance

Occasionally it is necessary to perform maintenance operations on a database due to data fragmentation or other damage. When you create your runtime application, you should build some database maintenance tools into your application. Access 97 provides the data compact and repair utilities, but in order for your customer to use them in a runtime application, you must build shortcuts to the utilities.

> **WARNING**
>
> In order to repair or compact the database, the end user must also have the database closed or the operations will fail.

This is simply a matter of creating shortcuts to the application startup icon with the `/compact`, `/repair`, or `/repair /compact` command line switches. The Setup Wizard can automatically create these shortcut icons for distribution with your application.

> **TIP**
>
> End users must have open exclusive permission for a secured database before they can run a repair or compacting operation.

Designing the Runtime Help File

ODE includes a tool named the Microsoft Help Workshop, which is a wizard-like tool that you can use to build help files for your applications. Some help features of the full release of Access are not available in the runtime; for example, the Microsoft Office Assistant is not available for inclusion in a runtime application.

> **TIP**
>
> After creating your help file, you must set the `AppHelpFile` key in the Registry under the `Runtime Options` key.

Creating Custom SetUp Programs

After you have finished building your Access 97 application, ODE provides a powerful tool for packaging your project for the end user: the ODE Setup Wizard. This tool takes your finished application and builds a deliverable package that is ready to be burned onto a CD-ROM or copied to disks for distribution.

The custom setup program that is included with the distribution product will provide a professional looking user installation interface that will allow the end user to install specified options. Figure 3.18 shows the user interface that is used to select this option, among others.

FIGURE 3.18.

A sample setup dialog screen for an Access 97 runtime application that was prepared for distribution with the Setup Wizard.

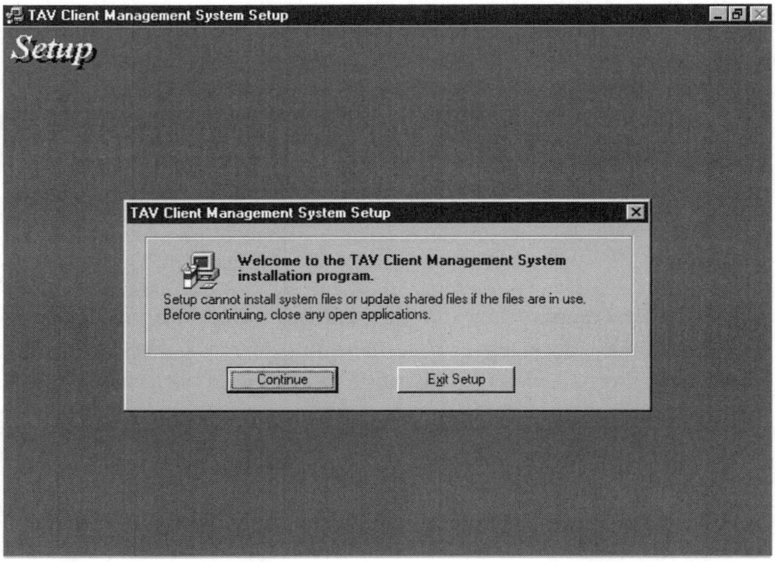

The Setup Wizard handles most of the logistic issues with regards to preparing your application for distribution in an end-user–installable form. It automates the process of modifying the user's Registry settings, and can install desired shortcuts.

The Setup Wizard obtains the information from you that is necessary to build the final distribution form and then creates disk images for the appropriate distribution medium.

One of the options that you can specify while running the Setup Wizard is whether you want to include the Access 97 runtime version for those users who don't have a full version of Access.

Creating a custom Setup program for your application is fairly simple, just follow the instructions below:

1. Start the Setup Wizard, which can be found in the Microsoft ODE Tools group.
   Follow the instructions.

2. Copy the file images to your distribution medium or to a network location for push or pull installations.

Automation and Access Runtime Applications

Using automation with Access 97 runtime applications requires some coding differences that may not be readily apparent to you from the outset.

The first step for your code is to check for a loaded instance of Access 97 or the runtime. If one is not loaded, specify a shell function path to Access and a database.

To close an Access 97 runtime application, use the `Quit` method of the application object.

The following example checks to see whether Access is already running. If it is not, it tries to open the full version of Access. If Microsoft Access is not installed, the procedure opens a runtime version of Access.

```
Sub OpenRunTime()
Dim objAccess as Object
Dim strAccPath As String, strDbPath As String
On Error Resume Next
strDbPath = C:\Databases\R&D\Customer Databases\
➥Book Collector\Book Collection1.mdb
Set objAccess = GetObject(strDbPath)
If Err <> 0 Then
If Dir(strDbPath) = Then
MsgBox ERROR iX 43, No iX Application Database Found.
Exit Sub
Else
strAccPath = C:\Program Files & \Microsoft Office\Office\MSAccess.exe
If Dir(strAccPath) = Then
MsgBox ERROR iX 11, Could Not Locate iX
➥ Application Full-Release Environment.
Exit Sub
Else
Shell pathname:=strAccPath &  & Chr(34) & strDbPath & Chr(34),
➥ windowstyle:=11
```

```
Do
Err = 0
Set objAccess = GetObject(strDbPath)
Loop While Err <> 0
End If
End Sub
```

Distributable File List for Runtime Applications

Microsoft allows you to distribute the following files free of royalty with your Access 97 runtime applications:

12520437.cpx	12520850.cpx	acme.exe
acmsetup.exe	acmsetup.hlp	acread80.wri
axdist.exe	books.gif	clouds.wmf
cnfdntl.bmp	comcat.dll	comct232.ocx
comct132.ocx	comdlg32.ocx	commtb32.dll
contacts.gif	ctl3d32.dll	dao350.dll
dbmusic.gif	dbnmpntw.dll	drvssrvr.hlp
ds16gt.dll	ds32gt.dll	eatdrink.gif
expand.exe	extract.exe	flax.bmp
globe.wmf	gr8409.dll	gr8aph8.exe
gr8galry.gra	graph8.olb	graph8rt.srg
hatten.ttf	hlp95en.dll	houshold.gif
invntory.gif	members.gif	mfc40.dll
mfcans32.dll	mfcuia32.dll	monytrak.gif
msacccah.dll	msaccess.exe	mscal.ocx
mscuia32.dll	msexcl35.dll	msinet.ocx
msjet35.dll	msjint35.dll	msjter35.dll
msltus35.dll	mso97rt.dll	msodeusa.dll
msothunk.dll	mspdox35.dll	msrclr35.dll
msrd2x32.dll	msrecr35.dll	msremr35.dll
msrepl35.dll	msrpfs35.dll	mssetup.dll
mstext35.dll	mstool32.dll	mstrai35.dll
mstran35.exe	msvcrt20.dll	msvcrt40.dll
mswinsck.ocx	msxbse35.dll	northwind.mdb
odbc16gt.dll	odbc32.dll	odbc32gt.dll

odbcad32.exe	odbccp32.cpl	odbccp32.dll
odbccr32.dll	odbcinst.hlp	odbcint.dll
odbcjet.hlp	odbcji32.dll	odbcjt32.dll
odbcjtnw.hlp	odbckey.inf	odbcstf.dll
odbct132.dll	oddbse32.dll	odex132.dll
odfox32.dll	odpdx32.dll	odtext32.dll
offsetup.ttf	olepro32.dll	orders.mdb
pattern.bmp	phonordr.gif	photos.gif
replman.exe	replread.doc	resource.gif
richtx32.ocx	rplman35.cnt	rplman35.hlp
school.gif	sea_dusk.wmf	setup.exe
setup.ini	setup.tdf	soa800.dll
solutions.mdb	sqlsrv32.dll	stone.bmp
swu8032.dll	tahoma.ttf	tahomabd.ttf
utility.mda	vba332.dll	vbajet32.dll
ven2232.olb	videos.gif	win351.exe
win95fiber	wininet.dll	workout.gif
wrkgadm.exe		

Source Code Control and Access 97

Source code control is a key strategy for multi-developer environments where numerous programmers are working on components of an application at the same time. One of the major problems encountered in the multi-developer paradigm is the coordination of the project development logistics and version controls. When a project is continually being enhanced and updated, especially by more than one person, it becomes imperative that some form of application development controls be implemented. Without some means of tracking chronological changes, components being worked on, and developer's individual activities within a project, this is very difficult.

One of the technologies born out of this need to control development efforts at the programming level was source code control. This technology and methodology answers many of the needs of development workgroups because of the ability to manage versions and components of applications at the source-code level, and is beginning to proliferate into multi-developer environments at a rapid pace. With the added emphasis on process management within organizations, through industry standards such as ISO-9000, source code control capabilities become all the more important.

> **NOTE**
>
> Because of the document tracking capabilities of Office 97 through tools such as binders and journals, companies are beginning to find ways to move their operations closer to the ISO-9000 standards certification mark. There are some good case studies on ISO-9000 certification and Office 97 document controls. Microsoft has even used Office 97 as a major keystone in the successful certification of one of their hardware manufacturing facilities.
>
> If you are developing applications for an industry in which your customers are starting to move toward ISO-9000 or a comparable standards certification, you must plan on implementing some form of development controls for quality and standards assurance. One of the primary requirements for ISO-9000 certification is that companies (especially manufacturers) must not only apply the standard to their internal operations, but they must also purchase supplies and products that are from companies that are ISO-9000 certified.
>
> That means that if your customers are ISO-9000 certified and your competition achieves certification but you don't, your customers are obligated to buy your competitor's products. The certification process is difficult, extremely expensive, and usually requires a major overhaul of a company's operations and management. It may not make much difference how much your customer likes you; if you aren't certified, they must look for someone who is. According to ISO guidelines, only after exhausting their options are they allowed to purchase products that will be used in their production from non-ISO-certified vendors.

A source code control utility that allows you to use any source code control product that uses the standard source code control interface is included with ODE in the Developer Edition Tools. The standard source code control interfaces were designed by the Microsoft Visual SourceSafe development team and have been shared as an industry standard.

If you develop Access 97 applications in a multiuser environment, you should consider the advantages of implementing source code control.

Source code control allows you to implement check-in and check-out controls so that your developers always know who is working on what components. Once an object is in a form that the administrator does not want to lose, the object can be checked out to prevent any further modifications. When a developer completes changes to an object, they can check it back in and allow the other members of the team to update their versions with the changes.

The administrator has an audit trail and chronological record of all changes that have been made to a project, and can roll the project back to any particular point in the history of the development process. Version changes can be compared, merged, and synchronized, and if necessary, rolled back to any previous version.

Working with source code control in Access 97 is similar to using it in VB. The source code control utility offers specific features during certain application events and allows you to perform code control operations within Access 97.

The Source Code Control Paradigm

A development team uses source code control to manage an up-to-date version of the master application objects. As each developer works on their own copy of the project, the master copies stay up-to-date by recording any changes when objects are checked back in. These changes are tracked and synchronized among all of the developers as they perform check-in and check-out operations. This does not allow more than one developer to alter an object at one time, but rather records the changes in an incremental fashion, maintaining version references within the master project. With the exception of modules, no one can check out an object until you have checked it back in. If you are working with a module, you have the option of merging changes from other developers with your own at check-in.

In our examination of source code control, we will use Microsoft Visual SourceSafe 5.0 (VSS) as the reference application. Within VSS, Access 97 objects (forms, macros, modules, queries, and reports) are stored as text files that are copied to your local machine when you check out an object. Access 97 then converts this text file definition of the object into an application object and loads it into your local project. When you check back in one of these objects, it is converted back to a text file and stored within VSS. Other Access 97 objects are stored as binary components of an Access database file that is managed by VSS.

As we mentioned previously, the source code control integration utility is part of the ODE Developer Edition Tools. In order to integrate source code control into your Access 97 development environment, you must have ODE installed and obtain a copy of a source code control application such as Microsoft Visual SourceSafe.

> **NOTE**
>
> Microsoft Visual SourceSafe 5.0 is available as either a licensed developer product that is purchased separately or as part of the Microsoft Visual Basic Enterprise Edition bundle. You must use VSS or a similar third-party source code control package that adheres to the standard interface in order to use source code control integration within your projects.

Source Code Control Functions in Access 97

Installing the source code control component with ODE enables the following functions on Access 97 menus:

- Add Database to SourceSafe
- Add Objects to SourceSafe

- Create Database from SourceSafe Project
- Check In
- Check Out
- Get Latest Version
- Undo Check Out
- Options
- Refresh Object Status

Add Database to SourceSafe

The add database to SourceSafe function adds the current database to a source code control project, and places it under source code controls.

When you place an Access 97 database under source code control, the icons in the database window reflect the control status of the various objects. The filename suffixes for objects added to VSS source code control are as follows:

Object	Suffix
Forms	`*.acf`
Macros	`*.acs`
Modules	`*.acm`
Queries	`*.acq`
Reports	`*.acr`
Tables and other objects	`*.acb`

Add Objects to SourceSafe

The Add Objects to SourceSafe function allows you to place Access 97 objects under VSS source code control.

Create Database from SourceSafe Project

A new Access 97 exclusive database is created from an existing VSS project when you use the Create database from SourceSafe project function. This is the normal means of joining a development team.

Check In, Check Out, Get Latest Version, and Undo Check Out

The Check in, Check out, Get Latest Version, and Undo Check Out commands allow you to interact with VSS source code control to perform object transactions and synchronize versions of Access 97 objects.

Options

The Options function allows you to customize the behavior of VSS in Access 97.

Refresh Object Status

The Refresh Object Status function allows you to refresh the display of Access 97 objects in the database window. This is done in order to see whether the VSS status of any of the objects has changed since you opened your project.

Other Functions

All other commands or functions that you use with VSS will call VSS code directly as if you were using the VSS interface instead of Access 97.

Run SourceSafe

This command opens the VSS Explorer.

Show Differences

This command compares your local Access 97 project to the VSS project and displays the differences. It will not compare objects stored in the VSS binary Access project file.

SourceSafe Properties

This command allows you to set VSS properties.

Share Objects

This command moves Access object from one VSS project into another, and allows you to update the shared object into your current Access application.

Show History

This command allows you to view the object or project history.

Changes to Microsoft Access Behavior Under VSS

When you use source code control, in this case Microsoft Visual SourceSafe 5.0, you need to be aware of some of the behavioral differences that you will experience while developing with Access 97.

Compacting Access Databases

Compacting a database is one of the ways of severing the source code controls on a database project. When you perform a compact operation, Access 97 asks you whether you want to remove the project from source code control. Access 97 then removes the properties of VSS from your Access 97 application.

Opening and Closing VSS Access 97 Applications

When opening an Access 97 project that is currently under VSS control, Access looks at the VSS browse option to determine when to refresh the database objects.

Projects under VSS control are only opened as exclusive databases to prevent conflicts between multiple developers.

Before closing the application, Access will ask you whether you want to check any objects back in to VSS.

Opening VSS-Controlled Access 97 Objects in Design View

Access 97 checks to see whether the object that you want to check out is available. If it is an exclusive check-out object, and it is not available, you are denied access. If it is a VB module that is already checked out, you are alerted to this fact and given the option of checking the module out. Any changes made at the same time by multiple developers on a module have to be merged using the source code control utility. If the object is available for check out, the object is checked out of VSS to you, Design View is opened, and the object is displayed.

Saving New Objects

When you create a new form, macro, module, query, or report, Access 97 asks you whether you want to place the new object under source code control.

Renaming Objects

You cannot rename any object under source code control unless you have it checked out.

Deleting Objects

You cannot delete objects under source code control unless they are checked out to you, or unless you have the VSS options set to allow specific automatic deletions.

Access 97 Objects Under VSS Source Code Control

This section describes the differences in Access 97 objects that might occur while the VSS source code control is in use. Being familiar with this information could save you a lot of trouble-shooting time.

Queries

Queries are stored as independent application objects under VSS control and can be checked out as separate objects. Queries can only be checked out by one developer at a time.

NOTE

When you place your project under source code control, Access 97 ignores any relationships involving queries. Access must do this in order to allow you to check out individual queries as separate VSS text files instead of as binary components of the VSS project.

Multi-developer work on a project would be impractical if VSS tried to enforce relationships with queries under source code control.

In order to save any changes that you make to a query's design properties, you must check out the query from VSS. If you do not do this, you will not be able to check-in any changes that you make while browsing the query.

Forms, Macros, and Reports

Forms, macros, and reports are saved as separate components under VSS, and the same rules regarding changes made while browsing the objects apply to forms, macros, and reports as with queries; they must be checked out to you in order for you to check your changes in to the VSS project.

Modules

As we mentioned before, unlike most of the other Access 97 objects, modules can be checked out by more than one user at a time.

After the first developer's module is checked in, any conflicts between versions that have been checked-in must be resolved by the subsequent developers. VSS simplifies this process with the visual merge dialog box.

Data and Miscellaneous Objects

VSS creates an Access database in which it stores all of the binary components of the Access project that are not stored as independently available text files. These objects include conditional compile arguments, data access specifications, relationships, start-up procedures, tables, and VBA references.

These objects must be checked out together and can only be checked out in an exclusive fashion.

WARNING

Any of these binary objects that you create without checking out data and miscellaneous objects will be deleted or overwritten without warning when you try to do a get or synchronize your version of the application with VSS.

Relationships, Toolbars, Database Properties, and VBA References

You must have Data and Misc. Objects checked out in order to design any of these objects under source code control. Access automatically prompts you to do this when you open the respective dialog boxes.

Because all of these objects are dependent items, they have to be worked on in concert with one another. The rules of referential integrity make versioning data a very complex operation. If you tried to implement independent object controls for these objects, the rules for check-in and check-out would enormously over-complicate the operations involved.

Source Code Control Limitations

Source code control has performance and logistic limitations that you should be aware of if you are administering a VSS project. If you do not become familiar with these limitations, you may innadvertently be creating a major technical headache for yourself or your development team.

> **TIP**
>
> If one of your developers leaves without checking an object back in that someone else needs, or if he suffers a system crash before checking in an object, the VSS administrator can use the VSS Explorer interface to retrieve checked-out items.
>
> In order to do this in VSS 5.0 with an Access 97 database project, you must edit the `srcsafe.ini` file. Delete the `Disable_UI = Yes` line and restart VSS Explorer. Then you will be able to perform the retrieval operation. The next time that you open the Access 97 database, Access will add the `Disable_Ui = Yes` line back to `srcsafe.ini`.
>
> If one of your developers leaves the company or loses his password while he still has objects checked out, the administrator can change the user's password and then use VSS Explorer under that developer's ID and password to check his files back in.

User Level Access

When you place a project under source code control, all user and workgroup permission settings are removed by VSS. These settings must be set up again after the project has been removed from source code control.

Replication

Replication is not supported under VSS source code control. The only form of replication that takes place in source code control is when objects are imported from one VSS project to the master of another, and then replicated out from the design master.

Application Changes Through DAO and Microsoft Jet

DAO changes performed on local versions of a VSS project through Microsoft Jet circumvent normal source code controls. These changes will be deleted without warning when you attempt to synchronize your project with the VSS project.

Access 2.0 or Access 95 Databases

Projects from earlier versions of Access cannot be placed under source code control until they have been converted to Access 97 projects.

Local Database File Operations

If you want to move or copy a local copy of a database under VSS control, you must check-in your database, delete the existing local copy, and then have VSS recreate a new local version where desired.

Integrating Source Code Control into Access 97

As we mentioned previously, in addition to ODE and the source code control add-in utility, you must also install a source code control application that conforms to the standard source code control interface. With ODE, Access 97, and VSS (normally a five-user license), each individual user must have licensed copies of the applications installed on his system.

VSS should be set up on the development server that all of your developers will have access to, and all of the developer clients will have to access the VSS network and run `netsetup.exe` in order for Access 97 to see the source code control provider in their Registries.

The Access source code control add-in must be installed through the ODE Developer's Toolkit setup. Then you should implement client installations of VSS on each developer's machine.

This will provide VSS source code control with Access 97, which is available through the SourceSafe selection in the Tools menu. Figure 3.19 shows you how to start VSS from Access 97.

FIGURE 3.19.
Starting Visual SourceSafe within Access 97.

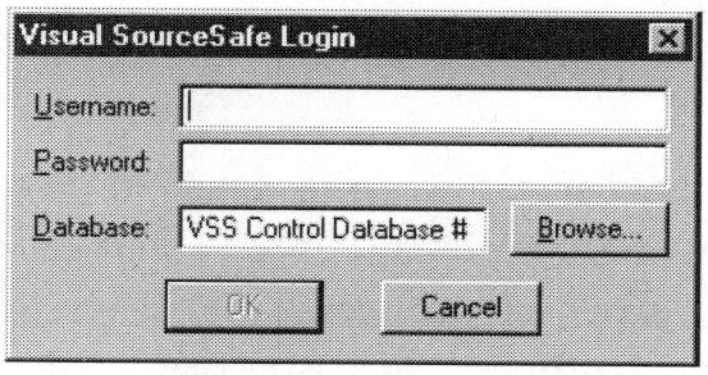

3
ACCESS 97
DEVELOPMENT
ISSUES

NOTE

One of the items installed with ODE Developer's Tools was the source code control White Paper. This is a valuable reference tool if you need a more in-depth understanding of the topic as it applies to Access 97.

Developing with Source Code Control

Source code control can help you organize your database applications as projects and subprojects with version controls, track and audit changes made to projects, allow project version rollback capabilities, study the changes between versions of objects, report project activity, synchronize projects from a design master, control access to components of a project under development, and avoid accidental deletion or overwriting of information.

Team development under source code control is a bit different than single-user development. Though you have less flexibility in general, with source code control you have far more control over the design process between developers. The following development steps should be added to your normal guidelines in order to take into account the particulars of working under source code control.

- After creating a new Access 97 database project, add it to source code control.
- After you create the various Access objects, taking into account the check-out requirements, add the objects to the source code control project when you save them.
- After objects have been added to source code control, you must check them out again before you can make any permanent changes through Design View or while browsing the object.
- Make your changes and updates available to the other developers by checking-in your work.

Remember to add objects to source code control after you have created them with a wizard. In some cases, you may have to use the Tools menu to tell Access 97 to add the new object to source code control.

> **TIP**
>
> If you want to work on an Access 97 database that is under source code control while you are not connected to the VSS server, just check out the objects that you want to work on before you disconnect.

The Access 97 source code control component that is part of ODE Developer's Tools is designed specifically to work with Access 97. Changes to Access projects under source code control should be managed through this tool rather than through the source code control provider alone. Otherwise, you will lose any object changes made when you close your database.

After you have finished development of your Access 97 project under VSS, you must remove it from source code control before you can distribute or replicate it.

VSS is like a security warehouse for your development project. The VSS security system controls access to the project, the VSS controls manage checked-in or checked-out projects, and VSS version control capabilities manage all records of changes and modifications to the project.

Each time a developer executes a command, VSS checks his user privileges to make sure that he is authorized. The VSS administrator has control over all user privileges on a project-by-project basis.

Many source code control systems work very well on individual source code files, but few of them actually establish relationships between files. This is a problem when you are developing for the Windows environment, because an application can consist of numerous library files and executable files that can be constructed from multiple source files that may already be distributed among a wide range of applications. If your source code control provider cannot manage relationships, it is possible that your source files themselves may not be protected.

VSS controls relationships through its version control system in order to present a project-oriented development environment instead of a file-oriented one.

VSS is the best source code control provider for Access 97 application development in a team environment and is fully integrated with Access, FrontPage, Visual Basic, Visual C++, Visual J++, and Visual FoxPro.

Source code control and VSS provide a valuable solution for managing development environments across enterprises or in small workgroups.

Turn of the Century Considerations

There is a potential problem looming on the horizon. What will happen when our computers try to change their internal clocks to January 1, 2000? You should take this issue into account at the development level in order to prepare your products for the 21st century.

OK, so what will actually happen?

According to some sources, on January 1, 2000, your computer clock will reset itself to January 4, 1980.

In the 1960s, due to system memory, mass-storage limitations, and high cost, computer scientists decided to use a two-digit code to manage internal system clocks and software chronological functions, never imagining that we would still be locked into a two-digit code thirty years later. This means that from that point forward, date references in code were made based on the last two numbers of the year according to the Julian calendar. For instance, in the simplest of terms, the change between 1977 and 1978 was referenced in the following way:

$$19(77)+(01)=19(78)$$

So, if we take what will happen in 1999, in a very simplified fashion, it will look a bit like this:

$$19(99)+(01)=19(??)$$

Some Information Technology professionals realized that this problem would arise, and in the 1960s and 1970s they developed methods of dealing with the issue. They employed various techniques, such as Julian to Gregorian calender conversions. The problem was that the additional processing memory, computing time, and disk-storage requirements were not seen as budget-worthy because, from a technology standpoint, the problem was still in the distant future. By the 1980s, most of the government and private industry sectors had become accustomed to managing system and data chronology in the default two-digit fashion, and they overlooked the issue until it was thrust upon them again by the approach of the 21st century. The penny-wise practices of past government and industry leadership will probably prove to be somewhat pound-foolish in a couple of years.

If your organization was one of those wise enough to solve this issue before it became a problem, you only need to worry about those organizations with whom you interface that haven't taken appropriate measures. The potential exists for a massive shock to our national and international information infrastructures. The likelihood of a debilitating technical crisis arising from this issue is rapidly dimishing due to increased awareness and proactive efforts. However, you should not trust someone else to take care of this potential problem for you. Prudence demands that you deploy basic strategies for dealing with the turn of the century issue both internally and externally.

To fix the problem, again in very simplified terms, we should reference our numeric calendar year in the following manner:

$$(1999)+(0001)=(2000)$$

> **NOTE**
>
> The mathematical samples shown are simplified to illustrate the problem and do not reflect the actual computational models involved.

According to Microsoft sources, Windows 95 Fat-16– and Fat-32–based operating systems will be functional through the year 2108. Using two digit shorthand for the calendar year in Access 95 and 97 will allow your applications to be viable through 2109. Access 95 and 97 have the theoretical ability to function through the year 9999, if you use four-digit year numbers.

As you can see, standalone Access 97 users should have no trouble working with their database applications from within the Access 97 environment. The problem will be for the systems external to Access 97. With so much distributed computing across LAN, WAN, and media such as the Internet, the task of keeping all of these integrated systems in sync is a major obstacle.

We recommend watching for technical articles and product enhancements from Microsoft and other major ISVs in order to stay on top of this issue.

Summary

The Access 97 development environment has a lot to offer even the most serious developer. With Visual Basic outgrowing its desktop application development role and establishing itself as a viable enterprise development platform, tools such as Access 97 and Office 97 will grow ever more popular.

II

PART

Programming the Access 97 Primary Components

Access 97 Tables

by Tony Gigliotti

IN THIS CHAPTER

This chapter provides information on the development, design, creation, and implementation of tables using Access 97. It begins by discussing the relevant points in determining the tables needed for a database application. Next, the chapter discusses the different table views supported under Access 97.

The chapter then considers issues around importing and linking tables and explores the basic elements in creating fields in tables. Included in this discussion are general table properties and the various data types and properties supported within Access 97.

After delving into how table fields are created, the chapter looks at primary keys and the creation of relationships among tables. Included in this discussion is a definition of referential integrity and the rules required to enforce it. The chapter concludes with some examples taken from the Northwind sample database. These examples include the use of validation rules and validation text properties, the use of the input mask property, and the use of the Lookup Wizard to provide end users with a list of data to choose from when entering information into a table.

Designing and Normalizing Tables

The first step in designing and developing a successful Access 97 application is to create tables. Everything going into the database and everything retrieved from the database must first be in a table. Determine all the information desired for the database before trying to divide it into tables. This process helps you figure out how many tables to create, what relationships to create, and how the tables will interact with the other objects in your database.

Designing Tables

It is always good practice to design the tables in hard copy form before trying to create them in Access. I prefer to do a complete table diagram before actually creating the database. I have found it easier to establish the tables and their relationships on paper before creating them electronically so that no fields, tables, or relationships are left out inadvertently.

Once you have determined generally which tables you need, you should also go through the process of normalizing them, to at least Third Normal Form.

Normalizing Tables

There are three good reasons to normalize the tables you create: size, efficiency, and ease of updates. The size of your database can grow rapidly if you allow data to be duplicated unnecessarily. This can make it difficult to retrieve accurate data if the duplicated data is updated in one table and not updated in another. To control the size of your database, try to make all the data in each table unique to that table. There is only one reason you should have any duplicate data in any of your tables, and that is to keep a history of what transpires in your database. For example, say you send out an invoice to a customer, and then your MIS department decides to change the description of one of the line items on that invoice in your Item master table. You will not be able to reprint that exact invoice later because the information no longer exists in the same form.

How lax or how strict you must be in defining your information depends on the rules governing your business. If your product line does not change very much, the need to record everything exactly as it happens diminishes greatly. Because creating an exact copy of an invoice record is more costly to program, store, and maintain, the benefits of such duplication are far outweighed by the detriments.

That's the case for controlling the size of your database. With the size of the database at a minimum, using normalization to ensure efficiency and ease of updates should be obvious.

Here are a few simple rules to remember about normalization:

- Pare your fields (data elements) down to their simplest forms. Never put more than one thing in one field. For example, street address, city, state, and ZIP code should never be bundled into one field called `Address`. That is considered bad style because you typically want to access each of those pieces of information separately. On the other hand, you can over-normalize your database. You don't need to store an area code, for example, separate from the rest of a phone number unless your application requires it. As a rule of thumb, if you find you are always concatenating two fields that you never need to process individually, they probably belong together.

- Only group fields that relate to each other into a table. For example, putting an order number in the customer table is not a good idea. That would mean that a customer could have only one order, and how many businesses would stay in business if that were the case?

- Add some dummy records to your tables. This helps to show any defects in the design of the tables and makes it easier to spot them. If you get repeated data or no data in some fields, those fields should be moved to an appropriate table. For example, you might create a database to keep information about school students and add a field to each record to indicate which students are veterans. Not all the students will be veterans, however, so it makes more sense to move that information to a separate, related table. Leaving the field in every record in one table would leave a lot of empty fields—not an efficient way of storing the data.

- Keep indexes to a minimum. Indexes should be placed on any field or group of fields that you sort, join, or search by. This speeds up data retrieval. In a multiuser environment, however, indexes can slow down changes to table data because Access must update all indexes across the network that point to the indexed field. This does not mean you should never use indexes. It just means you should not create any indexes you will not use. For example, you can create an index on a `ZipCode` field, but if you are not going to sort, join, or search by that field, the index will just slow you down.

Go into any table and add a field called `TableID`. Save it and look at your indexes. Notice that Access created an index for the new field. By default, Access creates a new index for every field you add or every table you import that starts or ends with `ID`, `KEY`, `CODE`, or `NUM`. This is very helpful in most cases. If you have a field called `number`, Access makes an index for you automatically. You can change this by selecting Tools | Options from the Access menu bar and clicking the Tables/Queries tab. The `Autoindex on Import/Create` property lets you change the character patterns for this new feature to reflect your naming conventions, or you can delete them totally.

Once you have the determined how many tables you need and what their design should look like, you can enter the Access 97 development environment and begin creating the tables.

Table Views

Access 97 provides two views of tables: Datasheet View and Design View. Datasheet View allows you to view the actual data in the table. Design View shows you the fields and field properties of a table. Most table development in Access 97 occurs in Design View.

Datasheet View

The Table Datasheet View allows you to view the raw data in each table. Each field name appears at the top of the view, with the raw data it contains shown below. In Datasheet View it is possible to add, delete, and edit data.

Design View

The Table Design View is where the basic construction of a table takes place. Figure 4.1 shows what this view looks like. You can use any field name you want. Make sure that the field name selected is short and easily identifiable because these names are used throughout Access 97 development. The field name should also be long enough to easily identify the field associated with it.

There is a limited number of data types that you can use in creating a table. The available data types include Text, Memo, Number, Date/Time, Currency, AutoNumber, Yes/No, OLE Object, and Hyperlink. A complete listing and description of the data types, along with the properties and values associated with each, follow later in this chapter. Figure 4.1 shows the Design View of the `Employees` table contained in the sample `Northwind` database.

FIGURE 4.1.

The Employees *table in Design View.*

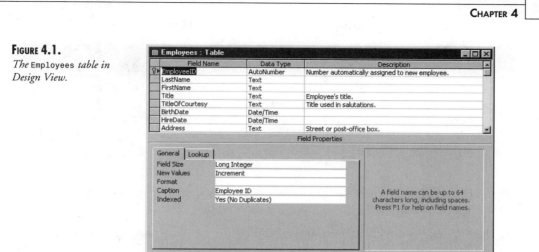

Table Wizard

The Table Wizard allows you to select the fields to include in a new table from a list of pre-defined tables. The predefined tables are broken into two categories: business and personal. The wizard walks you through the creation of a unique table based on the sample fields in each of these predefined tables. You can select multiple fields from multiple tables, and the wizard will create the table based on your selections.

> **TIP**
>
> The Table Wizard is a great tool for starting a table. It cuts down on the typing and setting up of your fields. It is a good idea to use the Table Wizard to start your table and then go into Design View and make any changes needed.

To invoke the Table Wizard, move to the Tables tab in the main database window and select New. On the list of available choices provided, select Table Wizard. The Table Wizard then starts and prompts you for the information it needs.

Import Table

Access 97 allows you to import the following types of tables: Microsoft Access (all versions), text files, Microsoft Excel, HTML documents, dBASE III, dBASE IV, dBASE 5, Microsoft FoxPro, Microsoft FoxPro 3.0, Paradox, or tables from any database structure with a 32-bit ODBC driver. Once you select the file containing the table, Access 97 prompts for the actual database objects that are to be imported. You can select to import relationships, menus and toolbars, Import/Export Specs, Definitions and Data, or Definitions Only. When importing queries, Access 97 allows you to import them as queries or as tables. To specify which import options to use, select the Options button on the Import Objects window.

> **TIP**
>
> It is always a good idea to try once to import a table from another application to see what questions Access 97 needs answered and what final output you can expect. Then you usually need to go into the original application and modify the table to be imported to make the best "fit" for the new Access 97 table. You do not need to do this if the table is already in an Access format.

There are two ways to import a table in Access 97: by using the Import option or by using the Import Table Wizard.

To import a table using the Import option, select File | Get External Data | Import from the menu bar. Once the table has been imported, Access 97 displays it in the Tables tab of the main database window.

To import a table using the Import Table Wizard, move to the Tables tab in the main database window and click the New command button. From the list of choices provided, select Import Table. Access 97 then provides a standard file-selection window. Find the file that contains the table you want to import. When you select the file, Access 97 provides a list of the tables available for import. Click on the table you want to import, and Access 97 imports it into the open database.

> **WARNING**
>
> You may need extra drivers to import some tables. Microsoft Access supplies most of the major drivers. If you can't import a table, you may need to contact the appropriate vendor for the latest 32-bit ODBC drivers that meet ODBC Level 1 specifications. Each ODBC driver has specific requirements for installing and setting up data sources.

Link Table

Access 97 allows you to link tables from another database when developing the database application. You do not have as many options when linking a table as you do when importing a table. When linking, you are only afforded the option of selecting the table to be linked.

There are two ways to link a table in Access 97: by using the Link Tables option or by using the Import Table Wizard.

To link using the Link Tables option, select File | Get External Data | Link Tables from the menu bar. Once the table has been linked, Access 97 displays it in the Tables tab of the main database window. You can identify a linked table by the icon associated with it.

To link a table using the Link Table Wizard, move to the Tables tab in the main database window and click the New command button. From the list of choices provided, select Link Table. Access 97 then provides a standard file-selection window. Find the file that contains the table you want to link. When you have selected the file, Access 97 provides a list of the available tables. Click on the table you want to link, and Access 97 links it to the open database.

Access doesn't care whether you run queries on linked or local tables. The location or type of table is transparent to you. You can create an Access query from an Excel spreadsheet of accounts and a dBASE table of clients and link them together in Access without knowing what they are or even where they are coming from. This is called a *heterogeneous join*.

Deciding Whether to Import or Link a Table

The decision whether to import or link a table should be made on the basis of how the table will be used in relation to the database. Importing data creates a copy of the table in the new Access 97 database. Linking a table allows you to read and, in most cases, update data in the external data source. Linking a table does not change the format of the original table, and the table can still be used with the program that created it. However, if the data in a linked table is modified in the Access 97 application, the external data changes in the other program as well.

Linking a table is an excellent choice when you are in the process of migrating from another database to an Access 97 database. You can link the table during beta testing of the Access 97 application and, upon final implementation, import the table so the Access 97 application can stand on its own when the other application is phased out. That way, the final implementation of the Access 97 application will contain the most recent data from the other application.

General Table Properties

Each table has a set of general properties that you can set. To view these properties, open the table in Design View and either click the Properties button on the toolbar or select Properties from the View menu bar.

The settings for the properties affect the entire table. The Description property provides information about the table in the database window. The table's description appears in the Description column in the Details View of the database window. A linked table shows the path and table type in this property.

The Validation Rule for a table is best used when importing data into the table and the data needs to be checked for consistency before being imported. The Validation Text is simply the text that appears when the Validation Rule is broken. If the Validation Text is not included, Access 97 uses generic text to report a validation rule error. The Filter property for a table allows you to filter table data before displaying it. The Order By property sets the order by which the data in a table is displayed.

Data Types and Properties

When setting the fields to be included in a data table, Access 97 allows you to set certain properties associated with each field. This section describes the properties that can be set when creating fields. Access 97 provides for the following data types: Text, Memo, Number, Date/Time, Currency, AutoNumber, Yes/No, OLE Object, and Hyperlink. The specific properties for each data type are different.

Each data type may have different properties associated with it. The properties for each data type appear on the lower half of the screen used to select the data type for a particular field. For example, suppose you want to create a new table. Select New Table on the Tables tab in the main database window. When the Design View of the table appears, enter the name of the first field. Select the data type. The properties associated with this type appear automatically in the lower half of the window.

Field Size

Field size is important to the program from a physical space perspective. The larger the size, the more physical space that Access 97 must allocate to the field. The Text data type can hold 0 to 255 characters. The Memo data type can hold up to 64,000 characters. For the Number data type, the storage size allocated for each field size is seen in Table 4.1. Incorrectly estimating your number field sizes can cost you a lot of hard drive space. If you need a field to store a number from 1 to 100 and you used a Double instead of a Byte, every 150,000 records will cost you approximately 1MB of space. That is an awful lot for just one mistake in one table.

Table 4.1. Storage size for data types.

Setting	Description	Decimal precision	Storage size
Byte	Stores numbers from 0 to 255 (no fractions).	None	1 byte
Integer	Stores numbers from -32,768 to 32,767 (no fractions).	None	2 bytes
Long Integer	(Default) Stores numbers from -2,147,483,648 to 2,147,483,647 (no fractions).	None	4 bytes
Single	Stores numbers from -3.402823E38 to -1.401298E45 for negative values and from 1.401298E45 to 3.402823E38 for positive values.	7	4 bytes

Setting	Description	Decimal precision	Storage size
Double	Stores numbers from -1.79769313486231E308 to -4.94065645841247E324 for negative values and from 1.79769313486231E308 to 4.94065645841247E324 for positive values.	15	8 bytes
Replication ID	Globally unique identifier (GUID)	N/A	16 bytes

Format

The Format property is used to display data in a field in a specific format; it does not affect the way the data is stored in a table. For example, if the Format property of a text field is (@@@) @@@-@@@@, to represent a phone number, and the user enters 0123456789, the data will be displayed as (012) 345-6789. However, the data in the table is still stored as 0123456789. To force the data to be stored in a particular format, use the Input Mask property.

Input Mask

The Input Mask property forces the literal characters used in the mask into the actual data entered. For example, if the Input Mask property is set to (___) ___-____, Access forces any string of 10 characters into this specific format for storage in the table. If the user enters 0123456789, the data in the table will be stored as (012) 345-6789.

The input mask definition can contain up to three sections separated by semicolons. The first section is the input mask. The second section determines whether to store the literal display characters. The third section is the character that is displayed for blanks in the input mask.

If a definition is set in both the Format property and the Input Mask property, Access uses the Input Mask property setting when adding or editing data, and the Format property setting when displaying the data. When using both the Format and Input Mask properties, be careful to avoid a conflict between the settings for each of them.

Caption

The Caption property is used for the column headings for a field in the table or a query in the Datasheet View. The Caption property is a string containing up to 2,048 characters. If a field is dragged from a field list, the Caption property follows as the label for the field.

Default Value

The Default Value property is simply the default setting for a particular field. For example, if the default value of a City field is set to New York, every new record created containing the City field is predefined as New York unless other data is specifically entered. This property is useful for predefining commonly used fields as they are created, so that the user does not have to enter the same information each time.

Validation Rule

The Validation Rule property for a field allows you to set rules for entering data into a specific field. This is very useful for limiting what a user can put in a particular field. For example, you can limit a number to between 1 and 100 or a date to earlier than today's date. As the user enters data, Access checks the Validation Rule before allowing the user to leave the field if you set the Validation Rule property at the field level. You also can use the Validation Rule property at the record level, preventing the user from leaving the record until bad data has been corrected. Record-level validation is specified in the Table property sheet; field-level validation is specified in the Field property page. If the Validation Rule is broken, Access displays an error message describing the problem. If the problem is not fixed, Access does not save the data. Here is an example of good record-level validation:

```
[DueDate]=[InvoiceDate]+15
```

You could use this code to compare values from one field to another. Now, here is an example of good field-level validation:

```
<=Date()
```

You could use this code to make sure that no user puts a date in that is later than today's date.

Validation Text

The Validation Text property is the message displayed when a validation rule is broken. If the validation rule requires that a number contain nine characters and the user enters only eight, the Validation Text property value appears when the user tries to save the data. If a validation rule has been set but no validation text has been set, Access displays a generic error message that the validation rule has been broken but does not provide any further explanation. Because of this, you should always set the Validation Text property when you set the Validation Rule property. You can set the Validation Text property at the field level and at the record level. You put the appropriate message on the appropriate Validation Text property.

Required

The Required property can be set to either yes or no. This property requires a user to enter data into the field before the record can be saved. In other words, a null value cannot be entered in a field if the Required property is set to yes.

Allow Zero Length

The `Allow Zero Length` property applies to the text, memo, and hyperlink data types. If this property is set to yes, an empty string can be entered into the field.

Indexed

The `Indexed` property can have the following values: `No`, `Yes (duplicates OK)`, and `Yes (no duplicates)`. Setting the `Indexed` property to yes speeds up queries based on the indexed field as well as sorting and grouping on this field. The index is automatically updated when the table is saved.

Decimal Places

The `Decimal Places` property is straightforward. This property is available for the Number and AutoNumber data types. The value for this property can be set by the user or set for `auto`. If the `Decimal Places` property is set for `auto`, Access uses the setting specified in the `Format` property of the data type. If the user has defined the number of decimal places, Access uses that number. The setting for a user-defined decimal place can be between 0 and 15.

New Values

The `New Values` property is only available for the AutoNumber data type. You can choose to have the new value of the AutoNumber be either `incremental` or `random`. If the `New Values` property is set to `incremental`, each new record is assigned in sequential order starting with 1. If the `New Values` property is set to `random`, Access randomly assigns a long integer value to the new record.

Primary Keys

Access databases are built on the relational database model. Because of this, each table must contain a field that uniquely identifies each record in the table. When creating a table in Access, you must specify a primary key. Upon exiting a table where no primary key has been specified, Access prompts you to specify a primary key or allow Access to create one. If Access creates the primary key, a new `AutoNumber` field is added to the table.

The primary key speeds up Access's ability to find a field in a given table. If a primary key is specified for a table, Access automatically checks the field for null values and duplicate values. Neither null values nor duplicate values are allowed in a primary key.

Primary keys are the main way for you to establish relationships between tables in a single database. Access allows for the creation of `AutoNumber` primary keys, single primary keys, or multiple primary keys in a table.

Relationships

Defining the relationships between tables in a database tells Access how each table should communicate and share data. Relationships are established between the primary keys in each table. It is not required for every table to have a relationship with another. Access allows you to create one-to-one, one-to-many, or many-to-many relationships. To create a relationship, choose Tools | Relationships. The Relationships window for the Northwind database is displayed in Figure 4.2.

FIGURE 4.2.

Northwind
relationships.

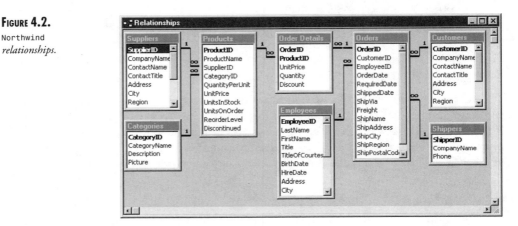

The primary keys in each table appear in boldface type. To create a relationship, click on the primary key and drag it to the table where the corresponding identifier resides. The window shown in Figure 4.3 appears.

FIGURE 4.3.

*The relationship
creation window.*

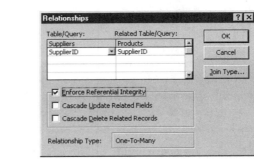

In this example from the Northwind database, a relationship is created between the SupplierID field in the Suppliers table and the SupplierID field in the Products table. After creating a relationship, click the Join Type button to tell Access what type of relationship is needed. Figure 4.4 shows the window used for selecting the type of relationship desired.

FIGURE 4.4.
*Selecting the type
of relationship.*

Select 1 to establish a one-to-one relationship. Select 2 to establish a one-to-many relationship from the Products table to the Suppliers table. Select 3 to establish a one-to-many relationship from the Suppliers table to the Products table.

One-to-One Relationships

A one-to-one relationship should be established when there is only one matching record in each table. One reason to establish a one-to-one relationship is to split a table because its size has become unmanageable. Another reason to create a one-to-one relationship is to split a table for security reasons to remove sensitive data to a more protected table. Also, you might want to store similar data in two different tables to speed up querying, grouping, and sorting functions.

One-to-Many Relationships

Most relationships are one-to-many relationships. This type of relationship is characterized by one unique field in one table relating to many like fields in another table. For example, there is one unique SupplierID in the Suppliers table of the Northwind database. Each supplier could be providing numerous different products, so the SupplierID field in the Products table could have many like SupplierIDs. A one-to-many relationship would establish a relationship between the SupplierID field in the Suppliers table and the SupplierID field in the Products table. Once the relationship is established, it becomes unnecessary to enter all the supplier information for each product in the Products table. The relationship ties the two tables together, so it is only necessary to include the SupplierID in the Products table.

Many-to-Many Relationships

A many-to-many relationship is really two one-to-many relationships with a third table. A many-to-many relationship is only necessary when you are trying to relate multiple records in one table to multiple records in another table. The only way to establish a many-to-many relationship is to create a third table with the foreign keys of the two original tables. The foreign keys are one or more table fields consisting of the primary keys from the other tables. The foreign keys must be identical to the primary keys in each table.

Referential Integrity

Referential integrity is used to ensure that the relationships between records in related tables are valid and that related data is not accidentally deleted or changed when the original data is deleted or changed by the user or programmer.

In order for referential integrity to work properly, certain conditions must be met. The primary table must include a matching field that is a primary key or a unique index. The fields where referential integrity is to be applied must have the same data type. Microsoft has allowed for two exceptions to this last condition. The first applies where an AutoNumber field is related to a number field. In this case, the Field Size property must be set to a long integer in both fields. The second exception applies where an AutoNumber field is related to a number field and the Field Size property is set to replication ID in both.

The final condition for getting referential integrity to work properly is that both tables containing the matching fields must be in the same Microsoft Access database. Linked tables will work if they both are in Microsoft Access format and both are open when referential integrity is set.

To enforce referential integrity, additional rules must be observed. There must be a value in the primary key in the primary table before a value can be entered in the foreign key field of the related table. In addition, records cannot be deleted from the primary table if matching records are in the related table. Finally, primary keys in the primary table cannot be changed if there is a related key in the related table.

Optimize General Table Performance

Once your tables and relationships have been created, Microsoft provides some helpful tips in optimizing the performance of the tables. One way to optimize the performance is to use the Performance Analyzer on specific tables in the database. To use the Performance Analyzer, choose Tools | Analyze. On the Analyze menu, choose Table to have Access 97 analyze the basic table structure for any defects. Choose Performance to have Access 97 analyze the performance of your tables and your database as a whole. The Access 97 Help files describe additional ways to enhance the performance of tables in an Access 97 database application.

The next section looks at some of the sample tables in the Northwind sample database to see how to create tables and how to set some of the properties associated with some of the data types.

Validation Rule/Validation Text Example

A good example of how the Validation Rule and Validation Text properties work can be found in the Employees table of the Northwind database. Figure 4.5 shows the properties associated with the BirthDate field in the Employees table.

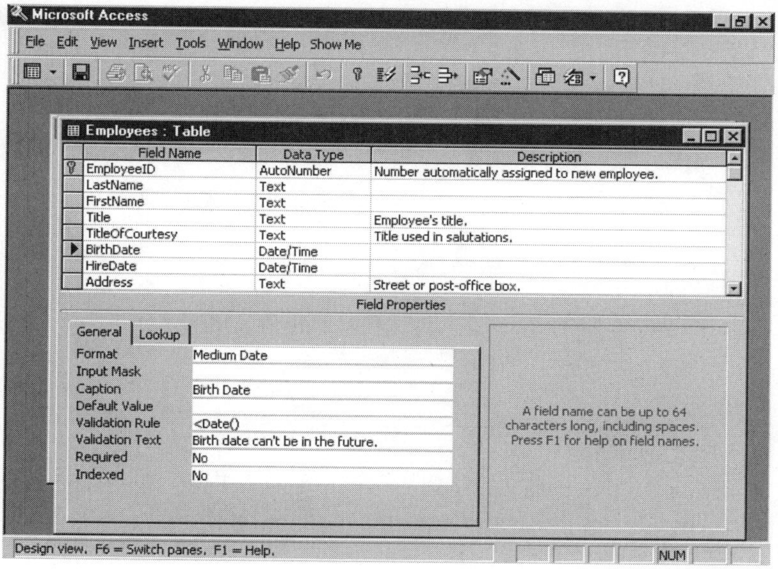

FIGURE 4.5.

The Employees *table* BirthDate *field's properties.*

The validation rule is set to ensure that any date entered into this field is earlier than the current date. If an attempt is made to enter either today's date or a future date, Access displays a window explaining that the rule has been violated (see Figure 4.6).

FIGURE 4.6.

The BirthDate *field validation rule violation window.*

When the user clicks the OK button, Access allows him or her to re-enter the date. If the new date violates the validation rule, the error message appears again. After three user attempts at entering an invalid date, Access tells the user that the data in the field cannot be saved, but the user is allowed to continue entering other data.

Input Mask Example

An example of using the Input Mask property of a Text data type can be seen in the Customers table for the CustomerID field. This input mask establishes a unique five-character identifier for a customer based on the customer name. Figure 4.7 shows the properties associated with the CustomerID field in the Customers table of the Northwind sample database.

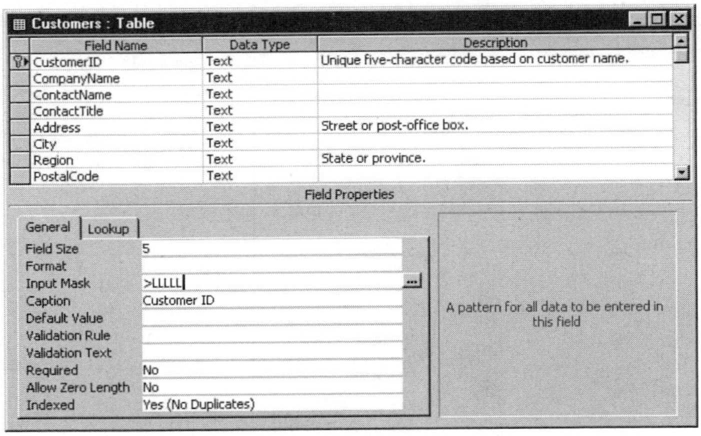

FIGURE 4.7.

The CustomerID *field's properties.*

Note that the Input Mask property is set to >LLLLL. The > sign forces the characters into upper-case. The L forces the user to type in five characters between A and Z.

Lookup Properties Example

Access 97 also allows you to create fields that display either of two kinds of lists to make data entry simpler. These lists can display values that resulted from a table lookup or query, or from a set of fixed values that were created when the field was created. The ProductID field in the Order Details table of the Northwind sample database is an example of a lookup list that dis-plays the values in an existing table or query. Figure 4.8 shows the lookup field properties for the ProductID field in the Order Details table.

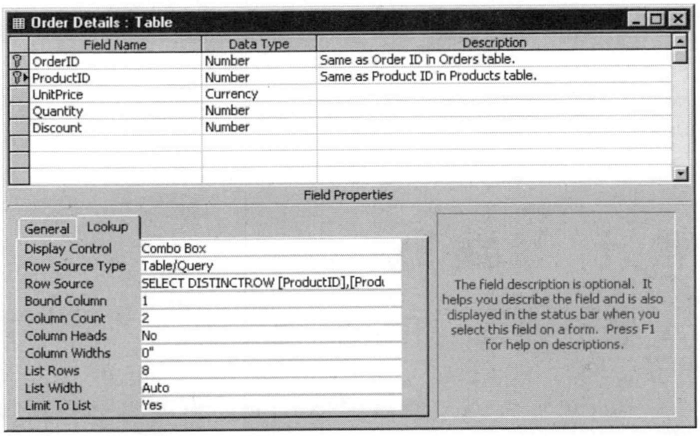

FIGURE 4.8.

Order Details *table* ProductID *lookup field properties.*

In the lookup properties, the Display property has been set to a combo box. Other choices for the Display property include a text box or a list box. The record source is set to Table/Query. The row source contains the following SQL statement:

```
SELECT DISTINCTROW [ProductID],[ProductName] FROM Products ORDER BY [ProductName];
```

This statement tells Access 97 to retrieve the ProductID and ProductName fields from the Products table and sort them based on the ProductName field. The Bound column property is set to 1. This tells Access 97 to bind the field to the ProductID value selected in the combo box. Notice that the ColumnWidths property has been set to 0. This allows Access to hide the ProductID field from view when accessing the ProductID combo box field in Datasheet View. Figure 4.9 shows the results of this lookup field when the table is opened in Datasheet View.

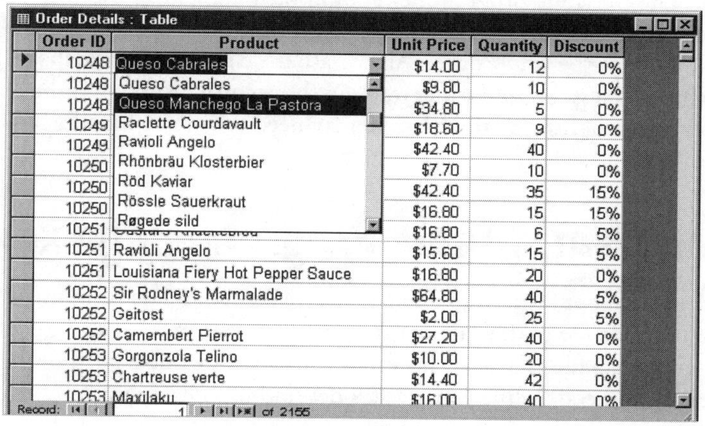

FIGURE 4.9.
The ProductID *lookup field in Datasheet View.*

Using a lookup field in a table allows the user to more easily enter data based on the lookup field properties. Rather than having to know the ProductIDs for every entry, the user can select a ProductID by simply knowing the product name.

Table Programming Tips

Envision your database. Know what you are trying to accomplish. It is your job as a database programmer to know the problems and provide a solution. Example: Suppose you have a client who has an Access database that keeps track of sales in a small TV store. He has a problem with applying the right amount of tax on a sale. The database works correctly until he sells a service and a TV on the same order. The state he is in does not allow taxes to be collected on services. Looking at his database, you conclude that the previous developer has applied the tax percentage on the whole order and not to each line item within the order. You have defined the problem. Now you have to supply a solution. One solution to this problem is to remove the tax percent field from the order table and move it to the order line item table. Now when your client sells a service and a TV on one order, you know that each line item will get its own tax percentage. This example illustrates one of the biggest issues in database programming: normalizing your tables correctly. The previous developer did not think the problem all the way through, and the client did not find the problem until he sold a TV with a service.

Always give your design a final walk-through before moving on to other tasks. You should have something in mind when you do this. In the preceding example, the previous developer could have walked through the tables with taxes in mind. This is done simply by looking at the structures of the tables that affect taxes and making sure that the fields are in the correct tables. The client should be able to explain what he needs. Use your resources to your advantage and not to your disadvantage. The client usually knows what he needs, and with his help when reviewing his methods of getting the job done, you should be able to provide a solution to the problem. The previous programmer should have looked at the way the client did his business before laying out the table designs. He would have seen that the client did not apply a tax percentage to the whole order. Always ask the client to provide the forms and reports he uses to run his business. His old paper trail can show you a lot about his business. You usually will find other pieces of information that he may need to collect, like the serial numbers of the TVs he sells.

Real-World Table Programming Example

In multiuser applications, you need to separate your data from the rest of your code. You then link the code file to the data file. You give everyone a copy of the code file and let them link to the same data file. This allows everyone to use the same data. The biggest problem with dividing data and code while you are still developing is having your client start to enter data in the data file when you discover you need to add or delete a field. This is what we discuss in this section.

Look on the CD-ROM that accompanies this book for a file called Chapter 4.MDB. This file contains some sample code that we can walk through. Open the database, and open the frmAddField form (see Figure 4.10). Let's set the scene. You are the programmer in charge of some database. You are almost through with building the database, and you let the client begin to enter valuable data. Suddenly you realize that you forgot a field and it needs to be added to the data side of the database. What do you do? The data file is 60MB+ in size and does not fit on a floppy. You can ask the client to back up the file and mail it to you so you can fix it and mail it back, but that is not very professional and will cause a lot of downtime for your client. You can walk the client through adding the field to the table, but that might be beyond his level of expertise. No, you need to make the change through code, and then when the user runs the code file, it will do the work for you.

FIGURE 4.10.

Form view of
frmAddField.

For test purposes, run another session of Access 97 and make a blank database in your root directory called C:\DB1.MDB. (It is OK to have two or more Access programs running at the same time.) Add a table named Table1 with a field called This is a test. Now, switch over to Chapter 4.MDB and, in the text box labeled Path and File Name on the form frmAddField, type the path and filename for the database you just made. Type Table1 in the Table Name text box. Enter the field name Memo Field and choose the field type Memo. Make sure that you are not in Design View of the table in the other session of Access 97 that is running and click the Add Field button on the form. Now go look at Table1 in DB1.MDB in Design View. Your table should look like Figure 4.11.

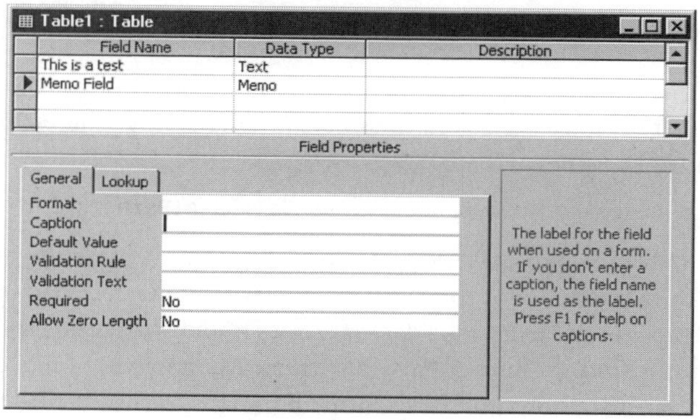

FIGURE 4.11.

Design View of Table1
after update.

Let's walk through the code that makes this work:

```
Public Function AddAField(Path As String, TableName As String,
➡FieldName As String, FieldType As String)
On Error GoTo err_AddAField

    Dim DB As Database
    Dim Mytable As TableDef
    Dim MyField As Field

    Set DB = DBEngine.Workspaces(0).OpenDatabase(Path)
    Set Mytable = DB.TableDefs(TableName)
    Set MyField = Mytable.CreateField(FieldName, FieldType)
    Mytable.Fields.Append MyField
    MsgBox "Done"

exit_AddAField:
    Exit Function
```

4

ACCESS 97 TABLES

```
err_AddAField:
    MsgBox Error
    Resume exit_AddAField
    End Function
```

The first thing that has to be done, which does not appear in the preceding listing, is to make sure that the text boxes on the form have data in them before you can proceed. Then the values on the form are passed to the function AddAField(). There are four arguments required for this function: Path, TableName, FieldName, and FieldType. (Do not get confused by the names of these arguments. I made them up when I wrote the function.)

> **TIP**
>
> Sometimes things in code look like they are part of Access when they were actually made up by the developer. This is one of the points that I am trying to convey. To tell easily whether something is a standard part of Access or, as in this case, a made-up entity, put your cursor on the object in question and press F1. If the entity is part of Access, you get help on it. If it is not part of Access, you get the message Keyword Not Found.

Notice that the first thing that happens in the preceding code is that all the variables are used with Dim. This makes space in memory to temporarily store values that you will need later in your code. The line

```
Set DB = DBEngine.Workspaces(0).OpenDatabase(Path)
```

opens a database and sets it equal to the variable DB. This is so you can refer to the database by DB, which makes it easier to program. Access looks for the database listed in the variable Path and attempts to open it. If the database does not exist, Access reports an error and tells you that it could not find the file. If Path is correct, Access gives you access to the database's objects. You can do just about anything to the database you want to—add database objects, rename them, or even delete them if you have the appropriate security clearance to do so. Next, the tableDef variable and the Field variable are set to what was specified on the form, and the code attempts to Append MyField. Notice I said "attempts." If there is any reason that this cannot be done (like the field already exists), Access reports an error through the function's built-in error-trapping capability.

You can do many things in code to tables. Let's look at the next example in Chapter 4.MDB. Open the frmAddAndDeleteField form. You can see that it is very similar to the other form. The difference is the extra button, Delete Field. This button runs another function that deletes a field from a table in another database. This function is called DeleteAField(). Type the information from Figure 4.11 into this form and click the Delete Field button. It removes the field you just put in.

TIP

Run two copies of Access. One is `Chapter 4.MDB` and the other is `C:\DB1.MDB`. That way you do not have to open and close your databases, which will slow you down when you go back and forth checking what is going on within Access 97. In Win95, the memory management is enhanced to allow you to run multiple copies of Access much more efficiently. It is common to run four or five copies of your application to test things like locking.

Now test this code on other databases and see how it reacts to other fields in other tables.

CAUTION

These deletions are permanent. Do not try this on any database that has valuable data in it—or you will quickly learn how valuable it is to back up your database!

If you tested well enough, you will find that you cannot delete a field that is part of an index. To get around this problem, type this code in the function `DeleteAField()` under the line `Set Mytable = DB.TableDefs(TableName)`:

```
'Loop through all the indexes and remove
'it if MyField Participates in it.
    Dim indLoop As Integer
    Dim IndFldLoop As Integer
    Dim MyIndex As Index
    Dim i As Integer

    i = 0
    Do Until i = 1
        i = 1
        For indLoop = 0 To Mytable.Indexes.Count - 1
            IndFldLoop = 0
            For IndFldLoop = 0 To Mytable.Indexes(indLoop).Fields.Count - 1
                If FieldName = Mytable.Indexes(indLoop).Fields(IndFldLoop).
➥Name Then
                    Set MyIndex = Mytable.Indexes(indLoop)
                    Mytable.Indexes.Delete MyIndex.Name
                    i = 0
                    Exit For
                End If
            Next IndFldLoop
            Exit For
        Next indLoop
    Loop
```

This code is not in the `Chapter.MDB file`. It is left out so you can get comfortable editing a function that in turn edits a table in a database you specify. The first step is getting into the function and starting the process of updating the existing code. The hardest part is starting. Most people worry about messing up the function to where it is unusable. If you do so, don't worry about it. Just get another copy off the CD-ROM and start over. Go to the database container and click the Modules tab. Select the `basEditTables` module and click the Design button. Go to the Procedure combo box and select the `DeleteAField()` function. Type in the preceding code under the `Line Set Mytable = DB.TableDefs(TableName)`, and then compile and save the function. Now try to delete a field that participates in an index. You should be able to, if you have typed in everything correctly.

Congratulations! You can now write functions that edit a table's structure. You can even set other properties of fields like the `Size`, `Required Y/N`, or even the `Indexed` property. You cannot edit some properties through Data Access Object (DAO). You can't edit the `Format`, `Decimal Places`, `Input Mask`, or `Caption` properties. This a limitation of the DAO environment. You may have noticed that if you try to delete a field that participates in a relationship, Access reports an error. You must delete the relationships that the field is in, delete the indexes, and finally delete the field itself. This can be done with the `Relations` object.

Summary

This chapter provided the necessary information for you to design, create, and implement tables in Access 97. Once you create the tables, you have the basic structure of the database done. This is the most important part of developing applications in Access 97. The rest of the development is easier as long as the tables and their relationships have been created properly. Now we are ready to discuss the queries needed for the application, and how to design and create them in Access 97.

Access 97 Queries

by Scott Billings

IN THIS CHAPTER

CHAPTER 5

Introduction

Queries are the fundamental vehicle in which data is retrieved for display in an Access 97 database. There are numerous ways to create queries in Access 97. The most common way to create a query is in the Access 97 Query Design View. While this is the most common way, Access 97 also provides a number of query wizards to help in the creation of queries. These wizards include the Select query, the Crosstab query, the Find Duplicate query, and the Find Unmatched query. While using the wizards can help in the creation of queries, using the Design View to modify a query created by a wizard is almost always necessary.

There are three development environments to create queries in Access 97. The first is to use the Access 97 Query Design View development environment. The second way to create a query is to write SQL statements in the SQL View in the query design windows. The third way is to use the query builder for individual controls located on Access 97 forms and reports. All methods work well.

This chapter defines the different types of queries supported within Access 97 and how to use the query wizards in Access 97 to aid in the initial steps of query creation. It then discusses the Query Design View and the objects and properties associated with creating queries manually.

 The chapter then discusses the creation of queries by providing examples from the Northwind and Query_Sample databases provided on the enclosed CD-ROM. I conclude this chapter with a look at the basic Structured Query Language (SQL) expressions and the syntax used when creating SQL statements. At the end of the chapter is a brief discussion of some specific SQL-type methodologies available in Access 97.

Query Types

There are three basic types of queries in Access 97. The most common type of query is the Select query. However, Access 97 provides programmers with the use of Crosstab queries and Action queries. The Action queries available in Access 97 are the Make-table query, the Update query, the Append query, and the delete query. In addition, Access 97 supports the creation of Parameter queries that allow the user to input certain parameters used by the query. Each of these queries will be discussed in the following sections.

Select Query

The most common type of query is a Select query. Using specified criteria, a Select query retrieves data from one or more tables and then displays this data. The Select query allows you to retrieve selected data for display in either controls, forms, or reports. It is often used to populate a combo box or list box field.

Crosstab Query

A Crosstab query is like a spreadsheet. This query allows functions to be performed on a field in a table. These functions include average, count, standard deviation, sum, and so on. The information is then grouped by one set of factors down the left side of the spreadsheet and another set of factors over the top of the spreadsheet. A good example of the Crosstab query in the Northwind database is the Quarterly Orders by Product query. This query will be discussed in detail in the "Quarterly Orders by Product Example" section later in this chapter.

Action Queries

As the name would explain, an Action query is a query that carries out a specific action in addition to the retrieval of data. There are four types of Action queries supported in Access 97. These queries include the Make-table query, the Update query, the Append query, and the Delete query.

Make-Table Query

A Make-table query can be used to archive records, make backup copies of tables, or make copies to export to another database or to use as a basis for reports that display data for a particular time period. This query can be made in one of two ways: through a direct SQL statement using the following syntax or by using the Access 97 Design View development environment.

The SQL syntax to be used for a Make-table query is as follows:

```
SELECT field1[, field2[, ...]]
INTO newtable [IN externaldatabase]
FROM source
```

To create a Make-table query in the Access 97 Design View, click the toolbar item used to define the query type. Figure 5.1 shows the drop-down menu available for selecting the query type to be used.

> **NOTE**
>
> Note that any of the standard queries supported by Access 97 can be created using this toolbar item.

FIGURE 5.1.

The query type menu.

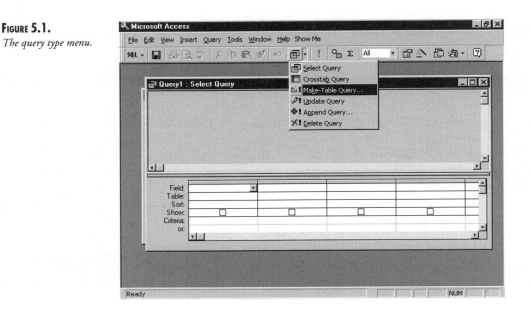

Update Query

An Update query makes global changes to a group of records in one or more tables. You can also use an Update query to change data in existing tables. You can create this query in the same fashion noted previously, by clicking the toolbar item used to define the query type.

A good example of how to use this query is in a help desk call-handling application. Suppose the form used to enter calls in this application also displays the total calls received and the total calls outstanding. This calculation would need to be made after every call is entered. A normal form will not do this calculation until the form is opened and the total calls at that time are displayed. To give this operation a more real-time appearance, use an Update query to update the table when the user clicks to save the information just entered. The Update query would then change the actual data in the table to reflect the newly entered information.

Append Query

An Append query adds a group of records from one or more tables to the end of one or more tables. Examples of the Make-table query and the Append query follow later in the "Creating Make-Table and Append Queries" section.

Delete Query

A Delete query deletes a group of records from one or more tables. Delete queries always delete entire records, not just selected fields within records.

Query Wizards

Rather than creating queries directly, Access 97 includes several wizards that walk you through the first steps of creating many queries. Experience has shown that wizards are a useful first step in initially creating the queries. You may always modify any query created by the wizards later.

Simple Query Wizard

The Simple Query Wizard creates a Select query. This wizard displays only two screens; the first screen allows you to select the table or query where the data is contained. It also provides you with a listing of the fields in the table for easy selection. Figure 5.2 shows the wizard window used to select the tables and fields to be used in the query.

FIGURE 5.2.

The Simple Query Wizard table and field selection dialog box.

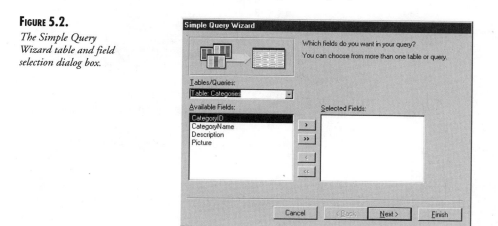

Use the arrows in the middle to select the fields to be included in the query. Once the fields have been selected, the wizard prompts you for the name of the query and provides either a display of the query results or a display of the query in Design View to make modifications to the query.

Crosstab Query Wizard

The Crosstab query displays information in a spreadsheet format. This wizard begins by allowing you to select multiple tables and queries for use in selecting the fields for the Crosstab query.

> **CAUTION**
>
> The table or query to be used must contain at least three numeric, date, or text fields. If the table you select does not contain enough of these fields, Access 97 will prompt you to enter a table containing the appropriate number of fields. The initial Crosstab Query Wizard screen is shown in Figure 5.3.

FIGURE 5.3.

The initial Crosstab Query Wizard screen.

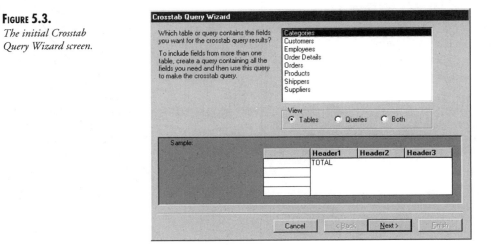

After the tables and queries have been selected, you are prompted to select the fields to be included in the query. Figure 5.4 shows the Crosstab Query Wizard field selection box.

FIGURE 5.4.

The Crosstab Query Wizard field selection box.

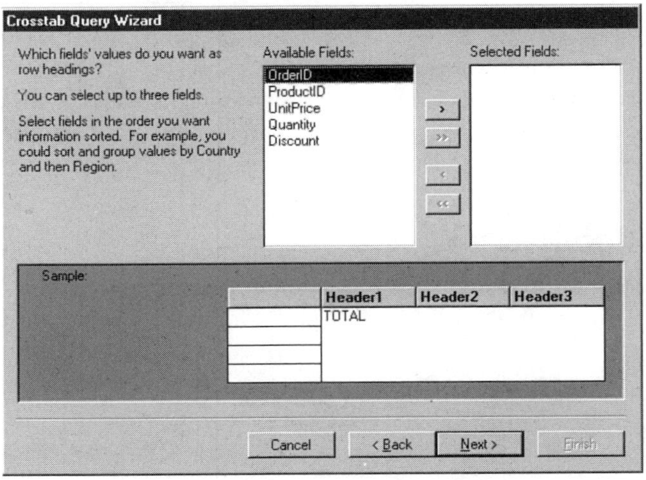

After you have selected the fields to be included in the new Crosstab query, the next step is to select the field to be used as the column heading. Figure 5.5 shows the Crosstab Query Wizard column selection box.

FIGURE 5.5.

The Crosstab Query Wizard column selection box.

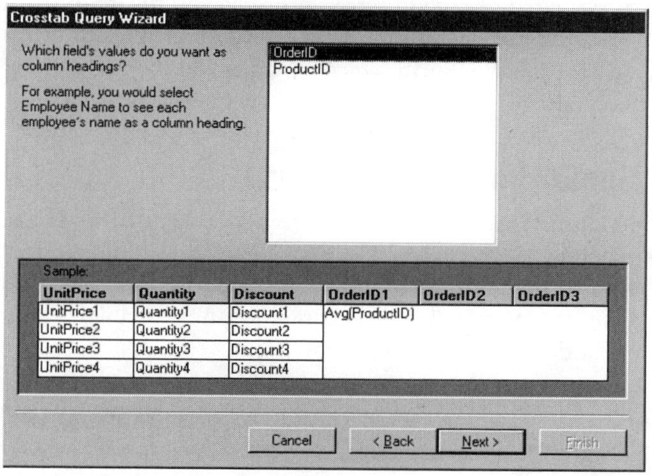

Once this is completed, the wizard allows the user to select which function the query is to perform. Figure 5.6 shows the Crosstab Query Wizard function selection dialog box.

FIGURE 5.6.

The Crosstab Query Wizard function selection dialog box.

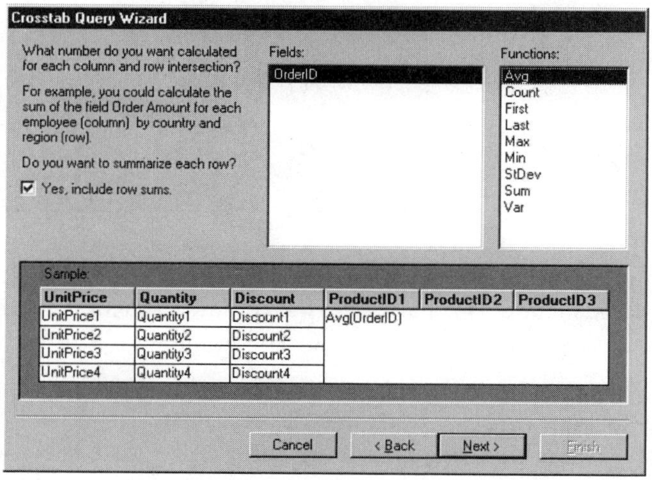

When these steps have been completed, the wizard prompts you for the name of the query and displays either the query results or the query in Design View so modifications can be made to the new query.

Find Duplicate Query Wizard

The Find Duplicate Query Wizard allows you to find records in tables or queries with duplicate values. This wizard consists of four screens. The first screen lets you select the table or query to be used. The second screen prompts you for the fields to be included in the query. The third screen enables you to include additional fields to be displayed in the results of the query. And finally, the fourth screen prompts you for the query name and allows you to view either the results or Design View of the new query.

Find Unmatched Query Wizard

The Find Unmatched Query Wizard creates a query that finds records in one table that do not have a match in another table. The first screen allows you to select the table where the records that should be matched are located. The second screen selects the table to be searched. The third screen lets you select the field contained in both tables. Figure 5.7 shows the Unmatched Query Wizard common field selection box.

FIGURE 5.7.

The Find Unmatched Query Wizard common field selection box.

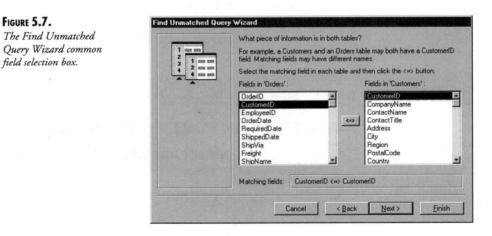

Once the matching fields have been selected, the wizard prompts you for the fields you want to be displayed in the query. The wizard then prompts you for the name of the query and whether the results should be shown or the design of the query displayed so modifications can be made.

All of the queries created by the query wizards can be created manually if desired. In practice it is easier to create the queries first with the wizards and later modify to get the optimum results. The query wizards provide a quick easy interface for the first pass of query creation.

Creating Queries Manually

Besides using the wizards, a number of different queries can be created manually. Access 97 provides a nice development environment to create queries manually. When creating a new query, the first thing to do is select the tables or other queries containing the data to be used in the new query. To help you select which tables or other queries to use, Access 97 displays the Show Table window. Figure 5.8 shows the window used to select tables or queries. The tables shown are those found in the `Northwind` database.

Figure 5.8.

The Show Table window.

Select the tables to be used in the new query by clicking the table and then clicking Add. After selecting the tables and queries to be used, the Query Design View window appears. Figure 5.9 shows the basic Query Design View used to create queries in Access 97.

Figure 5.9.

The Query Design View.

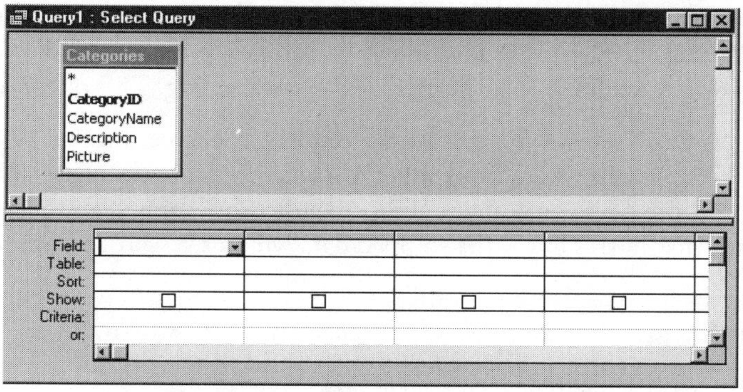

The tables selected will be displayed in the gray box on the top of this window. When creating a new query, Access 97 lets you create a Select query by default.

Product Sales for 1995 Example

Let's look at an example of a Select query that uses all of the standard features of Design View for queries. The `Product Sales for 1995` query is a good example of a query that uses many of the standard features of the Query Design View in Access 97. Figure 5.10 shows the Design View of the `Product Sales for 1995` query found in the `Northwind` database.

FIGURE 5.10.

The Product Sales
for 1995 *Design View.*

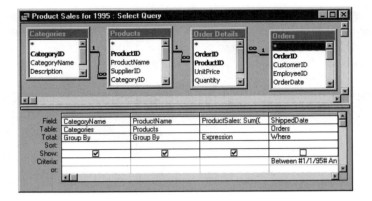

The top half of the Design View shows the tables used in this query. In this example, four tables are used: Categories, Products, Order Details, and Orders. The relationship for each table is illustrated by a line connecting the table boxes. To view all the relationships for the database application, select the Tools option on the menu bar and then choose Relationships. This window displays all the tables and their associated relationships.

The bottom half of the screen shows the mechanics of the query. The first row shows the fields in the queries: CategoryName from the Categories table, ProductName from the Products table, and ShippedDate, from the Orders table. Notice that this query also creates an expression—ProductSales. The Total row allows you to group the results of the query, create an expression, or tell Access 97 that a criteria exists for totaling. This query does all three.

The Sort row allows you to sort the results either in ascending or descending order. In this query, the results are to be grouped by both the category name and the product name. The Show row provides you with the ability to either show or hide the field in the results of the query. Notice that in this query the shipped date will not be shown in the results of the query.

The ProductSales column of the query is an expression. The actual expression is contained in the Field row. The expression for ProductSales is as follows:

```
ProductSales: Sum(CCur([Order Details].[UnitPrice]
➥*[Quantity]*(1-[Discount])/100)*100)
```

The expression name precedes the colon. The actual expression uses the Sum function to sum the total of the UnitPrice, times the Quantity, times the Discount percentage from the Order Details table. The CCur function converts the numeric values into currency.

The ShippedDate column sets the criteria for the query. The Where statement in the Total row tells Access 97 that a criteria exists for which values of the ShippedDate field are to be used in the query. The Criteria field establishes this criteria. For this query, the criteria is as follows:

```
Between #1/1/95# And #12/31/95#
```

This criteria tells Access 97 to use only those product sales that have a `ShippedDate` between January 1, 1995 and December 31, 1995. To run the query from within the Design View, click the toolbar icon with an exclamation point on it. This toolbar button runs the query from within the Query Design View and displays the results. Figure 5.11 shows the final results of the `Product Sales for 1995` query.

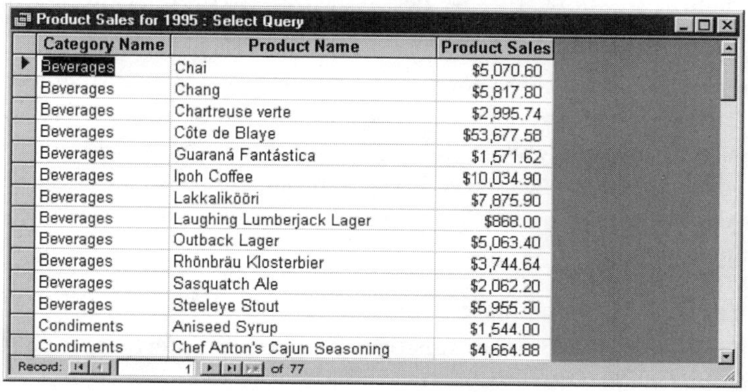

FIGURE 5.11.

The final results of `Product Sales for 1995` *query.*

This is a good example of a select query that uses almost all of the standard properties of the Design View for queries within Access 97.

Quarterly Orders by Product Example

The `Quarterly Orders by Product` query in the `Northwind` sample database is a good example of a Crosstab query.

Remember that a Crosstab query allows the display of summarized data determined by the function you selected. Figure 5.12 shows the `Quarterly Orders by Product` query in its Design View.

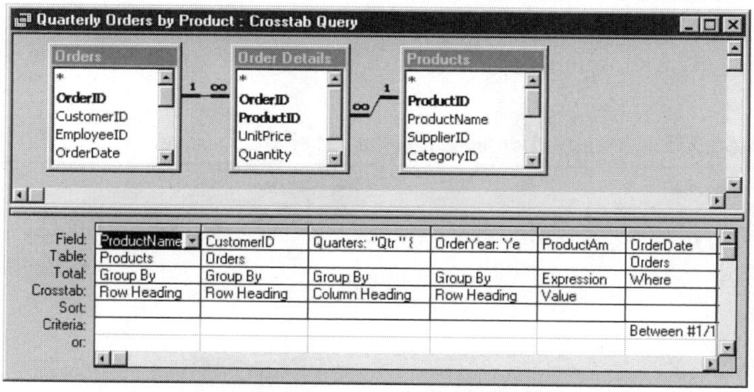

FIGURE 5.12.

The design view of the `Quarterly Orders by Product` *query.*

This Crosstab query uses the Orders, Order Details, and Products tables in the Northwind database. Let's look at each field individually. The first field is the ProductName field from the Products table. The query's final results are to be grouped by this field and will use the product name as a row heading.

The CustomerID field from the Orders table is to be used in the same fashion as the ProductName field; however, the CustomerID field is included so the query knows how to group the customers purchasing the same product in the same quarter.

The Quarters field is provided so the data is grouped according to the quarter in which the order took place. Notice that Quarters is followed by a colon. This syntax is used to establish an alias for what follows the colon. Because there is not a field in any of the tables containing the data grouped by Quarters, this field must be added to the query. In order to place this field on a form or report, Access 97 must know what to call this field. The alias Quarters is how this is done:

```
Quarters: "Qtr " & DatePart("q",[OrderDate],1,0)
```

This field uses the DatePart function to retrieve an interval of time. The syntax for this function is as follows:

```
DatePart(interval, date[,firstdayofweek[, firstweekofyear]])
```

The DatePart function arguments are described in Table 5.1.

Table 5.1. The arguments of the DatePart function.

Part	Description
interval	Interval of time to return.
date	Date to evaluate.
firstdayofweek	First day of the week. Sunday is the default.
firstweekofyear	First week of the year. January, week 1 is the default.

The interval argument settings are shown in Table 5.2.

Table 5.2. The interval arguments in the DatePart function.

Setting	Description
Yyyy	Year
Q	Quarter
M	Month
Y	Day of year
D	Day of month

Setting	Description
w	Weekday
Ww	Week
h	Hour
n	Minute
s	Second

The `firstdayofweek` argument settings are shown in Table 5.3.

Table 5.3. The `firstdayofweek` argument settings.

Constant	Value	Description
vbUseSystem	0	Use the NLS API setting.
vbSunday	1	Sunday (default)
vbMonday	2	Monday
vbTuesday	3	Tuesday
vbWednesday	4	Wednesday
vbThursday	5	Thursday
vbFriday	6	Friday
vbSaturday	7	Saturday

The `firstweekofyear` argument settings are shown in Table 5.4.

Table 5.4. The `firstweekofyear` argument settings

Constant	Value	Description
vbUseSystem	0	Use the NLS API setting.
vbFirstJan1	1	Start with week in which January 1 occurs (default).
vbFirstFourDays	2	Start with the first week in the new year that has at least four days.
vbFirstFullWeek	3	Start with the first full week of the year.

Let's take a look at the actual field in the Crosstab query again in light of the information provided:

```
Quarters: "Qtr " & DatePart("q",[OrderDate],1,0)
```

`Quarters` is the alias for the field, and `"Qrt"` is the column heading. The `DatePart` function uses the `"q"` to signify the time interval as quarters. The `[OrderDate]` tells the function to use the date in the `OrderDate` field of this query. The `1` tells the function to use Sunday as the first day of the week, and finally, the `0` tells the function to use the NLS API setting for the `firstweekofyear` argument.

The next column in the `Quarterly Orders by Product` Crosstab query is the `OrderYear`. This field uses the `Year` function:

```
OrderYear: Year([OrderDate])
```

The syntax for the `Year` function is `Year(date)`. This function returns a variant value representing the whole number for the date provided in the argument. In this example, the function uses the `OrderDate` field in the query for the date.

The next column is the `ProductAmount` field. This field represents an expression. The field calculates the sum of the orders and converts that number to a currency value:

```
ProductAmount: Sum(CCur([Order Details].[UnitPrice]*
➥[Quantity]*(1-[Discount])/100)*100)
```

Finally, the last column in this Crosstab query is the `OrderDate` column. This field tells the query what year to use as criteria for the overall query. The `Where` statement tells the query that a criterion exists, and the criterion used is as follows:

```
Between #1/1/95# And #12/31/95#
```

This criterion tells the query to use the dates between January 1, 1995 and December 31, 1995. This field is also used in both the `Quarters` field and the `OrderYear` field.

Now that all the fields required for this Crosstab query are in place, it is time to see the final results of the query. Note again that these results appear in a spreadsheet format. Figure 5.13 shows the final results of the `Quarter Sales by Product` query.

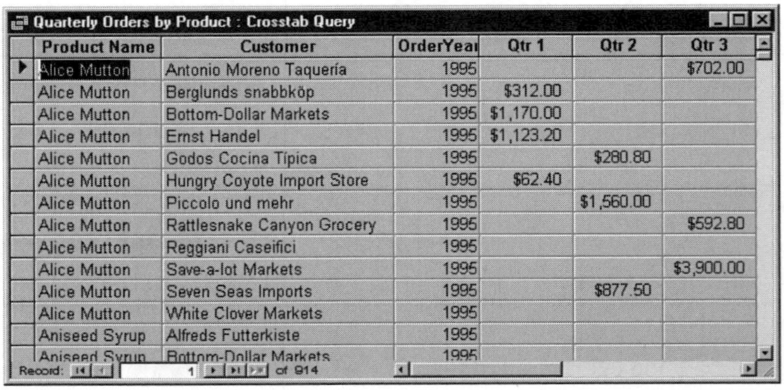

Figure 5.13.

The final results of Quarterly Sales by Product *Crosstab query.*

Product Name	Customer	OrderYear	Qtr 1	Qtr 2	Qtr 3
Alice Mutton	Antonio Moreno Taquería	1995			$702.00
Alice Mutton	Berglunds snabbköp	1995	$312.00		
Alice Mutton	Bottom-Dollar Markets	1995	$1,170.00		
Alice Mutton	Ernst Handel	1995	$1,123.20		
Alice Mutton	Godos Cocina Típica	1995		$280.80	
Alice Mutton	Hungry Coyote Import Store	1995	$62.40		
Alice Mutton	Piccolo und mehr	1995		$1,560.00	
Alice Mutton	Rattlesnake Canyon Grocery	1995			$592.80
Alice Mutton	Reggiani Caseifici	1995			
Alice Mutton	Save-a-lot Markets	1995			$3,900.00
Alice Mutton	Seven Seas Imports	1995		$877.50	
Alice Mutton	White Clover Markets	1995			
Aniseed Syrup	Alfreds Futterkiste	1995			
Aniseed Syrup	Bottom-Dollar Markets	1995			

These two examples show how easy it is to create Select and Crosstab queries in Access 97. Now let's look at creating some Action queries. Action queries, as the name implies, direct Access 97 to carry out some type of action based on the query.

Creating Make-Table and Append Queries

 This example is provided in the Query_Sample database provided on the CD-ROM that accompanies this book. Suppose a database is needed that tracks the passengers riding in a car. A data table has been created that includes the following fields: Last_Name, First_Name, Passenger_1, Passenger_2, Passenger_3, Passenger_4, and Passenger_5. Now, suppose your customer comes to you and wants a form built that will find records based on a passenger's name.

Sounds easy enough, but because you do not have all the passengers in one field, Access will have to look in five separate fields before finding the record you need. This is time-consuming. An easy way to accomplish this task is to use a Make-table query to create a new table and append the passenger fields associated with each driver to the newly created table. This creates one table with all the passenger names and their associated driver's names.

Creating a Make-Table Query

Let's take a look at how this is done. First, move to the queries windows in Access 97. Click New Query. When the Design View of the New Query window opens it asks you to select the table to be used in the query; select the Data table. Move up to the toolbar on the Query Type button and select Make-Table Query. Figure 5.14 shows the Make Table dialog window.

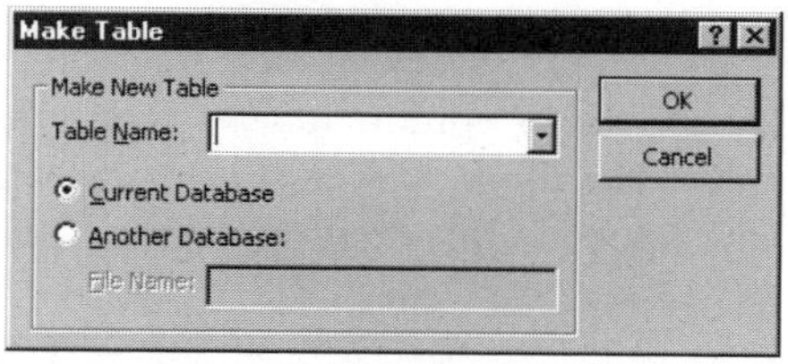

FIGURE 5.14.

The Make Table dialog window.

Enter the new table name. In this example, the new table is called Passengers. Note that you can choose to create the new table in the current database or another database. In this example, use the current database. If Another Database is selected, fill in the filename of the other database in the text box provided. Once this is done, Access 97 drops out to the Design View of the Make-table query. Figure 5.15 shows the new Make-table query in Design View.

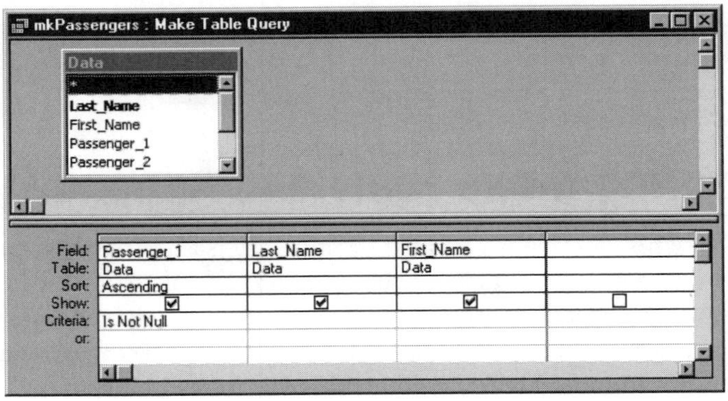

FIGURE 5.15.

*The Design View of the
Make-table query.*

In the Design View of the Make-table query, click on the Passenger_1 field in the Data table and drag it down to the first column on the lower half of the screen. In this example, the passengers names are to be sorted in ascending order. Note that the Criteria field includes the statement Is Not Null. This excludes any records that do not contain a passenger name in the Passenger_1 field of the Data table. Next, select the Last_Name field and drag it into the second column, and do likewise for the First_Name field.

The new Make-table query is complete. If the query were run now, a new table would be created in the database with the names contained in the Passenger_1 field of the Data table and the last and first names associated with them. This only gets part of the way there.

Creating Append Queries

The next step in solving our problem is to create multiple Append queries that will append the Passenger_2, Passenger_3, Passenger_4, and Passenger_5 fields to the new Passenger table created by the preceding query. To accomplish this, select the New button on the queries windows.

When the New Query Design window appears, it prompts you to select the table for the query. Select the Data table. Next, move up to the Query Type toolbar button for selecting the type of query and select the Append Query option. Figure 5.16 shows the Append dialog window.

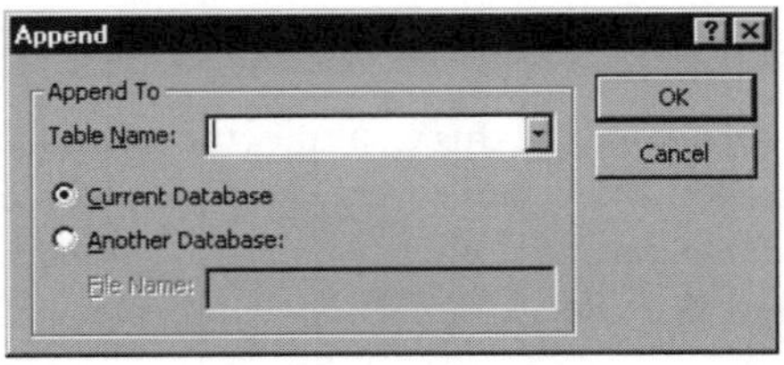

FIGURE 5.16.

*The Append
dialog window.*

Note that the Append Query window is set up in the same manner as the Make Table Query window. In the Table Name text box, type in the name of the Passenger table and click OK. Access 97 then displays the Design View of the Append query. Figure 5.17 shows the new Append query in Design View.

FIGURE 5.17.
*The Append Query
Design View.*

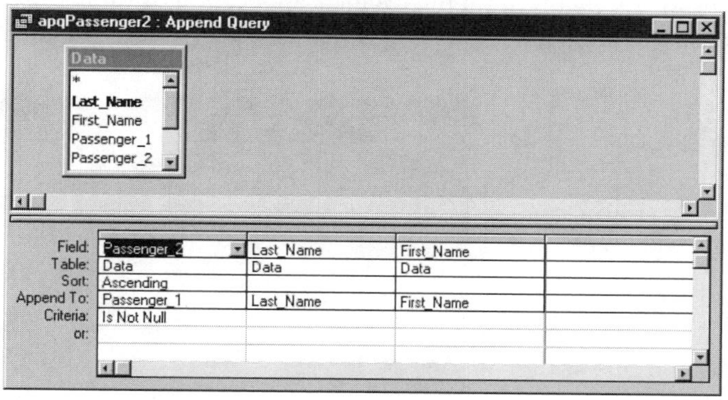

This looks exactly like the Design View of the Make-table query just created, with two exceptions: One difference is in the title bar, which now says apqPassenger2 : Append Query instead of mkPassnegers : Make Table Query. The second difference is that the Show row in the Make-table query has been changed to the Append To row, designating which row in the Passenger table to append the results of this query. Other than those differences, the Append Query Design View is the same as the Make-table Design View.

CAUTION

If the Append query is run now, it will append the results to the Passengers table. Note that the Make-table query must be run before the Append query. If this is not done, an error will occur, because the Append query will not have a table to append to when it runs.

Finally, to complete this example, simply follow the steps previously outlined to create three more Append queries in the same fashion, except append the Passenger_3, Passenger_4, and Passenger_5 fields from the Data table to the new Passengers table.

Once the remaining Append queries have been created, it is time to create the macro that will run the queries behind the scenes to create the Passengers table.

TIP

I prefer to create macros to run the queries in most cases because the macros can be called easily from many places within your database application.

Select the Macros tab from the Database window, and then select the New button. In the `Action` column select the `OpenQuery` action.

In the Action Argument section located on the lower half of this screen, tell Access 97 to open the Make-table query first and then the Append queries. You can now create the `Passengers` table from anywhere within the database application by calling this macro. Figure 5.18 shows this macro in Design View.

FIGURE 5.18.

The `mkTable` *macro Design View.*

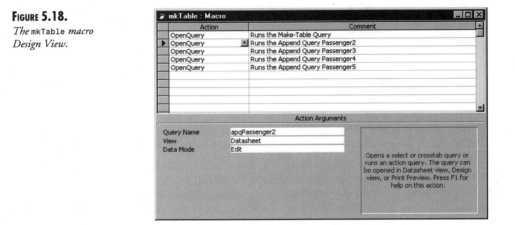

CAUTION

The warnings Access 97 provides when running Action queries are important. For example, if the `mkTable` macro is invoked from within the database application, Access 97 will display a warning message explaining that records are about to be appended and then display another message confirming that the records have been appended. Many users often get nervous about warning messages. Fortunately for these users, Access 97 provides several easy ways to turn off these warning messages.

When a Make-table query is run and the new table is already in existence, Access 97 will display a warning telling the user the Make-table query is about to delete an existing table. If the Make-table query is to be used to keep the most current information available in a temporary table, you can bypass this warning message in several ways. Likewise, when Append queries are run, Access 97 will notify the user that records are going to be appended to an existing table. After this message, Access 97 will display another window confirming how many records were appended.

The first option you can use to avoid these messages, and the one I recommend, is to add two lines to the macro. Simply add the `SetWarnings` action to the top and bottom of the `mkTable` macro. The first `SetWarnings` action will turn off the warnings, and the second will turn them back on again. This will turn off the warning messages while the macro is running and then turn them back on when the macro is through. The macro can now run without interruption from Access 97, the warning messages in this instance. Figure 5.19 shows the mkTable macro with the SetWarning actions added.

FIGURE 5.19.

The mkTable *macro with* SetWarnings *actions.*

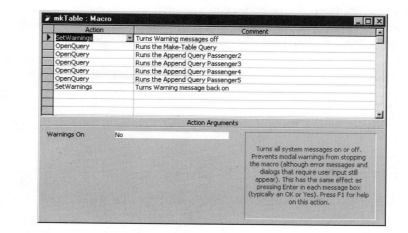

The second option you can use to avoid warning messages is to create another macro that will delete the table after exiting the form or report in which the Make-table query is being run. Because the table will be deleted, no warning messages will appear the next time the Make-table query is run. Figure 5.20 shows a DeleteObject macro named mkTable in Design View.

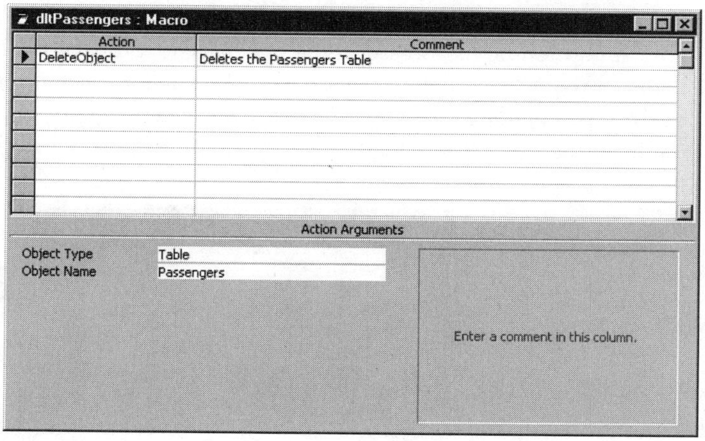

FIGURE 5.20.

The mkTable *macro in Design View.*

The third option, and not one I recommend, is to open the Edit/Find tab under Tools | Options and uncheck the Record Changes, Document Deletion, and/or Action Queries options in the Confirm option group. This method is not recommended because it is not isolated to just this instance of running action queries in this database. Turning off this confirmation turns it off in Access 97 until these options are rechecked. If you accidentally delete a form or report, there will not be a warning with an option to cancel the deletion. You can imagine what a problem this could cause.

To turn off the confirmation messages generated by Access 97 when running Action queries, open the Tools option on the menu bar. Select the Options from the drop-down menu, and then click on the Edit/Find tab. Figure 5.21 shows the Edit/Find tab on the Options window.

FIGURE 5.21.

The Access 97 Edit/ Find tab.

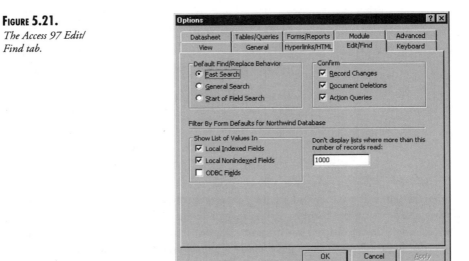

The Confirm option box is located in the upper-right corner of the Edit/Find tab. Note that the default for the Action Queries option is checked. Uncheck this option. The mkTable macro can now run without any warning or confirmation messages appearing. Figure 5.22 shows the final results of the Make-table query and Append queries just created.

FIGURE 5.22.

The final results of the Make-table and Append queries.

Passenger_1	Last_Name	First_Name
Clark, Joseph	Smith	Howard
Cooper, Frank	Jones	Phil
Smith, Henry	Doe	John
Thompson, Ste\	James	Alice
Franks, Mary	James	Alice
Hawkins, Patric	Jones	Phil
Johnson, Carl	Doe	John
Gates, Eleanor	Jones	Phil
Jones, David	Doe	John
Phillips, James	Doe	John
Carl, Hank	Doe	John

Record: 1 of 11

The Make-table query and Append queries of this example can be run from a number locations by simply calling the `mkTable` macro. The `mkTable` macro may be called from the `Click` event of a command button. It can also be called when a form is initially opened from the `OnLoad` or `OnOpen` events in the form properties, so the most current list of passengers can be used in a combo box or a list box.

These examples have shown you how to create a number of standard queries from within the Access 97 development environment. Another type of advanced query is the Parameter query.

Parameter Queries

Parameter queries prompt the user to enter parameters before the query is run. This prompt appears in a dialog box and allows the user to set the criteria for the query before the data is retrieved.

Parameter queries are useful for reports and forms. Many times these queries are used to prompt the user for dates the query will use. When the dates are entered, the query then returns the appropriate data based on the dates entered.

 An example of a Parameter query can be found in the `Query_Sample` database on the enclosed CD-ROM. In this example, the query is designed to prompt the user for two dates. A `HireDate` field has been added in the `Data` table. Figure 5.23 shows a Parameter query in Design View that can be used to find the first and last names of individuals hired between two dates specified by the user.

FIGURE 5.23.

A Parameter query in Design View.

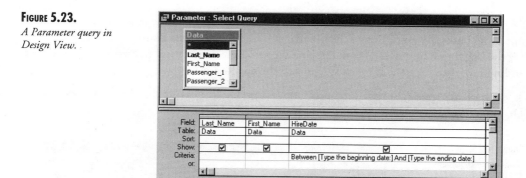

When this query is run, a dialog box appears prompting the user to enter the beginning date. When the user types in the date and clicks OK, a second dialog box appears that prompts the user to enter the ending date. When the user clicks OK after entering the second date, the query returns the results shown in Figure 5.24.

FIGURE 5.24.
The results of a Parameter query.

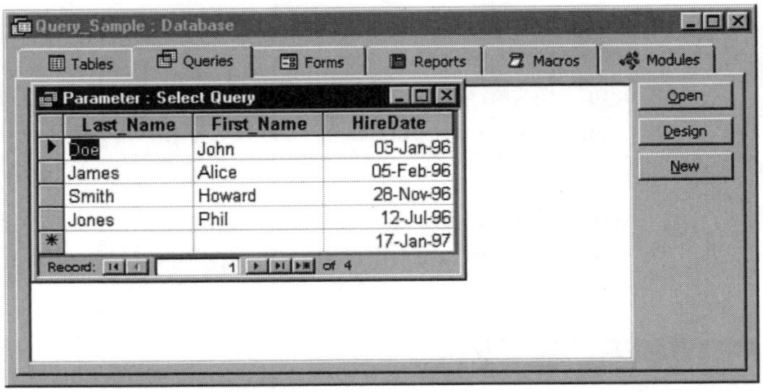

If you want to have the user enter the two dates on a single form instead of two, you must create a custom dialog window. A custom form has been created in the Query_Sample database on the enclosed CD-ROM. Figure 5.25 shows a custom dialog form for entering the parameters for a Parameter query.

FIGURE 5.25.
A custom Parameter query form.

As you can see, this form has one line of text, two text boxes, and one command button. The line of text asks the user to enter the hire dates. The first Text Box control named txtbegin is for the beginning hire date parameter. The second Text Box control named txtend is for the ending hire date parameter. Click OK to run the Custom query.

The Parameter query for this form is called Custom. Figure 5.26 shows the Custom query in Design View.

FIGURE 5.26.
The Parameter query Design View.

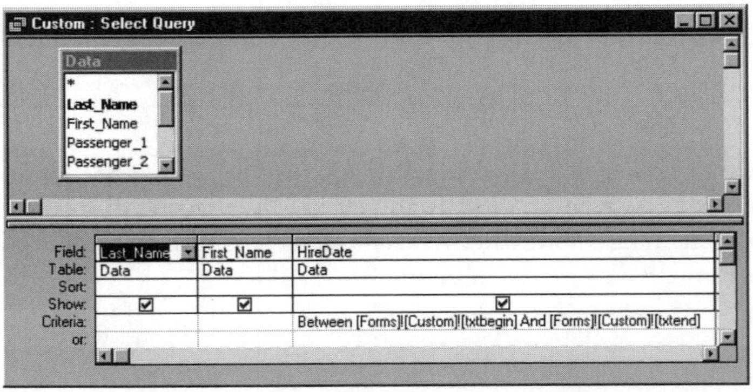

NOTE

Note that in the Criteria field for the HireDate field, the statement (Between [Forms]![Custom]![txtbegin] And [Forms]![Custom]![txtend]) tells Access to look in the txtbegin and txtend controls on the Custom form for the parameters of the query. When the user opens the form and enters the desired dates, the query will run and return the appropriate first and last names with the hire date.

CAUTION

Access will not be able to run the query without opening the form and entering the dates in the form. If this is done, Access will display a dialog box asking the user to enter the date for Forms![Custom]![txtbegin] and then open another dialog box asking the user for Forms![Custom]![txtend]. To avoid this, always open the form first and let it call and run the query.

SQL Basics

Microsoft SQL was designed to be a scalable, high-performance relationship database management system. Access 97 allows for the use of the basic SQL query statements from within its development environment. The following are some of the standard SQL statements and clauses available in Access 97:

```
SELECT

WHERE

ORDER BY

GROUP BY

HAVING
```

The SELECT statement is the most basic statement used to query data in SQL. The following is the full SQL SELECT syntax:

```
SELECT [ALL/DISTINCT] select_list
                [INTO [new_table_name]]
                [FROM {table_name/view_name} . . .]
                [WHERE clause]
                [GROUP BY clause]
                [HAVING clause]
                [ORDER BY clause]
                [COMPUTE clause]
                [FOR BROWSE clause]
```

Using an * in the SELECT statement designates all fields in a table. Microsoft recommends always using a WHERE clause with a SELECT statement so that system resources are not wasted. It is always advisable to be specific in your SELECT statement to maximize the efficiency of your query. The SELECT statement consists of the field name(s) where the desired data is located. For example, the following SELECT statement will retrieve the first and last names from a table called Clients.

```
SELECT Fname,Lname
  FROM Clients
```

The WHERE clause allows you to select the records to be returned in a query, based on some criterion. The search conditions that can be used in a WHERE clause are included in Table 5.4.

Table 5.4. WHERE statement search conditions.

Type	Conditions
Ranges	=,>,<,>=,<=,<>
Lists	Between/Not Between
String Matches	In/Not In
Unknown Variables	Like/Not Like
Combinations	And, Or
Negatives	Not

Some good examples of SQL expressions have been provided in the Access 97 help file.

Other SQL Query Types

There are also a number of queries that can be created using a Structured Query Language (SQL) statement. A SQL query is a query created using a SQL statement. Examples of SQL-specific queries are the Union query, Pass-through query, Data-definition query, and subquery.

Union Queries

A Union query takes fields from one or more tables and combines them into one field. A Make-table query can be based on a Union query to create a new table. An example of a Union query is the Customers and Suppliers by City query found in the Northwind database. The statement to create this query is as follows:

```
SELECT City, CompanyName, ContactName, "Customers" AS [Relationship]
FROM Customers
UNION SELECT City, CompanyName, ContactName, "Suppliers"
FROM Suppliers
ORDER BY City, CompanyName;
```

This query returns a table with three columns: `City`, `CompanyName`, and `ContactName`. The data in this table consists of all the records in both the `Customers` and `Supplier` tables. The `AS [Relationship]` portion of this query adds a column to the table and provides data as to which table each individual record came from. Figure 5.27 shows the results of the `Customers and Suppliers by City` Union query.

FIGURE 5.27.

Results of Customers and Suppliers by City *query.*

This query returns the following table:

City	CompanyName	ContactName	Relationship
Aachen	Drachenblut Delikatessen	Sven Ottlieb	Customers
Albuquerque	Rattlesnake Canyon Grocery	Paula Wilson	Customers
Anchorage	Old World Delicatessen	Rene Phillips	Customers
Ann Arbor	Grandma Kelly's Homestead	Regina Murphy	Suppliers
Annecy	Gai pâturage	Eliane Noz	Suppliers
Århus	Vaffeljernet	Palle Ibsen	Customers
Barcelona	Galería del gastrónomo	Eduardo Saavedra	Customers
Barquisimeto	LILA-Supermercado	Carlos González	Customers
Bend	Bigfoot Breweries	Cheryl Saylor	Suppliers
Bergamo	Magazzini Alimentari Riuniti	Giovanni Rovelli	Customers
Berlin	Alfreds Futterkiste	Maria Anders	Customers
Berlin	Heli Süßwaren GmbH & Co. KG	Petra Winkler	Suppliers
Bern	Chop-suey Chinese	Yang Wang	Customers

Record: 1 of 120

Pass-Through Query

This query will send a command to an Open Database Connectivity (ODBC)–compliant database. This query can be used to retrieve data from the other database. It can also be used to change data in another database.

Data-Definition Query

This query is used to create or alter database objects, such as tables.

Subquery

A subquery is a SQL SELECT statement inside another query. A subquery can be created in the Query Design View or the SQL view of a query. The subquery allows you to perform a function through a SELECT statement, as well as to establish other criteria on the query results before the data is actually displayed. In other words, a subset of the overall query is created that the original query then refines even more.

To build one of these SQL queries, click View and then SQL View in the Query Design View of the Access 97 development environment. Figure 5.28 shows the SQL Design View.

FIGURE 5.28.

The SQL Design View.

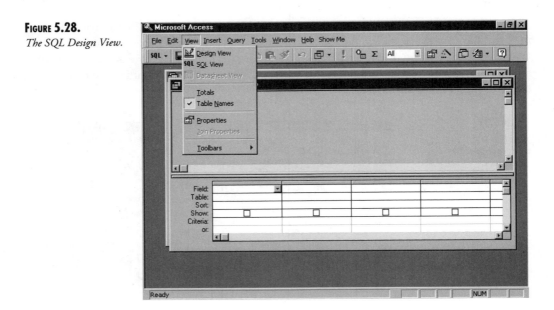

The SQL Design View is just a blank screen where the statements can be entered. You can view other Select queries as they would appear as a SQL statement by selecting SQL View. For example, the `Current Product List` Select query in the `Northwind` database would appear as a SQL statement as follows:

```
SELECT [Product List].ProductID, [Product List].ProductName
FROM Products AS [Product List]
WHERE (((([Product List].Discontinued)=No))
ORDER BY [Product List].ProductName;
```

Figure 5.29 shows the final results of the `Current Product List` Select query.

FIGURE 5.29.

The results of the
`Current Product List`
Select query.

Product ID	Product Name
3	Aniseed Syrup
40	Boston Crab Meat
60	Camembert Pierrot
18	Carnarvon Tigers
1	Chai
2	Chang
39	Chartreuse verte
4	Chef Anton's Cajun Seasoning
48	Chocolade
38	Côte de Blaye
58	Escargots de Bourgogne
52	Filo Mix
71	Fløtemysost

Record: 1 of 69

The `Quarterly Orders by Products` Crosstab query in the `Northwind` database would appear as a SQL statement like this:

```
TRANSFORM Sum(CCur([Order Details].[UnitPrice]*[Quantity]*(1-[Discount])
➥/100)*100) AS ProductAmount
SELECT Products.ProductName, Orders.CustomerID, Year([OrderDate])
➥ AS OrderYear
ROM Products INNER JOIN (Orders INNER JOIN [Order Details] ON Orders.OrderID
➥ = [Order Details].OrderID) ON Products.ProductID = [Order Details].ProductID
WHERE (((Orders.OrderDate) Between #1/1/95# And #12/31/95#))
GROUP BY Products.ProductName, Orders.CustomerID, Year([OrderDate])
PIVOT "Qtr " & DatePart("q",[OrderDate],1,0) In
➥ ("Qtr 1","Qtr 2","Qtr 3","Qtr 4");
```

Refer to Figure 5.14 for a picture of the result of this Crosstab query. As you can see from this example, in many cases it is easier to design a query using the Access 97 development environment rather than writing SQL statements. If any of this syntax is done incorrectly, the query will not run, or if it does run, it will return an incorrect result.

Summary

This chapter has shown you the various ways to create queries from within Access 97. It has discussed the different development environments for query creation. You can use either the Access 97 development environment or the SQL development environment.

I introduced the numerous types of queries supported by Access 97 and some examples of how to modify queries after first creating them with the wizards provided in Access 97. The various Action queries have been covered with examples of the Make-table query and Append query provided.

The next step in developing an Access 97 database application is the creation of forms. The next chapter will give an in-depth discussion on the creation of forms, while providing more examples along the way.

Access 97 Forms

by Tony Gigliotti

IN THIS CHAPTER

CHAPTER

6

This chapter discusses the design, development, and creation of a basic user interface for any Microsoft Access 97 database application. All Access 97 applications work on the event-driven model of programming, which is characterized by the need for certain events to occur that in turn prompt other events to occur. The user interface for Access 97 is centered on the use of forms, and on those forms are controls. *Controls* are objects designed to carry out certain functions. Each control has a set of properties that describe not only the physical characteristics of the control, but also the events associated with it.

The beginning of this chapter provides you with a brief look at the Access 97 form-design environment. It then briefly discusses the standard controls offered in Access 97.

The chapter continues with a brief look at the form wizards that come with Access 97: the Form Wizard, AutoForm: Columnar, AutoForm: Tabular, AutoForm: Datasheet, the Chart Wizard, and the PivotTable Wizard.

The chapter examines a number of examples taken from the Northwind sample database that comes with Access 97: the Main Switchboard form, the Customer Order form (including subforms), the Orders form (including subform), the Employees form, and the Customer Phone List form. These examples will provide a good walkthrough on the different ways of designing forms and how to maximize the efficiency of your forms. The examples also demonstrate many of the form controls within Access 97 and how they are commonly used.

The chapter concludes with a brief explanation of a new feature in Access 97: lightweight forms, which are forms that have had the code modules stripped from them. The benefit of lightweight forms is primarily found in the overall efficiency of the database, as you'll learn later.

The Form-Development Environment

All forms are windows. A *window* is something you see on the monitor, such as an application or a message box. That's why they call the OS (operating system) Windows 95. Windows are treated by the OS just as you treat documents; hence the phrase *multiple document interface* (MDI). Access 97 is an MDI application, which means that it can have multiple forms opened at one time. An MDI-type application will have a parent window (the application window) and multiple child windows (forms). If you close the parent window, the child windows will close as well. All the other objects that are opened into a window, such as tables, reports, and so on, are considered children to the parent.

Access 97 provides an easy-to-use form-development environment. To enter the development environment, move to the Forms tab in the database, click on New and select Design View. As in all previous versions of Access, the option of selecting the table that will provide the data for the form is provided in the Design View selection window. You can select the table here or select it later by going into the form properties and adding the table to the Record Source property. When the Design View of a new form is invoked, you are greeted by the screen shown in Figure 6.1.

FIGURE 6.1.

The Design View of the Access 97 development environment.

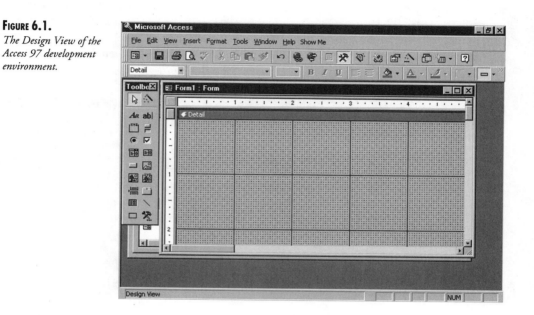

In this development environment, there are three basic areas to note. The first is at top of the screen: the toolbar. The toolbar has several useful buttons for working with the overall design of the form. It also has navigational buttons that allow you to move to different views of the form and to invoke several other windows that aid in form development.

The second area is the toolbox, which is located on the left side of the window. The toolbox contains buttons that allow you to insert controls on the form. Those controls are the basic building blocks of form creation.

The third area is the form design window, which is where the controls are placed and the actual development of form layout occurs.

I prefer to add one more area to the Form Design View. Because every object that is placed on a form contains properties, I have found it useful to call up the property window at the very beginning of the form-development process. This provides easy access to the property sheet throughout the creation of the form. Setting your video at a higher resolution will allow more room to work. Just make sure that when you go back to 640×480 resolution, your form will fit in the application window. You do not want to see any unnecessary scrollbars.

There are several ways to call up the property window in Access 97. First, look on the toolbar between the code button and the build button and notice the button that has a hand pointing to a white sheet. If you move the mouse over this button, a help tip appears that identifies this button as the properties button. Click the button to display the property window. Another way to view the properties of an object is to right-click on the object itself, which causes a pop-up menu to appear. The properties selection is usually located on the bottom of this menu. Yet another way to view the properties of an object is by selecting View from the menu bar at the top of the window. The Properties option is located in the second group; you invoke it by clicking on it. The property window is shown in Figure 6.2 on the right.

FIGURE 6.2.

The property window for Access 97 form development.

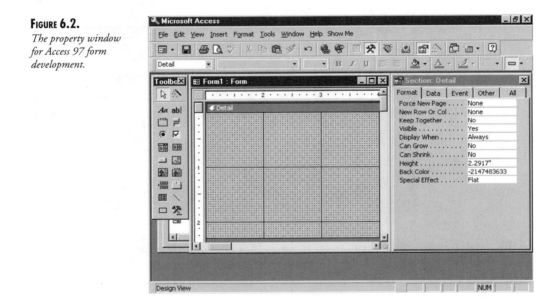

You can reposition the windows on the screen to provide a look and feel that you find the most comfortable for developing forms. I recommend that you play around with the windows to find the best environment for you. Figure 6.3 shows my preferred setup for designing forms.

This is the form-development environment in a nutshell. When a new form is created in the Access 97 environment, there are certain properties that Access 97 assigns to the form. These properties are explained in the following section.

FIGURE 6.3.
A basic custom design environment.

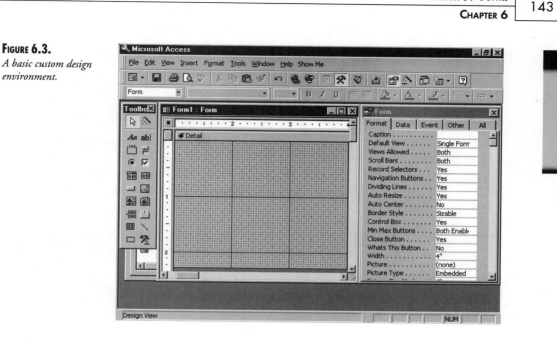

Form Properties

The form property sheet is divided into five tabs: Format, Data, Event, Other, and All. Tabs were added to the property sheet when Microsoft added the Tabs control to the toolbox in Access 97 and are a good use for that control. In Access 2.0, you had to take one of the selections from a combo box. In most cases, the combo box was hardly used because it took longer to use than just scrolling down the list of properties until you found what you were looking for.

The All tab shows a listing of all the properties at one time. It is always a good idea to set the form's properties before adding controls to the form. To view the form's properties, select Edit from the menu bar at the top of the window. When the Edit menu appears, choose the Select Form option. The form properties also can be viewed by using the hotkey (Ctrl+R) associated with this menu option. If the properties window is already open onscreen, the properties will change to the form's properties when you use the hotkey (Ctrl+R). If the properties window is not open, you need to open it before you can edit the form's properties.

Once the form properties are set, the controls can be added to the form. The controls are the means by which data is displayed and retrieved. The controls are also used to enhance the overall appearance of the form. Access 97 allows the use of standard controls that come with it as well as the use of additional controls that may be registered in the operating system Registry.

Standard Access 97 Controls

Access 97 provides 17 standard controls for form development. These controls are by no means the only controls that can be added to a form, but they are the most common controls used in developing forms. Two of them are new: the tab control and the image control.

Before we look at the individual controls, notice the button in the upper-right corner of the toolbox that looks like a magic wand with stars coming out of it. This is the Wizard button. If this button is pushed down, a wizard will invoke for every control created that has an associated wizard. These controls include the option group, combo box, list box, command button, and subform/subreport.

> **TIP**
>
> In many cases, I have found these wizards helpful for the initial creation of the control. Remember that modifications to control properties can always be made after the control has been created.

The first thing to do after a control is created is to name it.

> **TIP**
>
> Make sure that you do not have any code associated with the control before you change the name. The code will not transfer to the renamed control; you have to rename the code first and then rename the control. The code still may be not connected to the right event, so go to that event and click the Build button. If you rename the block of code properly, it will attach itself to the event. When renaming controls, you sometimes have to do this to get Access to recognize your code.

Microsoft has developed a standard naming convention for objects. Using this naming convention greatly enhances the ease with which you can identify certain objects in an application. A standard name also allows other programmers to easily recognize and manipulate an object in an environment where multiple programmers are working on the same project. Using a standard naming convention also aids in the consistency of an application should later modification be necessary.

As I continue with the discussion of each control, the Microsoft naming convention for each control is provided next to the control type. For those controls not included in the Microsoft standard convention, I have provided a name alternative. These names are denoted with an asterisk.

For example, the naming convention for a label is `lbl` followed by the specific name for that individual label. The `lbl` tells the programmer that the object is a label. Should another programmer need to call that object later in code, it can be easily identified as a label.

For each of these controls, the remainder of this section provides a general discussion followed by examples of its use.

Label (`lbl`)

The label control is used to display text on the form. It can be used for simple display or to trigger an event. An example of using a label to trigger an event would be similar to the hypertext convention for Web documents. Often, one can jump to another Web site by clicking on the words associated with that site. In Access 97, you can use a label in a different color to jump the user to a different form. All you have to do to set this up is to call a macro with the `OpenForm` action pointing to the form and place the call in the `OnClick` event of the label. When the user clicks on the label, the form designated in the `OpenForm` action argument will be opened.

Text Box (`txt`)

The text box control is used to display data from a table or to input data into a table. This is one of the most common controls used in form design. A text box may include a label, or it may not, depending on its use. The label, when clicked on in Form View, will put the cursor in the text box with which it is associated. If you have a text box without a label, you can connect another one to it: Just create another label and add the text you want. Now, cut the text by making sure the label is selected and choosing Edit | Cut from the menu bar. Now select the text box and choose Edit | Paste. That will connect the new label to your existing text box. Text box inputs may be used in parameter queries to provide the criteria for the query, such as dates.

Option Group (`optgrp`)*

Option group controls may contain option buttons, toggle buttons, or checkboxes. This control allows you to group other controls together. It is always recommended to use an option group with option buttons. By grouping the option buttons in an option group, you allow the user to select only one option. This control is used primarily for setting flags that represent or do certain things. You can store the flag's value in a table or just leave it unbound and allow the user to make certain choices on how to run your program. A good example is to make an option group with two option buttons: one called Print and the other called Preview. Then, when you print a report from that form, set the view on the `OpenReport` method to the appropriate value.

Toggle Button (`tgl`)*

A toggle button control allows you to invoke an event or function depending on the position of the toggle button. The easiest example for using a toggle button is a custom toolbar. When the button is pushed, an event is triggered that will continue until the toggle button is returned to its default position. If you need a custom toolbar in your application, you can create one easily with a single form containing nothing but toggle buttons on it. A toggle button control also can be included in an option group control.

Option Button (`opt`)

The option button control should be used from within the option group control. A label describing the option should always accompany an option button control. When the option is selected, an event can occur that changes some piece of the overall application. You can make the event occur either when the selection is made or by including a command button to invoke the event.

Checkbox (`chk`)

A checkbox control can be used from within an option group control or by itself. The difference between a checkbox and an option button control is that checkboxes normally are used when there are multiple choices to be made, and an option button is used to make only one choice between multiple choices. For example, you are doing a survey on categories of food that men and women buy. You would use an option button for the choices Male and Female and checkboxes for all the categories of food. The users can be only one sex but can buy from multiple categories of food. Queries then can be run on the values associated in the checkbox and return results based on those values.

Combo Box (`cbo`)

A combo box control is used to display a group of data taken from a table or query. The small arrow on the right side of the box can identify combo box controls. This arrow, when clicked, displays the data associated with the combo box below the box itself. A combo box is a text box combined with a list box.

Combo box controls can be either bound or unbound. A *bound combo box* is attached to a specific field in a table. The field to which it is bound is located in the `ControlSource` property. When data is retrieved or entered, the source or destination for the combo box is the bound field. In Access 2.0, if you had a combo box that was bound to a field in the `RowSource` other than the one you could see and you assigned a value to it and then tried to delete it, you would get an error. In that situation, you had just tried to delete what was in the text portion of the combo box. You had to write a function that would actually delete the value of the combo box and run it from the `BeforeUpdate` event. Access 97 eliminates that problem.

List Box (`lst`)

A list box control is very similar to the combo box control from a functional standpoint. A list box behaves like a combo box, except it requires the user to click on the arrow before it will display the data. The primary difference between a list box and a combo box is that the data in a list box is limited to the data in the list, whereas a combo box can allow the user to add data to the list. The other difference is simply the amount of space used to display the data. A list box takes up more room on the form than a combo box does.

Command Button (`cmd`)

The command button control is another often-used control. The command button is mainly used to move around the application by opening and closing forms. It is also used to fire off code at the user's convenience, which could be calculations of data or running of queries or any other type of code envisioned by the programmer. The common uses of the command button can be found by running the Command Button Wizard. These types of actions include record navigation, record operations, form operations, report operations, and application operations, as well as other types.

Image (`img`)

The image control allows you to include a bitmap image on a form. When you add an image control to a form, Access 97 automatically prompts you for the selection of the image to be included. By using the `Picture Type` property of an image control, you can select to either embed the image on the form or link the image to the form. This is very similar to the unbound object control. The main difference is that the image control is not updated by the user. If you want to put a picture on a form that the user needs to edit, use the unbound object frame control; otherwise, you can use the image control. If your computer is set up for the Internet, you can put a hyperlink on this control; when the user clicks it, he will go to that location on the Internet.

Unbound Object Frame (`uof`)*

The unbound object frame control should be used to contain an object that will be changed on a frequent basis. The `ControlSource` property of an unbound object frame is usually empty. The source of the frame is filled when the form opens or when the user selects an item from a list.

An example of an unbound object frame is a preview window. You can provide a list of choices to the user beside an unbound object frame. When the user selects an item from the list, a preview of the item is displayed in the frame. The `ControlSource` property for the unbound frame is also selected when the user makes his or her selection. Thus, the user is allowed to preview his or her choice before some action/event occurs.

Bound Object Frame (`bof`)*

The bound object frame control is associated with a specific field in a database table. The `ControlSource` property of a bound object frame will contain the location of the field in the table to which it is bound. The frequently used example of a bound object frame is an employee picture. You can put whatever you want in this frame, and whatever that is will be linked to the field or stored in it. For example, you can put an Excel spreadsheet into a field with this and store it inside the database instead of just store the location of where the file is.

Page Break (`pgb`)*

The page break control puts a horizontal break between controls on a form. When the user presses the Page Up or Page Down key, the controls change depending upon the page on which they are located. This control behaves similarly to the tab control but without the tabs.

Tab Control (`tab`)*

The tab control is new for Access 97. It allows you to place different controls on different pages inside the control. The user selects the different pages by clicking on the appropriate tab.

The number of controls you can put on one form has been greatly increased with this control. In the past, you were limited in the number of controls you could put on a form by the screen size. Good form design told you to limit the number of controls so the user would not get stuck on a single form or have to scroll continually up or down a form to see the information. Because of this limitation, you would have to create multiple forms and have the user click on buttons to move between them. The tab control does away with that necessity.

An example of the new tab control can be found in the `Employees` form in the `Northwind` sample database. In the "`Employees` Form Example" section of this chapter, you learn how the tab control can be used and how to program the various properties associated with it.

Subform/Subreport (`sub`)*

The subform/subreport control is used to include a mini-form or mini-report inside a larger form or report. The subform/subreport control is very useful in displaying information in a table-like fashion using data from another table and displaying it as a subsection on a form that displays data from a different table.

A good example of a subform can be found in the Northwind sample database. The Orders form contains the Orders subform. The Orders form retrieves its data from the Order query; the Orders subform retrieves its data from the Order Details table. Figure 6.4 displays the Orders form found in the Northwind sample database.

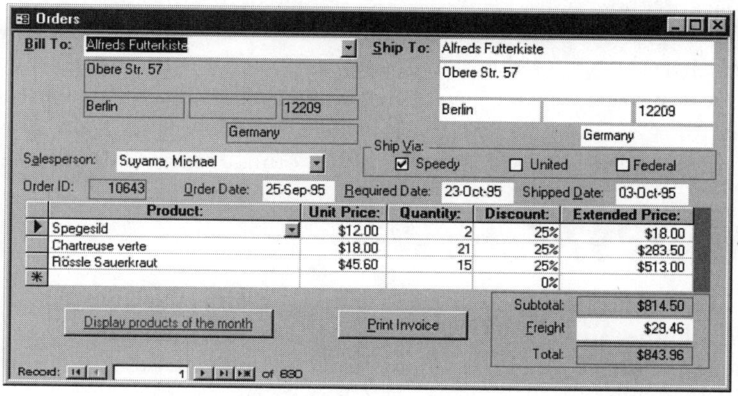

FIGURE 6.4.

The Orders *form from the* Northwind *database.*

On the lower half of the Orders form is a Datasheet View of the Orders subform. In order for the subform to properly communicate with the main form, Access 97 has provided the LinkChildFields and LinkMasterFields properties. The LinkChildFields property is the field identified in the subform that has a corresponding field in the main form. By setting these properties in the subform, a relationship is created between the two forms. In this example, the LinkChildFields and LinkMasterFields properties are set to the OrderID field. This is a common use of the subform/subreport control.

It is easy to create a subform/subreport using the wizard attached to the control. The wizard prompts for the selection of the table or form that will be the basis of the subform/subreport, and it then prompts for the selection of the LinkMasterFields and LinkChildFields properties.

Line (lin)

The line control simply displays a line on the form. You would use this to visually separate controls on the form to make your form easier to read.

Rectangle (rec)*

Similar to the line control, the rectangle control displays a rectangle on the form. You would use this just like the line control, except that you would group similar information together on the form.

More Controls

On the Access 97 toolbox window in the Form Design View is a button for displaying more controls. Clicking this button brings up a listing of all the other available controls you can place on an Access 97 form. The available controls are those registered in the Windows 95 Registry. To register new ActiveX controls, add the files for the control to the hard disk. To do this within Access 97, select Tools | ActiveX controls from the menu bar. A window will appear, listing all the currently registered ActiveX controls. To add a new control to the list, click the Register button. Provide Access 97 with the path to the files on the hard disk where the new ActiveX control is located. The new control will now be registered in the Windows 95 Registry, and you will be able to use the control in the normal Access 97 development environment.

Access 97 Form Wizards

Access 97 provides six form wizards to help you with initial form development. Like most other wizards, they are helpful in providing a quick starting point from which further form development can occur. The form wizards are the Form Wizard, Autoform: Columnar, Autoform: Tabular, Autoform: Datasheet, the Chart Wizard, and the PivotTable Wizard.

Form Wizard

There are four steps to using the Form Wizard. Step one is the selection of the table/query and fields to be included on the form. The first screen enables you to select both the table and query to be used for the form and the fields to be included on the form.

Step two is to select the appropriate layout for the form. The layout choices are columnar, tabular, datasheet, and justified. The columnar layout places the field labels down the left side of the form and the field values next to them on the right. An example of a form created from the Categories tables in the Northwind database using the columnar layout is shown in Figure 6.5.

FIGURE 6.5.

An example of columnar layout.

The tabular layout places the field labels across the top of the form with the field values down the length of the form. An example of a form created from the Categories tables in the Northwind database using the tabular layout is shown in Figure 6.6.

FIGURE 6.6.

*An example of
tabular layout.*

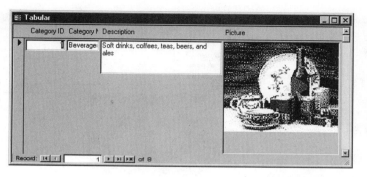

The datasheet layout is like a spreadsheet, with the field names across the top and the data below. An example of a form created from the `Categories` tables in the `Northwind` database using the datasheet layout is shown in Figure 6.7.

FIGURE 6.7.

*An example of
datasheet layout.*

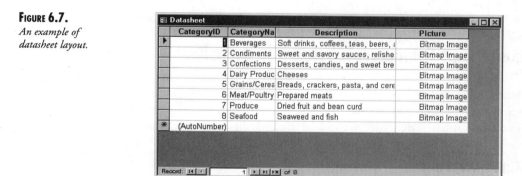

The difference between the tabular and datasheet layouts is that the datasheet will only display text like the Datasheet View of a table when it is opened. In the justified layout, the field names are put side-by-side on the form, and the data is displayed directly below the field name. An example of a form created from the `Categories` tables in the `Northwind` database using the justified layout is shown in Figure 6.8.

Step three is to select the style for the form. The style choices are clouds, colorful1, colorful2, dusk, evergreen, flax, international, pattern, standard, and stone.

TIP

My experience has taught me to always create the form using the standard style and then customize its style later.

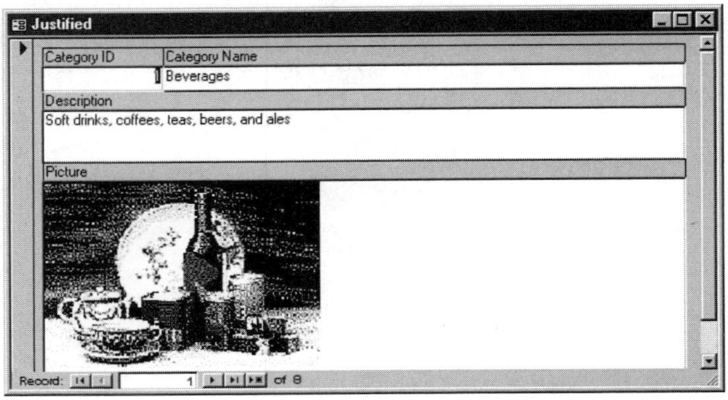

FIGURE 6.8.

An example of justified layout.

The fourth and final step is to give the new form a name and to choose between either opening the form for entering data or opening the form in Design View so modifications can be made. When you have completed these steps, Access 97 goes about creating the form.

AutoForm: Columnar, Tabular, and Datasheet

The AutoForm Wizards do the same thing as the Form Wizard, except that steps two through four are minimized depending on which autoform is selected. When using an autoform, you select the table/query to be used. The autoform assumes that all fields are to be included and uses the standard style. Once the table is selected, the form is created.

Chart Wizard

The Chart Wizard is a new wizard for Access 97. To use this wizard, you must select the table/query where the underlying fields are located. The wizard then prompts for the fields to be used in the chart. Next, the wizard allows you to select from 20 predefined chart styles, ranging from simple charts to scatter charts or 3D charts.

The wizard then prompts you to lay out the chart through an easy-to-use layout screen. Next, you must enter a name for the form. You are given the option of displaying a legend on the chart and also to open the form for viewing or further design. The form is then created, consisting of the chart only.

The PivotTable Wizard

The PivotTable Wizard creates an Access form with an Excel spreadsheet object on the form. The spreadsheet object is an Excel pivot table. (A *pivot table* is an interactive table that summarizes large amounts of data.)

When the wizard is run, you must select a table and then the fields from the table to be included in the pivot table. Once these selections have been made, the wizard opens Excel and runs the PivotTable Wizard from that application. Inside this wizard, you are asked to construct the pivot table by selecting the column, row, and data fields. Do this by selecting the field and dragging it into the appropriate box. When this is done, Excel calculates the pivot table and returns to Access 97 so the final form can be created.

When the wizard is through, a form is created with an Excel spreadsheet object consisting of the pivot table. To edit the pivot table, the user simply clicks the Edit Pivot Table button, and Excel opens, ready for editing.

Although the wizards are useful to create the first pass at form design, you should always make modifications to the form. The way to modify a form design is within the Form Design View in the Access 97 development environment. The best way to learn how to place controls on forms and how to set their properties is by looking at examples. The Northwind database in Access 97 is an excellent source on how to use the various controls in the creation and design of forms for a database application.

Form Examples

The following sections give examples of forms.

The Main Switchboard Example

Let's begin our look at some sample forms with the Main Switchboard form found in the Northwind sample database. Figure 6.9 displays the Main Switchboard form in its final form.

FIGURE 6.9.
The Northwind *database* Main Switchboard *form.*

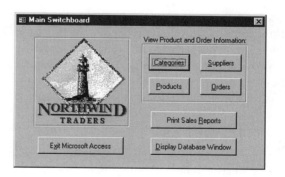

First, you need to look at the form properties for this form. To do this, open the form in Design View and click the Properties button on the toolbar. The following properties were set differently from the default form properties:

Property	Main Switchboard
Views Allowed	Form
Scroll Bars	Neither
Record Selectors	No
Navigation Buttons	No
AutoCenter	Yes
Border Style	Dialog

In addition to these properties, the help file was designated and the help index was changed. (Working with help files is covered later in Chapter 21, "Creating and Customizing Help Files.") The only other unique form property to this form is its size. In most cases, the size properties will always be different. To change the size of a form, simply drag the edges of the form in the Design View of the form.

Once you have set the form properties, you can add the controls to the form. This form consists of the following controls:

> One image
>
> One label
>
> One rectangle
>
> Seven command buttons

The image contained in this control is the logo image and is embedded in the database. The label is used to guide the user through his selection of the command buttons in the rectangle. These four command buttons will take the user to different forms within the database.

The best way to see what a command button is programmed to do is to look at the OnClick property of the control. The OnClick property is found on the Events and All tabs of the control's property sheet. If the property has an event associated with it, the phrase [Event Procedure] will show in the value of that property. To view the event procedure, click the button located to the right of the property value. The button will appear when the property value is selected. For example, the Categories button on the Main Switchboard form contains the following statement in its OnClick property: =OpenForms("Categories"). The other command buttons in the rectangle have a similar event procedure in their OnClick property, just pointing to different forms.

The Print Sales Report command button opens the Sales Report Dialog form. This is done through the following OnClick property: =OpenForms("Sales Reports Dialog"). The two remaining command button controls are used to invoke other events from within the application. Both of these buttons were created using the Command Button Wizard. As mentioned earlier, this wizard creates an event procedure that tells Access 97 what to do when the button is clicked. Let's take a look at the code behind these two buttons. (See Listings 6.1 and 6.2.)

Listing 6.1. The `DisplayDatabaseWindow_Click` event procedure.

```
Sub DisplayDatabaseWindow_Click()
' This code created in part by Command Button Wizard.
On Error GoTo Err_DisplayDatabaseWindow_Click

    Dim strDocName As String

    strDocName = "Categories"

    ' Close Main Switchboard form.
    DoCmd.Close

    ' Give focus to Database window; select Categories table
    '(first form in list).
    DoCmd.SelectObject acTable, strDocName, True

Exit_DisplayDatabaseWindow_Click:
    Exit Sub

Err_DisplayDatabaseWindow_Click:
    MsgBox Err.Description
    Resume Exit_DisplayDatabaseWindow_Click

End Sub
```

You can see from this code that this button closes the Main Switchboard form and moves the focus to the Categories table on the Tables tab of the database window.

Listing 6.2. The `ExitMicrosoftAccess_Click` event procedure.

```
Sub ExitMicrosoftAccess_Click()
' This code created by Command Button Wizard.
On Error GoTo Err_ExitMicrosoftAccess_Click

    ' Exit Microsoft Access.
    DoCmd.Quit

Exit_ExitMicrosoftAccess_Click:
    Exit Sub

Err_ExitMicrosoftAccess_Click:
    MsgBox Err.Description
    Resume Exit_ExitMicrosoftAccess_Click

End Sub
```

The code behind this command button simply exits Microsoft Access 97 using the Quit command. Note that both of these command buttons contain an error-handling mechanism. If an error occurs during the event specified by the code, a message box is displayed with the error description. It is always a good idea to include this type of error handling in code such as this.

In summary, this is a simple form to create. No new code creation was needed. The Command Button Wizard automatically generated the code behind the last two command buttons.

The Customer Orders Example

Now let's look at another simple form that uses the subform/subreport control. The Customer Orders form in the Northwind database is a good example of a form that uses the subform/subreport controls. The Customer Orders form appears to the user as shown in Figure 6.10.

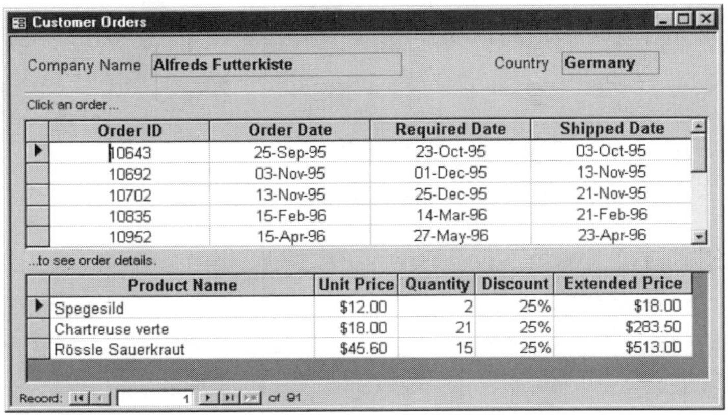

FIGURE 6.10.

The Customer Orders *form.*

This form consists of two text box controls and two subform/subreport controls. The text boxes appear at the top of the form and are bound to the CompanyName and Country fields in the Customer tables. To bind these text boxes, the ControlSource property in the form is set to the Customer tables, whereas the ControlSource property of the text boxes is set to CompanyName and Country, respectively.

The first Customer Orders subform is the Customer Orders Subform1. If this form were opened, it would appear as shown in Figure 6.11.

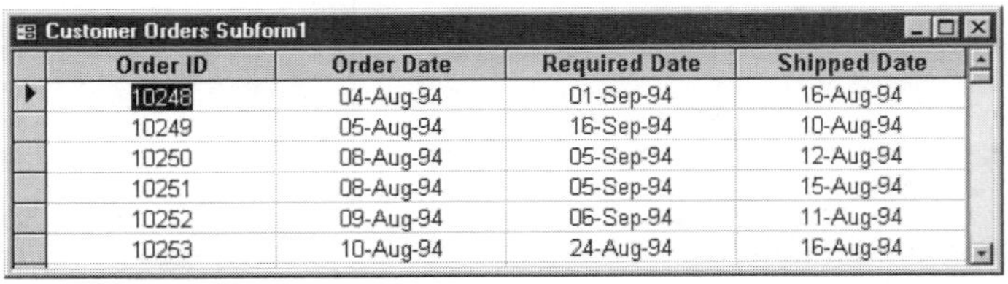

FIGURE 6.11.

Customer Orders *Subform1.*

The first thing to notice is that the form appears using the datasheet layout. If you view the subform in Design View, as shown in Figure 6.12, you can see that the form consists of four text boxes bound to their appropriate fields in the Orders table.

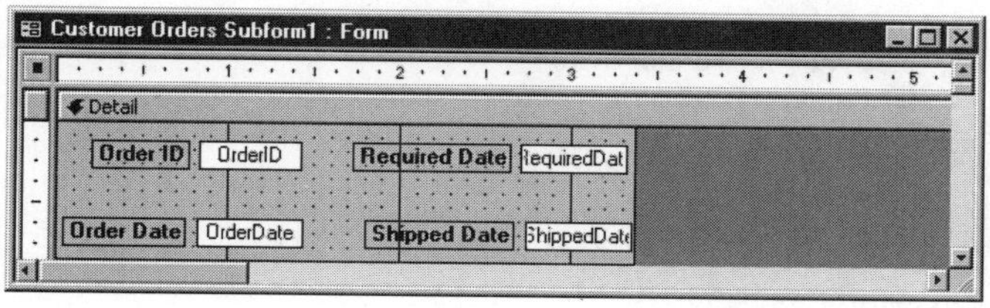

6

ACCESS 97
FORMS

Figure 6.12.
Design View of the
Customer Orders
Subform1.

By looking at the property sheet for this subform (see Figure 6.13), you can see that both the
Default View and Views Allowed properties have been set to Datasheet. These properties are
the ones that allow the form to be viewed as a datasheet when opened.

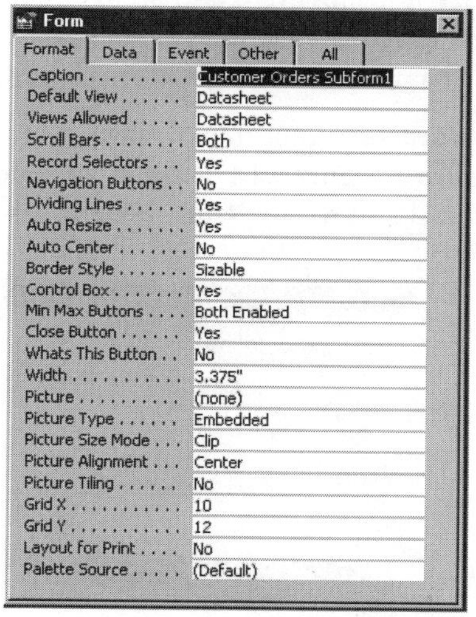

Figure 6.13.
The property sheet for
Customer Orders
Subform1.

Note also that the OnCurrent property of the Customer Orders Subform1 contains the following event procedure created by the Form Wizard. To view this information, move to the Events
tab of the form's property sheet. Notice that the OnCurrent property includes the phrase [Event
Procedure]. Click to the right of this property, and the event procedure will appear in the Code
Builder design window:

```
Sub Form_Current()
' This code created by Form Wizard.
    Dim strParentDocName As String

    On Error Resume Next
    strParentDocName = Me.Parent.Name

    If Err <> 0 Then
        GoTo Form_Current_Exit
```

```
    Else
        On Error GoTo Form_Current_Err
        Me.Parent![Customer Orders Subform2].Requery
    End If

Form_Current_Exit:
    Exit Sub

Form_Current_Err:
    MsgBox Err.Description
    Resume Form_Current_Exit

End Sub
```

The Current event is triggered when the focus in a form moves to a record. This makes that record the current record. This event also occurs when the form is refreshed or requeried. This piece of code is used to requery the Customer Orders Subform2 when the user moves to a different record in the Customer Orders Subform1.

When the Customer Orders Subform2 is opened, it appears very similar to the Customer Orders Subform1. You can see in Figure 6.14 that Customer Orders Subform2 is displayed in a datasheet view as well. Figure 6.15 shows the same form in Design View.

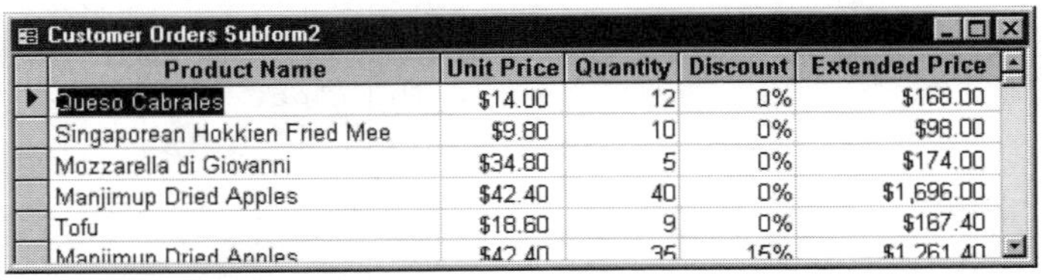

FIGURE 6.14.

Customer Orders
Subform2.

FIGURE 6.15.

Customer Orders
Subform2 in Design View.

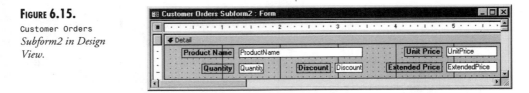

In Figure 6.15, you can see that this subform consists of five text boxes bound to their appropriate fields in the Order Details Extended Select query in the database. This query is shown in Figure 6.16 in its Design View. To view this query in Design View, select the subform by either choosing Select Form from the Edit menu or pressing Ctrl+R. After selecting the form, click the properties button on the toolbar or select Properties from the View menu.

The ExtendedPrice field in this query is a calculated field. The field syntax is as follows:

```
ExtendedPrice: CCur([Order Details].[UnitPrice]*
➡[Quantity]*(1-[Discount])/100)*100
```

FIGURE 6.16.
The Order Details Extended Select query in Design View.

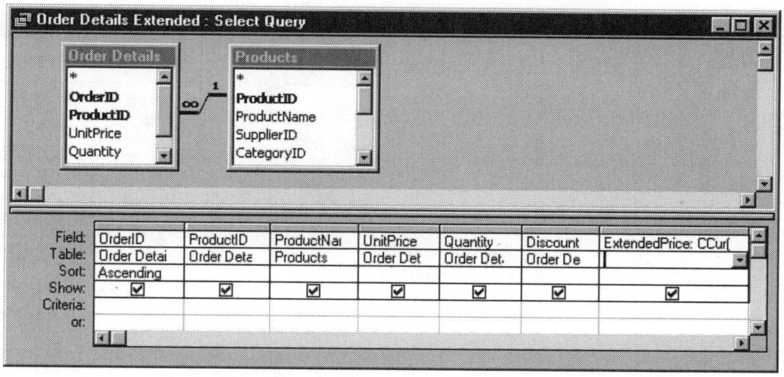

This field calculates the extended price of each order item. The subform has used this query as its basis, binding the display field desired in text boxes. It is worthy to note that no code was necessary for the creation of this subform.

The Orders Form Example

Another example of a form that uses the subform/subreport control as well as numerous other controls is the Orders form. This form is shown in Figure 6.17 in its final state. Figure 6.18 shows the form in its Design View.

FIGURE 6.17.
The Orders form in its final state.

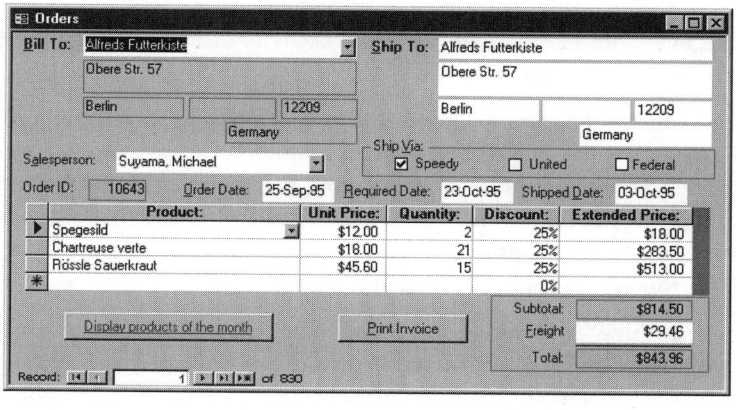

To describe the inner workings of this form, I must break it into parts for discussion purposes. First, you should look at the form properties. The first thing to notice is that the form is using data supplied to it by the Orders Qry query, but if you go to the Queries tab of the database, there is no Orders Qry query.

FIGURE 6.18.

The Orders *form in Design View.*

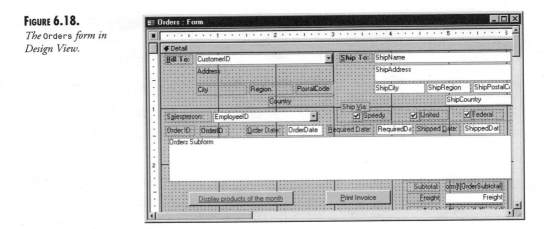

This is a good example of building a form based solely on a query that is built using the Query Builder. The Query Builder is like a wizard for creating queries. It is invoked in the RecordSource property of a form. With the value for this field blank, click the button with three dots. The Query Builder is automatically invoked and ensures that the proper syntax is used for the query. The Query Builder Design View is exactly like the regular Design View for creating queries.

For this form, the Query Builder uses the Orders and Customers tables from the database. The query is set up to show only those fields from these tables needed for the form. This is a good way to base a form on data from two tables at once. Typically, a form is based on only one table, but in practice there are numerous needs for data from two tables. Using the Query Builder is the way to solve this problem.

Now, back to the form design for the Orders form. First, you can look at the Bill To piece of this form. The Bill To section consists of one combo box and five text boxes. The text boxes are bound to their appropriate fields from the Order Qry record source in the form property. A closer look at the combo box in this section reveals how the combo box control operates. This combo box was probably created using the Combo Box Wizard. Figure 6.19 shows the Data property sheet for this particular combo box.

The first thing to examine on this combo box is the RowSource property. The RowSource property tells Access 97 where to get the records to be displayed in the combo box. To view the RowSource property, select the combo box by clicking on it. Open the properties sheet. On the Data tab, there is a property called RowSource. To view the query associated with this property, click to the right of the property to display the Query Builder.

In the RowSource property, you see that this combo box retrieves the CustomerID and CustomerName fields from the Customers table in the database. Note that there is only one bound column for this combo box: the field in the database table where the data is stored if entered by the user. But when the form is opened and the combo box is selected, only the customer name appears in the list. This is done because the CustomerID field in the Format property sheet for this combo box has the first column width set to 0. Figure 6.20 shows the Format property sheet for this combo box.

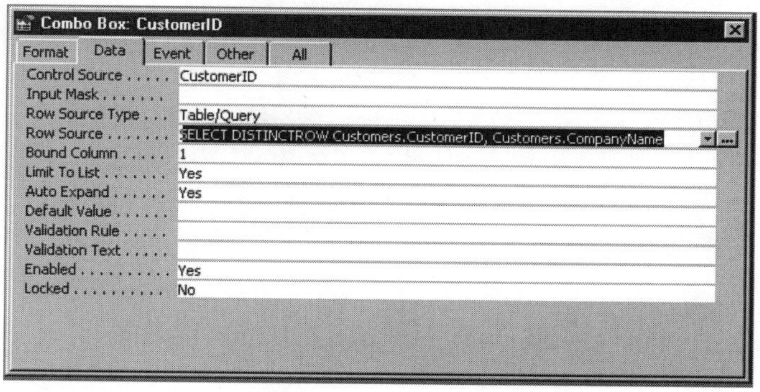

FIGURE 6.19.

The Data property sheet for the combo box.

Now that you know how the combo box gets its data and how it displays the data, let's see how it manipulates the data. With the properties sheet for the combo box already open, click on the Event tab to see what events are associated with this combo box. Figure 6.21 shows the Event property sheet for this combo box.

Notice that the BeforeUpdate and AfterUpdate properties contain event procedures. The first thing to think about is when these events are triggered. As the names would lead you to believe, the BeforeUpdate event is triggered before data that has changed in the combo box control is updated, and the AfterUpdate event is triggered after data in the combo box control has been updated.

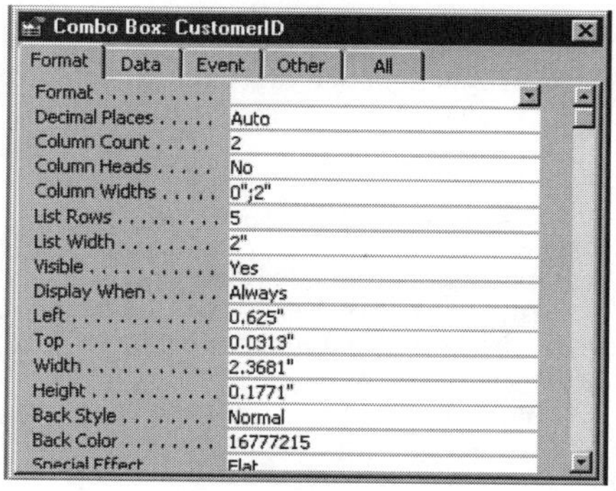

FIGURE 6.20.

The Format property sheet for the combo box.

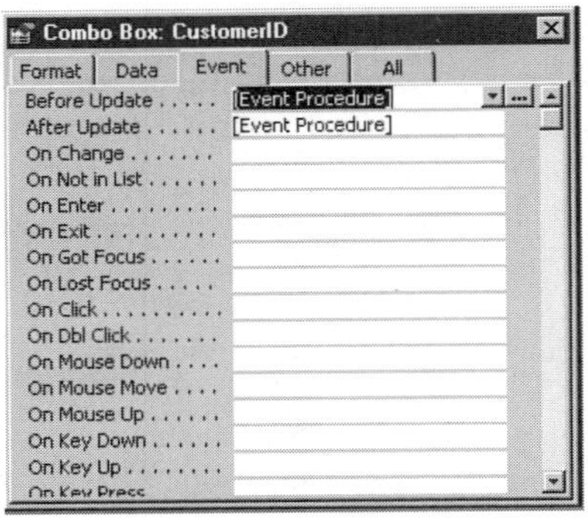

FIGURE 6.21.

The Event property sheet for the combo box.

Both of these event procedures were created with the Code Builder that you invoke by clicking the button with the three dots next to the event. When this button is first clicked, you have the option of choosing to use the Expression Builder, the Macro Builder, or the Code Builder. For this example, the Code Builder was used. The code behind this `BeforeUpdate` event procedure is as follows:

```
Private Sub CustomerID_BeforeUpdate(Cancel As Integer)
' Display message if CustomerID combo box is blank.

    Dim strMsg As String, strTitle As String
    Dim intStyle As Integer

    If IsNull(Me!CustomerID) Or Me!CustomerID = "" Then
        strMsg = "You must pick a value from the Bill To list."
        strTitle = "Bill To Customer Required"
        intStyle = vbOKOnly
        MsgBox strMsg, intStyle, strTitle
        Cancel = True
    End If

End Sub
```

As the comment line states, this procedure will display a message if the `CustomerID` combo box is blank. The event procedure begins by declaring three variables: `strMsg`, `strTitle`, and `intStyle`. These variables are used in the actual procedure within the code. The procedure checks the combo box for a null value or an empty string. The `strMsg` is given the value `You must pick a value form the Bill To list.`, the `strTitle` variable is provided the value `Bill To Customer Required`, and the `intStyle` variable is given the value `vbOKOnly`. The procedure is then told to display a message box using the appropriate variables as the arguments for the `MsgBox` function.

The `MsgBox` function uses the following syntax:

```
MsgBox(prompt[, buttons] [, title] [, helpfile, context])
```

The *prompt* argument is the string expression that is displayed in the message box. The *buttons* argument tells Access 97 which message box to use—that is, how many and which ones. The *title* argument is simply the title to be used in the message box. The options available for the *buttons* argument in Access 97 are shown in Table 6.1. Figure 6.22 shows the final result of this procedure. You can use the value itself: Just choose the things you want, add up all the values, and replace the variable names with the total. This is more complicated to do, but once you figure it out, it will save a lot of typing.

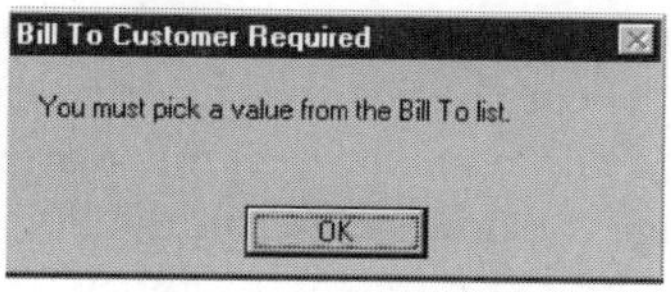

FIGURE 6.22.

*The message box form
for the event procedure
in the combo box.*

Table 6.1. The MsgBox buttons arguments.

Constant	*Value*	*Description*
vbOKOnly	0	Display OK button only.
vbOKCancel	1	Display OK and Cancel buttons.
vbAbortRetryIgnore	2	Display Abort, Retry, and Ignore buttons.
vbYesNoCancel	3	Display Yes, No, and Cancel buttons.
vbYesNo	4	Display Yes and No buttons.
vbRetryCancel	5	Display Retry and Cancel buttons.
vbCritical	16	Display Critical Message icon.
vbQuestion	32	Display Warning Query icon.
vbExclamation	48	Display Warning Message icon.
vbInformation	64	Display Information Message icon.
vbDefaultButton1	0	First button is default.
vbDefaultButton2	256	Second button is default.
vbDefaultButton3	512	Third button is default.
vbDefaultButton4	768	Fourth button is default.
vbApplicationModal	0	Application modal; the user must respond to the message box before continuing work in the current application.
vbSystemModal	4096	System modal; all applications are suspended until the user responds to the message box.

The event procedure assigned to the AfterUpdate property of this combo box is as follows:

```
Private Sub CustomerID_AfterUpdate()
' Update ShipTo controls based on value selected in CustomerID combo box.
    Me!ShipName = Me![CustomerID].Column(1)
    Me!ShipAddress = Me!Address
    Me!ShipCity = Me!City
```

```
Me!ShipRegion = Me!Region
Me!ShipPostalCode = Me!PostalCode
Me!ShipCountry = Me!Country

End Sub
```

This event procedure, as the comment tells you, updates the Ship To text boxes on the form based on the customer name that appears in the combo box. Note that the field the procedure uses to determine if the combo box data has changed is the `CustomerID` field. The first line of the procedure sets the ship name to the same name as that appearing in the combo box. The rest of the lines change the other values in the Ship To area of the form. Note that each text box value is preceded by the phrase `Me!`. This phrase tells Access 97 to use the current form when changing these values.

The last thing to notice about this combo box is the Other property sheet associated with it. To view the Other property sheet, simply select the combo box and open the properties sheet by clicking the properties button on the toolbar, right-clicking on the combo box to select properties on the pop-up menu, or selecting properties from the View menu on the menu bar. Once the property sheet has been opened, click on the Other tab. Figure 6.23 shows this property sheet.

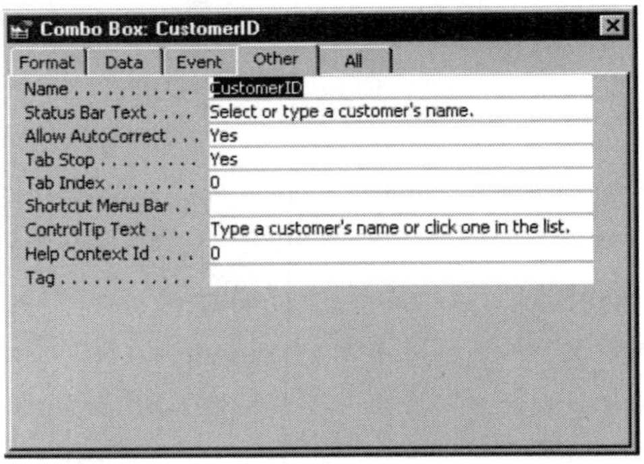

FIGURE 6.23.

The Other property sheet for the combo box.

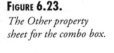

Notice on this property sheet the `StatusBarText` and `ControlTipText` properties. These properties provide useful information for the user to see. The `StatusBarText` property is displayed in the bottom-left corner of the window in the status bar when the combo box has the focus. The `ControlTipText` property is displayed when the user moves the cursor over the combo box in a little yellow box just like tooltips are displayed when you put the cursor over the icon on the toolbar.

The next piece of this form is the Ship To portion, located in the upper-right side of the form. This piece of the form consists of six text boxes. The values for the text boxes are determined initially by the Order Qry query on which the form is based. However, as noted earlier, in the `AfterUpdate` property of the combo box just discussed, there is an event procedure that changes the values in the text box depending on the value of the combo box.

The Ship Via portion of the form consists of one option box control and three checkbox controls. Remember, the importance of the option group control is to limit the number of possible selections from the group.

To the left of the Ship Via portion of the form is another combo box for the salesperson. This combo box was most likely created using the Combo Box Wizard. The data for this combo box is retrieved using the following statement in the RecordSource property of the combo box:

```
SELECT DISTINCTROW Employees.EmployeeID, [LastName] & ", " &
➥[FirstName] AS Salesperson
```

You can see from this statement that the combo box contains the EmployeeID field from the Employees table and the LastName and FirstName fields from the same table.

One additional comment about this statement is the formatting to be used when displaying the information in the list box portion of the combo box. The & symbol is an operator for Access 97; it is used to force string concatenation of two expressions. The quotation marks tell Access 97 to use the literal value of what is between them. Therefore, the end result of this formatting is the last name followed by a comma and a space, followed by the first name of the salesperson.

Directly below the salesperson combo box and across the form are four text box controls. The RecordSource property for these controls is provided through the Order Qry query.

Below these text boxes is a subform: the Orders subform. Figure 6.24 displays the Orders subform when opened, and Figure 6.25 shows the same form in Design View.

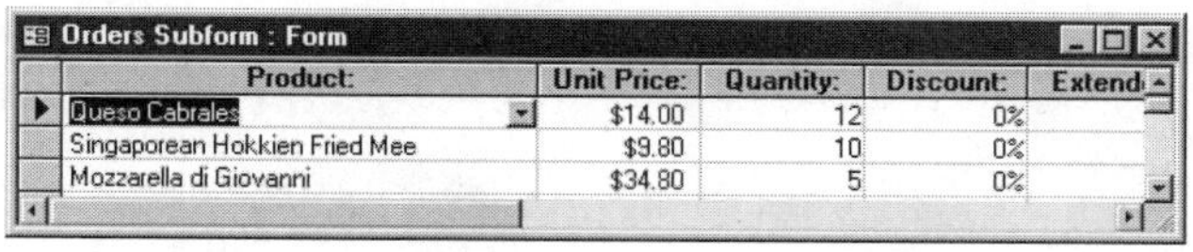

FIGURE 6.24.

The Orders *subform.*

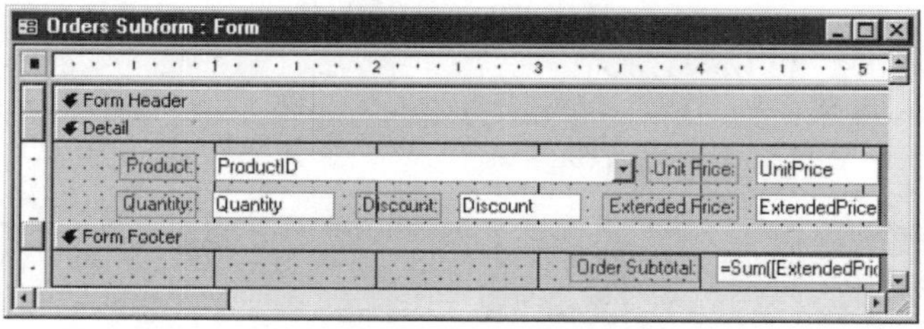

FIGURE 6.25.

The Orders *subform in Design View.*

There are two things to note about this subform that are different from a design standpoint from the subforms already discussed. The first is the OrderSubtotal text box. This text box has a RecordSource property with the following statement: =Sum([ExtendedPrice]). This property illustrates a calculated control using the Sum function.

The result of the calculation is the sum of the ExtendedPrice field from the Order Details extended select query. We know this field is from this query because the ControlSource property of the form is set to this query. The OrderSubtotal text box was placed in the footer of the subform because that enables it to calculate a total for all the extended price values in a single order. Because the form displays itself in Datasheet View, the footer is not seen.

The second thing of note in this subform is the use of a combo box to allow the user to either select the product name from the list provided or enter a new name. The RecordSource property for this combo box is as follows:

```
SELECT DISTINCTROW [ProductID],[ProductName],[Discontinued]
➥FROM Products ORDER BY [ProductName];
```

The only major distinction of this statement is the use of the ORDER BY clause to sort the data before it is viewed in the combo box. A minor distinction is that the combo box displays two columns instead of one, as do the other combo boxes on this form.

The only controls remaining on this form to discuss are the two command buttons located on the bottom-left of the form and the three text boxes located on the bottom-right. Let's start with the command buttons. The first command button is the Display Products command button, which is a good example of the HyperlinkAddress property. The Format property sheet for this command button is shown in Figure 6.26.

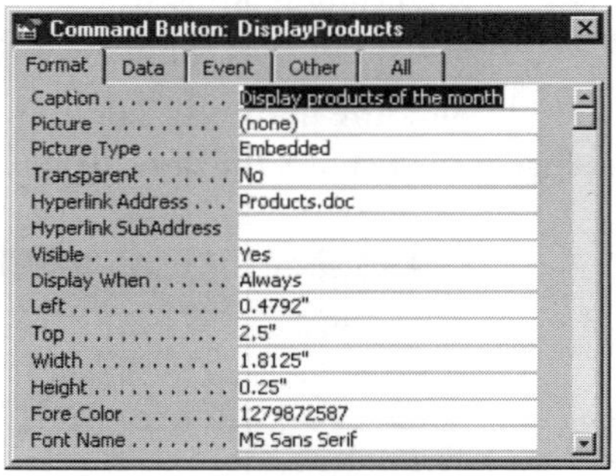

FIGURE 6.26.

The Format property sheet of the Display Products button.

Notice that the HyperlinkAddress property is set to Products.doc. This tells Access 97 to open Microsoft Word and display the Products document. This document is located in the same directory as the Northwind database.

> **WARNING**
>
> The thing to remember about hyperlink addresses is to always keep those called in a database in the same directory as the database. If the document is moved and the new location is not changed in the HyperlinkAddress property, Access 97 will not be able to find the document, and an error message will appear.

The next button to discuss is the Print Invoice command button. To see the event procedure associated with this button, select the button and open the properties sheet associated with it.

Once the property sheet has been opened, select the Event tab. The event procedure located in this button's OnClick property is as follows:

```
Sub PrintInvoice_Click()
' This code created by Command Button Wizard.
On Error GoTo Err_PrintInvoice_Click

    Dim strDocName As String

    strDocName = "Invoice"
    ' Print Invoice report, using Invoices Filter query to print
    ' invoice for current order.
    DoCmd.OpenReport strDocName, acViewNormal, "Invoices Filter"

Exit_PrintInvoice_Click:
    Exit Sub

Err_PrintInvoice_Click:
    ' If action was cancelled by the user, don't display an error message.
    Const conErrDoCmdCancelled = 2501
    If (Err = conErrDoCmdCancelled) Then
        Resume Exit_PrintInvoice_Click
    Else
        MsgBox Err.Description
        Resume Exit_PrintInvoice_Click
    End If

End Sub
```

The Command Button Wizard created this code. The first line in the code sets the error handling for the procedure. The next line declares a string variable with the name strDocName. The next line sets the string variable value to Invoice. The procedure then runs the line DoCmd.OpenReport strDocName, acViewNormal, "Invoices Filter". This command opens the report Invoice in the normal Report View and uses the Invoice Filter query to sort the data before it is displayed. (We discuss reports in detail in Chapter 7, "Access 97 Reports.")

The last controls on this report are the three text box controls located on the bottom-right of the report. Note that there is a rectangle control used to highlight the text boxes. The ControlSource property of the Subtotal text box contains the following statement:

```
=[Orders Subform].[Form]![OrderSubtotal]
```

The statement simply calls for the value located in the Order Subtotal text box in the Orders subform.

The Freight text box displays the value of the freight field in the Order Qry query.

The Total text box is a calculated control that uses the following statement to add the values in the Subtotal text box and the Freight text box:

```
=[Subtotal]+[Freight]
```

This concludes the discussion on the example of the Orders form. The next example examines a form that uses the tab control.

The Employees Form Example

The Employees form provides a good example of how the tab control is used in form design. Figure 6.27 shows the Employees form with the Company Info tab selected. Figure 6.28 shows the same form with the Personal Info tab selected.

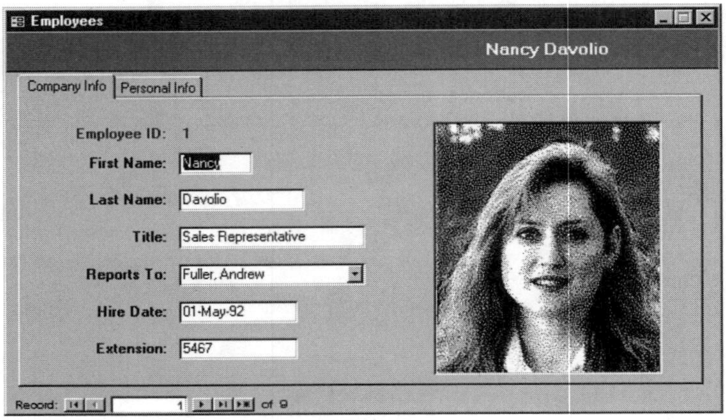

FIGURE 6.27.

The Employees *form—Company Info tab.*

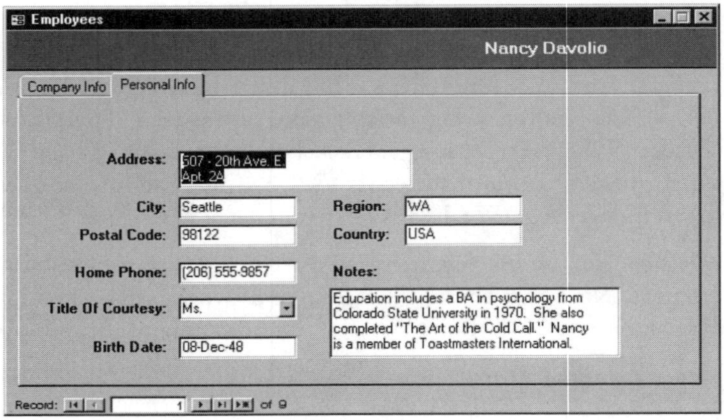

FIGURE 6.28.

The Employees *form—Personal Info tab.*

Now let's see what each of these looks like in the Design View of the Access 97 development environment. Figure 6.29 displays the Employees form in Design View with the Company Info tab selected. Figure 6.30 shows the same thing with the Personal Info tab selected.

FIGURE 6.29.
The Employee *form in Design View—the Company Info tab.*

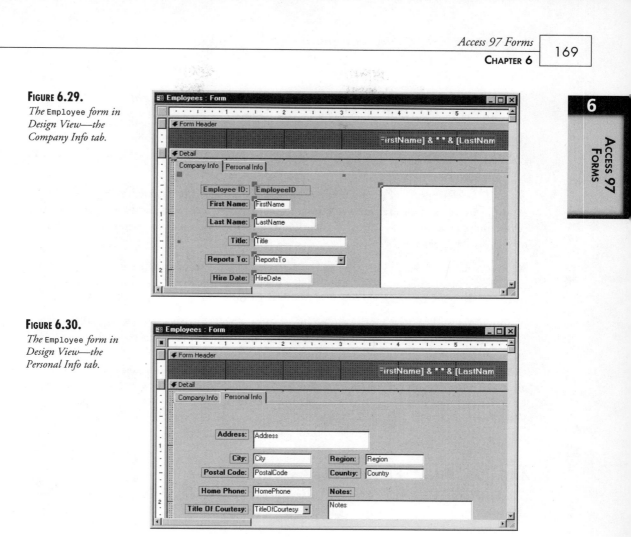

FIGURE 6.30.
The Employee *form in Design View—the Personal Info tab.*

The focus of this discussion is on the tab control and any other controls that have not been discussed in the previous two examples.

The first thing to note about the design of this form is the heading, which has been included in a form header. A form's header can be viewed by selecting View | Form Header/Footer. When using a tab control, it is always a good idea to use the header of a form to maintain a consistent look and feel to the form. The tab control would be created in the Details section of the form.

The text box control located in the header section of this form displays the employee's first and last names. But instead of using two text box controls (because the data is stored in two fields in the Employees table), the RecordSource property contains the following statement:

```
=[FirstName] & " " & [LastName]
```

As previously discussed, this statement tells Access 97 to concatenate two string expressions and displays the first name followed by a space followed by the last name.

Now let's discuss the tab control. When a tab control is first added to a form, it contains two pages. To add pages to the tab control, select the tab control and then select Insert|Tab Control Page from the menu bar.

The `MultiRow` property of the tab control tells Access 97 whether the tab control can contain multiple tab rows. This example contains a tab control with one row and two pages. To move between the pages, click on the page identifier on the top of the tab control. Each page has its own property sheet.

All that is necessary to add controls to the different pages is to select the page where the controls need to go. Other than that, it is just like having multiple forms contained within a single form. This greatly increases the amount of information that can be displayed in a single form.

A similar method of creating the same type of information display containing multiple pages can be accomplished by using the page break control. An example of this control can be found by viewing the `Employees` (page break) form in the `Northwind` database. The difference between using a form with page breaks and using a tab control is that a command button has to be added to allow the user to move between the pages on a form that uses page break controls. From a developer's standpoint, the tab control is easier to use because the design space is contained within the tab control. Moving between pages is easier, and the display of the controls is more efficient.

The `Customer Phone List` Form Example

The final form design example to discuss is the `Customer Phone List` form. Figure 6.31 shows this form when opened. Figure 6.32 displays the form in Design View.

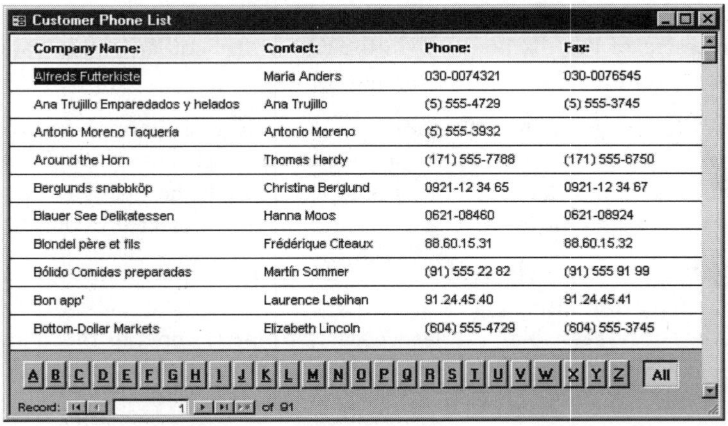
Customer Phone List
Company Name:
Contact:
Phone:
Fax:
Alfreds Futterkiste
Maria Anders
030-0074321
030-0076545
Ana Trujillo Emparedados y helados
Ana Trujillo
(5) 555-4729
(5) 555-3745
Antonio Moreno Taquería
Antonio Moreno
(5) 555-3932
Around the Horn
Thomas Hardy
(171) 555-7788
(171) 555-6750
Berglunds snabbköp
Christina Berglund
0921-12 34 65
0921-12 34 67
Blauer See Delikatessen
Hanna Moos
0621-08460
0621-08924
Blondel père et fils
Frédérique Citeaux
88.60.15.31
88.60.15.32
Bólido Comidas preparadas
Martín Sommer
(91) 555 22 82
(91) 555 91 99
Bon app'
Laurence Lebihan
91.24.45.40
91.24.45.41
Bottom-Dollar Markets
Elizabeth Lincoln
(604) 555-4729
(604) 555-3745
A B C D E F G H I J K L M N O P Q R S T U V W X Y Z All
Record: 1 of 91

FIGURE 6.31.
The `Customer Phone List` *form.*

FIGURE 6.32.

The Customer Phone
List *form in Design
View.*

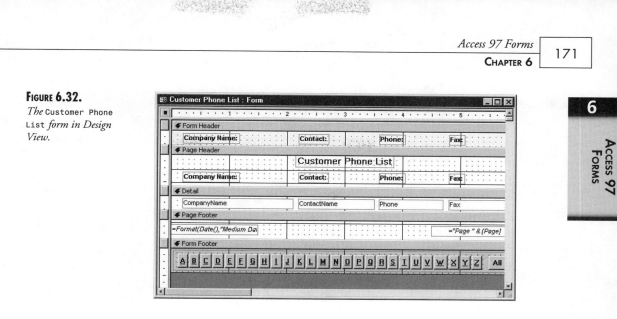

This form design is unique because it uses the page header function of the Access 97 form-development environment. As shown in Figure 6.32, this form contains a form header, page header, detail section, page footer, and form footer. The thing to remember about page headers and footers is that they are displayed only on a printed page, not in a form. For this reason, you will notice that Figure 6.32 shows the page header and Figure 6.31 does not show it. However, if this form were printed, the page header would appear.

The other unique feature of this form is the form footer. You may be wondering what will prevent the form footer from displaying on a printed page. To answer this, look in the form footer property sheet. On this sheet, you will find a property called DisplayWhen. This property tells Access 97 when to display the form footer. In this example, the DisplayWhen property is set to Screen Only. The other options for displaying a form footer are Always or Print Only.

In addition, this form footer contains a number of toggle button controls. Note that all the toggle button controls are contained in an option group control. Remember that the option group control allows only one of the options to be selected at a time. The option group also controls the event when the user selects a toggle button. Notice that in the Event tab of the option group control property sheet, the following statement is in the AfterUpdate property:

```
Customer Phone List.Alpha Buttons
```

What this statement does is call the Alpha Buttons macro contained in the Customer Phone List macro page. To view this macro, select the Macros tab in Database View. Select the Customer Phone List macro and then select Design. Figure 6.33 shows the Design View of this macro.

This macro filters the values that are displayed on the Customer Phone List form, depending on which one of the toggle button controls is selected. This macro is described in detail in Chapter 8, "Access 97 Macros."

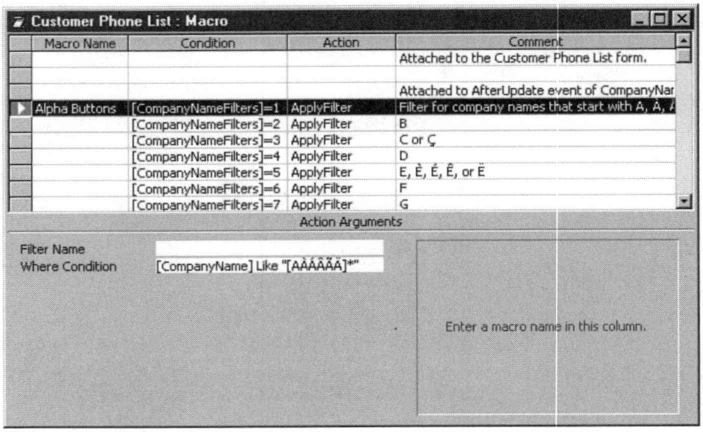

FIGURE 6.33.

The Alpha Buttons *macro in the* Customer Phone List *macro page.*

Lightweight Forms

One of the new features in Access 97 is the concept of lightweight forms. When Access 97 creates a form, it also creates a code class module, which contains the code associated with the form. Whenever an event procedure is created, it is stored in the class module. In many cases, a form can be created and used without ever using an event procedure. Because hyperlink addresses have their own property, an event procedure is not needed when using them.

> **WARNING**
>
> In an attempt to address some of the complaints Microsoft was receiving about the performance of Access 95, Microsoft Access developers created a new form property: the HasModule property. The default setting for this property is Yes. However, to create a lightweight form, simply change this property to No. When this property is changed to No, Access 97 deletes the associated code module with it. Let's say that again: *When the* HasModule *property of a form is set to* No, *Access 97 deletes the code module that was created with it. When the code module is deleted, all code in the module is deleted with it.*

Why is this a good thing? Well, many forms are created that do not use the code module created with it. But when Access 97 loads the form into memory, it also loads the code module. By deleting the code module, Access 97 is able to load the form much faster, thus improving the overall database performance. Deleting the code module also reduces the overall physical size of the database application.

Summary

This chapter focused on the Access 97 form-development features. After reading the chapter, you should be familiar with the Access 97 form Design View. In addition, you should now understand the various standard form controls and the properties associated with each control.

The chapter also took a brief look at the form wizards available in Access 97. The form wizards were discussed in light of what information was needed to use them and what features they provide for you.

Examples in this chapter were taken from the `Northwind` sample database that ships with every copy of Access 97. The examples were described in detail, examining most of the standard controls and how they can be used in form design. The examples include the `Main Switchboard`, `Customer Orders`, `Orders`, `Employees`, and `Customer Phone List` forms. These examples range from the simple form to the complex. The discussions of the examples deal in depth with how the controls are used to accomplish common tasks from within Access 97.

Finally, the chapter concluded with an examination of the new feature in Access 97 form designs, the lightweight form. The chapter described what this form is and how it is created. The discussion also included the benefit of using lightweight forms in an Access 97 database application.

Chapter 7 examines the creation of reports in Access 97.

Access 97 Reports

by Scott Billings

IN THIS CHAPTER

CHAPTER 7

This chapter examines the report-making features of Access 97. There are a few report basics that every programmer should be aware of when creating and developing reports from within the Access 97 development environment. These basics include building reports using a previously created form as the basis and converting reports to files for use in other applications.

This chapter also discusses the Access 97 design environment. Included in that section is a look at the fundamental elements that go into the creation of reports in Access 97. You will notice the similarity between the design environments Access 97 uses for forms and reports. This similarity begins with the use of the same controls for reports as are available for forms.

Following the design-environment evaluation, this chapter takes a look at the predefined report styles available in Access 97. This is followed by an examination of the Access 97 report wizards. The predefined report styles are initiated either after the report has been created (using the AutoFormat Wizard) or by using the report wizards to create the report initially.

The chapter concludes with an examination of several examples taken from the Northwind sample database. These examples include the Alphabetical List of Products, Catalog, Employee Sales by Quarter, Summary of Sales by Quarter, and Sales by Year reports. This discussion of the report examples will show you, the programmer, how reports are created and how the controls on the reports operate to retrieve data and display it.

Report Basics

Before a programmer begins to create and develop reports in Access 97, he should always survey the final users of the database application. The end users should provide the programmer with the needed detail on what to include in the reports and how to best organize the report for its intended uses.

Do not hesitate to get the most information possible from the end users. In most cases, the report is the final product of the database application, and usually the measuring tool of how useful the application is will be after completion.

The report function of the application should be taken very seriously. Its final product, the reports, will often be used to grade the primary functionality of any database. After all, the reports are usually the main reason for the development of the application in the first place. The storage of data, while important, is only one aspect of a database application. It is the reports and the ability of the application to retrieve and display information that will ultimately determine the database's usefulness in the eyes of the end user.

There are two basics in the creation of reports that every programmer should be aware of and make use of in report development: exporting a final report to a file that users can bring up and work with in other applications and converting a form to a report.

Exporting a Report to a File

Although Access 97 provides for the printing of reports directly from its own environment, many programmers will be asked to include the functionality to export a report to an external file for personalization by the end user. Exporting a report to a file in Access 97 is a relatively easy process. Once the report has been created, the programmer or user can simply select the report and choose SaveAs/Export... from the File menu.

To show an example of exporting a report to a file, let's export the Sales Total by Amount report from the Northwind database. Figure 7.1 shows the first screen displayed after the programmer or user has selected SaveAs/Export... from the File menu.

Figure 7.1.

The Save As dialog window.

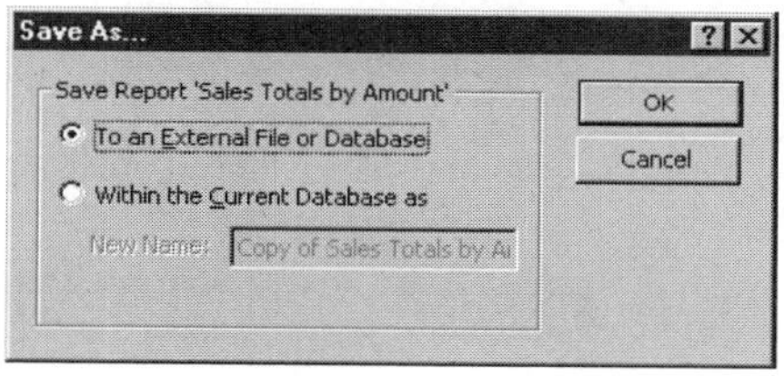

The default is to save the report to an external file or database. The user is then prompted for the location to save the file to, as shown in Figure 7.2. Note that at the bottom of this screen the user can select the appropriate file type.

Figure 7.2.

The Save As location screen.

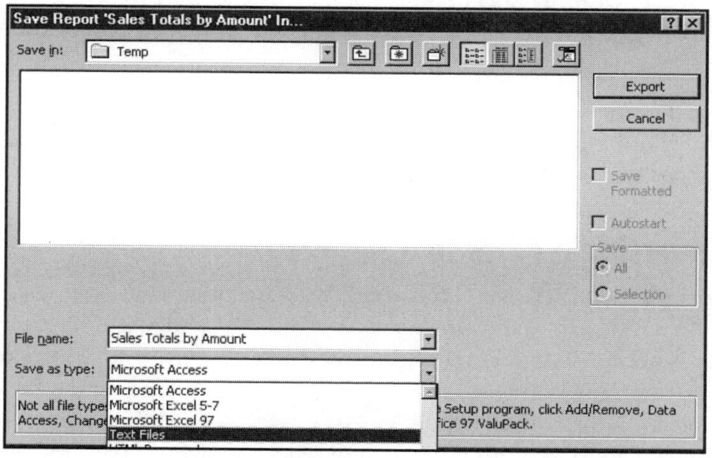

The file types supported under Access 97 for report exportation are Microsoft Access, Microsoft Excel 5–7, Microsoft Excel 97, Text File, HTML Documents, and Rich Text Format. The user selects the appropriate file type and location where he wants the file to go and clicks the OK button; Access 97 then exports the file to the appropriate location.

To include this functionality from within the application itself, all the programmer needs to do is create a macro to perform this function. Figure 7.3 is an example of a macro that exports the `Sales Total by Amounts` report to a text file called `SalesTotal` in the `C:\Temp` directory.

FIGURE 7.3.

The `ExportReport` *macro.*

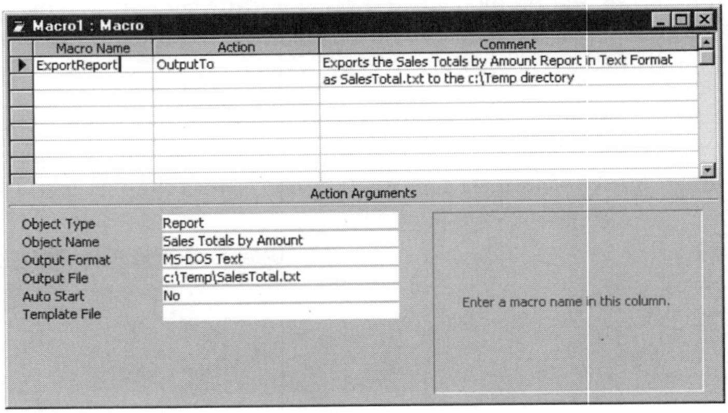

This macro uses the `OutputTo` action to accomplish the exporting. The available output formats for this action are HTML, Microsoft Excel, MS-DOS Text, and Rich Text Format.

For control purposes, you might want to set up a common shared network directory with the systems administrator that will initially receive all exported reports. This directory can then be periodically cleaned out. The other option is to leave the `OutputFile` property blank in the macro. This will cause Access 97 to prompt the end user for the location of where to output the report.

Once the macro has been created, the programmer can either create a command button on the main printing form created for the application or create a custom form used for all print requests to specifically allow the user either to print the report directly or export it to a file.

Converting a Form to a Report

Converting a form to a report is another report basic that is often used by programmers. Much time is devoted to developing forms in Access 97, and often the form design is very similar to what is needed for a report. The quickest way of converting a form to a report is by selecting the form on the Forms tab of the database, right-clicking on the form, and choosing Save As Report from the pop-up menu. Access 97 will ask for the name of the report desired. The programmer can move to the Reports tab in the database and either preview the report or make modifications to it.

This process takes the form and converts it directly to a report. If a lot of custom formatting was done (for example, colorization, increasing font size, and so on) to the form when it was created, in most instances this formatting should be removed from the report because most reports are printed in black and white and use standard fonts and font sizes. In addition, if the form displays the data one page at a time, the report version of the form will simply duplicate the form's formatting for each page of the report. In most cases, this is probably not what the end user wants.

Although converting a form to a report is easy and serves as a convenient means of not duplicating work, you should be careful in choosing which forms to convert to reports. Not all forms are appropriate and, depending on the amount of formatting used in the form, it may not be efficient to use this method. It could take more time reformatting a report that has been converted from a form than to simply create the report from the beginning. Logic should prevail in using this feature.

These are two of the most basic and most often used features in report development. The next section examines the design environment for report creation and development within Access 97.

The Design Environment

The design environment for creating reports within Access 97 is exactly like the form-design environment. (See Figure 7.4.)

Figure 7.4.

The Design View for a new report.

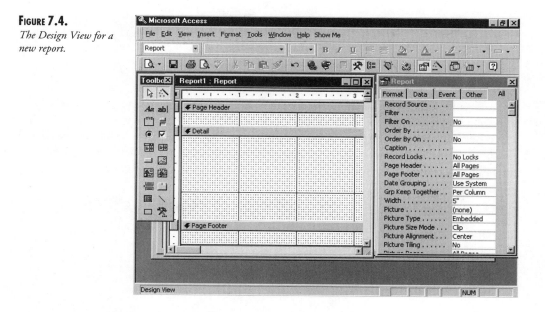

The toolbox that holds the available controls is on the left. The report design window is in the middle, and the property sheet is on the right. This should look very familiar.

When designing reports, you should be aware of the different properties associated with a report. Although the controls are the same and they work the same, the report properties are not entirely the same as the form properties. To view the properties associated with an individual report, open the report in Design View. Select the report by either selecting the report from the Edit menu bar or by using the hotkey (Ctrl+R) associated with this command. Once the report has been selected, click on the Properties button on the toolbar. Figure 7.5 displays a partial listing of the report properties.

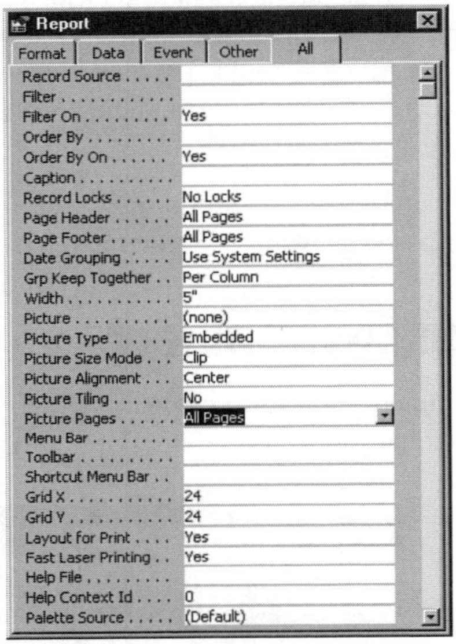

FIGURE 7.5.

A partial listing of report properties.

Report	
Format	Data	Event	Other	All
Record Source	
Filter	
Filter On	Yes
Order By	
Order By On	Yes
Caption	
Record Locks	No Locks
Page Header	All Pages
Page Footer	All Pages
Date Grouping	Use System Settings
Grp Keep Together . .	Per Column
Width	5"
Picture	(none)
Picture Type	Embedded
Picture Size Mode . . .	Clip
Picture Alignment . . .	Center
Picture Tiling	No
Picture Pages	All Pages
Menu Bar	
Toolbar	
Shortcut Menu Bar . .	
Grid X	24
Grid Y	24
Layout for Print	Yes
Fast Laser Printing . .	Yes
Help File	
Help Context Id	0
Palette Source	(Default)

 Another thing to be aware of about the report design environment is how to get Access 97 to sort and group data on a report. To do this, click on the Sorting and Grouping toolbar button. The other way of seeing the Sorting and Group properties for a report is to select Sorting and Grouping from the View menubar. Either of these methods invokes the Sorting and Grouping dialog box displayed in Figure 7.6.

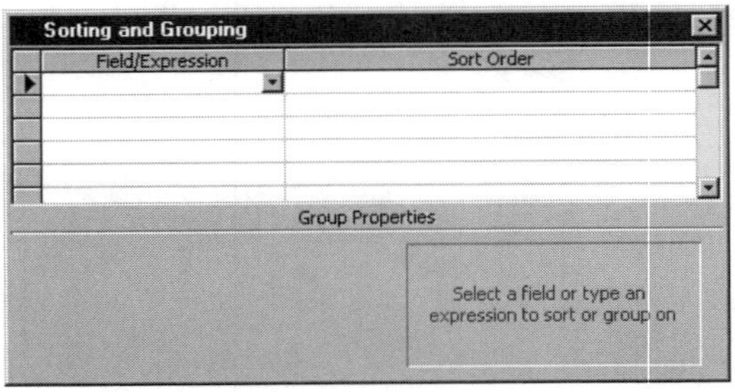

FIGURE 7.6.

The Sorting and Grouping dialog box.

Sorting and Grouping	
Field/Expression	Sort Order
Group Properties	
	Select a field or type an expression to sort or group on

To sort the data in a report, select the field or expression on the left and the sort order on the right. The grouping properties will appear on the lower portion of this dialog box. Sorting and grouping data is covered in more detail in the examples at the end of this chapter.

As you can see, the design environment for creating reports is just like the one used for creating forms. When a programmer is fluent in form design, the same skills can be used in report design.

Report Styles

Access 97 includes a number of predefined styles that can be used when creating reports. There are two ways to use report styles from within Access 97. When a report is created using the Report Wizard, the programmer is prompted for which style to use in creating the report. The second way to use a predefined report style is to use the AutoFormat Wizard.

The AutoFormat Wizard

The AutoFormat Wizard applies a predefined style to a report. There are two ways to invoke this wizard from within the report design view. The first is by selecting Format on the menu bar; the first choice on this menu is the AutoFormat Wizard. The second way is to click the button that looks like a wand sitting on top of piece of yellow paper. (This button is in between the Sorting and Grouping button and the Code button on the toolbar.) The AutoFormat Wizard can also be selected from the Format menubar.

Once the AutoFormat Wizard has been invoked, you are presented with a single screen that lists the available styles down the left side and shows a preview of the style in the middle. When you click the Attributes button, a drop-down form appears on the bottom of this screen. This screen is shown in Figure 7.7.

FIGURE 7.7.
The AutoFormat Wizard screen.

The Customize button on this screen allows you to create a new autoformat style, update the selected autoformat style with the values in the open report, or delete an autoformat style.

The autoformat features of Access 97 can be very useful to programmers. In a business environment, providing reports with a consistent format is very valuable to the end users. The autoformat component of Access 97 allows you to accomplish this with little frustration.

The best way to set up an autoformat style is to begin with an empty report. Add the controls and formatting elements that are to appear on all the reports. Start the AutoFormat Wizard and choose Customize. Select Create a new Autoformat from the dialog box displayed and provide the new name. Now when a new report is made, the programmer can select the new style either using the AutoFormat Wizard or by selecting it when running the Report Wizard.

Report Wizards

Microsoft Access 97 comes with the following report wizards: Report Wizard, Autoreport: Columnar, Autoreport: Tabular, Chart Wizard, and Label Wizard. As with other wizards, these report wizards provide an easy-to-use interface for initial report creation. After the wizard has run, you can go back into the report and make any necessary modifications to the report's design and functionality.

The Report Wizard

The Report Wizard is the most basic wizard used to initially create reports in Access 97. When the Report Wizard opens, you are prompted to enter the table/query that will serve as the basis for the report. In the same screen, you can select which fields from that table/query to include in the report.

The Report Wizard continues by asking if you would like to include any grouping levels. Figure 7.8 shows the window for adding these grouping levels.

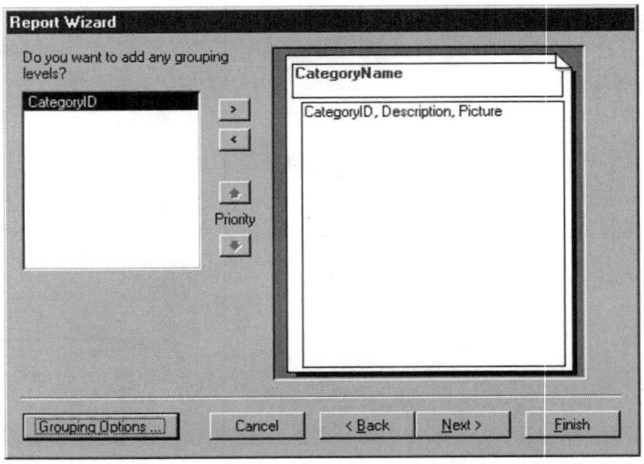

FIGURE 7.8.

Setting grouping levels in the Report Wizard.

If grouping levels are selected, you can set the grouping interval by clicking the Grouping Options button in the lower-left corner of this screen. Figure 7.9 shows the Grouping Intervals screen.

The Report Wizard then asks you if you want to add any sorting functions to the report. Figure 7.10 shows the screen used to enter sorting options.

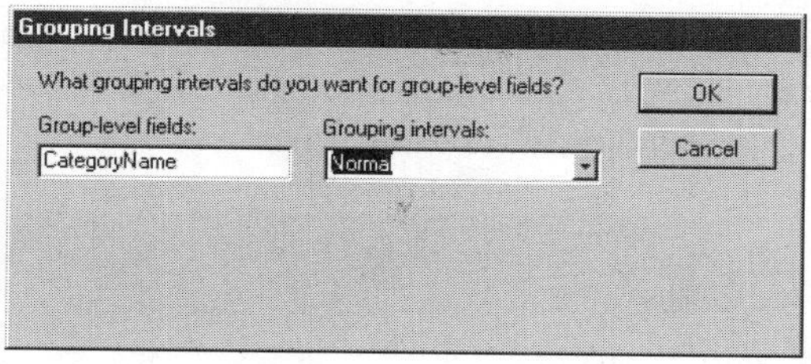

FIGURE 7.9.

The Report Wizard's Grouping Intervals screen.

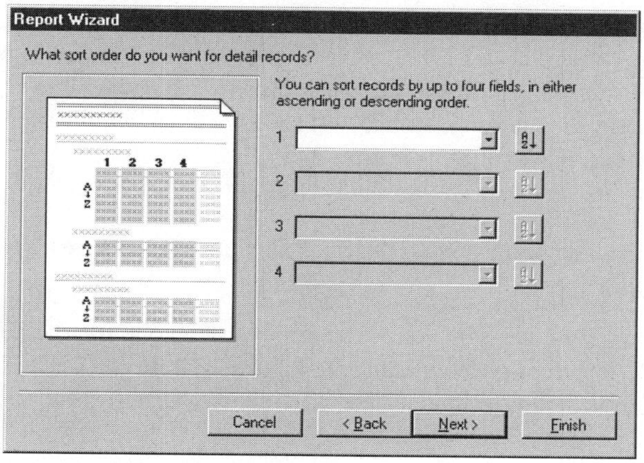

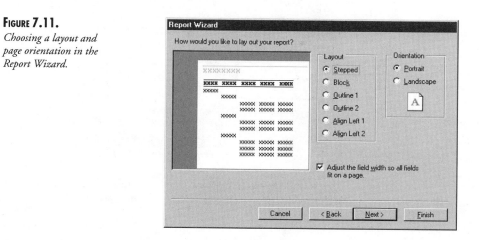

FIGURE 7.10.

Entering sorting options for the Report Wizard.

After you have selected the sorting options, the wizard prompts you for the desired layout and page orientation to be used for the report. (See Figure 7.11.)

FIGURE 7.11.

Choosing a layout and page orientation in the Report Wizard.

The Report Wizard allows the programmer to select one of six layouts predefined in Access 97: Stepped, Block, Outline 1, Outline 2, Align Left 1, and Align Left 2.

Note also the option on this screen that tells Access 97 to adjust the field width to fit on the page. This lets Access 97 decide how wide the field controls should be on the page so they will all fit, but it removes control from the programmer who wants to specify the field widths.

> **TIP**
>
> If you have a large number of fields to include in the report, it is a good idea to uncheck the Adjust field widths so all fields fit on a page box. With the box checked, Access 97 will automatically adjust the width of every field included on the report so that the fields fit across a single page. If a large number of fields are included on the report, the individual field widths will all have to be re-adjusted by the programmer to display the contents of each field. Unchecking this box will save time later when modifying the report; you'll spend less time stretching the controls to fit the information.

This screen also allows you to select either portrait or landscape for the page orientation used by the report.

The wizard then lets you select the appropriate style for the report. This is where any newly created autoformat style will appear. Figure 7.12 displays the screen you use to select the style for the report.

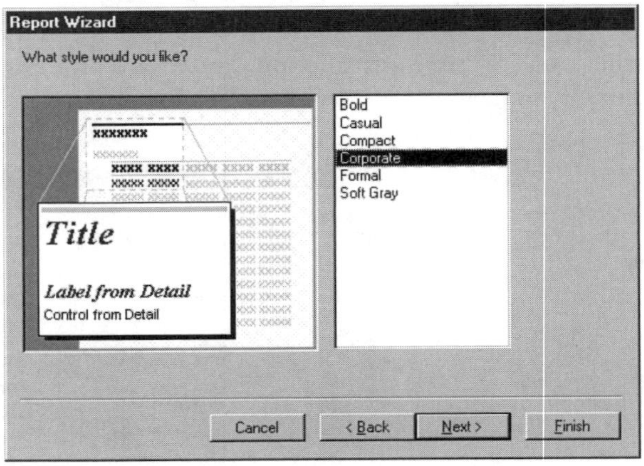

FIGURE 7.12.

Selecting a style in the Report Wizard.

The Report Wizard finishes with a screen for entering the name of the new report and provides the option of either previewing the report or opening for design modifications.

The AutoReport Wizards: Columnar and Tabular

The AutoReport wizards are condensed versions of the Report Wizard and do not allow for as much initial customization of the report. These report wizards just want to know what table to use as the basis for the report. Once this information is provided, the wizard creates the report and shows its preview. When the report preview is closed, you are given the option to save the report and to provide a name for it.

The columnar report shows the table name at the top and lists the fields directly below it. The field labels are listed down the left side of the report, with the data displayed to the right. Each record is shown below the preceding one.

The tabular report shows the table name as the page header. The field labels are spread across the top of the page, and the data is shown directly below them.

The Chart Wizard

The Chart Wizard is new for Access 97 and requires the selection of the base table before it will run. Once this is done, the wizard opens a screen for you to select which fields in the chosen table are to be charted. You are then prompted to select from among 20 predefined chart styles. Figure 7.13 shows the screen used for chart-style selection in the Chart Wizard.

FIGURE 7.13.
Selecting a chart type in the Chart Wizard style-selection screen.

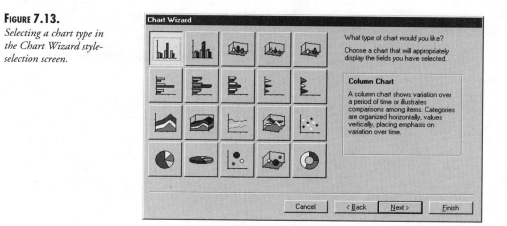

As you can see, the chart styles range from simple bar charts to 3D charts to scatter charts. The Chart Wizard allows you to modify the layout of the chart and to preview it before moving on to the final step. Figure 7.14 shows the screen used to modify the layout of the data for your chart.

When the layout is complete, the wizard prompts you for a name for the report. You can also add a legend to the chart and either preview the report or open it for modifications.

The Label Wizard

The Label Wizard is the fastest way to create a form that is nothing but labels. When you start this wizard, the first thing it does is prompt you for the kind of labels you want to use. (See Figure 7.15.)

FIGURE 7.14.
Modifying the data layout using the Chart Wizard.

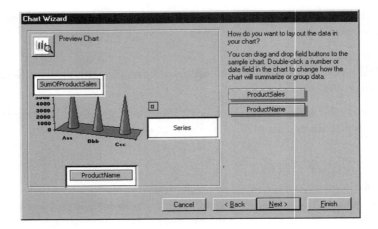

FIGURE 7.15.
Selecting a label type in the Label Wizard.

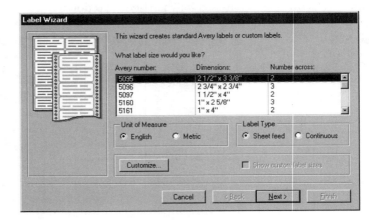

The Label Wizard allows you to select from many predefined Avery label formats or to create a customized label. This screen also provides for the selection of either sheet-fed labels or continuous-feed labels.

The Label Wizard's next step is to ask you to select the font and color for the text appearing on the label. Once these selections have been made, the Label Wizard allows you to create the layout of the fields on the label. Figure 7.16 shows this layout screen.

To create the layout, you must first select which line on the label to use before selecting the field to include on that line. Once the line is selected, you simply drag and drop the field over to the line. Spaces, dashes, and commas can be inserted between the fields where appropriate.

The Label Wizard then provides a screen for you to select which fields to use in sorting the data. You can sort by just one field or by multiple fields. The Label Wizard finishes by prompting you for the label report name and gives you the option to either preview the label report or open the label report for modifications. This is by far the easiest way to create label reports from within Access 97.

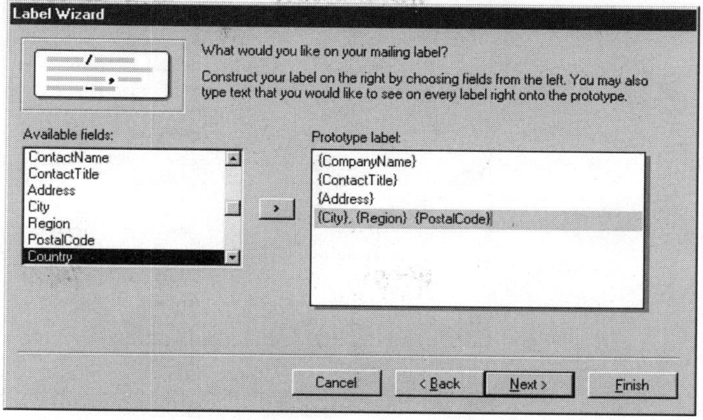

FIGURE 7.16.
The Label Wizard's
layout screen.

Report Examples

The following examples have been taken from the Northwind sample database that accompanies Access 97. The examples included in this section are the Alphabetical List of Products, Catalog, Employee Sales by Quarter, Summary of Sales by Quarter, Invoice, and Sales by Category reports. This discussion shows you how reports are created and how the controls on the reports operate to retrieve and display data.

The Alphabetical List of Products Example

The Alphabetical List of Products report is one of the simpler examples contained in the Northwind database. First, let's preview the final results of the report and look at the Design View of the report. Figures 7.17 and 7.18 show the report in these two different views.

This report uses the Alphabetical List of Products query as its base. This query was built with the Query Builder and can be viewed by clicking the button located to the immediate right of the RecordSource property on the report property sheet (when the RecordSource property has the focus). The button appears with an ellipse on it. Figure 7.19 shows the query in Design View.

Viewing the query shows the fields that are available to the report. In this example, all the fields from the Products table are included, as is the CategoryName field from the Categories table. The Discontinued field is shown separately because it is being used like a filter. Notice the No in the Criteria field. This is telling Access to not show (the Show checkbox is not checked) any products in the report that have been discontinued.

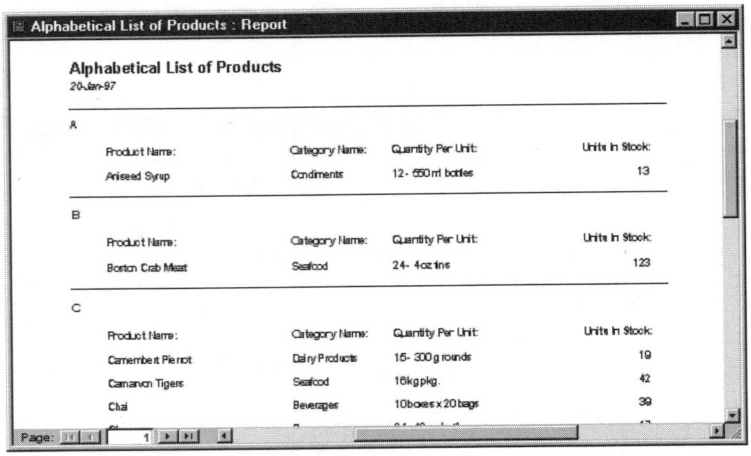

FIGURE 7.17.

The Alphabetical
List of Products
report preview.

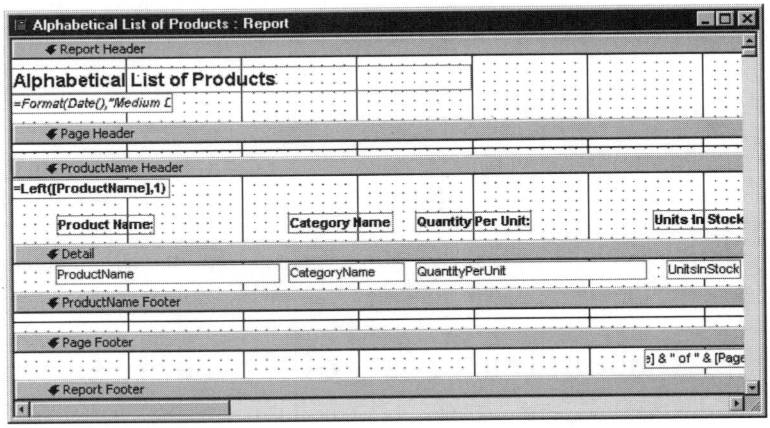

FIGURE 7.18.

The Alphabetical
List of Products
report in Design View.

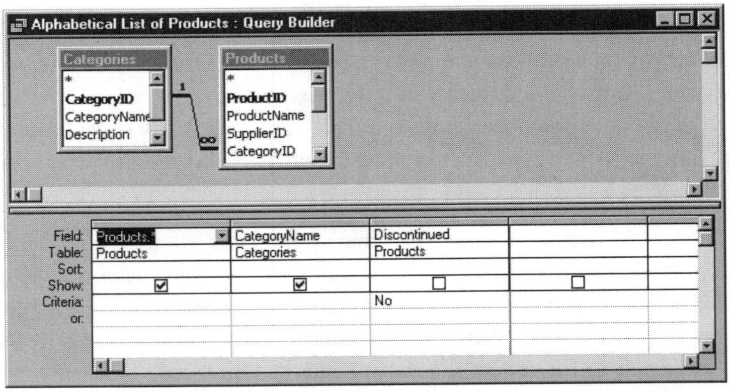

FIGURE 7.19.

The Alphabetical
List of Products
query in Design View.

Refer to Figure 7.18 and notice there are three headers and three footers on this report. The report header is displayed once at the beginning of the report. The page header is shown on every page, and the `ProductName` header appears before each listing of products defined by the grouping criteria. Likewise, the footers are at the bottom of each, respectively.

Refer to Figure 7.17 and note that the product listings have been grouped alphabetically by product name. To view the grouping criteria for this report, click the Sorting and Grouping button on the toolbar. Figure 7.20 shows the sorting and grouping criteria used for this report.

FIGURE 7.20.

The Alphabetical List of Products *sorting and grouping criteria.*

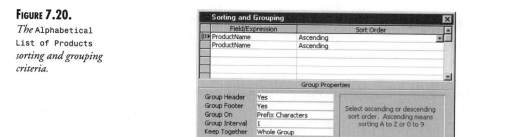

The data in this report is sorted twice by the same field name. Notice the grouping symbol to the immediate left of the first criterion. This tells Access 97 to group the data using the group properties shown on the lower half of this window. This is also where Access 97 gets the information to include a group header (note the Yes next to the first property in this part of the window). The first sort criterion groups the data by alphabetical prefix. The second sort criterion sorts the data in each group alphabetically.

The report header contains a label control and a text box. The label control shows the title of the report. The text box contains the following statement in its `ControlSource` property:

```
=Format(Date(),"Medium Date")
```

This is a common syntax for including a date on a report. This statement uses the `Format` function followed by an expression and the format to use in displaying the expression. The `Date()` is the expression used for today's date. The `Medium Date` format displays the date as `19-Jun-97`. Another way of accomplishing the same thing would have been to include `=Date()` in the text box `ControlSource` property and place the `Medium Date` value in the text box `Format` property.

The page header of this report consists of a single line control.

The `ProductName` header contains four labels describing the fields below it and one text box. The text box contains the following value in its `ControlSource` property:

```
=Left([ProductName],1)
```

This statement uses the `Left` function. The `Left` function displays a string value consisting of the specified number of characters starting from the left side of a string expression. The syntax to use is `Left(string, length)`. This statement tells Access 97 to display the first character of the `ProductName` field.

The Details section of this report contains four text boxes that display the respective fields from the `Alphabetical List of Products` query results.

The `ProductName` footer consists of a single line control.

The page footer contains one text box with the following statement in the `ControlSource` property:

```
="Page " & [Page] & " of " & [Pages]
```

This statement tells Access 97 to display `Page # of #` on the bottom of every page of the report. The `""` marks are used to tell Access 97 to display the literal values between them, including spaces. The `&` is used to tell Access 97 to concatenate the string. The `[Page]` and `[Pages]` tell Access 97 to print the `Page` and `Pages` properties of the report. The `Page` property is the current page number of the report when printed, and the `Pages` property is the total number of pages in the report.

The Catalog Example

The `Catalog` report in the `Northwind` database is a good example of using the report header for multiple pages combining graphics with text. The `Catalog` report also uses the report footer to create an order form that prints after the detail of the products is printed. Figures 7.21, 7.22, and 7.23 display the report in the preview format and show the overall layout of the catalog report.

FIGURE 7.21.

The Catalog *report header preview.*

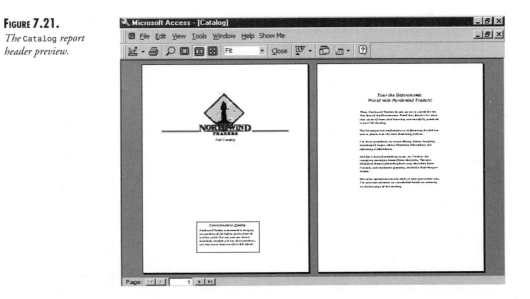

7

ACCESS 97 REPORTS

Figure 7.22.

The Catalog *report detail section preview.*

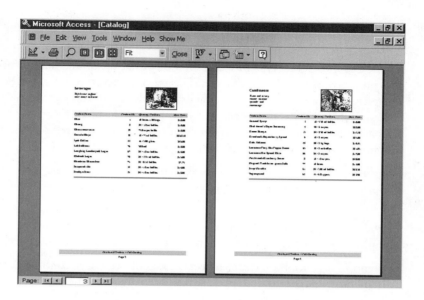

Figure 7.23.

The Catalog *report footer preview.*

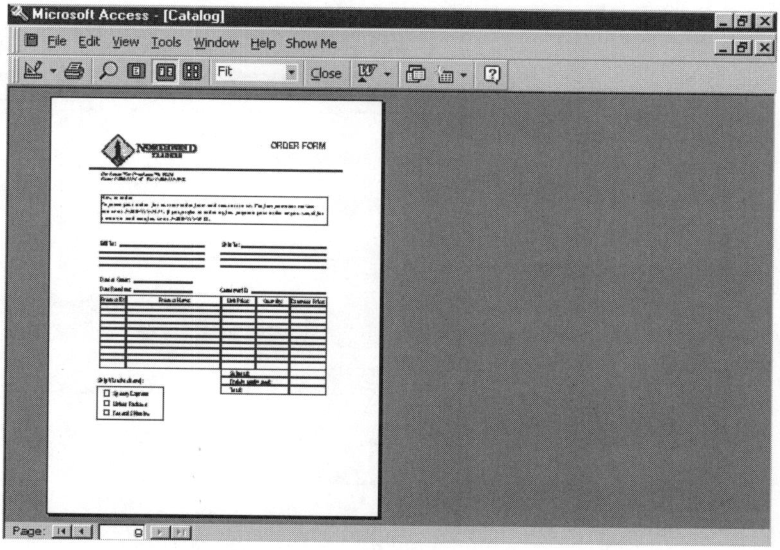

The Catalog report header consists of two pages. The first page contains an image control, two line controls, and one label control in the top-middle of the page, along with two label controls and one rectangle control on the bottom of the page.

While in Design View, select the image control. Notice the Picture property found on the Format tab of the image control property sheet. To select a different picture for this control, click the button with ellipses on it. This button will appear when the `Picture` property has the focus. This brings up the file dialog box where you can select a new picture.

Notice also the `PictureType` property on the Format tab of the image control property sheet. This property has been set to `embedded`. This means the picture will go where the database goes. The picture becomes a part of the database application. You can choose to link the picture instead. If the `PictureType` property is set to `linked`, the picture does not become a part of the database application. There is only a pointer to the picture; therefore, if the database is moved, you must remember to move the picture as well.

Using a `page break` control separates the second page in the report header from the first page. The `page break` control can be seen by viewing the report in Design View and is recognizable by six dots.

On the second page of the report header there are just two label controls. The text that actually appears in a label control can be entered in the `Caption` property of the label control.

The report footer for the `Catalog` report consists of two image controls along with many label, line, and rectangle controls. Once these have been designed, the actual detail of the report needs to be set up using the data contained in the database. Figure 7.24 displays the section of the `Catalog` report that provides the details of the catalog.

FIGURE 7.24.

The `Catalog` *report detail section in Design View.*

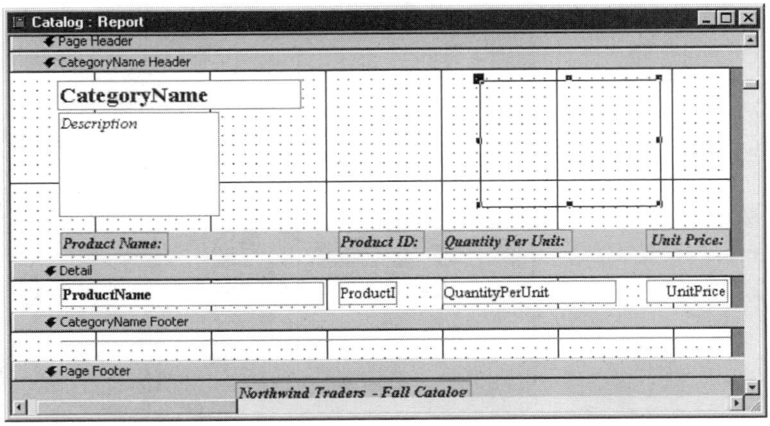

When analyzing the design for a report, the first thing to notice is what sources are used for the retrieval of data to be used by the report. For example, by viewing the `RecordSource` property of the `Catalog` report, you should notice that the report was based on the `Catalog` query created by the Query Builder.

The data to be used in the `Catalog` report comes from the `Categories` and `Products` tables. The data consists of eight fields from the two different tables, and the last field in the query tells Access 97 not to display any products that have been discontinued.

The next step is to establish the sorting and grouping properties for the data. Figure 7.25 displays the sorting and grouping property sheet for the `Catalog` report.

The data used in the `Catalog` report has two sorting and grouping criteria: The data is to be grouped according to the values in the `CategoryName` field of the `Catalog` query; and the data inside each group is to be sorted according the value contained in the `ProductName` field of the `Catalog` query.

Once the sorting and grouping criteria have been established, you can go about the task of placing the controls on the report in their appropriate places. For example, in the `CategoryName` header section, there are two text box controls, four label controls, one rectangle control, and one bound object frame control.

The bound object frame control is bound to the `Picture` field of the `Catalog` query. To determine which field is bound to a control, view the `ControlSource` property contained in the control property sheet. Notice also the `Size` property of the bound object frame control. In this example, the `Size` property is set to `stretch`. The other available options for the `Size` property of a bound object frame control are `clip` and `zoom`.

In the Detail section of the `Catalog` report there are four text boxes. Each text box is bound to the appropriate field in the `Catalog` query.

The page footer section of this report contains one text box control, one rectangle control, and one label control. The text box control uses the same `ControlSource` property discussed in the preceding example to display the page numbers on the report.

The Employee Sales by Country Example

The `Employee Sales by Country` report is a good example of a more complex form that contains some underlying code. It also shows a number of new things you can add to reports to enhance their appearance. Figure 7.26 shows a preview of the final result of the `Employee Sales by Country` report. Figures 7.27 and 7.28 display the Design View of this report.

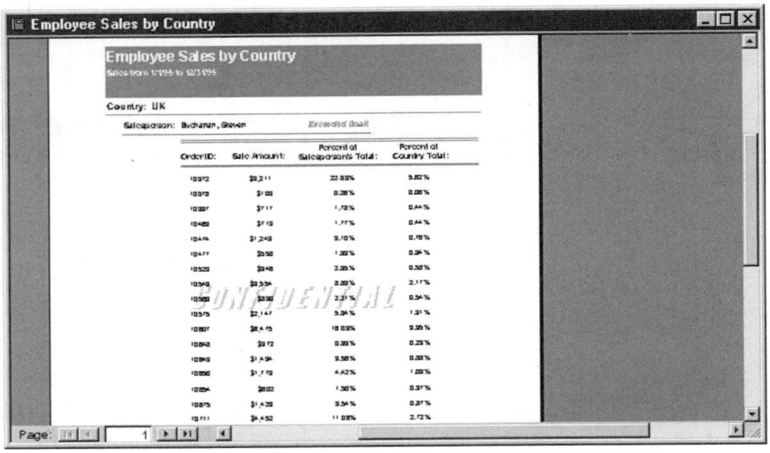

FIGURE 7.26.

The Employee Sales by Country *report preview.*

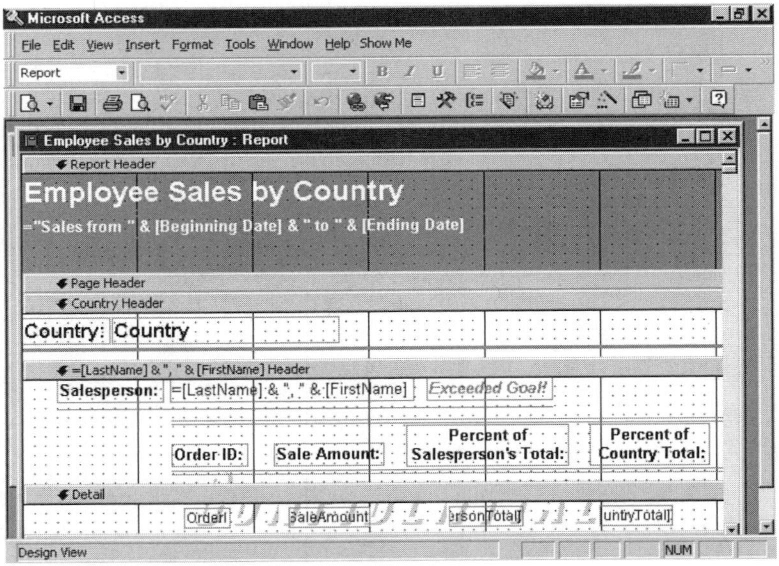

FIGURE 7.27.

Employee Sales by Country *in Design View (upper half).*

The first thing to notice about this report is that it is broken into nine different sections: four different header and footer sections and one detail section. Each section contains different controls except the page header section, which is empty.

The data used by the report is taken from the Employee Sales by Country query. You can view this query by clicking on the ellipses button located to the right of the RecordSource property of the report, or by selecting the query on the Queries tab on the main database window and then clicking the Design button. The query screen displaying the design of this query is shown in Figure 7.29.

FIGURE 7.28.

Employee Sales by Country *in Design View (lower half).*

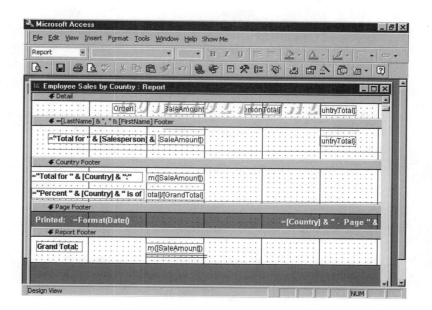

FIGURE 7.29.

The Employee Sales by Country *query screen.*

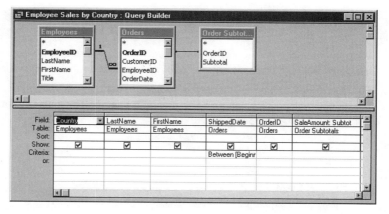

There are two things to notice about this query. First, the query is drawing data from two tables and one other query. The box in the upper portion of this query, entitled Orders Subtotals, is a query that has been previously created. This is a good example of a inner join. Let's take a look at the SQL code for the query to see the inner join better. You can learn more about inner joins from the help file that comes with Access 97. SQL is discussed briefly in the SQL Basics section in Chapter 5, "Access 97 Queries:"

```
PARAMETERS [Beginning Date] DateTime, [Ending Date] DateTime;
SELECT DISTINCTROW Employees.Country, Employees.LastName, Employees.FirstName,
) Orders.ShippedDate, Orders.OrderID, [Order Subtotals].Subtotal AS SaleAmount
FROM Employees
        INNER JOIN (Orders INNER JOIN [Order Subtotals] ON Orders.OrderID =
```

```
)[Order Subtotals].OrderID) ON
     Employees.EmployeeID = Orders.EmployeeID
          WHERE (((Orders.ShippedDate) Between [Beginning Date] And
)[Ending Date]));
```

Notice the indented area of this code. This portion creates an inner join on the `OrderID` fields between the `Orders` table and the `Order Subtotals` query, and on the `EmployeeID` fields in the `Employees` and `Orders` tables. This type of join takes records from two different tables/queries and combines them in another query's results when the right conditions are met. In this case, the condition is that records must have the same `OrderID` value.

The second thing to notice about this query is the `ShippedDate` field. Go to the Design View of this query. The following statement can be found in the `Criteria` property of the `ShippedDate` field:

```
Between [Beginning Date] And [Ending Date]
```

This establishes the parameters for the query. Because the statement does pull the values from a specific form, the end user will be required to input these values each time the query is run before generating the report. This parameter setting uses the default Access 97 form for entering the values of the beginning and ending dates.

TIP

A good thing to do when using parameters in a query is to provide a scenario that handles the situation when the data entered by the user is not available in the database.

To do this, look at the `NoData` property for the report. This property has an event procedure associated with it. Click the builder button to the right of the `NoData` property field and the following code will appear:

```
Private Sub Report_NoData(Cancel As Integer)
' Display a message if user enters a date for which there are no records,
' and don't preview or print report.
    Dim strMsg As String, strTitle As String
    Dim intStyle As Integer

    strMsg = "You must enter a date between 10-Aug-94 and 5-Jun-96."
    intStyle = vbOKOnly
    strTitle = "No Data for Date Range"

    MsgBox strMsg, intStyle, strTitle
    Cancel = True
End Sub
```

This procedure will produce a message box if the dates entered by the user produce a query with no data in the results. As you can see, the data for the `Northwind` sample database falls between August 10, 1994 and June 5, 1996. The message appears, and the user is allowed to run the report again using the appropriate dates.

There are two interesting things to note in this report's sorting and grouping criteria as well. Figure 7.30 shows the sorting and grouping criteria used for this report.

FIGURE 7.30.

The Employee Sales by Country *sorting and grouping.*

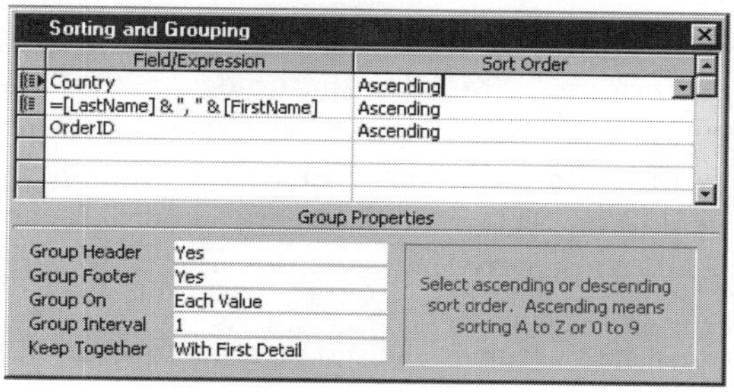

The first thing to note is that Access 97 allows the data underlying a report to be grouped multiple times. In this example, the data is first grouped by the Country field in the Employee Sales by Country query. The data is also grouped by the LastName and FirstName expression used in the report.

The second unique aspect of this sorting and grouping criteria is the use of an expression in the actual criteria. Up to this point, the sorting and grouping criteria have been based on a single field from the underlying table or query. This example shows the capability of Access 97 to group data based on an expression. The same expression is used in the actual report as the ControlSource property for the text box identifying this section in the report. Refer to Figure 7.28 to view the grouping footer based on this expression.

There are four headers used in this report. Likewise, there are four footers. The first header is the report header, which contains one label control and one text box control. The text box control demonstrates the capability of Access 97 to use an expression from the query used by the report. Notice that the query does not contain the beginning and ending dates as fields in the query; rather, these dates are the parameters used by the query. When the user enters the dates for the report, Access 97 stores these values until the report is run again. The text box control then uses the values in the parameter to display the beginning and ending dates used by the query.

The second header is the page header and is not used in this report. The third header contains a label control, a text box control, and a line control. The text box is used to display the value of the Country field from the query. Another thing to notice about this header is the code behind it. To view the code behind a report, select View from the menu bar and then select Code. The code for this header appears as follows:

```
Private Sub GroupHeader0_Format(Cancel As Integer, FormatCount As Integer)
' Set page number to 1 when a new group starts.
    Page = 1

End Sub
```

As the comment line explains, this code sets the page number to 1 when a new group is started. The new group is the one associated with the header, which is the Country field in this example.

The fourth header is the most interesting header on this report. This header contains six label controls, three line controls, and one text box control. The text box contains an expression that concatenates the LastName and FirstName fields from the underlying query and is also the source for the grouping criteria previously discussed.

The interesting features provided in this header are the SalespersonLine line control and the ExceededGoalLabel label control that appear in red on the report. These controls are to appear on the report only if a certain criterion is met. To set a criterion for controlling what is displayed when the report is printed, an event procedure (or code) must be created and associated with the Format property of the header. The code behind this header appears as follows:

```
Private Sub GroupHeader2_Format(Cancel As Integer, FormatCount As Integer)
' Display ExceededGoalLabel and SalespersonLine if salesperson's total
' meets criteria.
    If Me!SalespersonTotal > 5000 Then
        Me!ExceededGoalLabel.Visible = True
        Me!SalespersonLine.Visible = True
    Else
        Me!ExceededGoalLabel.Visible = False
        Me!SalespersonLine.Visible = False
    End If
End Sub
```

This code checks the value of the SalespersonTotal text box control appearing in the =[LastName] & ", " & [FirstName] footer. If the value in this text box is greater than 5,000, the ExceededGoalLabel and SalespersonLine controls will be visible on the report when printed. If not, the Visible property is set to False.

The Detail section of this report contains four text boxes. The values for three of these text boxes are provided directly from the query used by the report. The value for the PercentOfCountryTotal text box is provided by an expression: =[SaleAmount]/[CountryTotal]. The Sale Amount text box is in this section of the report. The CountryTotal text box appears in the =[LastName] & ", " & [FirstName] footer.

The =[LastName] & ", " & [FirstName] footer contains three text box controls and two line controls. The ControlSource property for each of the three text box controls is shown in Table 7.1.

Table 7.1. ControlSource properties for text box controls.

Text box name	ControlSource *property*
EmployeeTotalCaption	="Total for " & [Salesperson] & ":"
SalespersonTotal	=Sum([SaleAmount])
PercentofCountryTotal2	=[SalespersonTotal]/[CountryTotal]

These are examples of the various ways to manipulate data for display or to calculate values based on the data contained in the report or from the query underlying the report.

The `Country` footer contains four text box controls and one line control. The text boxes in this footer provide a good example of how a text box can be used to display label-type information or calculated values based on data in the report. Table 7.2 shows the `ControlSource` property for each of the four text box controls.

Table 7.2. `ControlSource` properties for text box controls.

Text box name	`ControlSource` *property*
CountryTotalCaption	="Total for " & [Country] & ":"
PercentOfGrandTotalCaption	="Percent " & [Country] & " is of Grand Total:"
CountryTotal	=Sum([SaleAmount])
PercentOfGrandTotal	=[CountryTotal]/[GrandTotal]

The first two text boxes in Table 7.2 are used to display label-type information as captions for the last two text boxes. Label controls cannot be used because they can only display literal information. Because these captions use data from the underlying report query, the only way to have the `Country` value displayed with other information as a caption for the other text box is to use a text box control.

The page footer contains two text boxes and a label. The text boxes contain the `ControlSource` properties shown in Table 7.3.

Table 7.3. `ControlSource` properties for text box controls.

Text box name	`ControlSource` *property*
DatePrinted	=Format(Date(),"Medium Date")
PageNumber	=[Country] & " - Page " & [Page]

These properties are similar to those that have been previously discussed in this chapter. The only difference is that the `Country` field is included in the page-numbering scheme for this report.

The final footer (`Report` footer) on this report contains one label control, one text box control, and one line control. The text box simply calculates a grand total of sales taken from the `SaleAmount` text box contained in the report.

The last thing to point out in this report is the way the footer controls the calculation of summary data in the report. In the `=[LastName] & ", " & [FirstName]` footer, `Country` footer, and `Report` footer are text boxes that contain the same property for their `ControlSource` (`=Sum([SaleAmount])`). Access 97 will calculate the value of this expression based on the grouping of the information. So, although the ControlSource property is the same, the value displayed in the report is different based on the grouping where the data is displayed.

This is a good example of a more complex report. It extensively uses calculated controls based on data contained elsewhere in the report. It also provides a good example of controlling the formatting of reports through code.

The Summary of Sales by Quarter Example

This example is included to demonstrate how Access 97 can subdivide data based on dates. Because many business reports are required to show data divided quarterly, this report is a good example of how to do that in Access 97. This section deviates from the previous sections in that each control on the report is not discussed. Rather, only the pertinent parts dealing with the date grouping are shown.

Figure 7.31 shows the Summary of Sales by Quarter report as it would be printed. Figure 7.32 shows the report in Design View.

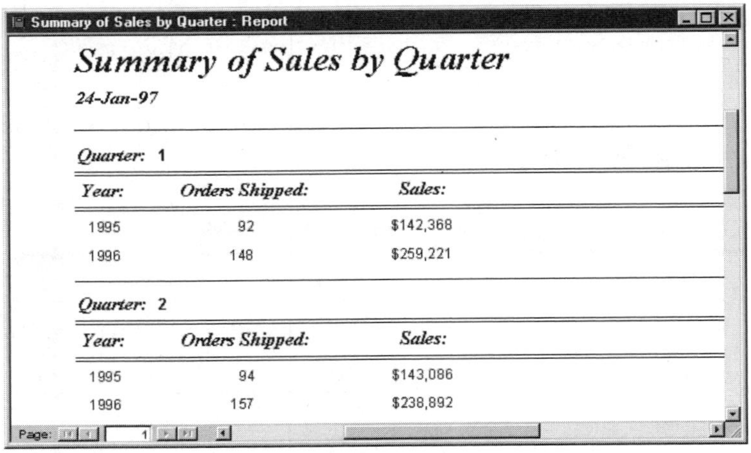

FIGURE 7.31.

The final version of the Summary of Sales by Quarter *report.*

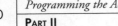

To get Access 97 to sort the data into date intervals, use the DatePart function. Refer to Chapter 5 and see Tables 5.1 through 5.4 for the appropriate syntax and arguments to use when using the DatePart function from within Access 97.

In this example, the data includes two grouping criteria. Figure 7.33 shows the sorting and grouping window used by this report.

As you can see, the first grouping is used by Access 97 to group the data into quarters. The statement =DatePart("q",[ShippedDate]) uses the DatePart function on the ShippedDate field with an interval of quarters ("q").

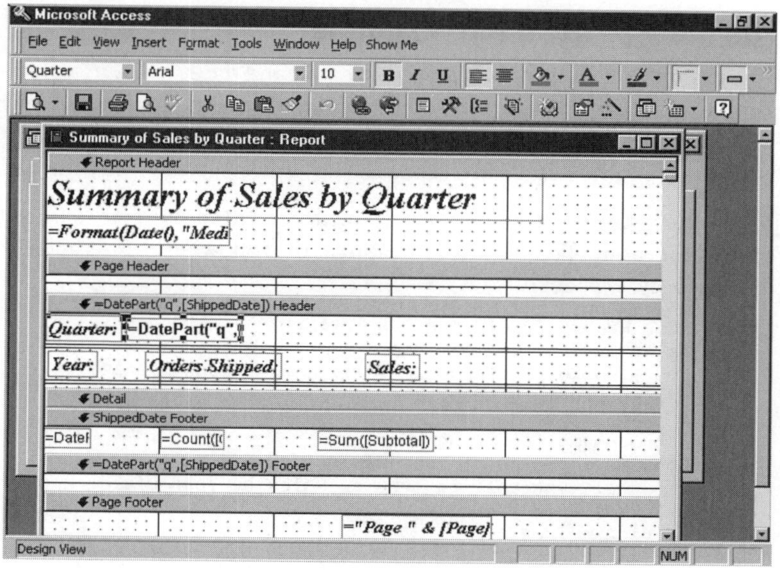

FIGURE 7.32.

The Summary of Sales by Quarter *report in Design View.*

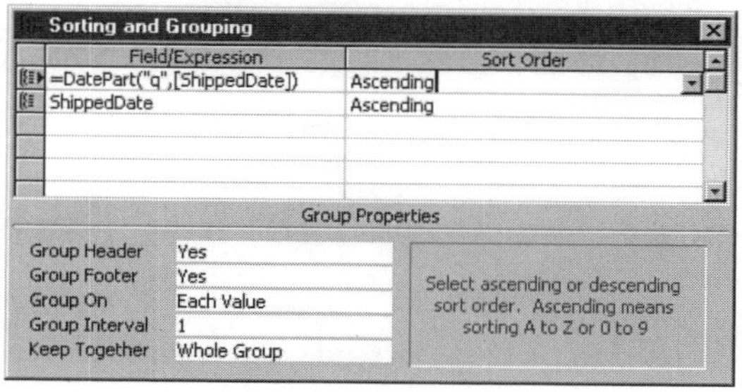

FIGURE 7.33.

The Summary of Sales by Quarter *sorting and grouping.*

Notice that the report does not have a ShippedDate header but does have a ShippedDate footer. This is done by setting the Header property to No for the ShippedDate group in the Sorting and Grouping window. By setting this property like this, it becomes unnecessary to include anything in the Detail section of this report. The data to be displayed is only that data grouped by the ShippedDate grouping. Therefore, the text boxes normally included in the Detail section of the report should be placed in the ShippedDate footer instead.

This is the most common way to create a report displaying data summarized by quarter. Variations of this formatting can also be done for weekly and yearly reports.

The Sales by Year Example

This example involves the Sales by Year report and the Sales by Year subreport in the Northwind sample database. These reports are examples of reports that use a dialog form for user input. This input determines which report to print and what dates the reports will use. The Sales by Year Dialog form was created separately to direct Access 97 to print the appropriate report.

When the Sales by Year report is opened, the Sales by Year Dialog form is automatically opened for input. To cause this to happen, the following code is added to the OnLoad event of the Sales by Year report:

```
Private Sub Report_Open(Cancel As Integer)
' Open Sales by Year Dialog form.
' IsLoaded function (defined in Utility Functions module) determines
' if specified form is open.

    Dim strDocName As String
    strDocName = "Sales by Year Dialog"
    ' Set public variable to True so Sales by Year Dialog knows that report
    ' is in its Open event.
    blnOpening = True

    ' Open form.
    DoCmd.OpenForm strDocName, , , , , acDialog

    ' If Sales by Year Dialog form isn't loaded, don't preview
)or print report.
    ' (User clicked Cancel button on form.)
    If IsLoaded(strDocName) = False Then Cancel = True

    'Set public variable to False, signifying that Open event is finished.
    blnOpening = False
End Sub
```

This procedure declares a string variable called strDocName. It then sets the value of that variable to Sales by Year Dialog. Following this, the procedure sets the blnOpening variable to True.

In the general declarations of the Sales by Year report, a public variable is created called blnOpening. This variable is set to True while the ReportOpen event is executing. If the ReportOpen event is executing, this variable has a value of True; if the ReportOpen event is not executing, the value is False. If this variable is False, the code will force an error message to be displayed. This entire code example forces the Sales by Year report to be open before the OK button is enabled for execution.

Setting this variable to True tells the Sales by Dialog form that the Sales by Year report is being opened. The procedure then uses the DoCmd (Do command) to open the form designated by the strDocName variable. It then checks to see whether the Sales by Year Dialog form is loaded; if it's not, the procedure cancels the report load. Finally, the procedure sets the blnOpening variable back to False.

When this procedure is run, the `Sales by Dialog` form opens on the screen. The end user may then enter the desired dates and check the box if details are desired. Figure 7.34 shows the `Sales by Year Dialog` form as the user would see it. Figure 7.35 shows the same form in Design View.

FIGURE 7.34.

The Final View of the `Sales by Year Dialog` *form.*

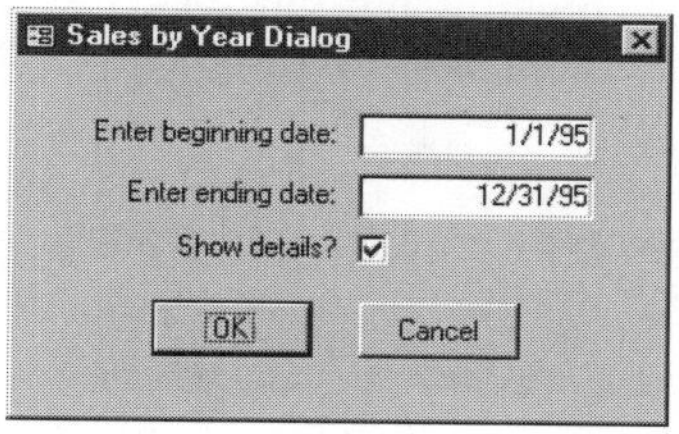

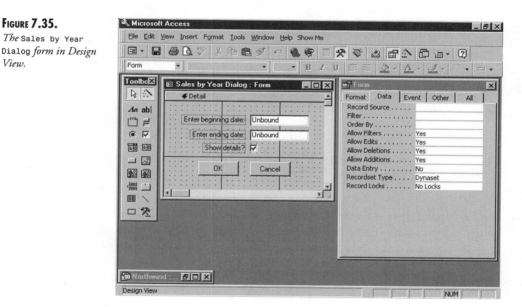

FIGURE 7.35.

The `Sales by Year Dialog` *form in Design View.*

In the Design View of this form, you can see two text box controls, one checkbox control, and two command buttons. The `RecordSource` property of this form is left empty because the form does not need data from any table in the database. The form's sole purpose is to allow the end user to enter the dates desired for printing the `Sales by Year` report.

The `DefaultValue` property of the beginning date text box is set to January 1, 1995 (`="1/1/95"`). This allows the report to print if the user double-clicks the report. Likewise, the `DefaultValue` property of the ending date text box is set to December 31, 1995 (`="12/31/95"`). If either of these properties were left empty, the form would have to open before the report would print. In addition, the `DefaultValue` property provides the end user with a standard entry to follow when providing the data.

The checkbox control is there to provide an option to the end user to show the details of the orders for the year if desired. The actual functionality of the check is determined by the code associated with it in the report. The DefaultValue property of the checkbox is set to True.

The code behind the OK command button can be seen by looking at the event procedure for the OnClick event. This code is as follows:

```
Private Sub OK_Click()
On Error GoTo Err_OK_Click
    Dim strMsg As String, strTitle As String
    Dim intStyle As Integer

    ' If Sales by Year report is not being opened for previewing
    )or printing,
    ' cause an error. (blnOpening variable is true only when report's
    )Open event
    ' is being executed.)
    If Not Reports![Sales By Year].blnOpening Then Err.Raise 0

    ' Hide form.
    Me.Visible = False
Exit_OK_Click:
    Exit Sub
Err_OK_Click:
    strMsg = "To use this form, you must preview or print the Sales by Year
    )report from the Database window or Design view."
    intStyle = vbOKOnly
    strTitle = "Open from Report"
    MsgBox strMsg, intStyle, strTitle
    Resume Exit_OK_Click
End Sub
```

The first part of this routine ensures that the Sales by Year report is being opened before this button can execute its code. It checks the blnOpening variable to ensure it currently is set to True. If this variable is False, the routine moves down to the Err OK Click subroutine, which displays a message telling the user that he must preview or print the Sales by Year report before accessing this form. If all conditions have been met, the procedure then hides the Sales by Year Dialog form using the Me.Visible = False statement.

The Sales by Year report then resumes its loading procedure and opens. The report then runs the Sales by Year query to generate the data for the report. Figure 7.36 shows this query in Design View.

The criteria property for the ShippedDate field has the following statement:

```
Is Not Null And Between [Forms]![Sales by Year Dialog]![BeginningDate] And
) [Forms]![Sales by Year Dialog]![EndingDate]
```

This statement tells the query to include the data between the dates entered on the Sales by Year Dialog form in the BeginningDate text box and the EndingDate text box. The expression in the criteria property also checks to ensure that a null value has not been entered. Notice also that the Year field uses the Format function to reformat the ShippedDate field when the query is run. To do this, the Year field contains the following statement:

```
Year: Format([ShippedDate],"yyyy")
```

FIGURE 7.36.

The Sales by Year *query in Design View.*

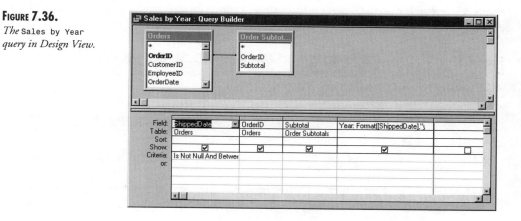

The report then checks the query results for data. If the query returns no data, the NoData event occurs. The event procedure associated with the NoData event is as follows:

```
Private Sub Report_NoData(Cancel As Integer)
' Display a message if user enters a date for which there are no records,
' and don't preview or print report.
    Dim strMsg As String, strTitle As String
    Dim intStyle As Integer

    strMsg = "You must enter a date between 10-Aug-94 and 05-Jun-96."
    intStyle = vbOKOnly
    strTitle = "No Data for Date Range"

    MsgBox strMsg, intStyle, strTitle
    Cancel = True
End Sub
```

If the report has no valid data, this procedure displays a message box directing the user to enter the appropriate data and cancels the report.

If there is data, the report header checks the value of the checkbox on the Sales by Year Dialog form. The following code accomplishes this from the OnFormat event in the report header:

```
Private Sub ReportHeader_Format(Cancel As Integer, FormatCount As Integer)
'If ShowDetails check box is cleared, set Show text box to False.
  If Forms![Sales by Year Dialog]!ShowDetails = False Then Me!
)Show.Value = False

End Sub
```

Figure 7.37 shows the Sales by Year report in Design View. On the left side of the page header is an unbound box. This box is the Show text box. The preceding code procedure sets the value of the Show text box in the page header to False if the checkbox value on the Sales by Year Dialog form is False. The Show text box in the page header is being used like a flag. The Show text box is not visible on the form at printing, but it allows for a flag to be raised if the ShowDetails checkbox value is set to False.

FIGURE 7.37.

The Sales by Year
report in Design View.

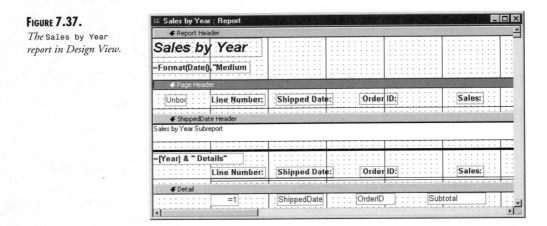

The following procedure is in the OnFormat event of the page header:

```
Private Sub PageHeader_Format(Cancel As Integer, FormatCount As Integer)
' If value of Show text box is False, don't print page header .
    If Me!Show.Value = False Then Cancel = True
End Sub
```

This procedure checks the value of the Show text box. If the Show text box value is False, the page header is not printed. If the Show text value is True, the page header is printed. The next event to occur is the ShippedDate header's OnFormat event. This event has the following procedure:

```
Private Sub GroupHeader0_Format(Cancel As Integer, FormatCount As Integer)
    Const conNone = 0

    ' If ShowDetails check box on Sales by Year Dialog form is checked,
    ' set value of Show text box to True so that page header will print on
    ' next page.
    If Forms![Sales by Year Dialog]!ShowDetails Then
        Me!Show.Value = True
    Else
    ' If ShowDetails check box on Sales by Year Dialog form is cleared, set
    ' ForceNewPage property to conNone and hide all labels for detail records.
        Me.Section(acGroupLevel1Footer).ForceNewPage = conNone
        Me!Line10.Visible = False
        Me!Line15.Visible = False
        Me!DetailsLabel.Visible = False
        Me!LineNumberLabel2.Visible = False
```

```
        Me!ShippedDateLabel2.Visible = False
        Me!OrdersShippedLabel2.Visible = False
        Me!SalesLabel2.Visible = False
    End If

End Sub
```

This procedure checks the checkbox on the `Sales by Year Dialog` form. If the checkbox's value is set to `True`, the procedure sets the value of the `Show` text box to `True`. If the `ShowDetails` checkbox has a value of `False`, the `ForceNewPage` value is set to `0`, and the `Visible` property of the controls in the `ShippedDate` header are all set to `False`. Notice also that the `ShippedDate` header contains a subreport control. Figure 7.38 shows the data properties to be aware of when using a subreport control.

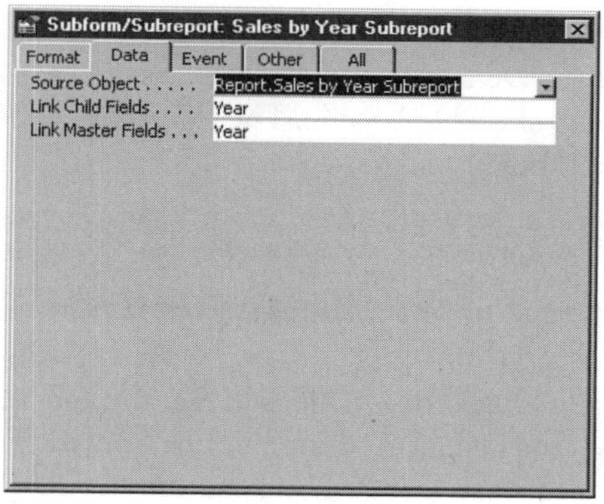

FIGURE 7.38.

The data properties of the Sales by Year *subreport.*

These properties tell the `Sales by Year` report how to handle the subreport. Figure 7.39 shows the `Sales by Year` subreport, and Figure 7.40 shows the `Sales by Year` subreport in Design View.

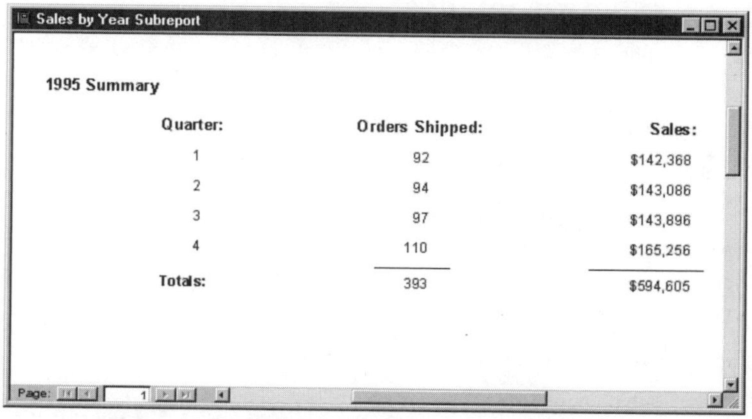

FIGURE 7.39.

The Sales by Year *subreport.*

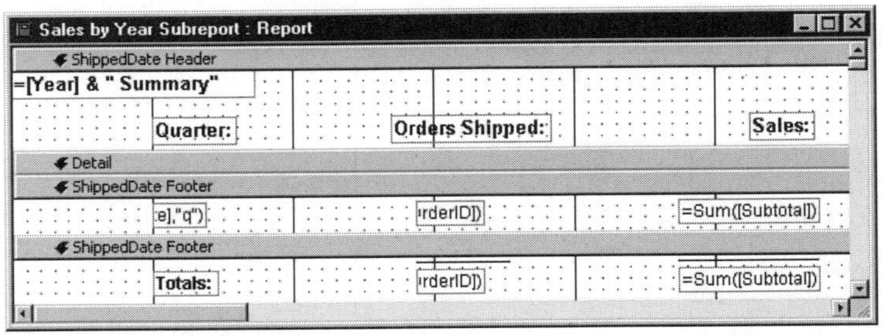

FIGURE 7.40.

The Sales by Year
*subreport in Design
View.*

The subreport is printed no matter what the value is for the ShowDetails checkbox on the Sales by Year Dialog form. In fact, if the ShowDetails checkbox value is False, the only thing printed is the Sales by Year subreport.

The printing of the Details section of the Sales by Year report is also contingent on the value of the ShowDetails checkbox's value. The following procedure is used to check the value of the ShowDetails checkbox:

```
Private Sub Detail_Format(Cancel As Integer, FormatCount As Integer)
' If ShowDetails check box on Sales by Year Dialog form is cleared,
' don't print detail section.
    If Forms![Sales by Year Dialog]!ShowDetails = False Then Cancel = True
End Sub
```

If the ShowDetails checkbox's value is False, the Cancel value of the Details section is set to True. This causes the Details section to not be printed. The next event to occur is the OnFormat event of the ShippedDate footer. This procedure contains the following code:

```
Private Sub GroupFooter1_Format(Cancel As Integer, FormatCount As Integer)

    ' If ShowDetails check box on Sales by Year Dialog form is checked,
    ' set value of Show text box to False so that page header won't print
    ' on next page.
    If Forms![Sales by Year Dialog]!ShowDetails Then
        Me!Show.Value = False
    Else
    ' If ShowDetails check box on Sales by Year Dialog form is cleared,
    ' don't print group footer.
        Cancel = True
    End If

End Sub
```

This code, as the comment lines explain, sets the value of the Show text box to False if the ShowDetails checkbox is True. This causes the page header to not print. If the ShowDetails checkbox is False, the Cancel property of the ShippedDate footer is set to True. This makes Access 97 not print the ShippedDate footer.

The following procedure is contained in the Retreat event of the ShippedDate footer:

```
Private Sub GroupFooter1_Retreat()
' If ShowDetails check box on Sales by Year Dialog form is checked,
```

```
' set value of Show text box to True so that page header will print on
' next page.
    If Forms![Sales by Year Dialog]!ShowDetails Then Me!Show.Value = True

End Sub
```

This procedure checks the value of the `ShowDetails` checkbox and sets the `Show` text box back to `True` if it is checked. This makes the page header print on the next page.

This example walked you through the code necessary to use a custom dialog box to allow the user to select specific print options for a single report. The methodology is fairly straightforward and should be followed when designing reports needing this functionality.

Summary

This chapter examined the report-making features available to the programmer in Access 97. You have learned how to use a form to build a report and how to convert a report to an external file. You were introduced to the Access 97 report design environment and you looked at the predefined report styles available in Access 97.

You walked through the Access 97 report wizards and how to set up a predefined style using the AutoFormat Wizard. You also examined several examples taken from the Northwind sample database.

Access 97 Macros

by Keith Roark

IN THIS CHAPTER

Macros are used to automate some of the more frequently used processes in Access 97. This chapter discusses when to consider using macros and how to create macros from within the Access 97 development environment. You can use this chapter as a reference guide for the predefined macros in Access 97 and the arguments associated with each. The chapter closes with a discussion of how to create special macros and a review of some sample macros found in the Northwind sample database, many of which can be used in developing other applications.

Using Macros

The beginning Access user quickly discovers the ease and convenience of macros. Access 97 provides 49 macro actions that can be used to quickly develop simple and even advanced applications without using code. This is a big advantage to the beginning programmer who is not required to learn all the syntax associated with a VBA action; macro arguments are graphically provided to the programmer in an easy-to-set format.

This format makes macros simple to use, but the problem is that macros have limitations when compared to using Visual Basic for Applications (VBA). The advantage of using macro programming is really only to the beginning programmer. VBA should be used when developing more professional and advanced applications because VBA can more readily handle the complex needs of programming.

VBA allows the programmer more control over the actions within a database. System-level calls can be made in VBA, but not with macros. In addition, custom error handling can be accomplished only with VBA. When VBA actions are added to a form or report, the VBA code goes with the form or report when copied. If the programmer uses macros to do the same thing, the macros must be included in any transfer of the form or report. The following are the limitations of macro programming versus VBA:

- Custom error trapping cannot be performed within a macro.
- A macro cannot perform system-level actions.
- Looping cannot be performed within a macro.
- A macro cannot move or perform operations one record at time within a recordset.
- Parameters cannot be passed from within a macro.
- Debugging macros is generally more difficult than debugging VBA code.
- Macros are separate from forms and reports, and when these objects are copied, macros are not transferred. VBA code, however, is transferred because it is a part of the original object.

It is apparent that VBA should be the preferred choice when serious applications are being developed. VBA is discussed in detail in Chapter 12, "Introduction to VBA for Access 97."

With this said, macros are still an important part of the Access 97 functionality and can be used by the advanced programmer when a rapid prototype of an application is needed. Macros provide a quick way for the advanced programmer to accomplish most tasks to ensure the viability of an application before the VBA code is created. In many instances, macros and VBA will both be used in the development of an application. It is recommended that every programmer, regardless of level, become familiar with how to use macro programming. Often a developer will discover the use of macros when enhancing or redesigning an application. A prior knowledge of macros can make this process a lot easier.

Another reason to consider using some macro programming is that certain actions can only be performed by macros. These macros are called special macros and are discussed in the "Special Macros" section, later in this chapter.

Creating Macros

Assigning actions to a new macro is accomplished in the macro development window. This window can be reached by clicking the New button on the Macro tab of the database window or by choosing the macro builder from a selected event in the property list of a control. Figure 8.1 shows the macro development window.

FIGURE 8.1.

The macro development window.

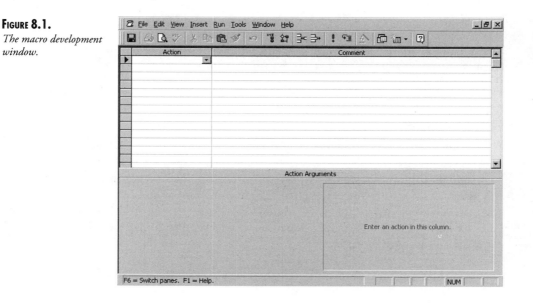

You simply select the action to be performed from the action list. To display the action list, click on the right side of the Action column. Figure 8.2 shows the drop-down list of macro actions. A complete listing of available actions and their arguments is provided in the "Action Arguments" section of this chapter.

FIGURE 8.2.

Available macro actions.

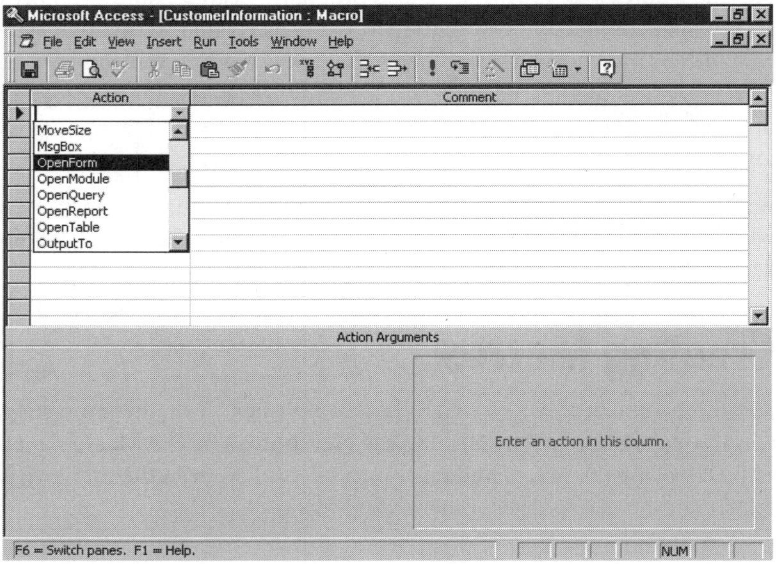

You can insert comments for the action in the Comment column. For this example, select the OpenForm action. The next step is to set the appropriate argument for this action.

Figure 8.3 shows the completed macro. From this figure, you can see that all arguments were not required; you needed to enter only three of them. This macro simply opens a form called Customer Information.

We did not apply any filters or where conditions. Close and save the macro as Customer. The final step is to assign the macro to a corresponding event. Open the Main Menu form in Design View, and then right-click the Customer button. Select Properties and click the Event tab. We will assign this macro to the Click event. To do this, click on the Available Macro list and select the Customer macro. Had we originally accessed the macro builder by clicking the button with three dots on the right side of the Click event field, the macro would have been automatically assigned to the event.

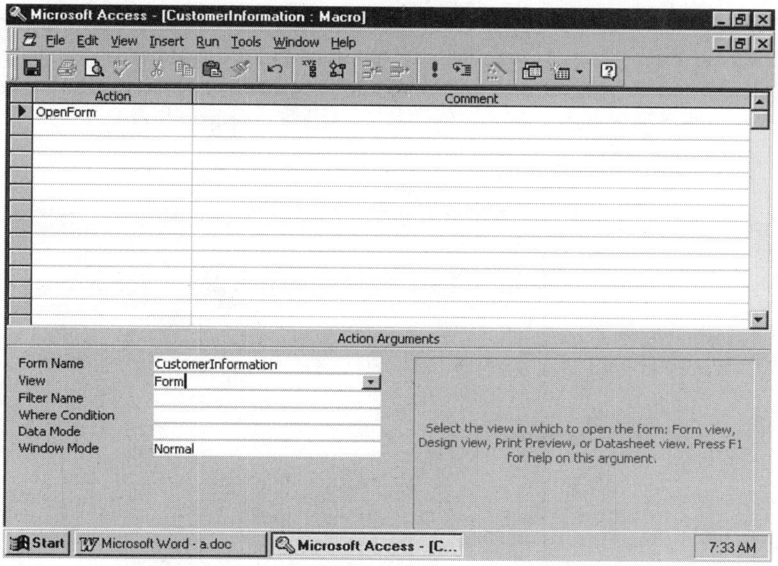

FIGURE 8.3.

The macro development window with the OpenForm action selected.

TIP

A very quick way to create the Openform macro is to drag the form name from the database window to the Action column of the macro. This will also work for reports, macros, queries, modules, and tables. It will automatically select the correct action and assign the object name to the corresponding argument.

TIP

You can automatically create a command button by dragging the macro from the database window to a form in Design View. This will create a command button with its caption defaulting to the macro name. A macro collection should not be used when doing this.

As you can see from the development window, many actions can be accomplished from within one macro. It is also possible to create a series of macros from within a single macro. To assign a specific name to a macro, select View | Macro Name from the menu bar. A Name column appears where you can insert the desired name.

Conditions can also be placed on macro actions. To see the Condition column in the Access 97 macro development window, select View | Conditions from the menu bar. The development window with the Macro Name and Condition columns is shown in Figure 8.4. The section called "Northwind Examples," later in this chapter, discusses how the Condition column can be used.

FIGURE 8.4.

The macro development window with the Macro Name and Conditions columns shown.

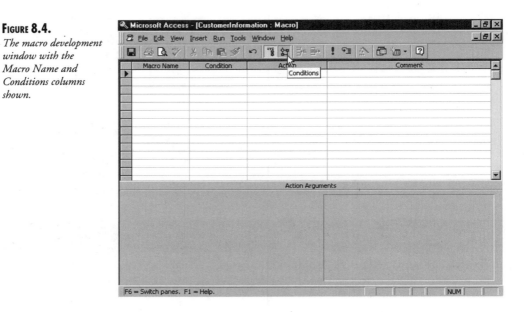

Predefined Macro Actions

Access 97 provides 49 predefined macro actions, as listed here:

AddMenu	ApplyFilter	Beep
CancelEvent	Close	CopyObject
DeleteObject	Echo	FindNext
FindRecord	GoToControl	GoToPage
GoToRecord	HourGlass	Maximize
Minimize	MoveSize	MsgBox
OpenForm	OpenModule	OpenQuery
OpenReport	OpenTable	OutputTo
PrintOut	Quit	Rename
RepaintObject	Requery	Restore
RunApp	RunCode	RunCommand

RunMacro	RunSQL	Save
SelectObject	SendKeys	SendObject
SetMenuItem	SetValue	SetWarnings
ShowAllRecords	ShowToolbar	StopAllMacros
StopMacro	TransferDatabase	TransferSpreadsheet
TransferText		

Most of these predefined macro actions contain specific arguments that must be set before the macro will perform the action correctly. The next section provides you with a quick reference to the arguments needed for each predefined macro action and the available choices for each argument.

Action Arguments

This section provides the action name followed by a brief description of what the action does:

AddMenu—Adds a custom menu bar or shortcut Menu Macro Name menu bar. The menu bar can be for a Status Bar Text specific form or report, or it can be global.

ApplyFilter—Applies a filter, query, or SQL WHERE condition clause to a table, form, or report.

Beep—Produces a computer beep.

CancelEvent—Cancels the event that caused the macro to run.

Close—Closes a specific window or the active window.

CopyObject—Copies a specific database object to another database or the same database.

DeleteObject—Deletes a specific database object. If no object is specified, it will delete the selected object.

Echo—Hides or shows the results of a macro while running.

FindNext—Moves to the next record specified in the Find dialog box or the FindRecord action.

FindRecord—Finds a specific record in the active form or datasheet.

GoToControl—Moves the focus to the specified control.

GoToPage—Moves the focus to the first control on a specific page.

GoToRecord—Selects the specified record.

HourGlass—Changes the pointer to an hourglass

Maximize—Maximizes the current window.

Minimize—Minimizes the current window.

`MoveSize`—Moves and sizes the current window.

`MsgBox`—Displays a specified message box.

`OpenForm`—Opens the specified form.

`OpenModule`—Opens the specified Visual Basic module.

`OpenQuery`—Opens the specified query.

`OpenReport`—Opens the specified report.

`OpenTable`—Opens the specified table.

`OutputTo`—Outputs the specified data.

`PrintOut`—Prints the current database object.

`Quit`—Quits Microsoft Access 97.

`Rename`—Renames the specified database object.

`RepaintObject`—Completes any pending updates or recalculations of the specified object.

`Requery`—Forces a requery of the specified control.

`Restore`—Restores the current window to its previous size.

`RunApp`—Runs the specified application.

`RunCode`—Runs the specified Visual Basic code.

`RunCommand`—Runs the specified Access 97 menu command. Replaces the `DoMenuItem` action. The command selected can be from a menu, toolbar, or shortcut menu.

`RunMacro`—Runs the specified macro.

`RunSQL`—Runs the specified SQL statement.

`Save`—Saves the specified database object.

`SelectObject`—Selects the specified database object.

`SendKeys`—Sends keystrokes to Access 97 or another application.

`SendObject`—Sends the specified database object in an electronic mail message.

`SetMenuItem`—Sets the state of menu items.

`SetValue`—Sets the value for a control, field, or property.

`SetWarnings`—Temporarily turns on or off the system warning messages.

`ShowAllRecords`—Shows all the records of the current table, query, or form.

`ShowToolbar`—Shows or hides the specified toolbar.

`StopAllMacros`—Stops all currently running macros. Also turns echo and display messages back on if previously turned off.

`StopMacro`—Stops the current macro. Also turns echo and display messages back on if previously turned off.

TransferDatabase—Transfers the specified database.

TransferSpreadsheet—Transfers the specified spreadsheet.

TransferText—Transfers the specified text.

As you can see, Access 97 predefined macros allow you, the programmer, to accomplish a wide variety of actions. These actions are easily programmed as macros and can be run from many different events. The next section discusses some of the more commonly used macros called special macros.

Special Macros

A special macro is not a macro action but a macro whose specific name is searched for and executed by Access without the need to assign the macro to an event or run the macro from code. The two types of special macros are AutoKeys and Autoexec. An example of how to create and use each is provided in the "Real-World Macro Examples" section.

The Autokeys Macro

The AutoKeys macro is used to globally map certain actions to key stroke combinations. This macro basically creates global hotkeys for application-wide use. Table 8.1 shows specific key combinations and their syntax. These combinations can be assigned to the AutoKeys macro and mapped to a specific action.

8

ACCESS 97 MACROS

Table 8.1. The AutoKeys macro naming syntax.

Macro Name	Key Combination
^A or ^9	Ctrl+any letter or number key
{F12}	Any function key
^{F12}	Ctrl+any function key
+{F12}	Shift+any function key
{INSERT}	Insert
^{INSERT}	Ctrl+Insert
+{INSERT}	Shift+Insert
{DELETE} or {DEL}	Delete
^{DELETE} or ^{DEL}	Ctrl+Delete
+{DELETE} or +{DEL}	Shift+Delete

The Autoexec Macro

The Autoexec macro provides a way for you to run a series of commands at the opening of a database. This macro automatically runs when the application is loaded. The Autoexec macro is a special macro but is no longer required in Access 97. Access 97 also provides the Startup dialog box, shown in Figure 8.5.

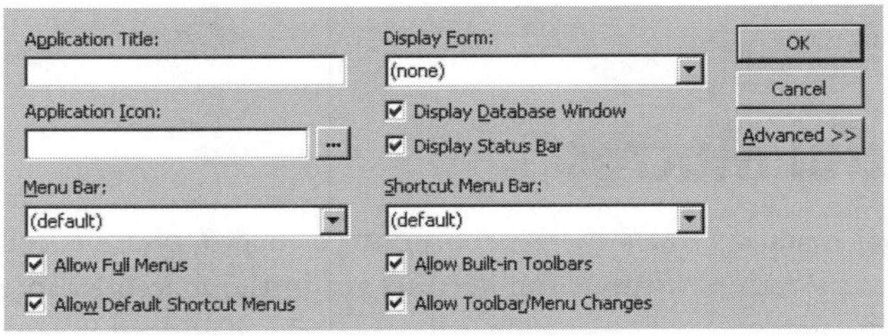

FIGURE 8.5.
The Startup dialog box.

The Startup dialog box can be used in place of the Autoexec macro. Any code called within Autoexec can now be moved to the Load or Timer event of the opening form. However, there can be times when you may want to run commands before opening a form. In this case, you would use Autoexec because the Startup dialog box currently does not provide a way to specify a module or macro as the starting point of an application.

There is another type of macro that is equally important in older versions of Access: the MenuBar macro.

NOTE

The user moving to Access 97 from previous versions will find that Access 97 has provided alternatives to some of the more common uses of macros. The Autoexec and MenuBar macros can still be used but are no longer required. Access 97 provides alternative ways of handling both.

Menu Bar Macros

In prior versions of Access, a user-defined menu bar could only be created with the use of macros. This has changed with Access 97. Access 97 still supports these menu bars, but during conversion it does not change them to the new CommandBar object. To accomplish this, you must select the macro from the database window and select Tools | Macro from the toolbar. Figure 8.6 shows the choices available during conversion of a macro.

FIGURE 8.6.

Macro conversion options available from the Database toolbar.

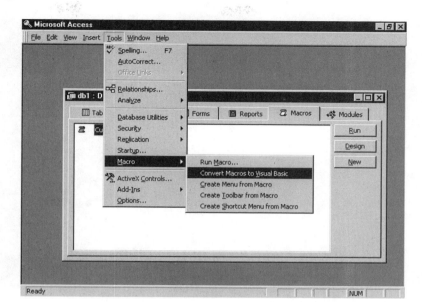

8

ACCESS 97
MACROS

TIP

You can also see in Figure 8.6 that a conversion option is listed to convert macros to VBA. This will convert a macro to a module. This can assist a developer who is modifying an existing database that heavily used macro programming. Access will also add error handling during conversion. The addition of error handling is a important reason to consider converting a macro to VBA.

Real-World Macro Examples

The "Real World Examples" section provides examples of how to create and use your macros in your own applications. It begins with creating special macros followed by a review of the Northwind macro examples that can be used as models for your own programming.

Creating an Autokeys Macro

In Figure 8.7, you can see the macro design window. To show or hide the Macro Name column, click the Macro Name button on the toolbar. The Macro Name column should contain the key combination that you want to map. In this quick example we will use the Ctrl and X keys to cancel changes when adding or updating a record. The first step is to put the key combination ^{Delete} in the Macro Name column.

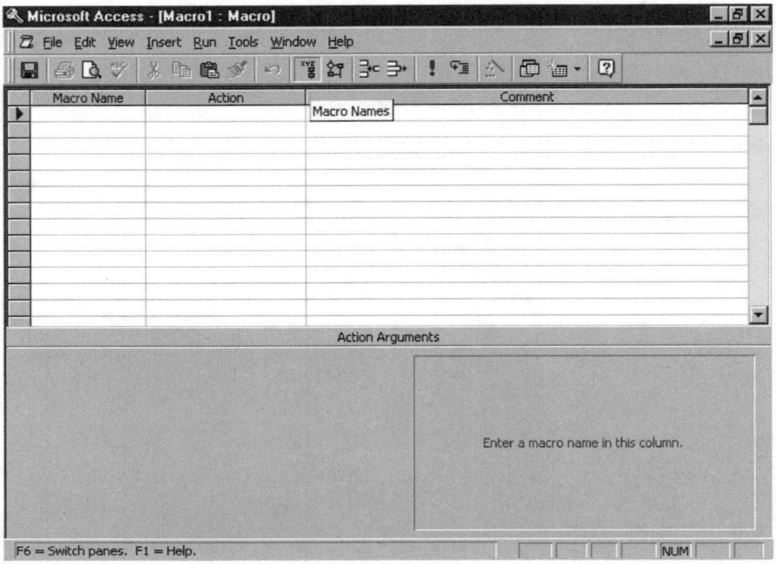

FIGURE 8.7.

Macro development window with the Macro Names column added.

> **NOTE**
>
> In a standard macro, the omission of the Name column will result in all rows of the macro being processed when the macro is run.

We will remove the Condition column by clicking the Conditions button on the macro design toolbar. The next step is to assign the correct action. Select the SendKeys action from the drop-down list. At the bottom of Figure 8.8, you can see the arguments for the selected SendKeys action.

There are two arguments for the SendKeys action. Enter {Esc}{Esc} for the Keystrokes argument. We will leave the Wait argument with the default of no. The {} symbols are used to mark a keystroke; by entering {Esc}{Esc} we will send two instances of the Esc key, which will clear the current changes. The final step is to save the macro as Autokeys.

As you can see, the macro Autokeys is really a macro collection. It contains the ^{Delete} macro. In Figure 8.9, you can see a standard Access form with a record for the Visual Access Corporation.

In Figure 8.10 shows what happens when we change the address and note fields and then press the Ctrl and Delete keys.

FIGURE 8.8.

SendKeys *Macro with the Ctrl+Del key remapped.*

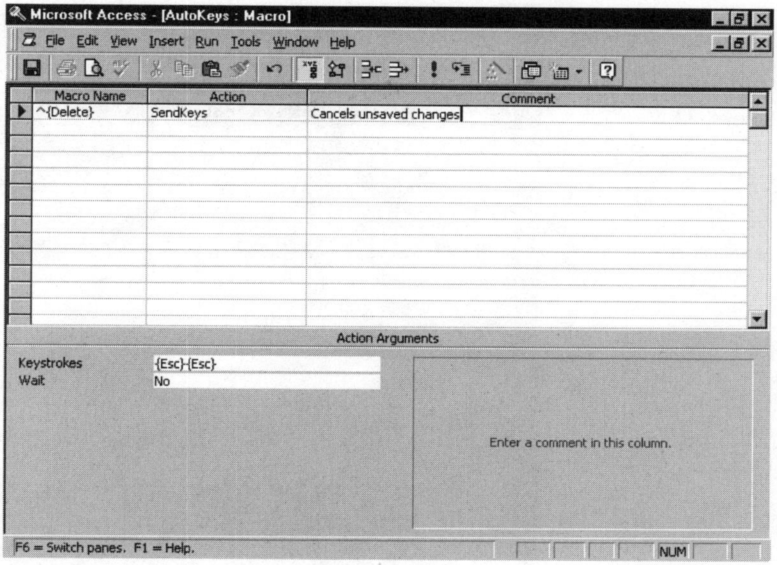

FIGURE 8.9.

The Customer Information *form.*

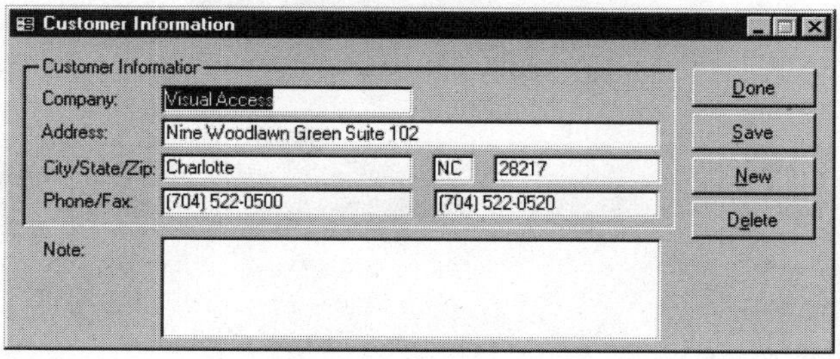

FIGURE 8.10.

The Customer Information *form with the Address and Note fields edited.*

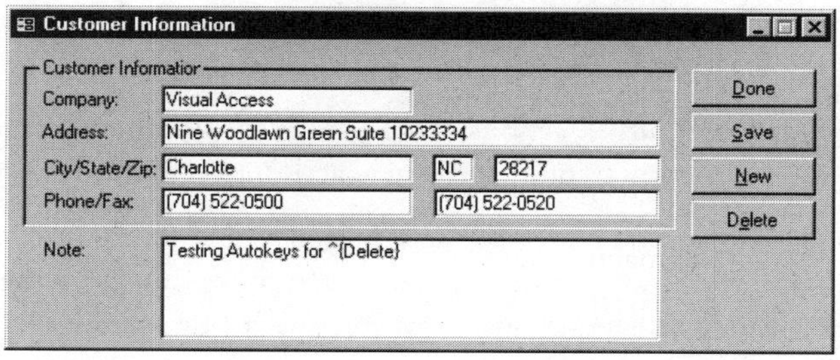

When this combination is pressed, Access finds the macro ^{Delete} and performs the sendkeys action. In Figure 8.11 you can see that our record changes have been canceled.

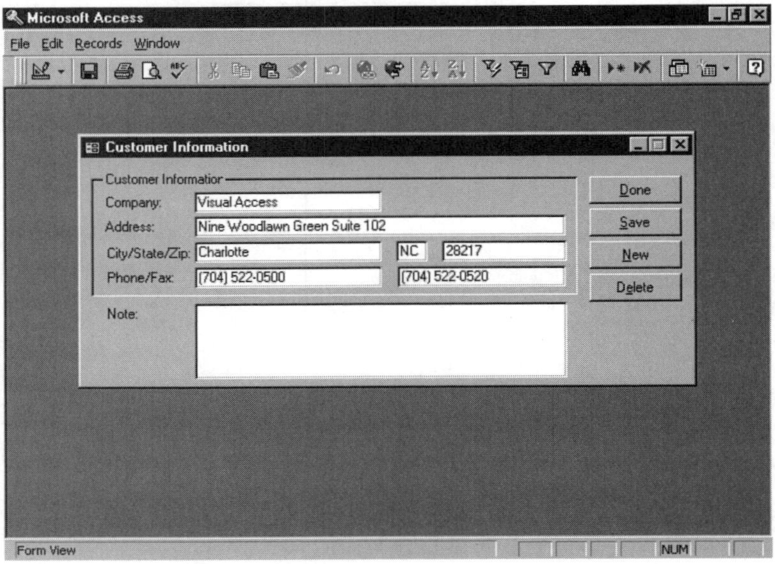

Figure 8.11.

The Customer Information *form after pressing the Ctrl+Delete key combination.*

NOTE

Many keys and key combinations are reserved for use by Access. For instance, the Ctrl+C combination is used to copy text, and the F11 key will bring the database window to the front. If Autokeys remapped any of the keys used by Access, AutoKeys will take precedence and override the default mapping. Access looks in the AutoKeys collection before looking at its own default internal mapping.

A macro can run multiple actions. If we wanted to display a message box stating that the changes have been canceled, we could add a new action to the ^{Delete} macro.

In Figure 8.12 we have added the action Msgbox, and its arguments are listed in the bottom left of the design window. In the Arguments section, we can enter the text of our message, turn on an audio beep, and assign a message icon and a title for the message box. The next time the Ctrl+Delete key combination is pressed, the changes will be removed and a message box will appear to inform the user.

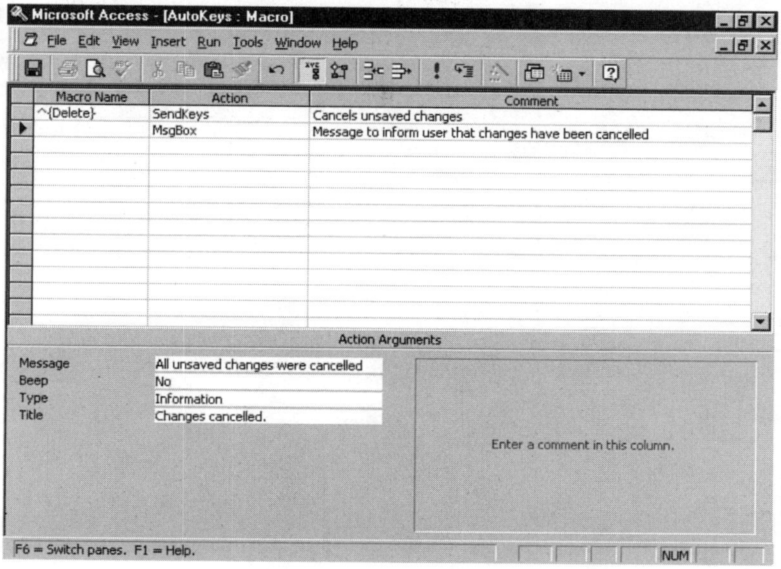

FIGURE 8.12.

The ^{Delete} macro with a message box added.

> **NOTE**
>
> Access validates the selected key or key combinations when saving the macro. Many combinations cannot be used by AutoKeys. If your selection is not allowed, Access will inform you that it is not a valid selection.

Finally, more than one macro can be created and run from inside the Autokeys collection.

In Figure 8.13 we have added a key combination to exit the application. The blank row has no purpose other than to make the design window easier to read. Access will process each row of the macro collection until the last row has been processed or a new macro name is found. The Ctrl+Q key combination is used to run the quit action. The quit action has one argument. The option argument is set to Prompt. This setting will prompt the user to save any unsaved changes before exiting the application.

Finally we will change the mapping of the {F11} key. The Access default for this key is to unhide and bring the window to front. As the programmer, you might want to hide this from the user. To accomplish this, hide the window when loading the database (see the following section about creating an Autoexec macro) and then change the default of the {F11} key.

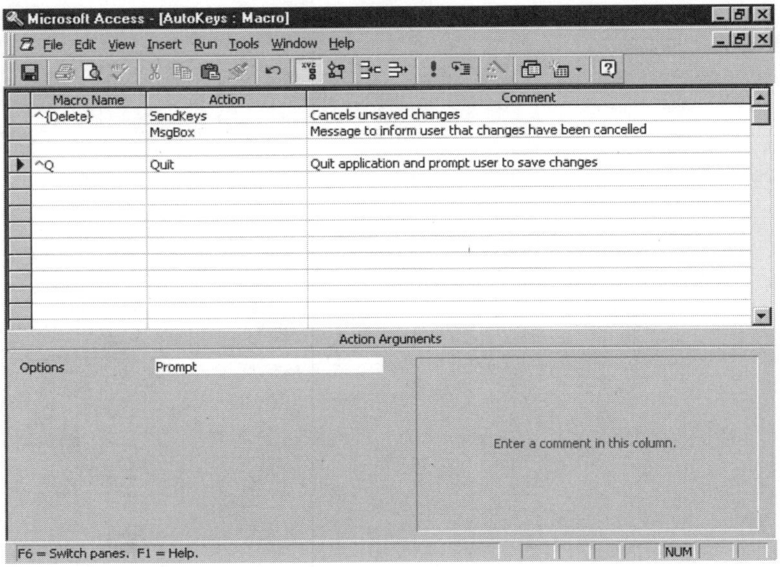

FIGURE 8.13.

The ^Q macro added to the SendKeys *macro library.*

In Figure 8.14 you see that macro {F11} has been added to the AutoKeys collection. We have not added an action for this macro. This will simply remove any default functionality from the key.

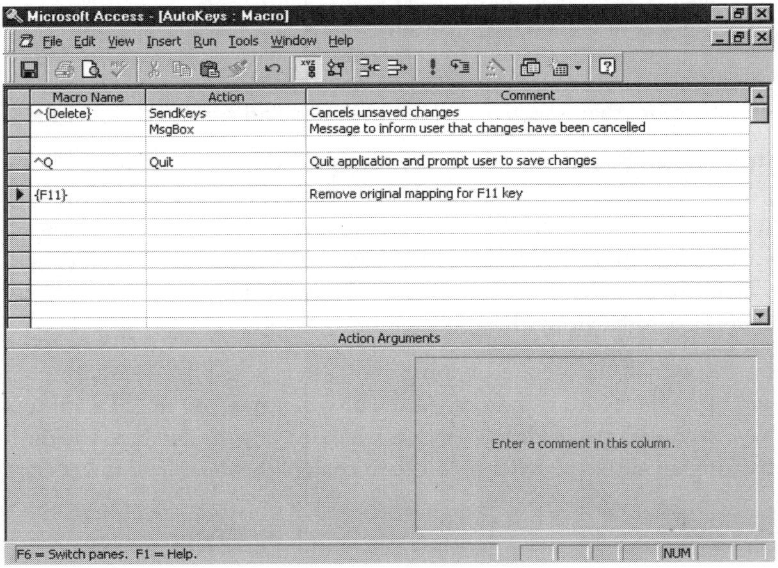

FIGURE 8.14.

The SendKeys *macro library with the* {F11} *macro added.*

Creating an Autoexec Macro

Next we will look at creating an `Autoexec` macro.

Figure 8.15 shows a standard `Autoexec` macro with two basic actions. The first is to hide the database window using the `RunCommand` action. The second is to open the main menu form. Unlike the `AutoKeys` macro, the `Autoexec` does not have to be a macro collection.

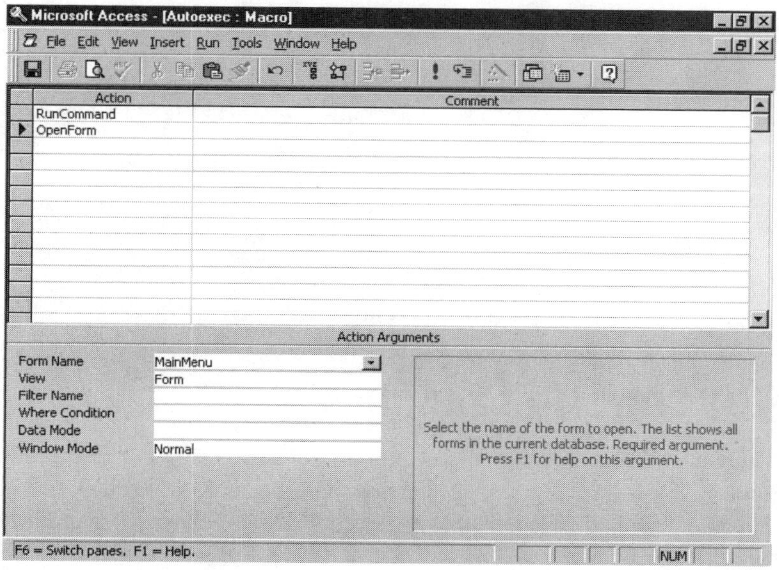

FIGURE 8.15.

The Autoexec *macro opening the* MainMenu *form.*

CAUTION

The `Autoexec` macro does not override or default to the form specified in the Startup dialog box. The `Autoexec` is still fired after the Startup dialog when an application is loaded.

Figure 8.16 shows another version of the `Autoexec` macro. It also hides the database window and then performs the `RunCode` action. The `RunCode` action runs a function. It is highly recommended that the `Autoexec` macro be as simple as possible, due to the lack of error trapping in macros. Most of the functionality should be passed to the `load` event of the first form or to a function. This same functionality could be done with the Statup dialog box by assigning a splash screen as the opening form and running code from the form events. This will also work if any type of linked table checking is done. The key is to use a splash form that will not be attached to any data.

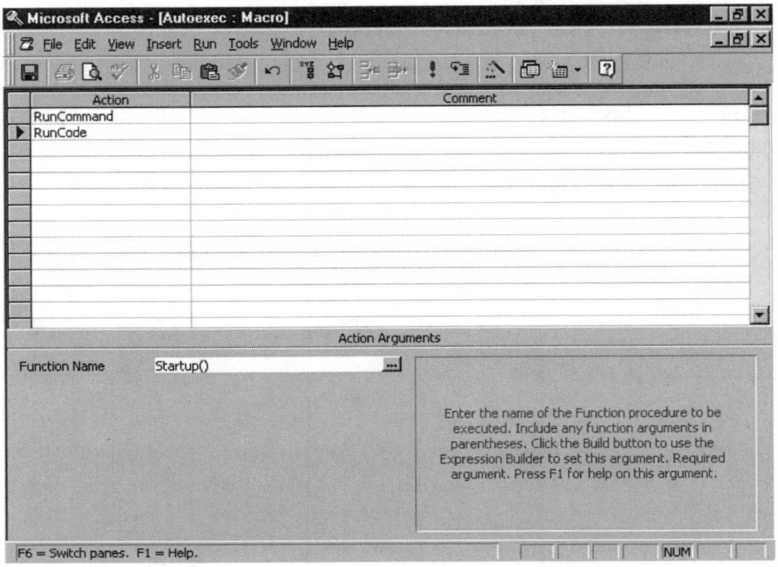

FIGURE 8.16.

The Autoexec *macro running the Startup module.*

Northwind Examples

This section examines some examples on how Access 97 uses macros to perform certain actions from within a database application. These examples are taken from the Northwind sample database provided by Microsoft in Access 97. The following examples include the Customer Labels Dialog, Customer Phone List, Employees (page break), Sales Totals by Amount, and Sample Autokeys macros.

The Customer Labels Dialog Example

The Customer Labels Dialog macro is actually a group of four macros. Figure 8.17 shows this macro in Design View.

Although not all macros can be seen, this is actually a group of macros consisting of the Enable SelectCountry, Preview, Print, and Cancel macros.

The first thing to be concerned with in creating a macro is the location of where the macro will be invoked or called. This macro group is attached to the Customer Labels Dialog form. The next thing that must be decided is which control contains the event that is to trigger the macro. Table 8.3 shows the location of the events that trigger the macros in the Customer Labels Dialog macro. All these macros are called from controls contained in the Customer Labels Dialog form.

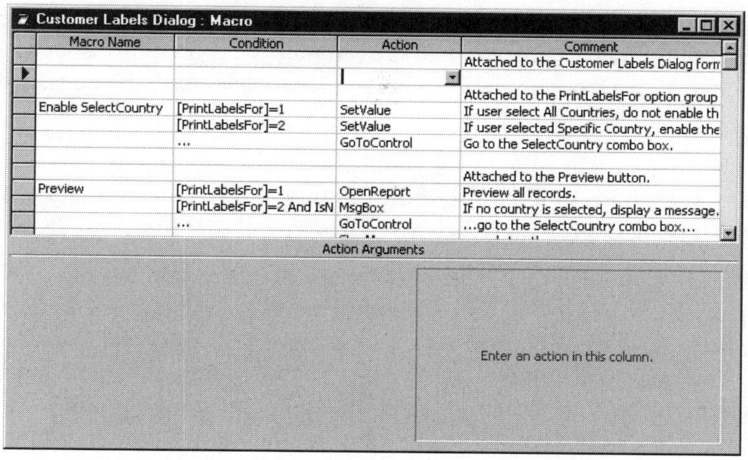

Figure 8.17.

The Customer Labels
Dialog *macro in
Design View.*

Table 8.3. The location of Customer Labels Dialog **macro calls.**

Control	Event	Call
PrintLabelsFor option group	AfterUpdate	Customer Labels Dialog.Enable SelectCountry
Preview command button	OnClick	Customer Labels Dialog.Preview
Print command button	OnClick	Customer Labels Dialog.Print
Cancel command button	OnClick	Customer Labels Dialog.Cancel

Notice the syntax of the call to the macro. The macro group name is listed first, followed by a period, followed by the macro name. If there is only one macro in a newly created macro, the macro call would only have to go to that specific macro; a macro group name would not be necessary.

The Enable SelectCountry macro is used to control the ability of the user to select a specific country. The SelectCountry combo box's Enable property has been preset on the form to No. This does not allow the user to select the control upon initial opening of the form. This macro controls when the SelectCountry combo box can be used.

The Enable SelectCountry macro consists of three actions, two SetValue actions, and one GoToControl action. The first SetValue action checks the condition of the PrintLabelsFor option group. If the value for this control is equal to 1, the SetValue action sets the Enabled property of the SelectCountry combo box to No. This prevents the user from using the combo box. The second SetValue action checks the condition of the same option group for a value of 2. If this is found, the value of the Enabled property for the combo box is set to Yes. The GoToControl then moves the focus on the form to the SelectCountry combo box, allowing the user to select a country.

The Preview macro contains six actions. The macro begins by checking the condition of the PrintLabelsFor option group. If the option group value is 1, the OpenReport action is done. The action opens the Customer Labels report and uses Preview View.

If the value of the option group is 2, the macro proceeds in one of two directions. The following condition is used to check whether there is a value in the SelectCountry combo box: [PrintLabelsFor]=2 And IsNull([SelectCountry]). This condition checks for a Null value in the SelectCountry combo box. If the condition is met, the macro uses the MsgBox action to display a message to the user directly, asking him to select a country. The macro then uses the GoToControl action to move the user back to the SelectCountry combo box and then uses the StopMacro action to stop the macro.

If the PrintLabelsFor option group contains a value of 2 and is not Null, the macro uses the OpenReport action to open the Customer Labels report in a Preview View. The OpenReport action also places the following statement in the Conditions argument on this action: [Country]=[Forms]![Customer Labels Dialog]![SelectCountry]. This condition sets the Country value in the report to the one selected in the SelectCountry combo box.

The Print macro does exactly the same thing as the Preview macro, except for one significant difference. The View argument of each OpenReport action is set to Print instead of Print Preview.

The Cancel macro uses the Close action to close the Customer Labels Dialog form.

The Customer Phone List Example

The Customer Phone List macro consists of two macros: Alpha Buttons and Print. The Print macro is used with the Sample Autokeys macro and will be discussed later in this chapter. The Alpha Buttons macro is an extremely useful macro that can be copied and used in other database.

In a nutshell, the Alpha Buttons macro is used to filter data based on the alphabet. Figure 8.18 shows part of the Customer Phone List macro in Design View.

The Alpha Buttons macro is called from the Customer Phone List form. On the Customer Phone List form footer is an option group control called CompanyNameFilters. This option group control contains 26 toggle button controls that represent the letters of the alphabet, plus one that is used to select all the records.

In the AfterUpdate event of the CompanyNameFilters is the call to the Customer Phone List Alpha Buttons macro (Customer Phone List.Alpha Buttons). This call triggers the macro to run. The filter to be used depends on the value of the option group property when the call is made to the macro. The value is determined by the user when a toggle button is selected. Each toggle button contains its own index value for the option group. The All toggle button has the index value of 27, which is also the `DefaultValue` of the option group.

FIGURE 8.18.

The Customer Phone List *macro in Design View.*

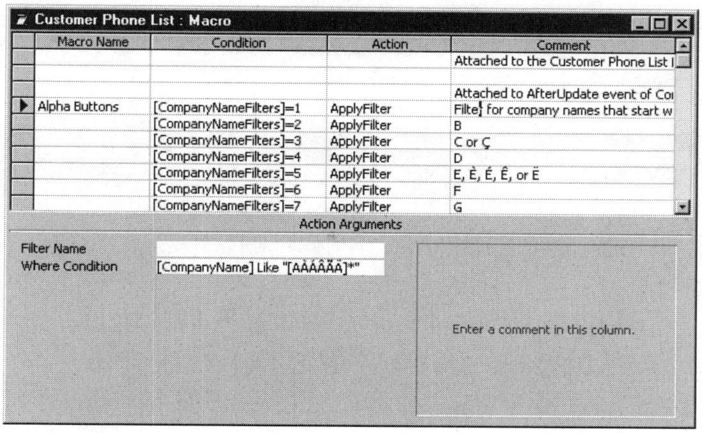

The user selects the toggle button that sets the option group value and triggers the `AfterUpdate` event. The `Alpha Button` macro is then run and, based on the condition of the value of the option group, filters the data using the `ApplyFilter` action.

In this example, suppose the A toggle button is selected, so the option group value is equal to 1. When the `AfterUpdate` event occurs, it triggers the `Alpha Buttons` macro. Looking at the first condition statement (`[CompanyNameFilters]=1`), the macro uses the `ApplyFilter` action and applies the filter name and `WHERE` condition arguments to the action.

For this example, the `WHERE` condition consists of the following statement: `[CompanyName] Like "[AÀÁÂÃÄ]*"`. This statement then filters the data on the `CompanyName` field where the first character of the name matches the string of A characters. The * after the string of A characters is used as a wildcard for the remaining characters of the company name in the `CompanyName` field. Each `ApplyFilter` action following this one simply modifies the `WHERE` condition for the different letters of the alphabet.

If the value of the option group is 27 (signifying the All toggle button), the macro uses the `ShowAllRecords` action to display all the records in the `CompanyName` field.

At the end of the `Alpha Buttons` macro, the programmers have included some action used to handle special circumstances that may arise while the macro is running. For example, the macro uses a condition placed on the `GoToControl` action to ensure that the `ApplyFilter` action results in a recordset with records in it.

The condition placed on this action is `[RecordsetClone].[RecordCount]>0`, which uses the `CompanyName` field as the argument. This condition ensures there is at least one record in the recordset that is returned. If the condition is met, the `Alpha Button` macro uses the `StopMacro` action to halt the macro.

The macro uses a condition on a `MsgBox` action to display a message box if the recordset returned contains zero records. This condition looks like this: `[RecordsetClone].[RecordCount]=0`. The `MsgBox` action results in an information message box appearing to the user, telling him there are no records for this selection. If this occurs, the macro uses the `ShowAllRecords` action to return all the records in the `CompanyName` field. The macro ends with the `SetValue` action to reset the `CompanyNameFilters` value back to 27.

> **TIP**
>
> This type of macro is extremely useful to the programmer when allowing the user to select specific filters for sorting data to be displayed in a form.

The `Employees (page break)` Example

The `Employees (page break)` macro is an example of a group macro that is used to move the user between different pages of a form. This macro is attached to the `Employees (page break)` form. Figure 8.19 shows this macro in Design View.

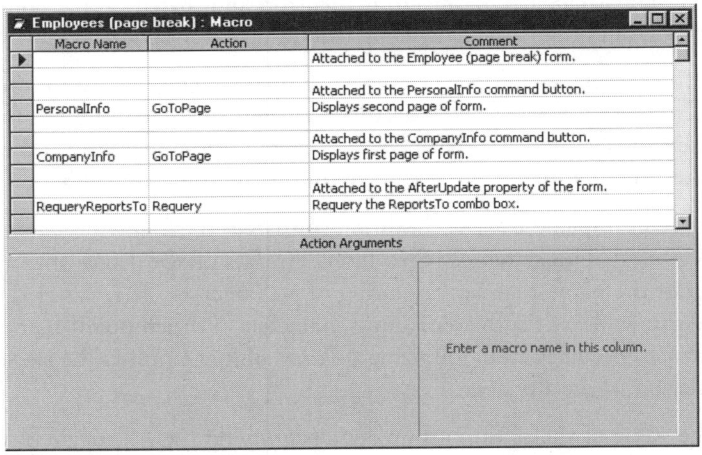

FIGURE 8.19.

The `Employees (page break)` *macro in Design View.*

This is a simple macro that uses the `GoToPage` action to move the user between different pages on a form. The `Employees (page break)` macro is a group macro containing the `PersonalInfo`, `CompanyInfo`, and `RequeryReportsTo` macros. The `PersonalInfo` and `CompanyInfo` macros are virtually identical. Both macros use the `GoToPage` action with the `Page Number` argument set to the different pages. These two macros are called from the `OnClick` event from the command buttons on the different pages.

The third macro in this group is `RequeryReportsTo`. This macro is called from the `AfterUpdate` event on the `Employee (page break)` form itself. The `RequeryReportsTo` macro uses the requery action to requery the ReportsTo combo box on the form, thereby regenerating the list of names that can be chosen from the box.

The Sales Totals by Amount Example

The Sales Totals by Amount macro group consists of five individual macros. These macros are used to manipulate some of the formatting functions associated with the Sales Totals by Amount report. This is a good example of how macros can be used to control printing options on reports. Figure 8.20 shows the Sales Totals by Amount macro in Design View.

FIGURE 8.20.

The Sales Totals by Amount *macro in Design View.*

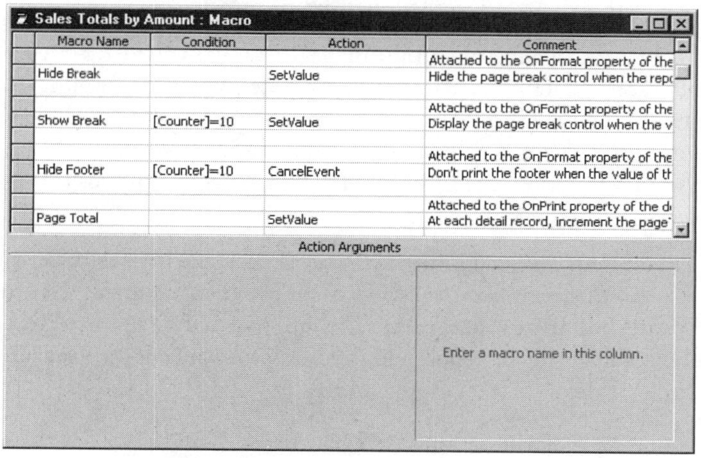

The objective of the report is to print a report listing each sale and its associated amount. The report requirements include a page total dollar amount to be displayed at the bottom of each page. In addition, the user requires the report to print only the top 10 sales on the first page, with the remaining sales on the following pages.

To accomplish this task, the programmers decided to use macros to tell Access 97 which orders to print on the first page using a counter. The first macro in the Sales Totals by Amount macro group is Hide Break. This macro is called from the OnFormat property of the page header in the Sales Totals by Amount report. The macro uses the SetValue action to set the page break control's Visible property ([HiddenPageBreak].[Visible]) to No. This action hides the page break when the report is doing its first pass to format the report.

The second macro in this group (Show Break) is called from the OnFormat property of the Details section. The report formats the report until the condition associated with this macro is met. In this example, the condition is [Counter]=10. The Counter is a text box control located on the report. The ControlSource property of this control is set to =1, which tells Access 97 to print a number for each record, beginning with 1 and continuing in sequential order. The Show Break macro waits until the counter gets to 10 and then uses the SetValue action to reset the page break control's Visible property to yes, thereby producing a page break.

The third macro in this group (Hide Footer) is called from the OnFormat property of the SalesAmount footer. The SalesAmount footer consists of a single line control used to separate the orders into groups. In the sorting and grouping criteria for the report, the data printed on the report is to be grouped in $1,000 intervals. For each $1,000 break in the data, the SalesAmount footer (a single line) should print.

This macro controls when to print this line. Because the first page is to consist of only the top 10 sales amounts, the end user does not want to see a line printed at the bottom of the top 10. The Hide Footer macro uses the same condition as the Show Page macro to keep track of when not to print this line. When the value of the counter control box reaches 10, the macro uses the CancelEvent action to stop the line from printing.

The fourth macro in this group (Page Total) is called from the OnPrint property of the Details section. This macro is used to increase the dollar amount shown in the PageTotal text box by the value in the SalesAmount text box. The report will add a record to the Details section until the page is full. Each time the report adds a record, the PageTotal text box needs to be adjusted to reflect the addition. This macro accomplishes this process using the SetValue action.

Two arguments are used in the SetValue action: the item to be set and the expression on how to set it. In this example, the property for the Item argument is set to the PageTotal text box. The expression ([PageTotal]+[SaleAmount]) adds the PageTotal text box and the SalesAmount text box. Each time the report adds a record, the value of the PageTotal text box is increased by the value of the SalesAmount text added.

The final macro in this group (New Page) is called from the OnPrint property of the page header. This macro is used to reset the value in the PageTotal text box to 0. The macro uses the SetValue action to set the value back to 0, so when the report moves to the next page it begins recalculating the PageTotal value.

Summary

This chapter focuses on the use of macros in Access 97. Some of the more common uses of macros in previous versions of Access have been relinquished by the release of Access 97. This chapter was developed as a reference guide to the predefined macros available in Access 97.

The chapter also covers the macro actions and their arguments, as well as how to use and create special macros. The chapter finishes with a walk through some of the more frequently used macros taken from the Northwind sample database. The use of macros in Access 97 has not gone away completely, and to the beginning programmer or in some circumstances they can still be a valuable part of more advanced applications.

Access 97 Modules

by Scott Billings

IN THIS CHAPTER

CHAPTER 9

This chapter focuses on using modules in Access 97. *Modules* are the place where programming code is stored. They are usually a set of Visual Basic for Application (VBA) declarations, functions and/or procedures that are put together as a unit. The intricacies of how to program using VBA are discussed in Part IV, "Visual Basic for Applications for Access 97" (Chapters 12–14) of this book.

The chapter begins with a discussion of the two types of modules used by Access 97. Following this, you'll look at the module design window and the components available for use in Access 97.

This chapter also examines the Object Browser available in Access 97 and how to find it and use it. It concludes by showing some examples of modules taken from the Northwind sample database and discusses their use in application development.

Types of Modules

There are two basic types of modules in Access 97: standard modules and class modules. *Standard modules* are associated with a specific object in the application and are used to create VBA procedures that are frequently used and can be run from anywhere in the database application. To view the standard modules in the database, click on the Modules tab in the database window.

Class modules, on the other hand, are not associated with any object in Access 97. Two types of class modules are form and report modules. These modules are associated with particular forms or reports in the database application.

A form or report module is created at the time the initial form or report is created. To view the code module for its associated form or report, click the Code button on the toolbar or select Code from the View menu on the menu bar. The following code snippet is an example of a form module. The example is taken from the Orders form of the Northwind sample database. The first part of the example is in the general declarations section of the module; the second part is located in the AfterUpdate section of the CustomerID combo box control.

```
Option Compare Database ' Use database order for string comparisons.
Option Explicit ' Requires variables to be declared before they are used.


Private Sub CustomerID_AfterUpdate()
' Update ShipTo controls based on value selected in CustomerID combo box.
    Me!ShipName = Me![CustomerID].Column(1)
    Me!ShipAddress = Me!Address
    Me!ShipCity = Me!City
    Me!ShipRegion = Me!Region
    Me!ShipPostalCode = Me!PostalCode
    Me!ShipCountry = Me!Country
End Sub
```

Remember that Access 97 introduces the concept of lightweight forms. A lightweight form is a form that contains no code behind it or associated with it. Each newly created form has the `HasModule` property. To create a lightweight form, simply change this property to `no`. When this property is changed to `no`, Access 97 deletes the associated code module with it. When Access 97 loads a form into memory, it also loads the code module, but many forms are created that do not use their code module. By deleting the code module, Access 97 is able to load the form much faster, thus improving the overall database performance. In addition, deleting the code module also reduces the overall physical size of the database application.

In Access 95, class modules are only available in the form and report varieties. Access 97 allows the programmer to create independent class modules. These modules are found on the Modules tab of the database window and can be used to create custom objects for Access 97.

Procedures

Procedures are the units of code residing in a module that perform an operation or calculate a value. There are two types of procedures. The `Sub` procedure is code that performs an operation and does not return a value. For example, the second part of the code snippet in the preceding section performs the operation of updating the value of the fields on the form. It does not return a value by itself.

The `Function` procedure performs a calculation and returns a value. Access 97 provides a number of the most commonly used functions that can be used in a database application. The following code is an example of a function and was taken from the `Function Utility` module in the `Northwind` sample database:

```
Function IsLoaded(ByVal strFormName As String) As Boolean
 ' Returns True if the specified form is open in Form view or Datasheet view.

    Const conObjStateClosed = 0
    Const conDesignView = 0

    If SysCmd(acSysCmdGetObjectState, acForm, strFormName) <>
➥conObjStateClosed Then
        If Forms(strFormName).CurrentView <> conDesignView Then
            IsLoaded = True
        End If
    End If

End Function
```

As you can see from the comment line, the function returns a `True` value if the specified form is open in Form View or Datasheet View.

The Module Design Window

Creating a new module in Access 97 is the same as creating any other object. Move to the Modules tab and click Create. Figure 9.1 shows a new module in Design View.

FIGURE 9.1.

A new module in Design View.

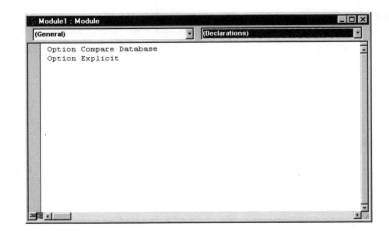

The module window is broken into three parts. In the upper-left corner is a combo box that displays the current object. The upper-right combo box displays the current procedure. The large window below these combo boxes is for typing the actual code to be used with the object or procedure selected.

The module toolbar provides the most frequently used menu items you will use when creating and debugging the code.

Access 97 allows the programmer to customize the way code is written in a module. To customize the programming environment, select Tools | Options from the menu bar. Figure 9.2 shows the Module tab of the Options dialog box.

As you can see, the options available for customization are broken into three categories: Code Colors, Coding Options, and Window Settings. The Code Colors and Window Settings options are self-explanatory. Access 97 has added three new options to the Coding Options: Auto List Members, Auto Quick Info, and Auto Data Tips.

Figure 9.2.

Module customization options.

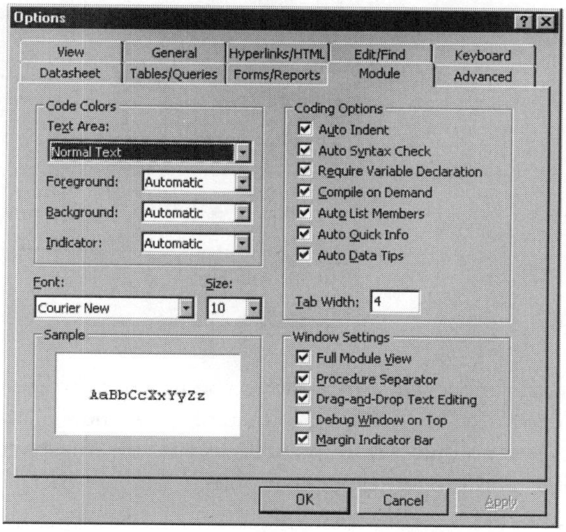

The Auto List Members option supplies a list of the possible objects, properties, and methods that can assist the programmer in completing a statement based on the name of the object typed. This is done while you are actually creating the code. You can click on the item listed or continue typing the code, whichever you prefer.

The Auto Quick Info option provides the appropriate syntax to use for a procedure or method in a temporary window that automatically appears directly below the line where you are typing the code. The suggested syntax includes the arguments needed to complete the code.

The Auto Data Tips option supplies the value of a variable or expression in the code while in break mode. The value is displayed when the mouse is moved over the variable or expression.

These options may or may not be useful to you, depending on the level of your knowledge of VBA. Extremely knowledgeable VBA programmers may find the options more cumbersome than helpful, while the more inexperienced VBA programmer will find the new option extremely useful in providing needed information without having to constantly check the help file for syntax and object names.

The Object Browser

Access 97 provides a utility called the Object Browser, which is used to easily find methods and properties for the objects available in Access 97. To open the Object Browser, open any module and click the Object Browser toolbar button. Figure 9.3 shows the Object Browser's initial window.

FIGURE 9.3.

The Object Browser window.

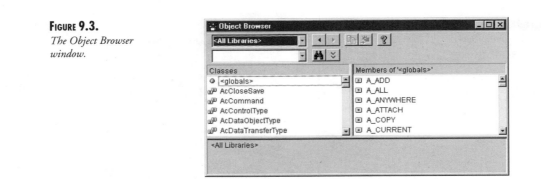

The box in the upper-left corner allows you to select the project or library to use. When you select what you need, the Classes box then fills with the available objects for that library. Then, when you select an object from the Classes window, the Members of box fills with the available methods and properties for that object. You can then select the object, click the Copy button, and then paste the object into the open module.

The Object Browser provides an easy-to-use method of finding and using the various objects available in Access 97 or in other libraries contained on the development system.

Sample Modules

The Northwind sample database contains a limited set of examples of modules. Some form and report modules have already been discussed in the previous chapters on forms and report. Part IV contains numerous examples of modules and how to use them, but following are some additional examples found in the Northwind sample database.

The Startup Module

The Startup module in the Northwind database is used in the Startup form. The Startup module consists of four separate functions: OpenStartup, HideStartupForm, CloseForm, and IsItAReplica. The comment lines contained in the module explain what each function does and how it works.

The overall purpose of the Startup module is to determine whether the database is a design master or a replica. If the database is a design master or replica, the module directs Access 97 whether the Startup form is or is not opened when the database is initially opened. To view the Startup module, go to the Modules tab in the main database window. Click on Startup, then click on the Design button. The Startup module will open in Design View. The code used in the Startup module is as follows:

```
Function OpenStartup() As Boolean
' Displays Startup form only if database is not a design master or replica.
' Used in OnOpen property of Startup form.

On Error GoTo OpenStartup_Err
    If IsItAReplica() Then
        ' This database is a design master or replica, so close Startup form
        ' before it is displayed.

        DoCmd.Close

    Else
        ' This database is not a design master or replica,
➥' so display Startup form.
        ' Set the value of HideStartupForm checkbox using the value of
        ' StartupForm property of database (as set in Display Form box
        ' in Startup dialog box).

        If CurrentDb().Properties("StartupForm") = "Startup" Then
            ' StartupForm property is set to Startup, so clear HideStartupForm
            ' checkbox.

            Forms!Startup!HideStartupForm = False

        Else
            ' StartupForm property is not set to Startup,
➥' so check HideStartupForm
            ' checkbox.

            Forms!Startup!HideStartupForm = True
        End If
    End If

OpenStartup_Exit:
    Exit Function

OpenStartup_Err:
    Const conPropertyNotFound = 3270
    If Err = conPropertyNotFound Then
        Forms!Startup!HideStartupForm = True
        Resume OpenStartup_Exit
    End If
End Function
Function HideStartupForm()
On Error GoTo HideStartupForm_Err
' Uses the value of HideStartupForm checkbox to determine the setting for
' StartupForm property of database. (The setting is displayed in Display Form
' box in Startup dialog box).
' Used in OnClose property of Startup form.

        If Forms!Startup!HideStartupForm Then
        ' HideStartupForm checkbox is checked, so set StartupForm
➥' property to (none).
            CurrentDb().Properties("StartupForm") = "(none)"

        Else
            ' HideStartupForm checkbox is cleared, so set StartupForm
➥' property to Startup.
```

```
            CurrentDb().Properties("StartupForm") = "Startup"
        End If

        Exit Function

HideStartupForm_Err:
    Const conPropertyNotFound = 3270
    If Err = conPropertyNotFound Then
        Dim db As Database
        Dim prop As Property
        Set db = CurrentDb()
        Set prop = db.CreateProperty("StartupForm", dbText, "Startup")
        db.Properties.Append prop
        Resume Next
    End If
End Function
Function CloseForm()
' Closes Startup form.
' Used in OnClick property of OK command button on Startup form.

    DoCmd.Close

End Function
Function IsItAReplica() As Boolean
On Error GoTo IsItAReplica_Err
' Determines if database is a design master or a replica.
' Used in OpenStartup function.

    Dim blnReturnValue As Boolean

    blnReturnValue = False
    If CurrentDb().Properties("Replicable") = "T" Then
        ' Replicable property setting is T, so database is a
➥' design master or replica.
        blnReturnValue = True

    Else
        ' Replicable property setting is not T, so database is
➥' not a design master
        ' or replica.

        blnReturnValue = False
    End If

IsItAReplica_Exit:
    IsItAReplica = blnReturnValue
    Exit Function

IsItAReplica_Err:
    Resume IsItAReplica_Exit
End Function
```

The Startup module is a good example of the use of function procedures in modules. As previously mentioned, modules can also be used to create sub procedures. The next section will show an example of a module that is used to contain sub procedures.

The Sales Analysis Form Module

The Sales Analysis form contains a form module consisting of a sub procedure. A form module is a module of code that is associated with a single form. In this case, the form module is contained in the Sales Analysis form. The sub procedure provides the option of opening a pivot table for editing. On the form itself is a button that the user can click to edit the pivot table on the form. To view this form module, go to the Forms tab in the main database window. Select the Sales Analysis form and click the Design button. Once the form is displayed, click the Code button on the toolbar. The following sub procedure is located in the Click event of this button:

```
Private Sub btnEdit_Click()
On Error GoTo btnEdit_Err
    Me!PivotTable.Verb = acOLEVerbOpen
    Me!PivotTable.Action = acOLEActivate
btnEdit_Exit:
    Exit Sub
btnEdit_Err:
    MsgBox Err.Description
    Resume btnEdit_Exit
End Sub
```

As you can see from the code, the procedure opens the pivot table, then activates it for editing. Note that the procedure includes an error-handling procedure should an error arise. The procedure opens a message box displaying the type of error and then exits the procedure. Including an error-handling routine is always recommended in developing code for a database application.

The Products Form Module

The Products form module is another example of a module containing sub procedures. This example contains two sub procedures. The first sub procedure is located in the Click event of the OutputToHTML button located on the form. To view this form module, go to the Forms tab in the main database window. Select the Products form and click the Design button. Once the form is displayed, click the Code button on the toolbar. The following is the code associated with the Click event of the OutputToHTML button:

```
Private Sub OutputToHTML_Click()
On Error GoTo Err_OuputToHTML_Click
' Outputs the Alphabetical List of Products report as an HTML
' document, and opens the document in an Internet browser.
' You must have Nwindtem.htm (template for Northwind) and NWLogo.gif
' (Northwind logo) in the same folder as the Northwind database.
    DoCmd.OutputTo acOutputReport, "Alphabetical List of Products",
➥acFormatHTML, "Products.htm", True, "Nwindtem.htm"
Exit_OutputToHTML_Click:
    Exit Sub
Err_OuputToHTML_Click:
    ' If action was cancelled by the user, don't display an error message.
    Const conErrDoCmdCancelled = 2501
    If (Err = conErrDoCmdCancelled) Then
```

```
        Resume Exit_OutputToHTML_Click
    Else
        MsgBox Err.Description
        Resume Exit_OutputToHTML_Click
    End If

End Sub
```

This procedure uses the Do command (DoCmd) to output the Alphabetical List of Products report to an HTML-formatted file entitled Products.htm using the Nwindtem.htm file as the template. The procedure uses the acOutputReport constant to tell Access 97 the object type for the OutputTo action and the acFormatHTML constant to set the format of the new document. Both of these constants can be easily found using the Object Browser. The procedure also includes an error-handling routine that preempts the error-message window if the user cancels the procedure.

The second sub procedure in the Products form module is found in the AfterUpdate event of the ProductName text box control. The code for this sub procedure is as follows:

```
Private Sub ProductName_AfterUpdate()
' If OpenArgs property isn't null, set SupplierID to value of form's OpenArgs
' property. OpenArgs will have a value if Products form is opened by clicking
' AddProducts command button on Suppliers form.
    If IsNull(Forms!Products.OpenArgs) Then
        Exit Sub
    Else
        Me!SupplierID = Forms!Products.OpenArgs
    End If

End Sub
```

This procedure is used to check whether the AddProducts command button was used to open the Products form. If it was, the SupplierID is taken from the Suppliers form value for SupplierID. If the Products form was opened a different way, the procedure is exited and the SupplierID is from the first record.

This procedure is a nice example of adding helpful features to your database application. Instead of having the user input all the supplier information from scratch each time the Products form is opened, the developers have added this procedure to take information from one form and transfer it to another so the user can save time when entering a new product.

The Suppliers Form Module

The Suppliers form module is another example of using a module to carry out Sub procedures. This module contains five sub procedures. Table 9.1 shows each sub procedure with the associated control and event that triggers the procedure.

Table 9.1. Suppliers form module summary.

Control name	Control type	Control event
AddProducts	Command Button	Click
Suppliers	Form	BeforeUpdate
Suppliers	Form	Close
Suppliers	Form	Current
ReviewProducts	Command Button	Click

```
Option Compare Database ' Use database order for string comparisons.
Option Explicit ' Requires variables to be declared before they are used.

Sub AddProducts_Click()
' This code created in part by Command Button Wizard.

On Error GoTo Err_AddProducts_Click
    Dim strDocName As String
    strDocName = "Products"
    ' Open Products form in data entry mode and store SupplierID in
    ' the form's OpenArgs property.
    DoCmd.OpenForm strDocName, , , , acAdd, , Me!SupplierID
    ' Close Product List form.
    DoCmd.Close acForm, "Product List"
    ' Give ProductName control focus.
    Forms![Products]!ProductName.SetFocus

Exit_AddProducts_Click:
    Exit Sub

Err_AddProducts_Click:
    MsgBox Err.Description
    Resume Exit_AddProducts_Click
End Sub
```

The Command Button Wizard created this sub procedure. The procedure simply opens the Products form, closes the Suppliers form, and sets the focus to the ProductName field on the Suppliers form. This is also the sub procedure that sets the value of the OpenArgs property in the Products form. As mentioned in the previous example, this part of the procedure is used to check whether the Products form was opened from this command button. If it was, the SupplierID field on the Products form is taken from the Suppliers field.

The next sub procedure checks the postal code entered with the country and displays an error message if the number of digits does not match for that particular country. The procedure is triggered by the BeforeUpdate event on the form. The code is as follows:

```
Private Sub Form_BeforeUpdate(Cancel As Integer)

' If number of digits entered in PostalCode text box is incorrect for value
' in Country text box, display message and undo PostalCode value.
```

9

ACCESS 97 MODULES

```
    Select Case Me!Country
        Case IsNull(Me![Country])
            Exit Sub
        Case "France", "Italy", "Spain"
            If Len(Me![PostalCode]) <> 5 Then
                MsgBox "Postal Code must be 5 characters", 0,
➥"Postal Code Error"
                Cancel = True
                Me![PostalCode].SetFocus
            End If
        Case "Australia", "Singapore"
            If Len(Me![PostalCode]) <> 4 Then
                MsgBox "Postal Code must be 4 characters", 0,
➥"Postal Code Error"
                Cancel = True
                Me![PostalCode].SetFocus
            End If
        Case "Canada"
            If Not Me![PostalCode] Like "[A-Z][0-9][A-Z] [0-9][A-Z][0-9]" Then
                MsgBox "Postal Code not valid. Example of Canadian code:
➥H1J 1C3", 0, "Postal Code Error"
                Cancel = True
                Me![PostalCode].SetFocus
            End If

    End Select
End Sub
```

This sub procedure is a good example of using the `SELECT CASE` statement to evaluate a field's value and perform an operation based on that value. The first line of the code tells the `SELECT CASE` routine which field to evaluate. In this example, the field is the `Country` field on the `Suppliers` form.

The sub procedure then moves down through three different cases. If the value in the `SELECT CASE` statement variable matches one of the cases, the statements directly below the case are executed.

In this example, suppose the supplier being entered is in Australia. When the `BeforeUpdate` event occurs, the sub procedure evaluates the `Country` field. When it finds the string `Australia`, the procedure then checks the number of digits in the `PostalCode` field to determine whether the total number of digits equals four.

If the `PostalCode` field does not contain four digits, the sub procedure displays a message box telling the user that the Postal Code for Australia must be only four digits. The sub procedure then sets the focus of the form to the `PostalCode` field so the user can make the appropriate changes. The `Sub` procedure is now through and will be run again when the `BeforeUpdate` event occurs.

The next sub procedure in the `Suppliers` form module simply checks to see whether the `Products List` or `Products` forms are open. If they are open, the procedure closes them. This sub procedure is called when the `Close` event occurs for the `Suppliers` form. The code used to accomplish this is as follows:

```
Private Sub Form_Close()

    ' Close Product List form and Products form if they are open.
    If IsLoaded("Product List") Then DoCmd.Close acForm, "Product List"
    If IsLoaded("Products") Then DoCmd.Close acForm, "Products"

End Sub
```

The next sub procedure in the `Suppliers` form module manipulates the way the `Products List` form displays the products. The procedure is triggered by the `Current` event on the `Suppliers` form. The code for this sub procedure is as follows:

```
Private Sub Form_Current()
On Error GoTo Err_Form_Current

' If Product List form is open, show current supplier's products.

    Dim strDocName As String
    Dim strLinkCriteria As String

        strDocName = "Product List"
        strLinkCriteria = "[SupplierID] = Forms![Suppliers]![SupplierID]"

    If IsNull(Me![CompanyName]) Then
        Exit Sub
    ElseIf IsLoaded("Product List") Then
        DoCmd.OpenForm strDocName, , , strLinkCriteria
    End If

Exit_Form_Current:
    Exit Sub

Err_Form_Current:
    MsgBox Err.Description
    Resume Exit_Form_Current

End Sub
```

The first part of this procedure declares two string variables, `strDocName` and `strLinkCriteria`. The sub procedure then sets the values for each variable. The `strDocName` variable is set to the following string `Product List`. The `strLinkCriteria` variable sets the `SupplierID` field on the `Product List` form to equal the value of the `SupplierID` field from the `Suppliers` form.

The second part of this sub procedure uses an `If...ElseIf` statement to check to see whether there is a value in the `CompanyName` field on the `Suppliers` form. If the `CompanyName` field is `Null`, the sub procedure is exited. If there is a value in the `CompanyName` field, the sub procedure then checks to see whether the `Product List` form is loaded. If the `Product List` form is not loaded, the sub procedure uses the `Do` command to open the `Product List` form using the `strLinkCriteria` variable to set the products shown on the `Product List` form to those matching the `SupplierID` value from the `Suppliers` form.

9

ACCESS 97 MODULES

This procedure is good way of providing the user with the most relevant information to the specific form he/she is viewing. The last sub procedure in the Suppliers form module is triggered from the Click event associated with the ReviewProducts command button. This is an example of using the Command Button Wizard to create a piece of a procedure and later modifying that procedure to accomplish a more specific task. The code for this sub procedure is as follows:

```
Private Sub ReviewProducts_Click()
' This code created in part by Command Button Wizard.
On Error GoTo Err_ReviewProducts_Click

    Dim strMsg As String, strTitle As String
    Dim intStyle As Integer
    Dim strDocName As String, strLinkCriteria As String

    ' If CompanyName control is blank, display a message.
    If IsNull(Me![CompanyName]) Then
        strMsg = "Move to the supplier record whose products you want to see,
➡then press the Review Products button again."
        intStyle = vbOKOnly
        strTitle = "Select a Supplier"
        MsgBox strMsg, intStyle, strTitle
        Me![CompanyName].SetFocus
    Else
    ' Otherwise, open Product List form, showing products for
➡' current supplier.
        strDocName = "Product List"
        strLinkCriteria = "[SupplierID] = Forms![Suppliers]![SupplierID]"
        DoCmd.OpenForm strDocName, , , strLinkCriteria
        DoCmd.MoveSize (1440 * 0.78), (1440 * 1.8)
    End If

Exit_ReviewProducts_Click:
    Exit Sub

Err_ReviewProducts_Click:
    MsgBox Err.Description
    Resume Exit_ReviewProducts_Click

End Sub
```

The first section of this sub procedure declares five variables: strMsg, strTitle, intStyle, strDocName, and strLinkCriteria. The next part of the sub procedure checks for a value in the CompanyName field on the Suppliers form. If there is not a value in this field, the sub procedure will display a message guiding the user to select a supplier. The sub procedure then sets the focus back to the CompanyName field so the user can enter the appropriate data.

If there is a value in the CompanyName field when the ReviewProducts button is clicked, the sub procedure opens the Product List form and uses the Do command to execute the MoveSize action to move the Product List form to the location specified in the MoveSize arguments.

This is another good example of making the database application more aesthetically pleasing to the user. The MoveSize action moves the Product List form directly below the Company Name on the Suppliers form.

If the user then moves the form to view additional information on the `Suppliers` form, the next time the `ReviewProducts` button is clicked the `Product List` form moves back to the most appropriate location.

These are just a few examples of how procedures within modules can be used. There is much more information about VBA and how to use it in Part IV.

Summary

This chapter was designed to give the programmer a glimpse of the Access 97 modules. In reality, modules are just the location where VBA code is stored for use within an Access 97 database application. While there are different types of modules and procedures, the actual module is nothing more than a container for VBA code.

The chapter did provide some examples taken from the `Northwind` sample database to illustrate what modules can accomplish. However, the use of modules in Access 97 is strictly up to the individual programmer. This chapter was only an attempt to illustrate how modules can be used.

III

PART

Access 97 Wizards and Add-Ins

Access 97 Database Wizards

by Teresa Bergman

IN THIS CHAPTER

CHAPTER 10

Wizards, builders, and menu add-ins are three types of add-ins supported by Access. This chapter explains the different kinds of wizards that are available and how to create your own wizard. Menu add-ins are discussed in Chapter 11, "Add-Ins."

Types of Wizards

The idea behind the creation of a wizard is to take a complex and sometimes repetitive process, and try to decrease the complexity by having the wizard do all the work behind the scenes. This is done to hide all the complex operations in creating a form, table, report, or query. Presenting the user with an interface of easy questions to answer helps the user decide what to do and how to present the results.

How to Use What Microsoft Has Already Created

Microsoft has included four types of wizards in Access 97: tables, queries, forms, and reports.

The Table Wizard

The Table Wizard can help create a table quickly, based on the type of information the user wants and the fields associated to the selected table. Figure 10.1 shows the first form you'll see when creating a new table.

FIGURE 10.1.

Creating a new table using the New Table dialog box.

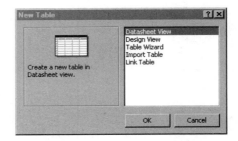

When Table Wizard is selected, the Table Wizard dialog box appears, as shown in Figure 10.2. This dialog box lists the types of tables that the wizard can build and the fields that are associated with each table.

FIGURE 10.2.
*The Table Wizard's
table and field choice
form.*

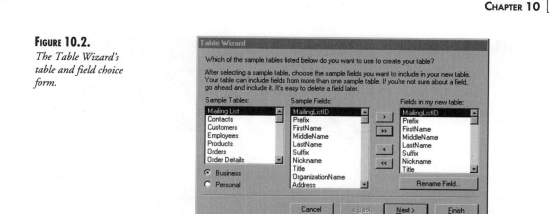

The Query Wizard

Query Wizards are used to create a query quickly. For the novice user, this is a great way to learn how to create a query. Figure 10.3 shows the first form that appears when you are creating a Simple query using the Simple Query Wizard.

FIGURE 10.3.
*The Simple Query
Wizard dialog box.*

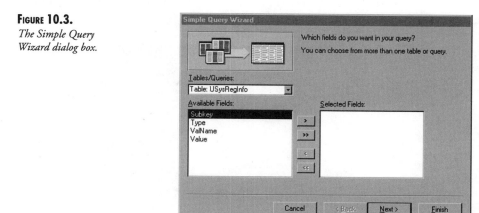

The Form Wizard

Need help creating a form? Use the Form Wizard to design your form. There are many combinations you can use to create a form using this wizard. This is ideal for a first-time developer, because it creates everything you need to start a form that can then be modified to suit your needs. Figure 10.4 shows the first form you'll see when using the Form Wizard option.

10

**ACCESS 97
DATABASE
WIZARDS**

FIGURE 10.4.
The Form Wizard dialog box.

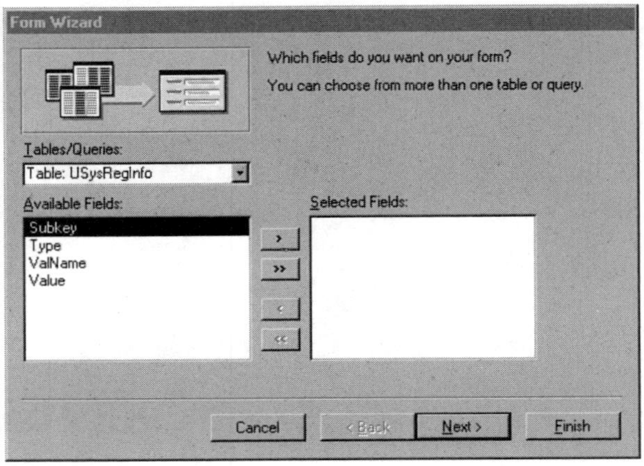

Report Wizards

For any developer, this is a quick way to create a report. Once the report is created, modifying it is easy. When the wizard asks questions on grouping, make sure that the choices and ordering are logical or the results of the report may not be as expected. Figure 10.5 is the first form to appear when the Report Wizard is chosen.

FIGURE 10.5.
The first form of the New Report Wizard.

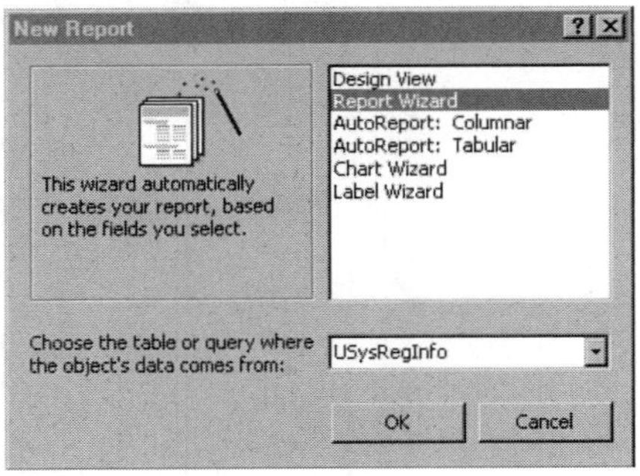

Figure 10.6 shows the report grouping form where the data is grouped with group headers and footers.

With the Report and Form Wizards, a record source must be selected before the report or form can be created. The same goes for the Query Wizard—a table or query must be made upon which the wizard can be based.

Figure 10.6.

The Report Wizard grouping and levels form.

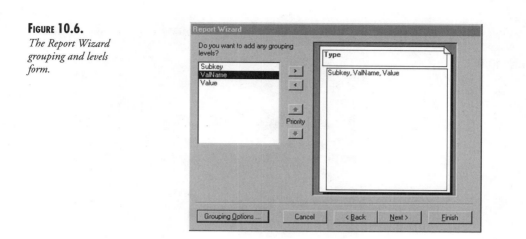

The Database Wizard

The Database Wizard incorporates the four wizards mentioned previously with creating modules and macros, as needed. This tool is an easy way to create a ready-to-use database or the building blocks of a more complex and customized database. By following all the instructions on each wizard's form, the complete database (with sub forms, sub reports, relationships, and code modules included) can be completed within 10 minutes. This is much faster than having to design the database from scratch. The one downfall is when it comes to customizing the database to meet your needs; in this case it can take longer.

Figure 10.7 shows the list of Database Wizards that Microsoft has already created. Each wizard creates a complete and fully functional database.

Figure 10.7.

The databases you can create with the Database Wizard.

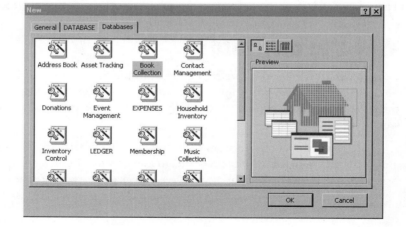

Figure 10.8 shows the first form that appears once the database has been created.

FIGURE **10.8.**

*The opening form of the
Database Wizard.*

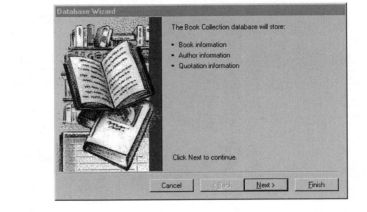

TIP

Microsoft has made the code available for the following wizards:

```
WZLIB80.EXE
WZMAIN80.EXE
WZTOOL80.EXE
UTILITY8.EXE
```

These downloads can be found at: http://www.microsoft.com/accessdev/accwhite/viewwiz.htm.

Why Use a Wizard?

Using a wizard is a personal preference. Most of the time a wizard is used if you're not sure how to create the table, query, form, report, or the entire database. Many developers rarely use the wizards, because they find them clunky, slow, and not as flexible as they (the developers) would like.

It's more of a personal preference as to whether to use a wizard. If it saves you time when creating an object—such as a company-standard menu form—by all means use it. The initial idea behind Access was to make creating a database quick and easy, hence the idea of using wizards.

How to Create Your Own Wizard

Microsoft can't provide everything to make the development of your application easier. To do so would take all the fun and challenge away from having a hands-on feel for the application.

> **NOTE**
>
> Keep in mind, a wizard is designed primarily to help create an object by asking a series of questions and then doing all the work behind the scenes.

What if there is no wizard to create an object—say a simple Data Definition query to drop a Make-table query? As a software development team, you may have a set of standards that specify how each type of form and report is to look. Is there a simple way to create them without having to import the object from another database and then delete the code and unnecessary controls? Can a wizard be used to create the objects? Certainly!

Guidelines

There are certain guidelines that should be followed when creating your wizard. Each wizard that Microsoft has included in Access looks similar in format, buttons, and questions. When creating your own wizard, keep this in mind. Make the layouts of your wizard's forms look similar to the wizards for that object that are included with Access. This gives a look of continuity to your wizard—almost as if Microsoft developed it. Microsoft has used the same formats for their wizards since the first version of Access came out. The only changes that have been made were made to reflect the new technology, so why change something that works?

Optimizing the wizard should be done as well. The user does not want a slow clunky wizard; this may deter him from using the wizard.

Use error trapping to trap errors that occur during the running of the wizard. If an error occurs and it wasn't trapped by code (no error handling on the code or a `Resume Next`), an ugly runtime error will occur. The error usually says that you don't have permission to view modules. The most common reason this occurs is that the user's code hasn't been compiled, and therefore produced an error. This runtime error is one you never want to have appear.

Part IX, "Performance, Optimization, and Troubleshooting," goes into more detail on improving the performance of your application, optimizing code, and error handling.

Another key point to consider when developing your wizard is whether you are going to sell the wizard. If you are planning to do so, think of international support—languages and program differences. These differences can cause some problems when using the wizard. The international development of a wizard is discussed in more detail at the end of this chapter.

The `SendKeys` statement can cause some potential problems and should therefore be avoided. If the user has set up an `AutoKeys` macro or changed the settings, your wizard can fail to respond as you had intended. The best solution is to not use the `SendKeys` statement or keep it to a minimum ("Y," "N," and so on) that the user won't usually modify. Always relying on a key combination to perform the same way in every application on every computer can be deadly!

The wizard should never modify the environment of the user's application. The following are the most common settings that are modified:

- Show Status Bar
- Built-In Toolbars (such as the Hide the database toolbar)

If the wizard needs to turn off these options, they should be restored when the wizard is closed or when an error exits the wizard. A good rule of thumb to follow is to *never* modify the database environment. If your wizard modifies the environment and an error occurs that terminates the wizard prematurely while the wizard is running, the user is going to wonder where their status bar and toolbars have gone.

Writing a Wizard: Two Real-World Examples

Once you have decided what you want your wizard to do, the next step is to jump right in and start designing. The code samples used here are found in `Chap10.mdb` on the CD-ROM. Two examples of wizards have been included: a simple Drop Table query and a `Menu` form. Along with these examples is an example of the `USysRegInfo` table, which is the key to your wizard.

Elements of a Wizard

A wizard is just like a regular database application, with the following additions:

- `USysRegInfo` table. A regular database application does not require this table for the application to run; however, a wizard requires this table to configure the wizard for use when it is installed.
- A code module is used to run the wizard application instead of an `AutoExec` macro or using the Startup command on the Tools menu option, which is used to start a regular database application.
- Database properties are set to display information about the database and its creators to the user. While this can be done for a regular database application, a wizard relies on this information when installing and displaying information on the wizard.

The `USysRegInfo` table determines what kind of add-in to install, how to start the wizard, and the environment of the wizard. This is a user-defined system object table and is therefore hidden to the user, unless the Show System Objects option is checked in the database's properties tab.

NOTE

Tables starting with Usys are user-defined tables, as opposed to tables prefixed with Msys, which are system-defined tables.

To display the hidden tables, do the following:

1. Select Options from the Tools menu.
2. A tabbed dialog box will now be displayed. Choose the View tab.
3. Under the Show option, select the System Objects checkbox.
4. Save the changes by clicking the OK button.

Now that the system tables have been displayed, the next step is to add the USysRegInfo table.

Instead of creating the table, import the table from the Wztool80.mda wizard. There are two versions of the table: Sample USysRegInfo and USysRegInfo. The first one has an example of how the table should be filled in, and the second one is a blank copy. How to fill in this table will be discussed later in the chapter.

Instead of running your application using an AutoExec macro or setting the startup options to open the form when the database is opened, a wizard only requires a module with a DoCmd.OpenForm "<form name>" statement. In the USysRegInfo table, one of the records is Function. This is the function that calls the first form and does any preliminary pre-processing that needs to be done.

NOTE

A macro is not used to start a wizard—use a code function procedure instead.

Changing the database properties is new with Access 95 and 97. In previous versions, the company name and such were included in the Usys table. Now this information is in the database properties. To set these properties from the database window, do the following:

1. Select Database Properties from the File menu.
2. A tabbed dialog box is displayed. Click on the Summary tab.
3. In the Title box, enter the formal name of your wizard, not the database filename.
4. In the Company box, enter the name of the company or individual(s) who developed the wizard.
5. In the Comments box, enter a description of the wizard—short and to the point, please.
6. Click the OK button to save the changes.

10

ACCESS 97
DATABASE
WIZARDS

Keep in mind that everyone sees this information when they install your wizard through the Add-in Manager dialog box.

Steps to Create a Wizard

Now that you're ready to create the wizard, you can begin the design process. This process is the same as designing a regular database application. Create the database, then create the tables, queries, forms, reports, macros, and modules needed. For a wizard, reports are not used because there is nothing to report on; you are just creating an object. The examples in the Chap10.mdb database only use forms and modules to gather and manipulate the data.

> **WARNING**
>
> Naming Conventions: When naming your wizard database, objects, controls, modules, fields, and so on, use names that would not usually be used for an application (such as prefixing everything with a "Z").

Forms

Figure 10.4 in the section "The Form Wizard" shows the opening form for creating a new form if you are using Access's built-in wizards. Using this as a model of how your forms should look, start creating your interface.

The form should be set as a modal dialog box, and the properties should be set as shown in Figure 10.9.

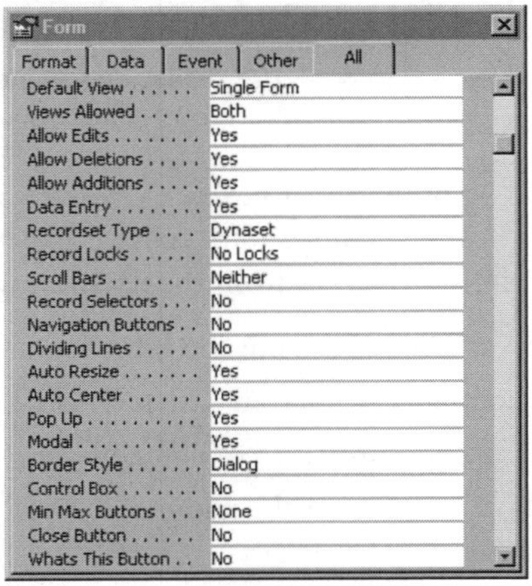

FIGURE 10.9.

Setting the form properties in the Form dialog box.

Form					
Format	Data	Event	Other	All	
Default View				Single Form	
Views Allowed				Both	
Allow Edits				Yes	
Allow Deletions				Yes	
Allow Additions				Yes	
Data Entry				Yes	
Recordset Type				Dynaset	
Record Locks				No Locks	
Scroll Bars				Neither	
Record Selectors . . .				No	
Navigation Buttons . .				No	
Dividing Lines				No	
Auto Resize				Yes	
Auto Center				Yes	
Pop Up				Yes	
Modal				Yes	
Border Style				Dialog	
Control Box				No	
Min Max Buttons				None	
Close Button				No	
Whats This Button . .				No	

Setting the form to modal and removing the Control Box and the Min, Max, and Close buttons means that the user can only either cancel the wizard or continue on with the wizard. This way, no unexpected features or bugs can pop up.

Code

Try keeping all your Visual Basic code local to the forms you are creating for your wizard. This will increase the performance of the wizard as well as make the form more "portable" and easy to incorporate into another wizard.

The form, wzfpopMainMenuStep1, in the Chap10.mdb database is the starting point to creating a menu form (for those developers who do not like to use the Switchboard option). The second form, wzfpopStep1, is used to create a Drop Table query.

The first wizard form (wzfpopMainMenuStep1) creates a form with controls using the Create functions, while the second form (wzfpopStep1) creates a querydef using the Create methods. Table 10.1 summarizes the functions you can use when creating a wizard that creates a form or report.

Table 10.1. Creating user-interface objects (reports, forms, and so on).

Function	Description
CreateForm	This creates the form itself.
CreateControl	This creates a control on the form.
CreateReport	This creates the report itself.
CreateReportControl	This creates a control on the report.
CreateGroupLevel	This creates a report group.

The syntax and constants for each function can be found by searching for the function itself in the Access help file.

Listing 10.1 is part of the code found in the wzCreateForm() module on the wzfpopMainMenuStep1 form. It first creates the new menu form and then adds two label boxes to the form.

Listing 10.1. Creating the new form and labels.

```
Sub wzCreateForm()
    Dim wzfrm As Form, I As Integer
    Dim wzctlLabel As Control, wzctlText As Control
    ' Create the form
    Set wzfrm = CreateForm
    wzfrm.Caption = Me!txtMnuFormTitle
    wzfrm.NavigationButtons = False
    wzfrm.RecordSelectors = False
    ' Create the label boxes
```

continues

10

ACCESS 97
DATABASE
WIZARDS

Listing 10.1. continued

```
Set wzctlText = CreateControl(wzfrm.Name, acLabel, , "", "", _
    wzTITLELEFT, wzTITLETOP, wzTITLEWIDTH, wzTITLEHEIGHT)
wzctlText.Caption = Me![txtMnuName]
wzctlText.FontSize = 24
wzctlText.FontName = "Times New Roman"
wzctlText.FontBold = True
wzctlText.SpecialEffect = 3
```

When using the `CreateControl` and `CreateReportControl` functions, the `Left`, `Top`, `Width`, and `Height` values are measured in twips. It takes some getting used to, but if you assign your `Left`, `Top`, `Width`, and `Height` values to constants, you'll find that there will be less confusion when modifying the code. Listing 10.2 shows the pre-set constants for the label control that was created in Listing 10.1.

Listing 10.2. Constants used for `Left`, `Top`, `Width`, and `Height`.

```
Const wzTITLEHEIGHT = 720 '* application title
Const wzTITLEWIDTH = 8640
Const wzTITLELEFT = 180
Const wzTITLETOP = 90
Const wzSPACER = 400
```

Table 10.2 shows how a twip is calculated.

Table 10.2. A basic twip conversion chart.

Inch	*Twip*
1 inch	1440 twips
$1/2$ inch	720 twips
$1/4$ inch	360 twips
$1/8$ inch	180 twips
$1/16$ inch	90 twips

The usual height for a label, text box, and command button is 240 twips, while most default to a width of 1440 twips. This makes it easy to create multiple controls, one under another. Part of the menu wizard is used to enter up to 10 buttons and labels from which the form will create buttons and labels on the new form, using the names entered on the wizard's form. These buttons and labels are to appear about two-thirds of an inch (400 twips) below the top of the previous button and label. By creating a spacer constant, the buttons and labels can be spaced vertically in even intervals on the form. Listing 10.3 demonstrates one way of placing the buttons on the form.

Listing 10.3. Using a For loop to create controls.

```
Const wzBUTHEIGHT = 240 '* button
Const wzBUTWIDTH = 240
Const wzBUTLEFT = 4320
Const wzBUTTOP = 900
Const wzLBLHEIGHT = 240 '* button's label
Const wzLBLTOP = 900
Const wzLBLWIDTH = 4600
Const wzLBLLEFT = 4600
Const wzSPACER = 400 ' space between controls
If Me!txtNoButtons > 1 Then
    wzstrCapCur = Left$(Me!lstCaption.RowSource, _
            InStr(Me!lstCaption.RowSource, ";") - 1)
Else
    wzstrCapCur = Me!lstCaption.RowSource
End If
wzstrCapRemain = Me!lstCaption.RowSource
For I = 0 To Me!txtNoButtons - 1
    If I = 0 Then '* the first time through
        Set wzctlButton = CreateControl(wzfrm.Name, _
            acCommandButton, , "", "", _
            wzBUTLEFT, wzBUTTOP, wzBUTWIDTH, wzBUTHEIGHT)
        Set wzctlText = CreateControl(wzfrm.Name, acLabel, , "", _
            "", wzLBLLEFT, wzLBLTOP, wzLBLWIDTH, wzLBLHEIGHT)
    Else '* second and subsequent times through
        Set wzctlButton = CreateControl(wzfrm.Name, _
            acCommandButton, , "", "", wzBUTLEFT, _
            wzBUTTOP + (wzSPACER * I), wzBUTWIDTH, wzBUTHEIGHT)
        Set wzctlText = CreateControl(wzfrm.Name, acLabel, , "", _
            "", wzLBLLEFT, wzLBLTOP + (wzSPACER * I), _
            wzLBLWIDTH, wzLBLHEIGHT)
    End If
    wzctlButton.Caption = " "
    wzctlText.Caption = wzstrCapCur
    wzctlText.FontName = "Times New Roman"
    wzctlText.FontBold = True
    If InStr(wzstrCapRemain, ";") > 0 Then
        wzstrCapRemain = Right$(wzstrCapRemain, _
            (Len(wzstrCapRemain) - (Len(wzstrCapCur) + 1)))
        If InStr(wzstrCapRemain, ";") > 0 Then
            wzstrCapCur = Left$(wzstrCapRemain, _
                InStr(wzstrCapRemain, ";") - 1)
        Else
            wzstrCapCur = wzstrCapRemain
        End If
    Else
        wzstrCapCur = wzstrCapRemain
    End If
Next I
```

10

WzLBLTOP and wzBUTTOP values are the amount of twips from the top of the form to the top of the first label or button. Taking the spacer constant (wzSPACER) times the value of I and adding that value to the value of wzLBLTOP or wzBUTTOP will give you the amount of space from the top of the form to the top of the next label or button. Once the control has been created, it is easy to assign an attribute such as a caption, color, or font to the form by accessing the Properties collection for the form or report.

> **WARNING**
>
> The report or form must be opened in Design View before a control or group level can be added.

When creating DAO objects such as databases, tables, queries, fields, indexes, users, and groups, the `Create` methods are used instead of the `Create` functions, which are used to create forms, reports, and controls. Table 10.3. contains the methods to create these objects.

Table 10.3. Methods used to create DAO objects.

Method	Description
CreateDatabase	Create a database object.
*CreateTableDef	Creates a new table definition.
CreateQueryDef	Creates a new query definition.
*CreateField	Creates a new field in a table.
*CreateIndex	Creates a new index on a table.
CreateRelation	Creates a relationship between fields and tables.
CreateWorkspace	Creates a new session for the Jet Engine.
*CreateUser	Creates a new user account.
*CreateGroup	Creates a new security group.

Methods marked with an * indicate that the `Append` method must be used to add the object to its proper collection (`tabledefs`, `indexes`, and so on).

The second wizard form, `wzfpopStep1`, uses the `CreateQueryDef` method to create the new query.

The first step when creating the Drop Table query is to get a listing of the available tables that can be used. This is done by accessing the `TableDefs` collection. Listing 10.4 shows you how to get a listing of tables.

Listing 10.4. Create a listing of available tables.

```
Private Sub Form_Open(Cancel As Integer)
On Error GoTo ErrwzTableDefNames
    '* list all the tables in the current database
    Dim wzdbCurrent As Database
    Dim wztdfTable As TableDef
    Dim wzstrTables As String
    Set wzdbCurrent = CurrentDb()
    With wzdbCurrent
        For Each wztdfTable In .TableDefs
            ' look in the tabledefs collection and find
```

```
              ' all the table names that don't start with
              ' Msy or Usy which are system tables.
              If Not (Left$(wztdfTable.Name, 3) = "Msy") And Not _
                  (Left$(wztdfTable.Name, 3) = "Usy") Then
                  '* if not a system table
                  If Len(wzstrTables) < 1 Then
                      ' is this the first table in the list?
                      wzstrTables = wztdfTable.Name
                  Else
                      ' not the first table in the list, string together
                      wzstrTables = wzstrTables & ";" & wztdfTable.Name
                  End If
              End If
          Next wztdfTable
          ' assign the table combo box's rowsource to the list of
          ' tables created above
          Me![wzcboTables].RowSource = wzstrTables
          Me![wzcboTables].Requery
          .Close
      End With
      Exit Sub
  ErrwzTableDefNames:
      '* error handling code - any error.
      MsgBox "The following error occurred:  " & _
              Err.Number & ":  " & Err.Description, _
              vbOKOnly, "Unexpected Error"
      Exit Sub
  End Sub
```

This code goes through the `TableDefs` collection and lists the names of every table in the current database, excluding the tables prefixed with `MSy` and `USy`, which are hidden tables. This list then becomes the base of the combo box that lists all the tables. If the wizard that you are creating is to include queries as well, access the `QueryDefs` collection in the same manner as in Listing 10.4, and add them to the list. This code is not only useful for creating a query, but for creating forms and reports as well.

Listing 10.5 shows how the query's SQL statement was developed. Because this is a relatively simple query with no joins involved, it takes one step to create the statement.

Listing 10.5. Creating the SQL statement.

```
Private Sub wzcboTables_AfterUpdate()
' create the SQL statement for the query
On Error Resume Next
    If IsNull(Me![wzcboTables]) Then
        ' if there is no table selected, cancel
        Me![wzcmdCancel].SetFocus
        Me![wzcmdFinish].enabled = False
    Else
        ' if there is a table, create the SQL statement
        Me![wztxtSQL] = "DROP TABLE " & Me![wzcboTables] & ";"
        Me![wzcmdFinish].SetFocus
    End If
End Sub
```

10

ACCESS 97 DATABASE WIZARDS

Now that the SQL statement has been created, the query definition can be created. Listing 10.6 shows how to use the `CreateQueryDef` method to create the new query. The syntax for this method, as well as the other methods mentioned in Table 10.3, can be found in the Access help files.

Listing 10.6. Using the `CreateQueryDef` method.

```
Private Sub wzcmdFinish_Click()
On Error Resume Next
    ' Create the querydef when the finish button
    ' is pressed.
    Dim wzdbCurrent As Database
    Dim wzqdfQuery As QueryDef
    Dim wzQName As String
    If IsNull(Me![wztxtSQL]) Then
        DoCmd.Close acForm, "wzfpopStep1"
    Else
        Set wzdbCurrent = CurrentDb()
        With wzdbCurrent
            wzQName = "qdef" & Me![wzcboTables]
            Set wzqdfQuery = .CreateQueryDef(wzQName, Me![wztxtSQL])
            .Close
        End With
        DoCmd.Close acForm, "wzfpopStep1"
    End If
End Sub
```

Creating the `USysRegInfo` Table

Once the forms have been created, the last design step is to create the entries in the `USysRegInfo` table. This table forms the cornerstone of the wizard, builder, or menu add-in. Without this table, the database is just a database; however, with the table it now becomes a useful development tool.

The `USysRegInfo` table contains the following fields found in Table 10.4.

Table 10.4. Fields contained in the `USysRegInfo` table.

Field name	Description
Subkey	Used to determine the type of add-in to install.
Type	Type of value created in the Windows Registry file.
ValName	The name of the value.
Value	The actual value.

The `Subkey` field always starts with either the `HKEY_CURRENT_ACCESS_PROFILE` or the `HKEY_LOCAL_MACHINE`.

The first option, `HKEY_CURRENT_ACCESS_PROFILE`, uses the user profile that is in use when the Add-in Manager was started and creates the Registry entries under that specific profile. The second statement is used if there is no profile in use.

> **NOTE**
>
> If the `HKEY_CURRENT_ACCESS_PROFILE` statement is used and there is no profile in use, the Registry entries will be created and stored under the `HKEY_LOCAL_MACHINE` profile instead of the profile in use.

The next part of the `Subkey` field is to add what category the add-in falls into. The following are the various types of wizards.

    Table Wizards
    Query Wizards
    Form Wizards
    Report Wizards

Table 10.5 lists the values for the remaining three fields (`Type`, `ValName`, and `Value`).

Table 10.5. Values For `Type`, `ValName`, and `Value` fields.

Type	*ValName*	*Value*
0		
1	Bitmap	Path to the bitmap for the wizard forms
4	Datasource Required	1 = Yes, 0 = No
1	Description	Description of the wizard
1	Function	The function that calls the first form of the wizard
4	Index	Order in the list that the wizard appears (first wizard in the list is 0)
4	Can Edit	1 = Yes, 0 = No. Can the query be edited?
1	Library	The location of the wizard

When the `Library` record is created, the value is

```
¦ACCDIR\<wizard name>.mda
```

This statement tells the Add-in Manager to look in the Access root directory to find the location of the wizard. It is important for the wizard to be installed in Access' root directory.

Table 10.6 shows the values of the completed USysRegInfo table for a Query Wizard. All Subkey fields start with

```
HKEY_CURRENT_ACCESS_PROFILE\Wizards\Query Wizards\Drop Table Query
```

where Drop Table Query is the name that will appear in the Query Wizard list box.

The first line of the USysRegInfo table *must* contain the HKEY statement with a type = 0. This signifies that this is the start of a new wizard. More than one wizard can be set up in the table, with each new wizard starting with the HKEY subkey and type = 0.

Table 10.6. Complete USysRegInfo Table.

Subkey	Type	ValName	Value
HKEY...	0		
HKEY...	1	Bitmap	c:\MSOffice\ddlwiz.bmp
HKEY...	4	Datasource Required	0
HKEY...	1	Description	Drop Table Query
HKEY...	1	Function	wzStart
HKEY...	4	Index	5
HKEY...	4	Can Edit	0
HKEY...	1	Library	¦ACCDIR\qrywiz.mda

For more information on creating the USysRegInfo table, consult the Knowledge Base in Microsoft's Web site, and look for article Q153858.

Testing, Debugging, and Error Handling

Now that the forms have been created, the code has been added, and the USysRegInfo table is filled in, the next step is to debug the wizard. The first stage of testing is to test to see whether the wizard works as a standalone database. This is the quickest way to get all the quirks and bugs found and removed before the form goes into production. At the same time, any extra error handling can be added to the code. (See Chapter 26, "Errors," for more information on error handling.) Once the wizard passes this initial testing, it is ready to be installed and tested as a wizard add-in.

Installing the Wizard

Installing the wizard is the same as installing a regular add-in through the Add-in Manager.

If you are not familiar with installing an add-in, the following steps may be beneficial:

1. Choose Add-ins from the Tools menu.
2. Next, choose Add-in Manager from the list of installed menu add-ins.
3. If your wizard add-in doesn't appear in the list, click the Add New button to add the wizard you want.
4. The wizard can now be installed by clicking on the wizard's name and then clicking the Install button. Once the wizard is installed, an x will appear beside the wizard's name.
5. To save the changes, click the Close button.

Now that the wizard is installed, you can continue testing the wizard by actually using it as a wizard. Open a database, and based on what kind of wizard you created, create a new object using the wizard.

When all testing has been completed, the final step, distributing the wizard, can be done.

Distributing the Wizard

The final phase in developing a wizard is to distribute the wizard. Whether it is for local use (may have to copy to other machines or install on the network) or for sale, there are some steps that must be done.

Remove any unnecessary code from the wizard. Chapter 25, "Optimizing Code," goes more into this topic; it is part of increasing the performance of the application.

Remove any obsolete objects that were used for testing purposes or are no longer used.

Compile and save all the modules. This will speed up the processing of the wizard.

Implementing security on your wizard is an option you may want to consider before distributing the wizard. If you don't want the user to change any part of the wizard or copy your code, make the wizard into an MDE file. Chapter 25 explains the context of an MDE file and how to create one. The other option is to remove the permissions to administer the wizard by the Admin account (see Chapter 22, "Security").

> **NOTE**
>
> Keep a master copy of your wizard in case you have to make changes. This copy should not be made into an MDE file or have security implemented.

If the wizard is going to be used by individuals or companies where there may be a difference in language, consider adding a reference table that contains all the forms label box information in each language. With a bit of redesigning, incorporate the code shown in Listing 10.7 to determine the language and which value goes into the label's caption.

Listing 10.7. Determining the language.

```
Function DetLang() as string
    On Error Resume Next
    Err.Raise 7
    Select Case Err.Description
        Case "<error description's value in English>"
            DetLang = "English"
        Case "<error description's value in French>"
            DetLang = "French"
        <Repeat case statements for other languages>
    End Select
```

The table can be set up as shown in Table 10.7.

Table 10.7. International table.

Field	Type	Description
Lang	Text	Language
FrmName	Text	Name of the form
LblName	Text	Name of the label
TranslationMemo		Translation from English to the language found in the Lang field

The caption of the label or button can be changed to find the correct translation by using a Dlookup statement.

This is a quick-and-dirty way of handling international support for your wizard, and it requires little modification to the wizard. You only need to add a few lines on the On Open event of the form to modify the label and button captions to reflect the language set up on the machine.

Summary

Wizards provide a quick way to create an object, whether it is a new database or a new form. By answering simple questions, the object can be created without the user having any prior programming knowledge.

A wizard can also reduce the repetitive task of importing an object and then redesigning it to suit the current need.

Add-Ins

by Joe Rhemann

CHAPTER 11

IN THIS CHAPTER

As mentioned in Chapter 3, "Access 97 Development Issues," *add-ins* are components that are used to enhance the Access 97 environment. They are usually third-party or custom-built enhancements that you can create yourself or obtain from an ISV. Often, add-ins are used to automate difficult or repetitive tasks and to add custom features to the Access user interface.

Add-ins are a special kind of database file with an .MDA extension. Add-in MDA databases contain VB code procedures and the objects that the procedures work with. These special databases can be integrated into the Access 97 GUI to enhance or remove certain capabilities and are managed through the Access Add-in Manager.

> **NOTE**
>
> All add-ins are installed and removed through the Access 97 Add-in Manager. You must build certain information into your add-in database in order for the Add-in Manager to recognize it and install it properly. Without the required database property settings and a USysRegInfo table, the Add-in Manager will not be able to install the add-in.

Add-ins can be installed in an application, distributed with applications as options, or sold to others for their use or distribution. They are saved with the .MDA file extension just like a library database file, but add-ins can also be saved as MDE files with all of the source code stripped out.

As you work with Access 97, you may find tasks that can be simplified through the use of automated tools in the form of add-ins. You should, however, be familiar with creating the different aspects of an Access 97 application manually before you begin building add-ins. You will draw upon a working knowledge of building VB code into Access 97 components to create effective add-ins that add value to your application.

Add-Ins Come in Three Flavors

Add-ins come in three basic types: builders, menu add-ins, and wizards. How your end user will use the add-in will be the primary factor in deciding which of the three categories your add-in falls into. How the add-in will be presented in the application's GUI will determine how it needs to be designed, distributed, and installed.

The following rules generally apply when you are deciding which type of add-in to create. How the add-in is registered during installation tells Access 97 which type of add-in you are integrating:

■ If you want your add-in to be available to the end user when he is setting properties within Design View, the add-in will be a builder. These add-ins will be available through Design View in the same fashion as other Access 97 builders.

■ If you want your add-in to be available to the end user when he is creating new controls, forms, queries, reports, or tables, the add-in will be a wizard. Wizard add-ins will be available in the same fashion as other Access 97 wizards.

■ If you want your add-in to be available to the end user when he is performing tasks other than setting properties in Design View or while creating controls, forms, queries, reports, or tables, the add-in is not context specific and will be a menu add-in. Menu add-ins will be available through the Add-Ins submenu under the Tools menu.

Builders and wizards are generally designed to create new controls; however, you can also use builders or wizards to change existing controls by modifying the properties of the control object.

Builder Add-Ins

Builders are relatively simple tools that are used to assist the end user in setting properties. Generally, they are presented as single dialog forms within Design View. An example of a builder is the Access 97 Field Builder, which is available through Design View when creating new fields within a table. In Figure 11.1, the Field Builder is available by selecting a table and then clicking the Design button. This brings up the table in Design View, and then you access the command bar by right-clicking in the empty cell where you want to insert your new field. The Field Builder is started by clicking on the Build… icon on the pop-up command bar.

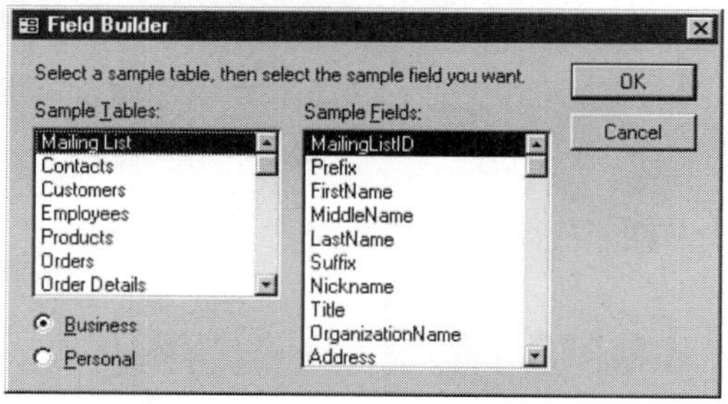

FIGURE 11.1.
*The Access 97 Field
Builder add-in.*

This add-in allows sample fields from a graphical interface to be selected for insertion into the table in which the user is working. This add-in allows the user to use one convenient point of reference when creating new fields, and then automates the process of entering the selected field into the table.

The following is a list of Access 97 builder add-ins and their functions:

■ Color Builder—Automates custom color selection.

■ Expression Builder—Automates the creation of expressions in macros, queries, and properties.

■ Field Builder—Automates the creation of new fields in tables.

■ ODBC Connection String Builder—Automates the creation of syntax strings for connections to an ODBC data source.

■ Picture Builder—A bitmap image builder for forms and reports.

■ Query Builder—Automates the creation of query syntax strings.

Access 97 supports many different types of builders, which you can create for any property. Because numerous builders can be defined for each property, your new builders can be added to the existing database environment without removing those that already exist. Your builders would be available through the standard interface from a list of available builders for the selected property.

Menu Add-Ins

Menu add-ins are non-specific tools that are created to manage changes to numerous application objects or to the application environment. If a task that you want to automate does not fit into the builder or wizard category, it will fall into this category.

For example, the Switchboard Manager add-in, shown in Figure 11.2, is used to manage switchboard forms within an application. It performs many functions that are similar to both wizards and builders, but doesn't completely fall within one category or the other. The command to start the Switchboard Manager is also accessed through the Add-Ins submenu.

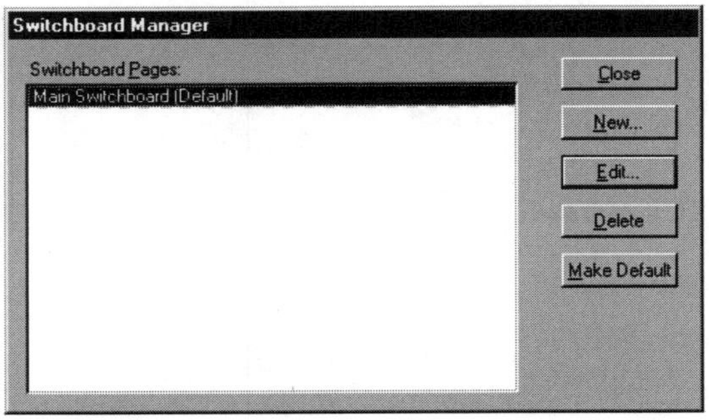

FIGURE 11.2.

The Switchboard Manager menu add-in.

Menu add-ins are available to the end user through the Add-Ins submenu under the Tools menu. Whenever the Tools menu is available to the end user in an Access 97 application, the menu add-ins are also available.

The following table shows the menu add-ins that are included with Access 97:

Menu Add-In	Description
Add-in Manager	The primary interface for managing builders, menu add-ins, and wizards.

Menu Add-In	Description
Linked Table Manager	Manages the connection between foreign tables (tables from different databases).
Switchboard Manager	Manages the creation and configuration of switchboard forms.

After you install your menu add-in, it is available in the Add-Ins submenu, but you can also add a button or control to any toolbar by using that toolbar's customizing features. You may notice that in some Access 97 applications, a command button has been added to the switchboard forms so that the user can run the Switchboard Manager straight from the switchboard.

Wizard Add-Ins

Wizards are tools that perform complex operations based on information obtained through a graphical interface. The wizard guides the end user through the processes of the complex operation.

An example of an add-in wizard is the Find Duplicates Query Wizard (see Figure 11.3), which is used to ferret out duplicated record fields within a table or query.

FIGURE 11.3.
The Find Duplicates Query Wizard.

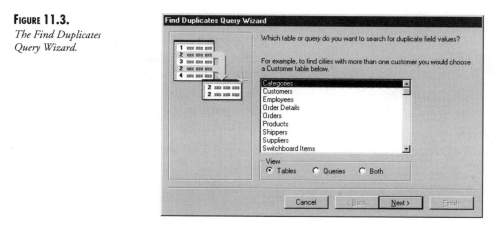

Add-in wizards are available through the same user interface as the included Access 97 wizards and will be available at the appropriate times according to the wizard's purpose.

Table 11.1 shows the wizards included in Access 97.

Table 11.1. Access 97 wizards.

Wizard	Description
Chart Wizard	Creates charts in forms or reports based on a table or query data source.
Combo Box Wizard	Creates combo box controls on forms.
Command Button Wizard	Creates command button controls on forms.
Conflict Resolver	Resolves conflicts when synchronizing replicated databases.
Crosstab Query Wizard	Creates a crosstab query.
Database Splitter Wizard	Splits a database's data back end from the user interface, which allows you to maintain central control of the data over a distributed network of users. They will have the user interface on their local machines linked back to the central data repository.
Database Wizard	Creates a new database from the ground up based on application templates supplied with Access 97.
Export Text Wizard	Exports source data to text files.
Find Duplicates Query Wizard	Creates queries that locate records with duplicate field values in tables or queries.
Find Unmatched Query Wizard	Creates queries that locate unrelated records between tables.
Form Wizard	Creates new forms.
Import HTML Wizard	Imports HTML data sources into Access tables.
Import Spreadsheet Wizard	Imports spreadsheet data sources into Access tables.
Import Text Wizard	Imports text files into Access tables.
Input Mask Wizard	Creates input masks for fields.
Label Wizard	Generates mailing label reports that can be directed to label printers to produce the desired label output.
Link HTML Wizard	Links HTML data sources to Access tables.
Link Spreadsheet Wizard	Links spreadsheet data sources to Access tables.
Link Text Wizard	Links text files to Access tables.

Wizard	*Description*
List Box Wizard	Creates list box controls on forms.
Lookup Wizard	Creates lookup columns in tables, which display lists of values.
Microsoft Word Mail Merge Wizard	Creates mail merge operations with Word 97 documents and Access 97 databases.
Option Group Wizard	Creates option buttons on forms.
Performance Analyzer	Analyzes databases and recommends performance improvements.
PivotTable Wizard	Creates Excel PivotTables on Access forms.
Publish to the Web Wizard	Generates dynamic or static HTML output from your Access applications.
Report Wizard	Generates Access 97 reports.
Simple Query Wizard	Creates standard Access 97 queries.
Subform/Subreport Field Linker	Links fields between primary forms or reports and their subordinates.
Subform/Subreport Wizard	Creates subordinate forms or reports on primary forms or reports.
Table Analyzer Wizard	Splits large monolithic tables into smaller related tables for increased efficiency.
Table Wizard	Creates new tables.
User-Level Security Wizard	Converts standard Access 97 databases to encrypted databases and implements user-level access control.
Web Publishing Wizard	Works in conjunction with the Publish to the Web Wizard. This wizard takes the HTML output generated by the Publish to the Web Wizard and uploads it to the desired server address on the Web.

11

ADD-INS

TIP

If you have developed wizards using Access Basic or VB for an earlier version of Access, your wizard code will have to be updated with referential changes that point to current Access 97 library database files. Check the names of the library databases that are referred to in your code and make sure that they reflect the names of the appropriate ones in Access 97.

Wizards are one of the most dynamic tools within the Access 97 environment. Using a well-designed wizard to create an Access application is a process that only takes a few seconds and requires little technical experience. Some Microsoft critics argue that the use of wizards has simply "dumbed down" the database application development process. In reality, using automated tools to generate the core components of an application gives the developer more time and energy to dedicate to the design of the application interface and other vital components. Instead of spending a large portion of your development window creating the basic application infrastructure, you can now spend the bulk of your time designing custom features (such as add-ins) that can be built into the core application. Wizards also provide an ideal vehicle for implementing your company's individual style and form by creating and using wizards as customized templates.

Creating Add-Ins

Creating an add-in is very similar to creating any other Access 97 application. You create the add-in as its own database, create and customize the objects, build the code, test and debug it, and give it a unique name that does not duplicate any other existing add-ins in the folder where it is going to be stored on the end user's machine.

Keep the various computing environments that will be used by your end user in mind, and build an add-in that will be compatible with the widest range of your customer's capabilities. Generally speaking, your basic environment will probably be standard VGA resolution. Build your application to work at 640×480 16-color resolution for the widest range of compatibility. Keep in mind that some of your customers may even be using monochrome displays.

Any new tables that are going to be in the add-in should be created within the add-in. If the linked files are moved around, linking tables can cause problems with your end user's application because the links would then be invalid.

Because of the way that Access 97 uses forms as its event-driven interface, it is best to try to build as much of your code into the form modules as possible.

> **TIP**
>
> Make sure that all the command buttons that were created using the Command Button Wizard in earlier versions of Access are replaced with buttons generated in the current version. Remove the older buttons from your converted databases and create new buttons in Access 97 because the earlier command button code is not compatible.

Try to break down large add-in processes into logical units that can be implemented as separate forms. Then build in the VB code modules that apply to each form. The code for each form can then be executed in an event-driven fashion when the forms open. Use the OnOpen or

OnLoad event to launch the code. Doing this will make your code much more manageable from a development standpoint.

Creating Add-In Database Objects

Visual Basic allows you to create and customize add-in GUI objects using functions, methods, and statements. In most cases, these VB tools are only available when you are in an object's design view, so add-ins created with them generally fit into the wizard category.

When an add-in VB module uses control-creating functions that return objects, you can set the control properties by defining the object's variables in the code as well. For instance, if you wanted to create a new label control on a form that was open in Design View and then specify the label control's layout properties, you could use a string similar to the following:

```
Set ctlNewLabel = CreateControl("cnf_frmCurrentForm", acLabel, acDetail,
➥ctl.Name, "", (3280 - twLabelWidth), twTop, twLabelWidth, twTextBoxHeight)
```

The VB functions shown in Table 11.2 can be used to create or delete GUI objects.

Table 11.2. VB functions that create or delete GUI objects.

VB function	Description
CreateForm	Does just what it says. Creates forms and returns form objects.
CreateControl	Creates controls on forms that are open in Design View and then returns control objects.
CreateReport	Creates reports and then returns report objects.
CreateReportControl	Creates controls on reports in Design View and then returns control objects.
CreateGroupLevel	Creates new group levels for reports in Design View and then returns new group index values.
DeleteControl	Deletes controls on forms in Design View.
DeleteReportControl	Deletes controls on reports in Design View.

Table 11.3 shows DAO methods that can be used to create databases, queries, security accounts, and tables.

Table 11.3. DOA methods used to create databases, queries, security accounts, and tables.

DAO method	Description
CreateDatabase	Creates database objects.
CreateTableDef	Creates `TableDef` objects that represent included or linked tables.
CreateField	Creates field objects.
CreateIndex	Creates index objects.
CreateQueryDef	Creates `QueryDef` objects, which represent queries.
CreateRelation	Creates relationship objects, which represent field relationships between tables or queries.
CreateWorkspace	Creates new session definition objects for Microsoft Jet. These are for Jet sessions in addition to any default open sessions.
CreateUser	Creates user objects, which add new user accounts to the users collection in secured databases.
CreateGroup	Creates group objects, which add new security groups to the groups collection of secured databases.
DeleteObject	A `DoCmd` object method used to delete database objects.

Designing the Add-In Interface

The same care and attention should be given to building your add-ins as when designing a standard Access 97 application. Plan your add-ins carefully and build upon a standard user interface in order to present to the end user a familiar look and feel. Try to stick with your application's standard interface style. If your applications do not have customized interfaces, you might want to use the standard Access 97 add-in styles in order to keep things consistent from the user's perspective. To conform to the Microsoft Access 97 add-in styles, make the following property settings in your add-in interface:

- Use a dialog box style for all of your forms in order to control the end user's progression through the called processes.
- Autocenter all of your add-in forms.
- Keep your control placement consistent for each form.
- Turn off built-in navigation buttons, record selectors, and scrollbars.

Calling Add-In Objects

Add-in databases are able to contain any object that can be contained in a standard Access database. Because of this, Access 97 has rules that apply when referring to add-in objects that must coexist with the standard database application objects.

Data sources for forms and reports are restricted to sources contained in the add-in database. Access 97 calls to an add-in form or report will result in an error if an internal data source is not found in the add-in for the object being called.

Access 97 looks for add-in macros in the internal add-in code first. Only after searching for the macro in the add-in code will Access move its search to the currently loaded database application. The same caution practiced when using macros in a runtime database should also apply to using a macro in an add-in. Macros do not have the facility for building in error handling, and they are difficult to debug, which means that the process of testing and debugging your add-ins will be greatly complicated.

Data references used in an add-in database, which are part of domain aggregate functions like `DLookup`, `DMax`, and `DMin`, are restricted to data sources located in the database that is currently open.

You can create custom toolbars within add-in databases. When the end user selects `ShowToolbar`, Access 97 looks in the add-in for the specified toolbar before it looks in the current database.

Add-ins are always opened in shared access mode and can be used by multiple users. In order to write information back to the add-in database, you have to open the add-in in read/write permission mode. The best rule of thumb is to configure the add-ins that don't need read/write access to be loaded in read-only mode in order to control access without having to establish locking protocols.

Verifying User Settings for Add-In Compatibility

Your add-in should have the ability to verify certain environmental parameters that are configured on the end user's machine. Because of the flexible user interface of Access 97, you will need to make sure that your add-in will be compatible with the end user's environment by having it check this when it loads.

One of the largest potential problems is with `SendKey` operations. Users can customize their user interface with the `AutoKeys` macro and remap certain keystrokes to different actions, or use the Options dialog box to change the function of their cursor arrow keys. The `SendKey` operation may cause a catastrophic error on the end user's machine.

Using the `RunCommand` operations instead of the `SendKeys` operations is the easiest and most effective way of avoiding this conflict. In cases where you have to use `SendKeys` actions or statements, you should have your add-in check the end user's database for the existence of an `AutoKeys`

macro and the cursor arrow key settings. If either one of these potential problems exists—
AutoKeys macros or customized cursor arrow key settings—you should have your add-in display an error message before your add-in loads, warning the end user of the potential conflict.
To check for an AutoKeys macro, have your add-in use the GetOption method of the application object to find the name of the end user's AutoKeys macro, and then search for that macro
name in the script's container object. If one is found, send the warning message.

Changing the End User's Access Environment

Try to avoid having your add-in change the environment of your end user's Access application. This can lead to a very disgruntled customer if you are not careful. As a rule of thumb, try
not to change his GUI settings unless you absolutely have to. If you have to, you can do this
using the SetOption of the application object to modify his Access 97 option settings.

> **NOTE**
>
> Make sure your add-in restores the end user's option settings if your add-in encounters an
> error, or before exiting, whether intentionally or unexpectedly.

Building Error Handling into Your Add-In

If you don't build error handling into your add-in, troubleshooting your application on end-
user systems will be more difficult. If your add-in will be used in the Access runtime environment, error handling is almost a requirement.

Generally, error-handling code will be built into your procedures and will take over when a
runtime error occurs. In this code, you build the alternate procedures that you want your application to go through as a way of recovering from the error. When this primary error-
handling code can't recover from an error, your add-in should call your public error-handling
code. Public error-handling code contains fall-back code procedures in a module that are public and viewable by the end user.

Your public error-handling procedures should close all application objects that have been opened
by your add-in, remove any created objects or files, restore any settings that have been changed,
and then display information on the error to the end user. The public information that is displayed to the end user should include an Access error number, the Err object description property value, and details about the error. You might want to consider incorporating custom error
messages into your public error-handling procedures.

Microsoft's Access error messages may seem cryptic to the end user, and your custom message
may be able to describe the problem more clearly or completely to the end user. A custom error
message may provide an explanation sufficient to solve the error at the end-user level. In

addition to a custom message, having your error-handling procedure build a text log file of unrecoverable errors is also a valuable troubleshooting strategy. You can have your procedures record all the system variables that were at play when the error occurred.

One of the error-handling obstacles that slows down the troubleshooting process is that Access doesn't retrieve the current procedure name when an error occurs. This is useful information for the troubleshooter, and you can build this feature into your public error procedures. Essentially, you will build a VB procedure stack into your application code as a public array. Each procedure will call a procedure that stores the name of the current procedure in the stack, which your public error-handling code can then retrieve when it is called.

Your VB public array procedure stack can look something like the following:

■ First, in the add-in's declaration section you will need to add strings similar to the following example in order to create a public array:

```
Public Const conStackSize = 40
Public strProcNames (1 to conStackSize) As String
```

■ Then you will have to build the stack procedures that manipulate the procedure names in the desired fashion. This example calls PushDebugStack with the current procedure name as the argument, and then calls PopDebugStack at the procedure's exit point to pop the name off of the stack:

```
Sub PushDebugStack(strSubOrFunction)
Dim iXInteger As Integer
For iXInteger = conStackSize To 2 Step -1
strProcNames(iXInteger) = strProcNames(iXInteger - 1)
Next
strProcNames(1) = strSubOrFunction
End Sub
Sub PopDebugStack()
Dim iXInteger As Integer
For iXInteger = 1 To (conStackSize - 1)
strProcNames(iXInteger) = strProcNames(iXInteger + 1)
Next iXInteger
End Sub
```

■ Once you have set up the public array and the procedure stack, you can use the following function to reference the current procedure:

```
Function SearchForm ()
PushDebugStack ("SearchForm")
.
. ' Main body of program.
.
PopDebugStack
End Function
```

■ Then your public error-handling code can reference the name of the current procedure and display it for the end user. Because of the public array conStackSize value, the following routine displays a list of up to 40 current procedures in a message box:

```
Dim iXStringMessage As String
Dim iXInteger As Integer
MsgBox "An error occurred in the following procedure: " & _
```

```
strProcNames(1)
iXStringMessage = "The following procedures were called: "
For iXInteger = 2 To conStackSize
iXStringMessage = iXStringMessage & strProcNames(iXInteger) & " "
Next iXInteger
MsgBox iXStringMessage
```

WARNING

Because Access 97 has some new error codes, error-handling routines that trap specific errors must be tested when you convert an add-in database from an earlier version of Access in order to ensure that the error codes have not changed.

Some code routines did not generate runtime errors in Access 95, but they may in Access 97. Look in the Access 97 help index for readme Microsoft Access, or in the file Acread80.wri, for further information on this subject.

Designing Your Add-In for Regional Support

When you are designing your solutions for multi-language support, you have to apply the same care to developing your add-ins with the same regional considerations. Because the Access menus and interface structure is the same regardless of which language version is being used, the interface of your add-in database will generally not be a problem as long as you take the text differences into account.

The menu text used in the interface will be whatever is standard for the region, so you will have to take that into consideration when designing add-ins that include SendKey menu operations or SendKey operations within dialog boxes.

The first step in dealing with a multi-language application environment is to have your add-in determine which language is being used as the standard, and then enable the appropriate text version. Figure 11.4 illustrates code within an add-in database module that uses the GetLanguage function to return the default language version.

After using a function to determine the appropriate language, you can use the appropriate SendKey operations based on the result. If you were going to use code to return the language version, you could call that result from all your future SendKey operations within that database. For example, if you wanted to initiate an event based on a profession dialog box in the appropriate language, you could use the following code:

```
Select Case GetLanguage()
Case "English"
SendKeys "Attorney", True
Case "Spanish"
SendKeys "Abogado", True
End Select
```

FIGURE 11.4.

An add-in database module that returns default language.

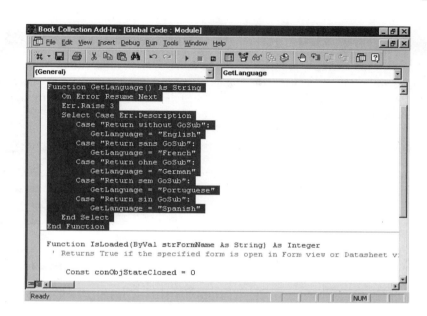

```
Book Collection Add-In - [Global Code : Module]
 File  Edit  View  Insert  Debug  Run  Tools  Window  Help

(General)                                    GetLanguage

Function GetLanguage() As String
    On Error Resume Next
    Err.Raise 3
    Select Case Err.Description
        Case "Return without GoSub":
            GetLanguage = "English"
        Case "Return sans GoSub":
            GetLanguage = "French"
        Case "Return ohne GoSub":
            GetLanguage = "German"
        Case "Return sem GoSub":
            GetLanguage = "Portuguese"
        Case "Return sin GoSub":
            GetLanguage = "Spanish"
    End Select
End Function

Function IsLoaded(ByVal strFormName As String) As Integer
    ' Returns True if the specified form is open in Form view or Datasheet v

        Const conObjStateClosed = 0

Ready                                                         NUM
```

International Support in Your Add-In

You can simplify multi-language support by translating all your text strings into the different languages that you want to support. By including the text used in the different Access messages and prompts in each respective language in a single module or table within the add-in database, you provide a central organized repository. Each message can be defined as a public constant within the module or a record within a table. When it is time to translate your application's text strings into a new language, you only have to look in one location.

If you have a lot of text strings and are concerned with your ability to organize them in a module, you can store them in a table and use the table's inherent grouping and sorting capabilities. This can be a lower-performance method of storing your text strings because of the resource overhead needed each time a table is accessed. However, if the localized strings are not going to be accessed very often, this is a more efficient method of storing them because they will not be loaded into memory unless they are needed. The primary advantage is that tables provide for better management of your localized text strings and faster application performance if they are not needed by the end user.

If you choose to store your localized strings in a module as public constants, they will automatically be loaded into memory. The problem with this is that if you have extensive localized strings, you will eat up your memory overhead and slow down overall performance. The more public constants that are stored in memory, the less memory that is available to Access 97. On the other hand, if you do use a module, your localized strings will be loaded into memory and therefore will be available very rapidly. If your end user will be using the localized strings constantly, this may be the best approach.

Setting Your Add-In Database Properties

Before you are ready to install your add-in for the first time, you must set the database properties and create the USysRegInfo table. To set the database properties, open the database window, select Database Properties under the File menu and then enter the appropriate values on the Summary tab, as illustrated in Figure 11.5.

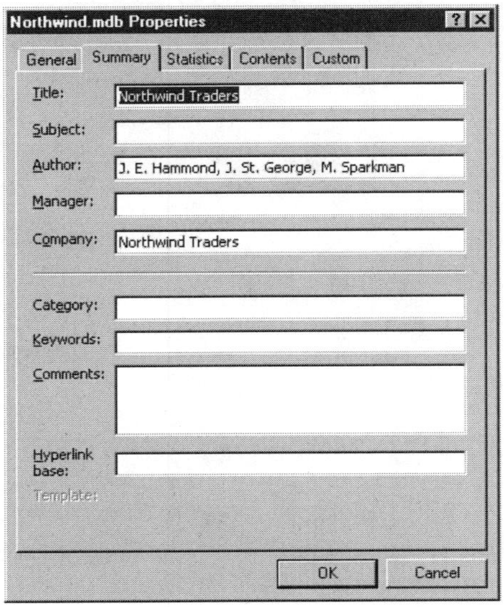

FIGURE 11.5.

Setting the database properties for your add-in database.

Once you have made these changes, it is time to create the USysRegInfo table.

Creating the USysRegInfo Table

The Access 97 Add-in Manager must find a USysRegInfo table, or else it will not install the add-in. This table is used by the Add-in Manager to determine the type of add-in that it is installing and to display add-in information to the end user. The simplest way to create a USysRegInfo table is to use an imported copy of a system table that is part of one of the included Microsoft Access 97 wizards. The normal procedure is to import the sample USysRegInfo table object from Wiztool80.mde, which is usually found in the C:/program files/microsoft office/office/ directory, as shown in Figure 11.6.

Once the sample USysRegInfo table has been imported, you can enter records that define four primary fields, which in turn registers your add-in.

Microsoft Access uses two primary types of system tables: intrinsic Access 97 system tables, which begin with the MSys prefix and user defined system tables, which begin with the USys prefix. These tables are displayed in the database window only if you have selected Options | View System | Objects in Access.

FIGURE 11.6.

Importing the sample
USysRegInfo *table into*
your add-in database.

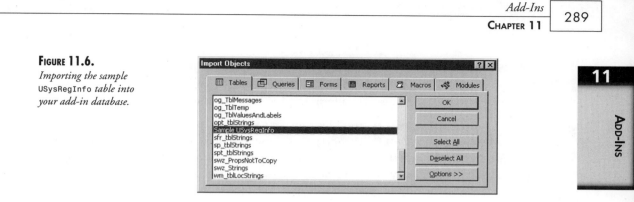

When users install your add-in, the Add-in Manager uses a table in the add-in's database named USysRegInfo to determine what type of add-in to install and to get general information about the add-in to display for your users. You create the USysRegInfo table in the database that contains the add-in, and then you add records that give the Add-in Manager the information it needs to install your add-in.

The four fields that need to be defined are shown in Figure 11.7.

FIGURE 11.7.

The new USysRegInfo
table containing the
four Registry definition
fields.

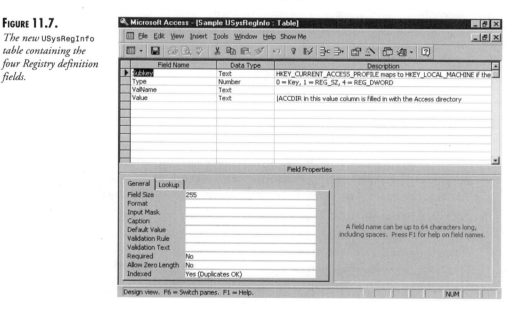

After you have imported this table, you need to define these field values. The value of Type field will always be 0, which tells the system to add this key, and the ValName and Value fields should always be left blank regardless of the type of add-in you are installing. The Subkey fields are the only fields that must be defined specifically in each record.

The Subkey Field

The SubKey value tells the Add-in Manager which Registry root key and subkeys to create to register your add-in, and must be uniform in all of the records in the table.

The Add-in Manager first creates the root key as either HKEY_LOCAL_MACHINE, or the HKEY_CURRENT_ACCESS_PROFILE, depending on the user system profile, and then creates the appropriate subkeys beneath the root key. If you want to ensure that your add-in is registered for all the users on a machine, you should have the root key created as HKEY_LOCAL_MACHINE. If you don't specify this, the Add-in Manager will create the root key based on whether Windows 95 has been started in a user profile. If it has been started in a user profile, the Add-in Manager will by default only create a root key in that profile Registry as HKEY_CURRENT_ACCESS_PROFILE.

Once the root key has been created, the Add-in Manager creates the subkeys based on the type of add-in that you are installing.

ActiveX Control Wizard, Builder, and Control Wizard Subkey Values

If your add-in is used to create controls or properties, you can specify the add-in type for ActiveX control wizards, builders, and control wizards by defining the subkeys as follows:

```
HKEY_LOCAL_MACHINE \SOFTWARE\Microsoft\Office\8.0\Access
➥\Wizards (Machine Global)
```

or

```
HKEY_CURRENT_ACCESS_PROFILE\Wizards\WizardType
➥\WizardSubType\WizardName (Profile)
```

The subkey wizard types and subtypes will be defined according to the following:

- Control Wizards: The control-creation tool that you want to call your wizard from. Can be one of the following: BoundObjectFrame, CheckBox, ComboBox, CommandButton, Image, Label, ListBox, Line, OptionGroup, OptionButton, PageBreak, Rectangle, Subform, Subreport, TabControl, TextBox, ToggleButton, or UnboundObjectFrame.

- ActiveX Control Wizards: The ActiveX control's class property value.

- Builders (Property Wizards): The name of the property that you want the builder to change or create. Standard Access 97 builders are BackColor, BorderColor, FieldName, ForeColor, InputMask, LinkChildFields, LinkMasterFields, MenuBar, ODBCConnectStr, Picture, and ShortcutMenuBar.

Object Wizard Subkey Values

If your add-in is an object wizard that is used to create a form, query, report, or table, it must be registered according to the following format:

```
HKEY_LOCAL_MACHINE\SOFTWARE\Microsoft\Office\8.0\Access
➥\Wizards (Machine Global)
```

or

```
HKEY_CURRENT_ACCESS_PROFILE\Wizards\WizardType
➥\WizardSubType\WizardName (Profile)
```

Object wizard subkey values are defined according to the following list:

- Form Wizards: The form wizard name that you define will be displayed as a choice in the New Form dialog box when the end user begins creating a new form.
- Query Wizards: The query wizard name that you define will be displayed as a choice in the New Query dialog box when the end user begins creating a new query.
- Report Wizards: The report wizard name that you define will be displayed as a choice in the New Report dialog box when the end user begins creating a new report.
- Table Wizards: The table wizard name that you define will be displayed as a choice in the New Table dialog box when the end user begins creating a new table.

Menu Add-In Subkey Values

If your add-in is a menu add-in that will appear in the Add-Ins submenu under the Tools menu, it must be registered according to the following format:

```
HKEY_LOCAL_MACHINE\SOFTWARE\Microsoft\Office\8.0\Access
➥\Menu Add-Ins (Global Machine)
```

or

```
HKEY_CURRENT_ACCESS_PROFILE\Menu Add-Ins\MenuAddInName (Profile)
```

MenuAddInName is where you enter the name of the add-in as you want it to appear in the Add-Ins submenu.

> **TIP**
>
> If you want to designate a keystroke from the keyboard that will call the menu add-in, place an & symbol in front of the letter that you wish to make the hotkey.

Adding Additional Records to the `USysRegInfo` Table

When you defined the `USysRegInfo` table's first record, you provided the system's instructions for registering the add-in. Additional records are added to the table to add values to the "last key" subkey in the Windows Registry.

In each subsequent record, you will keep the uniform definition of the subkey field by copying the subkey field value into each new record's subkey field. The subkey value must remain constant. These subsequent records are where you further define the `Type`, `ValName`, and `Value` fields.

The `Type`, `ValName`, and `Value` Fields

The `Type` field defines the value type that the Add-in Manager creates in the Registry. The value type can be either a string, which is type 1, or a `DWORD` value, which is type 4.

The `ValName` and `Value` fields define the name and the value of the `Value` field, respectively.

If you are registering an ActiveX control wizard, builder, or control wizard, you will have to add the following records to your `USysRegInfo` table:

■ Can Edit: (Type 4) Allows a builder or wizard to modify an existing control or property of the same type. (1=Yes, 0=No)

■ Description: (Type 1) This is the text string that you use to define the builder or wizard in the Choose Builder dialog box if you need to choose between more than one for the same control or property.

■ Function: (Type 1) This defines the function that calls the builder or wizard.

■ Library: (Type 1) This defines the name and location of the add-in database to the Add-in Manager. The Add-in Manager automatically defines the path to the Access directory; you only need to provide the name of the add-in database in the `AddInName.mda` position. (`¦ACCDIR\AddInName.mda`)

If you are adding an object wizard add-in, you will need to add the following records to the `USysRegInfo` table:

■ Bitmap: (Type 1) Defines the bitmap graphic that is displayed in the wizard dialog box.

■ Datasource: (Type 4) This record is required for form and report-building wizards, and specifies whether the end user must define a table or query for the object's data source before the wizard will continue running. (1=Yes, 2=No)

■ Description: (Type 1) Displays this text string on the left side of the wizard dialog box on top of the bitmap when the wizard is started.

■ Function: (Type 1) This defines the function that calls the builder or wizard.

■ Index: (Type 4) Defines the display order of the wizard functions as displayed on the start-up dialog box. (0 = first item on list)

■ Library: (Type 1) Defines the add-in databases name and location to the Add-in Manager. The manager automatically defines the path as the Access program path, but you must supply the name of the add-in database at the `AddinName.mda` position. (`¦ACCDIR\AddinName.mda.`)

If you are registering a menu add-in, you will have to add the following records to your `USysRegInfo` table:

- Expression: (Type 1) Defines the name of the function as an expression that calls the wizard or builder. (`"=FunctionName()"`)
- Library: (Type 1) Defines the add-in database's name and location to the Add-in Manager. The manager automatically defines the path as the Access program path, but you must supply the name of the add-in database at the `AddinName.mda` position. (`¦ACCDIR\AddinName.mda`.)

Debugging the Add-In

As you are developing your add-in, you should be testing and debugging the objects as they are being created. The application should be tested as an Access 97 database according to standard development guidelines, with a focus on user variables at the individual object and application level.

Once you have successfully debugged your add-in as an Access database, you can proceed to testing it as an installed add-in. If you are converting an add-in from an earlier version of Access, pay attention to your referenced library databases. Add-ins and library databases created in earlier versions of Access must be converted prior to use in Access 97. Access 97 also does not allow circular references between library databases. If you have circular references in your code, you must remove those references prior to conversion. As long as the specified library objects exist on each machine on which the add-in will be converted, the references will be retained. The default references for Office 97, VBA, Access 95, Jet SQL Help Topics, and DAO 2.5/3.0 Libraries are converted to Access 97 references during conversion. Any referenced libraries not found on the user's hard drive during installation may cause errors during compile operations.

When you are ready to install and test your add-in, use the following procedure to install it: Open the Add-in Manager from Tools | Add-Ins in Access, then open your add-in database, and install it (see Figure 11.8). If it installs properly, the Add-in Manager places an X beside the add-in's name in the dialog box. If the `USysRegInfo` table has a problem, or is missing, you will receive an error. Add-ins are easily installed and uninstalled through the Add-in Manager user interface.

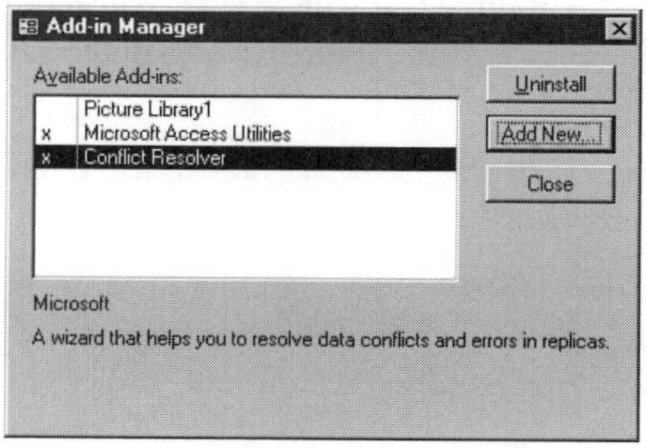

FIGURE 11.8.

The Microsoft Access 97 Add-in Manager.

Once you have completed the add-in installation with the Add-in Manager, the add-in will appear as an option in the appropriate circumstances when other add-ins of its type are being called.

At this point, you should thoroughly test and debug your add-in at each phase of its functionality, not forgetting to test its error-handling capabilities as well. I recommended that if you have the resources to do so, maintain a clean system for development, and perform your error trapping, configuration, and other potentially hazardous tests on a separate testbed system.

Once you have completed this final testing phase, you should streamline your add-in by removing unnecessary objects from the database and trimming excess components out of the other objects. Retest your add-in to make sure that you haven't removed anything that is needed, and then perform a compact and repair operation.

Important Finishing Touches

After you are satisfied with the add-in database, you should create a help file application to accompany it. A well-developed help file can add a lot to an application, and may save you from spending a lot of time troubleshooting or supporting your products after distribution. Refer to Chapter 21, "Creating and Customizing Help Files," for assistance on creating help files.

After all is said and done, and the add-in stands ready for distribution in its raw form, compile all VB modules. Keep both a compiled and an uncompiled version of your add-in in case you need to perform additional testing and debugging. Always make sure that your distribution version is fully compiled in order to avoid end-user errors.

Summary

Add-ins are one of the most flexible and useful tools that can be created with Access 97. As an Access developer, you should not overlook the opportunity to use add-ins to add value to your distribution products. This is perhaps one of the most neglected areas of Access database application development. Mastery of add-in design will give you a significant advantage over competitors without this ability. You will be able to develop incremental application updates and enhancements in a shorter time frame than that needed to create new, full-release versions of your application.

This chapter covered techniques that you can use to create your own custom builder, menu, and wizard add-ins with Access 97 and VBA.

You should also have a better understanding of some of the programming considerations that must be taken into account when designing add-ins and delivering them to a diverse customer base: localization, error-handling techniques, and environment control, among others.

Visual Basic for Applications for Access 97

Introduction to VBA for Access 97

by Dave Thompson

IN THIS CHAPTER

CHAPTER 12

Visual Basic for Applications (VBA) is the built-in programming language for Microsoft Office 97 (and its individual components, such as Access 97). VBA is included when you purchase Office 97. While you can accomplish many tasks without using VBA, it is the key to unlocking the full potential of Access 97.

Why VBA?

If Access 97 (and other Microsoft Office 97 components, such as Word, Excel, and PowerPoint) is indeed a feature-rich product with wizards, shortcut menus, and a wide variety of pull-down menus, what is to be gained from VBA?

VBA has more than 150 built-in functions that support classic programming tasks, financial calculations, date arithmetic, and statistical calculations. The help file for Access 97 lists 150 methods, 450 properties, 43 events, and hundreds of intrinsic constants. If you are new to VBA, the next chapter will explain these in more detail.

Using VBA, you can accomplish whatever you can accomplish through the Access 97 menu structure—and more. VBA is not only integral to Access 97, but to Office 97 as well.

Within Access 97, VBA's use is associated with the event model. Because the actions needed to respond to a single event are limited (most of the time, but not always), your programming will often entail writing just five to ten lines of code in a procedure specific to that one event. For example, to check that a user has not reversed a starting and ending date on a form, your code could as simple as the following:

```
If Me![StartDate] > Me![EndDate] Then
MsgBox "The Start Date is after the End Date."
Me![StartDate].SetFocus
End If
```

> **NOTE**
>
> Me is one those handy VBA shortcut techniques. In this case, it refers to the form where the user entered the dates.

This code would be attached to an event. For example, the OnClick event of a command button can be used to save the information on a form. Figure 13.1 in Chapter 13, "Getting Started with Access 97 VBA," shows an example of a code procedure attached to the OnClick event of a command button.

Figure 12.1 shows a simple form with a task number and associated start and end dates.

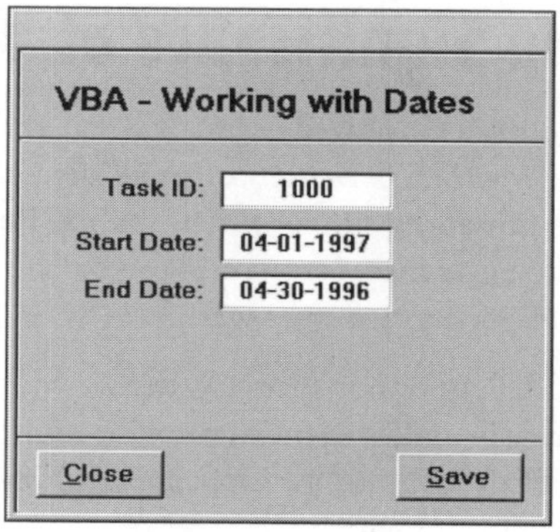

FIGURE 12.1.
The Task Dates form.

When the user clicks the Save button, the OnClick event occurs for that command button. By attaching the code to that event, you can give the user a warning message, as shown in Figure 12.2.

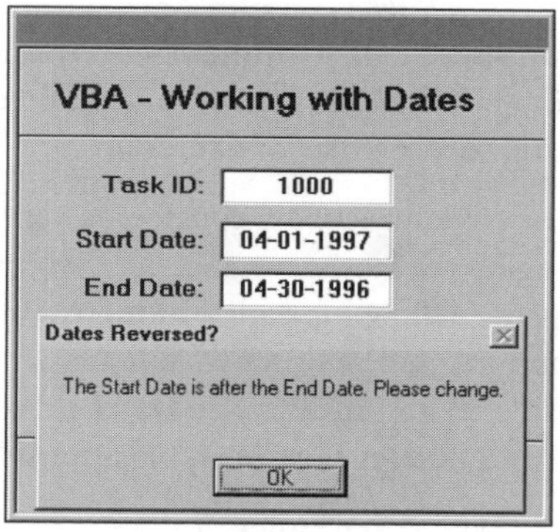

FIGURE 12.2.
A warning message to the user.

12

INTRODUCTION TO
VBA FOR ACCESS
97

> **NOTE**
>
> Typically your code will need to perform several data consistency checks before allowing a user to save new or edited information. This verification process can be done in whatever order you choose, warning the user at each error, and permitting corrections one at a time.

What Is the Significance of VBA?

For end user programmers (power users), VBA is the natural path of growth beyond macro programming. Code, which is written in small pieces called procedures, is easier to write and debug than macros providing similar functionality. Power macro programmers will appreciate the capability to trap and report errors, and to provide the user with recovery choices. No more suffering through `Macro Halted` messages!

For developers, VBA is an opportunity. Whether you are a corporate IT developer or an independent developer, VBA allows you to provide solutions for customers (internal or external) with a language tightly coupled to Office 97. Custom applications often involve a mix of requirements across components such as word processing, databases, spreadsheets, and graphics—in other words: the Office Suite. New to the Office Suite with Office 97, the IDE (Integrated Development Environment) gives you the capability to weave seamless, multi-component solutions.

For IT managers, VBA is a RAD (Rapid Application Development) tool. In addition to providing a multi-component development environment, Access 97 can front end Access databases and (through ODBC and now ODBCDirect with Access 97) a heterogeneous environment by attaching to a mixture of data sources.

While VBA does not contain as many controls as Visual Basic straight out of the box, consider that ActiveX is changing the landscape. Access 97 supports ActiveX controls. If you are responsible for development, achieving high productivity (translation: delivery schedules, defect ratios, end user support, and maintenance loads) can be an everyday battle. Do you count function points delivered and measure end user perceptions, which are negatively influenced by late deliverables and budget-busting applications?

While VBA may not be a silver bullet, it does provide a standardized development environment across most of the major categories for business applications: word processing, spreadsheet, presentation, and database.

 Take a look at the sample applications included on this book's CD-ROM. Conceal the words "Microsoft Access," and you might have difficulty deciding whether it is VB or VBA.

For those seeking to phase out older PC-based database applications, Access 97 allows you to develop the new application against the existing production data by attaching to either the live production data or copies of the production data. From there, queries can be used to copy the data into Access tables. Alternatively, you may choose to write your prototype forms and reports against the attached non-Access tables. Prototypes developed against existing table structures will provide a realistic view of conversion and implementation issues for the new production software.

For non-technical managers and business owners, VBA is an enabler for process innovation through information management. Moderately complex applications can be delivered in weeks instead of months. New reports can be created in hours instead of days. But remember that a high level of VBA proficiency will not be gained from a one-day seminar, nor is it realistic to expect your non-programmer professionals to become VBA experts in addition to their other tasks.

Failure rates on software development projects increase with the complexity of the project. End user programming failure rates rise dramatically with complexity. Enjoy the benefits that your power users gain from using VBA over macro programming, without expecting them to turn into professional application developers.

12

INTRODUCTION TO
VBA FOR ACCESS
97

VBA HISTORY

Microsoft was not the first software company to market an office suite. In the mid-eighties, several companies tried the concept, usually those with a particular strength in one component, such as word processing or database managers. For example, Innovative Software came out with the Smartware series: word processing, database, spreadsheet, and communications. These were PC-DOS–based packages. While they offered a graphical interface, graphics-intensive software typically performed poorly (was slow) on the available hardware of that time, such IBM AT class (80286 CPU) PCs.

Microsoft succeeded by building Word into a successful word processing package, eventually achieving market acceptance similar to Excel, which was not the dominant PC-DOS spreadsheet, but gained leadership as a Windows product.

Microsoft established a common menu structure in Word and Excel and began to build data exchange methods between the two programs. This made it efficient for users to use both Microsoft products.

The Microsoft Office Suite followed. It succeeded for many reasons, such as bundled pricing (the suite price was less than the sum of its parts), the relative ease of transferring data within its major components (such as from Excel to Word), and a uniform menu structure across these components.

Microsoft envisioned the need for a common programming language for application development using Word and Excel as the core products. The idea was first put forth in the PC-DOS era and described as a universal batch programming language.

Meanwhile, Visual Basic (VB) was winning over many application developers to the Windows environment. Microsoft first put VBA (almost a twin of VB, but tightly integrated into the host program) into Excel 5. Word for Windows received its own flavor of a VB-based program language: WordBasic.

Access 1.0 came out in late 1992 with yet another implementation called Access Basic.

So the picture was this: Excel had VBA; Word had WordBasic, and Access had Access Basic.

continues

continued

No more! VBA in Office 97 is a shared application language across Excel, Word, Access, and PowerPoint. Microsoft's is just that: VBA can drive a complete application from one component to complex projects using a combination of components. For those familiar with DDE, OLE, and now ActiveX, VBA is the glue for seamless development.

Two Access VBA/Access Basic Real-World Applications

While we are accustomed to accepting, even expecting, faster and more powerful PCs almost yearly, PC software is advancing as well. Access 97 is the fifth release of the database since 1992. This parallel progression of PC hardware and PC software is providing opportunities for custom applications in many areas. It just costs less today for a complete solution (hardware and software) than five years ago. Here are two examples, made possible because the total implementation costs were reasonable.

Emergency Room

A Microsoft Access database (controlled by VBA code) enables the doctors in a fast-paced, hospital ER (Emergency Room or trauma center) to find and print prescriptions in a matter of seconds. The doctor types the first few letters of the drug to be prescribed, and the Access-based program moves to the appropriate entry in a database of several thousand prescriptions. Then the doctor only has to point to the appropriate prescription (using a mouse or arrow keys), click (or press a function key), pick up the prescription from the printer, sign it, and he can now focus on other tasks.

Now what happens here? What are the benefits of this VBA-driven, Access database program to the people involved?

The doctor issues a legible prescription quickly. He does not have to recall or take the time to look up available packaging and dosages for the prescribed medication. A multi-part form is generated for record-keeping on hard-copy, and an electronic copy is sent to a patient history file on the computer. The doctor spends less than a minute or two on the computer, most of which is spent typing.

The patient then has a legible prescription, which is important to pharmacists. While they are skilled at reading doctors' hand-written prescriptions, pharmacists must call the doctor who issued the prescription if there is any question as to what it says. This type of phone call is the exception when the doctor uses the Access-based system.

This is a real world application. For those doubting how much productivity can be achieved with Access and VBA, consider the fact that this ER application started as an 11,000-line (executable statements), Microsoft PDS 7.1 (Professional Development System), single-workstation program. When the ER put in a five-station PC network, the application was rewritten in Access and was online in 16 days.

Corporate Advertising Department for National Chain

The corporate advertising department for a national chain plans and coordinates Sunday inserts in more than 200 newspapers for the chain's 400-plus stores. By implementing an Access database custom program (driven by VBA) instead of using the computer system of an off-site vendor, the chain shortened the process cycle time. It now has management reporting "at its fingertips" and is able to respond faster to a dynamic, competitive marketplace. There is also one unplanned advantage.

When a media planner leaves (through resignation or promotion), the training time for the new planner is reduced. The new planner need only learn the specific application, which happens to be written in Access VBA, rather than learning Microsoft Access.

Frequently Asked Questions for New Access VBA Users

The extent of VBA as integrated into Access has been seemingly a secret to some degree. Many users know about the Access macro language, and many PC users use or know about Visual Basic, the language.

Where Is VBA?

If you have Office 97, you have VBA.

Where Can I Use It?

You can use it within forms, reports, and general modules where the procedures you write are available throughout the database. For example, you can put procedures (such as functions and subs, or subroutines, which are discussed further in Chapter 13) in general modules, and call them from any form, even a macro (RunCode action).

How Does VBA Relate to the Event Model of Access 97?

Most VBA procedures are written as individual procedures that run upon the event occurrence. In the date example in this chapter (see Figures 12.1 and 12.2, along with accompanying text), the VBA code could be attached to the AfterUpdate event for the EndDate control.

As a Developer, Can I Protect My Source Code?

Yes. Access 97 supports creating an MDE file which strips the source code from your application. What remains, however, is a fully functional application. For additional information about MDE files, see Chapter 14, "Access 97 VBA for Developers," Figures 14.6 and 14.7 with accompanying text.

What Are Some of the Uses of VBA in an Application?

As you develop an application or program your own repetitive tasks, here are some areas where VBA can be useful:

Communicate with the user

> Report errors and offer suggestions
>
> Dynamically report database statistics
>
> Report successes

Navigate

> Open and close forms
>
> Print reports
>
> Move from record to record
>
> Move to a specific record
>
> Search for specific information
>
> Present only appropriate navigation choices

Control the user interface

> Lock individual controls on a form
>
> Present context-sensitive functionality
>
> Streamline user input dynamically

Ensure the consistency and integrity of your data

> Perform logical checks, such as for date reversals
>
> Check for missing information
>
> Test for duplicate information
>
> Require multi-step deletion procedures
>
> Avoid out-of-sequence processes

Security and auditing

> Write the username and date and time automatically

> **NOTE**
>
> Security in Access 97 generally works best when done through the Access Security Wizard and Access menu structure. Much of the security model is available through VBA, but should be approached cautiously to avoid breaches and maintenance headaches. It is much better to use the security model by reading (not writing) user and group information from within VBA, such as retrieving the username though the CurrentUser function.

Here is an example of using VBA to communicate with the user and control the user interface. While the form is part of a real application, remember that this form is intentionally simple and to the point. The overall application from which this example is drawn is relatively complex, involving more than 30 tables with referential integrity set.

Entering a New Client

Attorneys typically maintain a client database. Assume that each new client must have a unique client number and that no new client is entered unless the Social Security Number (SSN) is known.

The first criteria to enter a new client is:

> Client number must be entered
>
> Client number must be unique
>
> SSN must be entered
>
> SSN must be unique

If any of these elementary first criteria fail, there is no need to proceed. So the user is presented with the form shown in Figure 12.3.

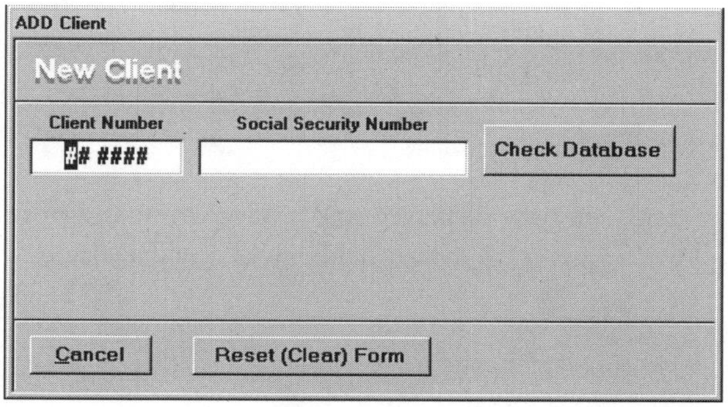

FIGURE 12.3.

The pop-up form for a new client.

ADD Client
New Client

Client Number   Social Security Number

`█# ####`   **Check Database**

Cancel   Reset (Clear) Form

Notice that initially the user is asked only for two pieces of information. Figure 12.4 shows the result of entering a duplicate client number (the same number is already assigned in the database) and clicking the Check Database button.

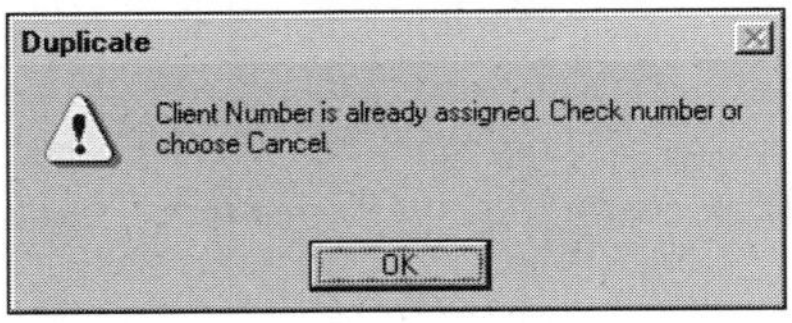

FIGURE 12.4.

This dialog box is displayed when a duplicate client number is entered.

The user is alerted to an error condition and given a chance to correct or cancel the entry. At this point, the process is under the control of VBA, and nothing in the database has been written or changed. The integrity of the data is protected.

The code for this and other examples from this chapter can be found in the CH12PAU.MDB file on the CD-ROM accompanying this book.

The VBA code attached to the Check Database button (actually attached to the OnClick event of the button) checks the entry against your initial criteria, reports any errors (such as missing or duplicate information), and enables you to take corrective action.

To finish this example with corrected information, let's dynamically alter the form and give the user a new context-sensitive choice, as shown in Figure 12.5.

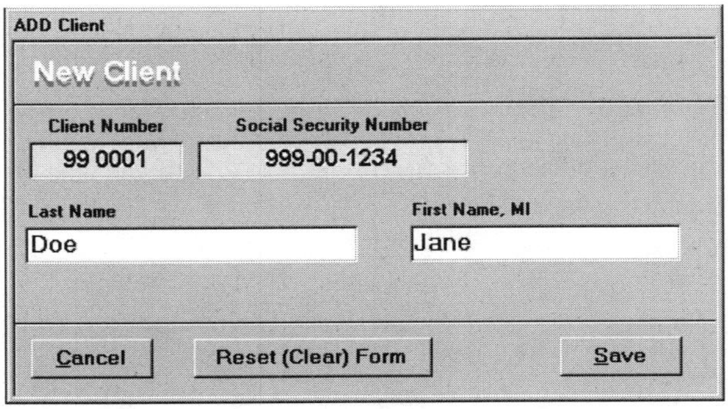

FIGURE 12.5.

The Save command is enabled after the database check succeeds.

The name fields are now displayed and a Save command button is visible. Also, the Client Number and Social Security Number fields have been locked and their background color changed.

Advice on Getting Started and Finding Help

 Start with a sample database and experiment. Use some of the examples from this book, available on the accompanying CD-ROM. Remember that you can always copy the original from the CD-ROM back onto your own drive and start over if necessary.

Getting Started

For macro users, Access 97 has a wizard to convert macros to VBA code. Run the wizard and study the code it produces. This should be great help in learning VBA.

For first-time users, just do it. Start with a very simple task, such as a form navigation system. Build your own main menu or switchboard form. Put some command buttons on it to open other forms. From those forms, add command buttons to close and return to your main menu.

Experiment with data verification, an important use of VBA. Write some code to verify the information on a form and attach it to the OnClick event of a command button to save the data. In other words, verify the information on the form. If an error exists, don't let the user save the record.

Experiment with context-sensitive functionality. An example might be a print command button placed on a form with client or customer information. If the client form is loaded, have the print command bring up a list of client reports. If the customer form is loaded, offer customer-specific reports.

For example, the user might want to print a report for the one client displayed, or print the entire client list in a short or long format.

A more advanced use of VBA might be to merge data from Access into a Word document. For example, a client's onscreen record might be merged to a form letter or contract. The power of VBA and Office really shines when you can place a command button on a client or customer form and instruct the user, "Click on the button and walk to the printer." The job's done.

Finding Help

Just a few places to find help about using VBA and Access 97 include:

- This book
- The help file included with Access 97
- *Alison Balter's Mastering Access 97, Second Edition* (Sams Publishing)
- Microsoft Developers Network

    United States and Canada: (800) 759-5474

    Outside North America: (510) 275-0763

    www.microsoft.com/msdn

MSDN has a tiered subscription service. The entry-level library one-year subscription provides a CD-ROM quarterly. For developers with any serious intent, joining MSDN is an excellent investment.

Technical Articles, Backgrounders and White Papers, Knowledge Base and Bug Lists, Product Documentation, and Conference and Seminar Papers are some of the major categories of information provided.

The Knowledge Base can be searched by keyword, similar to online Web search engines, and contains sample code for many common VBA uses. And would you believe, the CD-ROM has hyperlinks into Microsoft Web pages? If you click on the link, it initiates a login, and takes you to the site.

Microsoft Web sites:

`www.microsoft.com/accessdev`

`www.microsoft.com/msdn`

`www.microsoft.com/officedev`

`www.microsoft.com/kb`

Install the sample databases provided in the ValuPak for Access 97: `Northwind.MDB`, `Order.MDB`, and `Solutions.MDB`. See how the Microsoft in-house pros do it!

Summary

VBA for Access 97 and Office 97 is a feature-rich application development language. It is tightly coupled to the host components.

For end-user (power) programmers, VBA is a path of growth beyond the limitations of macro programming.

For developers, VBA is an opportunity to deliver polished applications to your customers.

For IT managers, VBA is a RAD (Rapid Application Development) tool. VBA offers fast cycle times, enjoys end-user acceptance, is extensible from simple to complex tasks, and can jump-start you into intranet and Internet publishing of both static and dynamic data. It is—in short—something that should be in your mix.

For non-technical managers and business owners, VBA for Access 97 offers the opportunity to have custom applications developed in a reasonable amount of time. Reasonable time means reasonable cost.

The world is changing. VBA offers significant potential in the real world of end-user demands for custom applications and streamlined processes delivered in short time frames. It can be done. Tomorrow—if not here already—is close.

Finally, remember that VBA, while new to many, is another classical Microsoft tenacity-and-talent success story. VBA has evolved into prime-time status over the past few years. After all, who remembers Windows 1.0 or Windows 2.0? Yet everyone knows about the success of Windows 3.*x*.

So it is with VBA. In Office 97, VBA has reached critical mass regarding the richness of its functionality, features, and components it will drive.

Getting Started with Access 97 VBA

by Dave Thompson

IN THIS CHAPTER

Visual Basic for Applications (VBA) is a built-in programming language for Access 97. It can control the features of Access and the features of other Office components, such as Excel, Word, and PowerPoint. VBA can provide additional capabilities that are not found through the Access menu structure.

VBA is a programming language. Your ability to communicate precisely in a foreign language depends on your proficiency in that language. VBA is no different. Your ability to use VBA to communicate with Access is a matter of proficiency.

It is not necessary to be fluent in a foreign language to gain benefit when traveling. Fortunately, it is the same with VBA. You will begin to enjoy the benefits of using VBA long before you achieve expert status.

If you have programmed in Access Basic (Access 1.*x* and 2.0) then you will find significant enhancements to the language. If you have programmed in VBA for Access 95, you will find new (and improved) functionality and more online help as you work (through the IDE or Integrated Development Environment). New to Access 97 is the ability to strip your code from applications in a format called MDE. (See Chapter 14, "Access 97 VBA for Developers," for a discussion of MDE files.)

Data Types

Data types correspond to the kind of information to be saved and what you want to do with it. For the most part, data types are intuitive, at least in their names.

As you create your own tables in Access, you will be asked to assign a data type to each field. Figure 13.1 shows the drop-down list for assigning a data type to a field in Access 97.

FIGURE 13.1.

The drop-down list of data types in Table Design.

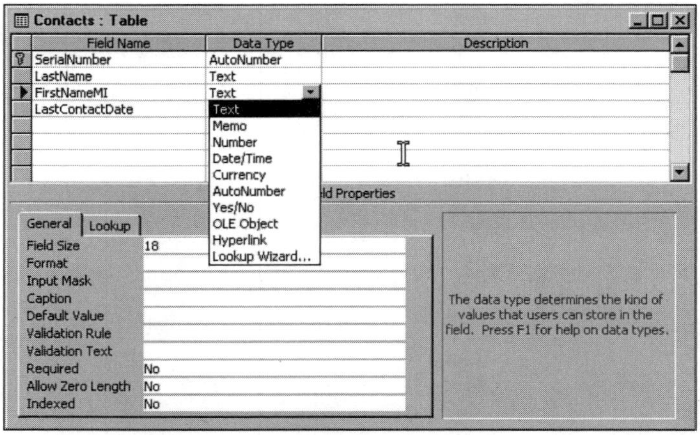

Similar to specifying a field data type when designing a table, VBA supports data types for your code variables and procedures. Table 13.1 shows the typical data types provided in the Access table Design View and the corresponding candidate data types for VBA.

Table 13.1. Data types in Access tables and VBA.

Table design	VBA
Text	String
Memo	String
Number	
Byte	Byte
Integer	Integer
Long Integer	Long
Single	Single
Double	Double
Replication ID	None
Date/Time	Date
Currency	Currency
AutoNumber	
Incremental	Long
Random	Long
Yes/No	Boolean
Hyperlink	String

CAUTION

It is important to understand that using VBA to manipulate the data in your database tables requires matching the VBA data type to the specific data type for each field. Mistakes in this area of programming lead to `Type Mismatch` errors when your program runs.

VBA supports a complete set of data types beyond those that appear in the field drop-down list in the table design view. For example, VBA supports user-defined data types. Variant is another VBA data type having many uses in VBA code.

TIP

The Variant data type can hold numeric, string, or date/time data. It is the only VBA data type that supports the assignment of `Null`. Data types not explicitly declared in VBA code are assumed to be Variant. A Variant data type is particularly useful when checking for empty text fields on forms.

The four most commonly used data types are

- Text (or String)
- Number (various types, depending on use)
- Date
- Logical (True/False, Yes/No)

Text

Text is perhaps the most easily understood. It is used to store names, addresses, titles, and descriptions. Access stores text fields as variable-length text.

This means that when designing tables, you can err on the safe side by making text fields as long as you think necessary. If you enter 30 characters of text into a `Text 50` field, Access will not use 20 extra spaces (field length of 50 minus the 30 characters entered) when saving the data to disk.

However, assigning text field lengths with some discipline is good programming practice. It will make report design easier, and your reports will hold fewer surprises when printed. Just as in printing spreadsheets it's frequently a battle to squeeze what you want on one line (and stay within the page margins); the same is true with Access reports. Assigning too much extra length to your text fields can cause your printed data to be truncated (meaning it won't all print on the page).

NOTE

If you use unbound forms to capture user input, failure to check text lengths against the field lengths will cause a `Data Too Long To Paste` error message when you attempt to save the record.

Number

Number fields are typically used when you want to perform calculations, such as extended prices on invoices (`Quantity` × `Unit Price` = `Extended`) or show sub-totals and totals on reports.

Using the Currency data type will avoid rounding errors in financial calculations.

Long is used in VBA to refer to AutoNumber fields.

Integer and Long can store whole numbers, but have specific limits as to the size of the number they can store. In approximate numbers, Integer can be used for numbers between -32,000 and +32,000, and Long for numbers between ±2 Billion.

NOTE

One conservative way to recall and use Integer and Long is to remember that Integer can contain any 4-digit whole number (-9,999 to +9,999), and Long can contain any 9-digit whole number (-999,999,999 to +999,999,999).

TIP

For a more complete comparison of data types available in Access 97, see Access Help | Contents and Index | Index and search for Replication IDs, comparison of data types.

Date

Date fields and the Date data type are a powerful and useful feature of Access 97 and VBA. The Date type supports date calculations in a common-sense way. For example, if you want to calculate the due date for an invoice with Net 10 terms, it can be as simple as:

```
Dim DueDate as Date
DueDate = Now() + 10
```

MICROSOFT ACCESS DATES—HOW DO THEY DO THAT?

Access displays dates in various standard (or user-defined) formats, such as 05/01/1997, or 01-May-97. However, the data is stored internally as a double-precision number. May 1, 1997 10:00:00 A.M. is stored by VBA as 35551.4166666667.

The portion to the left of the decimal point (in this case, 35551) is the days component of the date. The portion to the right of the decimal (in this case, 4166666667) represents the time component of the date down to individual seconds.

Day zero is December 30, 1899. Historians can take heart, because negative numbers are also stored. For example, the Battle of Hastings occurred on day −304324 (10/14/1066).

Date calculations are done internally by converting displayed dates to numbers, then adding or subtracting as necessary, and then converting the answer back to a date format.

TIP

Understanding that dates are stored internally as double-precision numbers is important to getting the results you expect from date comparisons and dates used as criteria in queries. VBA and Access provide a number of formatting options for date fields. Formatting date fields without the time component stores the date as a whole number without anything to the right of the decimal. Date comparisons then produce the results you expect. Alternatively, if you are dealing with data written (saved in the database) with the Access General Date format (which saves date and time to the second), use formatting functions to strip the time component when performing comparisons or using the data for query criteria.

VBA has built-in date functions and date intrinsic constants. I'll discuss intrinsic constants in greater detail later in this section.

Now() is a built-in VBA function that reads the computer (system) date and time. VBA's Format function has a number of uses to include working with Date data types. Table 13.2 shows some examples of formatting dates using VBA.

Table 13.2. User-defined formatting of dates.

Example	*Sample Result*
? Now()	6/30/97 3:28:53 PM
? Format(Now, "mm/dd/yyyy")	06/30/1997
? Format(Now, "m/dd/yy")	6/30/97
? Format(Now, "mmmm d, yyyy")	June 30, 1997
? Format(Now, "d-mmmm-yyyy")	30-June-1997
? Format(Now, "d-mmm-yyyy")	30-Jun-1997
? Format(Now, "h:mm AM/PM")	3:28 PM

Access provides several pre-defined date formats, as shown in the Table Design View, that can be used in VBA. Table 13.3 shows the results of using these formats.

Table 13.3. Access-defined formatting of dates.

Example	*Sample Result*
? Now()	6/30/97 3:28:53 PM
? Format(Now, "General Date")	6/30/97 3:28:53 PM
? Format(Now, "Short Date")	6/30/97

Example	Sample Result
? Format(Now, "Medium Date")	30-Jun-97
? Format(Now, "Long Date")	Monday, June 30, 1997
? Format(Now, "Medium Time")	03:28 PM

YEAR 2000 ISSUES

Handling date fields using four digits for the year will avoid any ambiguity or incorrect data. Many dates are used with a two-digit year format, as shown in Table 13.3. The explicit use of the yyyy format should be considered.

Access 97 makes some assumptions when storing dates entered in an abbreviated or two-digit format. Years entered as 30 through 99 (for example, 6/14/97) are assumed to be 1900s (1930–1999). Years entered as 00 through 29 are assumed to be 2000s (2000–2029).

VBA has several functions to support date calculations. One of them is the `DateAdd()` function, which permits adding or subtracting intervals (such as days, months, years, even weeks) to a date. `DateAdd()` returns a date as the answer.

Consider the following VBA code:

```
Dim StartDate As Date, EndDate As Date
'
StartDate = #6/30/97#
'
'now add 40 years and print the results
'
EndDate = DateAdd("yyyy", 40, StartDate)
'
Debug.Print "1. " & Format(EndDate, "Short Date")
Debug.Print "2. " & Format(EndDate, "m/dd/yyyy")
'
'but if the user types 6/30/37 into an abbreviated date
'control or field
'
Debug.Print "3. " & Format(#6/30/37#, "m/dd/yyyy")
```

The results are

    6/30/37
    6/30/2037
    6/30/1937

If a user enters StartDate onto a form and VBA is used to add 40 years to that date, the results will be accurate. If, however, the user manually enters 6/30/37 onto a form as the EndDate, then Access stores the result as 1937.

Some VBA functions useful for working with Date data types include:

- `Now()`
- `Date()`
- `DateAdd()`
- `DateDiff()`
- `DatePart()`
- `DateSerial()`
- `DateValue()`

One common use of date functions is to calculate a person's age. Age should not be stored in your database as a value, but rather calculated and displayed on forms and reports as needed. If you store a person's birthdate, you can use the following procedure to calculate age:

```
Public Function AgeInYears(vBirthDate As Variant) As Integer
If IsNull(vBirthDate) Or Not IsDate(vBirthDate) Then
 AgeInYears = 0
 Exit Function
End If
'note use of line continuation character in next line
AgeInYears = DateDiff("yyyy", vBirthDate, Now) + _
(Now < DateSerial(Year(Now), Month(vBirthDate), Day(vBirthDate)))
End Function
```

Another procedure that demonstrates the use of date functions is the following:

```
Public Function DaysUntilParty(vBirthDate As Variant) As Long
Dim BNum As Long, TodayNum As Long, DeltaDays As Long

BNum = DateDiff("d", vBirthDate, DateSerial(Year(vBirthDate), 1, 1))
TodayNum = DateDiff("d", Now, DateSerial(Year(Now), 1, 1))
DeltaDays = TodayNum - BNum - 1

Select Case DeltaDays
Case 0
 MsgBox "Happy Birthday!"
Case 1
 MsgBox "Tomorrow is the Birthday Party. Don't forget!"
Case Is > 1
 MsgBox CStr(NumberOfDays) & " days until Birthday Party."
Case Is < 0
 MsgBox "The party was " & CStr(-NumberOfDays) & " days ago."
End Select
End Function
```

CAUTION

If you use the `DateDiff()` function to calculate the number of weekdays (Monday–Friday), the function will not return the correct value. See Microsoft's Knowledge Base (www.microsoft.com/kb) for Article ID: Q95977 for additional information.

For more information on using dates and date math, see Access 97 Help | Contents and Index | Index | and search for Date fields.

Logical

Logical data types are used for those many real-world applications of Yes/No or True/False kinds of questions. For these situations, use the Boolean VBA data type. It can be assigned as either `True` (Yes) or `False` (No), nothing else.

> **NOTE**
>
> A Boolean data type cannot accept a value of `Null`. `Null` is sometimes used to mean not known, and sometimes used to mean unavailable. Boolean remains a two-value data type. Proceed carefully where there are three choices: Yes, No, and I don't know.

Constants and Variables

Constants are values that do not change. Your birthdate is a constant. However, variable values do change. For example, your age is a variable.

In VBA, constants are divided into three categories:

- Symbolic (something you specify)
- Intrinsic (something VBA has predefined)
- System (`True`, `False`, `Null`)

Symbolic

Symbolic constants can be user-defined and used throughout an Access 97 database. For example, you might want to change the back color property of controls on your forms in response to an event. In Chapter 12, "Introduction to VBA for Access 97," Figure 12.5, VBA is used to change the back color of the `Client Number` and `Social Security Number` controls.

Light gray was chosen as a back color for controls that the user cannot change. One way to accomplish this is to define a constant in a standard module as:

```
Public Const LightGray = 14935011
```

> **TIP**
>
> To find the value of a color (such as 14935011 for light gray), open a form in the Design View. Place a text control on the form and set its back color using the Fill/Back Color toolbar icon. The color value now appears in the properties for that control as its back color value. Write it down, or better yet, cut and paste the value into a standard module as in our example: `Public Const LightGray = 14935011`.

In the code for the New Client form, the Client Number control's back color property is changed from white to light gray with the following code:

```
Me![ClientNumber].BackColor = LightGray
```

Once it is defined as a public constant, light gray can be used on other forms, producing a uniform appearance throughout your application. VBA has eight predefined (intrinsic) color constants: `vbBlack`, `vbRed`, `vbGreen`, `vbYellow`, `vbBlue`, `vbMagenta`, `vbCyan`, and `vbWhite`.

> **NOTE**
>
> Public constants defined for use throughout a database should be defined in a standard code module.

Intrinsic

Intrinsic constants are predefined in VBA. For Access 97 there are hundreds of intrinsic constants with uses in major functional areas, such as DAO (Data Access Objects) constants, action constants, keycode constants, msgbox constants, security constants, and even color constants.

Lists of intrinsic constants are given in Access 97 Help | Contents and Index | Index, and search for constants.

You will find that you can use intrinsic constants in your VBA code in many ways, ranging from the simple to complex.

The `MsgBox()` function is used within VBA to inform users of events, such as errors, and to ask users to make decisions. It is a relatively simple function, but it can influence both the perception and the reality of how well you write VBA code. VBA also has about two dozen intrinsic constants for use with `MsgBox()`. The following line of code displays the message shown in Figure 13.2:

```
MsgBox "Hello world!", vbInformation, "Access 97"
```

FIGURE 13.2.

*This Hello World!
message box is displayed
using the* MsgBox
function.

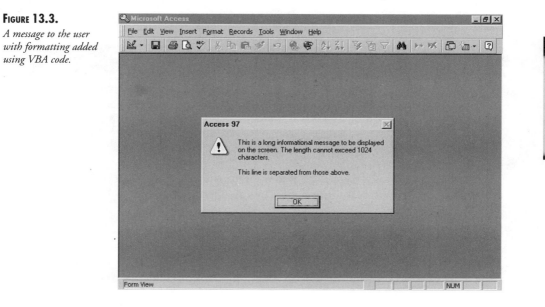

Additional icon choices are vbExclamation, vbQuestion, and vbCritical.

If you have a long message to display, vbCrLf is another helpful intrinsic constant (see Figure 13.3).

```
Dim msg as string
msg = "This is a long informational message to be "
msg = msg & "displayed on the screen. The length cannot "
msg = msg & "exceed 1024 characters."
msg = msg & vbCrLf & vbCrLf
msg = msg & "This line is separated from those above."
MsgBox msg, vbExclamation, "Access 97"
```

FIGURE 13.3.

*A message to the user
with formatting added
using VBA code.*

TIP

If you frequently use vbCrLf twice (as in the example above), declare a public constant such as

```
Public Const TwoCrLf = vbCrLf + vbCrLf
```

MsgBox() can ask the user a question and your VBA code can make decisions based on the result. This code can be attached to the On Click event of a command button on your main menu form:

```
Private Sub QuitCMD_Click()
Dim intButtons, x
intButtons = vbYesNo + vbQuestion
x = MsgBox("Do you want to exit the program now?", _
intButtons,"Confirm Exit")
If x = vbNo Then
 Exit Sub
  Else 'must be vbYes
    Application.Quit
End If
```

NOTE

When using MsgBox as a function that returns a value, use MsgBox with parentheses, as shown in the preceding code.

CAUTION

The underscore is used as a line continuation character. It can be used to break long code statements into two or more lines for readability, but use with caution. The underscore is preceded by a space (space, underscore) and is not used inside the text within quotation marks.

There are navigation tasks that can be accomplished with a line or two of code. Here are some examples where Access VBA intrinsic constants are used:

```
DoCmd.OpenForm "ClientList",,,,acReadOnly,acDialog
DoCmd.GoToRecord ,,acLast
DoCmd.OpenReport "rptTasks",acViewPreview
```

VBA can be used to control the look and functionality of your application. Many of the properties set through the Design View when creating new forms and reports can be changed by VBA as your application runs.

These kinds of changes are dynamic changes. When the user closes a form and then opens it again, your original, default design is restored. When opening forms such as client or customer forms, it is often best to open them as read-only. This keeps information from being accidentally changed. Either of the following code samples can be used to allow the user to edit information on a form opened as read-only:

```
forms![ClientList].AllowEdits = True
```

or

```
Me.AllowEdits = True
```

Remember that Me, as used here, is a reference shortcut to the form where the code procedure resides. For this reason, the keyword Me is not used in standard modules. Code procedures in a standard module can be used by more than one form. Me in a standard module is unknown.

System

There are three predefined constants that are universal to programming and programming languages such as VBA: True, False, and Null. These three system constants may be used anywhere within your VBA code (in the proper context, of course).

True/False

True/False are especially useful when setting control properties such as:

```
Me![MyControl].Visible = True
```

True/False are implicit in most logical constructs, but it is not necessary to explicitly use then. For example:

```
Dim x, y
x = 100
y = 10

If x > y Then
MsgBox "It is true that x is greater than y."
Else
MsgBox "x is not greater than y."
End if
```

The following code is equivalent to the code above:

```
If (x > y) = True Then
MsgBox "It is true that x is greater than y."
Else
MsgBox "x is not greater than y."
End if
```

> **NOTE**
>
> See Access 97 Help | Contents and Index | Index, and search for Not operator for additional information about a useful VBA language element often used with True/False expressions.

Boolean data types are either True or False. When converted to a number, false Boolean values are assigned the value 0; true Boolean values are assigned -1. The following code displays -1:

```
Dim xbln As Boolean, xInt As Integer
xbln = True
xInt = CInt(xb)
MsgBox CStr(xInt)
```

If `xbln` is false, then `xInt` is 0.

Many programmers are accustomed to using the -1/0 combination as equivalent to using `True`/ `False`. This is no longer good practice. The preferred practice is to declare Boolean data types and assign values as either `True` or `False`.

CAUTION

For those converting Access Basic applications (Access versions 1.x or 2.0) to Access 97, note that code such as the following should be changed:

```
(r is recordset in Access 97; a table or dynaset in 1.x or 2.0)
r![YesNoFieldName] = "-1"
```

Use the following code instead:

```
r![YesNoFieldName] = True
```

Null

`Null` is as much a concept as it is a value. For example, if a field is left blank on a form (in the absence of a declared default value), the field will assume the value of `Null`.

If the field is a Fax phone number, does this mean that there is no Fax number at all? Or do we just not have the Fax number to enter?

Sometimes `Null` means "does not exist;" at other times `Null` means "the information is not available—at this time."

`IsNull()` is a VBA function used to determine whether something (such as a field value or expression) has the value `Null`. `IsNull()` returns a value of either `True` or `False`. We can use `IsNull()` to determine whether a field has some value present before attempting to use the field value in calculations, for example:

```
If IsNull(me![OrderDate]) Then
MsgBox "Please enter the Order Date"
Else
'Code to run if the Order Date is present
End If
```

Procedures

A typical procedure can be thought of as a small, self-contained program. When you click on a command button, if you have added code to that event, Access will run that code, whether it's one line, or a hundred.

If there is no code associated with the On Click event of a command button, nothing will happen when the user clicks on the command button. Generally, you will assign VBA code to only a few of the events available for individual controls, forms, and reports.

Most procedures are short—less than 10 lines!

There are two types of procedures: function procedures and sub procedures. If you are new to Access VBA, the distinction between these two may not be obvious. Yet, you can write a lot of useful, working code before you feel comfortable deciding when to use a sub procedure and when to use a function procedure.

The word procedure is often dropped, and they are referred to as simply functions and subs.

> **NOTE**
>
> The context does matter because VBA has hundreds of built-in functions, whereas sub clearly implies a user-defined procedure.

13

Functions

Now() is a built-in VBA function that returns a value. On reports you can include a control (text box) and set its source to Now(). When the report prints, Now() returns the date and time from the computer clock.

In a multiuser environment with Access security applied, we can create our own (user-defined) function, such as follows:

```
Public Function DateTimeStampUser()
DateTimeStampUser = CurrentUser() & " " & Now()
End Function
```

Functions can be passed arguments that become part of the function's calculations to return a value. For spreadsheet users, think of functions as formulas. Spreadsheet formulas accept values and make calculations. Functions can be passed arguments and return values.

A frequent requirement when developing Access applications is to close the current form and open another. The following code demonstrates one way to do this:

```
Public Function CloseOpen(y As String)
On Error Resume Next
DoCmd.Close
DoCmd.OpenForm y
End Function
```

Place this function in a standard module. Standard modules are those listed under the Modules tab of the Access 97 database window. When you create a new database, the database window with the Modules tab selected will be empty.

To create a standard module, from the database window with the Modules tab selected, click on New. Choose Insert | Procedure. Name the procedure CloseOpen (do not include parentheses) and click OK.

Type the code as shown in the CloseOpen() example above. Be sure to type y as string within the parentheses that Access automatically adds to the procedure name. Now choose File | Save, and give your standard module a name, such as Utilities. CloseOpen() can now be used on any form in your database.

Figure 13.4 shows a form in the Design View, where CloseOpen() is used to close a form and return to the Main Menu form.

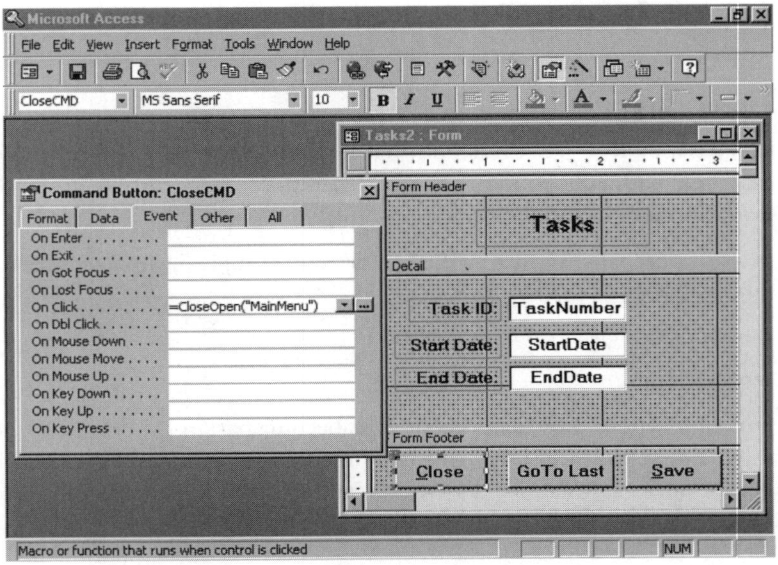

FIGURE 13.4.

Adding a function to a command button.

LIGHTWEIGHT FORMS

Experienced Access VBA programmers should note that Access 97 supports "codeless" forms (and reports) through a new form property, `HasModule`. A codeless form is considered a lightweight object. Codeless forms load faster and consume fewer resources than forms having an associated (class) module.

Depending upon your programming style, functions placed in standard modules may achieve new significance. From an event, you can call a public function located in a standard module while maintaining the form's lightweight status.

By default, new forms (and reports) are assigned a `HasModule` value of `No`. If the class module window is opened (even if no procedures are inserted), the `HasModule` property is automatically changed to `Yes`. If code is assigned to a control event, `HasModule` becomes `Yes`.

TIP

To maintain a form's status as lightweight, put any needed procedures in a standard module. You can assign standard-module procedures to an event on the form while maintaining the form's lightweight status. For example, the `On Click` event of a command button could have this entry in the command button's property sheet:

```
=CloseOpen("MainMenu")
```

Remember to use the = sign and note that only function procedures can be used—not sub procedures.

Access will convert a form to lightweight status if you change the value of the `HasModule` property from `Yes` to `No` in the Form Design View. This will strip the class module from the form. Move any needed code procedures to standard modules before setting `HasModule` to `No`.

Access provides a warning message when changing `HasModule` from `Yes` to `No`.

TIP

For menu forms, read-only forms, and other forms where little processing needs to done against control events, lightweight forms should be considered.

Sub Procedures

Sub procedures are the default style for the code builder used in the Design View of forms and reports. Access will name the sub automatically, appending the underscore character and the name of the event.

Unlike functions, subs do not return a value. You do not assign a value to a sub as done in the previous `DateTimeStampUser()` function example.

Otherwise, subs can be indistinguishable from a function. When a sub procedure runs (we say that a procedure is called), Access runs the code within the sub. As in the case of a function, the code executes, briefly becoming a mini-program.

To assign or attach VBA code to a form command button event, select the event from the object's property sheet. In Figure 13.5 we have selected the CloseCMD button to assign (or attach) code to its `On Click` event.

FIGURE 13.5.

Selecting an event in Form Design View.

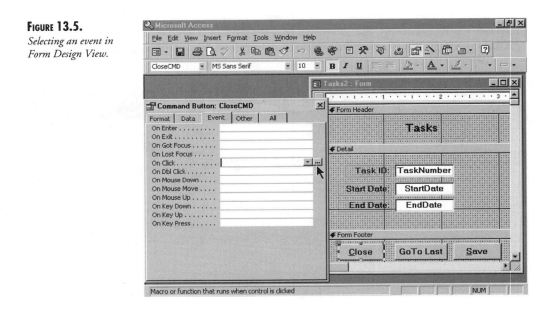

Next we select Code Builder from the Choose Builder list box, as shown in Figure 13.6.

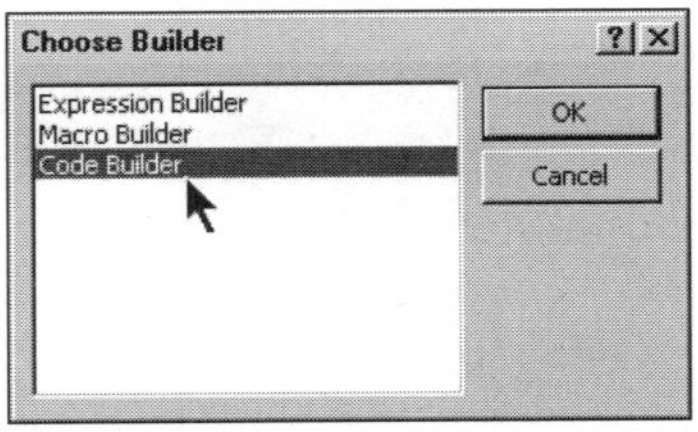

FIGURE 13.6.

Selecting Code Builder.

Finally we add our code, which in this case is only one line, as shown in Figure 13.7. Notice that Access named the sub `Private Sub CloseCMD_Click()`. Enter your VBA code after the sub name line and before the `End Sub` statement.

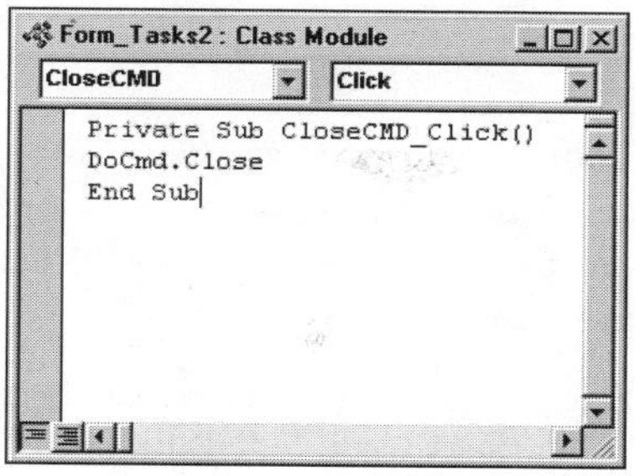

FIGURE 13.7.

*Entering code for the
sub procedure.*

Functions Versus Subs

Functions return a value, subs do not. Each serves as a mini-program, running the code within them.

Either functions or subs can be run from a form or report event, or from within other VBA subs or functions.

While functions return a value, we don't have to use it. In Figure 13.7, we could have entered the following code:

```
Private Sub CloseCMD_Click()
Dim x
x = CloseOpen("MainMenu")
End Sub
```

In the code for CloseCMD_Click(), you called a function from within a sub, and then passed the function CloseOpen() an argument ("MainMenu"). However, we did nothing with x, which is the returned value.

Functions and Data Types

If functions return a value, how do we determine the data type of the returned value?

The answer is by declaration. When creating and naming new functions that will be used to return values, we declare the data type as part of the function.

```
Public Function myDateRoutine(x,y) as Date
Public Function myLogicRoutine(x,y) as Boolean
Public Function myTextRoutine(x,y) as String
```

Declaring a procedure type, as Date for example, is not required. By default, VBA will assign a procedure type as Variant. In the CloseOpen() example used earlier in this chapter, no declaration was made.

In the case of CloseOpen(), we do not use the function to return a value. Declaring a type for the function in this case is unnecessary.

Modules

Procedures (VBA code) are grouped and saved in modules just as paragraphs are saved in a word-processing documents. When you open a word-processing document, you'll see all the paragraphs you have typed. When you open a VBA module, you'll find all the procedures (functions and subs) for that module.

This process of storing procedures in modules can be transparent when only working with form and report events using the Access Code Builder (refer to Figures 13.5 and 13.6). Access creates a module for your form or report code and saves it with the individual form or report. These are called *class modules*.

However, if you want to write procedures that are available throughout your application, use one or more standard modules. Standard modules are created in the database window with the Modules tab selected.

Deciding whether to place a given procedure in a standard or in a class module is not always evident. Sometimes it becomes a matter of style, because technical or performance reasons may not decisively favor one location (standard or class) over the other. Style is more subjective.

If you are an experienced macro programmer, you may find moving to VBA easier by working with standard modules first. They are analogous to macros in their general availability throughout your application.

Class modules may be more intuitive than standard modules, because you are writing specific code for a single event on an individual form or report.

> **NOTE**
>
> Class modules have a section where you can create procedures that are available throughout the single form or report. Access creates the `(General)` section automatically.

Code in standard modules is easier to maintain than code in class modules. In standard modules, there is only one place to change or debug the code. Code in class modules can be easier to write and debug.

In class modules the keyword `Me` can be used to refer to the object where the code resides. This saves a lot of typing and reduces mistakes.

Events

Events are discrete occurrences when Access checks for instructions, such as a procedure or a macro. If found, the instructions, which may be VBA code in a procedure or lines in macro, are executed.

Forms (or reports), sections of forms, and their controls, have events associated with them.

Events are ordered; for the most part, they occur in a specific sequence. Applications are usually written with VBA code assigned to only a few of the many possible event occurrences.

Table 13.4 lists the number of events for some typical objects.

Table 13.4. Objects and their number of events.

Object	Events
Form	31
FormHeader	5
FormDetail	5
FormFooter	5
Form Text Control	15
Form Label	5
Form Check Box	14
Combo Box	16
Command Button	12
Report	7
Report PageHeader	2
Report Detail	3
Report PageFooter	2

13

GETTING STARTED WITH ACCESS 97 VBA

Figure 13.8 shows the events for a text box control. The Format and Data tabs allow properties such as `format`, `input mask`, default values, and validation rules to be set. These properties can be used in the form Design View, which eliminates the need for VBA code.

A text box can be formatted to display uppercase by setting the `Format` property to > in the text box property sheet. However, as text is entered in the text box, the keyboard setting (upper- or lowercase) determines how the characters appear. Once the user tabs to the next field, the format is applied, forcing the text to uppercase.

For occasions where you would like forced uppercase (such as state abbreviations, alphanumeric customer IDs, and so on), this VBA assigned to the `On Key Press` event of a text box control will uppercase the text as it is typed:

```
Private Sub State_KeyPress(KeyAscii As Integer)
On Error Resume Next
Dim CHARACTER
CHARACTER = Chr(KeyAscii)
KeyAscii = Asc(UCase(CHARACTER))
End Sub
```

FIGURE 13.8.

Events for form text box control.

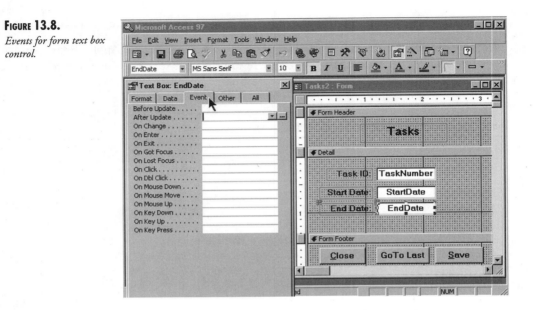

See Access 97 Help | Contents and Index | Index, and search for event procedures for additional (detailed) information.

Methods

Methods might best be accepted for what they do and learned as you need them. Much programming can be done in Access 97 using VBA without being overly conscious of object-oriented programming concepts.

For example, if you have a form in your database named Clients, then

```
DoCmd.OpenForm "Clients"
```

is a valid VBA code statement, which will execute without producing an error.

It happens that DoCmd is an object and OpenForm is a method (sometimes called an object function). The general format or syntax for using a method is:

```
object.method
```

NOTE

The DoCmd object supports 42 methods!

Some commonly used `DoCmd` methods are:

- `DoCmd.Close`
- `DoCmd.RunCommand`
- `DoCmd.FindRecord`
- `DoCmd.Hourglass`
- `DoCmd.Maximize`
- `DoCmd.OpenForm`
- `DoCmd.OpenReport`

> **CAUTION**
>
> In the examples above, only `DoCmd.Close` and `DoCmd.Maximize` can be used alone. The others require one or more arguments, such as a form or report name.

Remember that when a form name is used in VBA code, the form name should be a string data type. The following statements are equivalent:

```
DoCmd.OpenForm "Clients"
```

and

```
Dim strMyFormName
strMyFormName = "Clients"
DoCmd.OpenForm strMyFormName
```

> **TIP**
>
> When using `DoCmd.FindRecord` in VBA for a form, you must set the focus to the control to be searched before executing DoCmd:
>
> ```
> Me![strMfrCode].SetFocus
> DoCmd.FindRecord "ACME"
> ```

Methods are also used for recordsets, such as queries and tables, as in the following example:

```
Dim db as database, r as recordset
Dim fx as string, criteria as string

fx = InputBox("Please enter the Manufacturer Code", _
"Find by Code", "")

If fx = "" Then
 Exit Sub ' or Exit Function
End If
```

```
set db = CurrentDB
Set r = db.OpenRecordset("QryManufacturers")
criteria = "[strMfrCode] = " & Chr(39) & fx & Chr(39)
r.FindFirst criteria

If r.NoMatch Then
 MsgBox "Manufacturer Code " & fx & " not found.", _
 vbInformation, "No Match"
Else
 MsgBox "Manufacturer Code " & fx & " found.", _
 vbExclamation, "Found"
End If

r.close
```

The example above uses two methods (`OpenRecordset` and `FindFirst`) and one property (`NoMatch`).

If you already have a form open based on the recordset to be searched, then you could use this code:

```
Dim fx as string

fx = InputBox("Please enter the Manufacturer Code", _
"Find by Code", " ")

If fx = "" Then
 Exit Sub 'or Exit Function
End If

Me![strMfrCode].SetFocus
DoCmd.FindRecord fx

If Me![strMfrCode] <> fx Then
 MsgBox "Manufacturer Code " & fx & " not found.", _
 vbInformation, "No Match"
Else
 MsgBox "Manufacturer Code " & fx & " found.", _
 vbExclamation, "Found"
End If
End Sub 'or Function
```

Naming Conventions

Working with Access 97, you will make many naming decisions. It is not really much different from naming word-processing documents or spreadsheets. However, Access and VBA do impose some constraints.

Examples of things to be named by users within an Access application include:

- Tables
- Queries
- Forms
- Reports

- Macros
- Modules (standard)
- VBA code variables
- User-defined procedures
- User-defined constants
- Controls such as text boxes and combo boxes

Additionally, Access has a large number of names for intrinsic constants, properties, methods, actions, VBA language keywords, and more.

Choose names to avoid conflicts with VBA and Access. Be descriptive without being overly lengthy. Choose names that cause groups of related objects or collections to sort adjacent to one another. Following a naming convention style makes your project easier to maintain. Standard naming conventions are frequently used for large, multi-programmer projects.

TIP

Avoid assigning names that might duplicate, and therefore potentially conflict with, anything Access or VBA has named. This gets easier with experience.

You will notice that intrinsic constants have a pattern such as `acForm`, `vbCrLf`, and `dbReadOnly`. Easy enough. Within VBA, just avoid starting the names of your variables with the letters `ac`, `vb`, and `db`.

Do not name a user-defined function to conflict with a VBA built-in function or action such as `MsgBox`.

NOTE

Each release of Access (1.0, 1.1, 2.0, Access 95, and now Access 97) has been more forgiving of name conflicts. Access 97 will tolerate some duplicate names by searching in order, such as form (class) module first, and then standard module next. However, this can produce unexpected results. Moral: Name things with care and forethought.

There is one clear area of conflict to be avoided: tables and queries. Because Access treats queries as if they were tables, tables and queries share the same name space. You cannot have both a table named `Customers` and a query named `Customers`.

You might adopt your own naming convention for tables and queries, such as naming tables intuitively (for example, `Customers`) and naming your saved queries descriptively, such as `QryCustomers` or `QryCustomersByID`.

By default, when building a new form based on a recordset (table or query), Access assigns the field name as the control name. You might create a table named `Customers` and include a field named `CustomerID`. Access will assign `CustomerID` as the default name for the control bound to the `CustomerID` field on a new form.

TIP

Avoid spaces in your names. Access will allow spaces in the names of tables, queries, forms, reports, and controls. However, this opens the door to typing mistakes.

Access does not permit spaces to be used with the names for procedures.

There are other restrictions for procedure names. Special characters, such as &, $, #, and almost any other character found above the numbers on your keyboard are not allowed in procedure names.

TIP

Stick to letters, and use upper- and lowercase to make your names readable (for example, `MyOwnFunction`).

NAMING CONVENTIONS AND COMMON SENSE

Because matching data types is a necessary programming evil (although Access lets us fudge a bit by providing the Variant data type), rather strict conventions can be imposed for group (multi-programmer) projects. For learning purposes, naming a text box that is bound to a text field strCustomerName or intCustomerID informs the reader of the underlying field data type.

This is good practice, and good discipline.

The thought police will not audit your individual projects. It might be understood, for example, that a data field named `LastName` or `City` is a text field.

However, what is the data type of a field named `ID`? Is it a text field (perhaps ID can be A-1234) or is it a number field created by the Access AutoNumber feature (ID is 10010)?. It makes a lot of sense to name a control as either strID or sID for text and lngID (lowercase L + ng + ID) or even longID for numbers(as in Long Integer).

Rarely will you not know that a form is a form. But if it helps (or again for instructional purpose), you may decide to name your forms in a pattern such as frmClients.

If you decide to preface query names with qry, you may find it convenient to preface your table names with tbl.

Logic Constructs

VBA code can make decisions or choices. Some typical examples:

- If this is true then…

or

- If that's the case then…

or

- Please choose among the following choices:
  1. A
  2. B
  3. C
  4. None of the above

Making decisions based on conditions is supported in VBA through structured logic statements.

In programming parlance the spoken phrases "this is true," or "that is false" translate into the word "condition." And "choice" becomes "case."

Here is an example of a logic construct in VBA:

```
If Me![curAccountBalance] < 0 Then
 MsgBox "Customer has negative account balance."
End If
```

Another example:

```
If Me![curAccountBalance] < 0 Then
 MsgBox "Customer has negative account balance."
ElseIf Me![curAccountBalance] = 0 Then
 MsgBox "Customer account balance is zero."
ElseIf Me![curAccountBalance] > 0 Then
 MsgBox "Customer account balance is positive."
End If
```

CAUTION

Logical constructs are evaluated from top to bottom, just as they appear when typed. There can be only two outcomes: either one condition evaluates as True or none of the conditions evaluate as True (in which case the code does nothing).

Once a condition evaluates as True, no other conditions are tested, and the program skips to the end of your logical code construction.

When a condition is evaluated as `True`, the program no longer evaluates additional conditions. Because currency account balances are intuitively understood as possibly having only three conditions, our code is complete (we tested for all possible outcomes).

Remember that the program evaluates conditions in order. If it finds a `True` condition, its work is done. Any other conditions not already evaluated (that is, any tests below the line where the `True` condition is found) are not evaluated.

This says nothing about whether conditions not tested are `True` or `False`. They are just not evaluated. Here is an example of code you would not want to use:

```
If Me![curAccountBalance] < 0 Then
 MsgBox "Customer has negative account balance."
ElseIf Me![curAccountBalance] = 0 Then
 MsgBox "Customer account balance is zero."
ElseIf Me![curAccountBalance] > 0 Then
 MsgBox "Customer account balance is positive."
ElseIf (Me![curDeposits] - Me![curWithdrawals]) < 0
 MsgBox "Customer balance has declined."
End If
```

We will never know whether `Withdrawals` exceeded `Deposits`. One of the earlier conditions will evaluate as `True`, and the program skips to `End If`, or more precisely, the program jumps to the next executable statement after the `End If`.

Consider this slightly modified example:

```
If Me![curAccountBalance] < 0 Then
 MsgBox "Customer has negative account balance."
ElseIf Me![curAccountBalance] = 0 Then
 MsgBox "Customer account balance is zero."
ElseIf (Me![curDeposits] - Me![curWithdrawals]) < 0
 MsgBox "Customer balance has declined."
ElseIf Me![curAccountBalance] > 0 Then
 MsgBox "Customer account balance is positive."
End If
```

If `Withdrawals` exceeds `Deposits`, this code will not tell us whether `Account Balance` is still positive! Once `Deposits` minus `Withdrawals` evaluates as `True`, the code is finished.

There is a logical `If ... Then` construct which, if it can find no `True` conditions, permits you to specify code to run. In the following example, notice the use of the `Else` statement:

```
If condition1 Then
 'code to be executed
ElseIf condition2 Then
 'code to be executed
ElseIf condition3 Then
 'code to be executed
Else
 'code if no conditions above evaluate True
End If
```

The conditions we have used in the examples above are sometimes referred to as *expressions*.

Of course, logical constructs can be used for more meaningful work than simply displaying messages. You may create a form and set its `AllowDeletions` property to `No`, because you want to control deletions through VBA code.

```
Dim msg as String, Title as String
Dim DefAns as String, Answer as String

msg = "You have requested that a record be deleted."
msg = msg & " To delete the record, type YES [ENTER]."
msg = msg & vbCrLf & vbCrLf
msg = msg & " Otherwise, choose CANCEL."

Title = "Delete Record Request" ' Set title.

DefAns = "NO"  ' Set default return value.
Answer = ""
Answer = InputBox(msg, Title, DefAns) ' Get user input.
Answer = UCase$(Answer)

If Answer <> "YES" Then
 Exit Sub
End If
'code continues to delete record
```

The user must type the word yes (case insensitive) to delete the record. Otherwise the `If ... Then` construct evaluates as `True`.

If the answer is not equal to YES, we are finished with this entire procedure, so we `Exit Sub`.

Another logical construct is `Select Case`.

 See similar example on the `Clients` form in `PAU13VBA.MDB` on the accompanying CD-ROM.

```
Private Sub PrintCMD_Click()

Dim msg as String, Title as String
Dim DefAns as String, Answer as String

msg = "The report will be sent to the printer."
msg = msg & " Type the letter of your choice:"
msg = msg & vbCrLf & vbCrLf
msg = msg & " C - Sort by Code"
msg = msg & vbCrLf & " N - Sort by Name"
msg = msg & vbCrLf & vbCrLf
msg = msg & " Or click on Cancel."

Title = "Print Manufacturer List"
```

```
DefAns = "N"
Answer = ""
Answer = InputBox(msg, Title, DefAns)
Answer = Trim$(UCase$(Answer))

Select Case Answer
Case "C"
gReportType = 1

Case "N"
gReportType = 2

Case Else
Exit Sub

End Select

DoCmd.OpenReport "rptListManufacturers"
End Sub
```

`Select Case` supports decisions based on ranges. For example

```
Select Case intGrade

Case 90 - 100
MsgBox "Congratulations, you made an A!"

Case 80 - 89
MsgBox "Good work, you made a B."

Case 70 - 79
MsgBox "You made a C."

Case 65 - 69
MsgBox "D is your grade."

Case 0 - 64
MsgBox "See you next year."

End Select
```

`Select Case` is efficient for evaluating expressions because it calculates the test value once. For example

```
Select Case (intMidTerm + intFinal)/2
Case 90 - 100
'other cases
End Select
```

Error Trapping

Errors happen. It is best to accept reality and deal with them. VBA is a programming language, not a source of artificial intelligence.

Beyond five or six lines of code (and sometimes less), professional programmers accept the potential for coding errors. It can be a simple error such as a data type mismatch (If `ID > 1000`, but `ID` can be `ACME`, a string, not a number).

Errors can occur as the result of mistakes in logic, such as not anticipating all the cases in a logical construct.

Errors can happen dynamically, such as when a network is down and the program cannot find an attached database.

Sometimes you intentionally use error reporting to your benefit. Rather than look up a manufacturer code that is a primary key (that is, we do not want duplicate codes), before a user saves a new record, we can use the following code:

```
Private Sub SaveCMD_Click()
Dim Msg as String
On Error Goto TrapIT

'code to check and save new record

EnterHere:

Exit Sub 'important to keep from "falling into" error code
TrapIT:
If Err = 3022 Then
 msg = "The Manufacturer Code you entered is"
 msg = msg & " already assigned."
 MsgBox msg, vbExclamation, "Duplicate Code"
 Me![strMfrCode].SetFocus
Else
 MsgBox CStr(Err) & " " & Error$, vbCritical, "Error"
End If
Resume EnterHere

End Sub
```

`On Error Resume Next` is a valid statement. The program just ignores the statement where the error occurs and continues executing all the statements in the procedure until the program finds an exit or an end statement.

Use error trapping as you write and debug your code. After you have tested the application, you may go back to put in some `On Error Resume Next` statements where it is clear that any errors may safely be ignored.

A good example would be to use `On Error GoTo` to trap one-line procedures that open forms or reports. While you are developing your application, you may rename things. You may mistype names. Error trapping will tell you; however, the VBA development environment will not.

Common Mistakes

Programming is a science and an unforgiving one at that. Other than the occasional interruption caused by hardware failure, computers will execute a program exactly the way we type them.

If we introduce logic mistakes in our programming, the computer will follow right along attempting to execute the program logic, mistakes and all.

Programming is an art. Once the fundamentals of programming are mastered, creating a program can be a rewarding expression of personality and intellect.

This section discusses a few of the more common mistakes found in programming Access VBA.

1. Data type mismatch.

   ```
   Me![strMfrCode] = 100 'doesn't work.
   ```

   Here I am attempting to assign a numerical value to string field. While the Variant data type will accept numerical, string, or date information, Variant cannot be assigned as a field type for table. Here `strMfrCode` refers to a form control that is bound to a table (or query).

2. Data type size violations.

   ```
   Dim intCode as Integer
   intCode = 99,999 'Integer is +/- 32,000. Use Long.
   ```

   Integer data types are stored by the computer with just enough space to accommodate whole numbers only from -32,768 to +32,767. The range of values is limited, not unlike the fact that there are only so many seven-digit telephone numbers possible within one area code.

   The Long (or Long Integer) data type will accommodate whole numbers from –2,147,483,648 to +2,147,483,647.

   These whole number data types (Integer or Long) are used when appropriate, because the computer will perform mathematical calculations faster using whole numbers than it performs calculations using numbers with fractions. Also, whole number data types take fewer bytes to save the information to disk than do fractional numbers.

   For additional information, see Access 97 Help | Contents and Index | Index, and search for `Integer data type`.

3. Unable to reference an `AutoNumber` field.

   Use Long as your data type for variables or in other related tables.

   Often `AutoNumber` fields need to be referenced in your VBA code. There is no AutoNumber data type in VBA.

TIP

When you set referential integrity between two tables where the first table has an `AutoNumber` field, create a field in the second table and assign its field type to `Number`, `Long Integer`. Now you can relate the two tables from the `AutoNumber` field in the first table to the `Long Integer` field in the second table.

4. Violating table definition rules from a form.

   In a table design, you set `Required` as `Yes` for `FirstName`, then try to save a record without a `FirstName` from a form.

   When saving data on a form to the form's underlying table or query, any validation rules established in the table design must be followed. Otherwise, attempting to save the form (record) will produce an error. Similarly, fields specified as `Required` in the table design, cannot be blank (or `Null`) when saving a form based on that table.

5. Leaving multiple forms open.

   Returning to your `MainMenu` usually implies that you can close the form that you are leaving.

   For example, if you use the Toolbox Wizard to create a command button to open a form, the Wizard generates and assigns some VBA code to the command button's `On Click` event.

   While the code will open the target form, the wizard does not automatically include code to close the form where you placed the command button.

   In many cases, this is harmless. But in the case of multiuser applications, leaving a form open after the user is finished with that form can restrict the ability of other users to edit and add records. It is good practice to close forms through your code (especially data-entry forms) when they no longer need to open.

6. Incomplete logic constructs.

   Did you think of all the possibilities?

   Using Debug | Compile... will find many coding errors. But the Access VBA compiler cannot verify the completeness of your code. When using logic constructs such as `If ... Then` and `Select Case`, consider carefully the conditions tested. Have you identified all the possible conditions (or ranges of conditions)?

7. Trying to use too many events before understanding their meaning and sequence.

   Do you really know the difference between `After Update` and `On Change` for a text box?

   Access 97 is an event-rich programming environment. The command button, for example, has 12 events, each could be assigned a VBA procedure. But the reality is that you will normally use only one or two of them (`On Click` and `Dbl Click`).

   Do not think that you must learn every possible event. Choose a few, and master them.

8. No error trapping.

   Just do it!

   What you want to create are reliable applications. Error trapping will report errors as you develop your application, and error trapping will allow your users to recover from real-world happenings, such as network interruptions.

9. Focusing your development efforts on appearance before functionality.

   First you get it right, then you make it pretty.

   Many first time VBA developers conquer the aesthetics of putting graphic images on command buttons and creating forms with nice background images and unique color combinations. Just remember, that solid code is what makes the program useful (or even usable at all).

   Concentrate first on solid code.

10. Failure to think it through.

    All true programmers love to "lay down code." Think about what needs to be done first. With Access 97 it is easy to create a maze of forms and stored queries.

    Don't be in a hurry. For example, sometimes it is more efficient to create queries from within a class or standard module than it is to create and save a query for every occasion.

Summary

Access VBA is a language that you can learn at your own pace and comfort level. The Access 97 IDE (Integrated Development Environment) provides much help along the way. And speaking of help, the Access 97 Help file is extensive.

Learning VBA, then using it to assist you in developing applications, can be a lot of work. Proceed at your own pace. Over time, you will find that your efforts are rewarded with powerful user-friendly applications.

As you progress, you will likely find that the central question of your programming efforts is not "Can it be done?," but rather the discovery of *how* it can be done. Access 97 with VBA is a strong application development tool.

Access 97 VBA for Developers

by Dave Thompson

IN THIS CHAPTER

CHAPTER

14

This chapter assumes that you have some experience with Access Basic (Access versions 1.0, 1.1, and 2.0), Access 95 VBA, or both.

WHAT DO WE CALL IT?

In less than five years, Microsoft has shipped five versions of Access, three 16-bit (Windows 3.x) versions (1.0, 1.1, and 2.0), and now two 32-bit (Win 95/NT) versions (7.0 and 8.0). Fortunately, Microsoft has consistently provided a high degree of backward compatibility.

Access 7.0 was more commonly called Access 95, and Access 8.0 is most commonly referred to as Access 97. When searching the Microsoft Knowledge Base on the Internet (`www.microsoft.com/kb`), you might even see references to Access versions 2.0, 7.0, and 97.

Version numbers are consistently used when referring to Access 1.0, 1.1, and 2.0. With the release of Access 95 (that is, version 8.0), Access 95 references revert to its version number: 7.0.

New and Improved in Access 97

Because you may be upgrading from either Access 2.0 or Access 7.0 (Access 95), I will include changes from both 2.0 to 97 and from 7.0 to 97. Remember that although version 2.0 uses Access Basic, it is about as close to Access VBA as you can get without calling it VBA.

I might as well start with the really new stuff: hyperlinks!

Hyperlinks

Access 97 supports a new table field data type: hyperlink.

A *hyperlink* is a text field with three component parts delineated by the # sign. However, not all three parts are required.

Hyperlinks can point to a Web page (Internet or intranet) through its URL (Universal Resource Locator) or to a file, using the absolute or relative UNC (Universal Naming Convention) address.

The format of a hyperlink field is

`displaytext#address#subaddress`

The *displaytext* is what appears in a table or query datasheet view or on a form control. *displaytext* is always an optional entry (use # as a placeholder). If *displaytext* is blank (empty), Access will display the first nonblank entry looking at *address* first, and then at *subaddress*.

The *address* is a Web URL or UNC. It is optional only when a hyperlink is used to navigate within the same database; otherwise it is required.

The UNC address is used to navigate between files, such as Word documents, Excel books, or other Access databases. The files can be either local (to machine) or on a LAN. The following are some valid address examples (the middle part of the hyperlink field):

- `\\server\public\documents\Status.DOC`
- `D:\MSOffice97\Test.DOC`
- `D:\MSOffice97\Office\Samples\Northwind.MDB`
- `D:\MSOffice97\Test.XLS`

The *subaddress* is optional except when using a hyperlink to navigate within the same database. An example of the entire field for navigating within the same database is `##Form Customers` (note the space between the target object type, `Form`, and the target name, `Customers`).

The *subaddress* can be used to go to a bookmark in Word or to a range in Excel.

Figure 14.1 shows a sample table with entries for some uses of the hyperlink field.

FIGURE 14.1.
The table Datasheet View of `HyperLinkExamples`.

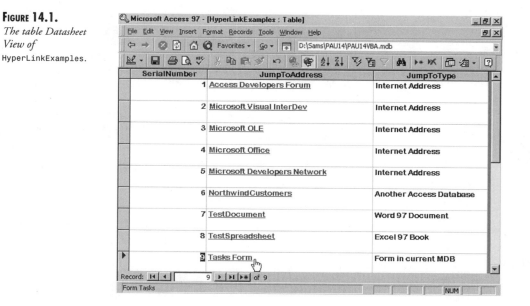

14

ACCESS 97 VBA FOR DEVELOPERS

> **CAUTION**
>
> To edit a hyperlink field from a Datasheet or Form View, tab to the field you want to edit, and press the F2 key. If you click on a hyperlink field or control to set the focus, the link will execute.

The full text of the data in the sample table is given in Figure 14.2. Access normally prints only the *displaytext* part of a hyperlink field, whereas the report uses a function to print the value of the field. The value is the entire entry for the field. For example,

```
FullHyperLinkField = Me![JumpToAddress].Value
```

In Figure 14.2, the function `FullHyperLinkField` is used to print the information labeled `Full text:` on the report.

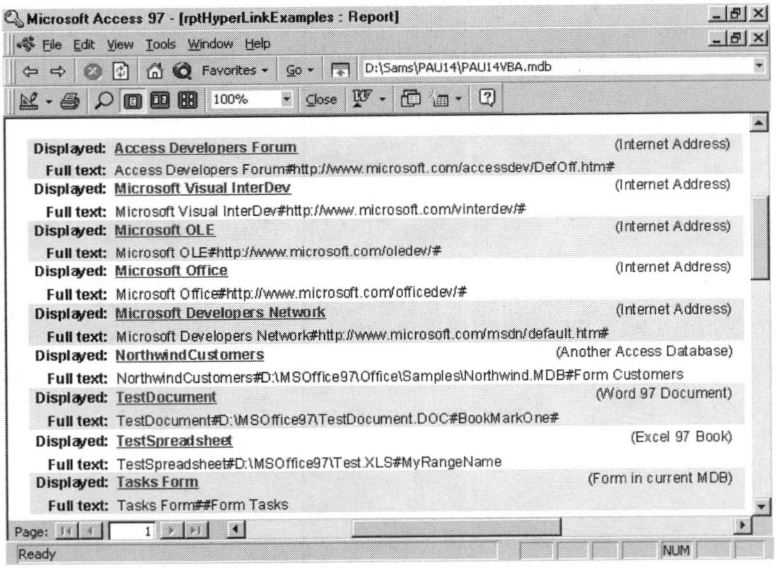

FIGURE 14.2.

Hyperlink entries for the sample table in Figure 14.1.

To support hyperlinks, the following properties are new to Access 97:

- ▪ `Hyperlink`
- ▪ `HyperlinkPart`
- ▪ `HyperlinkAddress`
- ▪ `HyperlinkSubAddress`

For the `Hyperlink` property, four new intrinsic constants can be used:

- `acDisplayedValue`
- `acDisplayText`
- `acAddress`
- `acSubAddress`

New methods have been added as well:

- `Follow`
- `FollowHyperlink`
- `AddToFavorites`

Hyperlink addresses and subaddresses can be assigned to these controls, which now support the *address* and *subaddress* properties:

- Label
- Image
- Command button

On reports, hyperlinks can be placed on label or image controls.

Of course, for bound forms, `Hyperlink` fields can be the control source for all controls supporting string data such as text, lists, and combo boxes. When displayed through bound controls, the control becomes a hot spot, and the link can be launched by clicking on the control in the form Normal (runtime) View.

USING HYPERLINKS ON FORMS WITH BOUND CONTROLS

When using hyperlinks on forms with bound controls, user interface issues might be considered. The style of *displaytext#address#subaddress* might not be intuitive for your users to edit. Also, it may be easy to launch a link accidentally.

Consider writing your own routines for users to dynamically add or edit link targets. You might even maintain reference tables of commonly used targets.

You may decide to overlay form hyperlink controls with a transparent command button. This allows you to write your own procedure to navigate the link. Here is an example of a procedure you can use to navigate a link that could be attached to the double-click event of a command button:

```
Private Sub GoToLinkCMD_DblClick(Cancel As Integer)
Dim vAdr, vSubAdr 'use variant
Dim intAdr As Integer, intSubAdr As Integer
```

continues

14

```
continued

'JumpToAddress is a bound text control

vAdr = HyperlinkPart(Me![JumpToAddress], acAddress)
vSubAdr = HyperlinkPart(Me![JumpToAddress], acSubAddress)

intAdr = Len(vAdr)
intSubAdr = Len(vSubAdr)

If intAdr > 0 Then 'have address
If intSubAdr > 0 Then 'plus subaddress
FollowHyperlink CStr(vAdr), CStr(vSubAdr)
 Else
FollowHyperlink CStr(vAdr) 'no subaddress
End If
Else
 MsgBox "Address not found.", vbExclamation, " "
End If
End Sub
```

This technique works especially well for continuous forms.

For help topics on hyperlinks, choose Access 97 Help | Contents and Index | Index, and search for `hyperlinks`.

Methods

If you are moving from Access 2.0 to Access 97, you will find dozens of new methods. Many of the help screens in the Access 97 help file list what's new for Access 2.0 users along with what's new for Access 95 (that is, version 7.0) users.

New objects or collections for Access 97 include the following:

- `Module` object
- `Modules` collection
- `Page` object
- `Pages` collection
- `Reference` object
- `References` collection

NOTE

For 2.0 users, these objects were first added or changed in 7.0 (Access 95):

- DoCmd (Now an object, `object.method` syntax)
- Debug (Changes made)

- Err object
- Errors collection (DAO)
- Connection object

Table 14.1 lists several new methods found in Access 97.

Table 14.1. New methods in Access 97.

Method	Where Used/Comment
AddFromFile	Module (standard or class)
AddFromFile	References collection
CreateEventProc	Class (form) module
Find	Module (standard or class)
Follow	Hyperlinks
FollowHyperlink	Hyperlinks
InsertLines	Module (standard or class)
InsertText	Module (standard or class)
RefreshDatabaseWindow	Application object
RunCommand	DoCmd method (replaces DoMenuItem)

DoCmd.RunCommand supports 334 intrinsic constants.

RefreshDatabaseWindow refreshes the display of collections shown in the database window, such as tables, queries, forms, reports, macros, and modules. If you've ever been adding to or deleting from collections through code and couldn't find the changes in the database window, look at this one.

> **NOTE**
>
> For 2.0 users, the help file methods reference file in 2.0 lists 64 methods. The help file methods reference file in Access 97 lists 150 methods. Later in this chapter, I address some coding issues to migrate your code from 2.0 to Access 97.

Properties

Access 97 adds several dozen properties to those available in Access 7.0. Many of these relate to ODBCDirect. Through ODBCDirect workspaces, you can access ODBC data sources without loading the Jet Engine.

Table 14.2 is a sample list of new properties not directly associated with ODBCDirect technology.

Table 14.2. New Properties in Access 97.

Property	*Where Used/Comment*
Assistant	Reference to Assistant object
Builtin	Tests whether reference required
CommandBars	Reference to collection
DatasheetBackColor	Read/Write (table, query, and form)
DatasheetForeColor	Read/Write in VBA
HasModule	Lightweight forms and reports
Hyperlink	Hyperlinks
HyperlinkAddress	Hyperlinks
HyperlinkSubAddress	Hyperlinks
IsBroken	Check reference against Registry
IsVisible	Check to see whether this is so (form, report)
Item	Collection member (position/name)
Kind	VBA project or type library
MDE	String (db.properties("MDE"))
MousePointer	Change it
OLEData	Copy it (ActiveX)
ProjectName	Read/Write
Style	Tab control
Toolbar	Custom displayed on form/report

> **NOTE**
>
> For a comprehensive list of properties, choose Access 97 Help | Contents and Index | Index, and search for properties, Visual Basic properties reference topics.

For a complete listing of `ODBCDirect` properties, select Access 97 Help | Contents and Index | Index, and search for `data access properties`.

Events

Access 97 adds few new events. For class modules, the `Initialize` event and `Terminate` event were added. To use with references added and deleted within a project, `ItemAdded` and `ItemRemoved` events were added, respectively.

For a comprehensive list of Access 97 events, select Access 97 Help | Contents and Index, and search for `events, listed alphabetically`.

NOTE

In the Form Design View for a 2.0 form, there are 59 events and properties listed for assignment. For Access 97 forms, there are 77 properties and events listed under View Properties | All in the Form Design View.

Constants

As Microsoft adds more functionality and features to Access, each new release has a more extensive list of intrinsic constants. Sometimes the old ones remain functional (as entered in your 2.0 code) for backward compatibility.

If you're moving from Access 7.0, look for additions to the list of available intrinsic constants. Also, check some of your old standbys. For example, `DoCmd.Close` with no arguments works. In Access 97, the recommended syntax to close the object where the statement resides (a form or report, for example) is `DoCmd.Close acDefault`.

Other changes for the everyday `DoCmd` methods of `OpenForm` and `OpenReport` are the action constants `acViewNormal`, `acViewPreview`, and `acViewDesign`.

Some of the changes and additions were prompted by the new Integrated Development Environment (IDE).

IDE

Because VBA is now consistently implemented across the major components of Office 97 (Access, Word, Excel, and PowerPoint), IDE certainly makes sense. VBers will appreciate the project-oriented approach of IDE.

14

ACCESS 97 VBA FOR DEVELOPERS

Access Basic and VBA users moving from version 7.0, will find IDE helpful. IDE has several customization options to alter the programming environment. By changing a few defaults here and there, you can establish a comfortable coding environment.

How far have we come? Figure 14.3 shows the dialog box for View | Options | Module Design called from the database window in Access 2.0.

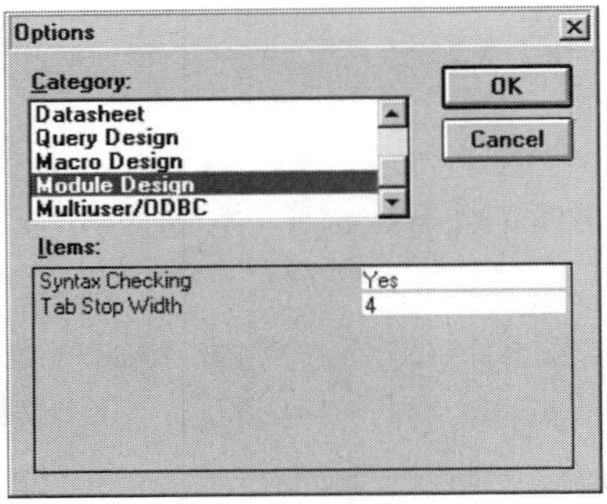

FIGURE 14.3.

Module design options in Access 2.0.

Figure 14.4 shows the Tools | Options | Module tab called from the database window in Access 97. As you can see, it's a bit different.

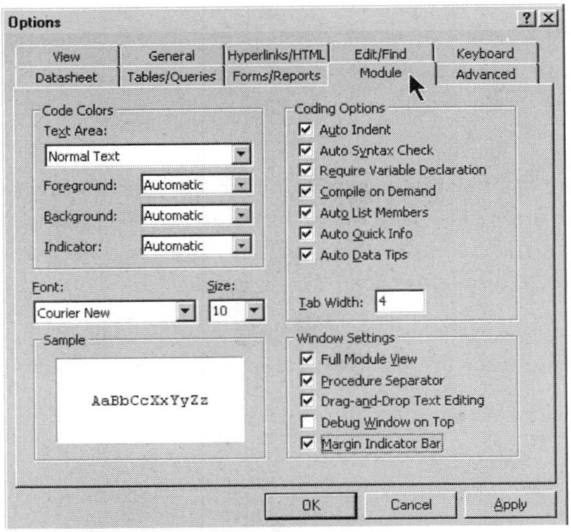

FIGURE 14.4.

The Module tab in Access 97.

One example of the enhanced environment for coding provided by IDE is Auto List Members, as shown in Figure 14.5. After entering `DoCmd.`, the auto list box opens. Auto Quick Info offers syntax and action constant help.

You can type through this help, meaning the help window automatically closes if you continue typing the full code without picking from the offered list.

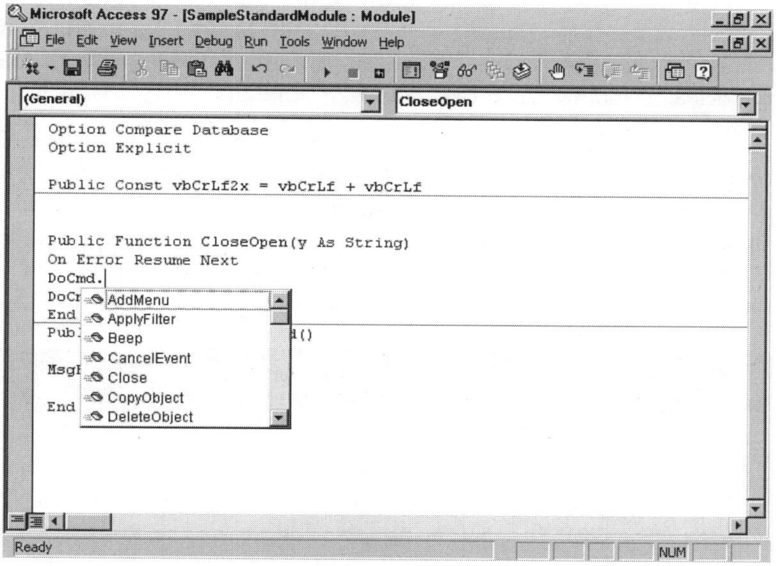

FIGURE 14.5.

The Auto List Members box in module Design View.

When you create a new database, Access assigns a project name that defaults to the database name. The project name can be changed through VBA code or set from the database window, Tools | Options, Advanced tab.

> **NOTE**
>
> If you copy a database to another name or rename a database, the project name will remain the same. If you want a new project name for the database, remember to change it from the database window, Tools | Options, Advanced tab.

For information about sharing project public procedures across databases (to include .MDB, .MDE, or .MDA), see Access 97 Help | Contents and Index and search for MDE files.

MDE

Access 97 supports saving a database as an MDE file instead of an MDB. An MDE database can be thought of as something between a full source code database and a runtime database created with ODE (or the Access Distribution Toolkit (ADT) for earlier versions). Creating an MDE database is much easier than creating a runtime with ODE 97 (or the ADT for Access 2.0 or 7.0).

14

ACCESS 97 VBA
FOR DEVELOPERS

An MDE file is created from the database window by selecting Tools | Database Utilities | Make MDE File.

This creates a fully functional database (with the extension .MDE) from which the source code has been stripped (leaving the p-code). The MDE does not permit design changes to forms, reports, or modules (the modules are empty of source code anyway). Additionally, a user cannot delete or modify any forms, reports, or modules.

P-code, or pseudocode (packed code for the C programmers), is essentially compiled binary code executed in an interpretive mode (that is, line-by-line). It is a Microsoft technology dating back to the "BASIC Wars" (see the following sidebar). P-code might be described as "binary interpretive," meaning that a PC processes the program code line-by-line (typical of interpretive languages) but doesn't have to compile each line because it is already compiled into its binary equivalent.

NOTE

Interpretive, compiled, object code and machine code are topics beyond the scope of our discussion. It is really not necessary to understand them to enjoy the benefits to you as an Access developer. For all Access applications using VBA, the benefit is speed. P-code, as integral to Access VBA, makes MDE possible.

In the Design View for modules (either class or standard), p-code is what is created when you choose one of the compile options from the Debug menu (Compile Loaded Modules, Compile All Modules, Compile and Save All Modules).

THE BASIC WARS

In 1981, the original IBM PC shipped with PC-DOS 1.0. Included with PC-DOS was BASIC 1.0, a BASIC interpreter written by Microsoft. Also included was a set of sample BASIC programs that, lore has it, was written in one weekend by Bill Gates. Gates, along with Paul Allen, first wrote a BASIC interpreter for the Altair personal computer circa 1975.

The first BASIC compilers for the PC were written by Microsoft and marketed by IBM as BASCOM 1.0 and BASCOM 2.0. Following that, Microsoft began marketing a BASIC compiler under the Microsoft name as QuickBASIC (and later as the Professional Development System).

During the QuickBASIC years, Borland International was marketing a BASIC product called Turbo BASIC. The products went head-to-head in the marketplace, and a features-and-performance shoot-out began.

The birth of p-code for BASIC occurred as Microsoft implemented an early version of the p-code technology in its QuickBASIC product. The result was astounding, for its time: numbers of lines-of-code compiled and executed per second in an interpretive development environment.

So today, as Access developers, we enjoy the benefits of VBA and can have some appreciation for its lineage.

Your forms or reports cannot be exported from an MDE database.

The project name associated with an MDE file is fixed when the MDE is created.

CAUTION

In some respects, an MDE is equivalent to a compiled executable. Remember, the MDB file is your source code. Forewarned is forearmed!

Figure 14.6 shows the Forms tab database window of an MDE database. Notice that the Design button and the New button are dimmed (not enabled). The same applies to reports and modules; their designs cannot be viewed. New forms, reports, or modules cannot be added from the database window.

Forms, reports, and modules cannot be deleted. Pressing the Delete key with one of these objects highlighted in the database window does nothing.

FIGURE 14.6.

The Forms tab in the database window for an MDE database.

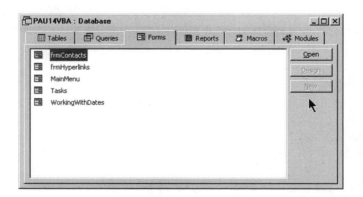

However, as Figure 14.7 shows, tables and queries are accessible from the database window of an MDE file. The table or query design can be viewed and changed. Tables and queries can be added or deleted.

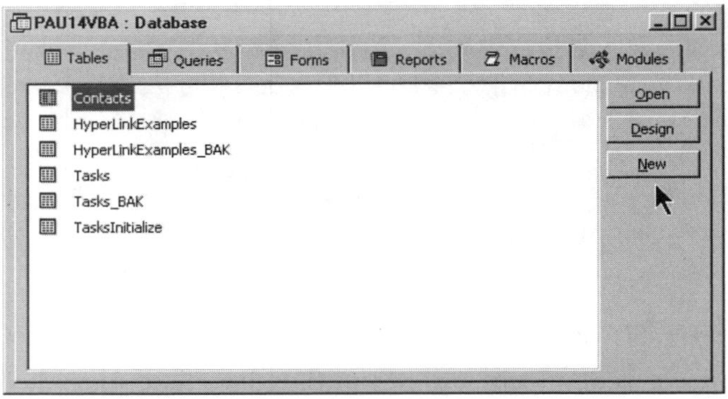

Figure 14.7.

The Tables tab in the database window for an MDE database.

> **NOTE**
>
> Using MDE with linked tables in a front-end/back-end configuration is less susceptible to inadvertent changes. Deleting a linked table does not delete the table, but instead deletes the connection reference to the table.
>
> This also applies to linked tables in a program module MDB file: Deleting a linked table just deletes the link reference, not the actual table.

MDE is not a silver bullet. Your forms, reports, and modules are protected, stored queries and tables within the MDE file are not.

For many projects, MDE can be the preferred method of distributing code (even beta) to users. MDE is straightforward to create. If you are accustomed to using the Access security model (workgroups) for source protection and stabilization of deliverables (once installed), MDE will save you a lot of time.

Sample Databases

The default installation of Office 97 or Access 97 may not install all available demo databases for Access 97. Select Access 97 Help | Contents and Index | Index, and search for `sample databases` and `applications` for additional information about installing and using the `Northwind`, `Orders`, and `Solutions` MDBs.

Migrating to Access 97

If you are migrating an application to Access 97 from Access 2.0, your Win APIs will be 16-bit and must be changed to their 32-bit equivalents.

To convert a database, choose File | Open Database from Access 97, select the old database, and then click Open. Now click the Convert Database button.

When converting code containing 16-bit calls, Access will notify you via the dialog box shown in Figure 14.8. The conversion usually will proceed, so you can edit out the 16-bit APIs from your 97 version database.

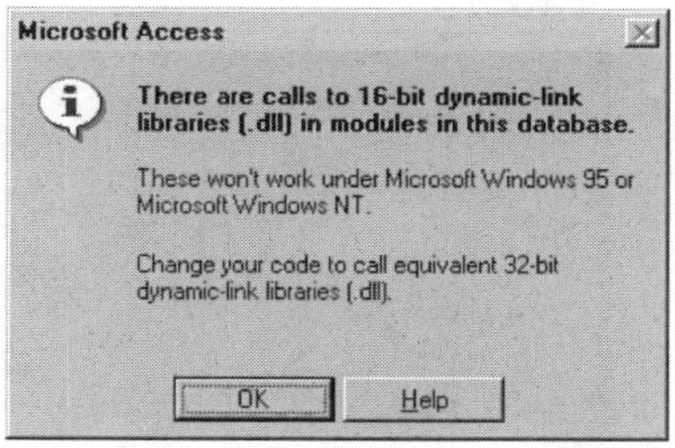

Figure 14.8.

A database conversion error message.

In the database converted in Figure 14.8, the conversion ran to completion after OKing the warning message. In this database, the 16-bit procedures were located in one module. With Access 97 still running, this module was loaded in Design View. Selecting Run | Go/Continue (or Debug | Compile All Modules) located the first error related to the use of 16-bit calls. This error is shown in Figure 14.9.

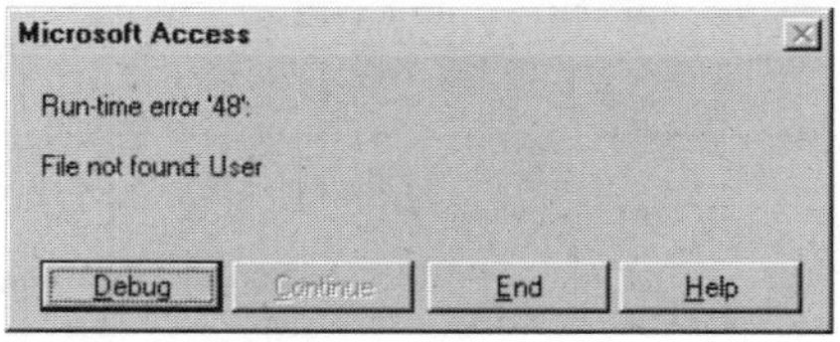

Figure 14.9.

A database conversion error flagged by Access 97.

Many conversion issues relate to obsolete methods or changes to Access objects. The way recordsets are handled has changed (albeit sometimes slightly) with each release.

Frequently, developers use the same technique throughout an application, such as table seeks or queries with `FindFirst`.

To edit all occurrences of an instance of code, open a module in Design View, and use Edit | Find (with Search Current Database checked) to search all the code in your database. In Figure 14.10, Find was used to locate the declaration for the offending `FindWindow` method shown in Figure 14.9.

For Access 7.0 migrations, expect few problems, if any. If your Access 7.0 database was itself migrated from Access 2.0, you might want to clean up the use of obsolete techniques that Access 97 supports (backward compatibility). If not, your code might be on borrowed time.

Table 14.3 lists a few areas to consider when converting Access 2.0 databases to Access 97.

14

ACCESS 97 VBA FOR DEVELOPERS

FIGURE 14.10.

Using Find to search the entire database.

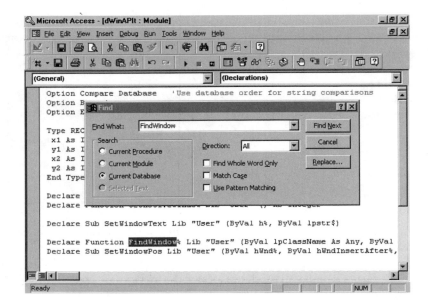

Table 14.3. Typical Access 2.0 conversion issues.

2.0 Example	Access 97
DoCmd OpenForm	DoCmd.OpenForm (DoCmd object)
DefaultEditing	AllowEdits, AllowAdditions, AllowDeletions
A_FORM	acForm (Style for constants)
DB_OPEN_TABLE	dbOpenTable
General module	Standard module (database window)
Global Const	Public Const
Global myVar as String	Public myVar as String
User, Kernel, GDI (.DLL)	User32.DLL, and so on (32-bit APIs)
Explicit transactions	Use Workspace object
set db = DBEngine(0)(0)	set db = CurrentDB
db.OpenTable	db.OpenRecordSet
DBEngine.FreeLocks	DBEngine.Idle
OpenQueryDef	QueryDefs collection

Table 14.3 shows that after converting, you should look around in all areas: properties, methods, constants, and especially recordset methods.

Access will fix a few things during conversion, such as converting `DoCmd OpenForm` to `DoCmd.OpenForm` (`DoCmd`, space, method becomes `DoCmd`, dot, method). However, it will not change `A_FORM` to `acForm`. The application will run, but consider using the new constructions uniformly. Remember that Edit | Find can search across the entire database.

CAUTION

Edit | Replace also can be set to make replacements across the entire database. Use with caution! If you select Current Database and then click Replace All, that is exactly what will happen. Remember that the operation is being performed against your VBA code only.

Consider the impact of globally changing something like `Cust` to `Customer`. `CustID` becomes `CustomerID`, but if `CustID` references a control name, the name is changed in your VBA code. Any related controls on your forms are not renamed.

`Me![CustomerID]`, used in VBA to refer to a control on a form, will produce a runtime error if you do not manually change the control name in the form's Design View.

For additional information, choose Microsoft Access 97 Help | Contents and Index | Index, and search for `converting databases` and `obsolete features in DAO`. Check out the Access Developers Forum on the Microsoft network (`www.microsoft.com/accessdev`) for articles discussing conversion issues. You can also search Microsoft's Knowledge Base (`www.microsoft.com/kb`) for `Access 97`.

NOTE

There is one solution that you can use in a worst-case scenario when you cannot get a database to convert: create a new Access 97 database. Start by importing your objects from the old version (maybe in groups, such as all forms). Compile and isolate!

CAUTION

If converting from 2.0, keep 2.0 on your machine or on a machine to which you have access until your applications are successfully converted.

Error Trapping and Recovery

Though not always the most riveting part of developing an application, handling errors is a necessity.

Informative error messages with suggested recovery will impact the reception your hard work receives from users.

During development, error trapping will save a lot of headaches and prevent code from stopping. Trapping can reveal many, but not all, logic errors in your code, such as cases not handled.

Errors can be used as a planned part of your code, such as allowing a save attempt on new records and trapping for Error 3022 (`Duplicate value in key ...`). This can save lots of `DCounts`, particularly when you know that the user wants to save the record and only made a mistake deciding upon a new unique key.

Err Object

The `Err` object reports VBA errors. As you might expect, `Err` has properties and methods. It even has a default property, `Number`, which is why the statement `MsgBox Cstr(Err)` works.

The `Err` object has six properties:

- Description
- HelpContext
- HelpFile
- LastDLLError
- Number
- Source

and two methods:

- Clear
- Raise

When an error occurs, the `Err` object returns its properties as variant, which is why `MsgBox Err.Number` does not itself return an error. (`MsgBox` is in this case expecting a string argument.)

The subtypes for the returned properties are

- Description is vbString
- HelpContext is vbString
- HelpFile is vbString
- LastDLLError is vbLong
- Number is vbLong
- Source is vbLong

For a list of VBA-trappable errors, choose Access 97 Help | Contents and Index | Index, and search for `trappable errors`. Data Access Objects (DAO) can produce errors that the `Err` object will report. DAO itself also supports an `Errors` collection.

Error Trapping within Procedures

VBA code is written procedure by procedure. That's where errors are trapped for, procedure by procedure. This may seem tedious at first, but it does become second nature (especially after a few crashes here and there).

Errors in code procedures occur when VBA cannot execute the code, or, in other words, cannot complete some code statement. If error trapping has been enabled through an `On Error` statement in your code, VBA will respond to an error as specified in the `On Error` statement.

There are two basic constructions for error-handling routines: `On Error GoTo` and in-line trapping. `On Error GoTo` jumps to the line label you specify, and VBA executes the next code it finds there.

For in-line trapping, tell VBA to ignore errors, but put code to check at specific points in the procedure to see if an error occurred. This works because, even though VBA is told to ignore errors, it does know when one occurs and will set an error code. Examples of both types of constructions for error-handling routines are presented in the following note.

> **NOTE**
>
> When a procedure is exited by either an exit statement (`Exit Sub` or `Exit Function`) or by reaching its end (`End Sub` or `End Function`), VBA clears its memory of any errors. You must start over with each new procedure. This is somewhat of a simplification because procedures can call other procedures (nested procedures). This gets into an area not covered here: calling trees or calls list.
>
> For more information on error handling in nested procedures, choose Access 97 Help | Contents and Index | Index, and search for `calls list`, searching for `error handler`.

Here is a basic example of using a `GoTo` style:

```
Private Sub SaveCMD_Click()
On Error GoTo TrapIT
'
' code to save record
'
EnterHere:  'line label, be sure to append colon
Exit Sub 'don't fall into error routine

TrapIT:
MsgBox Err.Number & " - " & Err.Description
Resume EnterHere 'no colon after line label as target

End Sub
```

CAUTION

Keep your error routines (for example, TrapIT) short and to the point. Do not introduce new errors while processing the last one.

If you know some specific errors that may occur based on the context of the procedure, use a logic construct to provide more information to the user, such as

```
TrapIT:
If Err.Number = 3022 Then
 'tried to save new record with duplicate primary key
 'MsgBox with information for user
 ' we could put a Resume statement here
 'and after each individual case
Else
 'something else
 MsgBox Err.Number & " - " & Err.Description
End If
Resume EnterHere
End Sub
```

Normally, it's informative to report the error number and description as returned by VBA or DAO. You can add your context-sensitive message or display only your custom message.

```
TrapIT:
MsgBox "An error occurred while saving the Record"
Resume EnterHere
```

or

```
TrapIT
strMsg = "An error occurred while saving the record."
strMsg = strMsg & " Please note the number and"
strMsg = strMsg & " description shown below."
strMsg = strMsg & vbCrLf & vbCrLf
strMsg = strMsg & Err.Number & " - " & Err.Description
MsgBox strMsg
Resume EnterHere
```

Here is an example of in-line error trapping using the Err object:

```
Private Sub SaveCMD_Click()
On Error Resume Next 'force procedure to continue
'
' code to save record
'
If Err.Number > 0 Then
 MsgBox Err.Number & " - " & Err.Description
 Err.Clear
End IF

End Sub
```

This example looks smooth and uses fewer lines of code, but if you have more than one error in your code when it executes, this will report only the last one.

Error-Message Text

Simulating the VBA error can discover the text of VBA errors. For example,

```
On Error GoTo TrapIT
Err.Clear
Err.Raise 91
```

will return `Object variable or With block variable not set` as `Err.Description`.

`Err.Raise` cannot be used to test for the text of DAO errors. Instead, use `AccessError()`, such as in this example:

```
MsgBox AccessError(3022)
```

This returns the full text of the DAO error, which begins as follows:

```
The changes you requested to the table were not successful because ....
```

Tricks, Traps, and Techniques

This section assumes you have a moderate amount of proficiency with Access and VBA. Many examples will be fragments of common tasks associated with developing Access projects. In some cases, I present a foundation giving the example a broader base and a more complete discussion.

Experienced developers will quickly recognize where the fragments can be used. Many developers already will have conquered the tasks illustrated, sometimes in a more elegant way.

It seems an almost invariant rule of programming that there is always more than one way to do something.

Linked Tables

Splitting an application into a program module (MDB/MDE) and a data module (MDB/MDE) is commonplace for experienced developers. The data module—as its name implies—has your data tables and only your data tables.

The program module contains your saved queries, forms, reports, macros, and standard modules. Depending upon your programming style, you may use the program MDB for temp tables.

If you've ever had to support production software in which the data was not split from the program, you might have uttered more than once, "Never again!" With the program split from the data, you can modify the application offline, replace the old program module with the new, check your table links (sometimes called attachments), and you're finished. However, if you make changes to the table structures or indexes, consider the impact on your program module.

For example, the table SEEK method requires an index name. Typically, you will hard code this name. If the index name is later changed in the data MDB, an error will occur.

Similarly, watch for field length changes, especially shortening text fields. This can produce `Data to long to paste` errors when editing or adding records.

If you change a field type in the data after the code is developed, you should carefully and thoroughly test it against your existing code.

> **NOTE**
>
> If the linked tables are in an Access database (that is, an MDB file), table type methods such as `Seek` can be used. Some older versions of Access restrict you to dynaset methods, even if the attached table was in an Access database. Access 97 opens data sets as recordsets using `db.OpenRecordset`.

> **TIP**
>
> Set referential integrity in the data MDB.

One of the issues of managing linked tables through VBA is finding the location of the data MDB. Its relative location usually changes from the development environment to the production (or customer) environment. In Chapter 18, "Empowering ActiveX Controls with VBA," I show how to use the ActiveX Common Dialog control to permit the user to navigate to and retrieve the path and filename of another database (such as the data MDB in a split database configuration). For now, I will give an example using the `Orders` sample database (which uses Win API calls).

The sample code to find a database through a dialog box is contained in the `Orders` sample database that comes with Access 97. Open `Orders.MDB` (or make a copy and open the copy).

> **TIP**
>
> Hold down the left Shift key when opening `Orders.MDB` to defeat the startup form.

From the database window Forms tab, open a new form and insert a command button. Add this code to the command button's `OnClick` event:

```
Private Sub FindMdbCMD_Click()
Dim strMyPath As String
strMyPath = FindNorthwind("")

If strMyPath = "" Then
 MsgBox "User canceled."
Else
```

```
 MsgBox strMyPath
End If

End Sub
```

Figure 14.11 shows the dialog box opened by the `OnClick` event.

Figure 14.11.

Using a dialog box to find MDB files.

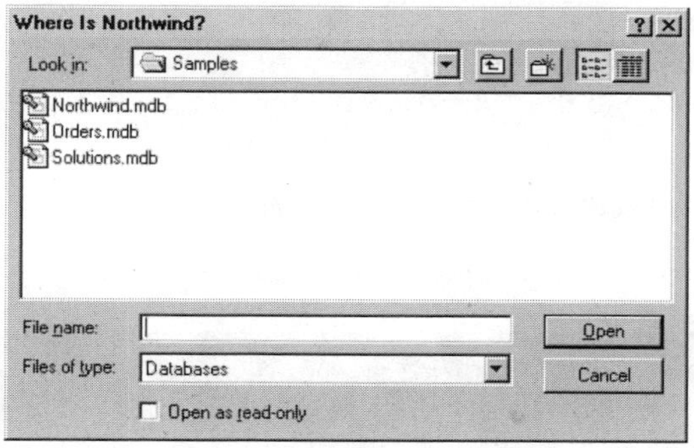

Figure 14.12.

The returned full path to the selected database.

Figure 14.12 shows the returned full path for this example.

The `Connect` property of linked tables will be needed for some of the examples that follow. It is a property of a `TableDef` object (one table), which in turn is a member of the `TableDefs` collection (one or more tables).

Open a linked table in the Design View and select View | Properties. The description tells something about the connect string. However, this string is not the exact connect string. Figure 14.13 shows the table properties for the linked table `Orders`.

Figure 14.13.

An example of the table description for a linked table.

The `TableDefs` property `Connect` can be used to find the connect string, as the following example shows:

```
Private Sub DisplayConnectCMD_Click()
Dim db As Database, td As TableDef
Set db = CurrentDb
Set td = db.TableDefs("Orders")
MsgBox td.Connect
End Sub
```

The `Orders` table in the `Orders.MDB` is a linked table, physically located in `Northwind.MDB`. The code, used from the `Orders.MDB`, shows the connect string to be (in this case)

```
;DATABASE=D:\MSOFFICE97\OFFICE\Samples\Northwind.mdb
```

The `;` (semicolon) is a placeholder indicating that the linked table is a Microsoft Jet database.

> **NOTE**
>
> In the examples that follow, linked tables are assumed to be Microsoft Jet (Access) databases.

Searching Recordsets with VBA

Saved (or stored) queries provide a lot of functionality, such as views of joined tables. Saved queries can also use parameters by asking for user input at execution time. Often you will know the parameter already (it may be a value from a form control), or you may want to provide your own user form to ask the user for information.

VBA can be used to run saved queries, even to provide them with parameter values. Some examples of using VBA to work with recordsets based on saved queries and linked tables are in the following sidebar.

> **SAVED QUERIES**
>
> The term saved (or stored) queries refers to queries created from the Queries tab in the database window. They are given names and saved.
>
> From within VBA, you can create queries on-the-fly and then open recordsets against them. These recordsets are closed when the procedure ends (although they should be explicitly closed as a matter of good practice).
>
> In the context of VBA and DAO code, the meaning of stored queries is clear.

The real work in the following example is in the `tbl.Index` and `tbl.Seek` lines. You must set `tbl.Index` beforeusing `tbl.Seek`. Here I used the `PrimaryKey` table design default for the table.

```
Private Sub SeekDemoCMD_Click()

Dim db As Database, aDB As Database
Dim tbl As Recordset, td As TableDef
Dim sCon As String, sPath As String
Dim sTable As String, criteria As Long
On Error GoTo TrapIT

criteria = 10250 'we will hard code for example

Set db = CurrentDb
sTable = "Orders" 'the name of the linked table
Set td = db.TableDefs(sTable)
sCon = td.Connect

sPath = Mid(sCon, InStr(1, sCon, "=") + 1)
Set aDB = DBEngine(0).OpenDatabase(sPath)
Set tbl = aDB.OpenRecordset(sTable, dbOpenTable)
 tbl.Index = "PrimaryKey" 'the name of the index
  tbl.Seek "=", criteria

If tbl.NoMatch Then
 MsgBox "Not Found"
Else
 MsgBox "Found" & " " & CStr(tbl![OrderID])
End If
EnterHere:
On Error Resume Next
tbl.Close

Exit Sub

TrapIT:
MsgBox Err.Number & " " & Err.Description
Resume EnterHere
End Sub
```

> **CAUTION**
>
> Once in place, it is best not to rename any indexes in your tables that will be used in your code for `Seek` methods. If you do forget to modify your VBA code, an error will result at runtime. Remember, the compile process will catch many coding errors but has no way to flag an incorrect index name.

Criteria must be the same data type as the field(s) in the index. Here are some examples:

```
Index = PrimaryKey
PrimaryKey is on a table field sMfrCode, a text field.
Use:

Dim criteria as string
criteria = "ACME"
...
tbl.Index = "PrimaryKey"
tbl.Seek "=", criteria

PrimaryKey is on a table field iMfrID, an AutoNumber field.

Dim criteria as Long
criteria = 10010
...

PrimaryKey is on two string fields:

Dim sMfrCode as String, sProdCode as String
sMfrCode = "ACME" : sProdCode = "WIDGETS"
t.Index = "PrimaryKey" 'ManufacturerCode, ProductCode
 t.Seek "=", sMfrCode, sProdCode
```

Saved Queries

Saved query in this context is used to indicate queries created in the QBE grid, named, and saved. `QueryDefs` can also be created on-the-fly in your VBA code.

The following is a procedure to open a saved Parameter query, pass a parameter using VBA, and see whether the resulting recordset has any records:

```
Public Function QryHasRecords(strQ, LongID) as Boolean
Dim db As Database, qd As QueryDef, r As Recordset
Set db = CurrentDb
Set qd = db.QueryDefs(strQ)
qd.PARAMETERS("zID") = LongID
Set r = qd.OpenRecordset()
If r.BOF Then
 QryHasRecords = False
Else
 QryHasRecords = True
End If
r.Close
End Function
```

The following code illustrates how to search with `QueryDef` using a wildcard:

```
'open QueryDef and Recordset
Dim criteria as String, strLetters
strLetters = "sm" 'hard code for example

criteria = "[LastName] like " & Chr(39) &  _
strLetters & "*" & Chr(39)
r.FindFirst criteria
```

```
If r.NoMatch Then
 MsgBox "Nothing found starting with " & strLetters
Else
 MsgBox "Found " & r![LastName]
End IF
r.Close
```

To look for a match in the previous example of code, change `criteria` to the following:

```
criteria = "[LastName] = " & Chr(39) & strFullLastName & Chr(39)
```

The following example demonstrates how to search using numeric data:

```
criteria = "[OrderID] = " & CStr(LongID)
```

Finding Information on Bound Forms

Here is an example of finding information on bound forms:

```
Dim LongID as Long
LongID = 10250 'hard code for example
Me![OrderID].SetFocus
DoCmd.FindRecord LongID
```

Remember to set the focus on the field to be searched before executing and to use the same data type.

There is no equivalent `NoMatch` here, so you can test the results by using the following code:

```
DoCmd.FindRecord LongID

If Me![OrderID] <> LongID Then
MsgBox "Not Found"
End If
```

The following code illustrates how to use a public (global) variable in a Parameter query by calling a procedure. Put the following procedure in a standard module:

```
Public Function QueryParam() as Long
QueryParam = gLongID
End Function
```

Next, put `=QueryParam()` in the `criteria` field on the QBE grid.

How to Dynamically Change Sort Order on Report

 A similar example of this technique is provided on the CD-ROM accompanying this book, in the PAU14VBA.MDB file. Select Client Example from the Main menu.

1. In a standard module, declare a public variable, such as

   ```
   Public gReportType As Integer
   ```

2. Ask users to supply the report sort order and assign their response (as a value) to `gReportType`.

3. Assign this procedure to the report's OnOpen event:

```
Private Sub Report_Open(Cancel As Integer)
            On Error Resume Next
            Me.OrderByOn = True
If gReportType = 1 Then
 Me.OrderBy = "[ManufacturerCode]"
ElseIf gReportType = 2 Then
 Me.OrderBy = "[MfrName]"
End If
End Sub
```

4. It is a good idea to put this on the report's OnNoData event:

```
Private Sub Report_NoData(Cancel As Integer)
MsgBox "Sorry, nothing found to print." & _
 "@Printing of the report is canceled." & _
            , vbOKOnly + vbInformation
            Cancel = True
            End Sub
```

5. If you want to change the back color of the field label that the report sorts on (assumes labels are in the page header section), use the following code on the OnPrint event of the PageHeader section:

```
On Error Resume Next
If gReportType = 1 Then
 Me![CodeLabel].BackColor = 14935011 'light gray
ElseIf gReportType = 2 Then
 Me![NameLabel].BackColor = 14935011
End If
```

6. If you want to "greenbar" (alternately shade the lines of the report for legibility) your report's detail section, do the following:

   - Put everything you need (text boxes from the report's data query or table record source) into the detail section.
   - Make sure that all controls are set to transparent back color.
   - Put an unbound text box control (a text box with Record Source blank) in the detail section and name the control LineNum.

> **NOTE**
>
> See the Hyperlink Report example in PAU14VBA.MDB.

   - Set the LineNum Visible property to No.
   - Set the Control Source to -1 on the Data tab of the LineNum property sheet.
   - Set the LineNum Running Sum property to Over All.
   - Add another unbound text box to the detail section and name this control GreenBar.

- The `GreenBar` control source should be left blank.
- Remove `GreenBar`'s label.
- Set the `GreenBar` back color to `14935011`.
- Size `Greenbar` to cover the entire detail section and send it to the back.

Add this code to the `OnPrint` event of the detail section:

```
If (Me![LineNum] Mod 2) = 0 Then
 Me.GreenBar.BackColor = vbWhite
Else
 Me.GreenBar.BackColor = 14935011
End If
```

Checking Forms with Code

Sometimes you want to use your own data verification routines on forms. Using table design to enforce business rules is a powerful feature of Access, but you can paint yourself into a corner.

Consider a workflow situation where various steps in a process are saved in the same table, as in the following example:

```
DefectReportID

strOriginatorID

strAssignedID

strProgrammerID

strQualAssureID

strApprovalID
```

As a defect item passes through the workflow process, an ID is required at each step. However, you can't set all the ID fields to `Required` in the table design. You start with one ID (`DefectReportID`), and new IDs are filled in as the defect item proceeds sequentially through the process.

One way to manage the workflow process is to provide a different data entry form for each step. Place a Save command button on each of these forms, and use code attached to the button's `OnClick` event to check the form's data before saving. If a defect item is being assigned, require `strAssignedID` to be non-blank before saving the data.

If you need to perform several data integrity checks before saving a form, you may want to add a checking routine `Sub` in the `(General)` section of the form's class module. Then your code for the Save command button may look something like the following:

```
Private Sub SaveCMD_Click()
Dim yOK as Boolean
CheckIT yOK
If Not yOK then
 Exit Sub
```

```
End If

'code to process save

End Sub
```

If you have other command buttons on the same form, (a Save and Edit Another command button, for example), they can share the CheckIT procedure.

To make CheckIT available to any command button on the form, add CheckIT to the form's class module in the (General) section.

```
Public Sub CheckIT(yOK)
yOK = True
Dim z
z = Me![strAssignedID]

If Len(z) = 0 Then
 MsgBox "Initials required for AssignedID."
 Me![strAssignedID].SetFocus
 yOK = False
 Exit Sub
End If
End Sub
```

A Few Considerations for Multiuser Development

Many projects that will be used in a multiuser environment are developed (written) on a standalone PC. You should take into account factors that will be important in the target, multiuser environment (such as record-locking conflicts/concurrency).

1. Are you working on a standalone development machine but want to test for multiuser behavior? Try loading multiple copies of the program module. Hot key between copies, setting a different context in each copy.

2. Jet 3.5 has several improvements to prevent locking conflicts. Changing the algorithm for storing index pages has enhanced concurrency. Nonetheless, consider the use of unbound forms to prevent conflicts, especially when adding new records.

Unbound forms are more work, but you can allow users all the time they need to enter a new record (especially in complex situations), perform all the integrity checks you desire, and then open your recordset and attempt a write.

Report any errors, and handle them.

Drill Down

Drill down is a technique that is still used, although less so as we move towards the hyperlink model. In drill down, the user selects an area (or control) on a form that is treated as a hot spot.

By clicking (or double-clicking) on the hot spot, more detail about the selected item is presented. This sounds similar to navigating to a linked page using a hyperlink, and it is.

Continuous forms are handy to allow users to find things (such as a customer record) by scrolling through or searching a list presented as a continuous form. When a specific customer or client is found in the list, the user may want immediate access to additional information for that one customer or client. The following example shows how to drill down to a client's full record.

For this example, I will use a client list. A continuous form will display only ClientNumber, SSN, LastName, and FirstNameMI. I'll let the user drill down to a client's full record of personal data, such as street address, city, and state.

 This example is included on the accompanying CD-ROM in the sample database PAU14VBA.MDB.

1. Set the form's Recordset type to Dynaset.

2. Add an unbound control named Dummy, remove its label, set its ForeColor and BackColor to be the same as the form, and make the Border transparent.

3. Set Enabled to No for all bound controls. The user then can tab to new records because only Dummy can accept focus.

4. Put a transparent command button over a hot zone such as customer ID, set tab stop to No, and bring to front.

Assign procedures to the transparent command button, as follows:

```
Private Sub GoToOverlayCMD_DblClick(Cancel As Integer)
On Error GoTo TrapIT
Dim criteria, z

z = Me![strClientNumber]

If IsNull(z) Then 'should not happen
 Exit Sub
End If

gCallingForm = "ClientNames": gIsDirty = False

criteria = "[strClientNumber] = " & Chr(39) & (Me![strClientNumber]) & Chr(39)
DoCmd.OpenForm "Clients", , , criteria, _
 acReadOnly, acDialog
On Error Resume Next
If gIsDirty Then 'the record was edited
 Me.Requery
 Me![strClientNumber].Enabled = True
 Me![strClientNumber].SetFocus
 DoCmd.FindRecord CStr(z)
 Me![Dummy].SetFocus
 Me![strClientNumber].Enabled = False
```

```
End If

RetFromErr:

Exit Sub
TrapIT:
MsgBox Err.Number & " " & Err.Description & ".",  vbExclamation, " "
Resume RetFromErr
End Sub
```

> **NOTE**
>
> Depending upon your style, you may find that drill-down techniques such as the one shown here may be preferable to using subforms. In a multiuser environment, this technique reduces network traffic by pulling only the data needed. Additional data is pulled across the network only if the user requests it.

Controlling When a User Can Exit Your Application

As a developer, you should always do what you can at the time of design to protect users from inadvertent mistakes that can impact the consistency or integrity of the data in the delivered application. Normally, you want an application to be closed in an orderly manner, and not by the user using control boxes or file menus.

Access provides different ways to do this, such as restricting the presentation of built-in (Access) menus. Here is a technique that can be used to require a user to navigate back to the main menu (or switchboard) and quit the application by choosing a command button labeled Quit.

Create a new unbound form. Assign your code to the form's On UnLoad event to ask the user about quitting the application. Hide the form. (Hint: Application.Quit.)

Summary

Access 97 is a powerful application development tool. VBA permits the development of professional applications and provides access to functionality not available through the menu structure or by using macros. This chapter gave some specific examples of using VBA to enhance your applications.

More importantly, you may gain a few insights which lead you to many ideas that you can implement in your own applications.

Data Access Programming

CHAPTER 15

Microsoft Access Object Model

In previous chapters you've read how to access data through the Access user interface. You've also been introduced to the programming language built into Access, Visual Basic for Applications (VBA). Data Access Objects (DAO) provides a set of objects and collections that enable an Access application developer to create and manipulate database components programmatically with VBA. Each object or collection has properties and methods that describe and manipulate these database components. These objects and collections form a hierarchy or hierarchical model of the database and its components that you, the developer, totally control.

This chapter covers Data Access Objects, the DAO hierarchical model, the differences between the Microsoft Jet hierarchy and the new ODBC Direct hierarchy, and the different types of objects and collections that compose the hierarchy. The text discusses the power of DAO, how to programmatically use the same capabilities of the user interface, and many more topics. When a topic discusses objects that are specific to one of the new workspace types, an indication is included in the title.

DAO Today

Access 97 includes a new version of DAO, DAO 3.5. It is an incremental but significant update to DAO 3.0, which was introduced with Access 95. DAO 3.5 is a fully host-independent set of OLE objects that any OLE-compatible client can use. New properties, methods, and objects have been added, and some have been changed. Probably the biggest addition is ODBC Direct.

DAO 3.5 is a shared resource (usually installed in the `\Program Files\Common Files\Microsoft Shared\DAO` directory). Any OLE-compatible client can use DAO 3.5, including C developers (using dbDAO and its SDK).

> **NOTE**
>
> DAO is 32-bit in Microsoft Access 97. That is, you can create only 32-bit applications with Access and thus can use only DAO 3.5 (which is 32-bit). New development with DAO 2.5 is not supported in Access 97.

What's Different in DAO 3.5?

Some major changes have been made to DAO. If you're converting or porting your application to Access 97, you'll probably want to take full advantage of this new functionality. Following are some of the changes made to DAO (for more information, see the later section "DAO Compatibility" or the online Help for DAO):

■ `DBEngine—IniPath` property: Windows 95 and Windows NT no longer support the use of INI files, but instead store INI-type information in the system Registry. `IniPath` now returns the PATH in the system Registry. Here's an example:

```
DBEngine.IniPath = "HKEY_CURRENT_USER\Software\VB and VBA Program
➥Settings\MYDBApp"
```

■ Recordset object: Rows from a `Recordset` object can now be retrieved into an array with the `GetRow` method. That is, to populate an array with records from a recordset, you normally would have to iterate through the recordset. With the `GetRow` method, shown in Listing 15.1, you can now retrieve whole blocks of records or smaller blocks.

Listing 15.1. An example of the GetRow method.

```
Public Sub GetRowsSample()
    Dim dbsDatabase As Database, rstSampleRecordSet As Recordset
    Dim varMyRecords As Variant, iCount As Integer

    Set dbsDatabase = CurrentDb()
    ' Place this all on one line
    Set rstSampleRecordSet = dbsDatabase.OpenRecordset("SELECT FirstName, " &
    ➥"LastName, Title FROM Employees", dbOpenSnapshot)

    varMyRecords = rstSampleRecordSet.GetRows(3)

    Debug.Print "First Name", "Last Name", "Title"

    ' The first subscript of the array identifies the Fields
    ' collection (moves horizontally across the record)
    ' Print the first field in the first record
    Debug.Print varMyRecords(0, 0),

    ' Print the second field in the first record
    Debug.Print varMyRecords(1, 0),

    ' Print the third field in the first record
    Debug.Print varMyRecords(2, 0)

    ' The second subscript of the array identifies the record number
    ' (moves vertically through records)
    ' Print the first field in the second record
    Debug.Print varMyRecords(0, 1),

    ' Print the second field in the second record
    Debug.Print varMyRecords(1, 1),

    ' Print the third field in the second record
    Debug.Print varMyRecords(2, 1)

End Sub
```

■ Container/Document object `AllPermissions` property: This property returns the permissions pertaining to each object (either a `Document` object or a `Container` object) that the user or the user's group has access to. `AllPermissions` differs from `Permissions` in that it includes the permissions for the group as well as permissions for the user. If the `UserName` property is set to a group, `AllPermissions` and `Permissions` function the same.

■ ODBC Direct: DAO 3.5 now supports a new workspace type, ODBC Direct, which exposes ODBC functionality through an extension to the fundamental DAO object model. This allows you to create high-performance client/server applications using familiar objects. Whenever you need to write an application that uses a remote database such as SQL Server or Oracle, use ODBC Direct. You use ODBC Direct by creating an ODBC Direct workspace. Listing 15.2 shows how to start working with ODBC Direct.

Listing 15.2. Creating an ODBC Direct workspace.

```
Dim wsODBC As Workspace
Set wsODBC = CreateWorkspace("ODBCWorkspace", "admin", "", dbUseODBC)
Workspaces.Append wsODBC
```

■ Backward compatibility: Access 97 supports both DAO 3.5 and DAO 2.5 and includes a compatibility layer for older applications. If you're porting your application to Access 97, the DAO 2.5/3.0 Compatibility Library is automatically selected. You can either use the DAO 2.5/3.0 Compatibility Library for compatibility with older version of DAO or deselect this reference to use the DAO 3.5 library only. The latter choice removes support for the older objects, properties, and methods.

The DAO Hierarchy

DAO in Access 97 is a set of OLE objects that represent the functionality of the Jet engine. This layer of objects sits between your application and the database you're trying to manipulate. This insulates you, the developer, from the complexities of database programming while providing a high level of flexibility and control.

Each object in the DAO is actually a class. A class is not unlike a datatype. You dimension an object as type class just as you dimension a variable as some datatype. Here's an example:

```
Dim MyWorkSpace As Workspace
Dim iCount As Integer
```

Because in this chapter most of the discussion is about objects you create and manipulate, the term *object* is used rather than *class* to keep things clear.

Each of the data access objects has its own properties that help define it and methods that manipulate it, and almost every object is part of a collection. Collections are simply a way to refer to groups of like objects. In other words, an object can have a collection that contains other objects with collections that contain other objects, and so forth. This is how the hierarchy is implemented—through collections. For more on objects, properties, methods, and collections, see Part IV, "Visual Basic for Applications for Access 97."

The DAO hierarchy can be confusing at times, but when you get the big picture, you can begin to see the ease of use and power of DAO. Figure 15.1 shows the DAO hierarchy when a Microsoft Jet workspace is used (each object/collection is represented by one object).

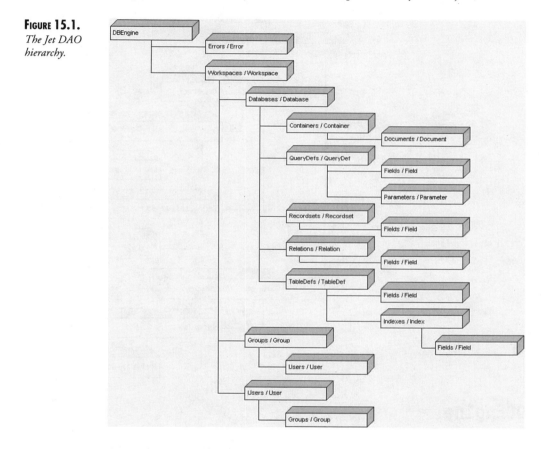

Figure 15.2 shows the DAO hierarchy when an ODBC Direct workspace is used.

Throughout the remainder of this chapter, object hierarchies will represent objects unique to one workspace type by the name of that workspace type.

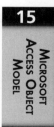

FIGURE 15.2.
The ODBC Direct DAO hierarchy.

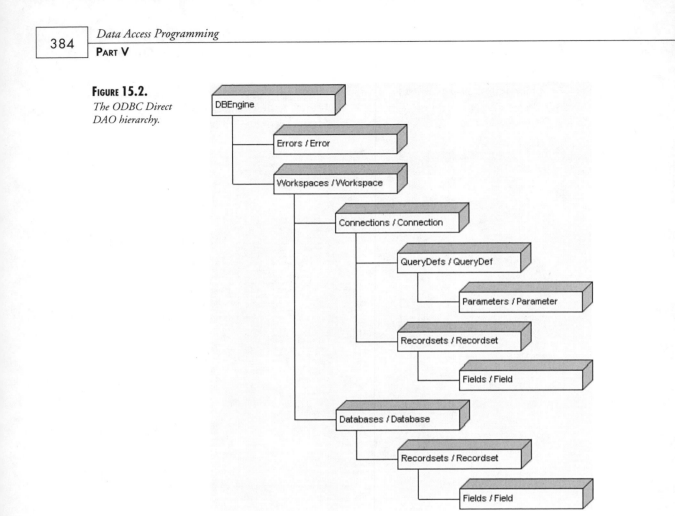

DBEngine

The DBEngine object, shown in Figure 15.3, is the top object in the DAO hierarchy. It is a predefined object, and it can't be created. The DBEngine object represents and directly man-ipulates the Jet database engine. There is only one instance of the DBEngine object per application. The DBEngine object therefore isn't an element of a collection; it is the object that contains everything else.

> **NOTE**
>
> Before version 3.0, you could have only up to 10 instances of the DBEngine object. Beginning with version 3.0, this limitation was removed, and you can run as many instances as you want.

FIGURE 15.3.
The DBEngine *object.*

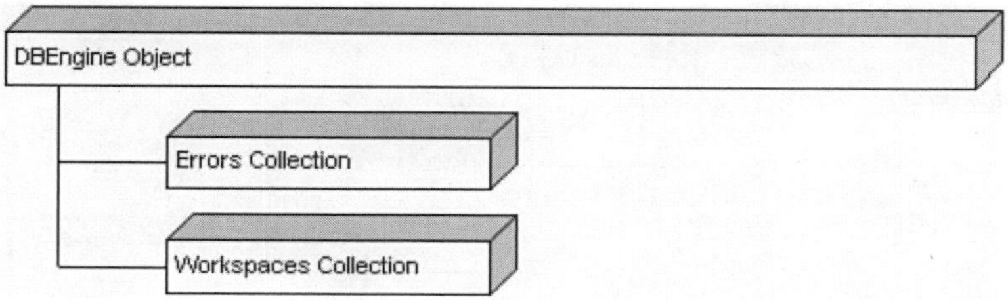

The DBEngine object can be used to compact or repair databases, register ODBC databases, get the Jet version number, and set the login timeout. Errors that occur from DAO actions will be placed into the DBEngine object's Errors collection. Table 15.1 shows the methods, properties, and collections of the DBEngine object.

Table 15.1. The methods, properties, and collections of the DBEngine object.

Methods	*Properties*	*Collections*
CompactDatabase	DefaultPassword	Errors
CreateWorkSpace	DefaultUser	Workspaces (default)
Idle	IniPath	Properties
RepairDatabase	Version	
RegisterDatabase	LoginTimeOut	
	SystemDB	

Errors

The Error object, shown in Figure 15.4, receives all errors when an action or activity performed by DAO fails. The collection is cleared, and all errors that occurred are placed into the collection. This action is taken because multiple errors might occur during a given activity or action by DAO. Errors in the Errors collection are ordered by error number; that is, the error with the lowest number is the first element, the next higher error is the next element, and so forth. Error handling for this collection is discussed later in this chapter. Table 15.2 shows the properties and collections of the Error object.

Table 15.2. The properties and collections of the Error object.

Properties	Collection
Description	Properties
HelpContext	
HelpFile	
Number	
Source	

If an error occurs in your Access application, it is useful to know how to find out what went wrong and to be able to gracefully handle the error. I'll show you more about this later in the section titled, imaginatively enough, "Handling Errors."

Workspaces

To define a session for the user, use the Workspace object, shown in Figure 15.5. This object contains all open databases for the user and a transaction scope for that user. A workspace also defines how Access will communicate with the database, whether it is Jet or ODBC Direct. Transactions within a Workspace object are global across all databases for that Workspace object. Access by default creates a Workspaces(0) object. If there is no security setup for the current database, the Name property is set to #Default Workspace#, and the UserName property is set to Admin. This is commonly referred to as the default workspace.

> **NOTE**
>
> It's important to note that, unlike with other collections, you *cannot* remove the default Workspace object. It can never be closed or removed from its collection, and it is always available.

The Workspaces collection is a collection of all Workspace objects. Table 15.3 shows the methods, properties, and collections of the Workspace object.

Figure 15.5.
The Workspaces collection and the Workspace *object.*

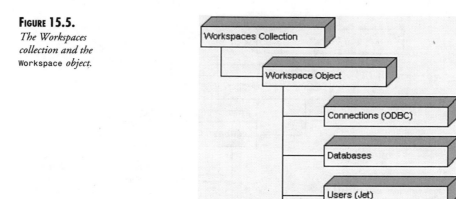

Table 15.3. The methods, properties, and collections of the Workspace object.

Methods	Properties	Collections
BeginTrans	DefaultCursorDriver	Connections
Close	(ODBC Direct)	ODBC Direct
CommitTrans	IsolateODBCTrans	Databases (default)
CreateDatabase	LoginTimeout	Groups
CreateGroup	(ODBC Direct)	Properties
CreateUser	Name	Users
OpenDatabase	Type	
(Jet)	UserName	
OpenConnection		
(ODBC Direct)		
Rollback		

Databases

The Database object, shown in Figure 15.6, represents a database that has been opened by or created with DAO. You use the Database object to connect to the current database or an ISAM database, such as an external Access database, FoxPro, or Paradox. You can also use it to connect to any ODBC datasource, such as SQL Server or Oracle, although it is recommended that you use the Connection object of an ODBC Direct workspace instead. If you use the CreateDatabase method of the Workspace object, the database is automatically appended to the Databases collection. Closing the Database object (using the Close method) removes it from the Databases collection.

15

MICROSOFT
ACCESS OBJECT
MODEL

FIGURE 15.6.

The Databases collection and the Database *object.*

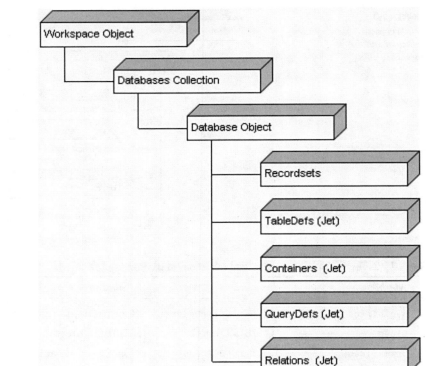

Connections

The Connection object, shown in Figure 15.7, represents a connection to a remote database through an ODBC Direct workspace. You use the Connection object in much the same way as the Database object discussed in the preceding section, except that the databases you can connect to are remote databases such as SQL Server or Oracle.

> **NOTE**
>
> If you use the Close method to close a Workspace, Database, or Connection object, all open Recordset objects close, and any pending transactions (updates or changes you have made) are rolled back. Also, it's important to note that if your Workspace, Database, or Connection object falls out of scope, any pending updates or changes are also rolled back. With this in mind, it is a good practice to explicitly close currently open Recordset objects before closing a Workspace, Database, or Connection object.

FIGURE 15.7.

*The Connections
collection and the
Connection object.*

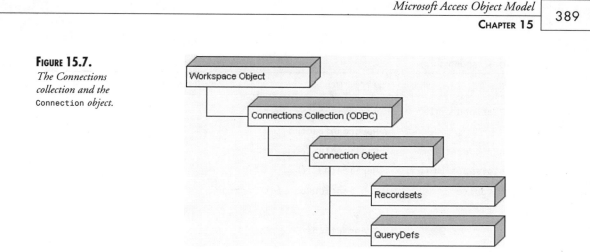

The Databases collection is a collection of all the Database objects opened by DAO, including the current database that was opened by Access. It's important to note that the "internal" or hidden databases (wizards, system.mda, and so on) used by Access aren't in this collection and aren't accessible through this collection.

> **NOTE**
>
> Databases(0) is the current database opened by Access every time. You can always use the CurrentDB object, which is the equivalent of DBEngine.Workspaces(0).Databases(0).

Table 15.4 shows the methods, properties, and collections of the Database object. Note that some of the methods and properties are specific to the kind of Workspace object the database is opened under.

Table 15.4. The methods, properties, and collections of the Database object.

Methods	Properties	Collections
Close	CollatingOrder	Containers
CreateProperty	Connect (Jet)	Properties
CreateQueryDef	Connection	QueryDefs
CreateRelation	(ODBC Direct)	Recordsets
CreateTableDef	DesignMasterID (Jet)	(default for ODBC Direct)
Execute		Relations
MakeReplica (Jet)	KeepLocal	TableDefs (default)
	Name	

continues

15

MICROSOFT
ACCESS OBJECT
MODEL

Table 15.4. continued

Methods	Properties	Collections
NewPassword (Jet)	QueryTimeout	
	RecordsAffected	
OpenRecordset	Replicable (Jet)	
PopulatePartial (Jet)	ReplicaID (Jet)	
Synchronize	ReplicationConflictFunction (Jet)	
	Transactions	
	Updatable	
	V1xNullBehavior	
	Version	

Users

In a Microsoft Jet workspace, each User object represents users that exist in the workgroup database (see Figure 15.8). Note that this object is not valid for an ODBC Direct workspace. The User object represents a user account as defined in the workgroup database. For more information on security, see Chapter 22, "Security." Table 15.5 shows the methods, properties, and collections of the User object.

FIGURE 15.8.

The Users collection and the User object.

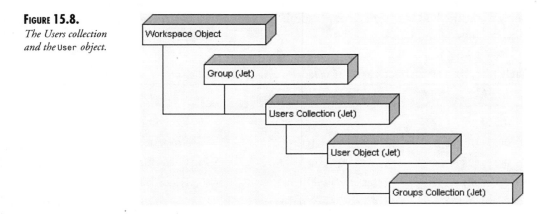

Table 15.5. The methods, properties, and collections of the User object.

Methods	Properties	Collections
CreateGroup	Name	Groups (default)
NewPassword	Password	Properties
	PID	

Groups

Like the User object, the Group object in a Microsoft Jet workspace (shown in Figure 15.9) represents groups that have been defined in the workgroup database. The Group object also is not valid for an ODBC Direct workspace. A Group object usually represents groups of users and their appropriate security. Each user in a group is represented by a User object in the Users collection of the group. For more information on security, see Chapter 22. Table 15.6 shows the methods, properties, and collections of the Group object.

FIGURE 15.9.
The Groups collection and the Group object.

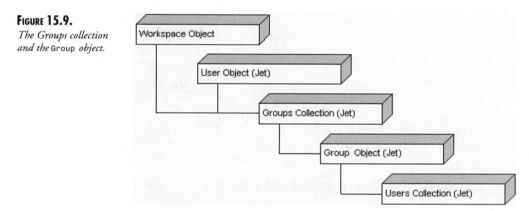

Table 15.6. The methods, properties, and collections of the Group object.

Methods	Properties	Collections
CreateUser	Name	Users (default)
	PID	Properties

15

MICROSOFT ACCESS OBJECT MODEL

QueryDefs

Each query that has been defined in Access or created using `CreateQueryDef` is represented by a `QueryDef` object in the QueryDefs collection (see Figure 15.10). With the `QueryDef` object, you can create `Recordset` objects, add your own properties (more on this topic later), look at the underlying SQL code, tell whether it returns records, or just execute it. Because QueryDefs are precompiled SQL statements, they generally run faster than dynamic SQL (Jet doesn't have to compile it on-the-fly). You can create queries with the `CreateQueryDef` method.

FIGURE 15.10.

The QueryDefs collection and the `QueryDef` *object.*

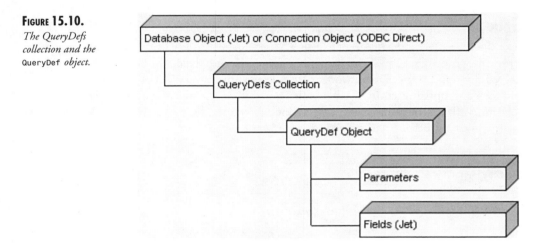

Similarly, a SQL Server database can have precompiled SQL statements called stored procedures that are represented by a `QueryDef` object when an ODBC Direct workspace is being used.

Table 15.7 shows the methods, properties, and collections of the `QueryDef` object.

Table 15.7. The methods, properties, and collections of the QueryDef object.

Methods	*Properties*	*Collections*
`Cancel`	`CacheSize`	Fields
(ODBC Direct)	(ODBC Direct)	Parameters (default)
`CreateProperty`	`Connect`	Properties
(Jet)	`Connection`	
`Execute`	(ODBC Direct)	
`OpenRecordset`	`Date Created` (Jet)	
	`KeepLocal` (Jet)	
	`LastUpdated` (Jet)	

Methods	Properties	Collections
	LogMessages (Jet)	
	MaxRecords	
	Name	
	ODBCTimeout	
	Prepare (ODBC Direct)	
	RecordsAffected	
	Replicable (Jet)	
	ReturnsRecords (Jet)	
	SQL	
	StillExecuting (ODBC Direct)	
	Type	
	Updatable	

TableDefs (Jet Only)

In a Microsoft Jet workspace, TableDef objects represent tables or stored table definitions in a given database (see Figure 15.11). The table can be in the current database or in an attached table from an external database. With the TableDef object, you can tell whether the table is attached, its validation rules, whether it is updatable, or the number of records in the table. Table 15.8 shows the methods, properties, and collections of the TableDef object.

> **NOTE**
>
> When a table is attached, the properties that define its definition are read-only. You must go back to the source database (where the table physically resides) and make changes there.

FIGURE 15.11.
The TableDefs collection and the `TableDef` *object.*

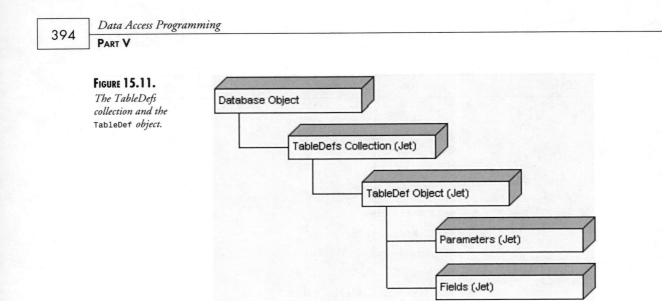

Table 15.8. The methods, properties, and collections of the `TableDef` object.

Methods	*Properties*	*Collections*
CreateField	Attributes	Fields (default)
CreateIndex	ConflictTable	Indexes
CreateProperty	Connect	Properties
OpenRecordset	DateCreated	
RefreshLink	KeepLocal	
	LastUpdated	
	Name	
	RecordCount	
	Replicable	
	ReplicaFilter	
	SourceTableName	
	Updatable	
	ValidationRule	
	ValidationText	

Indexes (Jet Only)

Indexes of a recordset or `TableDef` are represented by the `Index` object, shown in Figure 15.12. This way, you can set the index for a table, for instance, just by referring to an index in the Indexes collection. Table 15.9 shows the methods, properties, and collections of the `Index` object.

FIGURE 15.12.
The Indexes collection and the Index *object.*

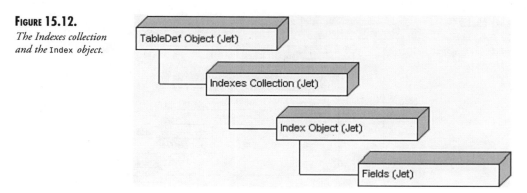

Table 15.9. The methods, properties, and collections of the Index object.

Methods	Properties	Collections
CreateField	Clustered	Properties
CreateProperty	DistinctCount	Fields (default)
	Foreign	
	IgnoreNulls	
	Name	
	Primary	
	Required	
	Unique	

Fields

Field objects represent common columns of data sharing similar properties and a common datatype (see Figure 15.13). Relation, Recordset, TableDef, QueryDef, and Index objects all have a Fields collection. For instance, if you're looking at a table using Access, each column of information is a field and is represented by a Field object. The attributes of a field are represented by the different properties (and can be modified) as well as the *value* of the field. Table 15.10 shows the methods, properties, and collections of the Field object.

FIGURE 15.13.
The Fields collection and the Field *object.*

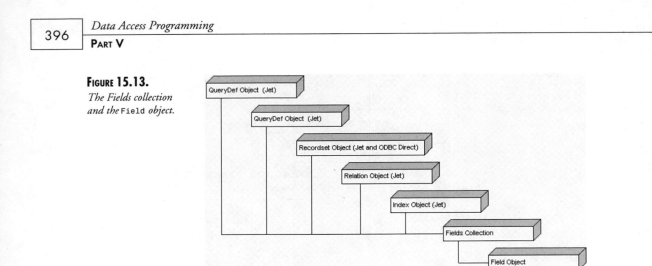

Table 15.10. The methods, properties, and collections of the Field **object.**

Methods	*Properties*	*Collection*
AppendChunk	AllowZeroLength	Properties
CreateProperty	(Jet)	
GetChunk	Attributes	
	CollatingOrder (Jet)	
	DataUpdatable	
	DefaultValue (Jet)	
	FieldSize	
	ForeignName	
	Name	
	OrdinalPosition	
	OriginalValue (ODBC Direct)	
	Required	
	Size	
	SourceField	
	SourceTable	
	Status (ODBC Direct)	
	Type	
	ValidateOnSet (Jet)	
	ValidationRule (Jet)	
	ValidationText (Jet)	
	Value	
	VisibleValue (ODBC Direct)	

Recordsets

The Recordset object, shown in Figure 15.14, is probably the most used and also the most powerful object DAO provides. With this object, you can programmatically access tables in the connected database. This type of object is somewhat different from the other objects in that it is created each time your application runs and you create recordsets. These objects are never stored on disk—or anywhere, for that matter. They're just temporary.

FIGURE 15.14.

The Recordsets collection and the Recordset *object.*

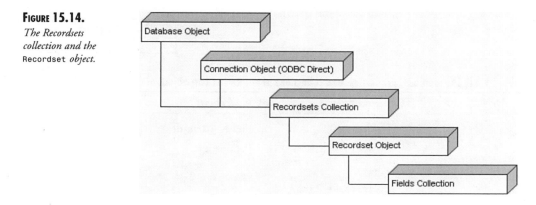

> **NOTE**
>
> The properties, methods, and collections of a Recordset object vary depending on the *type* of the recordset and the *type* of the current workspace. See the DAO online Help for a complete listing of properties, methods, and collections for this object.

Relations (Jet Only)

All relations of an Access database are represented by a Relation object, shown in Figure 15.15. A relation is defined as a relationship between fields in two or more tables. The Relations collection contains all the defined relationships for that Database object. Table 15.11 shows the methods, properties, and collections of the Relation object.

FIGURE 15.15.

*The Relations collection
and the* Relation
object.

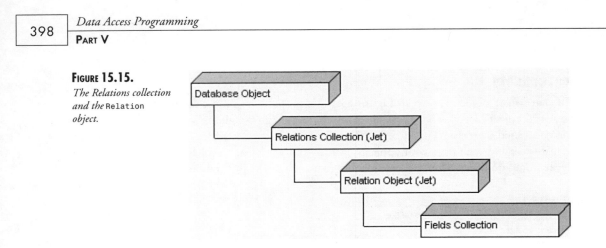

Table 15.11. The methods, properties, and collections of the Relation object.

Methods	Properties	Collection
CreateField	Attributes	Fields (default)
	ForeignTable	Properties
	Name	
	PartialReplica	
	Table	

Parameters

In Access, you can define queries that require formal parameters and supply these parameters at runtime. Formal or *explicit* parameters are parameters that have been defined in a query's SQL using the PARAMETERS keyword.

Similarly, a QueryDef object that represents a stored procedure in a remote SQL Server database can have parameters. A parameter in such a QueryDef can be either an input parameter (you pass the parameter to the QueryDef), an output parameter (the QueryDef returns information to you through the parameter), or a return value. The type of parameter is determined by the Direction property, which is specific to ODBC Direct.

These formal parameters are represented in the Parameters collection by the Parameter object, shown in Figure 15.16. It's important to note that *explicit,* not *implicit,* parameters are represented. The Parameter object only provides information on existing parameters. You cannot append or delete objects from the Parameters collection. Table 15.12 shows the properties and collections of the Parameter object.

FIGURE 15.16.
The Parameters collection and the Parameter *object.*

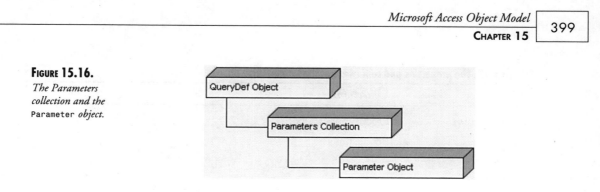

Table 15.12. The properties and collections of the Parameter object.

Properties	Collection
Direction (ODBC Direct)	Properties
Name	
Type	
Value	

Containers (Jet Only)

Using Container objects is one way DAO achieves its application independence (see the "Using DAO" section later in this chapter). The Container object, shown in Figure 15.17, stores such items as Access forms, databases, and modules. This object is generic enough to store these types of objects, yet flexible enough to maintain independence from any one application. Table 15.13 shows the properties and collections of the Container object.

FIGURE 15.17.
The Containers collection and the Container *object.*

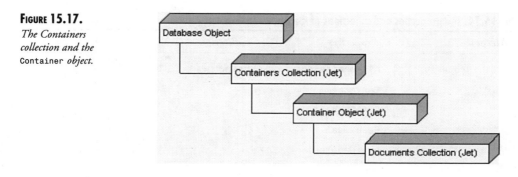

Table 15.13. The properties and collections of the `Container` object.

Properties	Collections
AllPermissions	Documents (default)
Inherit	Properties
Name	
Owner	
Permissions	
UserName	

Documents (Jet Only)

The `Document` object, shown in Figure 15.18, represents each *individual* application object (such as forms, modules, or tables). For instance, when you create your database, DAO creates a Forms container that contains a `Document` object for each form in the database. Table 15.14 shows the methods properties and collections of the `Document` object.

FIGURE 15.18.
The Documents collection and the `Document` *object.*

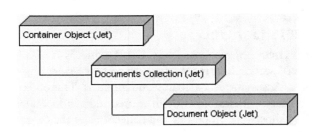

Table 15.14. The properties and collections of the `Document` object.

Method	Properties	Collection
CreateProperty	AllPermissions	Properties
	Container	
	DateCreated	
	KeepLocal	
	LastUpdated	
	Name	
	Owner	
	Permissions	
	Replicable	
	UserName	

Properties

A `Property` object represents the characteristics of an object (see Figure 15.19). Every object in DAO has a Properties collection, and each `Property` object can be a built-in or user-defined characteristic. You can manipulate these properties at runtime and can even add new properties using the `CreateProperty` method.

FIGURE 15.19.

The Properties collection and the `Property` *object.*

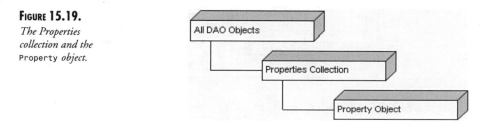

User-defined properties are properties added at runtime to a specific instance of an object. It's important to note that properties added to an object type are for only that instance of that object type and will disappear when the object is closed. You are responsible for setting and changing values in user-defined properties. This is the only type of property that can be deleted from the Properties collection; built-in properties cannot be deleted. Table 15.15 shows the properties and collections of the `Property` object.

Table 15.15. The properties and collections of the `Property` object.

Properties	Collection
Inherited	Properties
Name	
Type	
Value	

Using DAO

Now that you understand the hierarchy, you can get down to the basics of using DAO. By now you're comfortable with accessing data through Access 97's user interface or by using the built-in data control of a form. When you use the user interface to manipulate the database (creating queries, adding or creating tables, and so on), Access 97 calls Jet directly; that is, it doesn't hand off the request to DAO. The only time Access 97 uses DAO is in a code module. See Figure 15.20 to see where DAO sits in relation to your application or database.

DAO can now be accessed from any OLE-compatible client (Microsoft Visual Basic 4.0 32-bit, Microsoft Excel 95, or Microsoft Access 97). All the objects, properties, and methods are exposed to the developer as an OLE in-process server.

FIGURE 15.20.
The application object model.

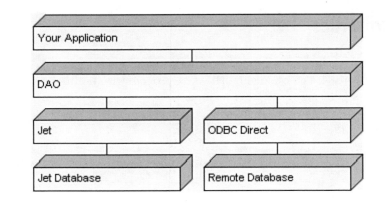

In-process servers are OLE Automation servers that are compiled as DLLs and that share the same process space as the calling (your) application. What is the difference between a DLL and an OLE server? An OLE server exposes all its objects, properties, and methods to you (just like a DLL), but an OLE server also exposes descriptions and explanations of each object, property, and method in an associated *type library*.

You can browse the type libraries of all the OLE servers in your application during design time by using the Object Browser, shown in Figure 15.21. You can activate the Object Browser from the Access 97 Toolbar, by pressing F2, or by selecting View | Object Browser.

FIGURE 15.21.
The Object Browser.

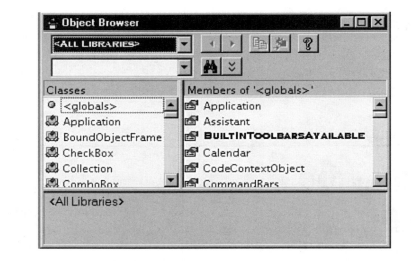

With the Object Browser, you can navigate through the DAO hierarchy and see each property and method for each object in the hierarchy. This feature is useful because it offers Help, an example, and a paste function that enables you to paste the method or property (or collection) into your code.

Objects and Collections

The concept of objects and collections is very important in DAO. In the hierarchy (refer to the earlier section "DAO Hierarchy"), most objects have collections which contain that object type's members. For instance, the DBEngine object has a collection of Workspaces that contain individual Workspace objects. Most objects are part of a collection that has objects, which in turn can have collections.

Usually in the OO (object-oriented) world, a collection is the plural of the object type that the collection contains. For example, the Workspaces collection contains Workspace objects. Notice that the collection (Workspaces) is the plural of the object (Workspace) it contains. This information is useful when you don't know the name of an object's collection—if, for example, the DBEngine has a collection of Workspace objects, and you want to use that collection (just make *Workspace* plural and you've got it).

Declaring DAO

To use DAO, you first must declare an object variable of whatever object type you want to use. As mentioned earlier, although DAO is actually a hierarchy of classes, this chapter refers to the classes as objects to avoid confusion. Classes are usually a type of object that you declare something as and can't use directly. For example, I don't have an object called Workspace, but instead have a variable wksMyWorkspace of the Workspace type or class:

```
Dim wksMyWorkspace as Workspace
```

Object Variables

Due to the nature of DAO's hierarchical structure, it could become cumbersome to keep referring to objects through the DAO hierarchy. This is where something called object variables comes in. Object variables are simply a pointer or reference to another object. Using an object variable instead of using the hierarchy directly will make your code more readable and easier to type (no more typing those long references!). The down side of using object variables is that dereferencing occurs at runtime, and this timing could cause some rather tricky debugging situations. Overall, the advantages outweigh the negatives, and you should always use object variables if you're referencing a property more than once. Here's an example:

```
Dim rstMyRecordset As Recordset, strName As String, strConnect As String
Dim iCount As Integer, strUpdatable As String, dbsMyDatabase As Database
Set dbsMyDatabase = CurrentDb
' This is the SLOW method (DON'T DO THIS)
' References get resolved through each iteration
```

```
For iCount = 1 To 10
    Debug.Print dbsMyDatabase.Name
Next

' This is the FAST method
' References get resolved just once
strName = dbsMyDatabase.Name
For iCount = 1 To 10
    Debug.Print strName
Next

' Use the With when refering to the same object a bunch of times
With dbsMyDatabase
    strUpdatable = .Updatable
    strName = .Name
    strConnect = .Connect
End With
```

DAO Unleashed

DAO is broken down into two parts: Data Definition Language (DDL) and Data Manipulation Language (DML). DDL is the part of DAO that *defines* the database, its objects, and its data, whereas DML *manipulates* the database, its objects, and its data. The following discussion covers how to create a database and then manipulate it using DAO.

Creating Databases

Creating databases with DAO is a fairly easy and straightforward process from a mechanics point of view. The effort is therefore in designing the data model for your database. If you have a good data model driving this process, things will flow much more smoothly. Too many developers design their data model "on-the-fly," and although this technique might satisfy some deadline, it will probably come back to bite you! The saying "A house is only as good as the foundation" also rings true for databases—a database is only as good as the data model it is designed from (database being a physical database, not a database application). That being said, let the process begin!

> **NOTE**
>
> Access can create only Access databases (MDBs). ODBC databases must be created in their native environments—Access has the capability only to manipulate these databases, not to create them. For help on creating Access ISAM databases, see the online Help.

Follow these steps to create an Access database using DAO:

1. Declare a Database object for the database you want to create:

   ```
   Dim MyNewDatabase as Database
   ```

2. Use the `CreateDatabase` method of the `Workspace` object to create an empty database and database file:

```
Set MyNewDatabase = WorkSpaces(0).CreateDatabase("MyNewDB")
```

3. Define each table in your new database. You should already know which fields and indexes should go into this table (from your data model).

4. Use the `CreateTableDef` method to create each table in the database:

```
Dim tdfNewTable as TableDef

Set tdfNewTable = MyNewDatabase.CreateTableDef("Employees")
```

5. Use the new `TableDef` object to create fields in the new table by using the `CreateField` method of the `Field` object. This example creates a few different fields:

```
Dim fldNewField As Field
Set fldNewField = tdfNewTable.CreateField("Employee_ID", dbLong)
fldNewField.Attributes = dbAutoIncrField
tdfNewTable.Append fldNewField

Set fldNewField = tdfNewTable.CreateField("First_Name", dbText, 25)
fldNewField.Attributes = dbAutoIncrField
tdfNewTable.Append fldNewField

Set fldNewField = tdfNewTable.CreateField("Last_Name", dbText, 25)
fldNewField.Attributes = dbAutoIncrField
tdfNewTable.Append fldNewField
```

6. Now that the table is defined, append it to the database. This step actually creates the table in your database and appends it to the Databases collection. After this step is done, though, you can't make any changes to the appended fields (you can, however, add and delete new ones):

```
MyNewDatabase.Append tdfNewTable
```

7. At this point, you can create one or more indexes using the `TableDef` object's `CreateIndex` method. Use `CreateIndex` to create an `Index` object:

```
Dim idxNewIndex As Index

Set idxNewIndex = tdfNewTable.CreateIndex("Employee")
```

8. Use the `CreateField` method of the `Index` object to create a `Field` object for every indexed field in the `Index` object, and append it to the `Index` object:

```
Set fldNewField = idxNewIndex.CreateField("Employee_ID")
fldNewField.Primary = True
idxNewIndex.Fields.Append fldNewField
```

9. Now append each `Index` object to the Indexes collection of the `TableDef` object using the `Append` method. Your table can have several indexes or no indexes:

```
TdfNewTable.Indexes.Append idxNewIndex
```

You have just created your first database. Using the Access user interface is a much easier way of accomplishing this task, but it's always good to know how to do it the hard way. For example, if you need to have your end users create a new database, such as a local lookup database, you can include a utility in your application to do this for them.

Using the Current Database

Normally, when developing Access applications, you are using the database that was opened from the design environment. DAO has a function called `CurrentDB` that is a pointer to the currently open database. This is a very handy little function to have around—whenever you need to reference the current database, a reference is already established.

`CurrentDB` references the database the same way `DBEngine.Workspaces(0).Databases(0)` does. You can't close `Databases(0)` as well as `CurrentDB`. (`CurrentDB.Close` has no effect and is ignored.) Although the second method is supported in Access 97 and probably will be supported in future versions, it is recommended that you use the `CurrentDB` function instead. Why? The `CurrentDB` function is a lot more friendly in multiuser environments than the older method. `CurrentDB` creates another instance of the open database (similar to using `OpenDatabase` on the current database) instead of referring to the open instance.

A Special Note on the `Close` Method

The `Close` method can cause lots of strange problems in an application. Strange problems normally don't pop up until final release of your application. In older version of DAO, the `Close` method would cause an error if it was used at the wrong time (when you had recordsets open) or if it wasn't used at all (problems were most likely to occur the next time your application was started).

This small section of text is devoted to the `Close` method because of its new behavior. The discussion starts with some of the new changes for this method. For the most part, the biggest change in this method is what happens when you use it. If you close an open database using the `Close` method, *all* objects referencing that database are dereferenced, *any* pending updates or edits are rolled back, and *all* recordsets against that database are closed. Any object that falls out of scope has similar results (if you don't explicitly close the object).

So the bottom line is that you should always explicitly close your `Database`, `Recordset`, `TableDef`, and `Workspace` objects.

Handling Errors

Error handling is done with the `DBEngine`'s Errors collection of `Error` objects. Whenever an error occurs, you can examine the Errors collection for all errors. Basically, the Errors collection holds all errors that occur during an action or transaction, and each error is represented by an `Error` object. If you're writing a generic error handler, you can examine the Errors collection and report errors (based on an `Error` table or a basic `Select Case` statement). Here's an example:

```
On Error Goto ErrorBlock_Err:
Dim dbsMyDatabase as Database, errErrorObject as Error

Set dbsMyDatabase = OpenDatabase("BogusDB.MDB")
dbsMyDatabase.Close
```

```
Exit Sub
ErrorBlock_Err:
    For Each errErrorObject in dbsMyDatabase.Errors
        Debug.Print errErrorObject.Description
        Debug.Print errErrorObject.Source
        Debug.Print errErrorObject.Number
    Next
Resume Next
```

In applications that use DAO, the most interesting error—the most specific error—is the last error in the collection. You could choose to log all errors but display only the one error you felt was most useful to your end users.

DAO Compatibility

With the new improved object model, some of the following DAO 2.5 objects, methods, and properties are no longer supported in DAO 3.5. Table 15.16 shows the object, method, or property and its corresponding replacement.

Table 15.16. DAO compatibility.

DAO 2.5 Functionality Not Present in DAO 3.5	Recommended DAO 3.5 Replacement
FreeLocks	Not needed in Access 97
SetDefaultWorkSpace	DBEngine.DefaultUser/DBEngine.DefaultPassword
SetDataAccessOption	DBEngine.IniPath
BeginTrans (Database object)	BeginTrans method of the Workspace object
CommitTrans (Database object)	CommitTrans method of the Workspace object
RollBack (Database object)	RollBack method of the Workspace object
CreateDynaset (Database object)	(Database.)OpenRecordSet of type Dynaset
CreateSnapshot (Database object)	(Database.)OpenRecordSet of type Snapshot
DeleteQueryDef (Database object)	QueryDefs collection's Delete method
ExecuteSQL (Database object)	Execute method and RecordsAffected property of the Database object
ListTables (Database object)	TableDefs collection of the Database object
OpenQueryDef (Database object)	QueryDefs collection of the Database object
OpenTable (Database object)	(Database.)OpenRecordSet of type Table
Table ListIndexes	Indexes collection of the TableDef object
CreateDynaset (QueryDef object)	OpenRecordset method of the QueryDef object

continues

15

MICROSOFT ACCESS OBJECT MODEL

Table 15.16. continued

DAO 2.5 Functionality Not Present in DAO 3.5	Recommended DAO 3.5 Replacement
CreateSnapshot (QueryDef object)	OpenRecordset method of the QueryDef object
ListParameters (QueryDef object)	Parameters collection of the QueryDef object
Dynaset object	Recordset object of type Dynaset
Snapshot object	Recordset object of type Snapshot
Table object	Recordset object of type Table
ListFields method (Table, Dynaset, and Snapshot objects)	Fields collection of the Recordset object
CreateDynaset (QueryDef and Dynaset objects)	OpenRecordset method of the object with type Dynaset
CreateSnapshot (QueryDef and Dynaset objects)	OpenRecordset method of the object with type Snapshot

If you have an Access 95 project, you should have no compatibility issues when you convert it to Access 97. If, however, you have an Access 2.0 project that contains some of the older objects, properties, or methods and you just want to convert to Access 97, you can use the Microsoft DAO 2.5/3.5 Compatibility Library. This library provides backward compatibility with older versions of DAO and Jet. To check whether you're using this type library, select Tools | References from a Module window, and look in the References dialog box for the Microsoft DAO 2.5/3.5 Compatibility Library option (see Figure 15.22).

It's important to note that applications or databases converted to Access 97 automatically reference this type library. Likewise, applications and databases created in Access 97 don't have this reference. If you have an older application and you're not sure whether you're using any of the older objects, deselect the Microsoft DAO 2.5/3.5 Compatibility Library option, and select Run | Compile All Modules while in a Module window. If your application recompiles without errors, you don't have to use the Compatibility Library.

To ensure proper compatibility with future versions of DAO, it is recommended that you convert to DAO 3.5. Your application won't have the additional overhead of another layer, and you won't have to distribute the Compatibility Library with your application.

> **NOTE**
>
> A note on version 2.5 of DAO and Jet: Access 97 won't use DAO 2.5 directly because it's a fully 32-bit environment and DAO 2.5 is 16 bit. Databases created as 2.5 can be converted to 3.5, or the developer can use the Compatibility Library.

FIGURE 15.22.

The References dialog box.

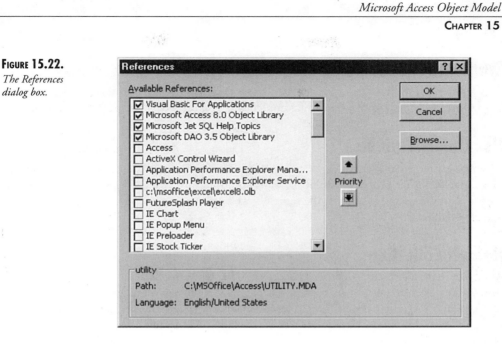

Bang (!) Usage Versus Dot (.) Usage

In the version of DAO prior to 3.0, you could use either the bang (exclamation point) or the dot (period) separator when referring to members of a collection. In DAO 3.5, most objects don't support the use of the dot separator. Eventually, support for the use of the dot separator will go away (and rolling over to new versions of DAO won't be as easy). Any future applications you develop should therefore use the bang separator only. Here's an example:

```
MyRS!Employee_ID ' This is OK
MyRS.Employee_Name ' This is OK, but not recommended
DBEngine.Workspaces(0) ' No longer supported
DBEngine!Workspaces(0) ' Correct usage
```

Optimizing DAO

The following sections cover some of the actions you can take to improve the performance of your application (strictly related to DAO). It's important to note that although some optimizations might provide a significant performance increase, some or all of the suggestions discussed here might not do anything for your application. Some external factors affect how much you can gain from each suggestion. Identifying key areas of functionality would be a good place to start optimizations—usually, only 10 percent of the code in an application provides 90 percent of the functionality. Start by concentrating on the 10 percent.

Start with a Good Database Design

First and foremost, make sure that the database is designed properly for its intended purpose. No amount of code optimization will completely overcome a deficient database design.

Use Object Variables

As stated earlier, whenever your application needs to reference a DAO property, store its value in a variable. This is probably one of the most common mistakes made by Access developers. Here's a simple rule of thumb: If the same object or property is used more than once, use an object variable.

Default Collections

All objects have a default property or collection. This setup might make your code difficult to read (some developers might get confused as to which property you're using if you're referring to the default property or collection). The code will run faster, however, because the compiler doesn't have to resolve an extra reference. For instance, the default collection of the DBEngine object is the Workspaces collection:

```
DBEngine.WorkSpaces(0).Databases(0)
```

You could use this instead:

```
DBEngine(0).Databases or DBEngine(0)(0)
```

The second version refers to the default collection of the DBEngine object. Confusing? Not really, after you learn what the default collections are for each object. After you have done one application using DAO, you get pretty familiar with data access objects.

Refreshing

Avoid refreshing unless you absolutely can't avoid it. Refreshing a collection gives you an up-to-date view of that collection's objects and properties or data, but in a multiuser environment or a speed-critical application, this is a very "expensive" method to use (in other words, it takes a lot of processor time or system resources).

Using Queries for Access Databases

Queries are precompiled SQL statements stored in your Access database. When your application uses dynamic SQL (SQL created in your code on-the-fly), Jet still needs to optimize and compile the SQL statement during runtime. If you use queries whenever possible, the optimization and compilation are done beforehand (when the query is created in Access), and you don't suffer the degradation in speed at runtime.

Using Stored Procedures for Remote Databases

If you are using a remote database such as SQL Server, use ODBC Direct and write your queries as stored procedures. Stored procedures are precompiled SQL statements in your remote database. When the stored procedure is compiled on your database, the server optimizes the query similar to how Access optimizes its own queries. The big difference here is that when you run the stored procedure, all the processing occurs on the remote server and only the data you asked for comes back to your workstation. If you use the Access query engine, much more data is returned to your workstation so the searching can occur there.

Recordset Snapshots

If your application doesn't need to update data in a recordset, use a snapshot rather than a dynaset. A snapshot's data is brought locally into your system's memory (except MEMO and OLE fields) and doesn't need the additional overhead a dynaset requires to update data. Additionally, if you're ever populating list boxes or combo boxes manually, use the `dbForwardOnly` option when creating the snapshot. This technique keeps links to only the next record (and realizes more memory savings) and can only go forward through the recordset.

Summary

This chapter discussed the use of Data Access Objects and Access 97, including the new ODBC Direct capabilities. With DAO, you have the tools to build feature-rich, robust database applications. Adding ODBC Direct positions Access 97 very well to be a solid client/server development platform.

Importing and Exporting Data

by Paul Anderson

IN THIS CHAPTER

CHAPTER 16

One of the most important features of any viable solution in the database market is connectivity. The strength of Access and the Jet Database Engine resides in their ability to accept, convert, and output data in a variety of formats. Importing and exporting data is accomplished through Access tools or the Jet Database Engine. The recent development in database connectivity, such as the Open Database Connectivity (ODBC) standard, has allowed data and its characteristics to be shared between database applications. Microsoft established ODBC within Access and continues to improve the functionality of ODBC in Access 97 with ODBC direct. As the industry progresses toward object database and Internet server technology, Access is quickly establishing methods and connectivity tools in these areas.

Importing Data

Access is designed to reference (attach) and import data from a wide variety of sources, including PC desktop applications, raw text data, or database origins. The Jet Database Engine can recognize and attach tables from sources such as the Index Sequential Access Method (ISAM) databases and legacy PC databases, such as dBASE or Paradox, while Access maintains compatibility with earlier versions of Access databases and other desktop products such as Lotus and Excel.

Before You Start

Rarely are database systems developed to encompass the entire set of data processed by an organization. Generally, maintaining an organization's ability to utilize data from external sources, such as accounting department forecasts from spreadsheet applications or remote office customer information, is a difficult process and valuable asset. However, there are requirements and regulations on the flow of information to individuals and groups inside and outside of the organization. For example, managers might want to share portions of customer databases with other departments or branch locations, and might even want to sell leads to other organizations. As the developer, you might be tasked with referencing data from many sources while maintaining appropriate rules and security in these operations.

Compatibility Issues When Working with Access Databases

When specifying a link or opening external Access tables directly, it is unnecessary to specify a source database type; use the same procedures to link or open other external databases. The dialog box for linking to an external database from the Tools | Add-ins menu is shown in Figure 16.1.

FIGURE 16.1.

*Linking to an external
data source.*

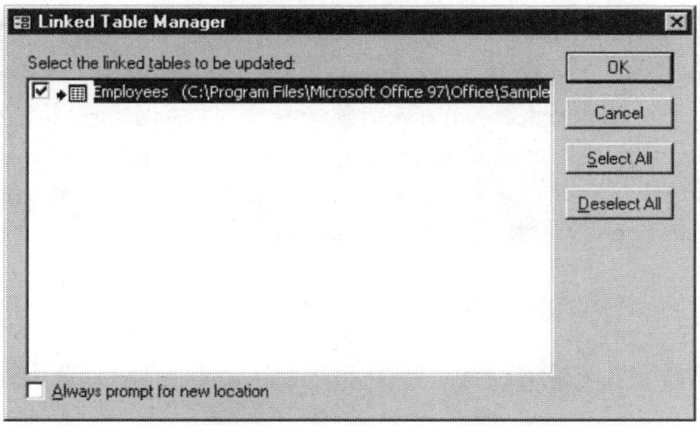

The dialog box for opening an external database from the File | Open menu is shown in
Figure 16.2.

FIGURE 16.2.

*Opening an external
data source with the
user interface.*

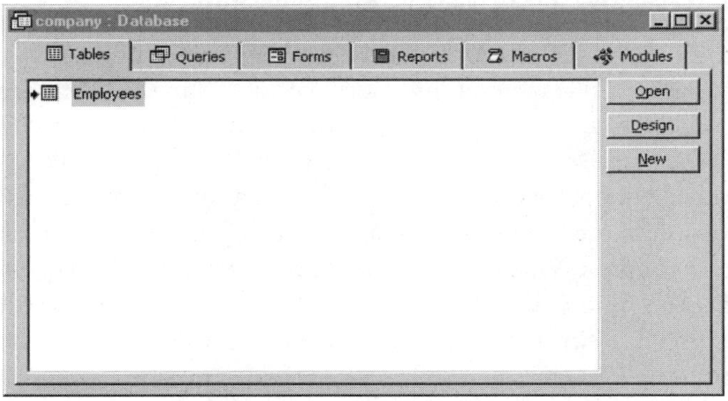

The CurrentDb function determines the active database and returns an object variable. The
connection string and source table name set the TableDef object to the external table and set its
SourceTableName property to the name of the external table. Use this method for the following
databases:

- Microsoft Access version 1.*x*
- Microsoft Access version 2.0
- Microsoft Access version 7.0
- Microsoft Access version 8.0

> **TIP**
>
> Specify the connection string and source table by using the connect and source arguments of the `CreateTableDef` method. Begin the connection string with a semicolon to hold a place for the database type, which is only used for the Jet Database Engine. Alternatively, the Access user interface can be used.

Opening an External Microsoft Access Table

The following is the simplest and most efficient way to open an external Microsoft Access table directly.

Create a database object and set the arguments of the `OpenDatabase` method to specify the full path to the external table and determine the option for sharing property of the database. It can be set to exclusive, read/write, or read-only permissions.

Linking to an external source can be accomplished using either the Access user interface or Visual Basic. While the user interface is consistent in the definition and handling of the external data, the source can be independently enabled with its own security and data-processing rules. The `TableDef` and `RecordDef` objects defined by the linking and opening processes can be enabled with password and security information parameters. Access provides a passthrough mechanism to provide this information as a default to the external data source. If you want to define a common set of security parameters across multiple software packages, Access will support this objective with this passthrough process. The procedure for linking is similar to opening a table directly. Figure 16.3 summarizes the key differences for referencing an external data source.

Figure 16.3.
Referencing an external data source.

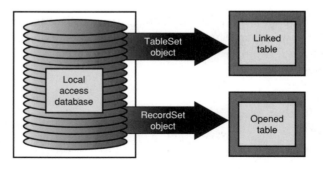

You must use Visual Basic to open external sources directly. When using Visual Basic to link a table or to open it directly, connection strings establish a reference to an external data source. The parameters passed to the external source reference the location of the source in the file system. The parameters may also pass security information.

TIP

Instead of specifying a connection string and source table name by setting properties of the TableDef object to a hard-coded location, you can specify them by using relative locations to the Access database using the connect and source arguments of the CreateTableDef method. You may even perform a search or query the user if the external source has moved as a part of the method routine.

Links define the connection information to reference the external data source. Connection information for linked data resides in the TableDef object for a particular table in the Access database. Moving or deleting the external data must be reflected in the corresponding TableDef object to maintain the external reference.

It is necessary to refresh the link of currently referenced tables that have been moved to maintain a connection to the data. First, reset the Connect property of the TableDef object to define a path to the table's new location. Then use the RefreshLink method of the TableDef object to update the link information.

An example of refreshing a link from the user interface is provided in Figure 16.4.

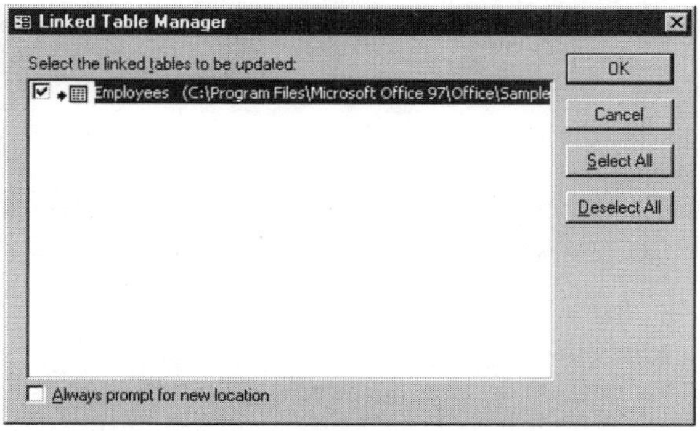

FIGURE 16.4.

Refreshing a link to an external data source.

Deleting the TableDef object associated with an external data source removes the icon from the Access table. The external data source record remains intact to external users; it is only flagged and unavailable to viewing by Access users.

In contrast to linking external data, the open process must be accompanied by the connection information at the beginning of each session. Access does not store any of the information needed to establish a connection to the external data, which may actually be an advantage in situations when the data is distributed. A query for customer information may be routed to the last known location and redirected to another server if it is not successfully connected on the first attempt. The user may intervene in the process, based on information from the customer or the employee handling the account.

> **TIP**
>
> When opening a table directly, specify the source and connection information as arguments of the `OpenDatabase` method instead of setting them separately as properties of a `TableDef` object. Use the dbname argument of the `OpenDatabase` method to specify the path and filename, and use the source argument of the `OpenRecordset` method to specify the table name.

The Jet Database Engine, installable ISAM driver, or ODBC direct driver determines which types of `Recordset` objects are available for the external data source you are referencing. Of these, only Jet recognizes the source and creates the type of `Recordset` that will result in the best performance. This intelligent link has a distinct advantage in reducing the effort and increasing efficiency in a heterogeneous database environment.

The Jet engine may also be fine-tuned as the process is running. Jet 3.5 does not have to be restarted to change operating parameters; a change in the characteristics of tasks generated in a mixed processing environment can be realigned with adjustments to the parameters. See Chapter 23, "Multiuser Development," for more information on these parameters. Microsoft Jet opens a table-type `Recordset` object.

> **CAUTION**
>
> Microsoft Jet opens a wide variety of external source file types. Be sure, however, to prevent the Jet engine from creating a table-type `Recordset` object for ODBC databases and linked installable ISAM tables. These external sources must be defined with ODBC direct, an appropriate ODBC driver, or an installable ISAM driver.

You must include the fully qualified path to an external file whether it is for a database, spreadsheet, text file, or HTML data source. On a local drive, the path must include the drive letter, all folders and subfolders, and the filename. The operating system may provide some flexibility to redirect the path by defining an alias or shortcut. If the external source were located in a folder on the user's workstation, it would be defined using the following syntax:

```
Drive:\Folder\Subfolder...\Filename
```

> **CAUTION**
>
> When referencing Paradox databases, the connection path must not be defined with an extension. Do, however, specify an extension for dBASE and FoxPro databases. External data sources that store multiple tables in a file require both the full path to the file defined as the dbname and the filename and extension in the source argument.

When you are referencing files over a network, the path must include a full path definition. Apply the following syntax:

```
\\Server Name\Share Name\Folder\Subfolder...\Filename
```

TIP

Map the network drive with one path per external source file. This will lend extra flexibility to your maintenance of file locations. ODBC data sources use a data source name (DSN) to indicate the path and filename. ODBC data sources require the DSN to be entered in their Windows Registry before the application attempts to reference external data.

Replica Set Synchronization

Replication is a valid feature for dealing with external data sources. A replica set contains one or more duplicate data files that can be distributed and updated independently. Periodically the replicas can be connected and resynchronized to share updates that have been made to any member of the replica set. A design master is a template for changes to the database structure. One or more replicas can be created from a design master replica. A design master can be created inside the current database for any external Access database source. A design master can also exist in a different Access database than the one running on the local workstation. The design master is usually found in the location designated as central to the resyncronization process with access provided to developers, whereas the replica would be stored at a remote location and cannot be modified structurally.

In either perspective, some consideration must be given to synchronization. *Synchronization* is the process of making some or all the data in the design master replica and in the replica(s) identical. This can be thought of as an import/export process; as changes are made to the existing records in one replica, updates are transferred to each of the other replicas that have that same record. New records added or records deleted from one replica are updated to the other replicas in the replica set.

You can synchronize one replica with another by using the Tools | Replication menu, as shown in Figure 16.5.

The synchronization process can also be driven by the Windows 95 Briefcase or Visual Basic code. Using Visual Basic, you can resynchronize the replicas each time an update occurs. Using the Briefcase, you use the Update All selection to synchronize replicas. You synchronize the replicas in Visual Basic by using the Synchronize method. Its syntax is

```
database.Synchronize pathname, exchange
```

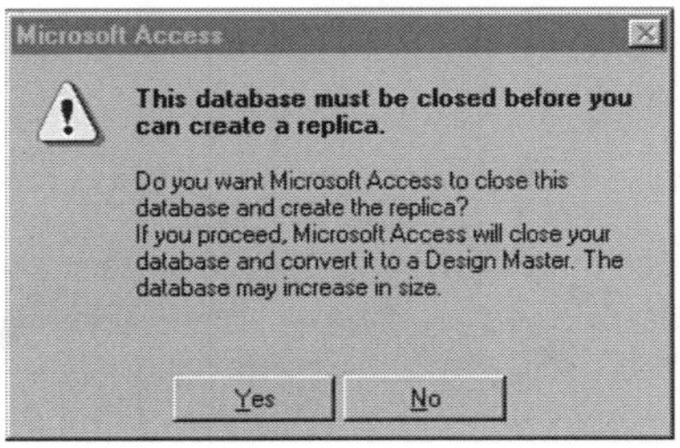

FIGURE 16.5.

The replica synchroni-
zation dialog box.

Here, *database* is an object variable that represents the database object that is the replica. You specify the path to the target replica in the *pathname* argument and use the *pathname* argument to synchronize one user's replica with another replica in the set. Set the exchange argument to a constant that indicates which direction to synchronize changes between the two replicas.

The exchange is bi-directional (import and export) unless an exchange argument is specified.

> **CAUTION**
>
> Microsoft Jet synchronizes design changes before it updates data. The design of replicas must be at the same version level before data can be exchanged. Do not make the replica on the network server the design master, because users will have permissions to change the design. Keep the design master replica on a local workstation that is restricted to developers. As changes are made to the development design master, the network server will be updated and will resynchronize other replicas in the set.

Compatibility Issues When Converting Tables from SQL Databases

Most database and other types of data-storage products have developed a range of compatible features that provide a mechanism for the transfer of data to another form. The advent of database standards has facilitated this process to the point where a common method and language have evolved.

The SQL developed for mainframe data retrieval and update has evolved into a general-purpose methodology for communicating data across disparate software platforms and as a client/server tool. In fact, among developers SQL has become erroneously synonymous with client/server strategies "unleashing" any application that can request and process data with a SQL interface to network services a contender in the marketplace. SQL is a tool through which components of the client/server strategy can be associated.

ODBC evolved as another standard within the SQL family that is promoted within Microsoft Access. ODBC uses SQL as the core language and facilitates client/server development over a network on inexpensive desktop workstations. SQL is not, however, a panacea in the quest for better data processing, and as an alternative more proprietary technologies are better suited to particular functions in data retrieval and updating. Several, such as ISAM, are derived from the method of data storage and retrieval used classically as an effective programming methodology.

Installable ISAM drivers for external data sources are provided for an array of databases using this approach. When accessing data from an external data source that does not use Microsoft Jet, you must specify the source database type in the connection string so that Access knows how to handle the data. It is not necessary to specify the source database type when you are accessing data from other data sources that use Microsoft Jet.

The import process is normally accomplished through the user interface. Figure 16.6 shows the dialog box for importing data from an external source.

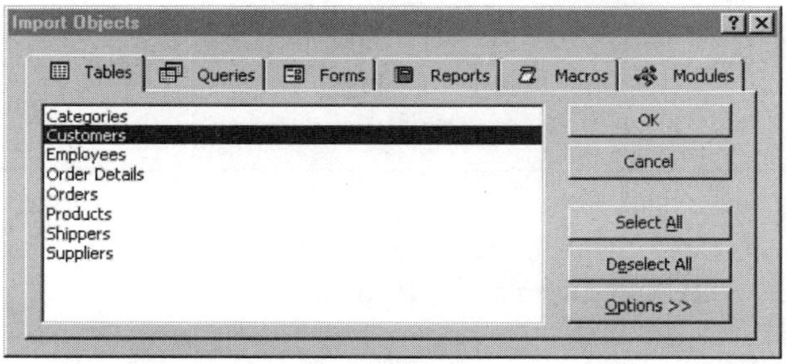

FIGURE 16.6.
The Import Objects dialog box.

A list of the external sources that can be imported by Access are represented in Table 16.1.

Table 16.1. External data sources that can be imported by Access.

Source	Version
dBASE	dBASE III
	dBASE IV
	dBASE 5.0
Microsoft Excel	Excel 3.0
	Excel 4.0
	Excel 5.0 (used for Microsoft Excel versions 5.0 and 7.0)
	Excel 8.0

continues

Table 16.1. continued

Source	Version
FoxPro	FoxPro 2.0
	FoxPro 2.5
	FoxPro 2.6
	FoxPro 3.0
	FoxPro DBC
Lotus 1-2-3	Lotus WK1
	Lotus WK3
	Lotus WKS
ODBC	ODBC
Paradox	Paradox 3.x
	Paradox 4.x
	Paradox 5.x
Text	Text
HTML	HTML Import

In the connection strings, enter the source external file type strings exactly as they appear in this table, including spaces and punctuation.

Referencing external data with Access is shown in Figure 16.7.

Figure 16.7.
Jet and installable ISAM external data sources.

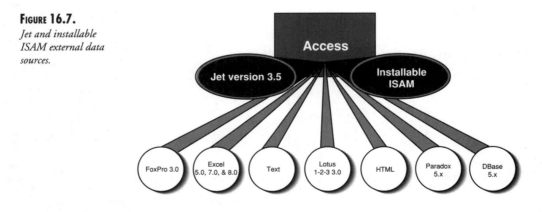

Passwords to External Data Sources

Rights to an external source that has been a password-protected table can be granted to the user by specifying them in the connection string. The PWD argument in the connection string is followed by a semicolon. Applications requiring network access must establish connections prior to attempting to access the external data, because the PWD argument can be used only to specify database passwords; it cannot be used to log on to a network. The PWD argument also cannot be used to open an encrypted Excel worksheet or workbook; you must unprotect and save the worksheet or workbook before you can open it with the Microsoft Excel installable ISAM driver.

It is best to avoid specifying the password in your code if sensitive data is stored in the external data source. If you must specify passwords in your code, consider either encrypting your database so that others cannot read the password with a text editor or disk utility, or establishing user-level or group-level security as the administrator on Windows NT.

> **TIP**
>
> Passwords may be saved as part of a linked ODBC table definition by setting the
> Attributes property of the TableDef object to dbAttachSavePWD.

When the user initially accesses the external data source, he is prompted for a password, which is then stored in Access. Access will attempt to use this password each time the user opens the linked tables. This is valuable because it gives the user access to the remote tables without having to input another password or worry about conflicting passwords. An application time-out feature can be used to detect a period of inactivity and then close the database on the workstation. This will resecure the external sources of data because the user must restart the application and supply the password(s) as needed to reconnect to the external sources.

> **TIP**
>
> If external data is extremely sensitive, create the MSysConf table in the external location
> instead of local storage of logon IDs and passwords. ODBC will automatically prompt
> users for any missing authentication information when they attempt to open the external
> database.

Data Access Objects and Performance

Improve application performance by using forward-only-type Recordset objects when the application requirements specify single-pass, read-only processing. Movement through the

`Recordset` object will be limited to one direction, and the following DAO methods and properties listed will remain unavailable:

The `Bookmark` property

The `Clone` method

The `FindFirst` method

The `FindLast` method

The `FindNext` method

The `Move` method (with any value other than 1)

The `MoveFirst` method

The `MoveLast` method

The `MovePrevious` method

The `OpenRecordset` method

This is not altogether a big disadvantage, because sometimes trade-offs must be made to increase performance when working with large external tables.

Other Databases

Installable ISAM drivers can enable linking or opening spreadsheets so that information can be manipulated as if the spreadsheets were database tables. Linking and opening spreadsheets is similar to the procedures for external databases. The following versions of Excel are supported by installable ISAM: 3.0, 4.0, 5.0, 7.0, and 8.0.

Data Access Objects can represent Excel spreadsheets to Access databases.

Lotus 1-2-3 files, including file types WK1, WK3, and WKS, may be similarly linked or opened using DAO methods.

The following operations cannot be performed on Excel worksheets or workbooks through installable ISAM:

- Deletion of rows
- Updating or clearing of cells that contain formulas
- Creating indexes
- Reading encrypted data
- Using the PWD (password) argument in a connection string to open an encrypted worksheet or workbook

TIP

Excel worksheets or workbooks can be decrypted through the Excel user interface to link or open them in your Access database.

Excel permits you to specify a subset of a data table when the worksheet or workbook is initially linked or opened. Visual Basic code can be used to link

- The whole worksheet
- A specified number of cells
- An unspecified number of cells

In a workbook file, you can link or open

- The whole worksheet
- A specified parameter anywhere in the workbook
- An unspecified parameter in a single worksheet

Microsoft Excel worksheet data links require the `Connect` property to be set to a connection string that includes the `DATABASE` argument and that has the `SourceTableName` property set to the name of the worksheet parameter specification of the cells to be accessed. When opening a worksheet or specified cell parameter directly, set the connection string in the `dbname` argument of the `OpenDatabase` method. This permits you to specify the name of the worksheet or cell parameters in the source argument of the `OpenRecordset` method. The conventions for these settings are shown in Table 16.2.

Table 16.2. Instructions for importing Excel data sources.

Object	Version	SourceTableName *or* source argument
Whole worksheet in a worksheet file	3.0 and 4.0	Specify `filename#xls`
Whole worksheet in a workbook file	5.0, 7.0, and 8.0	Specify `sheetname$`
Named range of cells in a worksheet or workbook file	3.0, 4.0, 5.0, 7.0, and 8.0	Specify the `NamedRange`
Unnamed range of cells in a worksheet file	3.0 and 4.0	Specify as `FirstCellInRange:LastCellInRange`

continues

Table 16.2. continued

Object	Version	SourceTableName *or* source argument
Unnamed range of cells in a single worksheet in a workbook file	5.0, 7.0, and 8.0	Specify the `sheetname$` and the range as `FirstCellInRange:LastCellInRange`

To access cells A1 through Z256 in a worksheet called `Employees`, for example, set the `SourceTableName` property or the source argument as follows:

```
Employees$A1:Z128256
```

> **CAUTION**
>
> Microsoft Excel will not permit a value to be specified for the worksheet or workbook with parameters that are larger than the number of rows, columns, or sheets.

Use the `CurrentDb` function to specify the full path of the Excel file to return an object variable representing the current Microsoft Access database. Set the connection string and source table name in a `TableDef` object. The `TableDef` object's `Connect` property should specify the source database type as well as the complete Microsoft Excel worksheet or workbook path. The `SourceTableName` property should be set to the worksheet's name or parameter specification.

Link external tables with the Microsoft Access user interface, or specify the connection string and source table by using the `Connect` and `Source` arguments of the `CreateTableDef` method, rather than setting properties of the `TableDef` object.

First define whether to open the worksheet or workbook exclusively, with read/write, or with read-only permissions. Then specify the source database type. Finally, specify the name of the worksheet or cell parameters as the `Source` argument of the `OpenRecordset` method.

The file formats of Excel versions 7.0 and 8.0 permit opening these files in read-only mode by Access.

The `HDR` argument in Excel and Lotus 1-2-3 contains the specification for the first row of the range opened as a record row or a definition of field names. Table 16.3 describes the `HDR` argument settings.

Table 16.3. HDR argument settings.

Setting	Value	Result
Yes	01	First row of a spreadsheet range is reserved for field names.
No	00	First row of a spreadsheet range is a record.

The Windows Registry contains the setting for the first row in the `FirstRowHasNames` parameter. Locate this setting in the following section:

```
\HKEY_LOCAL_MACHINE\SOFTWARE\Microsoft\Jet\3.5\Engines\Lotus key
\HKEY_LOCAL_MACHINE \SOFTWARE\Microsoft\Jet\3.5\Engines\Excel key
```

Converting Text Files

Text files are a valid data storage source; indeed, using them is by far the most common format. Delimited and fixed-width text files are simple and easy to reference directly from an Access database.

Text-format files, however, are rarely created with a structure consistent in structure for use in database processing. Text files created by a database such as Access are effective for storing small reference files, such as a list of values for a combo box or list box control. Rapid construction and ease of maintenance favor the use of text files in database applications.

Unfortunately, the performance of databases using text files quickly degrades as the file grows in size. Operations to add records or search to find a particular record are sources of performance degradation as text files grow.

Use the Text Installable ISAM to link a text file with an Access database for optimum performance. The procedure is similar to connecting to an external database. To link to the external file, define the source database type and the path specification for the text file in the `SourceTableName` property.

To open the text file, specify the source database type and the path of the text file in the `OpenDatabase` method arguments.

Text files can be linked to an Access database in four steps:

1. Use the `CurrentDb` function to return the object variable for the Access database.
2. Create a `TableDef` object and set the connection string and source table name.
3. Set the `TableDef` object's `Connect` property to the source type, and set the full path to the text file.
4. Finally, set the `SourceTableName` property to the name of the text file.

> **CAUTION**
>
> Access will use the information in the `Schema.ini` file only if it is placed in the same folder as the text file.

Before starting to organize the field values and delimiters of the text records, Access recognizes `Null` values in fixed-width text files by the absence of data (spaces) in the field, while in delimited text files, recognition is made by the presence of two consecutive characters. Carriage returns, commas, tabs, or user-defined delimiters are also valid.

The size limits for importing text are specified in Table 16.4.

Table 16.4. Size limits for importing text files.

Item	Maximum size per text file
Field	255 fields
Field name	64 characters
Field width	32,766 characters
Record size	65,000 bytes

> **CAUTION**
>
> Access does not support multiuser access to text files; instead, Access gives the user exclusive access to an opened file. Text files should be stored on the local workstation of each user or as clones, one for each user on the network. The latter method requires a workstation-specific variable to be specified in the argument of the `SourceTableName` property. This effort will be rewarded by allowing the maintenance of these text source files in one central location.

In Access, text file formats are determined either by directly reading the file or by using a schema information file that overrides the default settings in the Windows Registry. This schema information file is always named `Schema.ini` and must be stored in the same folder as the text data source. Fixed-width data cannot be accessed without a `Schema.ini` file, and should also be used when the text file contains the following data type:

> Date/Time
>
> Currency
>
> Floating-point numeric data

The `Schema.ini` file can be used whenever the developer wants formal control over data handling. A separate `Schema.ini` file for each text file being linked is not necessary. A `Schema.ini` file can be created with any text editor as long as one of five text-file characteristics is specified by each entry:

> Filename
>
> File format
>
> Field names, widths, and data types
>
> The character set
>
> Special data type formats and conversions

The name of the text source file is always specified first in a `Schema.ini` file. The following is an example:

```
Status.txt
```

Two basic text-file formats can be imported by Access: variable-length records and fixed-length records. Both can be used to store data, but the nature of computer storage and the constructs of programming languages are more suited to the use of fixed-length data formats. Storage sectors on magnetic disks are fixed in length. Memory storage buffers are fixed in the amount of data that can be stored. This extends itself to programming languages where a variable cannot exceed a certain length. The manifestation of this concept in Access results in the limitation of a record key to 50 characters and a maximum field length of 255 characters. The record must also not exceed 255 fields.

CAUTION

Although the number of fields that can be defined in Access is stated as 255, there are other considerations, such as the field name length, that may further limit the number of fields in a database record.

At the other end of the information systems spectrum, the nature of information is varied in length. Ask an American whose family immigrated to the United States in the early 1900s what he thinks about fixed-length data formats. The semiautomated data collection devices used to record the immigrants' names was limited. Family names from diverse cultures were not only compromised at the whim of overworked immigration officers, but could not be recorded by the primitive data storage devices that had been adapted from the carpet-manufacturing machines. Many families' names were truncated to allow for the entry of the data into forms and the storage systems. Through the later decades of this century, computing technology has been developed to allow larger and more variable-length information to be stored and processed.

As you can imagine, an organization would not want to limit its growth by the number of records that can be stored in a file or the range of numbers that can be stored in a field. On the other hand, certain processes are dependent on a fixed-length format. Numbers used for sorting must be a constant length to maintain the correct sort order. Significant characters for sorting must be in the same relative position to be sorted correctly. The dilemma about the year 2000 is a case in point (see the following Caution). When sorted from left to right, a fixed-length format will sort in a more predictable manner than a variable-length number or field. Sorting from right to left on numeric data in variable length data is always recommended.

CAUTION

As information changes and grows in complexity, the limitations of storage and data processing systems is challenged. Date field storage and processing is facing a major challenge as the year 2000 approaches. Database systems and programs are being scrutinized worldwide to see whether the date January 1, 2000 will result in erroneous data output.

The basic problem is that most external dates are stored and processed as a two-digit year with no reference to the century. Thus, the year 1999 is expressed as 99. When the year 2000 occurs, the year could be expressed as 00. Because 00 is technically before 99, all records would be out of sequence when the year field was processed. When the data is processed by the year, sorting algorithms output 00 before 99, which would be confusing when data from both years is included.

One solution is to program code to add the century to the beginning of the decade, and the year number as the data is retrieved for processing. If the year 99 was encountered, it would be processed as 1999. When encountering the number 00, the year would be processed as 2000. This method assumes that all records do not contain data that has dates near the beginning of the 19th century. If this assumption is correct, the algorithm could be extended to include the first quarter or half of the next century—or 2025 to 2050.

The Access database stores a date as a number of days before or after an arbitrary Day 0. The interpretation of this number is accommodated well past the year 2000. You must, however, be aware when date fields are not stored as Access date field types or when importing data that contains a date field. The year-2000 processing must be handled programmatically or converted into an Access date field well before the year 2000 occurs, especially in organizations that do long-range forecasting and may already be projecting data into the next century.

Hybrid-format files are used for internal database file formats where the majority of the fields are of fixed length but there are some fields that are designated as memo fields and must have more flexible lengths. In these hybrid formats, certain constructs, such as keys and indexed fields, are usually a fixed length. Sorting and subdividing data within fields is facilitated by using a fixed-length format.

Fixed-length fields must be padded or truncated to maintain relative position in the database. The format of the text file can be set to any of the values shown in Table 16.5.

Table 16.5. Format values for importing text files.

Format	Value
Tab delimited	`TabDelimited`
Delimited by commas	`CSVDelimited`
Delimited by any character (char)	`Delimited(char)`
Predefined record length	`FixedLength`

CAUTION

When specifying a character-delimited format, a double quote character (") is not allowed. Developers will commonly use an asterisk (*) to delimit text fields.

Delimited text files are useful in storing variable-length data for use in information systems. The nature of text-type data is variable, such as in an employee's name or address. Even postal code information, which may be a fixed length in certain locations, is a different fixed length for another purpose, such as for a mailbox or an address in another country. Delimited text fields require an instruction to find the end of the field delimiter. Consider reasonable limitations on the maximum field length to keep the overhead in processing variable-length fields to a minimum.

To import text data and use the records and fields, the location and structure must be defined to Access. The path, field names, and number of records are specifications for external source text files.

Field names for delimited text files can be specified in the following ways:

- Set the `ColNameHeader` entry to `True` and define the field names in the first record of the source text file.
- Specify each field by number and designate the field name and data type.
- Let Access determine the data types of the fields when the text file is linked or opened.

Set the `MaxScanRows` entry to the number of records to be scanned when field data types are determined. Access will scan the whole file when the max row entry is set to `0`. For example, an asterisk-delimited text source file with headings in the first record that had the first 50 lines as records would be specified as follows:

```
Format = Delimited(*)
ColNameHeader=True
MaxScanRows=0
```

Fixed-width record text files are common in data-processing applications. The consistent format allows database programs to reliably reference fields by determining the offset number of characters to the beginning of the field and field length to extract data from a record. This data-processing design methodology and programming is widespread use where the data is consistent in length and data type, because fewer processing instructions are necessary to locate and extract the field data for fixed-length records.

For fixed-width record files, specify each field by number and by the field name, data type, and width designated for fixed-width files. Set the `Coln` entry; the syntax of which is as follows:

```
Coln=ColumnName type [Width #]
```

Each entry begins with `Coln`, where the `n` is a positive integer. The `ColumnName` is the name of the field. If the field name contains embedded spaces, it must be surrounded by double quotation marks. The `type` is any of the following Jet SQL data types:

> Byte
>
> Long
>
> Currency
>
> Single
>
> Double
>
> DateTime
>
> Text
>
> Memo

Other ODBC data types:

> Char (same as Text)
>
> Float (same as Double)
>
> Integer (same as Short)
>
> LongChar (same as Memo)
>
> Date date format

The `Width` value specifies the width of the field (required for fixed-width files). The `#` is an integer that specifies the number of characters in the field (required if `Width` is specified).

The following example defines two fields: an 8-character `EmployeeID` text field and a 30-character `EmployeeName` text field.

```
Col1=EmployeeID Text Width 8
Col2=EmployeeName Text Width 30
```

The `CharacterSet` must be specified in the `Schema.ini` file for the character set of the computer used. The choices are ANSI and OEM. Add the following entry to the `Schema.ini` file for ANSI:

```
CharacterSet=ANSI
```

An optional number of entries in the `Schema.ini` file defines the data type formats and conversions. For example, set this to the character used to separate thousands in currency values:

```
CurrencyThousandSymbol
```

Set the following to the character used to separate the whole number from the decimal portion of a currency value:

```
CurrencyDecimalSymbol
```

Access will use the value in Windows Control Panel for any omitted entries.

Importing HTML Files

Hypertext Markup Language (HTML) is the standard interpreted language on the Internet. These files include the text that users will see, tags that specify formatting and data entry, and location references to program and graphics files. They are used to present and gather information as well. A variety of Internet browsers can be used to interpret and display the information in the HTML file to the user. HTML, which can also be used to create pages on workstations of an intranet, is a simple and effective way to provide a user interface across the major workstation operating system environments. See an HTML programming book for a complete guide.

One or more tables can be embedded in an HTML file using the HTML table data tags (`<TD>` and `</TD>`). Access can be used to import the tabular data in the HTML files. Use the text-installable ISAM driver to link to the table in the HTML file or to open it directly.

The procedure to link an HTML data source is similar to connecting to external databases. HTML files can be linked to an Access database in four steps:

1. Use the `CurrentDb` function to return the object variable for the Access database.
2. Create a `TableDef` object and set the connection string and source table name.
3. Set the `TableDef` object's `Connect` property to the source type and the full path to the HTML file.
4. Set the `SourceTableName` property to the name of the table in the HTML file. The source database type is HTML Import. The path is determined by the uniform resource locator (URL) address of the HTML file on the Internet or intranet.

TIP

Specify the connection string and source table name by using the `Connect` and `Source` arguments of the `CreateTableDef` method. Use the Access user interface to link to the external data.

To open a table in an HTML file directly from Access, use the `OpenDatabase` method. Set the arguments of the `OpenDatabase` method to specify the complete path to the HTML file. Determine whether to open the HTML file exclusively, with read/write, or with read-only permissions.

CAUTION

The local copy of the HTML file is read-only. You cannot modify tabular data in an HTML file. You can, however, open tabular HTML information as a recordset and export the table as an HTML file if the contents of the recordset are saved in a new table in your local Access database.

When you open an HTML file, the ISAM driver uses File Transfer Protocol (FTP) to copy the source file from the Internet server to the workstation requesting the data. The text-installable ISAM does not access the file on the server, but references this local copy of the file. A snapshot of the actual records in the file on the server is provided. Your application does not have access to any changes made to the server copy of the file until you reopen or re-link the HTML file. Any changes you make to the local copy will not modify the copy of the file on the Internet server.

A table inside an HTML file must be referenced with a name. A table with a caption uses the caption as a name. A singular table in a file or a table without a caption can use the HTML document title as its name. If more than one table without captions exists in the HTML file, reference the tables sequentially in the code as `Table1`, `Table2`, and so on. When the tables are imported, the text-installable ISAM will interpret these as "the first unnamed table in the file," "the second unnamed table in the file," and so on.

The text-installable ISAM interprets the cell content as it reads the data in the HTML file and chooses the data type for each field in the table. The text-installable ISAM selects the Long or Double data type when most of the values in a table are numeric, depending on whether the majority of the numbers are integer or floating-point values. When textual field values outnumber numeric values, the ISAM driver selects the Text data type, which is limited to a maximum field size of 255 characters.

CAUTION

The ISAM driver assigns the `Null` value to cells of the minority data type in fields that contain a combination of data types. You can override or bypass the driver and specify data types for fields by creating a schema information file. This file contains information about each field in the table. Remember to store your `Schema.ini` file in the same folder as the local HTML file you are linking or opening.

You can use HTML to embed graphics within table cells. Graphics are identified through the HTML `<IMG SRC ... >` tag. If a cell contains this tag and no text, the ISAM driver returns a `Null` value because it can't read graphics. If the cell contains a graphic image reference and text, the installable ISAM will return the text.

When a hyperlink tag of the form `<A HREF="...">TEXT</A>` is found by the installable ISAM, the text between the tags is displayed and the hyperlink information is omitted. If the text embedded in the hyperlink has fewer than 255 characters, the installable ISAM creates a text field. If the text has more than 255 characters, the ISAM driver creates a memo field. The ISAM driver reads the caption and the URL associated with the hyperlink when the cell contains no other embedded text.

When lists are embedded within a table in an HTML table, the text-installable ISAM will insert a carriage return and a line feed after each list item. Separate cells for the list items are not created. The installable ISAM interprets a list that isn't embedded in a table as a single-field table. Tables that are embedded within other tables are treated as separate tables. The cell that contains the embedded table is set to the `Null` value, and the embedded table must be associated with a separate recordset.

TIP

Processing performance is decreased slightly in Access when an external link or table is opened in the database. This is because the installable ISAM is just one more layer your data must pass through when accessed. Transferring and translating data or maintaining an external index in a foreign format will result in significantly slower performance.

CAUTION

You can improve application performance by using forward-only-type `Recordset` objects when the application requirements specify single-pass, read-only processing. Movement through the `Recordset` object will be limited to one direction, and the DAO methods and

continues

continued

properties will remain unavailable. This is not altogether a big disadvantage; sometimes trade-offs must be made to increase performance when working with large external tables.

Visual Basic Code for External Data Sources

Visual Basic gives the developer finer control of processing external data sources. Query and update processing can be staged in the local environment to limit the amount of data and type of processing between Access and a remote data source. Once an external source has been defined to an Access database, the CurrentDb function can be used to reference the source. From this point, processing functions in Visual Basic can be used, treating the external source as any Access table. Of course, the limitations outlined in other sections of this chapter and common-sense guidelines for efficient external data source processing should be followed.

To link to an external data source with code, define a subroutine call as follows:

```
Call LinkToEmployees("C:\data\company","Employees","tblemployees")
```

The subroutine to link the data could be written as follows:

```
Sub LinkToAccess(strLocation As String, strTable As String, strTable)
Dim db As DATABASE
Set db = CurrentDb
Dim td As TableDef
Set td = db.CreateTableDef(strTable)
td.Connect = ";DATABASE=" & strLocation
td.SourceTableName = strTable
db.TableDef.Append td
End Sub
```

This is a simple way to link an Access database. If the link were being made to another source, the subroutine call would include the filename in the path instead of the unextended Access file, and would have the external source designation in the connection string.

Processing performance is decreased slightly in Microsoft Access when an external link or table is opened in the database. This is because the installable ISAM is just one more layer the data must pass through when accessed. Transferring and translating data or maintaining an external index in a foreign format will significantly decrease performance.

To open an external Access source, the following OpenDatabase method can be employed:

```
OpenDatabase(DBname, Exlusive, Read/Write, Source)
```

This method identifies the external source, the rights, and the type/connection string. Employing Visual Basic to accomplish this could include the following call:

```
Call OpenExdb("c:\data\company","Employees")
```

Suppose the Employees table is located in the Company database. The Visual Basic code could be written as follows:

```
Sub OpenExdb(Name As String, Table As String)
Dim db As DATABASE
Set db = DBEngine.Workspaces(0).OpenDatabase(strDBName, False, _False, "")
Dim rs As Recordset
Set rs = db.OpenRecordset(Name)
Do While Not rs.EOF
Debug.Print rs.Fields(0).Val
rs.MoveNext
Loop
End Sub
```

Each record (Val) would be available to the local Access database for the current session. The routine would be applicable to Access and other compatible external sources.

Troubleshooting Tips

There is a common set of problems you will usually encounter when connecting to an external data source. The following actions may help resolve these problems:

- Determine whether access to the external table is available through a file manager such as Windows Explorer.

- Run the native application and make sure that the external source file can be opened without error and is the proper type.

- Make sure that the code establishing the connection to the external table follows the proper guidelines as outlined earlier in this chapter.

- If the connection originally made to the data source no longer works, use a file utility to make sure the table is in its original location. You may have to refresh the link, especially if the table is linked to the Access database.

- If you receive the message Unable to find installable ISAM, check the source database type specified in your code. Remember that Excel 7.0 is not a valid source database type as Excel 5.0 is.

- Check that the installable ISAM driver is located in the Windows Registry folder and in the \HKEY_LOCAL_MACHINE\SOFTWARE\Microsoft\Jet\3.5\Engines key.

- Check that the arguments are of the correct form (and case, for a case-sensitive data source).

- Make sure there is a surplus of disk space where the external data source resides.

- Make sure users have enough temporary space to handle any indexes Access creates when you run a query.

- The Temp subfolder should reside in the user's Windows folder, and there should be sufficient disk space for the Temp indexes.

> **CAUTION**
>
> If there is not enough available disk space for query indexes, abnormal application behavior may result.

■ If you are trying to access the table by using Visual Basic code, try to import the table.

■ Choose Get External Data from the File menu and click Import to verify the properties that were set in Design View for the imported table before writing Visual Basic code for the connection string.

Exporting Data

Exporting data to be used in other applications is, at best, a shotgun approach to data processing. Finer control of external file output can be achieved (if permitted) through writing to external data sources that have been linked or opened for import. All the techniques and methods used in the previous sections of this chapter are valid to output data to the external source.

Before You Start

The export process covered here is intended to create external format file types from Access internal tables and sources that are currently opened or linked to the local database. Understanding the characteristics of the external file types and the limitations of Access features to reflect those features in other products are important considerations. Extensive testing of the export process to the target data files is recommended before incorporating them formally in an information-systems strategy.

Compatibility Issues

Compatible data formats are difficult to ascertain without actual practice. Software on different platforms, written on different platforms, with newer versions, may present difficulties in exporting the correct file formats. For example, a dBASE file format written by Quicken may not be in the same format as a newer version of dBASE itself. Compatibility standards in Excel 5.0 are more difficult to interpret than in earlier or later versions. The following questions are suggested for review:

■ What format features are expected by the users of the target program?

■ What versions of the target software are used?

■ What interval will be used to export the database to keep it updated for user needs?

> **TIP**
>
> Use the earliest version of the target file type for export. This will not only assure compatibility with the later versions of the application software, but will result in the simplest and most trouble-free set of format characteristics in the exported file.

HTML File Export

You cannot modify tabular data in an HTML file. Tabular HTML information can be opened as a recordset and the table exported as an HTML file if the contents of the recordset are saved in a new table in your local Access database. The contents of the table, as well as the minimum necessary HTML header information, is included when you export the table. After updating the table in the local Access database, you can combine it with the surrounding HTML code and then write it in a file as a text string. After closing the connection to the original file, the operating system's copy function can then be used to overwrite the existing file—which, for all intents and purposes, updates the file.

Summary

Access is an important tool for viewing and updating information from both Access-based and external data sources. Referencing external data is important in communicating information from outside or between organizations. An information infrastructure may also have evolved as a heterogeneous data-processing environment, including workstation clients and a variety of database servers. As the scale of connectivity problems increases, so does the complexity. The key to effective data management lies in the ability to define standard simple interfaces and work toward normalization of database structures.

Two similar ways of referencing external data sources with a Microsoft Access database are available: External data sources can be linked and remain independent of Access, or they can be opened directly and become defined and normalized within the database rules defined by the Access developer. Both linking and opening are flexible in the type of source file referenced and powerful in the ability to control processing of the external data. The data sources in each case can be shared in a homogeneous data processing environment without compromising the constraints intrinsic to their sources.

VI
PART

ActiveX Controls

ActiveX Controls

by Dave Thompson

IN THIS CHAPTER

A technology definition based on Microsoft's Component Object Technology (COM) specification, ActiveX controls replace OLE controls, first introduced to Access in version 7.0 (Access 95). ActiveX controls are objects and are sometimes called OLE objects or COM objects.

These controls are distributed as files, typically with an OCX extension, such as MSCAL.OCX. They may also be found with DLL and EXE filename extensions.

ActiveX controls may best be understood by what they do.

What's in a Name?

The short answer is that, beginning with Office 97, the term ActiveX replaces the term OLE (Object Linking and Embedding). This is a simplification, but helpful for those who are new to ActiveX, but not new to OLE.

You may have first heard of ActiveX in the context of the Internet. You can use ActiveX to create active content, such as animation, for Web sites. This chapter (and the next) focuses on ActiveX controls used for Access 97 applications.

SOFTWARE AS TECHNOLOGY

For many of us, technology is a hardware thing. Technology in the PC arena is CPU clock speeds, modem bps (bits per second), and laser printer resolutions and speeds. We all know that as technology advances we get faster PCs, faster modems, and faster, higher-resolution printers.

We tend to think of software as a product that we use on our high tech PCs.

But technology can also apply to software as ideas that become entire product categories.

Access 97 is a relational database. In 1968 Dr. E. F. Codd first described the relational model in theory as an exercise of applying mathematical theory to database management.

ActiveX is part of the evolving OLE/COM software technology.

Used as a descriptive term, ActiveX covers ActiveX controls, ActiveX documents, Internet ActiveX controls, and more.

What Are ActiveX Controls?

ActiveX controls are objects having methods, events, and properties. They can be used to provide needed functionality for your applications in a consistent manner. Additionally, by using ActiveX controls, your applications will present a polished, professional appearance to the user.

ActiveX controls can be described as self-contained, packaged bundles of code to include a user's presentation (or user interface). For example, if you've built a form with some procedures such as VBA code, and used that form again in a new application, you understand the concept of reusable objects. By re-using a form in this manner, you've treated the form as an object making use of the same user interface and the same functionality in multiple locations (applications).

When cutting and pasting a favorite form from one application to another, you might add a procedure here and there to the form in the new application. Or you might modify a procedure in the form's `code` module (`code behind forms`, now known as a `class` module in Access 97).

This is not so with ActiveX controls. They are true to the object model of encapsulation. In other words, you can't modify the code inside the control object. The control is factory-sealed, in this regard.

What you can do is use the control's properties, events, and methods to tailor the use of the control to your specific need.

When you re-use a form from one application to another, you copy it into a new database (an MDB file). Just as the form is placed in the forms collection of the database, so must ActiveX controls have a home.

ActiveX controls are placed on individual forms or reports in your application. The form serves as a container for the control.

It is important to know that controls, unlike our forms, do not have a separate existence. That is, controls must always be sited or located in some host container, such as a form. Just as text boxes, list boxes, or combo boxes are controls placed on a form, ActiveX controls are essentially just that: controls. They function in the context of a form or a report, just like other controls.

In the examples from this chapter and the next, you will see that ActiveX controls can appear simple or complex. The more sophisticated controls appear form-like, requiring a significant amount of screen "real estate" to display. Some have built-in command buttons. The overall visual effect becomes that of a pop-up or modal form.

Some of the simpler controls with limited functionality occupy little room (display size) on your form. Visually, this makes them appear more like controls.

Remember that even though ActiveX controls can be thought of as self-contained bundles of code with their own user interface, they require a host container, such as a form.

ActiveX Controls Provided with Access 97

Most of the ActiveX controls that Microsoft provides with Access 97 ship with the Office 97 Developer Edition (ODE). The `Calendar` and `Web Browser` ship with all versions of Access 97. Table 17.1 lists the currently supported ActiveX controls from Microsoft for Access 97.

Table 17.1. ActiveX controls for Access 97.

Control Name	Supplied with	Description
Animation	ODE	Plays avi files (no sound)
Calendar	ALL	Displays a monthly calendar
Common Dialog	ODE	Gets/saves files and printer control
ImageList	ODE	Images for other controls
ListView	ODE	Lists in dialog box format
Rich Textbox	ODE	RTF text formatting
MSInet	ODE	Internet transfer (HTTP/FTP)
ProgressBar	ODE	Similar to status line progress
Slider	ODE	Drags pointer across linear scale
TabStrip	ODE	One or more Tab objects
ToolBar	ODE	Custom toolbar
TreeView	ODE	Looks like Windows Explorer
UpDown	ODE	Increment/decrement values
WinSock	ODE	TCP/UDP network services
TX Web Browser	VP	Installed with IE 3.*x*

ODE = Microsoft Office 97 Developer Edition

ALL = All retail versions of Microsoft Office/Access 97

VP = ValuPack on Microsoft Office 97 CD-ROM.

CAUTION

Article Q160126, available on Microsoft's Knowledge Base site at www.microsoft.com/kb/, verifies that the controls listed in Table 17.1 have been tested for use with Access 97. There are other Microsoft and third-party ActiveX controls. Use them with caution, and read what each manufacturer says about the control's compatibility with Office/Access 97.

Registering ActiveX Controls

Earlier I described ActiveX controls as self-contained objects that you can use across different applications, or several times within the same application. I also said that these controls are essentially factory-sealed.

The control objects are typically distributed as OCX files and placed in your `Windows\System` subdirectory (or `Windows\System32` for NT). Your application will need to find the OCX file when the control is used in your application. Because the same control may be used by many applications, it is a good idea to have one copy of the OCX file and share it among applications.

This is done by placing a single copy of the control on your computer drive and providing an entry for it in the Windows Registry. The default location for shared controls is `\Windows\System`.

The setup program for ODE (Office 97 Developer Edition) will register installed ActiveX controls for you, and third-party providers provide their own instructions.

There are two ways to register a control yourself. `Regsvr32.exe` is a program installed with the ODE that can register (and unregister) controls. You can also register controls from within Access.

Regsvr32.EXE

`Regsver32.exe` can be used to manually register a control. Examples of its uses are shown in the `acread80.wri` (Access 97 `Readme` file):

```
Windows 95: regsvr32.exe \windows\system\mscal.ocx
Windows NT: regsvr32.exe \windows\system32\mscal.ocx
```

THINGS MOVE FAST

Check Microsoft's online Knowledge Base (www.microsoft.com/kb) for the latest copy of the Access Readme file as Article Q161345.

Also, look for Q161983 to download the most recent version of `Regsvr32.exe`.

In the Knowledge Base, use the search phrase `ActiveX AND 97` to find the latest information on Access 97 and ActiveX controls.

Using Access 97 to Register a Control

To register a control, select ActiveX Controls... from the Tools menu, as shown in Figure 17.1. Highlight the control you want to register, and click on the Register... button, as shown in Figure 17.2.

FIGURE 17.1.

The Access 97 Tools menu.

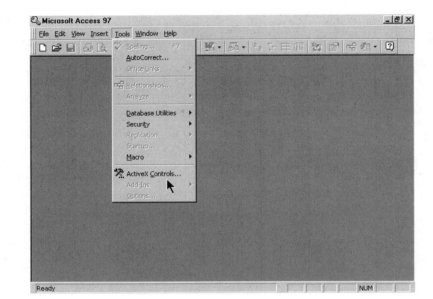

FIGURE 17.2.

The dialog box used to register ActiveX controls.

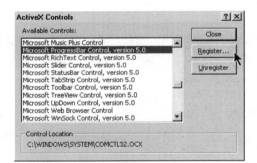

CAUTION

You will find that there are many controls listed in the Available Controls list box. The fact that a control shows up in this list does not imply that it is compatible with Access 97. Suggestion: At least initially, stick to the known quantities listed in this chapter and third-party controls specifically stated by the supplier of the control to be compatible with Access 97.

Table 17.2 shows the names of the controls listed in this chapter as they appear in the dialog box shown in Figure 17.2.

Table 17.2. ActiveX controls and how they are displayed in the register window.

Control Name	Appears in register window as
Animation	Microsoft Animation Control, version 5.0
Calendar	Calendar Control 8.0
Common Dialog	Microsoft Common Dialog Control, version 5.0
ImageList	Microsoft ImageList Control, version 5.0
ListView	Microsoft ListView Control, version 5.0
Rich Textbox	Microsoft RichText Control, version 5.0
MSInet	Microsoft Internet Transfer Control, version 5.0
ProgressBar	Microsoft ProgressBar Control, version 5.0
Slider	Microsoft Slider Control, version 5.0
TabStrip	Microsoft TabStrip Control, version 5.0
ToolBar	Microsoft Toolbar Control, version 5.0
TreeView	Microsoft TreeView Control, version 5.0
UpDown	Microsoft UpDown Control, version 5.0
WinSock	Microsoft WinSock Control, version 5.0
Web Browser	Microsoft Web Browser Control

The files containing the control objects are installed in Windows\System (or Windows\System32 for NT) and located within the files, as shown in Table 17.3.

Table 17.3. Filenames and internal file versions of controls.

Control Name	Filename	Internal version (Major)
Animation	COMCT232.OCX	5.0
Calendar	MSCAL.OCX	8.0
Common Dialog	COMDLG32.OCX	5.0
ImageList	COMCTL32.OCX	5.0
ListView	COMCTL32.OCX	5.0
Rich Textbox	RICHTX32.OCX	5.0
MSInet	MSINET.OCX	5.0
ProgressBar	COMCTL32.OCX	5.0
Slider	COMCTL32.OCX	5.0
TabStrip	COMCTL32.OCX	5.0

continues

Table 17.3. continued

Control Name	Filename	Internal version (Major)
ToolBar	COMCTL32.OCX	5.0
TreeView	COMCTL32.OCX	5.0
UpDown	COMCT232.OCX	5.0
WinSock	MSWINSCK.OCX	5.0
Web Browser	SHDOCVW.DLL	4.7

CAUTION

Check the Microsoft Web site (www.microsoft.com/ie/default.asp) for the latest update to Internet Explorer (IE) 3.01, if you are a Windows 95 or NT 4.0 user. The IE update will download the latest copy of SHDOCVW.DLL.

CAUTION

For developers distributing applications, most of the ActiveX controls in Table 17.2 have dependencies (other required files), such as ComCat.DLL. See Access 97 Help | Contents and Index | Index, and search for ActiveX controls, files required for.

Adding an ActiveX Control to a Form

There are two categories of ActiveX controls for when the control is visible and when the control is hidden, as used in Access 97 forms. The first category is a control that looks the same in both the form's Design View and Normal (runtime) View. The Calendar control is an example.

Another category is visible only in the Design View. The ActiveX control is placed on the form during design, but doesn't appear in the form's Normal (runtime) View. While not visible at runtime (or hidden), the ActiveX control's functionality is available to be used with the form.

The Common Dialog is an example of an ActiveX control that is hidden until invoked at runtime (for example: MyDialog.ShowOpen).

Inserting the ActiveX Calendar Control

In Figure 17.3 I have opened a new form in Design View and selected Insert | ActiveX Control…. After clicking on ActiveX Control…, the list of candidate controls appears, and you select Calendar Control 8.0, as shown in Figure 17.4, and then click OK.

FIGURE 17.3.

The form design Insert menu.

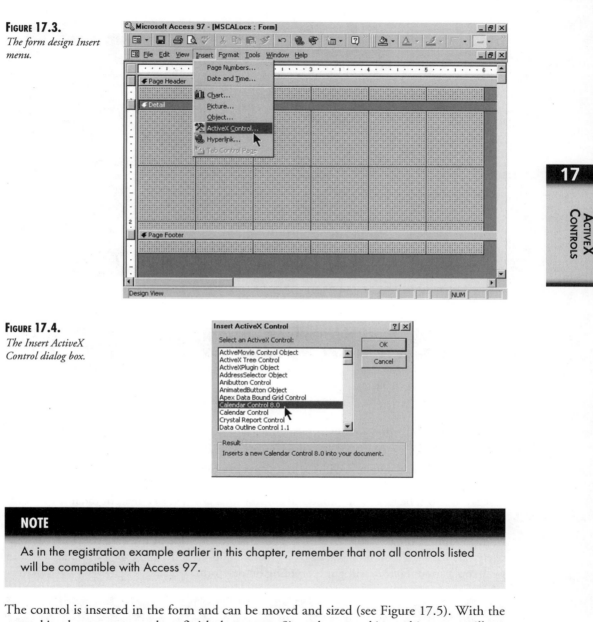

FIGURE 17.4.

The Insert ActiveX Control dialog box.

As in the registration example earlier in this chapter, remember that not all controls listed will be compatible with Access 97.

The control is inserted in the form and can be moved and sized (see Figure 17.5). With the control in place, you are ready to finish the process. Since the control is an object, you will use its properties, events, and methods to implement the functionality you need.

FIGURE 17.5.

The Calendar *control in form Design View.*

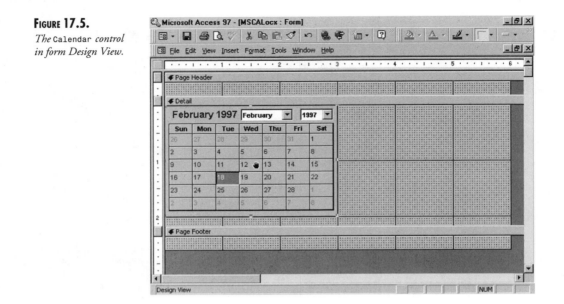

> **NOTE**
>
> The Calendar control will show MSCAL.Calendar.7 as its class property. It uses a version 7.0 Type Library, but is supported in Access 97.

For our example, I will name the control ATXCalendar and set its visible property to No in the usual manner. (Click on the control and then edit the property sheet.)

For the form's data source I will use the Contacts table having a NextContactDate field. ATXCalendar will be used to point-and-click, setting the NextContactDate field through VBA. ATXCalendar will be used as an unbound control (it is not tied to a field in the form's source table or query).

In this example, the Calendar control is positioned to the side of the data controls. Alternatively, the Calendar could be placed on a separate pop-up form and called from any form in your application. Here, I will put everything on one form.

> **TIP**
>
> You can also size the calendar and lay it over the other four controls. This makes for a smaller form, but is not convenient when working in form design.
>
> You can always temporarily resize the calendar while in form design to keep it out of the way, but you must remember to put it back to the desired size when you are finished.

Figure 17.6 shows the form for this example when first opened, and Figure 17.7 shows the result of clicking on the command button (with calendar icon graphic) to display the Calendar control.

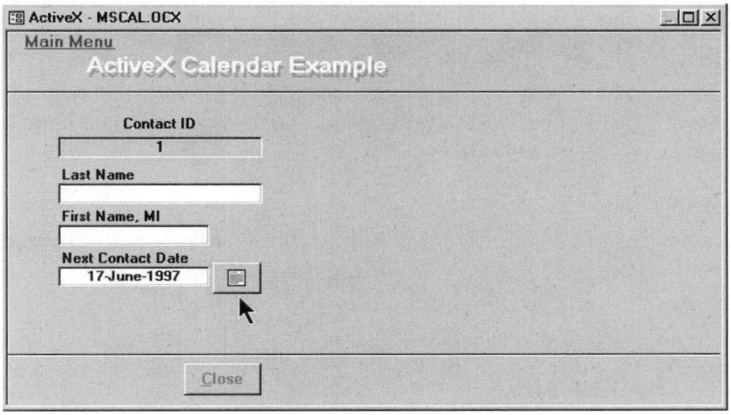

FIGURE 17.6.

The sample contact form.

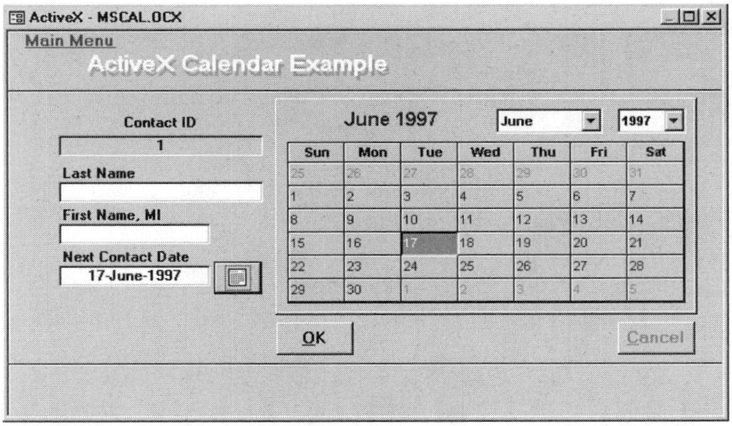

FIGURE 17.7.

The contact form with the Calendar control visible.

The command button to expose the calendar (see the arrow in Figure 17.6) has the following code attached:

```
Private Sub DateCMD_Click()
On Error Resume Next
Dim z
z = Me![NextContactDate]
'SEE general section this module
CalendarIsVisible True
If Not IsNull(z) Then
 Me![ATXCalendar].Value = z
End If
End Sub
```

Notice that when you display the calendar, you set its default value equal to the current value (if any) of NextContactDate control. If you do not supply a value, the control will default to the system date.

Because you will be showing and hiding the Calendar control from different command buttons, it is convenient to do this with one procedure. The general section of the form's class module has this procedure:

```
Public Sub CalendarIsVisible(ybln As Boolean)
'nothing of consequence to trap for on sample form
On Error Resume Next
If Not ybln Then
 'make sure move focus away from button before hiding
 Me![ID].SetFocus
End If
Me![ATXCalendar].Visible = ybln
Me![OKCalCMD].Visible = ybln
Me![CancelCalCMD].Visible = ybln
Me![ExitCMD].Visible = Not ybln
End Sub
```

Finally, you need to get the value of the calendar and set the date of the NextContactDate on our form, which you do with this procedure:

```
Private Sub OKCalCMD_Click()
Me![NextContactDate] = Me![ATXCalendar].Value
CalendarIsVisible False
End Sub
```

Calendar Properties, Events, and Methods

ActiveX controls have properties, events, and methods. Remember, though, that in Access 97 you work with the controls in a host container, such as a form. In this section, you will look specifically at the Calendar control, but the concepts are generally the same for working with other ActiveX controls placed in Access 97 forms.

Properties

The Calendar control has 22 properties (see Access 97 Help | Contents and Index | Index, and search for calendar control, properties).

All 22 properties appear on the property sheet (the Other tab) for the control in the form's Design View, as shown in Figure 17.8.

FIGURE 17.8.

The property sheet or Other tab for the Calendar *control.*

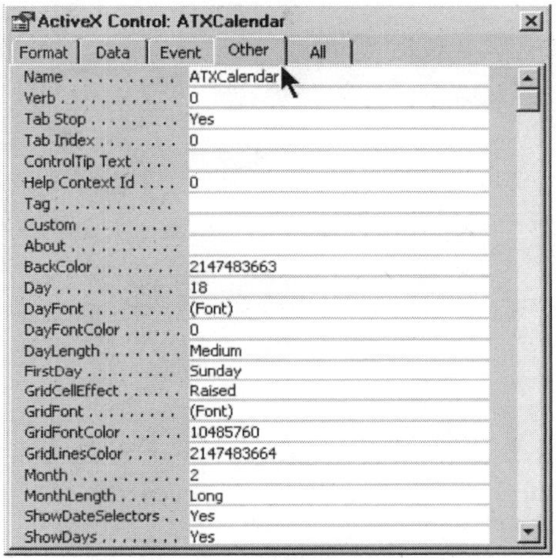

To view help file information about items appearing on the property sheet, select Help | What's This? The cursor changes to an arrow/question mark combination. Position the arrow on the name of a property (or within the ruled lines where the property value is set), and click.

Help for the specific property will be displayed, and then the cursor will be returned to normal.

Some controls support a custom property sheet. All the Calendar control properties are revealed in its Access 97 property sheet, but you may prefer to use the custom property sheet. To display the custom property sheet, click on the word Custom. (As you see in Figure 17.8, the Custom is eight lines down in the figure.) After clicking on Custom, a build button (three dots) will appear at the end of the line. Click on the build button to open the custom property sheet. (See also Figure 18.16 in Chapter 18, "Empowering ActiveX Controls with VBA.") Figure 17.9 shows the results of our example.

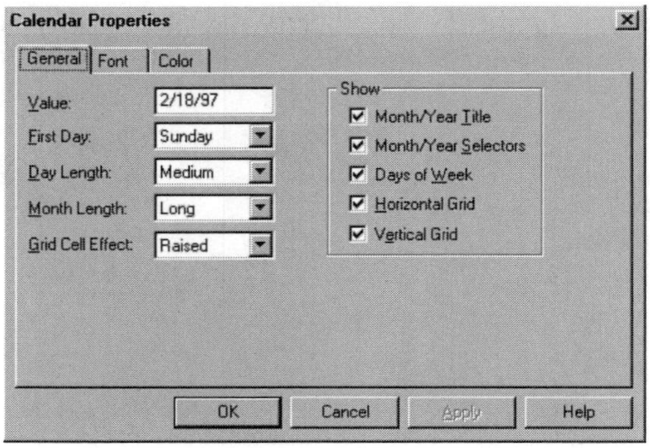

FIGURE 17.9.

The custom property sheet for the Calendar *control.*

Events

ActiveX controls can have events associated with them (not all ActiveX controls will have events). The Calendar control supports these nine events:

- AfterUpdate
- BeforeUpdate
- Click
- DblClick
- KeyDown
- KeyPress
- KeyUp
- NewMonth
- NewYear

If you look at the Event tab of the property sheet for the Calendar control (see Figure 17.10), you see only five events, none of which match with our list of nine events.

The five events on the property sheet are those for the Calendar control as a control on the form, and are not specific to the control's internal ActiveX events. Once the Calendar control has focus, its events as an ActiveX control are available to your VBA code.

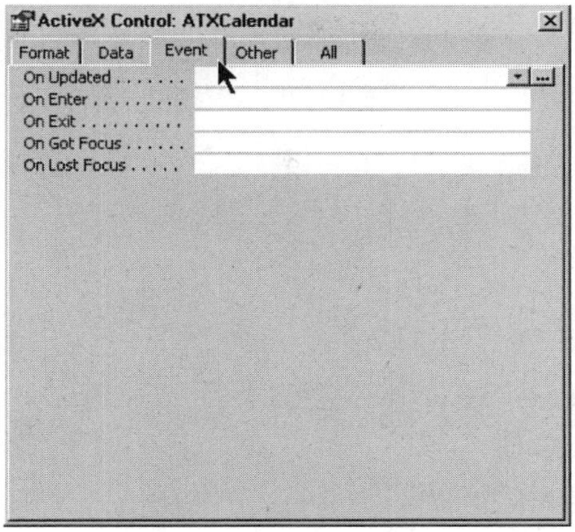

FIGURE 17.10.

The property sheet Event tab for Calendar *control.*

Question: Do you have nine events or five events?

Answer: Fourteen.

All the events for an ActiveX control can be viewed by selecting the ActiveX control from the object window in the `class` module (click View Code). Figure 17.11 shows the events in the procedure scroll box. (All fourteen events are available in the list.)

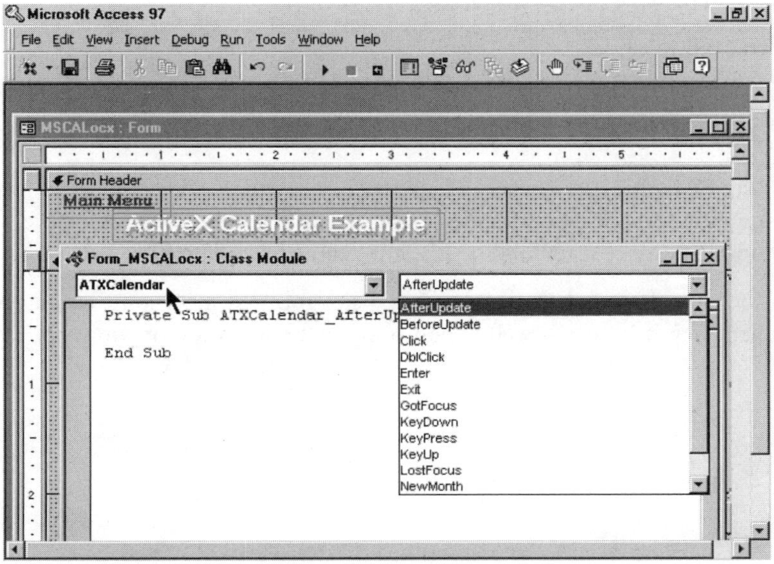

FIGURE 17.11.

The class *module design view of the* Calendar *event procedures.*

Methods

The Calendar control supports the following 11 methods:

- AboutBox
- NextDay
- NextMonth
- NextWeek
- NextYear
- PreviousDay
- PreviousMonth
- PreviousWeek
- PreviousYear
- Refresh
- Today

The familiar object.method syntax is used. You could assign code to a command button event (on our host or container form) to use the NextYear method as follows:

```
'ActiveX controls are dimensioned as control only
Dim atxCTRL As Control
Set atxCTRL = Me![ATXCalendar]
'moves the calendar to same day, next year
atxCTRL.NextYear
```

Summary

ActiveX controls for Access 97 are useful and can provide a polished, professional appearance for your applications. In some cases (such as in Common Dialog), ActiveX controls combine the functionality of several WinAPIs, a welcomed programming aid.

The next chapter discusses additional controls that meet some common application development requirements as well as polishing the presentation of your applications.

Empowering ActiveX Controls with VBA

by Dave Thompson

IN THIS CHAPTER

Objects—in this case ActiveX controls—are the building blocks of today's applications. But your programming objects don't just snap into place. They are fitted into place, finding their way into a framework designed and implemented through VBA by developers and end-user programmers.

This chapter shows you how to unleash the power of ActiveX controls through VBA.

Requirements

The examples in this chapter require several of the ActiveX controls that ship with the Office 97 Developer Edition (ODE), and the sample database for this chapter (PAU18ATX.MDB) requires that these ActiveX controls be installed on your computer. The ODE Setup program will install these controls for you from the ODE Tools CD-ROM.

> **NOTE**
>
> On the ODE Tools CD-ROM, you will find a sample application of ActiveX controls for Access 97 in
>
> \Msds\ODESmpl\Ode\Olecont\Actctrls.mdb
>
> You may want to check Microsoft's Office Developer site (www.microsoft.com/officedev) for the latest ODE Readme file.

If you do not have the ODE, you can download a copy of the Actctrls.MDB sample database along with the needed ActiveX controls. Visit the Microsoft Knowledge Base site at www.microsoft.com/kb, and search for the Article Q165437.

A Quick Review

ActiveX controls are objects with properties and methods. Some—not all—of these controls provide events that can be handled (or ignored) by the host container (a form or report in Access 97).

These controls are part of the ActiveX technology family, which is based on Microsoft's Component Object Model (COM). In earlier versions of Access, ActiveX controls were known as *OLE controls* and sometimes as *custom controls*. Access 97 supports only 32-bit controls.

> **NOTE**
>
> Those converting Access 2.0 applications to Access 97 should know that 16-bit OLE controls are not supported, just as 16-bit Win APIs are not supported. Visit the Microsoft Knowledge Base, and search for the Article Q138019 for additional information (www.microsoft.com/kb).

ActiveX controls require a host container such as a form or report in Access 97.

They can be thought of as factory-sealed bundles of functionality. In other words, for our purposes, I am concerned only with what they do, not how they do it.

To fit an ActiveX control into an application, you need Visual Basic for Applications (VBA). VBA is the language I use in this chapter to communicate with the control's properties, events, and methods.

> **NOTE**
>
> Although Visual Basic 5.0 supports creating custom ActiveX controls, VBA does not (yet).
>
> My focus here is on using available ActiveX controls, specifically those shipping with ODE 97.

If you've avoided Win API calls in your previous projects, ActiveX may be the solution you've been searching for. You will find the functionality of the more commonly used Win APIs in ActiveX controls. And sometimes it is convenient to use both ActiveX and Win APIs in the same procedure.

To summarize some key characteristics of ActiveX controls for Access 97, I can say they

- Are objects with properties and methods.
- Require a host container (a form or report).
- May have events (which the host must process).
- Are visible in the Design View.
- Are not always visible at runtime.
- Cannot be sized if they're visible only in Design View.
- Are 32-bit.
- Must be registered in the Windows Registry.
- Require VBA to implement full functionality.

The CommonDialog Control

> **NOTE**
>
> The CommonDialog control requires ComDlg32.OCX and ComCat.DLL.

Methods and Properties

The ActiveX `CommonDialog` control essentially presents a pop-up, modal dialog box with a familiar look. The possible uses for this control are indicated by the names of its six methods:

- `ShowColor`
- `ShowFont`
- `ShowHelp`
- `ShowOpen`
- `ShowPrinter`
- `ShowSave`

There are 20 properties for the `CommonDialog` control (see Access 97 Help Menu | Contents and Index | Index | `CommonDialog` control). There are no events for the `CommonDialog` control.

You can set some properties before calling the control and then check the value of other properties for returned values such as filenames after the control closes. Some of the examples that follow demonstrate both setting and reading `CommonDialog` properties.

CAUTION

Before attempting to use the VBA example code found in the Access 97 help file for the `CommonDialog` Control, read Article Q166291 found in the Microsoft Knowledge Base at www.microsoft.com/kb.

The CommonDialog ShowOpen Method

Windows application programmers use the `CommonDialog` control frequently. When you choose the File menu, and select Open from a typical Windows application, you are presented with a dialog box. This dialog box allows you to navigate among folders—even local and network drives—to find and select a file to open.

The `ShowOpen` method of the `CommonDialog` control will open such a dialog box within your application. One typical use would be to permit a user to find and select a database for opening.

To insert the `CommonDialog` control into a form, open a new form in Design View and select ActiveX Control from the Insert menu, as shown in Figure 18.1. Then select Microsoft CommonDialog Control, version 5.0, and click OK in the Insert ActiveX Control box (see Figure 18.2).

FIGURE 18.1.
The Insert menu while the form is in Design View.

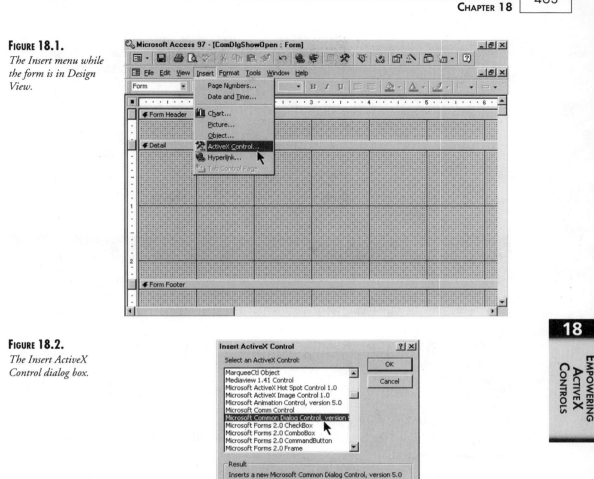

FIGURE 18.2.
The Insert ActiveX Control dialog box.

Figure 18.3 shows the CommonDialog control as it appears in Design View. I've added a form header and command button where I will attach my VBA code, and I have named the dialog control ATXDemo for this example.

As you will see, the dialog control is not visible in the form's normal (runtime) view. Therefore, even though the dialog control displays sizing handles (in the design view), I cannot resize the control.

INTRINSIC CONSTANTS

VBA has many intrinsic constants that you can use throughout your application for purposes such as indicating the icon for a message box (vbExclamation, vbInformation, and so on). They are also used for recordset operations (for example, dbReadOnly).

The CommonDialog control has almost 100 intrinsic constants defined in VBA. Fortunately, they are grouped by the method to be invoked (plus a group for error handling).

For a complete list, choose Access 97 Help | Contents and Index | Index | CommonDialog constants.

For this example, let's say I want to use the ShowOpen method to allow the user to locate a database. I have added the control to my form and have added a command button to open the CommonDialog control.

Now I will build my VBA procedure against the command button's OnClick event.

The basic steps for building this procedure are

1. Create Dim statements.
2. Set the error handler.
3. Set object references.
4. Set initial properties.
5. Activate the control.
6. Read and process returned properties.

The following sections explain these steps.

Dimension Statements

I use the Dim (Dimension) statement to declare variable and object types and names that I will use in my code procedure.

```
Dim ATX As Control
Dim strQualifiedFileName As String
Dim strFileName As String
```

Error Handling

For this example, I will use the `On Error GoTo` structure for error trapping (For more on error trapping, see Chapter 14, "Access 97 VBA for Developers").

```
On Error GoTo TrapIT
'more statements here .....
EnterHere:

Exit Sub

TrapIT:
If Err.Number = cdlCancel Then
 MsgBox "Cancel Pressed"
  Else
    MsgBox Err.Number & " - " & Err.Description & "."
End If
Resume EnterHere
```

Notice that I use one of the `CommonDialog` error constants—`cdlCancel`. For a complete list of available intrinsic constants for the `CommonDialog` control, choose Access 97 Help Menu | Contents and Index | Index | `CommonDialog` constants.

Setting Object References

In my `Dim` statements, I declared `ATX` as a control (such as `Dim ATX As Control`). Now I need to tell VBA that I am using `ATX` to refer to the control named `ATXDemo` on my form.

```
Set ATX = Me![ATXDemo]
```

In any code that follows in my procedure, I can refer to the control as simply `ATX`.

Setting Initial Properties

Before I open the dialog box, I will set a few of its properties. In my example, I want the dialog box to return an error if the user selects the Cancel button that is displayed while the control is running.

I will specify a filename filter similar to the Word for Windows file open dialog box where the user can restrict the filenames shown such as All Files (`*.*`) or Word Documents (`*.doc`).

```
With ATX

 'generate error if user selects Cancel in dialog box
 .CancelError = True

 ' Set flags. To set more than one use OR
 'such as cdlFlag1 OR cdlFlag2 OR ...
 .Flags = cdlOFNHideReadOnly
```

```
' Set filters, no spaces adjacent to "¦" symbol
' note line continuation (& {space} underscore) is used
.Filter = "All Files (*.*)¦*.*¦" & _
          "DLL Files (*.DLL)¦*.dll¦" & _
          "EXE Files (*.EXE)¦*.exe¦" & _
          "MDB Files (*.MDB)¦*.mdb¦" & _
          "OCX Files (*.OCX)¦*.ocx"

   ' Specify default filter as MDB, index base is 1
   .FilterIndex = 4

End With
```

In this example, because I am setting several properties for one object (ATX), I use the With statement. This simplifies typing the code.

Activating the Control

All the preceding steps lead to one line of code to do the work:

```
ATX.ShowOpen
```

Processing the Results

Now, let's examine two of the properties of the ATXDemo control on my form. These properties are set by ATX when the user closes the dialog box by clicking on the Open command button.

The following code is used after the dialog box closes:

```
strQualifiedFileName = ATX.FileName
strFileName = ATX.FileTitle
MsgBox "File name with path is " & strQualifiedFileName & _
       vbCrLf & vbCrLf & _
       "The file name alone is " & strFileName
```

NOTE

This code is not executed if the dialog returns an error. Instead, the error is trapped and reported, and the procedure resumes just before the Exit Sub statement (see the earlier section, "Error Handling," in this chapter).

Figure 18.4 shows the form in the normal (or runtime) view. The dialog box does not appear. In Figure 18.5 you see the dialog box that appears after you click on the command button labeled ShowOpen.

FIGURE 18.4.

A sample form to call the CommonDialog *control.*

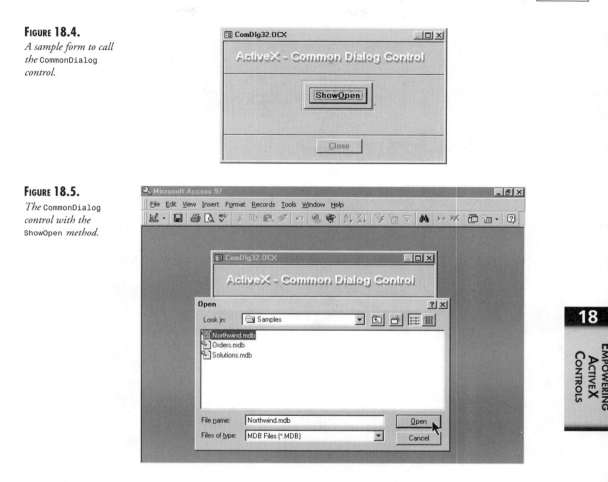

FIGURE 18.5.

The CommonDialog *control with the* ShowOpen *method.*

In the Open dialog box, navigate to a file, select it, and click the Open button. The dialog control returns both the fully qualified filename (that is, path + filename) and just the filename itself. These results are shown in Figure 18.6.

> **NOTE**
>
> The dialog box command button labeled Open does not actually open the file. Clicking on the Open command button closes the dialog box but takes no action against the file. I then examine the properties ATX.FileName and ATX.FileTitle. These two properties return the filename and path information so that I could open the file with additional VBA code, if desired. In this case, I am just displaying the returned information about the file.

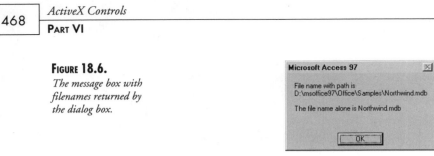

FIGURE 18.6.

The message box with filenames returned by the dialog box.

Other CommonDialog Examples

See the CD-ROM accompanying this book for additional examples using the CommonDialog control. One example uses both the CommonDialog control and Win APIs to return the version of ActiveX controls and associated files.

Figure 18.7 shows the version of ComDlg32.ocx used for the examples in this chapter.

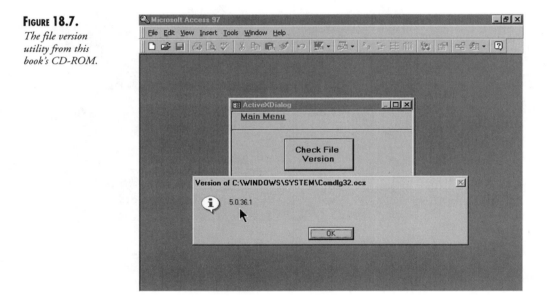

FIGURE 18.7.

The file version utility from this book's CD-ROM.

The ListView Control

Just as its name implies, the ActiveX ListView control is used to display lists. One advantage of the ListView control is its support for sorting on any displayed column, similar to the column heads in Windows Explorer.

ListView, as you will see, can look a lot like a continuous form, but it does not take a recordset as a data source. Instead, you fill the control with data using VBA. If you're a developer who works with arrays, think of ListView as a fast, scrollable viewport into a two-dimensional array.

Although you may use a recordset as the source data to fill a `ListView` control, you cannot bind the control to the recordset as you can bind a form to a recordset. In other words, the control will not read a table or query and display the data. The values displayed by the control are assigned to the `ListView` Items collection (the far-left column displayed) and SubItems (all other columns on the same row) through a VBA procedure that you must write.

Properties, Events, and Methods

`ListView` has 14 properties and four methods, and it provides four events.

The `ListView` control's properties are as follows:

Arrange	ListItems
ColumnHeaders	MultiSelect
DropHeight	SelectedItem
HideColumnHeaders	Sorted
Icons	SortKey
LabelEdit	SortOrder
LabelWrap	View

> **CAUTION**
>
> Article Q166912, available on Microsoft's Knowledge Base site at www.microsoft.com/kb, has information concerning the Microsoft `ListView` Control version 5.0 used with Access 97. When the `Visible` or `Enabled` properties (found on the standard property sheet for the control when the host form is in the Design View) are toggled (True/False) through VBA code, the control loses data. This requires that the control be cleared and refilled with data.

The `ListView` control's methods are

    FindItem
    GetFirstVisible
    HitTest
    StartLabelEdit

`ListView` provides the following events:

    AfterLabelEdit
    BeforeLabelEdit
    ColumnClick
    ItemClick

NOTE

ListView has 22 intrinsic constants defined to support its implementation. Choose Access 97 Help | Contents and Index | Index | ListView constants.

Implementing the Control

ListView, like all other Access ActiveX controls, requires a host container (form or report). That's where I will start. For this example, I use the same table of client information as used in Chapter 14, "Access 97 VBA for Developers."

The major steps to implement a ListView control are as follows:

1. Insert the control and size it.
2. Set the properties.
3. Add VBA code to fill the control.
4. Choose and code the events.

The following sections explain these steps in detail.

Inserting and Sizing the Control

Open a new form in Design View. From the Insert menu, select ActiveX Control. Find Microsoft ListView Control, version 5.0; select it and click OK.

For the sample list, I will use four fields from the Clients table: ClientNumber, SSN, LastName, and FirstNameMI. I will name the control ATXClientList, and for now, I'll size it to occupy most of the screen width (VGA resolution, 640×480).

Setting the Properties

The control will display rows of four columns (the four fields listed previously). I must allocate the width for each column individually.

In Figure 18.8, I have opened the custom property sheet for the ListView control (named ATXClientList in this example). I will use the property sheet (rather than VBA) to lay out the columns. Notice that for Width, the default value is 1440.00. What's that?

Twips are a logical unit of linear measurement defined with the intent of being device-resolution independent (for more information, choose Access 97 Help | Contents and Index | Find | twips). For our purposes, let's just accept that 1,440 twips equals one inch of printed output. I will use the scale across the top of the Access form in Design View to help estimate the number of twips to assign as the width of each of my four columns.

Figure 18.8.

Custom property sheet for the ListView *control.*

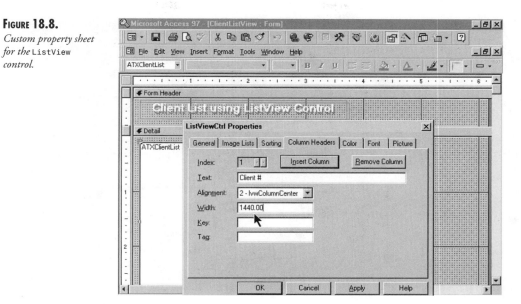

It is a more natural process to put text controls on a form in Design View and size the controls that way. So, to approximate my column widths, I will use a temporary form in Design View. After placing the four fields on the form, I will use the scale across the top of the form to determine "screen-inch widths" and multiply that value by 1,440 to calculate twips.

As shown in Figure 18.9, I can project a control's width onto the scale by pointing at the control with the mouse and holding down the left button. My results are shown in Table 18.1. I will round the calculated twips values to more convenient numbers as shown in the Use column.

Table 18.1. Column-width calculations.

Column Head	Screen Width	Calculated Twips	Use
Client #	0.7"	1,008	1,000
SSN	1.1"	1,584	1,500
Last Name	1.7"	2,448	2,500
First MI	1.2"	1,728	1,750

Adding Code to Fill the Control

ListItems is a property of the ListView ActiveX control. But ListItems is more than a single-valued property; it is a collection of ListItem objects.

FIGURE 18.9.

*Design View of form
used for Table 18.1.*

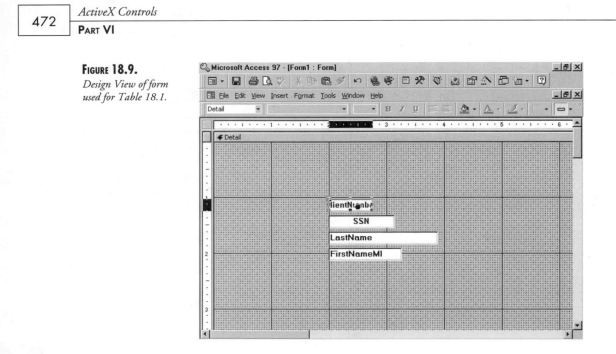

Because ListItems (with an *s*) is a collection, you should not be surprised to learn that it supports some of its own methods, such as Add, Clear, and Remove. ListItems also has two properties: Count and Item.

And if a ListItem is an object, then... it's time to take a quick look at the Object Browser. In Figure 18.10, I have launched the Object Browser from the menu bar of a module in Design View. In the figure, I selected ListItems and highlighted and right-clicked on Add to bring up the Help and Related Information dialog box. Clicking on Help at this point will bring up specific information.

In Figure 18.11, I am browsing the ListItem (no *s*) object and see that it has two methods and 13 properties. Fortunately, I will not be using all of them.

NOTE

A note for experienced VB developers: Access 97 does not support the following methods for the ListView control: Drag and ZOrder; nor these properties: Container, DragIcon, and DragMode; nor these events: DrapDrop and DragOver.

FIGURE 18.10.

ListItems, *as displayed in the Object Browser window.*

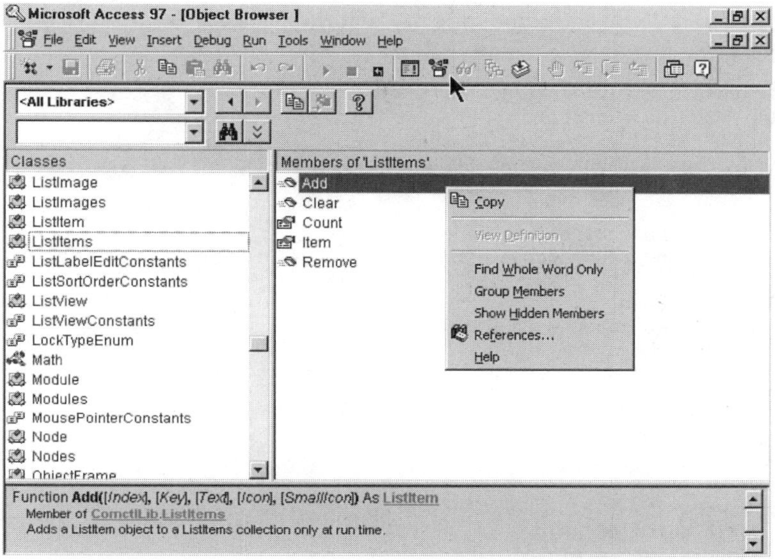

FIGURE 18.11.

ListItem, *as displayed in the Object Browser window.*

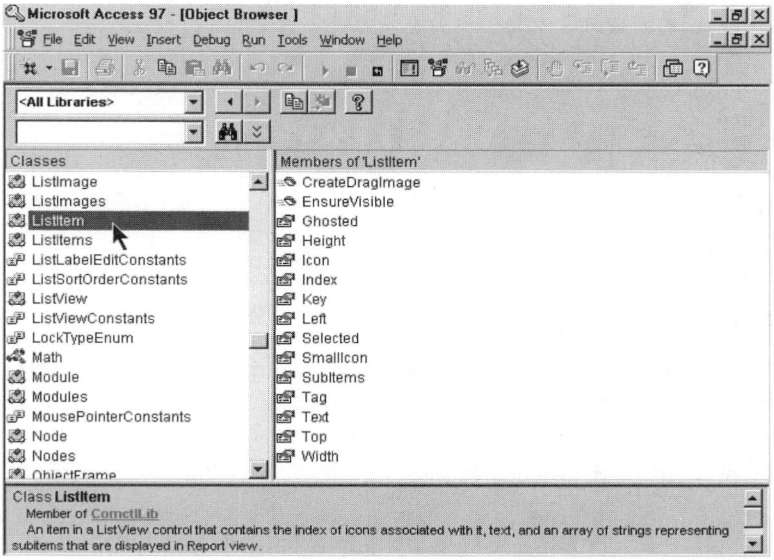

That said, I will add some code to the form's On Load event to fill the ListView control with data from the sample Clients table:

```
Private Sub Form_Load()
On Error GoTo TrapIT

Dim db As Database, r As Recordset, strSSN As String
Dim ATX As Control, lstItem As ListItem

Set db = CurrentDb
Set r = db.OpenRecordset("Clients")

If r.BOF Then
 MsgBox "No Records to Display"
 r.Close
 Exit Sub
End If

Set ATX = Me![ATXClientList]
ATX.View = lvwReport

r.MoveFirst
 While Not r.EOF
  Set lstItem = ATX.ListItems.Add()
  lstItem.Text = r!ClientNumber
   strSSN = Nz(Format(r![SSN], "@@@-@@-@@@@"), "None")
  lstItem.SubItems(1) = strSSN
  lstItem.SubItems(2) = r!LastName
  lstItem.SubItems(3) = r!FirstNameMI
   r.MoveNext
 Wend
r.Close
EnterHere:

Exit Sub

TrapIT:
MsgBox Err.Number & " - " & Err.Description & "."
Resume EnterHere
End Sub
```

At this point, my form will load and fill the control. I am a bit low on functionality, however, so let's add some.

Choosing and Coding Events

One of the neat features of the ListView control is the capability to click on a column head and have the list sort on that column. This is supported through the control's ColumnClick event. You may want to refer to Chapter 17, "ActiveX Controls," and Figure 17.11 for a discussion about how to find and add code to ActiveX control events. The event is found in the class module for the form as a procedure with the same name as the event, such as ColumnCLick.

With the class (form) module open for my form, I'll select the `ATXClientList` object and the `ColumnClick` procedure and add this code:

```
On Error GoTo TrapIT
' Sort items in column clicked.
' If I're already sorting by this column,
' alternate sort order.
' Otherwise, set to ascending.

Dim intCol As Integer, ATX As Control
Set ATX = Me![ATXClientList]

intCol = ColumnHeader.Index - 1

If (ATX.SortKey = intCol) Then
 If ATX.SortOrder = lvwAscending Then
  ATX.SortOrder = lvwDescending
   Else
  ATX.SortOrder = lvwAscending
 End If
Else
 ATX.SortKey = intCol
 ATX.SortOrder = lvwAscending
End If

ATX.Sorted = True
'EnsureVisible is a METHOD for the ListItem OBJECT
'(SEE Object Browser)
'It's use here is to scroll the list after sorting so that
'the Item selected before sorting remains visible
ATX.SelectedItem.EnsureVisible

EnterHere:

Exit Sub

TrapIT:
MsgBox Err.Number & " - " & Err.Description & "."
Resume EnterHere
```

Notice that the code uses some intrinsic constants for the `ListView` control, such as `lvwAscending`. For a complete listing of intrinsic constants for the `ListView` control, choose Access 97 Help | Contents and Index | Index | `ListView` constants.

Figure 18.12 shows the form with sample data.

Now that I have the list running with sort enabled (this is done in the code statement `ATX.Sorted = True`), I will add some additional functionality. `ListView` supports a `DoubleClick` event that I will use to open a client form. I need to add this code:

```
Private Sub ATXClientList_DblClick()
On Error GoTo TrapIT
Dim criteria As String
```

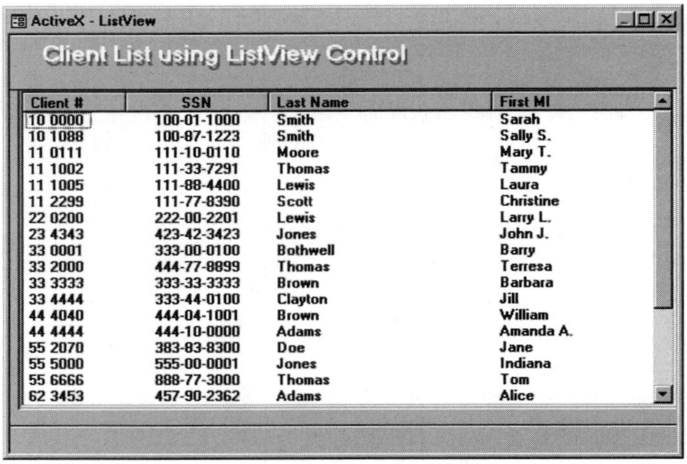

FIGURE 18.12.

The sample form with the ListView *control.*

```
gstrCallingForm = "ClientListView"
'Note: The line below uses the line continuation
'underscore. The line ending is '& {space} underscore'
criteria = "[ClientNumber] = " & _
Chr(39) & ATXClientList.SelectedItem.Text & Chr(39)

'acDialog holds code execution until called form is closed
DoCmd.OpenForm "ClientInfo", , , criteria, , acDialog
'code continues execution

EnterHere:

Exit Sub
TrapIT:
MsgBox Err.Number & " - " & Err.Description
Resume EnterHere

End Sub
```

By double-clicking on an item in the Client # column, I load the client form, as shown in Figure 18.13. In this case, I am allowing the editing of address information only. I could allow editing of the other fields, but then I must include code to trap for changes that affect list display and update the list accordingly. The code to do this is not included in my example.

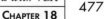

FIGURE 18.13.

The pop-up form called from ListView.

The ProgressBar Control

For many, it seems that the fastest computer is too slow. Although users must accept processing delays, developers have known since the earliest days of PCs the benefits of communicating with the user during processing delays. Longtime spreadsheet users may remember the Calc message that blinked while the spreadsheet recalculated the values in each cell across the entire spreadsheet.

For unavoidable delays, you can communicate to the user that the process is running and give some indication of its progress. Access does this through the status bar at the bottom of the screen that is displayed during lengthy queries, especially append and update queries.

With the ProgressBar control, you can provide your own onscreen display similar to the status bar feature of Access.

To periodically update a ProgressBar control that you have placed on a form, such as to display the progress of record-by-record processing, you might find the following VBA MOD() function useful:

```
Dim NumRecords as Long, Count as Long
Dim UpdateInterval as Integer
Dim r as Recordset
```

```
'... code to open recordset
'... code to set NumRecords = RecordCount()
'
'... begin record-by-record processing
UpdateInterval = 25
'open ProgressBar
Count = 0

While Not r.EOF()
Count = Count + 1
If Count MOD UpdateInterval = 0 then
 'code to update ProgressBar
 'remember to repaint form
End if
'... recordset operation
Wend
```

Figure 18.14 shows an example of the `ProgressBar` control from the `Actctrls.MDB` database provided with the ODE.

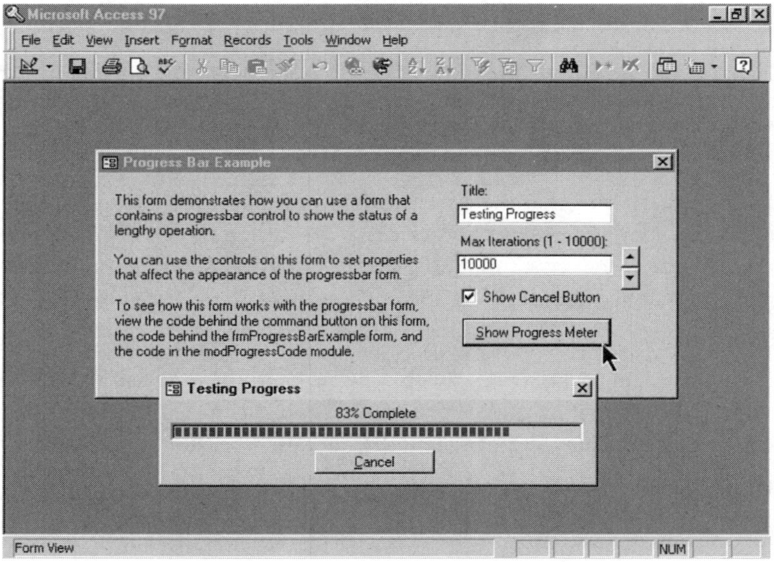

FIGURE 18.14.

A `ProgressBar`
example.

The UpDown Control

The `UpDown` control is similar to the record-navigation buttons at the bottom of Access forms. It can be used to increment and decrement values.

For Access 97, the `UpDown` control has seven properties:

> Alignment
>
> Increment

```
Max
Min
Orientation
Value
Wrap
```

> **CAUTION**
>
> The UpDown control has several "buddy" properties, but these properties are *not* supported in Access 97. See Microsoft Knowledge Base Article Q161402, at www.microsoft.com/kb.

The UpDown control has no methods but has three events:

```
Change
DownClick
UpClick
```

For this example, I will modify the Calendar control example from Chapter 17. Here, I will put a Calendar control on a pop-up form along with two UpDown controls to change the month and year.

When finished, I will have a reusable pop-up form that can be called from any form in my application or copied into other Access applications.

Earlier I said that the UpDown control has three events of its own. Remember that when ActiveX controls are placed on an Access form, the control property sheet will display some events for the control. These events (listed on the controls' property sheet) relate to the ActiveX control as being an object placed on the form. Such is the case for the UpDown control. Viewing its property sheet with the host form in Design View shows five available events (see Figure 18.15).

> **NOTE**
>
> The complete list of event procedures is available through the class module for the form. Select the control name from the object window and pull down the Procedures list. (Refer to Figure 17.11 in Chapter 17.)

To change the orientation of the UpDown controls I will use the custom property sheet for the two UpDown controls in my example. The custom property sheet is opened by clicking on the Build button on the Custom property as shown in Figure 18.16.

18

EMPOWERING
ACTIVEX
CONTROLS

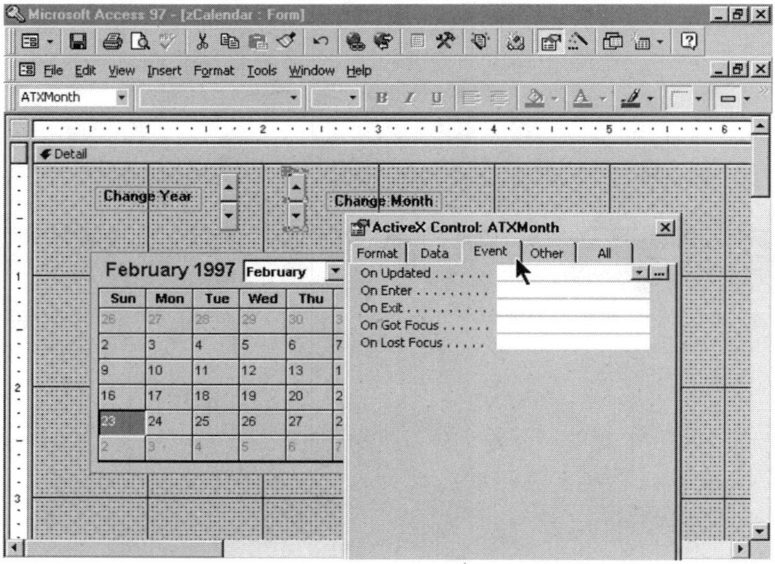

FIGURE 18.15.

Form control events for the UpDown control.

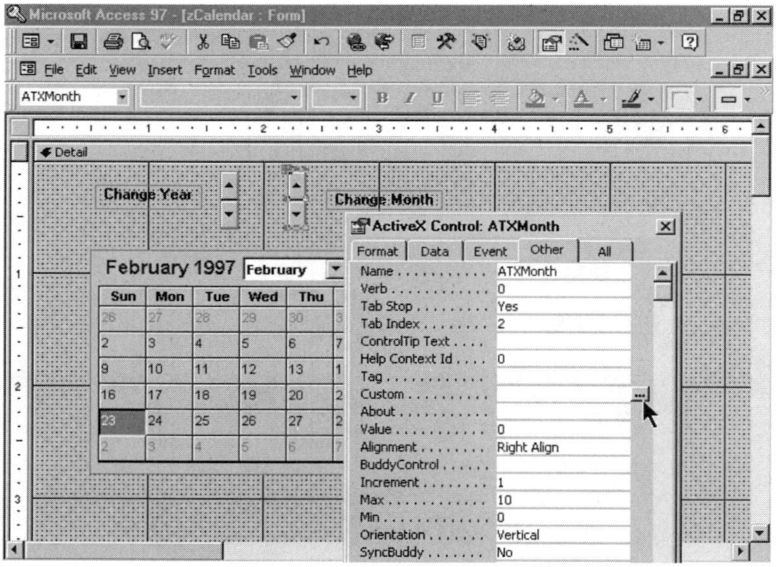

FIGURE 18.16.

Locating the Build button for the custom property sheet.

In Figure 18.16, I opened the control's property sheet and then selected the Other tab to find the Custom property.

For the two UpDown controls, select Horizontal Orientation and click Apply (see Figure 18.17).

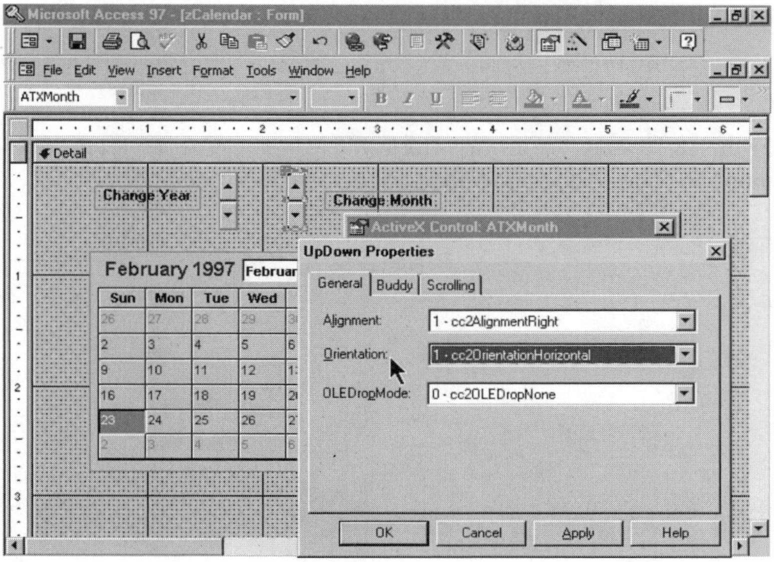

FIGURE 18.17.
The custom property sheet for the UpDown *control.*

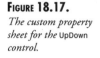

NOTE

Resize the controls after changing their orientation.

For this example, I will use two public (global) variables: gvDate and gblnRequery. To pass a date back and forth to my pop-up form, I will use gvDate (a variant). I will use gblnRequery (a Boolean) to indicate the user action taken to close the pop-up form (which button was clicked: OK or Cancel?).

I need to add VBA code to support the following program logic:

> Open Contacts form
>
> Select Calendar command button
>
> Set gvDate = NextContactDate
>
> Open form with Calendar control (dialog)
>
> If gvDate is Null, set Calendar control to system date
>
> Otherwise, set the Calendar control to gvDate
>
> User action
>
> User selects OK or Cancel
>
> If Cancel, set gblnRequery = False

18

If OK, set `gblnRequery` = `True` and `gvDate` = `Calendar` control value

Popup form is closed

Update Contacts form if `gblnRequery` = `True`

Figure 18.18 shows the `Contacts` form with command button for the calendar, and Figure 18.19 shows the pop-up `Calendar` form.

FIGURE 18.18.

The sample Contacts *form.*

FIGURE 18.19.

The sample pop-up Calendar *form.*

The ImageList Control

One of the more interesting ActiveX controls for Access 97 is the `ImageList` control. It is visible only when the host form is in Design View. The `ImageList` control is not visible at runtime.

`ImageList` allows you to gather a collection of images (`.bmp`, `.ico`) and bring them into the control (on one form). The control, in turn, makes these images available to other controls placed on the same form.

To demonstrate, open a new form. Select ActiveX Control from the Insert menu, select Microsoft `ImageList` Control, version 5.0, and click OK to insert the control. Name the control `ATXImageList`. Your next steps are as follows:

1. Select and places images into the image control.
2. Place additional ActiveX controls on the form.
3. Use the image control as source for other controls.

The following sections explain these steps in detail.

Placing Images into the Control

From the `ATXImageList` control's property sheet, choose the Other Tab and click on the Custom Build icon to open the custom property sheet, as shown in Figure 18.20.

FIGURE 18.20.

The custom property sheet for the `ImageList` *control.*

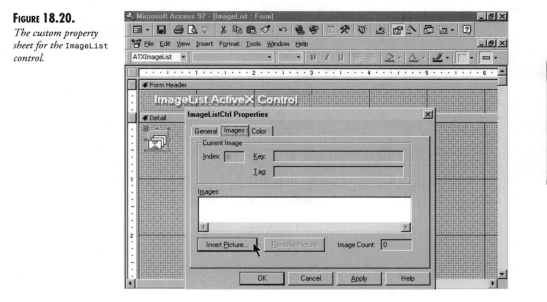

Click on Insert Picture and use the dialog box that opens to navigate and find some icon files, as shown in Figure 18.21.

The four icons (pictures) that I selected now appear in the custom property sheet for `ATXImageList` (see Figure 18.22). I set the `Tag` property for each picture as (in order) `Cloud`, `Earth`, `Snow`, and `Lightning`. The `Image Count` and `Index` are both `4`, telling us that images are indexed starting at the number 1.

FIGURE 18.21.
The dialog box for selecting a picture.

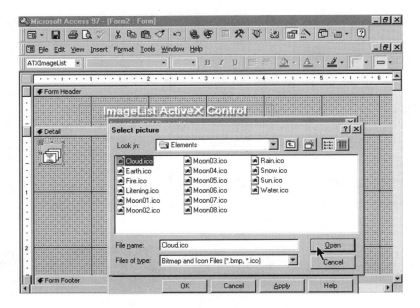

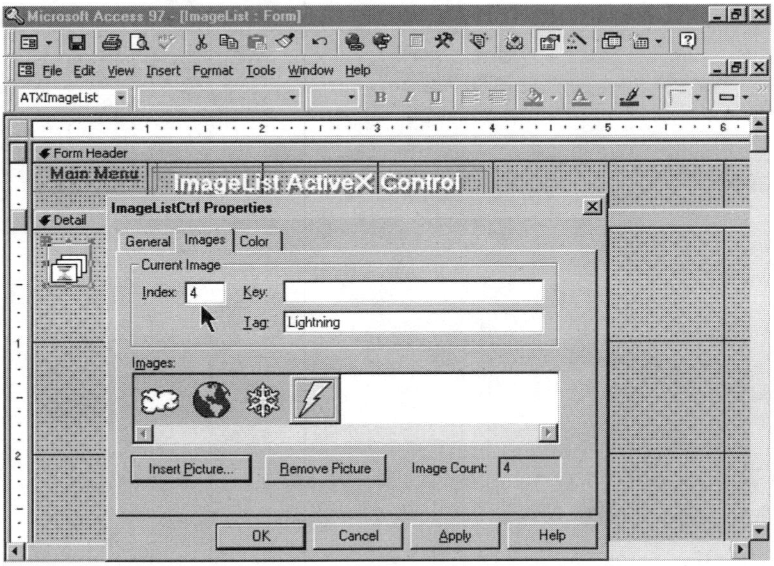

FIGURE 18.22.
The Images tab of the custom property sheet.

Next, add a `ToolBar` control to the form and add four buttons to the control using its custom property sheet. From the `ATXToolBar` control's custom property sheet, go to the General tab, pull down the Image List box, find `ATXImageList`, and select it (see Figure 18.23).

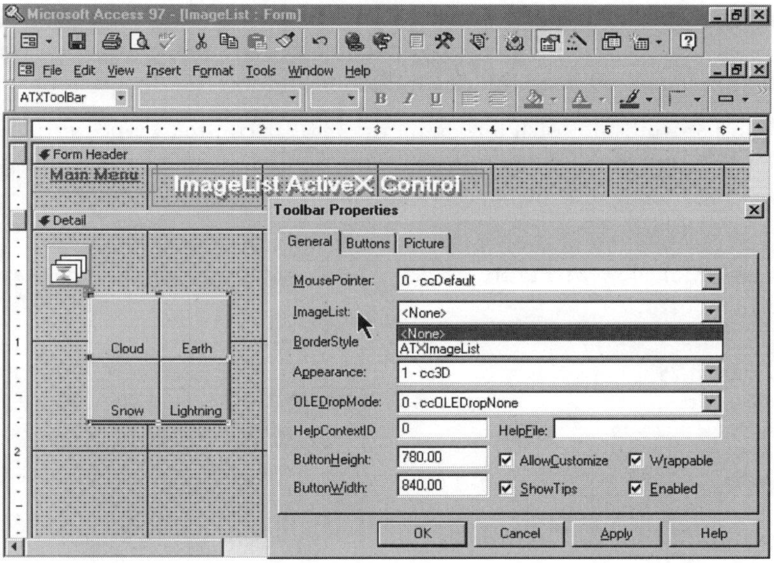

FIGURE 18.23.

The ImageList *property of the* ToolBar *control.*

In Figure 18.24, I have selected the Buttons tab of the ToolBar control's custom property sheet. By clicking on the arrow buttons adjacent to the Index text box, I stepped through the button list, setting the Caption property for each of the four buttons (that is, Cloud, Earth, Snow, and Lightning).

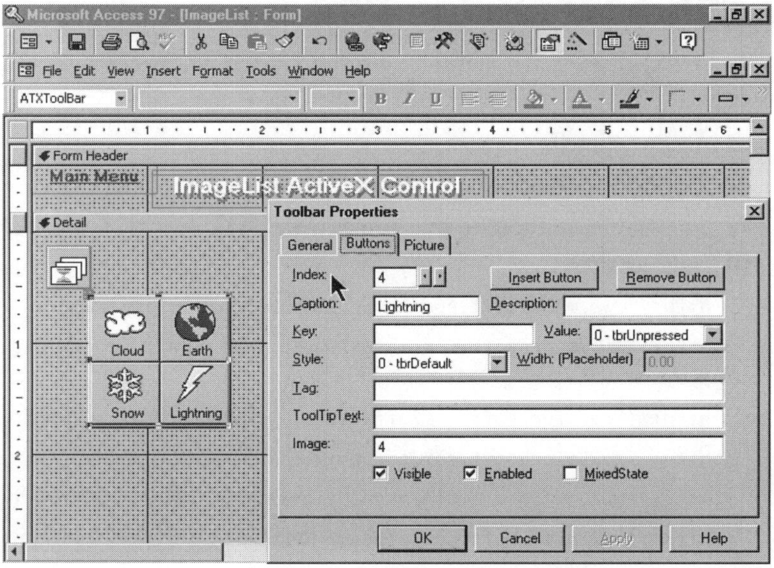

FIGURE 18.24.

Making button image assignments in the ToolBar *property sheet.*

At the bottom-left of the property sheet, you can see that I have set the Image property to the index number of the desired image as numbered within the ImageList control. In this case, the button index and image index are the same number, but that is not required.

In other words, for each button on the ToolBar control, I typed in a caption and selected an image to appear on the button above the caption. I could have left the caption blank for each button, leaving only the image to appear on the button.

The presentation of the ToolBar control using the ImageList control is shown in its normal (runtime) view in Figure 18.25. You could program the ToolBar itself to serve as a switchboard.

FIGURE 18.25.

The ToolBar *control using the* ImageList *control as an image source.*

Additional Information

Some sources for additional information about ActiveX, Access 97, Office 97, and OLE are as follows:

- Access 97 Help
- The Access 97 and ODE Readme files
- The sample application that comes with ODE: Actctrls.MDB
- Internet sites

    http://www.microsoft.com/kb (Microsoft Knowledge Base)

    http://www.microsoft.com/accessdev/DefOff.htm (Microsoft Access Developer Forum)

    http://www.microsoft.com/officedev/ (Microsoft Office Developer Forum)

    http://www.microsoft.com/support/ (Microsoft Support)

    http://www.microsoft.com/msdn/default.htm (Microsoft Developer Network Online)

    http://www.microsoft.com/oledev/ (MSDN OLE Development)

CHAPTER 18

Summary

ActiveX controls are objects based on Microsoft's COM (Component Object Model) specification. They replace the OLE and custom controls found in previous versions of Access.

As the trend toward component software continues, the importance of understanding and using "factory-sealed" software components such as ActiveX controls will increase. But building applications is not as simple as snapping these components into place.

Now, more than ever, VBA is important to the process of developing applications. VBA pulls the components together, facilitates communication between them, and controls program logic and flow.

VII
PART

Customizing Access 97

Customizing the Access 97 Development Environment

by Joe Rhemann

CHAPTER 19

This chapter briefly covers techniques for customizing your database environment for increased performance and usability with the built-in features of Access 97. The degree to which customization will yield increased performance and usability is dependent on your end user's system configuration and capabilities.

Hardware and operating system variables will affect your Access 97 environment. Many of these variables are obvious; they are not discussed here because it is assumed the readers of this book have the level of technical knowledge required of developers and programmers.

The following sections cover some of the technical aspects of the development and user environments as they apply to Access 97.

Assessing Hardware System Memory

With regard to system memory, keep in mind that Access performance is largely based on the amount of RAM that is available to the application. When you are running multiple applications or using automation in your applications, you can dramatically increase performance by using more than the minimum recommended amount of system memory.

> **NOTE**
>
> Access 97 requires a minimum of 12MB RAM to run as a standalone application under Windows 95, and a minimum of 16MB RAM to run under Windows NT.

Part of the process of ensuring adequate memory resources for your application is to make sure that your system has adequate hard disk space to effectively manage virtual memory. If you are using a dynamic swap file that is managed by Windows 95, the amount of virtual memory will increase and decrease according to the needs of your application. If Windows has plenty of hard disk space to use as virtual memory, overall system performance will be increased. The Windows 95 virtual memory settings are available through the Windows 95 Control Panel by clicking the System icon, selecting Performance, and then selecting Virtual Memory (see Figure 19.1).

Generally, allowing Windows 95 to manage your virtual memory settings is the best way to go; however, if you have another, higher-performance hard disk on your system, or if your primary hard disk is low on space, you can specify that Windows 95 use another drive for virtual memory.

If you have plenty of hard disk space, you might want to try setting your minimum disk space so that, combined with your primary RAM, your overall virtual memory will be at least 25MB or 30MB when using Access 97. If you are using several large applications concurrently with Access, you might want to set your minimum disk space even higher for optimal performance.

19

CUSTOMIZING THE DEVELOPMENT ENVIRONMENT

FIGURE 19.1.
The Windows 95 Virtual Memory settings.

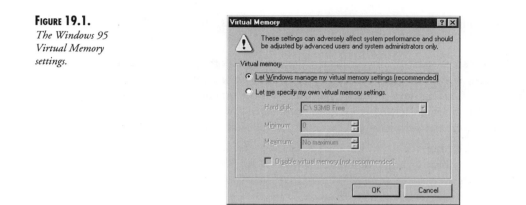

Customizing the Access 97 Software Environment

Access 97 allows you to customize the user interface through the Options dialog box, which is accessed through the Tools menu.

These settings are easily adjusted through this interface, and there is context-specific help for each setting. After you select your desired options, Access 97 saves the changes to your Workgroup Information File. Creating a Workgroup Information File is covered later in this chapter in the section titled "Workgroup Information File Definition," which is a subtopic to "Changing Windows Registry Settings for Access 97."

A number of Access environment options have changed or been removed since versions 1.*x* and 2.*x*. Refer to the Access 97 help file and look up Options in the Contents window for further information about these changes.

Using DAO Code to Customize Access 97 Settings

The most common method of changing Access 97 settings through DAO code is to use the SetOption method of the DBEngine object to change Registry settings. This allows you to make the changes while the application is running.

> **NOTE**
>
> This can be a useful way to modulate internal application settings when your database operations vary between large, bulk transactions and small, singular transactions. You can optimize these operations based on the transaction size by varying internal values for them. The changes are in effect only during the current instance of the DBEngine object and do not change the Registry settings.

The following internal settings can be changed with the `SetOption` method of the `DBEngine` object:

- `Threads`: `Threads` are independent software processes that run under multitasking operating system environments. Microsoft Jet uses multiple internal threads to perform background operations necessary for the function of your database application. The default setting is a maximum of three threads. This setting can be increased to enhance the performance of complicated database applications.

- `MaxBufferSize`: This specifies the size of the buffer in which non-explicit add, delete, or update record-transaction data is stored by Jet. Jet uses this buffer space as needed, up to the maximum as specified in `MaxBufferSize`. By default, this buffer size is set at `0`, which tells Jet to calculate the `MaxBufferSize` according to the formula [512KB + (RAM KB − 12,288)(4].

  Jet uses data in pages that are 2,048 bytes in size, and when the amount of data exceeds the `MaxBufferSize` or the maximum cache time (which is specified in either the `FlushTransactionTimeout`, `SharedAsyncDelay`, or `ExclusiveAsyncDelay` settings), it begins writing data to the database. This buffer size can be adjusted between 128KB and 8MB according to the complexity of the database application and the system resources.

  Setting the `MaxBufferSize` lower than 512KB or higher than 8MB will cause system performance to degrade. Additional threads are started to manage the writing of buffer data to the database, and reducing the `MaxBufferSize` below 512KB will require an excessive number of write operations. Creating a `MaxBufferSize` greater than 8MB will cause an excessive amount of system overhead to be dedicated to managing the large buffer and reach the point of diminishing return. If you do not use the `FlushTransactionTimeout` setting, you might need to increase or decrease the `SharedAsyncDelay` setting in direct proportion to the change in the `MaxBufferSize` setting.

- `UserCommitSync`: This Registry setting determines which write mode Jet uses to write explicit transaction changes. The default setting is `Yes`, which specifies synchronous mode and ensures that Jet does not relinquish control to the application code until the changes are written to the database. If you change this setting to cause Jet to use asynchronous mode to commit changes to the database, Jet will store the changes in its buffer and relinquish control back to the application code while writing the changes using a background thread. Using asynchronous mode can lead to application problems because there will be no mechanism in place to ensure that asynchronous changes are made to the database before the application code attempts to perform a new operation on the database.

- `ImplicitCommitSync`: This Registry setting determines which write mode Jet uses to write add, delete, or update record operations in non-explicit transactions. In this case, Jet automatically saves the results of internal transactions in its buffer. This setting determines whether the resulting internal transactions are written to the database in synchronous or asynchronous mode. The default setting is No, which allows these particular changes to be written in asynchronous mode. If you change the setting to Yes, you will receive the integrity benefit of synchronous mode, but the performance of Jet will be significantly impaired.

■ FlushTransactionTimeout: This determines the number of milliseconds that Jet will wait before writing cached asynchronous changes to a database, unless the size of the cache exceeds the MaxBufferSize setting. The default setting is 500 milliseconds; you should not increase this unless your database is updated over a slow network connection. This setting supersedes the ExclusiveAsyncDelay and SharedAsyncDelay settings and is generally the best method of controlling this delay. Setting FlushTransactionTimeout to 0 disables this method of control and allows you to use the ExclusiveAsyncDelay and SharedAsyncDelay settings.

■ ExclusiveAsyncDelay: This setting specifies the delay before asynchronous mode changes are made to a database that has been opened in exclusive mode. The default setting is 2000 milliseconds. If you want to ensure that changes are written faster, you can decrease this setting, but doing so will decrease performance as well. You should not increase this setting unless the user system has 32MB RAM or more, and you have specified a larger MaxBufferSize setting. The FlushTransactionTimeout setting supersedes this setting.

■ SharedAsyncDelay: This setting specifies the delay before asynchronous mode changes are made to a database that has been opened in shared mode. The default setting is 50 milliseconds. Changing this setting should be done in such a way as to balance the number of disk I/O operations against the number of concurrent users. The fewer the concurrent requests on a database, the larger your SharedAsyncDelay setting can be. This reduces the number of disk I/O operations required but holds the changed pages in the buffer longer while waiting to write to the database. Jet locks pages that are stored in the buffer so concurrent access performance will be reduced. The FlushTransactionTimeout setting supersedes this setting.

■ PageTimeout: This setting tells Jet how long to wait before checking for user changes to a database. If Jet detects a change, the data in the buffer is refreshed. The default setting is 5000 milliseconds. This setting should be adjusted with respect to the desire to reduce disk read operations while still keeping the changes up to date. The smaller the delay, the slower the performance but the faster that changes are available to the user. This setting can be overridden either by changing the Refresh Interval setting in the Advanced options dialog box in Access 97 or by using the dbRefreshCache argument of the DBObject Idle method in DAO code to refresh user changes to the database immediately.

■ LockDelay: This setting tells Jet how long to wait before trying to lock a page in a shared database that it was unable to lock on first or subsequent attempts. The default setting is 100 milliseconds. This setting helps reduce the number of lock request retries across networks that do not have an NOS that manages locking retries. Windows 95 peer-to-peer networks do not have a mechanism for central control of lock requests and retries, and they can lose a significant amount of bandwidth due to locking retry bombardment. Using the LockDelay setting reduces the number of locking retries that Jet will repeat within a specified period of time, protecting precious network bandwidth. If you want to change this setting, adjust the delay setting in proportion to the frequency of lock requests per user and the average number of records locked per user. If the NOS in use has locking-management capabilities, as does Windows NT, this Registry setting is redundant and does not need to be changed.

- MaxLocksPerFile: This setting specifies the maximum number of locks that Jet will allow per file. The default setting is 9500. This setting should be adjusted according to the maximum number of locks per file supported by the NOS server. The problem lies with having a MaxLocksPerFile setting in your Registry that exceeds the maximum locks-per-file capability of the NOS server. If your system tries to commit more than the maximum supported by the NOS server, an error will likely be generated when performing large transactions. If the number of locks needed to perform an operation exceeds the MaxLocksPerFile setting, Jet processes the data that is locked, clears the locks, and then locks and commits the remaining data.

- RecycleLVs: Long value (LV) pages store data in fields with the Memo, OLE Object, and Hyperlink data types, along with data that defines forms, reports, and modules. Databases that are open in shared mode can grow in size when data, forms, modules, and reports are deleted or changed in such a way that the current LV page must be discarded and replaced with a new one. The RecycleLVs setting specifies when old LV pages are available for reuse. The default setting is 0, which specifies that old LV pages become available for reuse after the last user closes the database. This setting can be changed to 1, which tells Jet to make old LV pages available after new LV data has been added and when there is only one user left in the database in shared mode. Old LV pages are removed when you run a compacting operation on a database.

One of the customization options available to you is the capability to set initialization parameters for your Access 97 application through VB code using the GetOption and SetOption methods of the Application object.

GetOption will allow you to have the application object return the current value associated with an Access 97 option setting, and the SetOption method allows you to change Access 97 options as they appear in the Options dialog.

CAUTION

If you are an Access 1.x or 2.x developer, and you plan to use the GetOption or SetOption method of the application object, avoid generating runtime errors by reviewing these changes.

If you are developing localized applications, or if your application is going to be run on a language version of Windows 95 or NT that is different from your development system language, you will need to pass the appropriate arguments through these methods in English.

Setting an option with these methods is not tab specific as relates to the dialog; you do not need to specify this in your strings. In other words, when writing your option-specific strings that are going to be passed through the GetOption or SetOption methods, you do not need to specify which tab an option appears on in the Options dialog. The only exception to your being able to work with your option settings through DAO code is that the settings for the Module tab are not available to you through the GetOption or SetOption methods. Settings for the Module tab must be made within the Access 97 user interface through the Options dialog.

Some option settings require that the GetOption method's return values be assigned to variables described as variants in your VBA code. If the return value of a GetOption method is assigned to a variable, the variable must be specified as a variant.

If you expect to change user options through the user dialog box during your sessions but you want to protect your default startup options, specifying initialization options this way will help you to do this. You can also use VB code to reset the original environment options after your session. The SetOption method can be used to reset Access 97 options to their defaults (original state) when your application is closed.

TIP

By creating public variables to store the default settings, you can create a convenient library of settings to refer to from your code in a close event procedure or special exit procedure.

The proper VB syntax to use with the GetOption or SetOption methods is as follows:

```
application object.GetOption(option name)
application object.SetOption option name, desired setting
```

The arguments for these strings are defined as follows:

- *application object*: This is where you enter the name of the application object whose options you want to change.

- *option name*: This argument specifies the name of the option that you want to change.

- *desired setting*: This is a variant value corresponding to the option setting. The value of the setting argument depends on the possible settings for a particular option. These can be one of three types, Yes/No, string or numeric value, and predefined values.

As specified, there are three basic types of option values. In the case where the option is set by using a checkbox, the `GetOption` method will use `-1` to signify `Yes` and `0` to signify `No`. When you are specifying these settings in your strings, use `True` and `False` as the argument settings, not `-1` and `0`.

If, for example, you want to use the `GetOption` method to return the value for the Title Bar option, you could use the following strings:

```
Dim varSetting As Variant
varSetting = application object.GetOption("Title Bar")
```

If you want to set this value using the `SetOption` method, you could use the following string:

```
Dim varSetting As Variant
varSetting = application object.SetOption "Title Bar", "Desired Title"
```

If you are going to use `GetOption` or `SetOption` to work with values for selections from lists of choices in list boxes or combo boxes, the value of the desired selection will correspond with its position on the list. For example, if a list box has four choices, `GetOption` will index the choices beginning with `0` for the first choice on the list, `1` for the second, and so on. This option is identified to `SetOption` by using its numeric position on the list.

The same basic principles apply to setting options for button positions in option groups. The desired selection is specified to `GetOption` and `SetOption` as a numeric value, starting with `0`, that corresponds to its position in the group.

Startup Properties

An Access 97 database consists of a Jet 3.5 DAO object, with startup, user-interface, and similar properties specified by Access 97. For this reason, Jet does not automatically recognize the startup properties of an Access database. If you want to use VB code to handle startup properties, you have to create the properties that you want and add them to the Properties collection of the database object. If you are not sure that a property exists in the object's Properties collection, you should use error-handling code when you set startup properties from VB in order to verify this.

Object Collections

An object collection such as a Properties collection, contains all the properties, or property objects, for a database object that specify the operational parameters of that particular application object.

You can work with Properties collections through the `Append`, `CreateProperty`, `Delete`, and `Refresh` methods. Essentially, you will create and define a custom property using the `CreateProperty` method and then add it to the Properties collection using the `Append` method. Then you can reference that property object from DAO code.

> **CAUTION**
>
> You must create and add a property to the Properties collection before you can reference that property from VB code. Failing to do this will generate an error. You will also generate an error if you try to append a property object to the Properties collection if one with that name already exists.
>
> This is best dealt with by incorporating error-handling code into your VB code to verify that a property exists in the Properties collection of the database object. Bear in mind that if you distribute your application as a standalone application that uses the Access 97 runtime engine, it is imperative that you build error-handling code into your application. The Access 97 runtime engine has no built-in error-handling capabilities, and an unhandled error will usually cause the runtime application to shut down immediately with no warning.

You can use the `Delete` method to remove unwanted custom properties from the Properties collection. You cannot remove built-in properties from the Properties collection.

These customized or user-defined properties will be specific only to the particular application object for which they have been created. They will not affect any other application objects.

Any changes that you make to the Properties collection must respect the context and use of the property objects being created, added, or removed. Attempting to append properties to a collection that have inappropriate values, or manipulating properties out of context, will result in an error. For instance, if you tried to define the `StartupMenuBar` property with the name of an unrelated image file, or if you tried to read the value from a write-only password property, you would be attempting to use out-of-context properties and would generate an error.

To work with built-in properties in a collection, you should refer to them by their `Name` property settings or their ordinal number. It is not necessary to use the full `Name` property syntax as you must do with custom property objects.

To refer to a custom user-defined property object or its value property, you must use the full syntax as follows, respective to the desired context:

```
Object.Properties("name")
```

Any of the following four syntax strings can be used with built-in properties:

```
object.Properties(0)
object.Properties("name")
object.Properties![name]
object.name
```

When you refer to startup properties in VB, you will use different property object names than those that appear in the Access 97 Startup properties dialog. The startup property objects that can be used in VB code are shown in Table 19.1.

Table 19.1. The startup property objects used in VB code.

VB Property Object	Access 97 Startup Property Settings
AllowFullMenus	Allow full menus
AllowShortcutMenus	Allow default shortcut menus
AllowBuiltInToolbars	Allow built-in toolbars
AllowToolbarChanges	Allow toolbar/menu changes
AllowBreakIntoCode	Allow viewing code after error
AllowSpecialKeys	Use Access special keys
AppTitle	Application title
AppIcon	Application icon
StartupForm	Display form
StartupShowDBWindow	Display database window
StartupShowStatusBar	Display status bar
StartupMenuBar	Menu bar
StartupShortcutMenuBar	Shortcut menu bar

The Append Method

The Append method is used to add a new DAO object to a collection. This appended object is permanently stored in the collection until you use the Delete method to remove it. The exception to this is if the collection is a Workspaces collection that only resides in memory. In this case, the appended object is removed by the Close method.

The appended object will be present immediately, but the Refresh method should be used on any other object collections that are affected by this type of change to the database application object.

Before you can append a new object to a collection, it must be fully developed, and all properties in any related objects must reflect the appropriate values. Otherwise, you will generate a runtime error.

The proper syntax is

```
collection.Append object
```

The Append method's syntax is broken down as follows:

Syntax Element	Definition
collection	Specifies an application object variable that contains objects such as startup property setting objects.
object	Specifies an application object variable that represents the object to be appended.

Table 19.2 illustrates the object collections contained in application objects and indicates whether they can be appended.

Table 19.2. Appending object collections in application objects.

Application Object	Object Collection	Append Limit
DBEngine	Workspaces	New custom objects can be appended to this collection.
DBEngine	Errors	New custom objects cannot be appended to this collection. Error objects are created and appended internally at the time of occurrence.
Workspace	Connections	New custom objects cannot be appended to this collection. The OpenConnection method acts internally to automatically create and append new objects.
Workspace	Databases	New custom objects cannot be appended to this collection. The OpenConnection method acts internally to automatically create and append new objects.
Workspace	Groups	New custom objects can be appended to this collection.
Workspace	Users	New custom objects can be appended to this collection.
Connection	QueryDefs	New custom objects cannot be appended to this collection. The CreateQueryDef method acts internally to automatically create and append new objects.

continues

19

CUSTOMIZING THE DEVELOPMENT ENVIRONMENT

Table 19.2. continued

Application Object	Object Collection	Append Limit
Connection	Recordsets	New custom objects cannot be appended to this collection. The OpenRecordset method acts internally to automatically create and append new objects.
Database	Containers	New custom objects cannot be appended to this collection.
Database	QueryDefs	Conditional. Allowed if the object is new, not previously appended, and unnamed.
Database	Recordsets	New custom objects cannot be appended to this collection. The OpenRecordset method acts internally to automatically create and append new objects.
Database	Relations	New custom objects can be appended to this collection.
Database	TableDefs	New custom objects can be appended to this collection.
Group	Users	New custom objects can be appended to this collection.
User	Groups	New custom objects can be appended to this collection.
Container	Documents	New custom objects cannot be appended to this collection.
QueryDef	Fields	New custom objects cannot be appended to this collection.
QueryDef	Parameters	New custom objects cannot be appended to this collection.
Recordset	Fields	New custom objects cannot be appended to this collection.
Relation	Fields	New custom objects can be appended to this collection.
TableDef	Fields	Conditional. Allowed if the Updateable property of the object is set to True or has not been previously appended.

Application Object	Object Collection	Append Limit
TableDef	Indexes	Conditional. Allowed if the Updateable property of the object is set to True or has not been previously appended.
Index	Fields	Conditional. Allowed if the object is new, not previously appended, and unnamed.
Database	Properties	Conditional. Allowed when these objects are in a Jet workspace.
Field	Properties	Conditional. Allowed when these objects are in a Jet workspace.
Index	Properties	Conditional. Allowed when these objects are in a Jet workspace.
QueryDef	Properties	Conditional. Allowed when these objects are in a Jet workspace.
TableDef	Properties	Conditional. Allowed when these objects are in a Jet workspace.
DBEngine	Properties	New custom objects cannot be appended to this collection.
Parameter	Properties	New custom objects cannot be appended to this collection.
Recordset	Properties	New custom objects cannot be appended to this collection.
Workspace	Properties	New custom objects cannot be appended to this collection.

19

The Delete Method

The Delete method is used to remove a DAO object from a collection. The exception to this is if the collection is a Databases, Recordsets, or Workspaces collection that resides only in memory. In this case, an active object can be removed only by the Close method.

The deleted object will be removed immediately, but the Refresh method should be used on any other object collections that are affected by this type of change to the database application object.

> **NOTE**
>
> Deleting a `TableDef` object from the TableDefs collection will also delete the table definition and the data in the table.

The proper syntax is

`collection.Delete object`

The `Delete` method's syntax is broken down as follows:

Syntax Element	Definition
`collection`	Specifies an application object variable that contains objects such as startup property setting objects.
`object`	Specifies an application object variable that represents the DAO object to be deleted within the specified collection.

Table 19.3 illustrates the object collections contained in application objects and indicates whether you can delete from them.

Table 19.3. Deleting from object collections in application objects.

Application Object	Object Collection	Delete Limit
`DBEngine`	Workspaces	The `Delete` method cannot be used to remove objects from this collection. The objects are removed by the `Close` method of the application object.
`DBEngine`	Errors	The `Delete` method cannot be used to remove objects from this collection.
`Workspace`	Connections	The `Delete` method cannot be used to remove objects from this collection. The objects are removed by the `Close` method of the application object.
`Workspace`	Databases	The `Delete` method cannot be used to remove objects from this collection. The objects are removed by the `Close` method of the application object.
`Workspace`	Groups	New custom objects can be deleted from this collection.
`Workspace`	Users	New custom objects can be deleted from this collection.

Application Object	Object Collection	Delete Limit
Connection	QueryDefs	New custom objects cannot be deleted from this collection.
Connection	Recordsets	New custom objects cannot be deleted from this collection. This collection is deleted when the active object is closed.
Database	QueryDefs	New custom objects can be deleted from this collection.
Database	Recordsets	New custom objects can be deleted from this collection. The collection is deleted when the active object is closed.
Database	Relations	New custom objects can be deleted from this collection.
Database	TableDefs	New custom objects can be deleted from this collection.
Group	Users	New custom objects can be deleted from this collection.
User	Groups	New custom objects can be deleted from this collection.
Container	Documents	New custom objects cannot be deleted from this collection.
QueryDef	Fields	New custom objects cannot be deleted from this collection.
QueryDef	Parameters	New custom objects cannot be deleted from this collection.
Recordset	Fields	New custom objects cannot be deleted from this collection.
Relation	Fields	Conditional. Allowed if the object is a new object that has not been previously appended.
TableDef	Fields	Conditional. Allowed if the Updateable property of the object is set to True or if it has not been previously appended.
TableDef	Indexes	Conditional. Allowed if the Updateable property of the object is set to True or if it has not been previously appended.

continues

19

CUSTOMIZING THE DEVELOPMENT ENVIRONMENT

Table 19.3. continued

Application Object	Object Collection	Delete Limit
Index	Fields	Conditional. Allowed if the object is a new object that has not been previously appended.
Database	Properties	Conditional. Allowed when these are custom objects.
Field	Properties	Conditional. Allowed when these are custom objects.
Index	Properties	Conditional. Allowed when these are custom objects.
QueryDef	Properties	Conditional. Allowed when these are custom objects.
TableDef	Properties	Conditional. Allowed when these are custom objects.
DBEngine	Properties	New custom objects cannot be deleted from this collection.
Parameter	Properties	New custom objects cannot be deleted from this collection.
Recordset	Properties	New custom objects cannot be deleted from this collection.
Workspace	Properties	New custom objects cannot be deleted from this collection.

The Refresh Method

The DAO Refresh method is used to update and refresh the objects in an object collection. This method is used to initialize changes that have occurred in one collection to other collections.

When you have made a change to an application object's object collection, you might want to use this method to make sure that the changes are reflected throughout any other related object collections in the application object.

> **NOTE**
>
> The Refresh method can be used only on *non-persistent* collections, or collections that have not been recorded permanently on the hard disk.
>
> Workspaces, Connections, and Recordsets are examples of non-persistent collections.

In a multiuser environment, the `Refresh` method can be used to refresh the Groups collection when a Users collection has been changed.

Although using the `Refresh` method in a multiuser environment will slow performance somewhat, it is a good idea when you think that other users might make a change to a collection. Before you perform any functions in an application object, use the `Refresh` method on any collections where you rely on the presence of certain objects and you suspect that other users may have changed the collection. This will ensure that your collections will be as up to date as possible.

The proper syntax for the `Refresh` method is as follows:

`Collection.Refresh`

In this syntax, `Collection` represents a persistent collection that has been stored permanently on the hard disk.

Properties Collection DAO Routines for Application Objects

To create and define a custom property object and append it to the Properties collection for your currently open database object, you can use the following code:

```
Sub PropertyX()
Dim dbsBookstore As Database
Dim prpNew As Property
Dim prpLoop As Property
Set dbsBookstore = OpenDatabase("Bookstore.mdb")
With dbsBookstore
Set prpNew = .CreateProperty()
prpNew.Name = "Custom"
prpNew.Type = dbText
prpNew.Value = "This is a custom user-defined property object."
.Properties.Append prpNew
Debug.Print "Properties of " & .Name
For Each prpLoop In .Properties
With prpLoop
Debug.Print "     " & .Name
Debug.Print "          Type: " & .Type
Debug.Print "          Value: " & .Value
Debug.Print "          Inherited: " & _
.Inherited
End With
Next prpLoop
' This sample Property Object will now be deleted.
.Properties.Delete "Custom"
End With
End Sub
```

The following code example illustrates the use of the `CreateObject` method to modify the value of a custom property object. If the property object does not exist in the database object collection, the `CreateProperty` method creates and defines the property object, and then the `SetOption` method is used to define the value of this property object in the Properties collection:

```
Sub CreatePropertyX()
Dim dbsBookstore As Database
Dim prpLoop As Property
Set dbsBookstore = OpenDatabase("Bookstore.mde")
SetProperty dbsBookstore, "Archive", True
With dbsBookstore
Debug.Print "Properties of " & .Name
For Each prpLoop In .Properties
If prpLoop <> "" Then Debug.Print "    " & _
prpLoop.Name & " = " & prpLoop
Next prpLoop
'Since "Archives" is a test, it will now be deleted
.Properties.Delete "Archive"
.Close
End With
End Sub
Sub SetProperty(dbsTemp As Database, strName As String, _
booTemp As Boolean)
Dim prpNew As Property
Dim errLoop As Error
On Error GoTo Err_Property
dbsTemp.Properties("strName") = booTemp
On Error GoTo 0
Exit Sub
Err_Property:
If DBEngine.Errors(0).Number = 3270 Then
Set prpNew = dbsTemp.CreateProperty(strName, _
dbBoolean, booTemp)
dbsTemp.Properties.Append prpNew
Resume Next
Else
For Each errLoop In DBEngine.Errors
MsgBox "iX dBApp Error number: " & errLoop.Number & vbCr & _
errLoop.Description
Next errLoop
End
End If
End Sub
```

The following code calls VB code that sets a property object's value within an object's Properties collection.

This VB code calls the value-setting procedure:

```
Sub CallPropertySet()
Dim dbs As Database, tdf As TableDef
Dim blnReturn As Boolean
Set dbs = CurrentDb
Set tdf = dbs.TableDefs!Employees
blnReturn = SetAccessProperty(tdf, _
"AllowFullMenus", dbBoolean, True)
If blnReturn = True Then
Debug.Print "Property set successfully."
Else
Debug.Print "Property not set successfully."
End If
End Sub
```

The preceding code calls the following procedure, which acts upon the property object's value:

```
Function SetAccessProperty(obj As Object, strName As String, _
intType As Integer, varSetting As Variant) As Boolean
Dim prp As Property
Const conPropNotFound As Integer = 3270
On Error GoTo ErrorSetAccessProperty
obj.Properties(strName) = varSetting
obj.Properties.Refresh
SetAccessProperty = True
ExitSetAccessProperty:
Exit Function
ErrorSetAccessProperty:
If Err = conPropNotFound Then
Set prp = obj.CreateProperty(strName, intType, varSetting)
obj.Properties.Append prp
obj.Properties.Refresh
SetAccessProperty = True
Resume ExitSetAccessProperty
Else
MsgBox Err & ": " & vbCrLf & Err.Description
SetAccessProperty = False
Resume ExitSetAccessProperty
End If
End Function
```

Assessing and Customizing System Policies

Although you can make a number of user environment changes within Access 97 using the Options dialog, as a network or workgroup administrator, you can also use the Systems Policy Editor to effect custom changes to your user environments to achieve increased performance and usability. This application can be found on your Windows 95 distribution CD-ROM in the `Poledit` subfolder under the `Admin` folder. The Office 97 Resource Kit and Windows NT 4.0 contain the latest version of the System Policy Editor. The Windows 95 System Policy Editor is shown in Figure 19.2.

FIGURE 19.2.

The Windows 95 System Policy Editor.

19

CUSTOMIZING THE DEVELOPMENT ENVIRONMENT

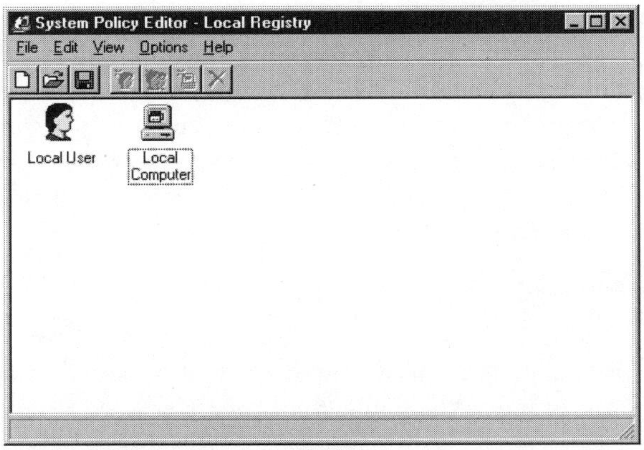

Using the Policy Editor saves you the trouble of administering individual changes to each Windows 95/NT 4.*x* system connected to your network and helps to provide a central mechanism for maintenance and control.

As I mentioned earlier in this chapter, Windows uses Registry key settings to manage system options and configuration information. *System policies* are options that are represented by Registry keys; they are specified in template files that are managed with the Windows System Policy Editor.

When you create a system policy file with the desired user settings, it can be placed on your network server for users to download. Because all users on the network will use the same system policy file, you can manage all the user environments from a central location.

> **NOTE**
>
> On Windows NT 4.*x* networks, name the customized policy file `Config.pol` and save it to the `Netlogon` folder of your client system's primary domain controller.
>
> On NetWare networks, copy `Config.pol` to the public folder on the client system's primary server.

User policies are system policies stored in the `HKEY_USERS` portion of the user's Windows Registry that represent application options for the user.

Computer policies are system policies stored in the `HKEY_LOCAL_MACHINE` portion of the Windows Registry that represent options relevant to particular computers.

If you add multiple groups, you can set the relative priority between the groups. Users who are members of more than one group have their highest priority settings processed last so that their priority settings don't override the lower-priority groups.

In order to use system policies, the end-user client machines will have to have Windows 95 or NT 4.*x* installed, as I mentioned previously, and they must have user policies enabled if you want to set user policies. If you want to set group policies, the client machines must have group policy capability installed. Client for Microsoft Networks must be the specified Windows Logon client, and the preferred server must be defined in order to download policies automatically on NT networks. Client for NetWare Networks must be the specified logon client, and the preferred server must be defined in order to download policies automatically from NetWare networks.

Windows automatically checks for the policies file based on user name or computer name and then copies the policies into the Registry.

The default policy file is called `Config.pol` and is located in the `Netlogon` folder on the preferred NT server and in the public folder of a NetWare server.

Office Policy Templates

Because of Access 97's tight integration with Office 97, we should briefly look at policy files for the Office 97 environment. As a system administrator or developer, you should already have either the Office 97 Developer's Edition or a copy of the Office 97 Resource Kit Tools and Utilities. Included with these resources are sample copies of Office template files that you can use to develop your own Office 97 system policies.

The policy files of particular interest are Access97.adm, Query97.adm, and Off97w95.adm or Off97nt4.adm. These policy files allow you to establish templates for Access 97, Microsoft Query and ODBC, and general Office 97 settings under Windows 95 or NT 4.x.

Most of the system policies correspond to user-selectable options within each application. Therefore, it is possible to establish a common template for user options across networked environments. As you can appreciate, this significantly reduces the administrative load on system administrators.

Those policies that are not user selectable within Access 97 are managed through the general Office 97 policies.

Changing Windows Registry Settings for Access 97

The Windows 95 or NT 4.x environment can be changed with respect to Access 97 by using the Registry Editor that is included with the operating systems.

Starting the Registry Editor is done from the command line. Click Start and choose Run. Type regedit and then click OK. (In Windows NT, run regedt32.) (See Figure 19.3.)

FIGURE 19.3.
The Windows Registry Editor.

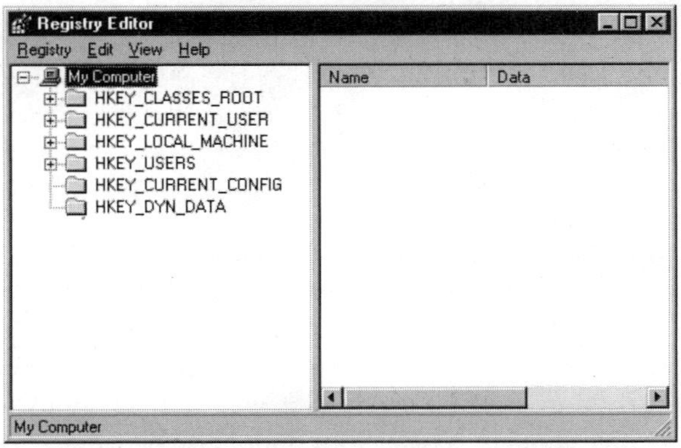

19

CUSTOMIZING THE DEVELOPMENT ENVIRONMENT

Once you have opened the Registry Editor, proceed to the appropriate key. In the case of Access 97, you are concerned with the following two keys:

```
"\HKEY_LOCAL_MACHINE\SOFTWARE\Microsoft\Office\8.0\Access"
"\HKEY_LOCAL_MACHINE\SOFTWARE\Microsoft\Jet\3.5"
```

> **CAUTION**
>
> As with other Office 97 and Windows applications, Access 97 stores its initialization parameters in the Windows Registry database. Generally speaking, changing Access Registry settings is not a good idea because it can lead to unpredictable errors or results. It is strongly recommended that you not change Access 97 settings in the Windows Registry, but, if you do want make Registry changes, use `regedit.exe`, and make sure that you make a backup copy before proceeding. Incorrect Registry changes may lead to a situation where you need to restore the original Registry settings or reinstall Access 97 to recover from the problem.

After making a change to the Registry, the new settings take effect the next time Access is started. Close and restart Access 97 to initialize the changes.

Direct Registry Settings for Microsoft Jet Version 3.5

To make direct changes to the Registry settings for Microsoft Jet version 3.5, open the `\HKEY_LOCAL_MACHINE\SOFTWARE\Microsoft\Jet\3.5\Engines\Jet\3.5` key and make the desired changes. Or, if you want to isolate your settings to Access 97 only, open the key `\HKEY_LOCAL_MACHINE\SOFTWARE\Microsoft\Office\8.0\Access\Jet\3.5\Engines\Jet\3.5`.

> **NOTE**
>
> You can also manipulate Jet 3.5 through the DAO code `SetOption` method of the `DBEngine` object. This method is described later in this section and is a good way to implement dynamic changes to the Access 97 environment without effecting permanent changes to the system Registry.

Keep in mind that changing these settings in the system Registry represents a permanent system environment change. The Registry is not the place to start messing around with Windows 95 or NT environment settings to see what happens next. If you don't have an isolated testbed system lying around waiting to be experimented on, the best method for researching changes to the Registry is to use DAO code to dynamically manipulate the `SetOption` method of the appropriate object, or else look at your options on paper. Even though you might be able to go back into the Registry and reverse any changes that you have made, you might not be able to reverse the unseen effects of those changes. Make sure that you make a backup copy of your Registry, but also be prepared to reinstall Access 97 to correct the changes.

At Access 97 installation time, `MSJET35.dll` and `MSRD2X35.dll` are automatically registered in the system Registry under the `\HKEY_LOCAL_MACHINES\Software\Microsoft\Jet\3.5\Engines` section using the `SystemDB = <path>\System.mdb` and the `CompactBYPkey = 01` entries.

Jet 3.5 uses the following Registry settings:

`SystemDB`	Specifies the path and filename of the workgroup information file. The default setting is the path and filename `System.mdb`.
`CompactByPKey`	Specifies that if Jet 3.*x* tables have a primary key, they are copied in primary-key order when they are compacted. Tables that do not have a primary key are copied in base-table order. `0` specifies that the tables should be copied in base-table order when they are being compacted; a `DWORD` value other than `0` specifies that the tables should be copied in primary-key order.

The following initialization settings are created under the `\HKEY_LOCAL_MACHINES\Software\Microsoft\Jet\3.5\Engines\Jet 3.5` Registry key when Jet is registered at installation:

- ■ `FlushTransactionTimeout`: This determines the number of milliseconds that Jet will wait before writing cached asynchronous changes to a database, unless the size of the cache exceeds the `MaxBufferSize` setting. The default setting is `500` milliseconds and should not be increased unless your database is updated over a slow network connection. This setting supersedes the `ExclusiveAsyncDelay` and `SharedAsyncDelay` settings and is generally the best method of controlling this delay. Setting `FlushTransactionTimeout` to `0` disables this method of control and allows you to use `ExclusiveAsyncDelay` and `SharedAsyncDelay` settings.

- ■ `ExclusiveAsyncDelay`: This setting specifies the delay before asynchronous mode changes are made to a database that has been opened in exclusive mode. The default setting is `2000` milliseconds. If you want to ensure that changes are written faster, you can decrease this setting, but doing so will decrease performance as well. You should not increase this setting unless the user system has 32MB RAM or more, and you have specified a larger `MaxBufferSize` setting. The `FlushTransactionTimeout` setting supersedes this setting.

- ■ `SharedAsyncDelay`: This setting specifies the delay before asynchronous mode changes are made to a database that has been opened in shared mode. The default setting is `50` milliseconds. Changing this setting should be done in such a way as to balance the number of disk I/O operations against the number of concurrent users. The fewer the concurrent requests on a database, the larger your `SharedAsyncDelay` setting can be. This reduces the number of disk I/O operations required but holds the changed pages in the buffer longer while waiting to write to the database. Jet locks pages that are stored in the buffer so concurrent access performance will be reduced. The `FlushTransactionTimeout` setting supersedes this setting.

- `PageTimeout`: This setting tells Jet how long to wait before checking for user changes to a database. If Jet detects a change, the data in the buffer is refreshed. The default setting is `5000` milliseconds. This setting should be adjusted with respect to the desire to reduce disk read operations while still keeping the changes up to date. The smaller the delay, the slower the performance but the faster that changes are available to the user. This setting can be overridden by using the Refresh Interval setting in the Advanced options dialog box in Access 97 or by using the `dbRefreshCache` argument of the `DBObject Idle` method in DAO code to refresh user changes to the database immediately.

- `LockDelay`: This setting tells Jet how long to wait before trying to lock a page in a shared database that it was unable to lock on first or subsequent attempts. The default setting is `100` milliseconds. This setting helps reduce the number of lock request retries across networks that do not have an NOS that manages locking retries. Windows 95 peer-to-peer networks do not have a mechanism for central control of lock requests and retries, and they can lose a significant amount of bandwidth due to locking retry bombardment. Using the `LockDelay` setting reduces the number of locking retries that Jet will repeat within a specified period of time, protecting precious network bandwidth. If you want to change this setting, adjust the delay setting in proportion to the frequency of lock requests per user and the average number of records locked per user. If the NOS in use has locking-management capabilities, as does Windows NT, this Registry setting is redundant and does not need to be changed.

- `MaxLocksPerFile`: This setting specifies the maximum number of locks that Jet will allow per file. The default setting is `9500`. This setting should be adjusted according to the maximum number of locks per file supported by the NOS server. The problem lies with having a `MaxLocksPerFile` setting in your Registry that exceeds the maximum locks-per-file capability of the NOS server. If your system tries to commit more than the maximum supported by the NOS server, an error will likely be generated when performing large transactions. If the number of locks needed to perform an operation exceeds the `MaxLocksPerFile` setting, Jet processes the data that is locked, clears the locks, and then locks and commits the remaining data.

- `RecycleLVs`: Long value (LV) pages store data in fields with Memo, OLE Object, and Hyperlink data types, along with data that defines forms, reports, and modules. Databases that are open in shared mode can grow in size when data, forms, modules, and reports are deleted or changed in such a way that the current LV page must be discarded and replaced with a new one. The `RecycleLVs` setting specifies when old LV pages are available for reuse. The default setting is `0`, which specifies that old LV pages become available for reuse after the last user closes the database. This setting can be changed to `1`, which tells Jet to make old LV pages available after new LV data has been added and when there is only one user left in the database in shared mode. Old LV pages are removed when you run a compacting operation on a database.

- ■ `Threads`: Threads are independent software processes that run under multitasking operating system environments. Jet uses multiple internal threads to perform background operations necessary for the function of your database application. The default setting is a maximum of three threads. This setting can be increased to enhance the performance of complicated database applications.

- ■ `MaxBufferSize`: This specifies the size of the buffer in which non-explicit add, delete, or update record transaction data is stored by Jet. Jet uses this buffer space as needed, up to the maximum as specified in the `MaxBufferSize`. By default, this buffer size is set to `0`, which tells Jet to calculate the `MaxBufferSize` according to the formula [`512KB + (RAM KB - 12,288)(4)`]. Jet uses data pages that are 2,048 bytes each, and when the amount of data exceeds the `MaxBufferSize` or the maximum cache time that is specified in the `FlushTransactionTimeout`, `SharedAsyncDelay`, or `ExclusiveAsyncDelay` setting, it begins writing data to the database.

  This buffer size can be adjusted between 128KB and 8MB according to the complexity of the database application and the system resources. Setting `MaxBufferSize` lower than 512KB or higher than 8MB will cause system performance to degrade. Additional threads are started to manage the writing of buffer data to the database, and reducing the `MaxBufferSize` below 512KB will require an excessive number of write operations. Creating a `MaxBufferSize` greater than 8MB will cause an excessive amount of system overhead to be dedicated to managing the large buffer and reach the point of diminishing return. If you do not use the `FlushTransactionTimeout` setting, you might need to increase or decrease the `SharedAsyncDelay` setting in direct proportion to the change in the `MaxBufferSize` setting.

- ■ `UserCommitSync`: This Registry setting determines which write mode Jet uses to write explicit transaction changes. The default setting is `Yes`, which specifies synchronous mode and ensures that Jet does not relinquish control to the application code until the changes are written to the database. If you change this setting to cause Jet to use asynchronous mode to commit changes to the database, Jet will store the changes in its buffer and relinquish control back to the application code while writing the changes using a background thread. Using asynchronous mode can lead to application problems because there will be no mechanism in place to ensure that asynchronous changes are made to the database before the application code attempts to perform a new operation on the database.

- ■ `ImplicitCommitSync`: This Registry setting determines which write mode Jet uses to write add, delete, or update record operations in non-explicit transactions. In this case, Jet automatically saves the results of internal transactions in its buffer. This setting determines whether the resulting internal transactions are written to the database in synchronous or asynchronous mode. The default setting is `No`, which allows these particular changes to be written in asynchronous mode. If you change the setting to `Yes`, you will receive the integrity benefit of synchronous mode, but the performance of Jet will be significantly impaired.

19

CUSTOMIZING THE DEVELOPMENT ENVIRONMENT

Table 19.4 lists the ISAM settings that are made under the `\HKEY_LOCAL_MACHINES\Software\Microsoft\Jet\3.5\ISAM` Registry section.

Table 19.4. Jet 3.5 ISAM Registry settings.

Setting	Value Type	Value
Engine	String	Jet 3.5
ExportFilter	String	Access "*.mdb"
ImportFilter	String	Access "*.mdb"
CanLink	Binary	00
OneTablePerFile	Binary	00
IndexDialog	Binary	00
CreateDBOnExport	Binary	00
ResultTextLink	String	LinkedDataSource.* The filename and path to an external data source file that will be used to create a linked table in the current database. Data changes to the local file will also be reflected in the external data source.
ResultTextImport	String	ImportDataSource.* The filename and path to an external data source that will be imported into the current database, limiting the changes to the local database only.
ResultTextExport	String	ExportDataSource.* The filename and path to an external data source that will have data from the current database exported into it. All changes to the current database will be reflected as appropriate in the external source.

Customizing Lotus Driver Settings

Microsoft does not recommend changing the Lotus driver settings manually because it may lead to unpredictable behavior or errors. Any Registry changes for this driver should be handled through the driver's setup utility.

If you decide to customize the Lotus driver setting, edit the values under the key `\HKEY_LOCAL_MACHINE\SOFTWARE\Microsoft\Jet\3.5\Engines\Lotus`. Or, if you want to restrict your settings to Access 97, edit the values under the key `\HKEY_LOCAL_MACHINE\SOFTWARE\Microsoft\Office\8.0\Access\Jet\3.5\Engines\Lotus`.

The Registry settings are as follows:

`\HKEY_LOCAL_MACHINES\Software\Microsoft\Jet\3.5\Engines\Lotus\`*setting*

- `win32`: Specifies the location of the `Msltus35.dll` file.
- `TypeGuessRows`: Specifies the number of rows to check for the data type. The default is `8`.
- `ImportMixedTypes`: Specifies how columns of mixed data types will be managed. `MajorityType` specifies that the predominant data type will be the delineator. `Text` specifies that the columns will be delineated as `Text` upon being imported.
- `AppendBlankRows`: Specifies the number of blank rows to append to the end of a Lotus 1-2-3 WK1 worksheet prior to importing new data to it.
- `FirstRowHasNames`: Specifies whether the first row of the table contains column names. `01` indicates yes; `00` indicates no.

Table 19.5 shows the ISAM settings for the `\HKEY_LOCAL_MACHINES\Software\Microsoft\Jet\3.5\Engines\Jet 3.5\ISAM Formats\Lotus WK1\`*setting* section.

Table 19.5. Jet 3.5 ISAM Lotus WK1 Registry settings.

Setting	Value Type	Value
Engine	String	Lotus
ExportFilter	String	Lotus 1-2-3 WK1 (*.wk1)
ImportFilter	String	Lotus 1-2-3 (*.wk*;*.wj*)
CanLink	Binary	00
OneTablePerFile	Binary	00
IsamType	DWORD	1
IndexDialog	Binary	00
CreateDBOnExport	Binary	01
ResultTextImport	String	ImportDataSource.* The filename and path to an external data source that will be imported into the current database, limiting the changes to the local database only.
ResultTextExport	String	ExportDataSource.* The filename and path to an external data source that will have data from the current database exported into it. All changes to the current database will be reflected as appropriate in the external source.

Table 19.6 shows the settings for the `\HKEY_LOCAL_MACHINES\Software\Microsoft\Jet\ 3.5\Engines\Jet 3.5\ISAM Formats\Lotus WK3` section.

Table 19.6. Jet 3.5 ISAM Registry settings for Lotus WK3 source files.

Entry name	Value Type	Value
Engine	String	Lotus
ExportFilter	String	Lotus 1-2-3 WK3 (*.wk3)
CanLink	Binary	00
OneTablePerFile	Binary	00
IsamType	DWORD	1
IndexDialog	Binary	00
CreateDBOnExport	Binary	01
ResultTextExport	String	ExportDataSource.* The filename and path to a Lotus 1-2-3 version 3.*x* worksheet external data source that will have data from the current database exported into it, overwriting existing data. All changes to the current database will be reflected as appropriate in the external source.

Table 19.7 lists the settings for the `\HKEY_LOCAL_MACHINES\Software\Microsoft\Jet\3.5\ Engines\Jet 3.5\ISAM Formats\Lotus WK4` section.

Table 19.7. Jet 3.5 ISAM formats Registry settings for Lotus WK4 source files.

Setting	Value Type	Value
Engine	String	Lotus
CanLink	Binary	00
OneTablePerFile	Binary	00
IsamType	DWORD	1
IndexDialog	Binary	00
CreateDBOnExport	Binary	01

Excel Driver Settings

This is another of the automatically set-up Registry entries that Microsoft discourages you from making direct modifications to. However, if you must, open the `\HKEY_LOCAL_MACHINE\`

`SOFTWARE\Microsoft\Jet\3.5\Engines\Excel` key, or the `\HKEY_LOCAL_MACHINE\SOFTWARE\` `Microsoft\Office\8.0\Access\Jet\3.5\Engines\Excel` key if you want to restrict your settings to Access 97.

The following are the initialization settings for the `\HKEY_LOCAL_MACHINES\Software\` `Microsoft\Jet\3.5\Engines\Excel` section, which is used to initialize the `Msexcl35.dll` Excel external data source driver:

- `TypeGuessRows`: Specifies the number of rows to check for the data type. The default is `8`.

- `ImportMixedTypes`: Specifies how columns of mixed data types will be managed. `MajorityType` specifies that the predominant data type will be the delineator. `Text` specifies that the columns will be delineated as text upon being imported.

- `AppendBlankRows`: Specifies the number of blank rows to append to the end of an Excel version 3.5 or 4.0 worksheet prior to importing new data to it.

- `FirstRowHasNames`: Specifies whether the first row of the table contains column names. `01` indicates yes; `00` indicates no.

- `win32`: Specifies the path to `Msexcl35.dll`.

Table 19.8 lists the ISAM settings for the `\HKEY_LOCAL_MACHINE\SOFTWARE\Microsoft\` `Jet\3.5\ISAM Formats\Excel 3.0` section.

Table 19.8. Jet 3.5 ISAM Registry settings for Excel 3.0 data sources.

Setting	Value Type	Value
Engine	String	`Excel`
ExportFilter	String	`Microsoft Excel 3 "*.xls"`
CanLink	Binary	`01`
OneTablePerFile	Binary	`00`
IsamType	DWORD	`1`
IndexDialog	Binary	`00`
CreateDBOnExport	Binary	`01`
ResultTextExport	String	`ExportDataSource.*` The filename and path to an Excel 3.0 external data source that will have data from the current database exported into it. All changes to the current database will be reflected as appropriate in the external source.

19

CUSTOMIZING THE
DEVELOPMENT
ENVIRONMENT

Table 19.9 shows the settings for the `\HKEY_LOCAL_MACHINE\SOFTWARE\Microsoft\Jet\3.5\ISAM Formats\Excel 4.0` section.

Table 19.9. Jet 3.5 ISAM Registry settings for Excel 4.0 source files.

Setting	Value Type	Value
Engine	String	`Excel`
ExportFilter	String	`Microsoft Excel 4 "*.xls"`
CanLink	Binary	`01`
OneTablePerFile	Binary	`00`
IsamType	DWORD	`1`
IndexDialog	Binary	`00`
CreateDBOnExport	Binary	`01`
ResultTextExport	String	`ExportDataSource.*` The filename and path to an Excel 4.0 external data source that will have data from the current database exported into it. All changes to the current database will be reflected as appropriate in the external source.

Table 19.10 shows the settings for the `\HKEY_LOCAL_MACHINE\SOFTWARE\Microsoft\Jet\3.5\ISAM Formats\Excel 5.0` section. These are the settings that correspond to Excel versions 5.0 and 7.0.

Table 19.10. Jet 3.5 ISAM Registry settings for Excel 5.0 and 95/7.0 source files.

Setting	Value Type	Value
Engine	String	`Excel`
ExportFilter	String	`Microsoft Excel 5-7 "*.xls"`
ImportFilter	String	`Microsoft Excel "*.xls"`
CanLink	Binary	`01`
OneTablePerFile	Binary	`00`
IsamType	DWORD	`1`
IndexDialog	Binary	`00`
CreateDBOnExport	Binary	`01`
ResultTextLink	String	`LinkedDataSource.*` The filename and path to an Excel 5.0 external data source

Setting	Value Type	Value
		file that will be used to create a linked table in the current database. Data changes to the local file will also be reflected in the external data source.
ResultTextImport	String	ImportDataSource.* The filename and path to an Excel 5.0 external data source that will be imported into the current database, limiting the changes to the local database only.
ResultTextExport	String	ExportDataSource.* The filename and path to an Excel 5.0 external data source that will have data from the current database exported into it. All changes to the current database will be reflected as appropriate in the external source.

Table 19.11 shows the settings for the `\HKEY_LOCAL_MACHINE\SOFTWARE\Microsoft\Jet\3.5\ISAM Formats\Excel 8.0` section. These settings apply to Excel 97/8.0.

Table 19.11. Jet 3.5 ISAM Registry settings for Excel 97/8.0 source files.

Setting	Value Type	Value
Engine	String	Excel
ExportFilter	String	Microsoft Excel 97
CanLink	Binary	01
OneTablePerFile	Binary	00
IsamType	DWORD	1
IndexDialog	Binary	00
CreateDBOnExport	Binary	01
ResultTextExport	String	ExportDataSource.* The filename and path to an Excel 97/8.0 external data source that will have data from the current database exported into it. All changes to the current database will be reflected as appropriate in the external source.

Customizing Text Driver Settings

When the text data source driver is added to your system, changes are automatically made to the Registry, and Microsoft does not recommend changing any of these settings manually. Changes to the Registry should be made in the driver installation process.

If you choose, against recommendations, to edit the text driver Registry key, use the Registry Editor to edit the \HKEY_LOCAL_MACHINE\SOFTWARE\Microsoft\Jet\3.5\Engines\Text key and make your desired changes.

> **CAUTION**
>
> These changes will affect all applications on the system that use Jet to access text data. If you want your changes to affect Access 97 only, edit the \HKEY_LOCAL_MACHINE\SOFTWARE\ Microsoft\Office\8.0\Access\Jet\3.5\Engines\Text key if it exists, or create the key and add the desired values.

The following text data source settings are for the Mstext35.dll driver, which is used to access external text based data sources:

- win32: This provides the path to Mstext35.dll that is determined when the driver is installed.

- MaxScanRows: Specifies the number of rows to be scanned when setting up table columns. Setting this to 0 forces a search of the entire text source. The default value is 25.

- FirstRowHasNames: 00 specifies that there are no column names in the first row, whereas 01 specifies that there are. 01 is the default setting.

- CharacterSet: Specifies how text pages are stored. OEM indicates that OEM-to-ANSI and ANSI-to-OEM conversions are performed. ANSI indicates that the conversions are not done. The default setting is OEM.

- Format: Specifies either CSVDelimited, Delimited (single character), or TabDelimited format. CSVDelimited is the default value.

- Extensions: Specifies the filename extensions to search for text-based data. The default settings are asc, csv, tab, and txt.

- ExportCurrencySymbols: Specifies the status of currency symbols in exported data fields. 00 indicates that no currency symbol is included, and 01 indicates that currency symbols are included.

The ISAM settings stored under the \HKEY_LOCAL_MACHINE\SOFTWARE\Microsoft\Jet\3.5\ISAM Formats\Text category are listed in Table 19.12.

Table 19.12. Jet 3.5 ISAM Registry settings for text-based source files.

Setting	Setting Type	Value
Engine	String	Text
ExportFilter	String	Text Files (*.txt; *.csv; *.tab; *.asc)
ImportFilter	String	Text Files (*.txt; *.csv; *.tab; *.asc)
CanLink	Binary	01
OneTablePerFile	Binary	01
IsamType	DWORD	2
IndexDialog	Binary	00
CreateDBOnExport	Binary	00
ResultTextLink	String	LinkedDataSource.* The filename and path to an external data source file that will be used to create a linked table in the current database. Data changes to the local file will also be reflected in the external data source.
ResultTextImport	String	ImportDataSource.* The filename and path to an external data source that will be imported into the current database, limiting the changes to the local database only.
ResultTextExport	String	ExportDataSource.* The filename and path to an external data source that will have data from the current database exported into it. All changes to the current database will be reflected as appropriate in the external source.

Customizing HTML Driver Settings

The HTML driver is another one whose Registry settings Microsoft discourages you from tampering with. The company recommends managing changes to these settings through the driver's setup utility.

If you want to modify these settings manually, open the \HKEY_LOCAL_MACHINE\SOFTWARE\ Microsoft\Jet\3.5\Engines\Text key, or the \HKEY_LOCAL_MACHINE\SOFTWARE\Microsoft\ Office\8.0\Access\Jet\3.5\Engines\Text key if you want to limit your Registry changes to Access 97, and make the desired changes.

19

CUSTOMIZING THE DEVELOPMENT ENVIRONMENT

Jet uses the following settings in the `\HKEY_LOCAL_MACHINE\SOFTWARE\Microsoft\Jet\3.5\` `Engines\Text` section of the Registry:

- `win32`: This provides the path to `Mstext35.dll` that is determined when the driver is installed.

- `MaxScanRows`: Specifies the number of rows to be scanned when setting up table columns. Setting this to `0` forces a search of the entire text source. The default value is `25`.

- `FirstRowHasNames`: `00` specifies that there are no column names in the first row, whereas `01` specifies that there are. `01` is the default setting.

- `CharacterSet`: Specifies how text pages are stored. `OEM` indicates that OEM-to-ANSI and ANSI-to-OEM conversions are performed. `ANSI` indicates that the conversions are not done. The default setting is `OEM`.

- `Format`: Specifies either `CSVDelimited`, `Delimited` (single character), or `TabDelimited` format. `CSVDelimited` is the default value.

- `Extensions`: Specifies the filename extensions to search for text-based data. The default settings are `asc`, `csv`, `tab`, and `txt`.

- `ExportCurrencySymbols`: Specifies the status of currency symbols in exported data fields. `00` indicates that no currency symbol is included; `01` indicates that currency symbols are included.

HTML import ISAM Registry settings are stored under the `\HKEY_LOCAL_MACHINE\SOFTWARE\` `Microsoft\Jet\3.5\ISAM Formats\HTML Import` category. They are listed in Table 19.13.

Table 19.13. Jet 3.5 ISAM Registry settings for HTML import data sources.

Setting	Value Type	Value
Engine	String	Text
ImportFilter	String	HTML Files "*.ht*"
CanLink	Binary	01
OneTablePerFile	Binary	00
IsamType	DWORD	2
IndexDialog	Binary	00
CreateDBOnExport	Binary	00
ResultTextLink	String	LinkedDataSource.* The filename and path to an external data source file that will be

Setting	Value Type	Value
		used to create a linked table in the current database. Data changes to the local file will also be reflected in the external data source.
ResultTextImport	String	ImportDataSource.* The filename and path to an external data source that will be imported into the current database, limiting the changes to the local database only.

HTML export ISAM Registry settings are stored under the \HKEY_LOCAL_MACHINE\ SOFTWARE\ Microsoft\Jet\3.5\ISAM Formats\HTML Export category. They are shown in Table 19.14.

Table 19.14. Jet 3.5 ISAM Registry settings for HTML export data sources.

Setting	Value Type	Value
Engine	String	Text
ExportFilter	String	HTML Files "*.htm"
CanLink	Binary	00
OneTablePerFile	Binary	01
IsamType	DWORD	2
IndexDialog	Binary	00
CreateDBOnExport	Binary	00
ResultTextExport	String	LinkedDataSource.* The filename and path to an external data source that will have data from the current database exported into it. All changes to the current database will be reflected as appropriate in the external source.

Customizing Xbase Driver Settings

The Xbase drivers are another category of drivers whose Registry settings you are encouraged to leave alone. If you choose to edit these settings, open the \HKEY_LOCAL_MACHINE\SOFTWARE\ Microsoft\Jet\3.5\Engines\Xbase key or the \HKEY_LOCAL_MACHINE\SOFTWARE\Microsoft\ Office\8.0\Access\Jet\3.5\Engines\Xbase key, and then modify the desired values.

19

CUSTOMIZING THE DEVELOPMENT ENVIRONMENT

dBASE-Specific Xbase Section Settings for the Jet Key

The following Registry settings initialize Jet to work with various dBASE version external source files:

- **win32**: Specifies the path to `Msxbse35.dll`.

- **NetworkAccess**: Specifies the file-locking preference. `00` specifies exclusive access; `01` specifies shared access. This setting overrides the `OpenDatabase` and `OpenRecordset` method settings. The default value is `01`.

- **PageTimeout**: This specifies how long each page of data, which is 2,048 bytes in size, is held in the cache before it is invalidated. The default value is 600×100 millisecond units, or 60,000 milliseconds.

- **INFPath**: Specifies the path to the `.inf` file directory. If Jet does not find an `.inf` file in the same directory as the external source table, it searches the specified directory in this setting before defaulting to the index files in the database directory.

- **CollatingSequence**: Specifies the collating sequence for any dBASE tables opened by Jet. The default value is `ASCII`; the other setting available is `International`.

- **DataCodePage**: Specifies how text data pages are stored. The default setting is `OEM`, which specifies that the OEM-to-ANSI and ANSI-to-OEM conversions are performed. Selecting `ANSI` specifies that the conversions are not performed.

- **Deleted**: This setting specifies how Jet will treat records that have been marked for deletion. `00` specifies that Jet will act in accordance with the dBASE command `SET DELETE OFF` and will treat deleted records the same as any other. `01` tells Jet to act in accordance with the dBASE command `SET DELETE ON`, where it is not to retrieve or access deleted records. The default value is `00`.

- **Century**: Specifies how Jet should format the century part of dates in order to be compatible with the date-to-string functions used in the dBASE file index expressions. The default setting of `00` tells Jet to conform to the dBASE `SET CENTURY OFF` command. `01` tells Jet to conform to the `SET CENTURY ON` command.

- **Date**: Specifies the date format to use in order to be compatible with dBASE index expressions that use date-to-string functions. Possible settings for this entry that conform to the dBASE `SET DATE` command are `American`, `ANSI`, `British`, `French`, `DMY`, `German`, `Italian`, `Japan`, `MDY`, `USA`, and `YMD`. The default setting is `MDY`.

- **Mark**: Specifies the decimal value of the ASCII character used to separate the parts of date expressions. The default value is decided by the `Date` setting, as described in the preceding item. The most common are (`"/"`, American, `MDY`), (`"."`, `ANSI`), (`"/"`, British, French, `DMY`), (`"."`, German), (`"-"`, Italian), and (`"/"`, Japan, `YMD`), (`"-"`, USA). The normal default value is specified as `0`. This tells Jet to use the separator that properly corresponds to the `Date` setting.

■ Exact: Specifies the binary indicator used for string comparisons. The default setting is 00, which tells Jet to behave in accordance with the dBASE command SET ACTION OFF. 01 tells Jet to conform to the dBASE command SET ACTION ON.

The settings for the \HKEY_LOCAL_MACHINE\SOFTWARE\Microsoft\Jet\3.5\ISAM Formats\dBASE III section are shown in Table 19.15.

Table 19.15. Jet 3.5 ISAM Registry settings for dBASE III data sources.

Setting	Value Type	Value
Engine	String	Xbase
ExportFilter	String	dBASE III "*.dbf"
ImportFilter	String	dBASE III "*.dbf"
CanLink	Binary	01
OneTablePerFile	Binary	01
IsamType	DWORD	0
IndexDialog	Binary	01
IndexFilter	String	dBASE Index "*.ndx"
CreateDBOnExport	Binary	00
ResultTextLink	String	LinkedDataSource.* The filename and path to an external data source file that will be used to create a linked table in the current database. Data changes to the local file will also be reflected in the external data source.
ResultTextImport	String	ImportDataSource.* The filename and path to an external data source that will be imported into the current database, limiting the changes to the local database only.
ResultTextExport	String	ExportDataSource.* The filename and path to an external data source that will have data from the current database exported into it. All changes to the current database will be reflected as appropriate in the external source.

The settings for the \HKEY_LOCAL_MACHINE\SOFTWARE\Microsoft\Jet\3.5\ISAM Formats\dBASE IV section are shown in Table 19.16.

19

CUSTOMIZING THE DEVELOPMENT ENVIRONMENT

Table 19.16. Jet 3.5 ISAM Registry settings for dBASE IV data sources.

Setting	Value Type	Value
Engine	String	Xbase
ExportFilter	String	dBASE IV "*.dbf"
ImportFilter	String	dBASE IV "*.dbf"
CanLink	Binary	01
OneTablePerFile	Binary	01
IsamType	DWORD	0
IndexDialog	Binary	01
IndexFilter	String	dBASE Index "*.ndx", "*.mdx"
CreateDBOnExport	Binary	00
ResultTextLink	String	LinkedDataSource.* The filename and path to an external data source file that will be used to create a linked table in the current database. Data changes to the local file will also be reflected in the external data source.
ResultTextImport	String	ImportDataSource.* The filename and path to an external data source that will be imported into the current database, limiting the changes to the local database only.
ResultTextExport	String	ExportDataSource.* The filename and path to an external data source that will have data from the current database exported into it. All changes to the current database will be reflected as appropriate in the external source.

Table 19.17 shows the settings for the `\HKEY_LOCAL_MACHINE\SOFTWARE\Microsoft\Jet\3.5\ISAM Formats\dBASE 5.x` section.

Table 19.17. Jet 3.5 ISAM Registry settings for dBASE 5.x data sources.

Setting	Value Type	Value
Engine	String	Xbase
ExportFilter	String	dBASE V "*.dbf"
ImportFilter	String	dBASE V "*.dbf"
CanLink	Binary	01

Setting	Value Type	Value
OneTablePerFile	Binary	01
IsamType	DWORD	0
IndexDialog	Binary	01
IndexFilter	String	dBASE Index "*.ndx", "*.mdx"
CreateDBOnExport	Binary	00
ResultTextLink	String	LinkedDataSource.* The filename and path to an external data source file that will be used to create a linked table in the current database. Data changes to the local file will also be reflected in the external data source.
ResultTextImport	String	ImportDataSource.* The filename and path to an external data source that will be imported into the current database, limiting the changes to the local database only.
ResultTextExport	String	ExportDataSource.* The filename and path to a dBASE 5 external data source that will have data from the current database exported into it. All changes to the current database will be reflected as appropriate in the external source.

Microsoft FoxPro-Specific Xbase Section Settings for the Jet Key

The following Registry settings initialize Jet to work with various FoxPro version external source files:

- **win32**: Specifies the path to Msxbse35.dll.

- **NetworkAccess**: Specifies the file-locking preference. 00 specifies exclusive access; 01 specifies shared access. This setting overrides the OpenDatabase and OpenRecordset method settings. The default value is 01.

- **PageTimeout**: This specifies how long each page of data containing 2,048 bytes is held in the cache before it is invalidated. The default value is 600×100 millisecond units, or 60,000 milliseconds.

- **INFPath**: Specifies the path to the .inf file directory. If Jet does not find an *.inf file in the same directory as the external source table, it searches the specified directory in this setting before defaulting to the index files in the database directory.

- **CollatingSequence**: Specifies the collating sequence for any FoxPro tables opened by Jet. The default value is ASCII; the other setting available is International.

■ `DataCodePage`: Specifies how text data pages are stored. The default setting is `OEM`, which specifies that the OEM-to-ANSI and ANSI-to-OEM conversions are performed. Selecting `ANSI` specifies that the conversions are not performed.

■ `Deleted`: This setting specifies how Jet will treat records that have been marked for deletion. `00` specifies that Jet will act in accordance with the FoxPro command `SET DELETE OFF` and will treat deleted records the same as any other. `01` tells Jet to act in accordance with the FoxPro command `SET DELETE ON`, which means it is not to retrieve or access deleted records. The default value is `00`.

■ `Century`: Specifies how Jet should format the century part of dates in order to be compatible with the date-to-string functions used in the FoxPro file index expressions. The default setting of `00` tells Jet to conform to the FoxPro `SET CENTURY OFF` command. `01` tells Jet to conform to the `SET CENTURY ON` command.

■ `Date`: Specifies the date format to use in order to be compatible with FoxPro index expressions that use date-to-string functions. Possible settings for this entry that conform to the FoxPro `SET DATE` command are `American`, `ANSI`, `British`, `French`, `DMY`, `German`, `Italian`, `Japan`, `MDY`, `USA`, and `YMD`. The default setting is `MDY`.

■ `Mark`: Specifies the decimal value of the ASCII character used to separate the parts of date expressions. The default value is decided by the `Date` setting, as described in the preceding item. The most common are (`"/"`, `American`, `MDY`), (`"."`, `ANSI`), (`"/"`, `British`, `French`, `DMY`), (`"."`, `German`), (`"-"`, `Italian`), and (`"/"`, `Japan`, `YMD`), (`"-"`, `USA`). The normal default value is specified as `0`. This tells Jet to use the separator that properly corresponds to the `Date` setting.

■ `Exact`: Specifies the binary indicator used for string comparisons. The default setting is `00`, which tells Jet to behave in accordance with the FoxPro command `SET ACTION OFF`. `01` tells Jet to conform to the FoxPro command `SET ACTION ON`.

The settings for the `\HKEY_LOCAL_MACHINE\SOFTWARE\Microsoft\Jet\3.5\ISAM Formats\FoxPro 2.0` section are listed in Table 19.18.

Table 19.18. Jet 3.5 ISAM Registry settings for FoxPro 2.0 data sources.

Setting	Value Type	Value
Engine	String	Xbase
ExportFilter	String	Microsoft FoxPro 2.0 "*.dbf"
ImportFilter	String	Microsoft FoxPro "*.dbf"
CanLink	Binary	01
OneTablePerFile	Binary	01
IsamType	DWORD	0
IndexDialog	Binary	01
IndexFilter	String	FoxPro Index "*.idx", "*.cdx"

Setting	Value Type	Value
CreateDBOnExport	Binary	00
ResultTextLink	String	LinkedDataSource.* The filename and path to an external data source file that will be used to create a linked table in the current database. Data changes to the local file will also be reflected in the external data source.
ResultTextImport	String	ImportDataSource.* The filename and path to an external data source that will be imported into the current database, limiting the changes to the local database only.
ResultTextExport	String	ExportDataSource.* The filename and path to a FoxPro 2.0 external data source that will have data from the current database exported into it. All changes to the current database will be reflected as appropriate in the external source.

Table 19.19 lists the settings for the `\HKEY_LOCAL_MACHINE\SOFTWARE\Microsoft\Jet\3.5\ISAM Formats\FoxPro 2.5` section.

Table 19.19. Jet 3.5 ISAM Registry settings for FoxPro 2.5 data sources.

Setting	Value Type	Value
Engine	String	Xbase
ExportFilter	String	Microsoft FoxPro 2.5 "*.dbf"
CanLink	Binary	01
OneTablePerFile	Binary	01
IsamType	DWORD	0
IndexDialog	Binary	01
IndexFilter	String	FoxPro Index "*.idx", "*.cdx"
CreateDBOnExport	Binary	00
ResultTextExport	String	ExportDataSource.* The filename and path to a FoxPro 2.5 external data source that will have data from the current database exported into it. Pre-existing data will be overwritten. All changes to the current database will be reflected as appropriate in the external source.

The settings for the `\HKEY_LOCAL_MACHINE\SOFTWARE\Microsoft\Jet\3.5\ISAM Formats\FoxPro 2.6` section are shown in Table 19.20.

Table 19.20. Jet 3.5 ISAM Registry settings for FoxPro 2.6 data sources.

Setting	Value Type	Value
Engine	String	Xbase
ExportFilter	String	Microsoft FoxPro 2.6 "*.dbf"
CanLink	Binary	01
OneTablePerFile	Binary	01
IsamType	DWORD	0
IndexDialog	Binary	01
IndexFilter	String	FoxPro Index "*.idx", "*.cdx"
CreateDBOnExport	Binary	00
ResultTextExport	String	ExportDataSource.* The filename and path to a FoxPro 2.6 external data source that will have data from the current database exported into it. All changes to the current database will be reflected as appropriate in the external source.

Table 19.21 shows the settings for the `\HKEY_LOCAL_MACHINE\SOFTWARE\Microsoft\Jet\3.5\ISAM Formats\FoxPro 3.0` section.

Table 19.21. Jet 3.5 ISAM Registry settings for FoxPro 3.0 data sources.

Setting	Value Type	Value
Engine	String	Xbase
ExportFilter	String	Microsoft FoxPro 3.0 "*.dbf"
CanLink	Binary	00
OneTablePerFile	Binary	01
IsamType	DWORD	0
IndexDialog	Binary	01
CreateDBOnExport	Binary	00
ResultTextExport	String	ExportDataSource.* The filename and path to a FoxPro 3.0 external data source that will have data from the current database exported

Setting	Value Type	Value
		into it. All changes to the current database will be reflected as appropriate in the external source.

The settings for the `\HKEY_LOCAL_MACHINE\SOFTWARE\Microsoft\Jet\3.5\ISAM Formats\FoxPro DBC` section are shown in Table 19.22.

Table 19.22. Jet 3.5 ISAM Registry settings for FoxPro DBC data sources.

Setting	Value Type	Value
Engine	String	Xbase
ExportFilter	String	Microsoft FoxPro 3.0 "*.dbc"
CanLink	Binary	00
OneTablePerFile	Binary	00
IsamType	DWORD	0
IndexDialog	Binary	00
IndexFilter	String	FoxPro Index "*.idx", "*.cdx"
CreateDBOnExport	Binary	00
ResultTextExport	String	ExportDataSource.* The filename and path to a FoxPro DBC external data source that will have data from the current database exported into it. All changes to the current database will be reflected as appropriate in the external source.

Customizing Paradox Driver Settings

The Paradox driver is another Registry section whose values Microsoft discourages you from tampering with. If you choose to do so, open the `\HKEY_LOCAL_MACHINE\SOFTWARE\Microsoft\Jet\3.5\Engines\Paradox` key, or if you want to restrict your Registry changes to Access 97, open the `\HKEY_LOCAL_MACHINE\SOFTWARE\Microsoft\Office\8.0\Access\Jet\3.5\Engines\Paradox` key and make the desired changes.

Jet uses the following settings in the Paradox Registry section:

- `win32`: Specifies the location of `Mspdox35.dll`.
- `PageTimeout`: Specifies the length of delay between the time that data is cached into the Jet buffer and when it is invalidated. The default value is 600×100 millisecond units, which equals 60,000 milliseconds, or 60 seconds.

19

CUSTOMIZING THE DEVELOPMENT ENVIRONMENT

- CollatingSequence: Specifies the collating sequence that Jet uses when it opens or creates Paradox tables. The default value is ASCII. The choices are ASCII, International, Norwegian-Danish, and Swedish-Finnish. This sequence setting must match the sequence used when the table was created.

- DataCodePage: Specifies how text pages are stored. The default setting is OEM, which specifies that the OEM-to-ANSI and ANSI-to-OEM conversions are performed. ANSI specifies that the conversion is not done.

- ParadoxUserName: Specifies the name that is displayed by Paradox if a table is currently locked by the Paradox ISAM or if a Paradox user tries to place an invalid lock on the table. If the computer is not on a network, this setting will not be added. If this setting is specified, a ParadoxNetPath and ParadoxNetStyle setting must also be specified. Failing to do so will generate an error when you try to access external Paradox data sources.

> **TIP**
>
> Here's an exception to the "don't tamper with the Registry settings" rule:
>
> If you want to access a Paradox database over a network in multiuser mode, you might have to modify these Registry settings (ParadoxUserName, ParadoxNetPath, and ParadoxNetStyle) manually.

- ParadoxNetPath: Specifies the path to the Paradox.net file (in the case of Paradox 3.*x*), or the Pdoxusrs.net file (in the case of Paradox 4.*x*). This setting is added only if your system is connected to a network. When the driver is set up, the initial setting of ParadoxNetPath is based on a general setting that might not be correct. You may have to edit this path setting to reflect the proper path to these files on your network. This path setting must be the same for all the users of the database. You must also specify a ParadoxUserName and ParadoxNetStyle if you use this setting, or you will encounter an error when trying to access external Paradox data sources. This setting might need to be edited manually in order to reflect the proper path information.

- ParadoxNetStyle: Specifies the network access style to use when accessing Paradox data sources. The default value is 4.*x*, which provides Paradox 4.*x*- and 5.0-compatible locking methods. The other choice is 3.*x*, which provides Paradox 3.*x*-compatible locking methods. This setting should correspond to the appropriate version of Paradox that is in use, and must be set consistently for all users of a database. This setting is installed at setup only if your system is connected to a network. A ParadoxNetPath and ParadoxUserName must also be specified when you are using this setting, or you will receive an error when you try to access external Paradox data over a network.

Table 19.23 shows the settings for the \HKEY_LOCAL_MACHINE\SOFTWARE\Microsoft\Jet\3.5\ISAM Formats\Paradox 3.x section.

Table 19.23. Jet 3.5 ISAM Registry settings for Paradox 3.*x* data sources.

Setting	Value Type	Value
Engine	String	Paradox
ExportFilter	String	Paradox 3 (*.db)
ImportFilter	String	Paradox (*.db)
CanLink	Binary	01
OneTablePerFile	Binary	01
IsamType	DWORD	0
IndexDialog	Binary	00
CreateDBOnExport	Binary	00
ResultTextLink	String	LinkedDataSource.* The filename and path to an external data source file that will be used to create a linked table in the current database. Data changes to the local file will also be reflected in the external data source.

The settings for the `\HKEY_LOCAL_MACHINE\SOFTWARE\Microsoft\Jet\3.5\ISAM Formats\Paradox 4.x` section are shown in Table 19.24.

Table 19.24. Jet 3.5 ISAM Registry settings for Paradox 4.*x* data sources.

Setting	Value Type	Value
Engine	String	Paradox
ExportFilter	String	Paradox 4 (*.db)
ImportFilter	String	Paradox "*.db"
CanLink	Binary	01
OneTablePerFile	Binary	01

continues

19

CUSTOMIZING THE
DEVELOPMENT
ENVIRONMENT

Table 19.24. continued

Setting	Value Type	Value
IsamType	DWORD	0
IndexDialog	Binary	00
CreateDBOnExport	Binary	00
ResultTextExport	String	ExportDataSource.* The filename and path to a Paradox 4.*x* external data source that will have data from the current database exported into it. All changes to the current database will be reflected as appropriate in the external source.

Table 19.25 shows the settings for the \HKEY_LOCAL_MACHINE\SOFTWARE\Microsoft\Jet\3.5\ISAM Formats\Paradox 5.x section.

Table 19.25. Jet 3.5 ISAM Registry settings for Paradox 5.*x* data sources.

Setting	Value Type	Value
Engine	String	Paradox
ExportFilter	String	Paradox 5 (*.db)
CanLink	Binary	01
OneTablePerFile	Binary	01
IsamType	DWORD	0
IndexDialog	Binary	00
CreateDBOnExport	Binary	00
ResultTextExport	String	ExportDataSource.* The filename and path to a Paradox 5.x external data source that will have data from the current database exported into it. All changes to the current database will be reflected as appropriate in the external source.

Customizing ODBC Driver Settings

To edit the ODBC Driver settings in the Registry, open the \HKEY_LOCAL_MACHINE\SOFTWARE\Microsoft\Jet\3.5\Engines\ODBC key, or if you want to isolate your changes to the Access 97 environment only, open the \HKEY_LOCAL_MACHINE\SOFTWARE\Microsoft\Office\8.0\Access\Jet\3.5\Engines\ODBC key and then make the desired changes.

Jet uses the following ODBC settings:

- `LoginTimeout`: Specifies the time limit for logon attempts in seconds. The default setting is `20` seconds.

- `QueryTimeout`: Specifies the time limit for query operations before they time-out. The default setting is `60` seconds. If the `DisableAsync=0` setting exists, the time-out delay is based on the number of seconds required to wait for a response from the server between polling requests to determine query completion status.

- `ConnectionTimeout`: Specifies the idle time-out setting in seconds for cached connections. The default is `600` seconds.

- `AsyncRetryInterval`: Specifies the millisecond delay between server polling to determine query completion status. This setting specifies the number of milliseconds between polls to determine if the server is done asynchronously processing a query. The default value is `500` milliseconds.

- `AttachCaseSensitive`: Specifies whether Jet should match table names exactly when linking. The default setting is `0`, which specifies that Jet should link the first matching table regardless of case. The other choice is `1`, which tells Jet to link tables only if their names match exactly.

- `AttachableObjects`: Specifies a list of server objects that allow linking. The default list is `TABLE`, `VIEW`, `SYSTEM TABLE`, `ALIAS`, and `SYNONYM`.

- `SnapshotOnly`: Specifies whether `RecordSet` objects are snapshot types or dynasets. The default setting is `0`, which allows dynasets. `1` specifies snapshots only.

- `TraceSQLMode`: Specifies whether Jet will trace SQL statements sent to an ODBC data source in `SQLOut.txt`. The default is `0`, which specifies no. `1` specifies yes. This setting may be used in place of an `SQLTraceMode` setting.

- `TraceODBCAPI`: Specifies whether Jet should trace ODBC API calls in `ODBCAPI.txt`. The default value is `0`, which specifies no. `1` specifies yes.

- `DisableAsync`: Specifies whether to force synchronous query execution. The default setting of `1` forces synchronous execution. `0` allows Jet to use asynchronous query execution if possible.

- `JETTryAuth`: Specifies that Jet should attempt to log in to the server with the Access 97 user name and password before prompting. The default setting of `1` specifies yes. `0` specifies no.

- `PreparedInsert`: Specifies whether to use a prepared `INSERT` statement that inserts data into all columns. The default setting of `0` specifies that Jet should use a custom `INSERT` statement that inserts only non-null values. `1` specifies that Jet should use a prepared `INSERT` statement. If you use prepared `INSERT` statements, it might cause nulls to overwrite server defaults and cause triggers to execute on columns that weren't inserted explicitly.

- `PreparedUpdate`: Specifies whether Jet should use a prepared `UPDATE` statement or a custom `UPDATE` statement. The default value, `0`, specifies that Jet should use a custom `UPDATE` statement that sets only columns that have been changed. `1` tells Jet to use a prepared statement, which can cause triggers to execute on unchanged columns.

- `FastRequery`: Specifies whether Jet should use a prepared `SELECT` statement. The default value of `0` specifies no. `1` specifies yes.

Workgroup Information File Definition

Microsoft discourages you from changing your Workgroup Information File in the Registry. Instead, Microsoft recommends using the Workgroup Administrator to accomplish this task.

If you want to specify a new Workgroup Information File manually, open the `\HKEY_LOCAL_MACHINE\SOFTWARE\Microsoft\Office\8.0\Access\Jet\3.5\Engines` key. Then make the desired changes to the `SystemDB` value to reflect the name and path to the new Workgroup Information File.

Specifying the OLE Version for OLE Links

You can specify whether Jet saves OLE links in version 1.0 or 2.0 format. Version 2.0 format saves absolute and relative link source references; version 1.0 format saves only absolute references. Use version 1.0 format if you are using Access 97 and Access 1.0 in the same shared environment.

To do this, open the `\HKEY_LOCAL_MACHINE\SOFTWARE\Microsoft\Office\8.0\Access` key; then open the `\Options` key, enter the new `DWORD` setting `AllowOLE1LinkFormat`, and give it a value of `1` for version 1.0 or `0` for version 2.0 format.

Customizing User Profiles

Microsoft recommends that you use the Setup Wizard included with Office 97 Developer's Edition to create the desired user profiles to be distributed with your applications.

User profiles are custom sets of Registry keys that you can create to include with your application. They specify custom Access, Jet, and Runtime settings for the end user that override the default settings. User profiles are a useful tool for application developers because it allows you to provide automatic custom settings on your end user's systems.

If you have specific Access, Jet, or Runtime settings that are needed by your application, you can ensure that they are installed properly and not overridden by other applications by using these profiles.

You then use the `/profile` command-line option to specify this user profile when you start your application.

If you want to create a user profile manually, open the `\HKEY_LOCAL_MACHINE\SOFTWARE` key in the Registry Editor and include a three-tiered, nested key that includes your company name, application name, and version number, similar to `\Company Name\Application Name\Version Number`. Then re-create all the keys under the `\HKEY_LOCAL_MACHINE\SOFTWARE\Microsoft\Office\8.0\Access` key that need to be modified, and then copy the appropriate values under each key.

Next, open the `\HKEY_LOCAL_MACHINE\SOFTWARE\Microsoft\Office\8.0\Access` key and add a new string named `\Profiles`. Add the string value and give it the name that you want to use on the command line when starting Access 97. Assign the string value the string information that indicates the locations of the three-tiered, nested keys. Now enter a command-line string inside double quotation marks that specifies the `\Profiles` name.

If you want to override any of the default Jet settings, open the `\HKEY_LOCAL_MACHINE\SOFTWARE\Company Name\Application Name\Version Number` profile key and create a key named `\Jet¦3.5\Engines` with subkeys for any of the drivers whose settings you want to override. Then add the appropriate settings and values to those keys.

When working with user profiles, you can use the `acSysCmdProfile` argument of the `SysCmd` function to determine whether your application has loaded your user profile.

Access 97 uses a `ConnectionTimeout` value of `100` when it is started with a custom user profile and a value of `300` when it is started without one.

Setting the Access 97 Runtime Options

If you want to specify runtime options in a user profile, create a key called `\Run-Time Options`, and then add the settings shown in Table 19.26.

Table 19.26. Registry settings for Access 97 runtime options.

Setting	Description
`AppTitleBar`	Title text for your application's main window.
`AppIcon`	Specifies the application icon to be displayed on your title bar when your application is minimized.
`AppHelpFile`	The default application help file that loads when the end user invokes Help.
`AppStartupScreen`	The splash screen bitmap image file that is displayed at application startup. You can also cause your system to load an image for the splash screen if it has the same name as the application, has a `.bmp` filename extension, is placed in the database application directory, and is specified as a command-line argument.

19

CUSTOMIZING THE DEVELOPMENT ENVIRONMENT

Creating the UsysRegInfo Table in Add-In Databases

Add-in databases must have a UsysRegInfo table in order for the Access 97 Add-In Manager to know what kind of add-in it is, how to install it, and how it is to be accessed through the user interface. This topic is covered in greater depth in Chapter 11, "Add-Ins."

Assessing Your Application with the Performance Analyzer Wizard

Although this seems to be more appropriate to Chapter 24, "Improving Performance with Access 97 Database Utilities," it is covered here briefly because of the beneficial customization tips that this wizard generates in the Analysis Results Report.

The Performance Analyzer Wizard is a tool that Microsoft included with Access 97 to assist you in creating higher-performance databases. This wizard is available by selecting Analyze and then Performance under the Tools menu. It allows you to analyze all or some of the components of your database application. The Performance Analyzer is shown in Figure 19.4.

FIGURE 19.4.

The Access 97 Performance Analyzer.

CAUTION

The Performance Analyzer might attempt to make certain logical changes to your application automatically. For this reason, it is a good idea to run a test copy of your application through the Performance Analyzer Wizard. This will allow you to safely review and test changes made to your application without fear of damaging your application.

After the Performance Analyzer digests the selected components of your database as specified in this initial object selection window, it generates an Analysis Results window that acts as an optimization control interface for you to manage performance changes to your application (see Figure 19.5).

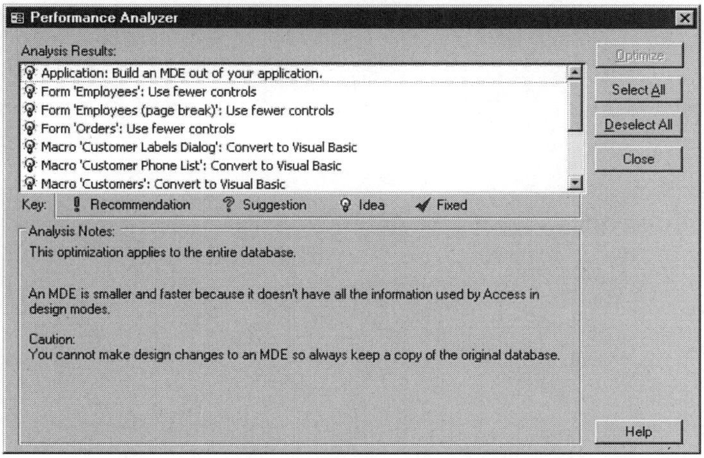

FIGURE 19.5.
The Performance Analyzer Analysis Results display and customization interface.

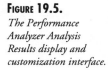

When you are using the Performance Analyzer, you can have Access 97 complete custom changes based on optimizations that fall into the Recommendation or Suggestion categories by selecting the desired changes and then clicking the Optimize button.

Any of the recommended changes that fall under the Idea category are manual operations that you must perform. Select the recommended change and then follow the instructions outlined in the Analysis Notes section of the window.

> **NOTE**
>
> Each optimization change will have its own advantages and disadvantages. When you are studying the results of the Performance Analyzer Wizard, make sure you look at the Analysis Notes section of the window for a description of the pros and cons.

Summary

A significant number of options are available to allow you to customize the operating environment for Access 97. As you have been repeatedly warned in this chapter, exercise caution when making changes to the Windows Registry. Some changes can lead to unexpected behavior and serious errors.

It is also a good idea to use an isolated test-bed system before making any changes that may adversely affect your local system or network environment.

19

CUSTOMIZING THE
DEVELOPMENT
ENVIRONMENT

Customizing Menus and Switchboards

by Joe Rhemann

IN THIS CHAPTER

CHAPTER 20

This chapter covers methods of designing and implementing customized menus and switchboards. Bearing in mind that forms are the most visible—and, interface-wise, the most important—component of your database application, it would be an excellent idea to review the topics covered in Chapter 6, "Access 97 Forms," before continuing with this chapter.

Design Standards

For this chapter, we will assume you have followed our previous guidelines and sketched a blueprint of your application on paper before beginning the actual design process. In this blueprint, you will have established the forms strategy that will be used in your application. With this strategy in mind, consider the best method of presenting your application's features at startup.

One of the most effective means of doing this is to design a startup form and use it as the primary switchboard for your application.

On this form, you should provide access to all the functions of your application, including controls that refer to additional switchboards.

> **TIP**
>
> When you have sub-switchboards to your primary switchboard, make sure that your links go both ways. Otherwise, if you have an end user who is not proficient at navigating through Access forms, he might find your submenus confusing.

The best strategy in designing your application is to avoid burying application features beneath the surface of the application. Present your application tools and capabilities as early as possible, and with as few layers as possible without cluttering your forms needlessly. This makes for a much friendlier application from the end user's perspective, and for a faster and generally more productive interface.

When your application contains a large number of forms, and you are unable to predict which form will be most utilized, consider designing a startup form that acts as a central switchboard or directory to the other forms in your application.

Creating Switchboard Forms

A *switchboard form* is like a control panel for your application. When you create a new application, this is the basic control form around which you will build your Access 97 forms interface. Although you can have multiple switchboards in an application, you should have one primary switchboard from which you have full access to your application's features.

One useful strategy is to develop multiple Access 97 forms interfaces for each application. Let's look at a sample customer site: a medium-sized bookstore company with numerous employees who perform diverse functions. (See Figure 20.1.)

FIGURE 20.1.
The organization chart for the La Fitte's Lair bookstore company.

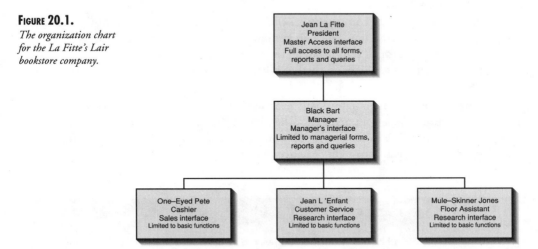

In this fictitious company, the Access database functionality is split among the separate job functions according to the individual user's needs. Individualized form interfaces are developed for each user level and linked back to the main database application on a network server. In this scenario, the degree of access to database information cascades down the company hierarchy. The president, Jean La Fitte, has unlimited access to all data, forms, reports, and queries, while the manager and other employees have access only to those database resources they need.

When you create a database application with an Access 97 Database Wizard, Access automatically generates the appropriate switchboards and other forms.

Creating a Switchboard Form Using the Switchboard Manager

When you use the Database Wizard to create a database, the wizard creates a switchboard that makes it easy to navigate among the forms and reports in your database. If you want to build the same type of switchboard for a database you created yourself, you can use the Switchboard Manager:

1. In the Tools menu, choose Add-ins, and then click Switchboard Manager.
2. If Microsoft Access asks whether you'd like to create a switchboard, click Yes.
3. In the Switchboard Manager dialog box, click Edit.
4. In the Edit Switchboard Page dialog box, type a name for the switchboard in the Switchboard Name box, and then click New.

5. In the Edit Switchboard Item dialog box, type the text for the first switchboard button in the text box, and then click a command in the Command box. For example, type `Review Products` in the text box, and then click Open Form In Edit Mode in the Command box.

6. Depending on which command you click, Microsoft Access displays another box below the Command box. Click an item in this box, if necessary. For example, if you clicked Open Form In Edit Mode in the Command box in step 5, click the name of the form you want to open in the Form box, such as `Review Products`, and then click OK.

7. Repeat steps 4 through 6 until you've added all the items to the switchboard. If you want to edit or delete an item, click the item in the Items On This Switchboard box, and then click Edit or Delete. If you want to rearrange items, click the item in the box, and then click Move Up or Move Down.

8. Click Close.

> **NOTE**
>
> You can use the Switchboard Manager to create a switchboard that branches to other switchboards. Use the preceding procedure to create one or more switchboards. To make a switchboard the switchboard that's automatically opened when you open the database, click the switchboard name in the Switchboard Manager dialog box, and then click Make Default. To have a switchboard branch to another switchboard, choose the Go To Switchboard command in the Command box in step 5 in the preceding procedure, and then specify the switchboard you want to go to.
>
> When you create a switchboard with the Switchboard Manager, Microsoft Access creates a `Switchboard Items` table that describes what the buttons on the form display and do. If you make changes to the `Switchboard` form later in Form Design View, the application might no longer work. If you expect to customize your switchboard form extensively, it's better to create the form from scratch and then specify it as the startup form.

Creating a New Switchboard That You Can Open from the Opening Switchboard

The following list describes the procedure for creating a new switchboard that can be opened from the opening switchboard of your Access 97 application:

1. Open the database.

2. Do one of the following to open the Switchboard Manager dialog box:

   If you created the switchboard by using the Database Wizard, click Change Switchboard Items in the opening switchboard.

If you created the switchboard by using the Switchboard Manager, select Add-ins from the Tools menu, and then click Switchboard Manager.

3. Click New.

4. Type the name of the new switchboard, and then click OK.

   Microsoft Access adds the switchboard to the Switchboard Pages box.

5. Click the new switchboard, and then click Edit.

6. Click New.

7. Type the text for the first switchboard item in the text box, and then click a command in the Command box. For example, type `View Recording Artists`, and then click Open Form In Edit Mode in the Command box.

8. Depending on which command you click, Microsoft Access displays another box below the Command box. Click an item in this box, if necessary. For example, if you clicked Open Form In Edit Mode in step 7, click the name of the form you want to open in the Form box, such as Recording Artists, and then click OK.

9. Repeat steps 6 through 8 until you've added all the items to the switchboard. If you want to edit or delete an item, click the item in the Items On This Switchboard box, and then click Edit or Delete. If you want to rearrange items, click the item in the box, and then click Move Up or Move Down.

10. When you've finished creating the switchboard, click Close.

Making a Change to an Existing Switchboard

The following list describes the procedure for making changes to existing switchboards in your Access 97 application:

1. Open the database.

2. Do one of the following to open the Switchboard Manager dialog box:

   If you created the switchboard by using the Database Wizard, click Change Switchboard Items in the opening switchboard.

   If you created the switchboard by using the Switchboard Manager, click Add-ins on the Tools menu, and then click Switchboard Manager.

3. Click the switchboard you want to edit, and then click Edit.

4. Click the item on the switchboard you want to change, and then do one of the following:

   To change the text of the item, the command performed by the item, or the object that's opened or run when you click the button, click Edit.

   To add an item, click New, type the text for the item, and then click a command in the Command box. Depending on which command you click, Microsoft Access displays another box below the Command box. Click an item in this box, if necessary. For example, if you click one of the form commands in the Command box, click the name of the form you want to open.

To delete an item, click Delete.

To move an item, click Move Up or Move Down.

5. When you've finished changing items, click Close.

Changing Which Switchboard Automatically Displays When You Open the Database

The following list describes the procedure for changing which switchboard appears when you start your Access 97 application:

1. Open the database.

2. Do one of the following to open the Switchboard Manager dialog box:

   If you created the switchboard by using the Database Wizard, click Change Switchboard Items in the opening switchboard.

   If you created the switchboard by using the Switchboard Manager, click Add-ins on the Tools menu, and then click Switchboard Manager.

3. Click the switchboard that you want to use as the opening switchboard if it is displayed in the Switchboard Pages box. Otherwise, create the switchboard.

4. Click Make Default.

The next time you open your database, Microsoft Access will automatically display the switchboard you specified.

Deleting a Switchboard

The following list describes the procedure for deleting a switchboard from your Access 97 application:

1. Open the database.

2. Do one of the following to open the Switchboard Manager dialog box:

   If you created the switchboard by using the Database Wizard, click Change Switchboard Items in the opening switchboard.

   If you created the switchboard by using the Switchboard Manager, click Add-ins on the Tools menu, and then click Switchboard Manager.

3. Click the switchboard you want to delete in the Switchboard Pages box, and then click Delete.

Displaying a Startup Form When a Database or Application Opens

The following list describes the procedure for displaying a startup form when you open an Access 97 application:

1. On the Tools menu, click Startup.

2. In the Display Form box, click a form from the current database.

3. If you don't want users to see or use the Database window, which appears behind the form, clear the Display Database Window checkbox.

Even if you clear the Display Database Window checkbox, the Database window may still be accessible.

> **NOTE**
>
> Changes to these settings in the Startup dialog box won't take effect until the next time the database or application is opened.
>
> The Northwind sample database has a startup form. It also has the Main Switchboard form, an example of a form you might use to control navigation in your database. To view these forms, open the Northwind database in the Samples folder. The startup form appears automatically when you open Northwind, but you can view it or the Main Switchboard form whenever you want by clicking the Forms tab in the Database window, clicking Startup or Main Switchboard, and then clicking Open.

Command Bars: Menu Bars, Toolbars, and Shortcut Menus

In Access 97, the internal workings of menu bars, shortcut menus, and toolbars have been unified into a single object called a *command bar*. Because they now share the same underlying technology, you have more flexibility when you customize existing Microsoft Access menu bars, toolbars, and shortcut menus, and when you create new ones for your application.

Menu bars and toolbars are two ways to present commands on command bars: a *menu bar* typically presents drop-down menus of commands as text, and a *toolbar* typically presents commands as buttons. A *shortcut menu* is a subset of a menu bar, presenting one menu of commands when a user right-clicks most objects and controls in Access. You can create new shortcut menus and associate them with the forms, reports, or controls in your application.

Because menu bars, toolbars, and shortcut menus share the same internal workings, you can use most of the same controls on all three. For example, in addition to their typical controls, a top-level menu bar can use buttons, a drop-down menu can use combo box controls, and a toolbar can use drop-down menu buttons that display text-only commands. In this respect, command bars can be too flexible. Putting menu bar and toolbar controls in unusual locations or configurations may confuse the user. Instead, model your custom command bars after the ones used in Access.

The simplest way to work with command bars is by using the Customize dialog box (accessed through the Toolbars submenu under the View menu). You can use the Customize dialog box to customize existing command bars or to create new ones. New command bars can contain existing commands or new commands that run the event procedures or macros you define.

By default, users can customize command bars. They can also make menu bars and toolbars free-standing by dragging them into the work area, or they can dock them to the sides or the bottom of the work area. In addition, users can resize or hide menu bars and toolbars. You can prevent users from customizing all command bars in your application in the Startup dialog box (accessed through the Tools menu). To prevent users from customizing, moving, or resizing an individual menu bar or toolbar, set the options in the Toolbar Properties dialog box. You can access the Toolbar Properties dialog box by clicking on the Properties button on the Toolbar tab of the Customize dialog box, which is accessed through the Access 97 View menu.

The objects, methods, and properties of the CommandBars collection in Visual Basic code can be used to create and work with command bars.

For more information, see the section titled "Working with Command Bars in Code," later in this chapter.

Changes to existing command bars are always stored in the Windows Registry in the \HKEY_CURRENT_USER\Software\Microsoft\Office\8.0\Access\Settings\CommandBars key. When you create a new command bar, it is saved in a system table in the current database and is available in that database only. But if you create an add-in database and store new command bars in it, they will be available from any installation of Microsoft Access that has the add-in installed.

Once you have customized an existing menu bar or toolbar, or created a new one, you can attach it to a form or report by specifying it by name in the MenuBar or Toolbar property for the form or report. To attach a shortcut menu to a form, report, or control, specify it by name in the ShortcutMenuBar property for the form, report, or control. You can also specify a global menu bar or a global shortcut menu to be available throughout your application by using the Startup dialog box (accessed through the Tools menu).

> **NOTE**
>
> Earlier versions of Microsoft Access use the AddMenu and DoMenuItem actions in macros to create custom menu bars and shortcut menus and to carry out standard Access menu commands. If you convert a database created in a previous version of Access to Access 97, the macros that contain the AddMenu and DoMenuItem actions will still run; however, Access 97 converts DoMenuItem actions in the macros to the new RunCommand action. For more information on the RunCommand action, search the Help index for "RunCommand action."

Although these menu bar macros created with a previous version of Access will run from the forms, reports, or controls they are attached to, they won't be available in the Customize dialog box. You can, however, create an Access 97–style menu bar or shortcut menu from a menu bar macro created in a previous version of Access. For more information on how to do this, search the Help index for "macros, using to work with menus."

Creating New Menu Bars, Toolbars, and Shortcut Menus

All command bars, whether they are menu bars, toolbars, or shortcut menus, are created using the Customize dialog box (accessed under the Tools submenu of the View menu). You create the different kinds of command bars by setting their properties and, if necessary, by setting properties for the commands within them to control how they appear and behave. The procedures outlined in the following sections show how to create new menu bars, toolbars, and shortcut menus.

Creating New Command Bars and Setting Their Properties

The first step in creating a new menu bar, toolbar, or shortcut menu is to create and name an empty command bar, set its type, and set other properties that control how it can be used.

To create an empty command bar and set its properties, follow these steps:

1. From the View menu, point to Toolbars, and then click Customize.
2. On the Toolbars tab, click New.
3. In the Toolbar Name box, type a name for the new command bar, and then click OK.

   Microsoft Access creates an empty, floating command bar, which you can specify to be a toolbar, menu bar, or shortcut menu.
4. In the Customize dialog box, click Properties to display the Toolbar Properties dialog box.

20

CUSTOMIZING MENUS AND SWITCHBOARDS

5. In the Type box, click the kind of command bar you want to create:

To create a menu bar, click Menu Bar.

To create a toolbar, click Toolbar.

To create a shortcut menu, click Popup.

NOTE

The Popup setting of the Type property is used for a shortcut menu because in the command bar object model, menus (on both menu bars and toolbars), submenus, and shortcut menus are all of this type. However, if a command bar has its Type property set to Popup, the Customize dialog box user interface only allows you to work with it as a shortcut menu. Additionally, as soon as you set a new command bar's Type property to Popup, it disappears because a shortcut menu can't display as free-standing. To add commands to your custom shortcut menu, you must display it. For more information, see the section titled "Adding Menus and Submenus to Command Bars," later in this chapter.

---

6. If you are creating a menu bar or toolbar, in the Docking box, click the kind of docking you want to allow (these settings don't apply to shortcut menus):

Allow Any: Allows users to dock the menu bar or toolbar, both horizontally and vertically

Can't Change: Prevents users from changing how the menu bar or toolbar is docked

No Vertical: Allows users to dock the menu bar or toolbar horizontally only

No Horizontal: Allows users to dock the menu bar or toolbar vertically only

7. Clear the following checkboxes whose default behavior you want to change:

Allow Customizing: Allows users to make changes to the command bar by using the Customize dialog box

Show On Toolbars Menu: Allows the new command bar to appear on the Toolbars submenu (View menu)

8. If you are creating a menu bar or toolbar, clear any of the following checkboxes whose default behavior you want to change (these settings don't apply to shortcut menus):

Allow Moving: Allows users to change how a menu bar or toolbar is docked

Allow Showing/Hiding: Allows users to show or hide the menu bar or toolbar

Allow Resizing: Allows users to resize the menu bar or toolbar

9. When you are finished specifying properties for the new command bar, click Close. To continue working with your new command bar, leave the Customize dialog box open.

At this point, you have an empty command bar of the type you specified in step 5. If you created a menu bar, you need to add menus to it and then add commands to those menus. If you created a shortcut menu, you need to add commands to it. If you created a toolbar, you need to add buttons or other controls to it.

Adding Menus and Submenus to Command Bars

If you are creating a menu bar, you must add and name top-level menus, and then add commands to those menus. If you want an additional menu to open from a menu command, you can add a submenu to it. You can also add menus and submenus to toolbars, and submenus to shortcut menus.

> **NOTE**
>
> In previous versions of Access, you had to add a single top-level menu to create a shortcut menu. This is not necessary in Access 97.

To add a menu or submenu to a command bar, follow these steps:

1. If the Customize dialog box isn't open, choose Toolbars from the View menu, and then click Customize.

2. If the menu bar, toolbar, or shortcut menu you want to work with isn't displayed, open it.

> **NOTE**
>
> To display a custom shortcut menu, select the Shortcut Menu checkbox in the Toolbars list of the Customize dialog box. On the Shortcut Menu toolbar, click Custom and then click the name of your custom shortcut menu.

3. In the Customize dialog box, click on the Commands tab.

4. In the Categories box, click New Menu.

   New Menu appears in the Commands box.

5. Drag New Menu from the Commands box to your menu bar or toolbar:

   To create a top-level menu, drag New Menu to the top row of your menu bar or toolbar.

   To create a submenu, you must have an existing top-level menu, or you must be adding a new menu to a shortcut menu. Drag and hold New Menu over a top-level menu (or shortcut menu) until it drops down; then drag New Menu to the location you want and release the mouse.

6. Right-click New Menu on your menu or toolbar, and then type the name for your menu in the Name box.

TIP

You can create an access key for your menu names so that users can access your menus with the keyboard. To do so, type an ampersand (&) in front of the letter you want to use. For example, to use F as the access key for a menu named File, type &File. The F in your menu name will be underlined, and users will be able to open the menu by pressing Alt+F.

---

7. To further customize your new menu or submenu, set other properties in the Control Properties dialog box. To display the Control Properties dialog box, right-click the new menu or submenu, and then click Properties.

For more information on the settings in the Control Properties dialog box, see the section titled "Setting Properties for Command Bar Controls," later this chapter.

Once you have added all the menus and submenus to your command bar, you have the basic framework to contain the commands that you want to be available. If you are creating a menu bar, you have top-level menus and perhaps some submenus. If you are creating a toolbar, you may have added top-level menu buttons and possibly submenus within them. If you are creating a shortcut menu, you may have added submenus. The next step is to add commands to your menus and submenus, or buttons that carry out commands to your toolbar.

Adding Existing Menu Commands, Buttons, and Other Controls to Command Bars

By using the Customize dialog box, you can add any existing Access menu command, toolbar button, or other control to your new command bar. This includes all standard Access menu commands and toolbar buttons, as well as drop-down combo box controls, such as the Font box, and special formatting controls, such as the Fill/Back Color and Special Effect controls.

To add an existing Access menu command, button, or other control, follow these steps:

1. If the Customize dialog box isn't open, choose Toolbars from the View menu, and then click Customize.

2. If the menu bar, toolbar, or shortcut menu you want to work with isn't displayed, open it.

3. In the Customize dialog box, click on the Commands tab.

4. In the Categories box, click the category that contains the menu command, button, or other control you want to add to your command bar. For example, to add a command that appears on the File menu, click File. To add an entire menu of commands at once, click Built-in Menus.

5. Drag the menu, menu command, button, or other control you want from the Commands box to the appropriate location on your command bar.

   To add the command or control to a menu or submenu, drag it and hold the mouse over the menu or submenu name until it drops down, and then drag the command or control where you want it on the menu or submenu and release the mouse.

> **NOTE**
>
> If you place the command or control in the wrong location, you can drag it to the correct location.

6. To further customize your command bar, you can change the images that appear on toolbar buttons and next to menu commands, and you can set other properties that determine how your menu commands, buttons, and other controls appear and work. To display a menu of customization options, right-click on the menu command, button, or control.

For more information, see the sections titled "Working with Button Images on Command Bars" and "Setting Properties for Command Bar Controls," later in this chapter.

Adding Custom Menu Commands and Buttons to Command Bars

There are three ways to add menu commands and buttons that perform custom actions to a command bar. You can

- ■ Add a menu command or button that opens a table, query, form, or report.
- ■ Create a macro and then add a menu command or button to run the macro.
- ■ Create a Visual Basic function procedure, and then add an existing menu command or button and customize it to run the function procedure.

Creating a Command or Button That Opens a Database Object

To create a command or button that opens a table, query, form, or report, drag the name of the database object from the appropriate category in the Customize dialog box to your command bar.

This method is equivalent to opening the object from the Database window; you can't specify additional parameters such as the mode in which Microsoft Access opens the object, and you can't perform other actions when opening the object. If you want to specify additional parameters or perform a series of actions when opening an object, you must create a macro or a Visual Basic function procedure and add it to your menu or toolbar, as described later in this section.

To add a custom command or button that opens a database object, follow these steps:

1. If the Customize dialog box isn't open, choose Toolbars from the View menu, and then click Customize.

2. If the menu bar, toolbar, or shortcut menu you want to work with isn't displayed, open it.

3. In the Customize dialog box, click on the Commands tab.

4. In the Categories box, click the category for the type of object you want to open: All Tables, All Queries, All Forms, or All Reports.

5. Drag the object you want to open from the Commands box to the appropriate location on your command bar.

   To add the command that opens the object to a menu or submenu, drag it and hold the mouse over the menu or submenu name until it drops down, and then drag the command where you want it on the menu or submenu and release the mouse.

> **NOTE**
>
> If you place the command in the wrong location, you can drag it to the correct location.

6. To further customize your command bar, you can change the images that appear on toolbar buttons and next to menu commands, and you can set other properties that determine how your menu commands and buttons appear and work. To display a menu of customization options, right-click the menu command or button.

For more information, see the sections titled "Working with Button Images on Command Bars" and "Setting Properties for Command Bar Controls," later in this chapter.

Creating a Command or Button That Runs a Macro

To create a command or button that runs a macro, create the macro and then drag its name from the Customize dialog box to your command bar. For example, you can create a macro that uses the OpenForm action to open a form and set the Data Mode argument to Add. Add the macro to a menu, and when a user clicks the custom command, Access runs the macro, opening a blank form ready to add a new record.

To add a custom command or button that runs a macro, follow these steps:

1. Create a macro that performs the action you want.

   (For information on creating macros, search the Help index for "macros, creating.")

2. If the Customize dialog box isn't open, choose Toolbars from the View menu, and then click Customize.

3. If the menu bar, toolbar, or shortcut menu you want to work with isn't displayed, open it.

4. In the Customize dialog box, click the Commands tab.

5. In the Categories box, click All Macros.

6. Drag the macro you want to run from the Commands box to the appropriate location on your command bar.

   To add a command that runs the macro to a menu or submenu, drag the command and hold the mouse over the menu or submenu name until it drops down, and then drag the command or control where you want it on the menu or submenu and release the mouse.

> **NOTE**
>
> If you place the command in the wrong location, you can drag it to the correct location.

7. To further customize your command bar, you can change the images that appear on toolbar buttons and next to menu commands, and you can set other properties that determine how your menu commands and buttons appear and work. To display a menu of customization options, right-click the menu command or button.

For more information, see the sections titled "Working with Button Images on Command Bars" and "Setting Properties for Command Bar Controls," later in this chapter.

Creating a Command or Button That Runs a Visual Basic Function Procedure

For the greatest flexibility, you can create a Visual Basic function procedure and run it from a menu command or toolbar button. To do so, add the Custom command to your command bar, and then customize it to run your function procedure.

> **NOTE**
>
> You can run only Visual Basic function procedures from a command bar, not subprocedures.

Follow these steps to add a custom command or button that runs a Visual Basic function procedure:

1. Create a Visual Basic function procedure that performs the action you want.

   For information on creating function procedures, search the Help index for "Visual Basic code, function procedures."

20

CUSTOMIZING
MENUS AND
SWITCHBOARDS

2. If the Customize dialog box isn't open, choose Toolbars from the View menu, and then click Customize.

3. If the menu bar, toolbar, or shortcut menu you want to work with isn't displayed, open it.

4. In the Customize dialog box, click on the Commands tab.

5. In the Categories box, click File and then drag the Custom command from the Commands box to your command bar.

6. Right-click the new command on your menu or toolbar, and then click Properties. Microsoft Access displays the Control Properties dialog box.

7. In the Caption box, delete the current name and then type the new name for your command.

TIP

You can create an access key for your command so that users can access it with the keyboard. To do so, type an ampersand (&) in front of the letter you want to use. For example, to use I as the access key for a Print Invoice command, type `Print &Invoice`. The I in your command name will be underlined, and users will be able to carry out the command by pressing Alt+I.

---

8. In the On Action box, type an expression to run your Visual Basic Function procedure. The expression must use the following syntax: `=functionname()`. For example, to run a function named `PrintInvoice`, you would type `=PrintInvoice()`.

9. To further customize your command bar, you can change the images that appear on toolbar buttons and next to menu commands, and you can set other properties that determine how your menu commands and buttons appear and work. To display a menu of customization options, right-click the menu command or button.

For more information, see the sections titled "Working with Button Images on Command Bars" and "Setting Properties for Command Bar Controls," later in this chapter.

Working with Button Images on Command Bars

Most Access command bar controls have a button image that is displayed when the control is on a toolbar and sometimes appears next to the control when the control is on a menu. You can customize these button images by doing any of the following:

■ Changing the image to one of a set of predefined images.

■ Copying a control's image and pasting it into another control.

■ Copying an image from a graphics program and pasting it into another control.

■ Editing the image by using the Button Editor dialog box.

Whether a control appears with a button image, text, or both is determined by the setting of the control's `Style` property and by whether the control is on a toolbar or a menu.

> **NOTE**
>
> A control's `Caption` property text is identical to the text in the Name box on the shortcut menu that appears when you right-click a control while the Customize dialog box is open.

> **NOTE**
>
> By default, some Access command bar controls don't have a button image associated with them and won't display an image regardless of the `Style` property setting. You can, however, add an image by using one of the methods described in the following procedure. Also, some Access command bar controls have their `Style` property set to `Text Only (In Menus)` by default so that they don't display their image on menus. If you want to display the image on menus, set the `Style` property to `Default Style`.

For information on setting the `Style` property and other command bar control properties, see the section titled "Setting Properties for Command Bar Controls," later in this chapter.

To customize a button image on a command bar control, follow these steps:

1. If the Customize dialog box isn't open, choose Toolbars from the View menu, and then click Customize.

2. If the menu bar, toolbar, or shortcut menu that contains the control you want to work with isn't displayed, open it.

3. Do one of the following:

   Right-click the control, point to Change Button Image, and then click on the image you want.

   Copy and paste another control's button image.

   Right-click the control that has the image you want to use, and then click Copy Button Image. Right-click the control whose image you are customizing, and then click Paste Button Image.

   Copy and paste an image from a graphics program.

   Open the image you want to copy in a graphics program. Select and copy the image (preferably a 16×16-pixel image or portion). Switch back to Microsoft Access. Right-click the control, and then click Paste Button Image.

   Edit the control's current button image.

Right-click the control, and then click Edit Button Image. In the Button Editor dialog box, you can change the color and shape of the image, adjust the image's position on the control, and preview your changes to the image. When you have finished editing the button image, click OK.

Reset a control to use its original button image.

Right-click the control and then click Reset Button Image.

4. When you have finished working with the button image, click Close.

Setting Properties for Command Bar Controls

Microsoft Access provides some additional menu and control properties that you can use to further customize menus, menu commands, and toolbar buttons. You set each of these properties in the Control Properties dialog box.

> **NOTE**
>
> Depending on the kind of control you're working with, some properties will not be available.

To set control properties for a menu, a menu command, or a toolbar button, follow these steps:

1. If the Customize dialog box isn't open, choose Toolbars from the View menu, and then click Customize.
2. If the menu bar, toolbar, or shortcut menu that contains the control you want to work with isn't displayed, open it.
3. Right-click the control, and then click Properties.
4. In the Control Properties dialog box, set the properties you want. They are described in Table 20.1.

Table 20.1. Control properties for menus, menu commands, and toolbar buttons.

Property	Description
Caption	The name that is displayed for the command. This is identical to the text entered in the Name box on a menu or control's shortcut menu.
Shortcut Text	The text that is displayed next to a menu command and that indicates its shortcut key; for example, Ctrl+P.
	This property only creates display text to prompt the user. To define the shortcut key, you must create an AutoKeys macro.

Property	Description
ToolTip	The text of the ToolTip that appears when a user rests the pointer on the control. If this setting is blank, Access uses the text from the Caption property as the ToolTip.
On Action	The name of a macro or Visual Basic function procedure that runs when a user clicks the control. When using a function procedure, you must enter the name of procedure as an expression, using the syntax =functionname().
Style	Controls how a command is displayed. The Style property settings are also available from a control's shortcut menu. For information on the Style property, see the "Working with Button Images on Command Bars" section, earlier in this chapter.
Help File	The help file that contains the What's This Tip topic specified by the Help ContextID property.
Help ContextID	The context ID of the topic to display as a What's This Tip for this command.
Parameter	An optional string associated with the control that your application can reference or set. For example, the Visual Basic function procedure specified in the On Action property can refer to the Parameter property to determine how it works, or the Parameter property can be used to store information about the control, much like the Tag property. The Parameter property isn't generally used by built-in menu and toolbar controls. The Parameter property for a menu command or toolbar button used to add an ActiveX control, however, is set to the ActiveX control's class identifier (CLSID), which is the Registry value that uniquely identifies that control. If you delete or modify the CLSID, the command or button won't work. Similarly, the Parameter property for a menu command or toolbar button used to open a particular database object is set to the name of the object.
Tag	An optional string that can be used later in event procedures.
Begin A Group	Select this checkbox to indicate the beginning of a group of controls. On menus, a separator bar appears above a command that has this property set. On toolbars, a vertical separator bar appears in front of the command. If you resize a floating toolbar and the entire group of controls doesn't fit on the current line, the whole group is bumped to a new line.

20

CUSTOMIZING
MENUS AND
SWITCHBOARDS

You can also set and read each of the properties in Visual Basic code. Most of the corresponding Visual Basic property names are the same as those listed in the preceding table, although the words are concatenated: for example, `ShortcutText` property. There are two exceptions: the Visual Basic properties that correspond to the `ToolTip` and `Begin A Group` properties in the Control Properties dialog box are `ToolTipText` and `BeginGroup`.

For more information on creating and customizing command bars, search the Help index for "toolbars" or "menus."

Importing Custom Command Bars

If you want to use the custom command bars from one application in another application, you can import them. You cannot import a single custom command bar, however; you must import all the custom command bars in an application, but Access doesn't import command bars that have the same name as existing command bars.

To import all custom command bars from another application, follow these steps:

1. Open the application into which you want to import the custom command bars.
2. From the File menu, choose Get External Data; then click Import.
3. In the Import dialog box that appears, select the application that contains the command bars you want to import, and then click Import.
4. In the Import Objects dialog box, click Options.
5. Select the Menus And Toolbars checkbox, and then click OK.

Using Custom Menu Bars and Shortcut Menus

You can use custom menu bars and shortcut menus in your application in three ways:

- Attached to a form or report. Access displays your custom menu bar whenever you open the form or display the report in Print Preview.
- As a shortcut menu attached to a form, a control on a form, or a report. Access displays your custom menu whenever you right-click the form, control, or report it's attached to.
- As your application's global menu bar. Access displays your custom menu bar in all windows, except in forms or reports that have their own custom menu bar. (A form or report's custom menu bar overrides a global custom menu bar.)

Attaching a Custom Menu Bar to a Form or Report

The easiest way to create a menu bar that's attached to a form or report is to create a new menu bar and then specify that menu bar in the form or report's `MenuBar` property so that Access displays the menu bar whenever the form or report is active.

To attach a custom menu bar to a form or report, follow these steps:

1. Create a custom menu bar, as described earlier in this chapter.
2. Open the form or report in Design View.
3. On the toolbar, click Properties.
4. In the MenuBar property box, enter the name of the menu bar you created in step 1.

You can attach the same menu bar to more than one form or report.

Attaching a Custom Shortcut Menu to a Form, to a Control on a Form, or to a Report

You can attach custom shortcut menus to a form, to a control on a form, or to a report. After you create the shortcut menu, set the ShortcutMenuBar property for the form, control, or report to the name of the shortcut menu. Access displays the custom shortcut menu whenever a user right-clicks the form, control, or report.

To attach a custom shortcut menu to a form, to a control on a form, or to a report, follow these steps:

1. Create a custom shortcut menu, as described earlier in this chapter.
2. Open the form or report in Design View.
3. Click the form, control, or report to which you want to attach a custom shortcut menu.
4. On the toolbar, click Properties.
5. In the ShortcutMenuBar property box, enter the name of the shortcut menu you created in step 1.

You can attach the same shortcut menu to more than one form, control, or report.

Specifying a Global Menu Bar or Shortcut Menu

You can specify a menu bar to use throughout your application by using the Startup dialog box.

To specify a global menu bar to display when your application starts, follow these steps:

1. Create a custom menu bar, as described earlier in this chapter.
2. Choose Startup from the Tools menu.
3. In the Menu Bar box, enter the name of the menu you created in step 1.
4. Click OK.

The next time you start your application, Microsoft Access displays your custom menu bar instead of the default menu bar.

You can change the global menu bar while your application is running, without having to restart your computer. To do so, set the `MenuBar` property of the `Application` object to the name of the menu bar.

For more information on specifying global menu bars in Visual Basic, search the Help index for "MenuBar property."

Using Custom Toolbars

You can use one or more custom toolbars in an application: Create the toolbars you want, and then use the appropriate method to display your custom toolbars:

- If your application has only one custom toolbar, simply use the Toolbars command (from the View menu) to display it, and it will appear each time your application starts.

- If your application has different custom toolbars for different forms or reports, you can specify a toolbar for each form or report in the form or report's `Toolbar` property.

- If you need to work with more than one custom toolbar for a form or report, or if you want to hide or show Access built-in toolbars, you can use the `Visible` property of the `CommandBar` object in Visual Basic code or the `ShowToolbar` action in macros to hide and show the toolbars.

- If you want your application to display only custom toolbars, you can hide all built-in toolbars by choosing the Startup command (from the Tools menu) and clearing the Allow Built-in Toolbars checkbox.

Attaching a Custom Toolbar to a Form

When using the Orders application, `Northwind` sales representatives want to click a button on the toolbar to print the invoice for the current order. You can create a custom toolbar for the `Orders` form with a button that prints invoices, and use the custom toolbar instead of the built-in toolbar.

1. Create the custom toolbar. Create a custom toolbar for the `Orders` form that includes a button that runs the `PrintInvoice` macro, as well as any other commands you want to provide, such as the Cut, Copy, and Paste commands in the Edit category of the Customize dialog box (in the Toolbars submenu under the View menu). Name this toolbar Orders Form Toolbar.

> **NOTE**
>
> The custom toolbar attached to the Orders form in the Orders sample application includes a Design View button. You can use this button to easily switch between Form View and Design View while you're looking at the sample application. However, if you don't want users to switch to Design View in your own application, don't put the Design View button on your custom toolbars.

2. Set the form's Toolbar property to the name of the custom toolbar. Open the Orders form in Design View, open the property sheet for the form, and then enter Orders Form Toolbar in the Toolbar property box of the form's property sheet.

> **NOTE**
>
> There is no need to create event procedures for the Activate and Deactivate events of the form to show and hide toolbars as is required in previous versions of Microsoft Access. Setting the Toolbar property to a custom toolbar automatically hides the built-in Form View toolbar when your form is opened, and hides your custom toolbar when a user closes the form or switches to another form.

Preventing Users from Customizing Your Application's Command Bars

You can control whether users can add or remove commands on all the menus and toolbars in your application.

To prevent users from customizing all command bars in an application, follow these steps:

1. Choose Startup from the Tools menu.
2. In the Startup dialog box, clear the Allow Toolbar/Menu Changes checkbox.
3. Click OK.

The next time your application starts, users won't be able to add or delete menu or toolbar commands. They will, however, still be able to move and resize toolbars.

> **NOTE**
>
> If you want to prevent users from customizing an individual command bar, you can clear the Allow Customizing checkbox in the Toolbar Properties dialog box. For more information, see the section titled "Creating New Command Bars and Setting Their Properties," earlier in this chapter.

20

CUSTOMIZING MENUS AND SWITCHBOARDS

Working with Command Bars in Code

You can work with menu bars, toolbars, and shortcut menus in Visual Basic code by using the properties and methods of the CommandBars collection and the objects associated with it. In the command bars object model, each menu is a CommandBar object. This is true of menus and submenus on all three types of command bars. For example, to refer to the Tools menu on the standard menu bar, use the following statement:

```
CommandBars!Tools
```

The following code uses the Add method and several command bar control properties to add a new, hidden Print Invoice command to the bottom of the Tools menu:

```
Private Sub AddInvoiceCommand()
    Dim cb As CommandBar, ctl As CommandBarControl
    ' Set a reference to the Tools menu.
    Set cb = CommandBars!Tools
    ' Create new CommandBarControl object on the Tools menu
    ' and set a reference to it.
    Set ctl = cb.Controls.Add(Type:=msoControlButton)
    ' Set properties of the new command.
    With ctl
        .BeginGroup = True
        .Caption = "Pri&nt Invoice"
        .FaceID = 0
        .OnAction = "=PrintInvoice()"
        .Visible = False
    End With
End Sub
```

You refer to a command bar control by name within a command bar's Controls collection. You must use the exact case and characters specified for the command's Caption property, but you can omit the ampersand (&) that designates the command's access key. For example, to use the Execute method to carry out the Options command on the Tools menu, you use the following statement:

```
CommandBars!Tools.Controls![Options...].Execute
```

To refer to a command on a submenu, you refer to the submenu as a member of the Controls collection of the menu that contains it. For example, to use the Execute method to carry out the Add-in Manager command on the Add-ins submenu, which is on the Tools menu, you use the following statement:

```
CommandBars!Tools.Controls![Add-ins].Controls![Add-in Manager].Execute
```

The following code makes the hidden Print Invoice command created with the AddInvoiceCommand Sub procedure visible:

```
Private Sub ShowInvoiceCommand()
    Dim cb As CommandBar, ctl As CommandBarControl
    ' Set a reference to the Tools menu.
    Set cb = CommandBars!Tools
    ' Set a reference to the control.
```

```
    Set ctl = cb.Controls![Print Invoice]
    ' Make the control visible.
    ctl.Visible = True
End Sub
```

For information on how to write and use Visual Basic functions, see Part IV, "Visual Basic for Applications for Access 97."

Summary

This chapter covered the various aspects of customizing menus and switchboards. Customizing these components of your applications is perhaps one of the best ways of creating applications that present a unique image for your company's Access 97–based products. You can develop a style for your applications that is identified with your company.

This is also one of the most crucial areas of Access 97 application design because these are the interface tools that your customers will be using to work with their data. Good menu and switchboard design complements a well-planned database application blueprint.

This can be one of the more enjoyable development tasks, so have fun customizing your user interface.

Creating and Customizing Help Files

by Joe Rhemann

IN THIS CHAPTER

CHAPTER 21

This chapter will teach you how to create a custom help file for your Access 97 application. In order to use the techniques described in this chapter, you should have the Microsoft Help Workshop that is installed with the Office 97 Developer's Edition, ODE tools, and certain other Microsoft developer products.

Custom Help Files

For obvious reasons, you might want to provide your end users with customized help files that are tailor-made for your product. Access 97 allows you to customize the application help environment by specifying various tips, shortcut-key text strings, and help files for your application's toolbar buttons, menu commands, controls, forms, and reports.

Specifying tips and shortcut-key text strings is accomplished easily in Access 97 by setting the appropriate properties for the toolbar button or menu command that you want to modify. Creating custom help files, though, cannot be done within the Access 97 environment. To create a custom help file for Access 97 applications, you must have the Microsoft Help Workshop or another application that allows you to compile your help project into a WinHelp version 4.0–compatible format.

This chapter briefly covers the internal help utility features of Access 97 and the process of creating custom help files using the Microsoft Help Workshop version 4.02.*x* for use with Microsoft WinHelp version 4.*x*. The version number can be viewed, as seen in Figure 21.1, by using the Help | About selection.

FIGURE 21.1.

The Microsoft Help Workshop version information.

Access 97 Internal Help Utility Features

Generally, Access 97 applications use the included Microsoft Access 97 help file (`Acmain80.hlp`), which is installed on the end user's system during Access 97 setup. The most noteworthy exception to this, of course, is the Access 97 runtime version, which does not include any help files by default. If you are going to be distributing your application using the runtime version, you need to plan on developing your own custom help files or make sure that Microsoft will allow you to distribute the individual files you are considering. If you refer to Chapter 3, "Access 97 Development Issues," you will see a brief listing of the Access 97–related files that you are allowed to distribute within your end-user license agreement (EULA).

At this time, you do not have the ability to distribute Microsoft's Office Assistant with your applications, but the ability to design your own custom Office Assistant may be realized in the near future.

Access 97 allows you to set the `AppHelpFile` settings in the Windows Registry under the Run-Time Options key. Where this setting and others were specified in the application `.ini` file in Access versions 1.*x* and 2.0, they are now recorded in the system Registry.

Custom Help Settings in the Registry

Assuming that a user profile exists, the first step in creating custom help settings is to create a Registry key named Run-Time Options.

You can then begin creating subkeys beneath the Run-Time Options key that specify the following four settings as illustrated in Figure 21.2:

- `AppHelpFile`: Uses the specified file as the default help file.
- `Icon`: Uses the specified icon for the application.
- `StartupScreen`: Displays the specified bitmap when your application starts.
- `TitleBar`: Displays the specified application title.

Figure 21.2.

Windows Registry key settings.

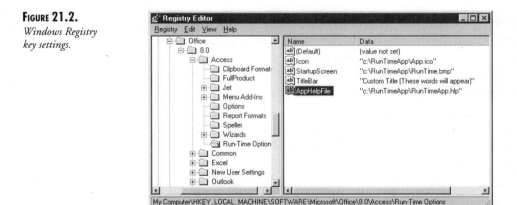

Specifying values for the `TitleBar` and `Icon` keys in the Windows Registry will prevent users from seeing "Microsoft Access" in the title bar and the Microsoft Access icon when your application starts. In addition to setting the properties this way, Microsoft Access 97 also provides some database startup properties that provide functionality similar to that provided by the Run-Time Options key in the Windows Registry. These properties include `AppTitle` and `AppIcon`.

You can set database startup properties by choosing Startup from the Tools menu and then setting the properties in the Startup dialog box.

If you do not want to specify the startup splash screen setting in the Registry, you can display a customized bitmap by renaming the bitmap of choice `YourApplicationName.bmp` and copying it into your application's folder. Then create a shortcut to start your application and place the name of the bitmap on the command line as an argument. Access 97 will use this bitmap as the splash screen graphic that is displayed at startup.

When the end user calls Help within your application, the help file specified in the `AppHelpFile` setting in his system Registry is displayed by WinHelp 4.0. The exception to this is the custom help settings you specify in your application for Access 97 controls, forms, and reports.

Custom Help Settings for Controls, Forms, and Reports

Access 97 allows you to use built-in features to create tips and status bar help for controls, forms, and reports. The following are the two types of custom help, other than compiled custom help files, that are supported:

- Control Pop-Up Tips: These appear as pop-up tips when the user moves his mouse pointer on top of the control. These tips are created using the `ControlTipText` property.
- Status Bar Help Information: This displays helpful information about controls and forms on the status bar, using the `StatusBarText` property.

Creating Custom Tips for a Toolbar Button

When you move your mouse pointer over a button or combo box control on a toolbar and pause for the specified time, your application displays a ToolTip. ToolTips are the small pop-up boxes that appear automatically and contain helpful or descriptive information about the specific control.

To create this type of helpful tip from within your application, choose Toolbars | Customize… from the View menu, and then select the toolbar that you want to customize. This brings up the toolbar customization dialog box shown in Figure 21.3.

After you have opened the toolbar customization dialog box, you can go directly to any of the buttons on the currently displayed toolbars and right-click with your mouse to bring up the customization menu for that control. Click on the Properties button to bring up the Database Control Properties dialog box, which displays the current settings for that control (see Figure 21.4).

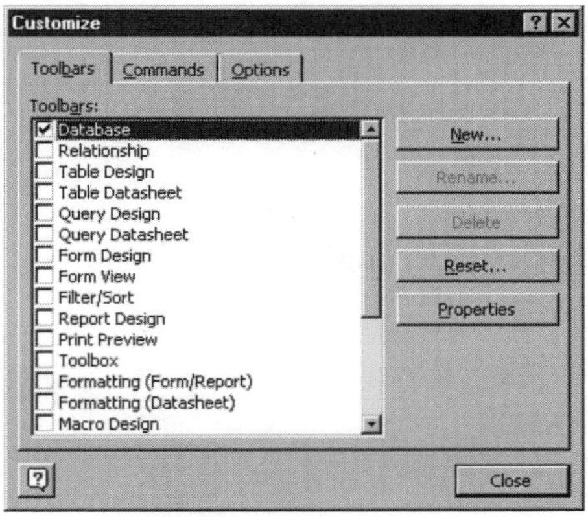

FIGURE 21.3.
*The toolbar
customization interface.*

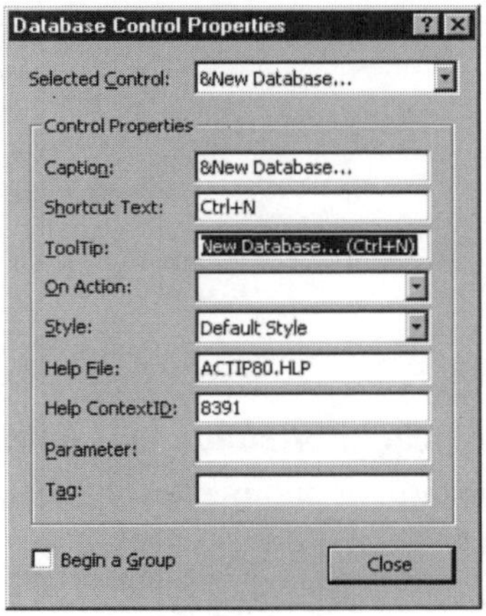

FIGURE 21.4.
*The Database Control
Properties dialog box,
where you can
customize any of the
currently displayed
toolbar controls.*

NOTE

You do not use the Customize dialog box to customize the controls; you have to move your mouse to the actual toolbar that is being displayed in your application interface. You can click on the Button command in the Customize dialog box all day long, and you won't change a thing.

Change the information in the ToolTip text box to reflect the information you want displayed to the end user. If you don't specify anything, Access 97 will display the contents of the Caption text box by default.

Creating Pop-Up Tips for Controls

The helpful pop-up tips for controls appear when the user moves his mouse pointer over a form control that has a pop-up tip assigned to it.

To create this kind of help tip, open the form that you want to work on in Design View, and then right-click the control to which you want to assign a pop-up tip. Then choose Properties from the customization menu that pops up and select Properties to bring up the control customization dialog box. (See Figure 21.5.)

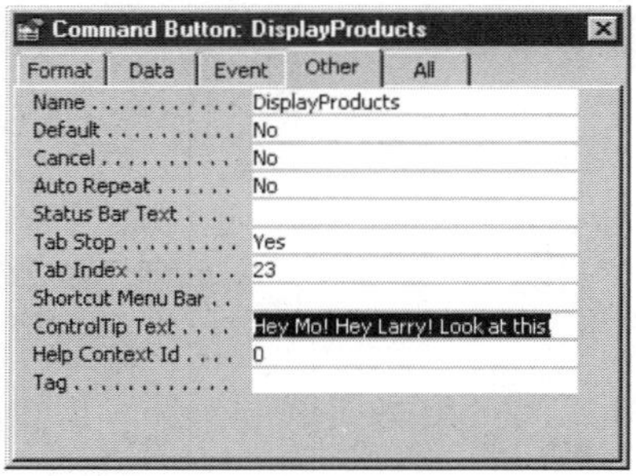

FIGURE 21.5.

The Command Button customization dialog box for the DisplayProducts *control on the* Orders *form in the* Northwind *sample database.*

Enter the information you want your users to see, up to a maximum of 255 characters, in the ControlTip Text text box.

Creating Status Bar Help Information for Controls

Status bar custom help displays information on the status bar when a user right-clicks the mouse pointer over a form control.

To create a status bar information message, you need to open the desired form in Design View and right-click on the control you want to work with. On the pop-up customization menu, click Properties to bring up the control customization dialog box you saw in Figure 21.4.

In the Status Bar Text text box, enter the information you want to display, up to 255 characters (or fewer, depending on the font and resolution used to display your application window). Figure 21.6 and Figure 21.7 show you the process and results of setting status bar help text.

WARNING

Keep in mind that if your status bar text has too many characters, Access 97 will only display the portion that fits into the screen width. Even if the status bar text fits in the window at standard VGA resolution on your machine, keep in mind that an end user might be using a larger system font or a different window size, either of which may cause some of the text to be cut off.

Creating and Customizing Help Files

CHAPTER 21

575

21

CREATING AND
CUSTOMIZING
HELP FILES

FIGURE 21.6.
*Setting the status bar
help text.*

FIGURE 21.7.
*The results of setting a
status bar text property
as a helpful hint.*

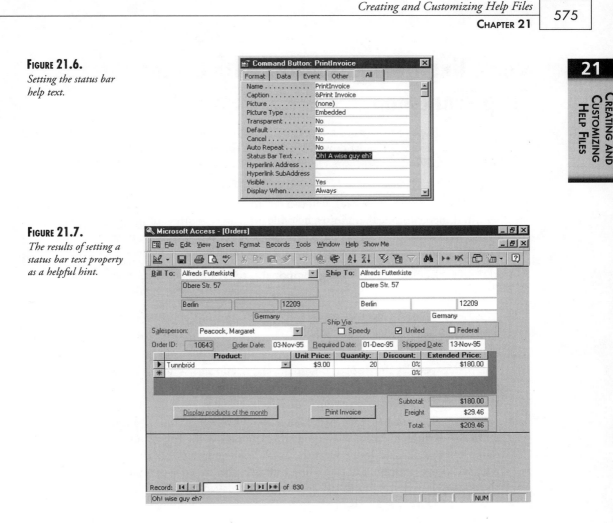

Custom Help Files Require a Help Compiler

Custom help files that appear when the end user invokes the help function, and other custom
help features such as "What's This?" tips that require a compiled help file, must be created
with the Microsoft Help Workshop, which is available as a standalone product, or bundled
with some of the developer tools from Microsoft. Creating custom help files can be a relatively
complex process and should be approached in much the same fashion as creating any other
embedded application.

The Help Workshop is covered in the following portions of this chapter. If you are considering creating professional, well-developed help resources to distribute with your application, the
Help Workshop is the way to go.

Compiling Help Resources with the Microsoft Help Workshop

The Help Workshop is a help project development application that is included with Microsoft Office 97 Developer's Edition, Microsoft Visual Basic for Applications, Microsoft Visual C++, and the Microsoft Windows Software Developer's Kit (SDK). It is also available from Microsoft as a developer's resource.

With the Help Workshop (hcw.exe), you can create each of the components of a help project, test them, and then compile them into a help file for delivery with your product, or to offer to the end user as an after-delivery update or option. The Help Workshop compiler consolidates all the project components into a single file that is compatible with Microsoft WinHelp.

A Workshop project uses the following components to create an *.HLP file that can be viewed with WinHelp:

- *.hpj files: Help project control files.
- *.rtf files: Help project topic files.
- *.bmX files: Help project bitmap images that are to be included in the help file. The X parameter specifies the display alignment justification to WinHelp. .bmc specifies that WinHelp should use the existing content justification for the image; .bml and .bmr specify left and right justification, respectively.
- bmc *mono.bmp;*16.bmp;*256.bmp;*16bit.bmp;*24bit.bmp files: Multiple bitmaps of an image in different color resolutions that can be specified as a single help-file image. WinHelp will automatically select the appropriate graphic from the specified bitmaps. The bmc at the beginning of this string indicates the presence of a bitmap image and the appropriate alignment justification when displayed by WinHelp.
- *.cnt files: Help project container files.
- *.avi files: Video image files that can be included using the MCI command in an *.rtf topic file. The MCI command specifies the multimedia control properties that will be available within the help file. Currently, WinHelp version 4.0 supports only .avi multimedia files. Microsoft has stated that future releases will support other formats.
- *.shg files: Help project multi-hotspot bitmaps.
- *.mrb files: Multi-resolution graphic files.
- Windows Metafile: WinHelp allows you to specify hexadecimal data that represents a metafile image. WinHelp then uses either the default or a specified image-mapping mode to generate the metafile image. You specify the metafile hexadecimal image data using the \wmetafile picture statement in the \pict token in an .rtf file.
- Binary Images Data: You can specify a string of binary data as an image file by including the \bin picture statement in the \pict token in an .rtf file.
- Other source files.

21

Microsoft Help Workshop Components

The following are the individual files that make up the Help Workshop product:

- `hcrtf.exe` and `hcw.exe`: These are the primary Help Workshop executable files that edit the individual components, compile these components into a tested help file, and then generate reports on the help file.

- `hcw.hlp`: This is the primary help file and tutorial for help-file authors.

- `mrbc.exe`: This is the Microsoft Multi-Resolution Bitmap Compiler version 1.1, which allows you to create multi-resolution images that can be combined into a single image. This allows you to create help-file illustrations that will be viewable regardless of the end user's display resolution.

- `shed.exe`: This is the Microsoft Hotspot Editor version 2.0, which allows you to create an interactive image file with multiple hotspots.

Help Limitations Under WinHelp 4.0

WinHelp 4.0 has the following capabilities and limitations:

- Maximum of 2GB for help-file size.
- Maximum of 50 characters for browse strings.
- Maximum of 259 characters for filenames.
- Maximum of 50 characters for window captions.
- Maximum of 9 indented content-level headings.
- Maximum of 255 characters for content topic strings.
- Maximum of 127 characters for content topic strings in DBCS language.

    DBCS stands for Double-Byte Character Set, and represents a new value that can be set in the [OPTIONS] section of a help project (`*.hpj`) file. This value specifies whether the files to be compiled use a DBCS. This value can be set to either YES or NO, according to the format DBCS=value and depending on the LCID (Language ID) option specified.

    LCIDs that force DBCS equal to NO.

LCID	Localized Region
0x0409	American
0x0C09	Australian
0x0C07	Austrian
0x042D	Basque
0x080C	Belgian
0x0809	British

continues

LCID	*Localized Region*
0x0402	Bulgarian
0x1009	Canadian
0x041A	Croatian
0x0405	Czech
0x0406	Danish
0x0413	Dutch (Standard)
0x0C01	Egyptian
0x040B	Finnish
0x040C	French (Standard)
0x0C0C	French Canadian
0x0407	German (Standard)
0x042E	German
0x0408	Greek
0x040E	Hungarian
0x040F	Icelandic
0x0801	Iraqi
0x1809	Irish
0x040D	Israeli
0x0410	Italian (Standard)
0x2C01	Jordanian
0x3401	Kuwaiti
0x0426	Latvian
0x3001	Lebanese
0x1001	Libyan
0x1407	Liechtenstein
0x0427	Lithuanian
0x140C	Luxembourg (French)
0x1007	Luxembourg (German)
0x042f	Macedonian
0x080A	Mexican
0x0819	Moldavian
0x0818	Moldavian
0x1801	Moroccan
0x1409	New Zealander

LCID	Localized Region
0x0414	Norwegian (Bokmal)
0x0814	Norwegian (Nynorsk)
0x2001	Omani
0x0415	Polish
0x0416	Portuguese (Brazilian)
0x0816	Portuguese (Standard)
0x0418	Romanian
0x0419	Russian
0x0401	Saudi Arabian
0x081A	Serbian
0x041B	Slovakian
0x0424	Slovenian
0x0C0A	Spanish (Modern Sort)
0x040A	Spanish (Traditional Sort)
0x0430	Sutu
0x041D	Swedish
0x100C	Swiss (French)
0x0807	Swiss (German)
0x0810	Swiss (Italian)
0x2801	Syrian
0x041E	Thai
0x0431	Tsonga
0x041f	Turkish
0x3801	U.A.E.
0x0422	Ukrainian
0x0420	Urdu
0x0436	Zulu

LCIDs that force DBCS equal to YES.

Identifier	Locale
0x0411	Japanese
0x0404	Taiwanese
0x1004	Singapore
0x0C04	Hong Kong

- Allows up to 64,000 topics per keyword.
- Maximum of 31 characters for font names.
- Maximum of 20 font ranges.
- 64KB error log file display in Windows 95; unlimited error log size.
- 1MB error log file display in Windows NT; unlimited error log size.
- Maximum of 4,095 characters for hotspot hidden text.
- Maximum of 127 characters for help and topic title strings.
- Maximum of 50 characters for window title strings.
- Maximum of 8 characters for window names.
- Maximum of 255 characters for the copyright string.
- Maximum of 2,000 characters for citation strings.
- Allows for 255 window definitions per project file.
- Maximum of 16,383 characters for topic footnotes.
- Maximum of 255 characters for keyword length.
- Maximum of 65,535 referenced bitmaps per help file.

Creating Custom Help Files

Once you have successfully installed the Windows Help Workshop, it's time to create your application's help system.

Creating a help system is essentially the same as creating another application within an application. This chapter does not cover many of the WinHelp 4.0 technical reference topics, however; that information is available to you in the online user documentation that is included on the Help Workshop distribution CD-ROM. You should be somewhat familiar with WinHelp 4.0 before you attempt to create your help application. The Help Workshop simplifies the creation of help applications, but a working knowledge of WinHelp 4.0 will be of great assistance to you.

Stage 1: Planning Your Help File Application

The first step to creating a help application is no different from any other application. Plan it on paper first. Draft a simple outline and a topical organizational chart that lay out the essential elements of an adequate help system for your application. Then establish the basic content requirements of each topical section and plan your links, hotspots, and other special elements.

Now that you have a good blueprint of your help system, it's time to start the actual design process.

Stage 2: Creating Your Topic Files

When you have finished the planning stage, it's time to begin building your topic files.

Your topic files can be generated on any word processor that supports RTF (Rich Text Format). Make sure you are using an editor or word processor that supports RTF-formatted text. The general guidelines to follow when writing your topics are: Use hard page breaks when separating your topics; add your footnotes at the beginning of the file; and save it as an RTF file.

When you are creating your help topic file, you must give each topic an identification text label. You do this by inserting a pound sign (#) as a footnote mark at the beginning of each topic, and then entering your identification string as the footnote text. Do not exceed 255 characters or use the !, @, #, %, *, +, or = characters or leading or trailing spaces in the ID label. Topic IDs also should not begin with numbers if they will be used in the [MAP] section. Using the prefix IDH_ in your topic ID will enable the Help Workshop to track errors, list undefined topics in the [MAP] section of the project file, and warn of any topics not listed in the [MAP] section.

Topic IDs that are assigned to context-sensitive help topics should begin with IDH_, because Help Workshop recognizes that a program will call topic IDs beginning with these characters. While compiling the project, Help Workshop displays a list of any topic IDs that are in your topic (.rtf) files but are not mapped to numeric values, or that are mapped to numeric values but are not in your topic files. Prefixes other than IDH_ should be designated in the Map dialog box.

Topic IDs are also used as place markers to allow your users to skip directly to desired locations in your topics.

Keywords

WinHelp 4.0 uses three types of keywords to index data in topic files: A-keywords, K-keywords, and multi-index keywords. Each of the three types of keywords must have its own individual topical footnotes, and each individual keyword must be separated by semicolons (;). The following list describes the three types of keywords:

- A-keywords: These keywords are denoted by the A footnote mark, do not appear in WinHelp indexes, and are used only by the ALink macro. A-keywords in your content files allow ALink macros to perform intertopical jumps. The example below shows you how to create one or more topical A-keywords:

```
A{\footnote keyword;[keyword;]...}
```

- K-keywords: These keywords are used for searches and topical links called from the Index button in the WinHelp user interface, or they are used by the KLink macro to jump between topics containing the specified K-keywords. A K footnote mark is used to specify a K-keyword in the contents file. The example below shows you how to create one or more topical K-keywords:

```
K{\footnote keyword;[keyword;]...}
```

■ Multi-index keywords: Multi-index keywords are used to specify alternate indexes. They are denoted by any alphabetic character except A or K and allow WinHelp to provide similar index capabilities to K-keywords. The example below shows you how to create one or more multi-index keywords that are part of an index that is referenced to B-keywords:

```
B{\footnote keyword;[keyword;]...}
```

ALink Targets

An ALink target is a topic that is associated with other similar topics by an A-keyword footnote. This gives WinHelp the ability to allow intertopical jumps from within a topic, instead of forcing the user to refer to a topical index. When an end user invokes a topical search, WinHelp will use the ALink macro to search the specified help files for any ALink targets, or topics, containing the specified A-keywords.

To designate a topic as an ALink target, place an A as a footnote mark at the beginning of the topic, and enter the desired keywords as footnote text.

Make sure that you do not use any carriage returns, spaces before or after the keywords, or more than 255 characters. All the keywords must be separated by semicolons, and you must account for case sensitivity.

If your topic does not contain any A-keywords, the ALink macro will not search it for results.

Title Footnotes

You can insert a title footnote by inserting a dollar sign ($) at the beginning of the topic where you want to locate it and then typing the text of the title footnote (up to 255 characters, or 127 characters for DBCS characters).

KLink Topical Index Entries

Use K-keywords to add a topic to a topical index that can be displayed in WinHelp when the user clicks on the Index button. The KLink macro searches for all topics that contain K-keyword footnotes and adds those topics to the index.

To create an index entry for a topic, insert a K footnote at the beginning of the topic, and enter a list of keywords.

Make sure that you do not use any carriage returns, spaces before or after the keywords, or more than 255 characters. All the keywords must be separated by semicolons, and you must account for case sensitivity.

If your topic does not contain any K-keywords, the KLink macro will not search it for results.

Second-Level Topical Index Entries

Second-level index entries are used to create subtopics under primary index topics in an outline fashion; they are displayed alphabetically.

To create a second-level index entry for a topic, insert a K footnote at the beginning of the topic, and enter a list of keywords separated by semicolons. After each keyword that needs a second-level index entry, enter a semicolon; type the keyword again, followed by a colon and a space; and then enter the second-level keyword and a semicolon in the following fashion:

Keyword1;Keyword1: 2ndLvlKeyword1;Keyword2;Keyword3;Keyword4

Topical Browse Sequences

If you want to add a topic to a browse sequence, insert a + footnote at the beginning of the topic, and enter a browse code as the footnote text. (If you want WinHelp to generate an automatic browse sequence, however, you do not have to enter a browse code for your topics.)

For content files that have only one browse sequence, use the word auto as the browse code for each of their topics so that Help Workshop knows to automatically create only one browse sequence based on the topic placement in the .rtf file.

> **WARNING**
>
> Make sure you do not use any of the !, @, #, %, *, +, or = characters, spaces in topical keywords, or individual keywords over 50 characters in length.

Make sure the browse buttons are enabled in the help project file in order for browse functions to be available.

When you are creating the browse codes, using numbers can complicate the process of updating the help file topics. Large help files can have many topics, and you will have to manually renumber each topic if you change the sequence. The other popular method is to use a name as the browse code and have all the topics in the browse sequence share that name. If you use names in the footnotes instead of numbers, WinHelp will display the browse sequence in the order in which each topic appears in the content file. Adding and deleting topics, and changing the order around, is merely a matter of moving the topics.

Tagging a Topic for Exclusion from the Compiled Help File

If you want to exclude certain portions of your topic content files from your compiled help files, you will need to mark them for the Help Workshop.

You must also make sure that you have specified which topics you want to include in the compile in the help project file. If you do not specifically exclude a topic from a compile, it will be added to the help file build.

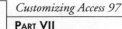
Exclusion tagging can be done by inserting an asterisk (*) as the first footnote tag at the beginning of the topic files that you want to exclude and then entering the appropriate build tags separated by semicolons. Build tags are not case sensitive.

Entry Macros for Help Topics

When you want to have a macro run automatically when the user opens the topic file, insert the exclamation point (!) footnote tag at the beginning of the topic and then enter the macro commands as the footnote text, separating each macro command with a semicolon. Do not use carriage returns.

Topic Display Windows

When you open a help topic from an `ALink` or `KLink` macro, or from an Index or Find tab, WinHelp looks at your help file settings to determine which type of window to display the help topics in. These display settings must be made in the help project file, and then you must use the window type specified in the project file as the footnote text with the > footnote tag.

Enter the topical footnote tag (>) at the beginning of the topic, and then enter the name of your window type as specified in the `.hpj` file.

Adding Non-Scrolling Regions to Topics

To add non-scrolling regions to a topic, situate the topic paragraphs that you want to include in these regions at the beginning of the topic and use the Keep With Next paragraph formatting, which can be found on the Format|Paragraph menu.

You should not use non-scrolling regions in help files that are displayed in pop-up windows. If you want to add custom colors or transparent bitmaps to a topical display, WinHelp automatically adjusts the background colors according to your specifications.

End users will not be able to select, copy, or print both the scrolling and non-scrolling portions of a topic unless they right-click on the topic with the mouse.

Suppressing Word Wrap when Displaying a Topic

If you have information that you do not want WinHelp to automatically word wrap to fit the display width, you must use the Keep Lines Together paragraph formatting (Format|Paragraph|Keep Lines Together) on the lines where you do not want a word wrap.

To do this, place the insertion point in the desired lines and apply the formatting. WinHelp will automatically display a left-to-right scrollbar in the bottom of the display window.

Creating Topical Links

Creating links between topics is one way of making your help application more user-friendly and functional. A link is essentially a hotspot within your topic content file that contains a link to the associated topic ID. When a user activates the hotspot, he is automatically sent to the linked topic.

To set up a link, place an insertion point immediately after the text or image that you want to designate as a hotspot. Then enter the topic ID to which you want to link. Do not leave a space between the link ID and the hotspot. Select the hotspot and apply the appropriate underline formatting, depending on the type of link topic. If you want to link to another topic, use the double-underline style. If you want to link to a pop-up topic, use the single-underline style. Once this is done, select the linked topic ID in the insertion point and apply the hidden-character format style.

If you are creating a link to another help file, insert an @ symbol behind the linked topic ID at the insertion point, followed by the name of the new help file.

You can specify the window type and text color characteristics by inserting an asterisk (*) in front of the linked topic ID for default color, a percent sign (%) for default color minus the underline, and a > symbol after the topic ID, followed by the desired window type name to tell it to display the linked topic in a specific window type.

> **TIP**
>
> Make sure you include all the text in a textual hotspot when you apply the underline formatting styles to designate the type of linked topic. If you leave out any punctuation marks or characters, your hotspot link will not display properly.

Hotspots That Run Macros

If you want WinHelp to automatically run a macro when a user selects a hotspot, you should create a hotspot followed by a macro command.

To set up a hotspot that runs a macro, you place an insertion point immediately after the text or image that you want to designate as a hotspot. Enter an exclamation point (!) followed by the macro command. You can specify more than one macro by separating the macro commands with a semicolon. Do not leave a space between the exclamation point and the hotspot. Next, select the hotspot and apply double-underline formatting; then apply the hidden-character style to the macro command string.

Adding Bitmap Images

Select the desired insertion point for your bitmap image, and then either use the Paste command or create a link to the image file with the appropriate display parameters.

Linked bitmaps are designated using the following syntax string:

```
bmX BitmapImageFileName.bmp
```

In this syntax string, you specify the display parameters for the linked image by replacing the X with the appropriate character:

Parameter	Definition
c	For text-character alignment.
l	To indicate left-justified text.
r	To indicate right-justified text.
t	Tells WinHelp to change the display of the bitmap's white background colors to match the background color of the window. This is used to try to eliminate the background frame from the original image. This is only used with 16-color bitmaps and can be used in conjunction with one of the other display parameters.

Multi-Color Depth Bitmaps

Creating multi-color depth bitmaps is a useful feature to build into your help files. This way WinHelp can select the appropriate image color depth for the end user's computer. Essentially, you will need to create a separate bitmap file for each of the display resolutions and color depths that you want to support, and then tell WinHelp how to find them.

At the appropriate insertion point, create a statement that includes each filename separated by a semicolon. WinHelp will then automatically select the appropriate image from the listed files. For example:

```
bmX 16ColorImageName.bmp;256ColorImageName.bmp,TrueColorImageName.bmp
```

> **WARNING**
>
> Make sure you do not repeat color depths and resolutions between image files that are listed in the same statement. This could confuse WinHelp and cause an error.

Hypergraphic Bitmap Images

To create *hypergraphic bitmap images* (images with one or multiple hotspots that can link or run macros), you need to use the Microsoft Hotspot Editor to edit the desired image. This tool (see Figure 21.8) is accessed by selecting SHED (Segmented Hypergraphics Editor) from the Help Workshop Tools menu.

FIGURE 21.8.

The Microsoft Hotspot Editor.

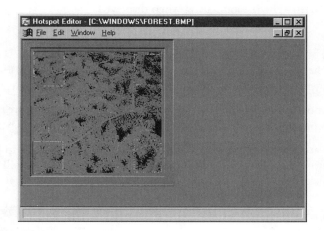

The Hotspot Editor allows you to create multiple hotspots on an image and then specify the hotspot's context string, link type, border visibility, and ID. The Hotspot Editor saves the hypergraphic image in a compressed .shg format.

Video and Animation

If you want to include video and animation in your help topics, place an insertion point at the desired location and create an mci link to the desired file. Currently WinHelp 4.0 supports only .avi files, but Microsoft has stated that it will support other video file formats in future releases. Create the mci command using the following syntax string and the appropriate mci display parameters (if you do not specify any optional parameters, WinHelp will automatically display a playbar with a menu button, a graphical interface toolbar that has buttons used to control multimedia playback, and will not play the video or animation file until the user requests it):

```
mci _left ¦ _right OPTION OPTION OPTION FileName.Extension
```

For example, if you wanted to automatically play an AVI multimedia file named forest.bmp, which remains external to the help file, without a menu button on the playbar, you would use the following code:

```
mci EXTERNAL NOMENU PLAY forest.bmp
```

The mci command inserts an .avi video or animation file into a topic and uses the following syntax parameters:

> EXTERNAL—The file remains external to the help file.
>
> NOPLAYBAR—No user playbar control is displayed.

> NOMENU—No menu button is shown on the playbar.
>
> REPEAT—Auto-repeat.
>
> PLAY—The file auto-plays when displayed.

Stage 3: Building Your Project Files

Now that your topic files are complete, you should create your project file. The project file is where you establish the administrative features of your help system.

Project files are designated by the .hpj filename extension and are used by the Help Workshop to compile and build your help files properly, according to the parameters you specify.

To create a new project file, make sure that you are in the Help Workshop, and then select New from the File menu. The New window (see Figure 21.9) will pop up; select Help Project and click OK.

FIGURE 21.9.
Creating a new help project file.

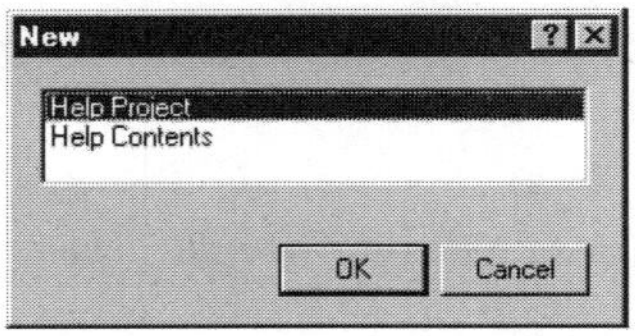

Help Workshop will automatically create a project file with the minimum settings necessary for a new project. Figure 21.10 shows a new help project file.

FIGURE 21.10.
The new help project file.

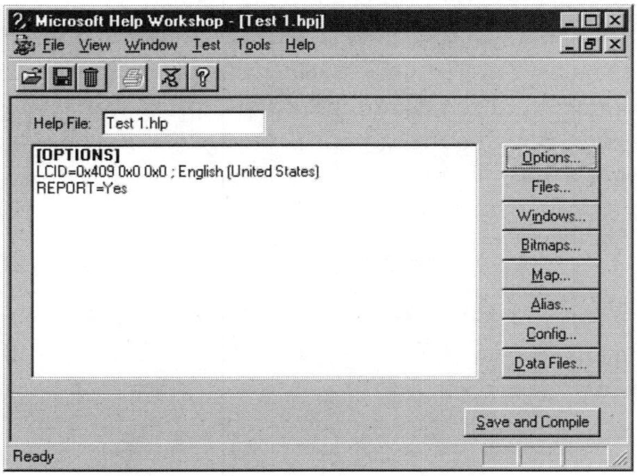

As you can see, the project file screen allows you to customize all the features of your help project. This is one of the most valuable features of the Help Workshop because it automates the process, saving a great deal of time and troubleshooting.

Creating and Customizing Help Files

CHAPTER 21

589

21

CREATING AND
CUSTOMIZING
HELP FILES

> **TIP**
>
> Getting into the practice of adding developer comments to your code is very useful, especially when you are involved in ongoing projects involving more than one developer. To add comments to your help file project files, use semicolons (;) to indicate your comments. Microsoft Help Workshop does not look at any text on a line following a semicolon. The exception to this is the [MACROS] section. You cannot use the semicolon to enter comments in the [MACROS] section.

The following list describes the different section components that make up a help file project file:

Section	Description
[ALIAS]	This section gives you the ability to alias one topic ID to another.
[BAGGAGE]	Help files have their own internal file systems, and this section lists all of the files that make up the help file.
[BITMAPS]	This section specifies bitmap files for backward WinHelp compatibility.
[BUILDTAGS]	This section specifies build tags for backward WinHelp compatibility.
[CONFIG]	This section specifies author-defined menus and buttons used in the help file and Registry DLLs and DLL functions used as macros within the help file. This section is required if these features are used.
[CONFIG:name]	This section provides the same function for individual window configurations as the [CONFIG] section does for the help file.
[EXCLUDE]	This section specifies build tags that identify topics that are to be excluded from the help file.
[FILES]	This required section specifies topic (.rtf) files to be included in the compiled help file.
[FONTS]	This section specifies fonts in topic files to be replaced with different fonts, point sizes, or character sets.
[INCLUDE]	This section specifies the build tags that identify the topics that should be included in the help file.
[MACROS]	This section specifies macros to run when a user selects one of the keywords listed in this section from the index.
[MAP]	This section associates topic IDs with context numbers that a program can use to call the specified help file.

continues

Section	Description
[OPTIONS]	This required section specifies options that control the build process.
[WINDOWS]	This section defines the characteristics of the main help window and secondary window types used in the help file.

Displaying Help Topics Individually

In the project file, click the Map button and add the topic that you want to have displayed, along with any context-sensitivity settings.

Aliasing Topic IDs

If you want to redirect your links without changing all the links specified in the topic files, simply establish an alias for the desired link target and apply it to the project. You can also use aliasing to correct topical displays that have been improperly redirected by a mapped numerical value without having to edit the program.

Bitmap Image Locations

In the project file, you can specify the location of your bitmap images through a simple interface by clicking the Bitmap button and adding the appropriate directory.

WinHelp will automatically search for images in the current working directories where the project (.hpj) and topic (.rtf) files are located, in any directory specified for topic files, and in any directory added through the project interface.

Providing a Title

The help file's title is displayed when a user invokes help and opens the help file. This is another simple setting that you can specify by entering the appropriate title text in the Help Title text box on the General tab of the Options menu (remember that the title cannot exceed 127 characters). You can set the help file title and other settings for your custom help file from within Microsoft Help Workshop.

Running a Macro for Index Entries

If you want to run a wizard, display specific help tools, reference a DLL, or run other operations that can be specified in a macro when a user clicks on an index entry, you can associate a macro with an index keyword through the Options button.

Click on Options, choose the Macros tab, and fill in the blanks. Figure 21.11 shows how to set up event-driven macros, which are invoked by clicking on an indexed entry.

FIGURE 21.11.
*Setting up macros to
run when a user clicks
on an index entry.*

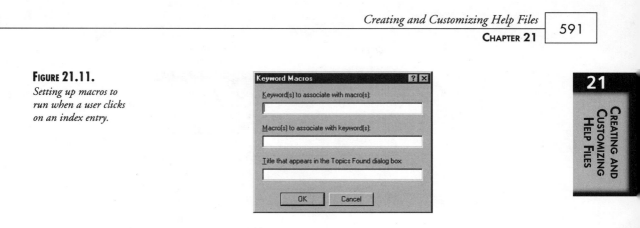

Any keywords associated with a macro will appear in the index even if they are not specified as
κ footnotes in the topic file.

> **NOTE**
>
> The title you specify is not displayed unless the user double-clicks on a keyword that is
> linked to a macro and to a topic.

Browse Buttons and Other Help Window Options

You add Browse buttons and other help window button options such as Print and Copy simply by enabling the optional control under the Buttons tab after you create a new window.
Figure 21.12 shows you how to enable browse buttons in a help window.

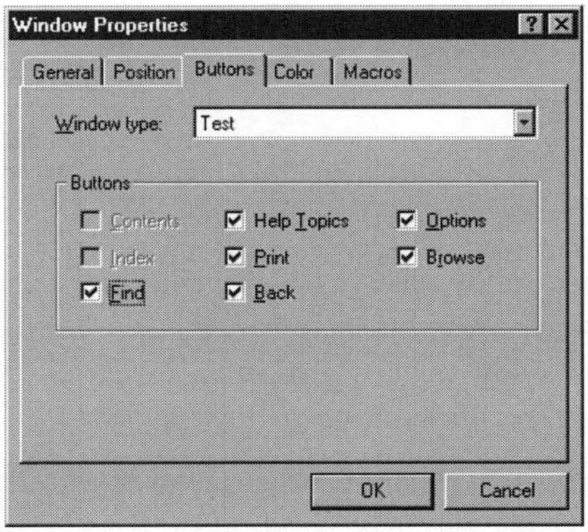

FIGURE 21.12.
*Enabling browse
buttons in a help file
window.*

Associating Contents Files to Help Files

You relate your contents file to your help file through the Options dialog interface as illustrated in Figure 21.13.

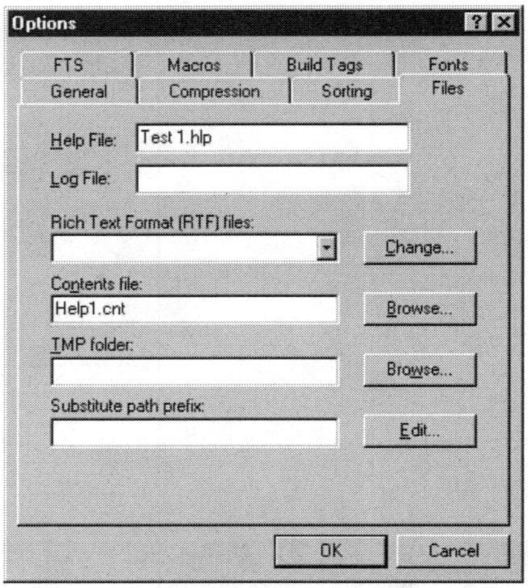

FIGURE 21.13.

*Specifying the name of
the contents file.*

Help Window Support

Help Workshop provides a convenient interface for adding support for secondary windows in your help file.

You add secondary windows through the Add a New Window Type dialog box, under the project's Windows menu. (See Figure 21.14.)

FIGURE 21.14.

*Adding new secondary
windows to your help
file. WinHelp supports
up to 255 additional
secondary windows per
help file.*

The Windows menu allows you to define a wide range of options, including the ability to specify a default window type for your help file. If you want to customize your default help file window, add a new window as illustrated in Figure 21.14, give it the name main, and then specify the various settings to suit your needs.

Secondary windows that do not have specified titles will display the title that is specified in the contents file associated with that window; or, if one is not specified in the contents file either, no title will be displayed.

WinHelp will determine the positions of all secondary windows automatically if you select the Default Positions option. Otherwise, you should either specify the manual size and position settings or select the Auto-Size Height option.

Users can override your specified window background colors by changing the window or text colors in Display properties or right-clicking a topic and then selecting the Use System Colors option.

Adding Buttons to a Secondary Window

You can create custom buttons by adding `CreateButton` macros to the window using the Macros tab.

> **NOTE**
>
> If you do not have any standard WinHelp buttons enabled, WinHelp disables button support in your help file and will not support adding custom buttons to any of your windows.

You can add buttons to the primary help window by customizing the Main window settings.

Specifying Macros for Windows

You can specify a macro that you want to run when a window is opened so that when the user opens the help file window, WinHelp launches the macro automatically. See Figure 21.15 for an illustration of adding a startup macro to a help window.

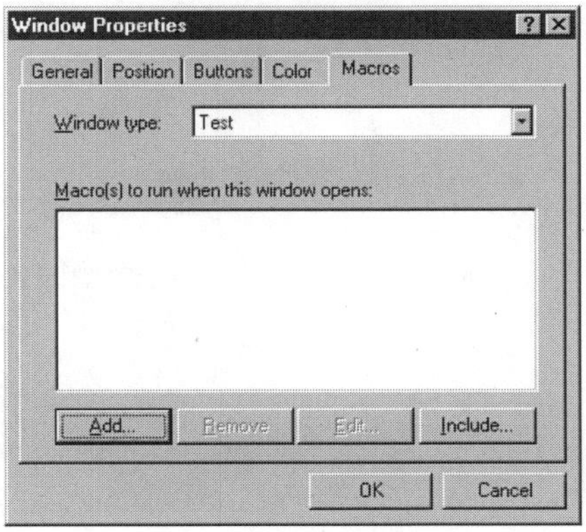

FIGURE 21.15.
Adding a startup macro to a help window.

Default Topics, Versions, and Copyright Information

Specifying the default topic, version information, and copyright information is simply a matter of specifying these settings in the General tab of the Options dialog box. (See Figure 21.16.)

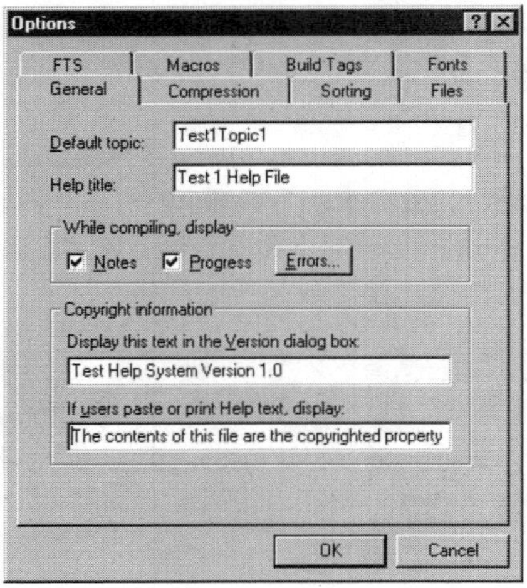

FIGURE 21.16.

Setting the general custom properties for your help file.

Adding a Startup Macro to a Help File

You can specify a macro to run at startup when a user invokes help and your help file is opened. You make this setting in the Macros tab of the Options dialog box, as illustrated in Figure 21.17.

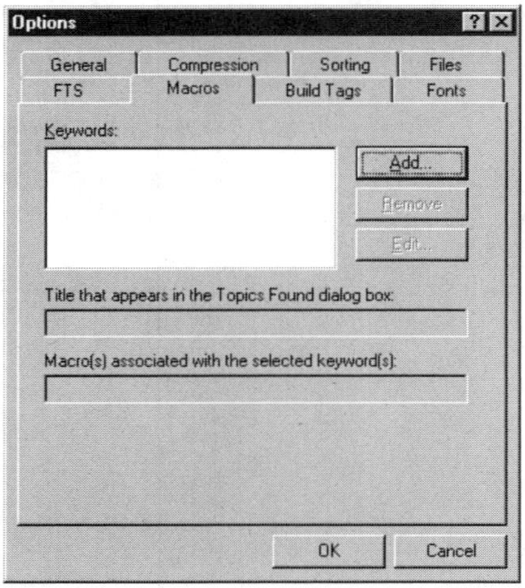

FIGURE 21.17.

Setting a startup macro to run when your help file is opened.

DLL Data Files

If you need to place DLL-related data in your help file, use the Data Files option in the Help Workshop project file editing window, as illustrated in Figure 21.18.

FIGURE 21.18.

Setting up DLL data files for use with your help file.

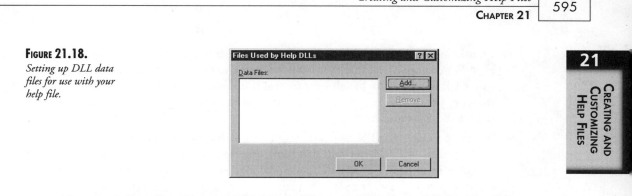

> **WARNING**
>
> These DLL filenames are case sensitive, so make sure that you use the appropriate case when specifying your data source files.

WinHelp 4.0 provides callback support for DLL files so the user can access the DLL data in a help file from his active application.

Localization Support in WinHelp Project Files

As I mentioned before, the Help Workshop allows you to compile the project in any language that is supported by the development system's operating system.

The localization support features of Help Workshop and WinHelp 4.0 offer the following:

- Compiling in Specified Languages—The regional settings that are supported on the system on which you are compiling your help file specify the default language that is used to compile the help file. You cannot specify a language that is not supported on your opepÇ4ing system. Change the Compiling in Specified Languages setting through the Options menu in the project file.

- Concurrent Language Support—WinHelp 4.0 allows you to run more than one language translation of a help file at the same time. This is a very useful tool for multilingual developers who are preparing the help file for distribution. This is easily accomplished by displaying the default language version of a main window help file topic and then pressing the Ctrl+Shift+J keystroke. You then type the following command string and click OK:

  ```
  !Compare(c:\\localized\\LocalizedHelpFileName.Extension)
  ```

  It is a good idea to rename the content files of the original help file and then load it with

  ```
  Winhlp32-g OriginalContentFileName.Extension
  ```

  If your localized help file is built properly, any movements in the original are reflected in the localized when you use the Ctrl+Shift+left arrow or Ctrl+Shift+right arrow keystroke.

■ Translating the Content Files—You create this setting under the File menu within Help Workshop. Make sure that Translation is checked. Before you do this, however, you need to make sure that all your topical IDs, help filenames, and window names are set to the desired language. Once you select the Translation option, you cannot change these parameters.

■ WinHelp Dialog Box Fonts—WinHelp will look for the specified font on the end user's system. If it does not find that font, WinHelp will use the closest match. If you are going to ship your product to a regional market without providing localized support, you might want to specify your own font to account for changing font sizes. Create this setting through the Options menu in the project file.

Step 4: Creating Your Contents Files

Contents files are ASCII text files that are the command source for the Contents tab in the Help Topics WinHelp dialog box. This is where you set up the display parameters for the Help Topics tab so that your users can view an interactive table of contents for your help file. The contents file specifies which keywords from help files are listed on the Index and Find tabs.

NOTE

You must have a valid link between a topic and an existing help file before WinHelp will display the Contents tab to the end user.

Creating the Contents File

You create new contents files in Help Workshop by selecting New from the File menu (see Figure 21.19).

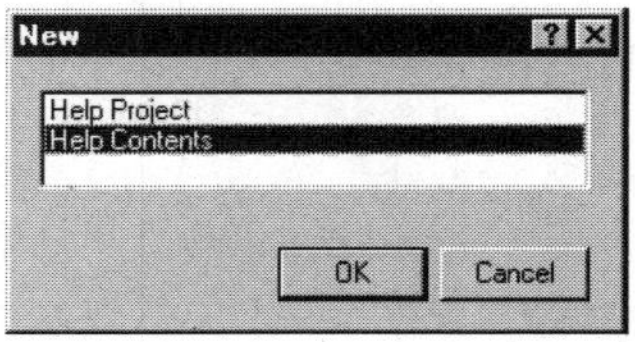

FIGURE 21.19.
Creating a new
contents file.

Selecting Help Contents and then clicking OK will bring up the contents file interface in Help Workshop (see Figure 21.20).

Now you can specify the settings to build your contents file. Adding headings and topics to your contents file is relatively easy using the Add Above/Below buttons, and you can specify keywords from more than one help file. Essentially, if you have a series of help files that addresses a general topic, you can use the contents file to draw them all together into one help system by displaying their keywords on the Contents tab. This provides a common interface for your users from which they can jump to any of the help files listed. Specify the index filenames for any other help files whose keywords you want to include in the Index tab.

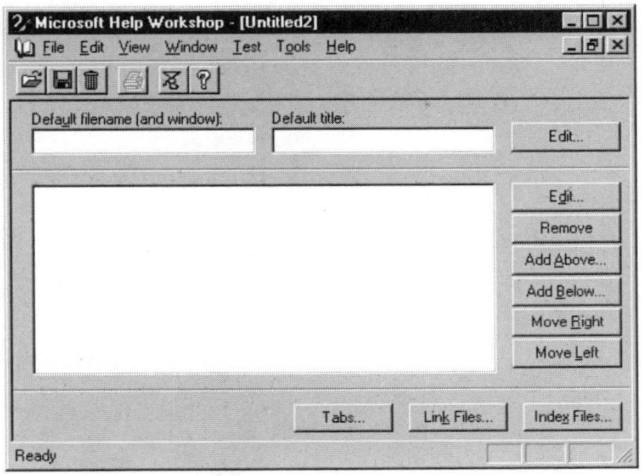

FIGURE 21.20.

The contents file interface in Help Workshop.

WinHelp supports a heading depth up to nine levels. You can change heading levels easily by selecting the heading that you want to promote or demote and then clicking the Move Right and Move Left buttons. All of the heading's subheadings and topics are migrated appropriately when you promote or demote a heading.

If you want to include the contents of additional contents files in your primary contents file, simply add them at the appropriate insertion point using the Add Above and Add Below buttons. Additional contents files are not displayed on the help file Contents tab if they are not present when WinHelp initializes the help file. If you specify a default help filename in the additional contents files, the default settings in those files remain local to that contents file and do not affect the primary contents file's default help file setting.

When several help files are listed in one contents file, they are automatically searched anytime an ALink or a KLink macro is run. If you want to create ALink or KLink links to other help files that are not included in the primary help file Index Files text box, you simply add their filenames using the LinkFiles button. For further information on keywords and ALink and KLink macros, see the "Keywords" section earlier in this chapter.

If you want to translate your contents file to offer localized support, check Translation under the File menu, open the contents file that you want to translate, and use the Edit command to change any headings or topics that you want to translate.

Adding New Custom Tabs to the Help Topics Dialog Box

To add new custom tabs to the Help Topics dialog box, you have to have a DLL file that specifies the dialog procedures that will be used with the new tab.

You do this by opening the contents file that you wish to customize with Help Workshop, selecting the Tabs button, and then specifying the desired information, as shown in Figure 21.21 and Figure 21.22.

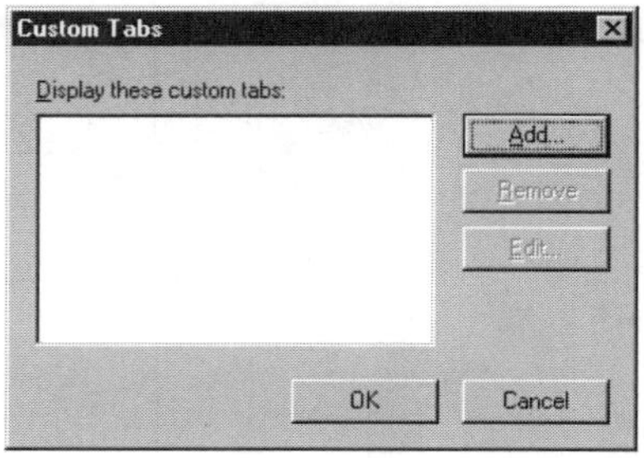

Figure 21.21.

The Custom Tabs dialog box.

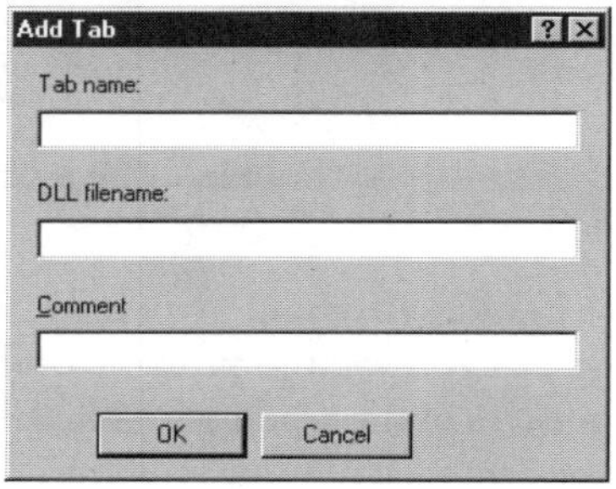

Figure 21.22.

The Add Tab dialog box, which pops up when you select the Add button in the Custom Tabs window.

Step 5: Compiling Your Help File

Compiling is the final step in creating your help file. The compile process takes your topic files, project files, and contents files and builds a finished help file application. Calling this a "help file application" is not inappropriate because it is characteristically similar to any other application that has to be designed, built, tested, and compiled. The process is simple and straightforward.

Save all your component files before compiling to ensure that you have a good backup of the core files in case something goes wrong in the compile process and there is resulting damage. The help file compiler is available by selecting Compile… under the File menu in Help Workshop, or by clicking on the Save and Compile button at the bottom of the Help Workshop window. The project file does not have to be open for you to compile it. If the project file is open, the Save and Compile button is available. See Figures 21.23 and 21.24.

FIGURE 21.23.

Click the Save and Compile button to compile the selected project file into a help file, or select the Compile... option under the File menu.

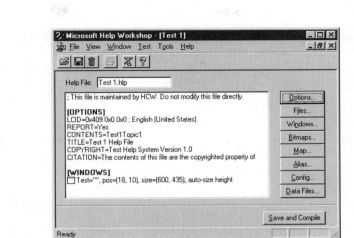

FIGURE 21.24.

The Help Workshop help file compile options window.

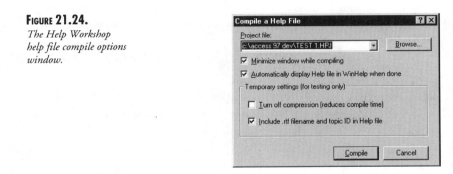

The compile options you can specify in the help compiler and in your project window are as follows:

■ Temporary File Storage—Help Workshop uses the temporary directory that you specify through the project file's Options menu, regardless of your TEMP system environment setting.

■ Specify Topics to Compile Into Help File—You specify the build tags for your topics in the project file in the Build Tags tab in the Options dialog box. Only topics that contain the build tags that you specify are included in the build. All topics containing a build tag that is in the Exclude field are excluded from the build.

■ Index File Generation—This setting tells Help Workshop whether to generate a full text search index. The Index File Generation setting can be changed under the Options menu of the project file. Compression must always be applied when generating a full text search index. If you do not generate a full text search index, the user is prompted to do so when he attempts to search the help file.

- Font Setting Changes—This allows you to change the font in a help file without having to make the font change in each of your topics. The Font Setting Changes setting can be changed under the Options menu in the project file.

- Source File Path Changes—This provides a simple way to change all the file paths if you have to relocate the project. The Source File Path Changes setting is made under the Options menu in the project file.

- Second-Level Index Entry Identifier Changes—This provides a simple way to change all the file paths if you have to relocate the project. The Second-Level Index Entry Identifier Changes setting is made under the Options menu in the project file. Although the comma (,) and the colon (:) are the default characters used in index sorting, Help Workshop will use whichever character you specify.

- Compression—This reduces the size of the help file to aid in distribution, but increases the compile time significantly.

- Suppress Compiler Messages—This prevents the compiler from displaying progress notes while compiling. You make the Suppress Compiler Messages setting under the project file's Options menu.

- Saving Compile Messages to a File—Help Workshop will store the progress message files in the log file that you specify in the project file Options menu.

If you want to compile more than one help file at a time, you need to create an ASCII text file that lists the full path of each project file that you want to compile, on separate lines and in the order in which you want to compile the help files. Save this file with an *.hmk extension. Then select Compile… from the File menu and specify the *.hmk file that you created as the project file to be compiled in the compiler options window that pops up. Help Workshop recognizes this as a compile list file and begins compiling the help files one after another, just as they are listed.

You can then view your compiled help files by choosing Run WinHelp… from the File menu and specifying the name of the file to be viewed. If it is a help file whose topic IDs have been mapped to numeric values in their project files, you will need to enter the path and filename for the project file and click the Refresh button to load the numeric values into the WinHelp queue. Then click the View Help button and display your help file, as shown in Figure 21.25.

Help Workshop gives you the ability to generate a report on your help file by selecting Report from the File menu and entering the name of the help file you want to see a report on in the Help Filename text box. You also need to specify the report output file for the results. Enter the desired name and path into the Output Filename text box. In Figure 21.26, you can see how to tell Help Workshop which help file to generate a report on and specify the information you want the report to display. Figure 21.27 shows a sample report generated on the file named Unimdm.hlp by Help Workshop.

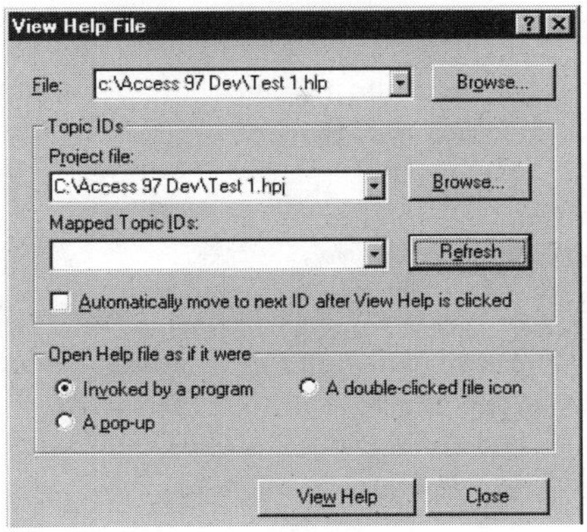

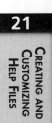

FIGURE 21.25.

The WinHelp help file viewer interface.

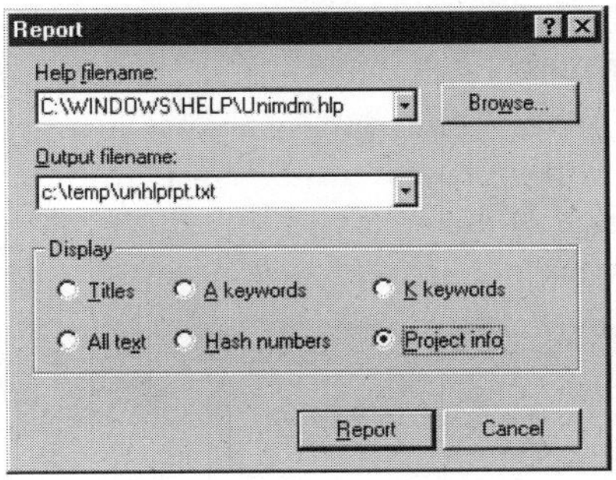

FIGURE 21.26.

The Help Workshop help file report interface.

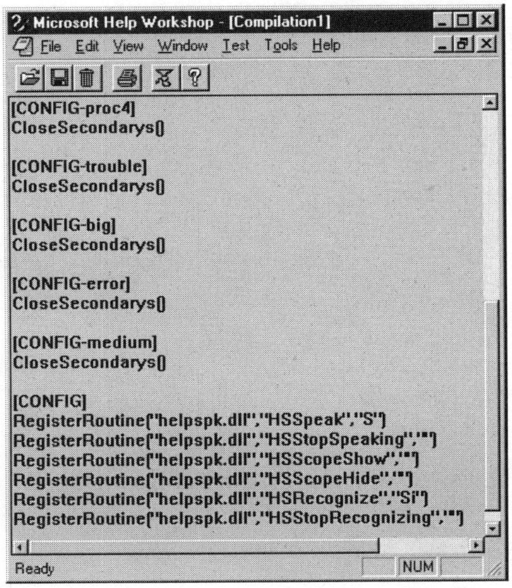

FIGURE 21.27.

A sample report generated by Help Workshop, showing the project file information for the file Unimdm.hlp.

Testing Your Help File

Help Workshop has some important help file component test functions built in that will enable you to test and debug your help application.

This part of the compile process should always be carried out prior to distribution.

TIP

It is a good idea to maintain copies of your help file and its components during each stage of the development and compile process. This is a manual form of source code version control that gives you the ability to roll back your project to a previous state if you encounter any difficult errors after making changes.

Testing Your Contents Files

Help Workshop can test your contents file for correct syntax usage and proper linking. When you tell Help Workshop to test a file, it will automatically analyze all the syntax for proper form and then locate all the links and actually test the physical jumps between topics and files to make sure there are no errors.

NOTE

Before you tell Help Workshop to test a contents file, make sure that all the specified links, including any that are in additional contents files, are included in the tested file. If the linked files or topics that are in the additional contents files are not available, Help Workshop will generate an error.

Testing the contents file is relatively easy. Just make sure that all the needed files are available, and then enter the name in the contents file's test window, which is available from the Test menu. This menu appears when you click on the Test button, as seen in Figure 21.28.

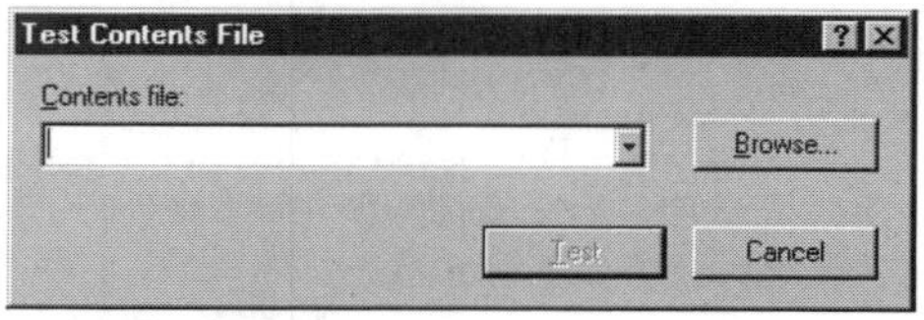

FIGURE 21.28.
The Test Contents File dialog box.

This is one of the most important test functions that you should complete prior to final distribution.

Creating and Customizing Help Files

CHAPTER 21

603

21

CREATING AND
CUSTOMIZING
HELP FILES

Simulating WinHelp API Program Calls

Simulating WinHelp API program calls is easily accomplished by selecting WinHelp API from the Test menu, which brings up the dialog box shown in Figure 21.29. Enter the path and filename of the file that you want to test, select the command and command value that you want to send in the API, and then click Call.

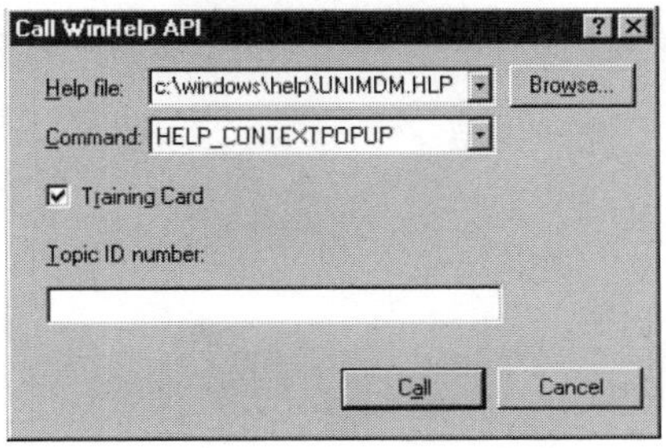

FIGURE 21.29.
The Call WinHelp API dialog box.

Other WinHelp Test Functions

WinHelp allows you to monitor an assortment of WinHelp messages by selecting WinHelp Messages from the Help Workshop View menu, as shown in Figure 21.30, and then selecting Message Options from the View menu.

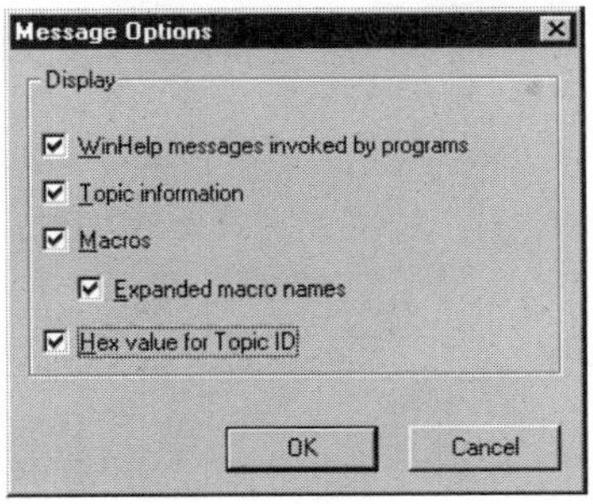

FIGURE 21.30.
The WinHelp Message Options dialog box.

If you are testing help files and loaded instances of WinHelp are causing problems, you might want to unload all active WinHelp events.

You do this by clicking the Close All Help button under the Help Workshop Test menu.

Summary

The Help Workshop development tool greatly simplifies and speeds up the help file development process. The possible exception to this is that in the past, many developers chose to include simple, single-facet help files for their applications, and now they have the tools to create complex help systems that can add significant value to their products. Instead of including simple help text files or basic help for forms, reports, or controls, Help Workshop developers might be inclined to add a new dimension to their application development strategy: including a sophisticated user help and tutorial environment.

Security and Multiuser Development

VIII

PART

Security

by Brad Darragh

IN THIS CHAPTER

CHAPTER 22

This chapter describes how security in Access 97 works and how to implement it in real-world situations. First, the major components of Access security are examined, and I discuss how they relate to each other. Next, the methods of manipulating security using the Security Wizard, the Access user interface, and code are discussed. The last part of this chapter describes how to use Access security to protect your code from unauthorized changes and how to protect your intellectual property from being copied.

Security Basics

This section covers the major components of Access security. A good understanding of how these components work and how to manipulate them will make the task of protecting your database easier.

Turning on Security

One of the most common questions that I am asked about security is, "How do I turn on Access security?" The answer is that Access security is always turned on.

Admin User Account

When you installed Access, one of the things that the setup program did was to create a user account called Admin. This user account is universal to all installations of Access. Initially the password is set to nothing (a zero-length string " ").

When you start Microsoft Access, it tries to log on with Admin and assumes that the password is blank. Normally, this part of the startup process works, and you would then be prompted to open or create a database.

Changing Passwords

Let's say you want to change the password for the Admin user account. After you start Access, click the Cancel button in the database window. Then select Tools | Security | User and Group Accounts and click on the Change Logon Password tab. You should see a dialog box similar to the one in Figure 22.1.

Leave the Old Password field blank, type your new password in the New Password and Verify fields, click OK, and shut down Access.

WARNING

All passwords are case sensitive.

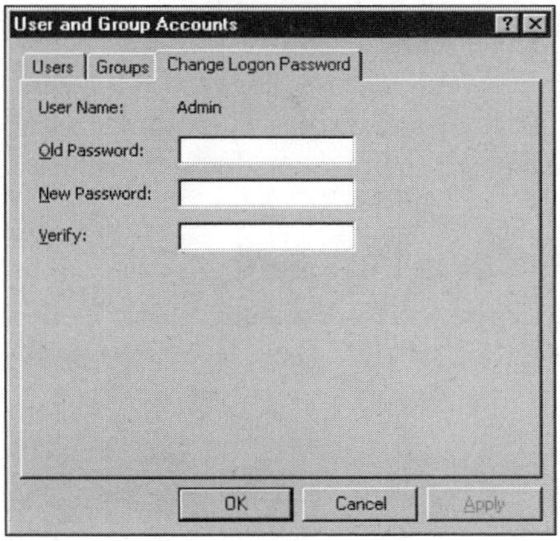

FIGURE 22.1.

This dialog box allows you to change the password for the Admin user account.

Logging On to the System

When you startup Access, it cannot automatically complete the normal startup process because the Admin user account now has a password. It will then prompt you to enter the password for Admin by displaying the dialog box shown in Figure 22.2.

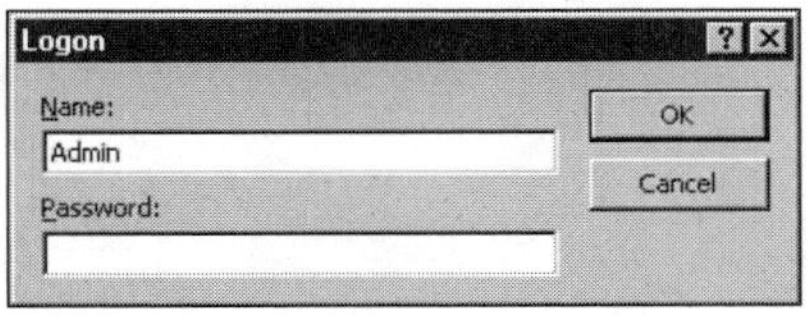

FIGURE 22.2.

The Logon dialog box.

Incorrect Password

If you enter an incorrect password, you will see a dialog box similar to the one in Figure 22.3. This dialog box may seem a little confusing. You know that Admin is a valid user account. So why doesn't the dialog box just say that the password is wrong?

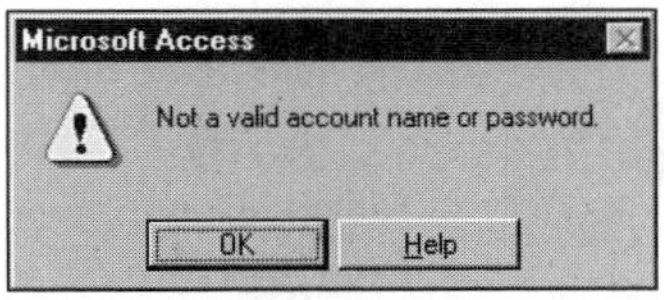

FIGURE 22.3.

The dialog box displayed when an incorrect user account or password is entered.

The message is worded this way to prevent someone from breaking into your database by identifying any valid user accounts. If someone knew the user account that created a protected database, he could create a program to repetitively try a series of passwords until he finds the correct one and breaks into your system. By not identifying whether it is the user account name or password that is incorrect, the possibility of breaking into a database is reduced.

Database Password

The capability to create a database password was a new feature introduced in Access 95. This is one of the simplest ways to restrict who can open your database. When this password is set, it makes the database virtually impossible to open unless you enter the correct password.

Setting the Database Password

To set the database password, select Tools | Security | Set Database Password, and a dialog box like the one in Figure 22.4 will appear. Enter the password twice to verify it.

FIGURE 22.4.
Setting the database password.

By setting this password, the next time anyone tries to open this database, a dialog box (similar to the one in Figure 22.5) will be displayed, asking for the database password. If the password is correct, the database will open.

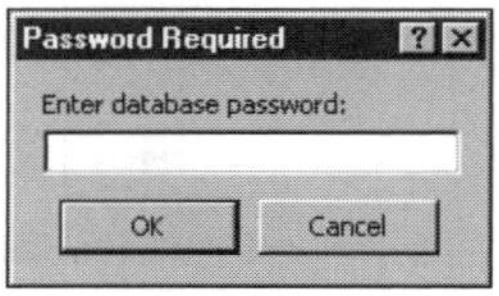

FIGURE 22.5.
Enter the database password.

NOTE

Database passwords can be up to 14 characters long and are case sensitive. They are stored as an encrypted string in the `.mdb` file where they were created.

Unsetting the Database Password

If you want to unset a database password, select Tools | Security | Unset Database Password, and enter the current database password. If the password you entered is correct, the old database password is erased.

NOTE

In order to set or unset the database password, a database must be opened exclusively.

Access 97 Security Model

A database password is suitable if you want to allow only a certain number of users to open a database. However, once the database is open, they will have full control over it. Another type of security is called user-level security.

But before I describe what user-level security is, let me quickly describe the more traditional security methods that other database engines use, namely share-level security.

Share-Level Security

For example, suppose you have a table called `Sales`, and you want to grant read-only access to it to the Operations department for reporting purposes. At the same time, you also want to grant read/write access to the Sales department. In a share-level environment, there would be one password for read-only access and a different password for read/write access.

The problem with this is it makes changing passwords very difficult because every time a password is changed, you must notify all the users of the change. The problem is compounded if there are numerous tables, which means numerous passwords.

User-Level Security

User-level security, which Access uses, centers around authenticating users rather than allowing anyone with the correct password to read or write to a table, form, report, query, macro, or module.

For example, let's use the same `Sales` table example. When you start Access, you log on with a valid user account and the matching password. If you attempt to read the `Sales` table, Access looks at the permissions associated with the table and determines whether your user account, or any of the group accounts that your user account is a member of, has at least read permission. If so, you will be able to read the table. If not, a dialog box similar to Figure 22.6 will appear.

Figure 22.6.

Read-permission-denied dialog box.

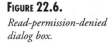

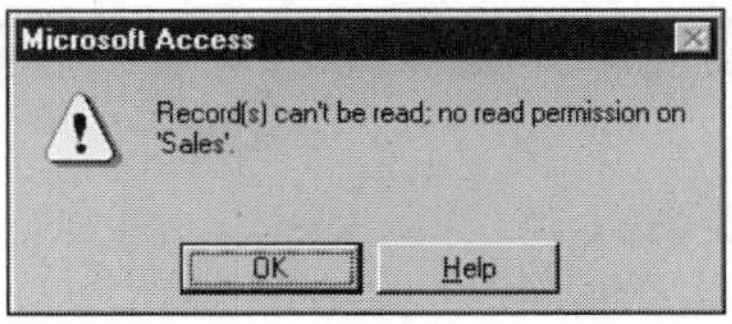

The point is that as a user of the system, you only have to remember your own password. You can even change your own password, and it will not affect any of your permissions. The administrator of the database simply tells Access what kind of permission, if any, all the user or group accounts have to all, some, or none of the objects in that Access database.

Securing Objects

When you create a new database, the user account logged on at that time (usually Admin) becomes the owner of that database. As the owner, you have complete control over all the tables, queries, forms, reports, macros, and modules (database objects) contained in that database. You also have control over who has access to these objects, even the database itself.

For example, let's say you want to restrict the access to the `Sales` table in your database so that only the Operations group account has read access. To do this, select Tools | Security | User and Group Permissions. You will see a dialog box similar to the one in Figure 22.7.

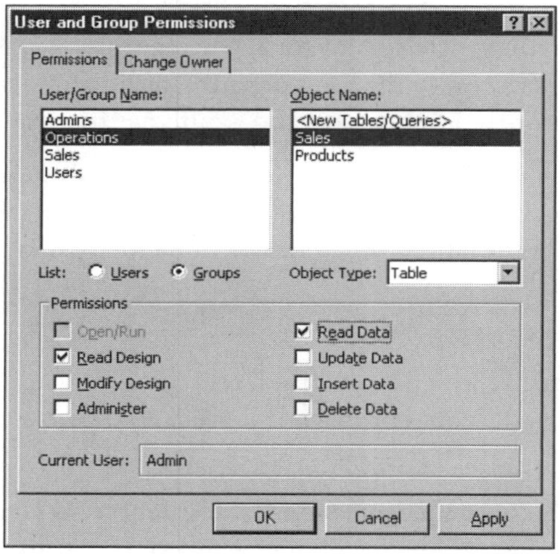

FIGURE 22.7.

User and Group Permissions dialog box.

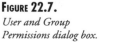

By clicking the Read Data checkbox while the Operations group account is highlighted, you effectively grant any user account that is a member of the Operations group account read access to the `Sales` table.

NOTE

You will notice that as you click the Read Data checkbox, the Read Design checkbox will also be checked. This is because in order to read a table, either by a report object, form object, or simply by displaying it in datasheet mode, Access needs to know the datatypes of all the fields in that table.

To emphasize these types of implied permissions, click the Administer checkbox. You will immediately notice that all permissions suddenly become checked. Obviously, if you have Administer permission on a particular object, you need all these permissions.

A detailed description of all access permissions is provided later in this chapter.

User and Group Accounts

You create new user and group accounts by selecting Tools | Security | User and Group Accounts. After clicking the New button on either the Users or Groups tab, you will see a dialog box like the one in Figure 22.8.

FIGURE 22.8.
This dialog box prompts you to enter a name and personal identifier.

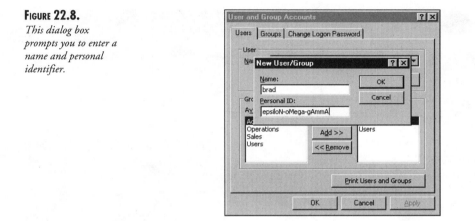

Enter the name of the new user or group along with a personal identifier (PID). The PID is used to ensure the uniqueness of the new account. Together, the name and PID are used to create a system identifier (SID). The SID is a 128-bit number that Access uses to uniquely identify all user and group accounts.

> **NOTE**
>
> User or group account names are not case sensitive, but personal identifiers (PIDs) are. As in the previous example, it is good practice to use unique PIDs with both upper- and lowercase letters.

> **NOTE**
>
> After you create a new user account, the password is set to a zero-length string. Be sure to set passwords for all new user accounts; otherwise, a user could log on to Access with this user account by simply leaving the password blank.

The Workgroup File

The workgroup file is where all user and group accounts, passwords, SIDs, and the relationship between these accounts, are stored.

All workgroup files are actually Access databases with special tables and queries, and they typically have the .MDW file extension. When Access is installed, a default workgroup file called SYSTEM.MDW is created. You can open this file just like any other Access database.

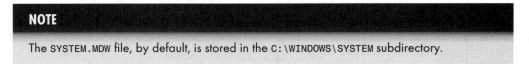

NOTE

The SYSTEM.MDW file, by default, is stored in the C:\WINDOWS\SYSTEM subdirectory.

User and group accounts are stored in a table called MSYSAccounts. Figure 22.9 illustrates the data that is contained in the MSYSAccounts table of a newly created SYSTEM.MDW.

FIGURE 22.9.

A sample MSYSAccount table.

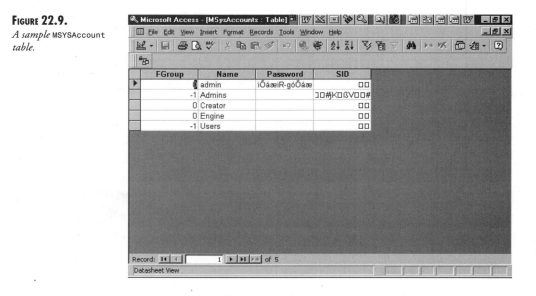

TIP

MSYSAccount is a system object, and all system objects do not appear in the database window by default. You can allow system objects to appear in the database window by selecting Tools | Options from the menu bar and clicking the System Objects checkbox.

As you can see, the MSYSAccounts table is a relatively simple table of four fields and five records. The field names of this table are described in Table 22.1.

Table 22.1. The MSYSAccount table.

Field name	Description
Fgroup	A Yes/No field indicating whether the account is a group account (-1) or a user account (0).
Name	An alphanumeric representation of the object.
Password	A 128-bit number representing the alphanumeric password for this object.
SID	Short for system identifier, this field identifies the object as a 128-bit number.

You will notice that there are three user accounts. The Admin user account is the default user that is used when Access is started, as discussed earlier. Creator and Engine are special user accounts that are used by the system and cannot be used to log on.

You also will notice that the only user account that seems to have a password is the Admin user account. Because Creator and Engine are used strictly by the system and cannot be used to log on, they do not need passwords.

So why does Admin seem to have a password when we know that the password is a zero-length string ("")? The reason is because even a zero-length string has a 128-bit representation.

The two other accounts (Admins and Users) are group accounts. Group accounts do not need a password because you cannot use them to log on anyway.

Before leaving the workgroup file, you may have also noticed the SID column and observed that all the SIDs ("") seem to be the same except for the Admin group account. The SIDs for the Admin, Creator, and Engine user accounts, and the Users group account are the same for all installations of Access. This allows you to create a database on one machine, and open it on another. All user accounts must belong to at least one group account. That account is the Users group account. So if you were to assign permissions to the user account for a particular database, you could then use Access on a different machine with a different workgroup file to open that database and still have it function the same way.

The Admins group account has a different SID for the opposite reason. Every workgroup has an Admins group, and the system is designed to allow any users that belong to the Admins group to have full access to a database. However, because the SID for each workgroup is different, a user on a different machine with a different workgroup file does not have full access to a database.

The Workgroup Administrator

So how does Access ensure that the SID for each Admins group account is unique? The answer is the Workgroup Administrator (WRKGADM.EXE) program.

This program is used to create new workgroup files or change to another existing one. It comes with Access and is stored in the C:\Windows\System subdirectory.

When you run the Workgroup Administrator program, a dialog box like the one in Figure 22.10 will appear.

FIGURE 22.10.

The Workgroup Administrator dialog box.

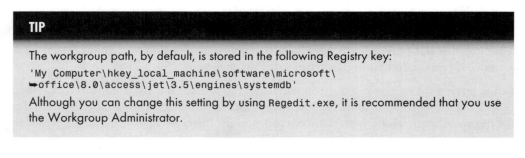

From this dialog box, you have the option of either creating a new workgroup file or joining an existing one. This dialog also displays the name, company, and current workgroup path stored in the Windows Registry.

TIP

The workgroup path, by default, is stored in the following Registry key:

`'My Computer\hkey_local_machine\software\microsoft\`
`➥office\8.0\access\jet\3.5\engines\systemdb'`

Although you can change this setting by using `Regedit.exe`, it is recommended that you use the Workgroup Administrator.

Creating a New Workgroup

When you select the Create button from the Workgroup Administrator, a dialog box like the one in Figure 22.11 will appear. This dialog box will prompt you for three pieces of information: your name, organization, and a workgroup ID.

This is how the Workgroup Administrator uses these three pieces of information to create a unique SID for the Admins group account for the new workgroup file that you are creating.

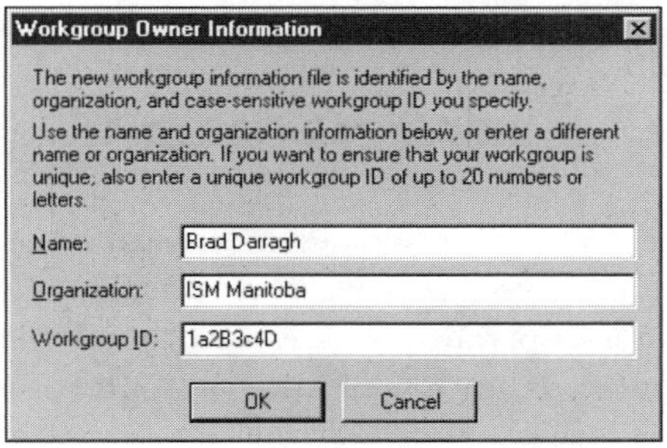

FIGURE 22.11.

The Workgroup Owner Information dialog box.

TIP

It is extremely important that you record and store the name, company (organization), and workgroup ID for all your workgroup files in a safe, secure place. If a workgroup file becomes corrupt, you will need this information in order to recreate the workgroup file. If you cannot recreate this workgroup file, you may potentially be locked out of your own database and never get back in.

Joining an Existing Workgroup

To join an existing workgroup, click the Join button from the Workgroup Administrator window (refer to Figure 22.10). A dialog box like the one in Figure 22.12 will appear and prompt you for a valid workgroup file. Once you select the file, Access will indicate that you successfully joined the new workgroup.

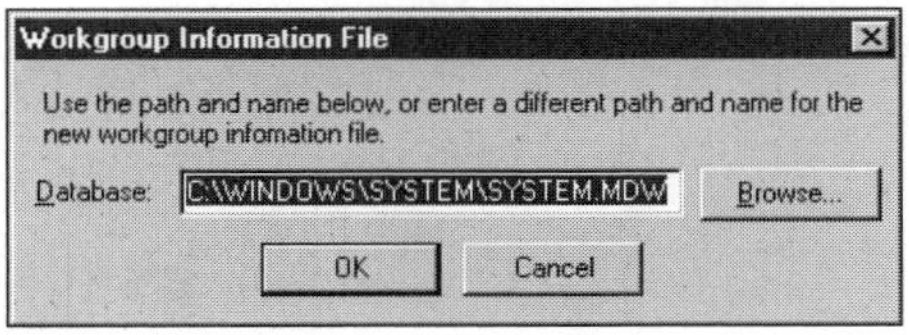

FIGURE 22.12.

Selecting an existing workgroup file.

Object Permissions

As explained earlier in this chapter, there are basically two group accounts (Admins and Users) and one user account (Admin) that are created and stored in the SYSTEM.MDW workgroup file when you first install Access.

When you change permissions for objects in your database, that information is stored directly in the database, not the workgroup file that is in use.

Both user and group accounts can have permissions to objects in a database. If you grant a user account access to a table, that user can access that table. However, if a user account does not have access to a table, but the Users group account has access to it, that user account can still access it.

This is because when a user account attempts to access an object, Access looks to see if that user account has permission to that object. If it does, Access opens the object in the normal manner. If it does not have permission, Access will check all the group accounts of which the user account is a member. If any one of these accounts has access to the object, the user account assumes the same permissions.

Assigning and Removing Permissions

Assigning and removing permissions for a database and for database objects is a key part of security. The following sections discuss ways that this can be accomplished.

The User Interface

The user interface method is the easiest and most common way to assign permissions. As shown previously in this chapter, by selecting Tools | Security | User and Group Permissions and clicking the Permissions tab, a dialog box with list boxes, similar to the ones in Figure 22.13, will appear.

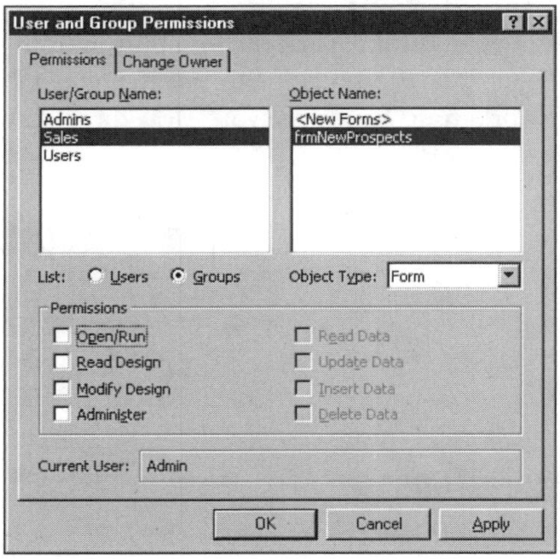

FIGURE 22.13.

The User and Group Permissions dialog box.

By selecting the Sales group and `frmNewProspects` form, you will see all the permissions that are available as well as the ones that are selected. Permissions that are dimmed are not applicable to the type of object selected. In this case, the Read Data, Update Data, Insert Data, and Delete Data permissions are dimmed because they apply only to table and query objects. You also will notice that there are no permissions for the Sales group for this particular form.

Table 22.2 lists all the permissions that are available for databases and database objects, along with a description of each permission.

Table 22.2. Permissions for databases and database objects.

Object	Permission	Description
Database	Open/Run	Open a database.
	Open Exclusive	Open a database exclusively.
	Administer	Set or unset a database password, change database startup properties, and replicate a database.
Table	Read Design	Open in Design View but not allowed to save changes.
	Modify Design	Open in Design View and allowed to save changes.
	Administer	Complete access to this object.
	Read Data	Read records only.
	Update Data	Modify records only.
	Insert Data	Insert records only.
	Delete Data	Delete records only.
Query	Read Design	Open in Design View but not allowed to save changes.
	Modify Design	Open in Design View and allowed to save changes.
	Administer	Complete access to this object.
	Read Data	Read records only.
	Update Data	Modify records only.
	Insert Data	Insert records only.
	Delete Data	Delete records only.
Form	Open/Run	Open in Form View only.
	Read Design	Open in Design View but not allowed to save changes.
	Modify Design	Open in Design View and allowed to save changes.
	Administer	Complete access to this object.
Report	Open/Run	Open in Report View only.
	Read Design	Open in Design View but not allowed to save changes.

continues

22

SECURITY

Table 22.2. continued

Object	Permission	Description
	Modify Design	Open in Design View and allowed to save changes.
	Administer	Complete access to this object.
Macro	Open/Run	Run this macro.
	Read Design	Open in Design View but not allowed to save changes.
	Modify Design	Open in Design View and allowed to save changes.
	Administer	Complete access to this object.
Module	Read Design	Open in Design View but not allowed to save changes.
	Modify Design	Open in Design View and allowed to save changes.
	Administer	Complete access to this object.

> **TIP**
>
> Always try to assign permissions for databases and database objects at a group account level rather than a user account level. It is much easier and good maintenance practice to assign, for example, the Sales group permission to read a table rather than selecting each user account within that group and assigning the permission.

VBA Code

The VBA programming method of assigning and removing permissions requires a certain level of skill but is very useful in tailoring security to fit certain situations.

Granting Open/Run Permission to a Group for a Form

For example, let's say I want to allow the Sales group to run a form called `frmNewProspects` that I just created. I want to allow them to open the form but not necessarily to open it in Design View. To programmatically change the permissions for the form, I could use the function shown in Listing 22.1.

Listing 22.1. The `AllowFormOpen()` function.

```
Function AllowFormOpen(sFormName$, sGroup$)
Dim db As Database
Dim doc As Document
```

```
Set db = CurrentDb
Set doc = db.Containers!Forms.Documents(sFormName)
doc.UserName = sGroup
doc.Permissions = doc.Permissions Or acSecFrmRptExecute
Set doc = Nothing
Set db = Nothing
End Function
```

As you can see, the code is not very complex (only eight lines). Here's what's happening.

The first four lines set up a database and document object. The database object (`db`) is simply pointing to the active database. The document object (`doc`) is pointing to the form `frmNewProspects`, which is what I passed as the variable `sFormName`. I then say that for the Sales group (`sGroupName`), I want to grant Open/Run permission (`acSecFrmRptExecute`). Notice the `OR` in the statement. This adds the permission that is to the right of the `OR` to the existing permissions that this group already has.

You can check to see if this function worked by selecting Tools | Security | User and Group Permissions and selecting the `frmNewProspects` form. The Open/Run option should be checked.

Removing an Open/Run Permission for a Form

You remove permission from an object virtually the same way, as in Listing 22.2.

Listing 22.2. The `DisallowFormOpen()` function.

```
Function DisallowFormOpen(sFormName$, sGroup$)
Dim db As Database
Dim doc As Document
Set db = CurrentDb
Set doc = db.Containers!Forms.Documents(sFormName)
doc.UserName = sGroup
doc.Permissions = doc.Permissions And Not acSecFrmRptExecute
Set doc = Nothing
Set db = Nothing
End Function
```

The only difference in this code is where the permissions are set, or in this case, where they are not set. This line of code assigns to the group specified by `sGroup` all the permissions that it already had, except for `acSecFrmRptExecute` permissions.

Now, you may be asking yourself, "Where is he getting constants like `acSecFrmRptExecute` from?" Access comes with a standard set of security constants. They are listed in Table 22.3, along with a brief explanation of what they are. For the sake of readability and maintenance, I strongly suggest that you use these constants rather than using the decimal values.

22

SECURITY

Table 22.3. Constants used to set the permissions property.

Security Constant	Decimal Value	Description
acSecFrmRptExecute	256	Allows users or groups to open a form or report in Form/Report View.
acSecFrmRptReadDef	4	Allows users or groups to open a form or report in Design View but does not allow them to make or save changes to that object.
acSecFrmRptWriteDef	65548	Allows users or groups to open a form or report in Design View and allows them to make or save changes to that object.
acSecMacExecute	8	Allows users or groups to run a macro object.
acSecMacReadDef	10	Allows users or groups to open a macro in Design View but does not allow them to make or save changes to that object.
acSecMacWriteDef	65542	Allows users or groups to open a macro in Design View and allows them to make or save changes to that object.
acSecModReadDef	2	Allows users or groups to open a module in Design View but does not allow them to make or save changes to that object.
acSecModWriteDef	65542	Allows users or groups to open a module in Design View and allows them to make or save changes to that object.
dbSecCreate	1	Allows users or groups to create new database objects.
dbSecDBAdmin	8	Allows users or groups to replicate a database or change a database password.
DbSecDBCreate	1	Allows users or groups to create new databases.
dbSecDBExclusive	4	Allows users or groups to open a database exclusively.
dbSecDBOpen	2	Allows users or groups to open a database.
dbSecDelete	65536	Allows users or groups to delete a database object.
dbSecDeleteData	128	Allows users or groups to delete records in a table or query object.

Security Constant	Decimal Value	Description
dbSecFullAccess	1048575	Allows users or groups to have full access to a database object.
dbSecInsertData	32	Allows users or groups to insert records into a table or query object.
dbSecNoAccess	0	Allows users or groups to have no access to a database object.
dbSecReadSec	131072	Allows users or groups to read security-related information for a database object.
dbSecReadDef	4	Allows users or groups to open a table or query in Design View but does not allow them to make or save changes to that object.
dbSecReplaceData	64	Allows users or groups to modify records in a table or query object.
dbSecRetrieveData	20	Allows users or groups to read records in a table or query object.
dbSecWriteDef	65548	Allows users or groups to open a table or query in Design View and allows them to make or save changes to that object.
dbSecWriteOwner	524288	Allows users or groups to change the owner of a database object.
dbSecWriteSec	262144	Allows users or groups to change access permissions for a database object.

Implementing Access 97 Security

Now that I have explained some of the basics of Access security, before I get too deep into the implementation of it, I want to spend a little time on some shortcuts that I use to shorten the amount of time it takes to test whether security is working the way I want it to. I am talking about the use of command-line switches.

Command-Line Switches

The only way to ensure that the security you set up for your database works the way you want is to log on to the various user accounts that will be using the system.

Some very useful command-line switches make the process of shutting down Access, restarting, and logging on with a different user account less tedious and error prone. Table 22.4 lists the command-line switches that you normally would use during testing.

22

SECURITY

Table 22.4. Useful security command-line switches.

Switch	Description
/excl	Opens the selected database exclusively.
/user	Starts Access with the specified user account.
/pwd	Starts Access with the specified password.
/wrkgrp	Starts Access with the specified workgroup file.

Some examples of these command-line switches are as follows:

- Open Access Database with user account jpicard

  `"C:\Program Files\Microsoft Office\Office\MSACCESS.EXE" "C:\My Documents\Sams Publishing\Security Examples.mdb" /user jpicard /pwd`

  Because the user account jpicard has a zero-length string (`""`) for a password, there is no parameter after /pwd.

- Open Access Database with user account Admin exclusively

  `"C:\Program Files\Microsoft Office\Office\MSACCESS.EXE" "C:\My Documents\Sams Publishing\Security Examples.mdb" /user Admin /pwd ORANGE /excl`

> **NOTE**
>
> It is important to include the path to Access (`"C:\Program Files\Microsoft Office\Office\MSACCESS.EXE"`). If this portion of the command line is omitted from your shortcut, Access will start, but the Logon dialog box will appear.

The Security Wizard

The Security Wizard that comes with Access speeds up the process of securing an unsecured database. Whenever a new database is created, the owner of the database and all of the database objects (tables, queries, forms, reports, macros, and modules) is the user account that was active at the time the database was created. In most cases, that user account is the Admin user account.

Access security is based on the rule that the owner of a database or database object has full permission to that object, regardless of whether or not all permissions have been removed. In other words, if Admin is the owner of a database or database object and you remove all permissions from Admin for that object, Admin still will have an implied permission for that object because it is the owner.

Because the Admin user account's SID is the same for every installation of Access, the owner of the database and all of its objects must be changed to a different user account; otherwise, these objects will remain unprotected, whether the Admin user account is removed from the Admins group account or not.

Therefore, the key to securing a database and all of its objects is first to change the owner. The best way to do this is to import all the objects that you want to be secured into another database while you are logged on to the user account that you want to be the owner. In essence, you are creating a new database with a user account other than Admin.

TIP

To ensure that the user account that will become the new owner of the database and all its objects has the authority to export these objects, grant the Users group account Administer permission for all database objects in the database.

NOTE

There is another way to change the owner of a database object. By selecting Tools | Security | User and Group Permissions and then selecting the Change Owner tab, you can select the object you want and change the owner to either a user or group account.

However, you cannot change the owner of the database itself. If you select Database from the Object Type drop-down list, you will notice that the Change Owner button is dimmed. Even if a user account does not own a particular object, or have permissions for it, it can grant itself permission for that object because it owns the database that contains the permission.

Therefore, it is better to use the Security Wizard, to change the owner of the database.

When you select Tools | Security | User-Level Security Wizard, a dialog box similar to the one in 22.14 appears.

FIGURE 22.14.

The User-Level Security Wizard dialog box.

This screen displays who the current user is and also displays the workgroup file that is currently in use. You can select the objects that are to be imported into the new database as well. For this example, I want to import all the objects into the new database, so all the checkboxes should be selected.

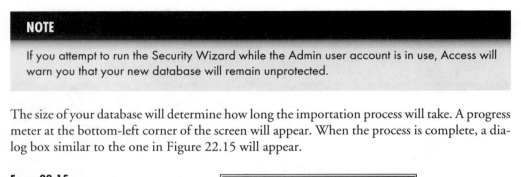

NOTE

If you attempt to run the Security Wizard while the Admin user account is in use, Access will warn you that your new database will remain unprotected.

The size of your database will determine how long the importation process will take. A progress meter at the bottom-left corner of the screen will appear. When the process is complete, a dialog box similar to the one in Figure 22.15 will appear.

FIGURE 22.15.
User-Level Security Wizard summary information.

In this example, the Brad user account is the owner of the database Brads Database.mdb and all its objects. However, all user accounts that are part of the Admins group also have permissions for this database, namely the Admin user account. The final step in protecting this database is to remove the Admin user account from the Admins group account and set the password to Admin.

Now if someone sits in front of your machine and tries to open Brads Database.mdb, Access will prompt the user for a logon password because the Admin user account is password protected. Even if he was able to enter the correct password, he still wouldn't get in because Admin is no longer a part of the Admins group account and therefore does not have any permissions for this database. A dialog box similar to the one in Figure 22.16 will appear.

FIGURE 22.16.
The database access-denied dialog box.

Restricting Access at the Object and Record Levels

Database objects, such as tables, queries, forms, reports, macros, and modules, can be protected in various ways. Permissions can vary from most restrictive (no access at all) to least restrictive (administer rights over the object). This is adequate for when you want to protect objects, but what if you want to restrict access at a record level?

For example, let's say you have a Sales table that contains records from four different sales regions, and you want to allow the managers for each of these regions to access the information. You could grant the managers permission to the Sales table, but then each manager could see the information of the other region.

The other alternative is to deny all access to the Sales table and create four queries against it. Each query would return records from the table for a specific region. You would then grant permission for each of these queries to the associated manager.

Each manager would be able to read or update the records that they are responsible for, yet all the information from all four regions can be stored in one place.

The Run Permissions Property

If you want to give access only to certain fields or records in a table, the Run Permissions property is important. Obviously, it's an all or nothing situation when granting permission to a table. If permission to read the table is granted, the user can read all fields and records in that table.

However, the alternative is to create a view of the table. To do this, remove all permissions from the table for all user and group accounts. Next, create a new query against the table and select only the fields and records that you want to display. Change the Run Permissions property from User's to Owner's, as shown in Figure 22.17. Save the query, grant read-only permission for the Users group account, and remove all other permissions.

Now restart Access and log on with a different user account (something other than the owner of the database). Try to open the table. You should get a dialog box saying that you do not have permission. Now try to open the query you just created. You should be successful, but you will be able to see only the fields that you selected, and you will not be able to change the records.

FIGURE 22.17.

The Run Permissions *property.*

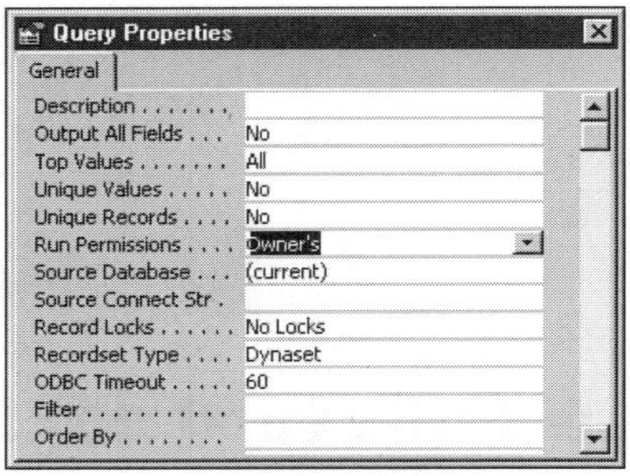

Here is an explanation of what is happening. First, you obviously can't open and read that table because the user account does not have permission and is not the owner of the table. However, you do have permission to open the query. This is because you set the Run Permissions property of the query to Owner's, which tells Access that anyone that has permission to this query has complete access to all tables and queries in the database. However, you restricted the permissions for the query to read-only. This allows you to view, but not change, any records.

> **NOTE**
>
> Only the owner of the query can set the Run Permissions property, and only the owner can save changes to the query.

> **NOTE**
>
> Do not grant Administer or Modify Design permissions to queries that have the Run Permissions property set to Owner's. An unscrupulous user could open the query in Design View, change it so he could look at any table or query, and view your data (assuming that the owner of the query has access to the table and query).

Database Encryption

User-level security controls how users open and view the objects in your Access database, but there is one other aspect that must be considered. Your database is just like any other file. In essence, it is a bunch of bytes arranged in a logical order. Nothing can prevent a user from opening your database using Microsoft Word or any other text editor. This is why database encryption is so important.

Start Microsoft Word and open the Northwind.mdb sample database. Immediately, your screen will be filled with a bunch of junk. Press Ctrl+F and find the phrase Maria Anders. You will actually be able to see the information stored in the Employees table in this sample database, as shown in Figure 22.18.

FIGURE 22.18.

The Northwind
database opened in
Microsoft Word.

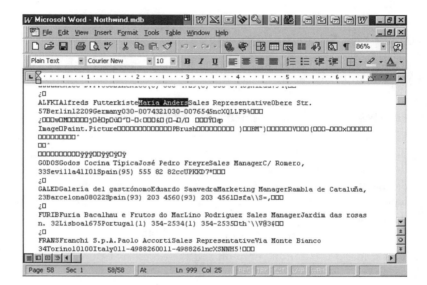

Using Access security prevents users from opening and viewing this information only from within Access. To prevent users from viewing information through some other program, you must encrypt your database.

Encrypting your database actually rewrites what is physically stored in your .mdb file by using a security algorithm. If you try to open an encrypted .mdb file with Word, your will see nothing but what looks to be garbage characters, therefore preventing anyone from seeing your data.

NOTE

In order to encrypt or decrypt a database, you must be either the database owner or a member of the Admins group.

However, there is a trade-off. Every time you read a table, run a query, or read information from your .mdb file, the data must first be decrypted. The data must also be encrypted whenever you attempt to write to your .mdb file. In order to perform all this extra work, database performance will drop 10–15 percent.

Of course, the decision to encrypt a database at the expense of database performance must be weighed against the sensitivity of the data. It is conceivable that users with some knowledge of Access could uncover the SID of the database owner or of the Admins group. Once they have the SID, they could grant themselves complete control over your database and view all your code as well.

Real-Life Security Examples

This section descibes some common security scenarios that I have encountered in various Access projects in the past.

Let Users Run Your Application but Not See the Code

You have just spent a large amount of time designing and constructing a database application. Your application is split into a front-end/back-end arrangement with all the non-table objects in the front end and all the table objects in the back end. You want users to download your two databases from a Web site, but you do not want them to see your VBA code stored in the form, report, and module objects. You also do not want the workgroup file that was used to create these databases to be downloaded in order to open these databases, and you do not want to force users to log on before starting your application.

This scenario is the most common and the easiest to set up. Refer to the following steps to secure your database:

1. Log on to a user account other than Admin, and run the Security Wizard for both databases. This changes the owner of the databases and all the database objects to something other than Admin.

2. Remove the Admin user account from the Admins group account. This prevents the Admin user account members from granting themselves permissions in your database.

3. Grant Administer permissions for all table, query, and macro objects to the Users group account. The Users group account will let any user account have permissions to these objects because all user accounts belong to the Users group account.

4. Grant the Users group account only Open/Run permissions for all form and report objects. This lets users open your forms and report in Form/Report View, but not in Design View.

5. Grant no access for all your module objects to the Users group account. Users still will be able to call all the functions and sub procedures in your module objects but will not be able to view or change them.

6. Encrypt your front-end database. This prevents someone from opening the database with a word processor and viewing the code.

Now your databases can be opened by any installation of Access, but the VBA code stored in the form, report, and module objects cannot be viewed or changed.

Using the Workgroup Approach

You have a database application that is to be used only by users in your company. These users are in different departments, and the computers they use are connected to the network. Each department has different uses for the database, and you want to secure the database appropriately.

To secure this database, follow these steps:

1. Create a new workgroup file and create all the group and user accounts that you will need. Join the user accounts to the appropriate group accounts.

2. Log on to the user account that will be the owner of this database (again, something other than Admin) and run the Security Wizard. This changes the owner of the database and all the database objects to something other than Admin.

3. Remove the Admin user account from the Admins group account. This prevents the users in the Admin user account from granting themselves permissions in your database.

4. Set a password for the Admin user account.

5. Assign the permissions for the database and each database object to the appropriate group accounts. For example, the Human Resources group should get full access to the HR tables, whereas the Sales group account should get no access to the HR tables.

6. Ensure that each computer that will use this database has a connection to the network, and store the workgroup file that you created on the network.

7. Create a shortcut that will start your database with the /wrkgrp switch, and ensure that each user can copy the shortcut from the network. For example, a shortcut to start a database called `ACME Sales.MDB` might look something like this:

   ```
   "C:\Program Files\Microsoft Office\Office\MSACCESS.EXE" "N:\Acme Sales.mdb"
   ➥/wrkgrp "N:\Acme Workgroup.mdw"
   ```

   Now when users start the application, they will first be asked to enter an account name and password. After that, the application will start, and they will be able to use the application according to the permissions that the groups that they belong to have.

Unlocking a Secure Application

Let's say you have created an application that you want to distribute freely, but after a number of uses, you want to have it lock up the application and prompt users to register the application if they want to continue to use it.

This scenario is similar to the one that I discussed previously in this chapter (in the section "Let Users Run Your Application but Not See the Code") except for one slight addition.

First, create a sub procedure that increments a counter in a protected table to count the number of times the application is started. The sub procedure will then check to see whether the counter is greater than the number of times that the user is allowed to open the database. If not, the database will open as normal. If so, the database will lock up by setting the database password.

The code in Listing 22.3 will set or unset the database password for a database.

Listing 22.3. Changing a database password.

```
Sub ChangeDatabasePassword(sOldPassword$, sNewPassword$)
Dim ws As Workspace
Dim db As Database
Dim tempdb As Database
Set db = CurrentDb()
Set ws = DBEngine.CreateWorkspace("", "DBA", "ORANGE")
Set tempdb = ws.OpenDatabase(db.Name)
tempdb.NewPassword sOldPassword, sNewPassword
Set tempdb = Nothing
Set db = Nothing
Set ws = Nothing
End Sub
```

This code temporarily creates a new workspace object with the owner (DBA) as the current user. It sets the new database password by passing it the current one along with the new one (or a zero-length string to erase the database password). After the sub procedure completes, the workspace is deleted, and the current user reverts back to the original user.

After the user registers with you (pays you, in other words), you can give him or her the database password, and he or she can unlock the application.

As you can see, the owner of this database and the password (DBA and Orange) are clearly visible. This code will set or unset the database password, depending on the situation. The important thing to remember is to place this code in a secure module object so that even if the database is unlocked, users cannot open this module, get the owner user account and password, and steal your secrets.

Stripping Your Code from Your Distributable Database

Let's say you have just created an application used to track accounting information. You obviously want to protect your intellectual property (your code) but at the same time let the users of the application enter their own information (data). This section describes how to accomplish this task and why it is so important.

Securing a Split Database

By definition, a *split database* is a situation where all the tables of an application are stored in one database (let's call it Data.mdb), and all the queries, forms, reports, macros and modules are stored in another (let's call it Code.mdb). Also stored in Code.mdb are linked tables that point to all the tables in Data.mdb.

The main reason for arranging an application in this fashion is it is very easy to maintain. If any changes need to be made to any of the non-table objects, they are applied only to Code.mdb; Data.mdb is left undisturbed. This can also make upgrading to a new version of an application very easy because the user needs to replace only the old Code.mdb with the new one, without having to import all of his existing data.

Also, testing becomes very easy because you can test your application changes against a test version of Data.mdb. When you are satisfied that the application is working the way you want, just change the linked tables to point to the unchanged, production version of Data.mdb by using the Linked Table Manager from the Add-ins menu.

Securing your Code.mdb would follow the same rules that I have discussed so far in regard to using user-level security. The trick is to secure your data so that no one with full access can simply open and look at or change your data but at the same time to let authorized users start up Code.mdb and use the data stored in Data.mdb.

This might seem like a difficult task, but it really isn't. If you used the Database Splitter Wizard from the Add-ins menu, Access already would have created a new back-end database that contains all your tables. In your application database, there are now linked tables to the new database. If user-level security was already in place before you split your database, you're halfway home. If not, secure your front-end database. To secure your back end, open it directly using the same workgroup file as your front-end database, and grant the permissions to all the tables to the appropriate group accounts.

Defining security permissions for the linked tables in the front-end database is not necessary. This is because whenever you attempt to access these tables, Access looks for the permissions in the database where the tables are physically stored. Therefore, in your front-end database, even though it might appear that the linked tables are unsecured, they really are secured because Access is checking the back-end database for the permissions.

TIP

If you want to prevent users from even opening back-end databases (even though they would not be able to view or change data), you can set a database password. Once you do that, you will have to relink all the tables in your front-end databases. When you try to

continues

continued

open one of the linked tables (provided you have permission to do so), Access looks for the database password for the back-end database in the linked table. It won't find it, and you will get a password error.

If you reattach all your tables, Access prompts you for the database password for the back-end database. You have to enter it only once because it is stored encrypted in the linked table. Now, when you try to open the linked table, it displays information correctly, but you are prompted for a database password when you try to open the back-end database directly.

NOTE

As always, remember that the passwords that you set are case sensitive. Also, when working with database passwords, take extra effort when creating your passwords. A forgotten password may lock you out of a database permanently.

MDE Databases

A new feature of Access 97 is the capability to create an executable database called an MDE database. This feature is well suited for a front-end/back-end type of application where all the data is contained in a back-end database, and all the queries, forms, reports, macros, and modules are contained in a front-end database.

You can create an MDE database by selecting Tools | Database Utilities from the menu bar. Access copies all the objects in the original database to another database with a .mde extension. After Access copies all the objects, it compiles and compacts the database and removes all editable source code.

What you are left with is a much smaller database, depending on how much source code you had. But the biggest advantage is that there is no source code to view or change. If you open the database, you will notice that you can't create or open any forms, reports, or modules in Design View.

NOTE

Always keep the original .mdb file that was used to create the new .mde. If changes are to be made, you have to change the .mdb file and re-create the .mde file.

Accessing a Secured Access Database with Visual Basic

Another common question that I am asked and that I feel should be discussed is the question of how to protect an Access database and still allow a Visual Basic application to open it.

Let's say that you have created a database called `Data.mdb` and you want to distribute it with a Visual Basic application called `MyApp.exe`. You would first protect the database by going through all the steps that I covered in this chapter. The key is to set up your database so that only one user account (the owner) can open the database.

Next, in a `Sub Main` procedure in your `MyApp.exe`, place the three lines in Listing 22.4.

Listing 22.4. The Sub Main procedure.

```
Sub Main()
DBEngine.SystemDB = "c:\windows\system\YourWorkgroupFile.mdw"
DBEngine.DefaultUser = "brad"
DBEngine.DefaultPassword = "orange"
End Sub
```

What you are really doing is changing the default user and password from `Admin` and `""` to `brad` and `orange`, respectively. Because this user account is the owner of the database and all its objects, you can now open all the objects unrestricted.

Because the Visual Basic application is a compiled `.exe` file, these lines are not visible. Therefore, users can't log on to the account and open the database with full access.

> **NOTE**
>
> In order for this scenario to work, you must ship the workgroup file along with the database and Visual Basic application.

Summary

In summary, this chapter described what I believe is one of the most misunderstood components of Access: security. It covered the major components of security and points out some of the features that are sometimes overlooked. I cannot stress the importance of securing your database applications enough.

With the huge investment that today's companies are putting into the development of applications, it is very important to protect that investment by putting the appropriate safeguards in place to prevent data loss and the theft of intellectual knowledge. Using the security methods this chapter outlined will reduce this risk considerably, if not completely, and in the long run will pay considerable dividends.

Multiuser Development

by Paul Anderson

IN THIS CHAPTER

CHAPTER 23

This chapter presents strategies and practical techniques in multiuser database management. The simplest and cleanest approach to this type of development is to start from scratch. Although rarely an option, creating a new application allows resource and program allocation toward the anticipated user environment. You can pay closer attention to network mapping, sharing, locking, and replication techniques when developing from scratch. When you're dealing with existing applications, you must consider additional factors in moving from the single-user desktop toward a client/server environment. These factors include database splitting, importing data for use with several Access versions (see Chapter 16, "Importing and Exporting Data"), and Jet Database Engine configuration issues.

Data Access

You can facilitate providing data to multiple heterogeneous users with careful planning and execution of information systems strategies. The Access toolset is useful in systems development and should be considered in several areas of multiuser data access. To match the functionality required, it is important to structure the database and properly enable the users on the basis of the task to be performed.

Sharing a Database on a Network

The Access environment contains tables where the data is stored; queries that present a logical view of the data; and application programs to retrieve, manipulate, and update the tables. An Access database exists as one or more files, depending on the arrangement of applications, queries, and tables in physical and logical relationships. The combinations may be expressed as shown in Table 23.1.

Table 23.1. Access database relationships.

Form/Report	Query	Table
Single	Single view	Single file
Single	Multiple views	Single file
Single	Multiple views	Multiple files
Multiple	Single view	Single file
Multiple	Single view	Multiple files
Multiple	Multiple views	Multiple files

You should carefully consider the positioning of the physical components in a client/server framework in the shared environment. The logical view is the link between the application and physical files. Distribution of the components over a networked environment is more or less flexible based on the ability to separate the components linked through the logical component. For example, the developer can send a client application query specified in Access on workstations to any SQL-compatible database server. The user interface for Pass-through queries is illustrated in Figure 23.1.

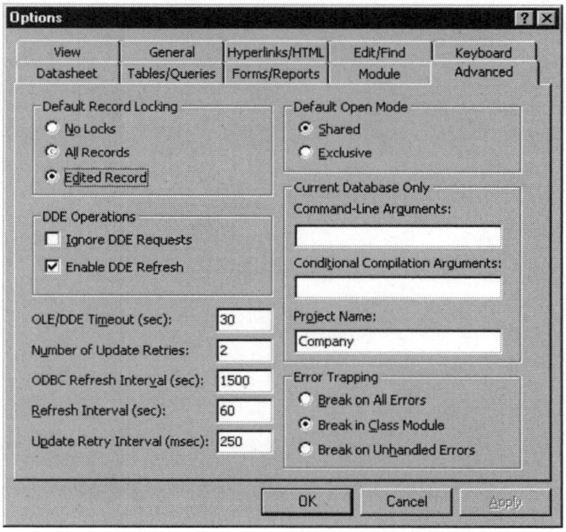

FIGURE 23.1.

A Pass-through query.

Viewing and Managing Replicated Jet Databases

The Jet Database Engine is optimized for retrieving and updating data external to the Access application. Jet initializes temporary data caches to manage large volumes of transactions in a multiuser environment. Figure 23.2 shows the caches maintained by Jet.

As the number of transactions increases, Jet buffers the flow of data in these areas. The type of query determines the character and performance of the process. Local client-based queries generate dynasets, whereas Pass-through queries result in snapshots returned from the server. The read-ahead cache processes record keys from the dynasets and entire records as snapshots. Jet 3.5 allocates up to 64KB of disk space at a time for sequential reads. The working cache stores data for internal processes, and the write-behind cache provides a buffer for data waiting to be written to disk. Transactions can be committed and rolled back within this scheme.

FIGURE 23.2.
Jet multithreaded
services.

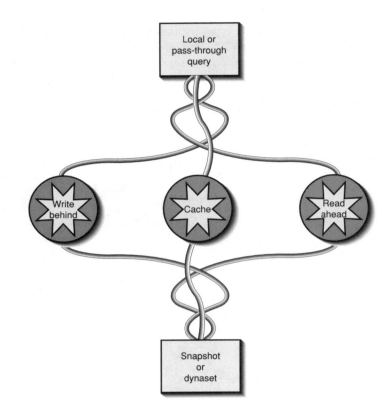

Sharing the Entire Database

When sharing an entire database, you must consider the juxtaposition of the users to the data and security. You can share an Access database simply by enabling sharing of the folder in which the database (.mdb) file resides. The advantage of this approach is in the single point of connection and maintenance. Backing up the file for disaster recovery only takes the time it takes to copy one file.

Another approach is to use a common point of access, which would manifest as an Access database available to all users, and then connect all the tables from other sources to this Access database. You would use this method instead of the single source to organize the database tables for later development and expansion to a multiserver environment. You must be careful to provide two-way external links that will not only reflect changes from the external source, but that are update-enabled from the central database manager. The mechanism that tags files for deletion as in the dBASE external links will be valuable if the Access link is used to erroneously purge data. There is no recovery except from a replica or backup if an internal Access database record is deleted.

Sharing the entire database is a security risk, however, if an open environment gives users the ability to span several job functions without the encumbrance of passwords and network server rights. The physical location of the workstation is the important consideration in having an open database environment. In a locked office, there is likely to be much less chance of tampering than in the office lobby. A workstation or network password is probably sufficient in small organizations where users need maximum accessibility and serve in many different data-processing capacities. Consider the physical location of the server to be the major concern. Then consider access to certain data and processes, such as employee records and payroll. Replication can be used to back up transactions and preserve images of the database files at certain critical points in processing. Before any batch processing such as month-end roll-up, synchronize your working copy of the current data to another on a separate server that has limited access. This will provide evidence of the preprocessing state of the data if it's necessary after a batch update. Finally, make sure that user activity is tracked by stamping each update to a record with the time, date, and user ID.

Sharing Only the Tables in the Database

Separating tables into back-end database files and maintaining database files exclusively for tables is useful in multiuser applications. Links from those objects to front-end application objects provide an economy of scale and flexibility to support multiuser development and operation. Efficient use of server resources results from passing only data objects across the network to workstations. Local workstation resources are used for forms, reports, updates, and modules. Records from tables are a shared resource and must receive more attention in the timing of transactions and how data set processing occurs to ensure database integrity. A simple tool for splitting application components from the database is shown in Figure 23.3.

FIGURE 23.3.

Splitting the database.

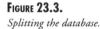

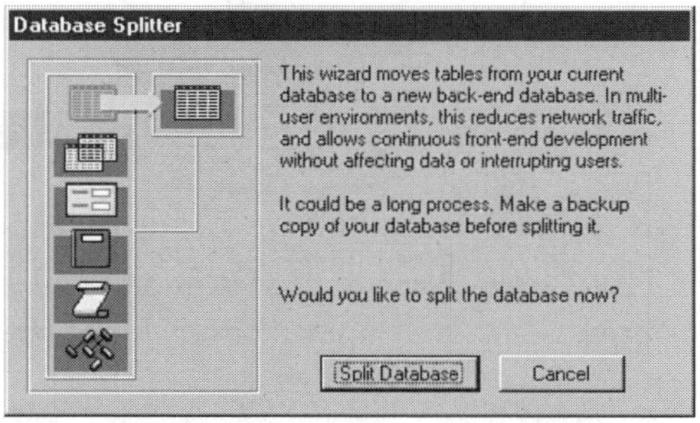

The Database Splitter Wizard is an aid to this process after a single database has been established to divide tables from other objects in the application. Existing applications can be roughly cut between the data objects and the objects that manipulate them. In the development of multiuser applications, this may only be a first step. Tables must be positioned for best use within the component structure of the network. It might be best to position some tables in intermediate locations such as workgroup servers or on local workstations based on an analysis of use and performance versus maintenance. Beginning the application development with an idea of positioning tables based on these considerations requires manual linking of tables and other objects in an array of locations. The result of a properly distributed database is appropriate allocation of resources and extended use of components over the application life cycle.

Sharing the Database on the Internet

The Internet has been established as an interconnection of computer networks for military, educational, and (more recently) commercial use. Commercial organizations have found e-mail for communication, Web sites for customer contact and advertising, and data file transfer between offices to provide cost-effective solutions in these areas. An Internet connection asynchronously transfers data. In cases in which the communication points are farther away than a local phone charge, the Internet is a ready-made wide area network with intermittent availability at minimum cost. Access replication sets maintain duplicate copies of the database in each locale. When a connection is established between locales, the duplicates can be resynchronized. You can use the Internet with replication to maintain a distributed database in decentralized, remote, and mobile computing environments. An Internet connection contributes to a dual strategy in networking multiple users, as shown in Figure 23.4.

FIGURE 23.4.

Replication sets.

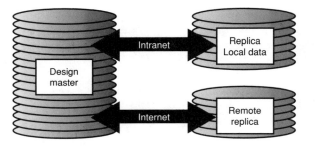

An HTTP or FTP connection can be used to import and link or export any Access-compatible file. This is performed as a single upload or download transaction.

CAUTION

Access uses local memory cache to temporarily store the file being transferred. Be sure the client has sufficient capacity for this operation, and be aware that this results in a read-only version of the file.

Using replication between files over the Internet requires several elements. First is the Internet connection. Second, using the Internet to store the database requires the establishment of an FTP site. Establish an FTP site with the appropriate security for sensitive files or commerce. To ensure the availability of your data request, you need one or more IP addresses at several Point of Presence (POP) locations for reliable operation. Next, use the Replication Manager Wizard to create a file replica on the communications server. Finally, create a process that confirms the exchange to or from the FTP site of the replicant file. This process will trigger resynchronization of the replica set.

Replication

Sharing a database with users in remote locations presents an array of problems and solutions. You can extend the network over dial-up lines and maintain a centralized database in a location best suited to communication charges and maintenance considerations, or you can replicate the entire database and maintain multiple copies for users at remote locations. An intermediate solution might be obvious when tables can be separated and stored locally, which requires a minimum number of queries and updates from multiple remote locations. Some tables desired from a single source will be maintained in a central location and require communication resources to service all queries and updates from remote sites. Restricted transactions in the local environment allow scheduled updates of shared tables. You'll need to resynchronize the master copy of the database with the transaction database table. These solutions require knowledge and activities in several areas of database and communication expertise that may not be practical to plan and implement in one stage of development.

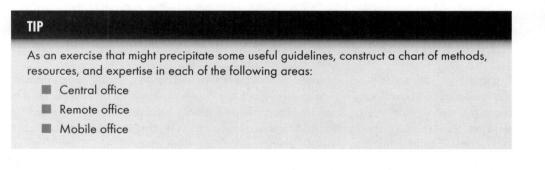

TIP

As an exercise that might precipitate some useful guidelines, construct a chart of methods, resources, and expertise in each of the following areas:

- Central office
- Remote office
- Mobile office

Synchronization

Replication is a process that allows several copies of a data set to exist and self-maintain a degree of synchronization. One template is designated as the *design master*; it maintains the design characteristics for all the replicas. The design master functions as the source and central point of distribution of structural changes to the database. Once a replica set has been created, additional replicas can be created from any replica. Replicas can be created through the

Replication submenu of the Tools menu. The design master function can be switched to any database in the replica set; however, only one design master can exist at any one time.

The duplication of replicas may also be generated from code using the make replica method. To make a replica that cannot be modified by the user, specify the `dbRepMakeReadOnly` option. This would allow a current view of sensitive data such as employee information available for read-only access. Another argument, `dbRepMakePartial`, can be used to create a replica subset. This could be used to exclude from the replica data such as salary information about particular employees.

Jet adds new properties, including the following, to the design master it creates:

```
ReplicaID

ReplicableBool

DesignMasterID
```

`ReplicaID` is created for each new replica. The database can be replicated once `ReplicableBool` is set to `True` by Access. Each replica set has one design master that initiates resynchronization. If a new design master is required, you can set this value.

CAUTION

The resynchronization of data in a replica set may be invalidated if a second design master exists. Only one design master should exist in the replica set, and it is only necessary to generate a design master if it is deleted. If the location of a replica is changed, the path to the replica must be reestablished before resynchronizing is possible. The connection string in the `Connect` property is used to define the path to the replica. This is an exception to the prohibition on design changes to replicas.

Using the original nonreplica database to generate a replica will create a second design master. The `DesignMasterID` property is used to distinguish the design master from other replicas. It is recommended that the design master be protected and moved infrequently. A replica can be used instead of the design master on the Access database server. The design master replica should be controlled by storing it on a development workstation with proper backup and security measures.

CAUTION

You should remove password protection from the database prior to replication synchronization because replicas cannot synchronize when they're protected by passwords. Setting permissions with Access security does not affect synchronization because replicas automatically inherit the design master properties.

You can convert an Access database to a design master using Jet. In this process, the characteristics used to differentiate this replica are established. The first step in the replication process attempts to identify a data type that could be a replication ID. The format is as follows:

```
{9999XX99-9999-9999-9999999999999999}
```

Failing to find a candidate field, the replica process adds a field called s_GUID. As additional replicas are created, these characteristics guide the synchronization process. Replicas maintain the same values for each record's s_GUID. A number of fields defined specifically for replication are described in Table 23.2.

Table 23.2. Replication fields.

Field	Value
s_GUID	Replication ID AutoNumber
s_Lineage	ReplicaID
s_Generation	Groups of changes
Gen_FieldName	Binary large object (BLOB)

A 16-byte value stores the replication ID. It is recommended that the s_GUID field also be designated as the record key. Every record has a unique identifier to a particular replica set through the s_Lineage field. The synchronization status of larger object fields is defined in Gen_FieldName. The value for the Gen_FieldName field is the field name appended with a binary (0 or 1) value. This value is set to 0 to indicate the need for resynchronization. Fields are also generated for each memo field, OLE object, and BLOB.

TIP

Memo fields and OLE objects can be reserved during dynaset queries across a network. You might want to limit the data traffic across the network from characteristically larger fields. Simply place the fields on a second page of a form to prevent initial display of these fields, and they will remain on the server until the page is selected.

A successful multiuser database management strategy includes a comprehensive backup and disaster recovery plan. Frequent synchronization of replicas can contribute to the maintenance of multiple copies of records if error recovery or comparison is needed. When a design master is inadvertently deleted or a replica is lost, any replica can be used as a backup copy to replace the original.

23

MULTIUSER DEVELOPMENT

> **TIP**
>
> If a replica is the design master or a partial replica, those characteristics unique to the replica must be reestablished. By making a replica of the specialized replica, you will be able to recover the loss of the original replica by simply modifying the properties of the backup replica. In any case, frequent synchronization after records have been updated is the best way to ensure integrity of replica sets.

Briefcase replication in Windows 95 affords a simple method to apply replication. This strategy is useful where there is intermittent connectivity between replicas. To implement replication with the briefcase, first connect the local computer to the network. Next, place the database file in the briefcase folder. This action automatically converts the database to a design master and creates a replica on the local system. Finally, disconnect from the network. Now updates will be local. When you reconnect the computer to the network and select Update All from the Briefcase menu, the replicas will resynchronize. This mechanism is not only useful for portable computing applications, but once you are disconnected from the network, all security issues over the network are removed from consideration.

Data access objects (DAO) provide a method for self-contained functionality across environments. Features of DAO methods for replication are as follows:

- Create or convert a database to a design master with any number of replicas
- Flexibly populate full and partial replicas
- Synchronize replicas at intervals based on time or events
- Change replication properties and table-level rules
- Handle conflicts and errors

A situation might arise that warrants a modification to a partial replication scheme. The growth of an organization may result in additional locations or consolidation of data that had previously been excluded. Removing or modifying the filters will result in population changes on the next data synchronization. To obtain a full view of the replicated data, set the `ReplicaFilter` property method to `False`, and then execute the `PopulatePartial` method.

> **TIP**
>
> Filters process all data set records to derive a subset of records that populate the partial replica. You can enhance synchronization performance by specifying indexed fields in the `ReplicaFilter` property.

You use DAO methods and properties to create a partial replica. Relationships and filters provide a mechanism for partial replication. The `ReplicaFilters` property of the `TableDef` method can be used to distinguish the criteria for the record subset. This is similar to an SQL WHERE clause. Specify the `dbRepMakePartial` option for the `MakeReplica` method. The subset of records with the desired criteria will be replicated with the `PopulatePartial` method.

> **CAUTION**
>
> When creating full or partial design replicas, make sure the database is opened exclusively for this purpose.
>
> Errors during synchronization may occur if table-level validation rules are established after replicas become asynchronous. Implementing a rule without testing it on the data set before synchronization is not recommended.

Using a unique string in the key assignment designating its origin is highly recommended. An error may occur during synchronization when records are generated using the same key. Do not rely on the generic counter to generate keys for table records in replica sets.

To correct errors that have occurred in synchronization, check the `MSysErrors` table. The following information is recorded:

- Table name
- Record key
- Replica or replicas affected
- Replica that last changed the record
- Type of operation that failed
- Reason it failed

Errors such as locks will be removed, by Jet, as the replicas are synchronized, if the lock is not encountered on a subsequent attempt.

> **CAUTION**
>
> You should correct errors between synchronizations. If errors are not removed from the `MSysErrors` table, the same error will occur during the next synchronization attempt, even though the data has been corrected.

Locking Features

Access shares the database for multiple users by default. It assumes that you want to share a snapshot view of the tables in lookup mode. Even after establishing this mode of operation, you can initiate another view in select or update mode to add, change, or delete records (rows of a table).

You maintain referential integrity within a replica set by setting replica relationships. If relationships between tables are important when populating a partial replica, use the `PartialReplica` property. This will combine all the records from both tables in an additive fashion. Use the `ReplicaFilter` and `PartialReplica` properties to limit which data is replicated. During synchronization, first the data records are copied from the partial replica, next the partial replica is purged of records, and finally the full replica is used to repopulate the partial replica. This prevents orphan records from being maintained in the partial replica.

Record-Locking Strategy

To ensure database capture in a multiuser environment, at least you must add a stamp or reference number to a record field when the transaction is completed and you must automatically generate a printed form or report. The record locking for transaction processing is handled automatically within the Access process unless code is written to change the update logic. In this case, programming logic must be used to verify the completion of an update. Figure 23.5 suggests a page-lock handling scheme in a flowchart format.

FIGURE 23.5.

A page-locking scheme.

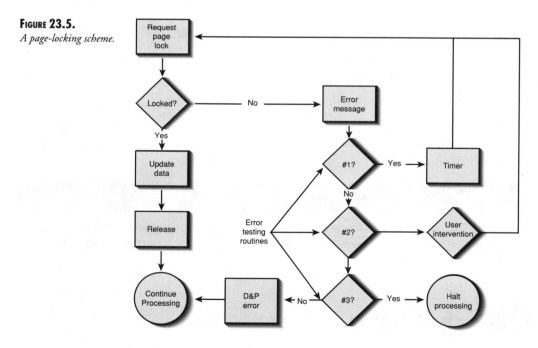

Read locks have been removed from indexed pages in Access 97. This enhances multiuser performance with less conflict.

Once a record is established, retrieval of that record for modification may be required by the process. You accomplish this change by first copying an image of the data from one or more records in the database. Next, the user or process interacts with the data and the underlying application of business rules to update the image. Then a transaction is completed, which copies the changes back to replace the original record(s).

As a default, called *no locks*, the attempted retrieval of data for modification will set a flag and identify your process to others as a transaction is completed. Three options are displayed:

- Overwrite the other users' changes
- Copy changes to the Clipboard
- Discard changes

These options should be used where changes to the same data by multiple users is infrequent and where you need processing to continue despite conflict.

With the Edited Records option set in the Advanced Options dialog box, restrictions are placed on users attempting to retrieve those records that are already in use by others. As the first user to retrieve data, your process locks records until the update transaction completes. Another user attempting to retrieve records will be locked out from editing the data. This option ensures that transactions are completed before others can retrieve the data for update. A process can be timed in an attempt to police the edit and periodically release records that are left unattended.

Setting the All Records property in the Advanced Options dialog box indiscriminately locks the entire data set, including tables that will not be accessible to any others while they're open to you. Use this option for periodic updates to entire tables or when superuser status is required for exclusive use.

CAUTION

The No Locks setting is automatically assigned, overriding any option set by the developer, if the data is derived (linked) to an SQL database using ODBC rules for updating the database.

Interval variables can be set to automatically refresh values that have been updated in place. In a multiuser environment this provides a method of reflecting changes to data sheet and form view users. A value of 1–32,776 seconds can be set to refresh either Access or ODBC records.

When a record is locked by another user, parameters can be set to determine how many times or how often updates to records will be attempted. Up to 10 retries can be set for 1–1,000 millisecond intervals.

Measuring the average length of user sessions is meaningful when setting these parameters. The automatic refresh values should be set up within the range of the length of the users' sessions. This would catch a majority of conflicts in updates. You can set the number and frequency of update retries to allow for the completion of user sessions before retrying the update.

Each user in a multiuser environment wants to have complete control of data and resources as if he were the only user. Conflicts in a multiuser environment are predictable and resolvable. Rules governing the retrieval and update processing should be enforced automatically. Notification of conflicts in processing should be accompanied by the available options for resolution. Predetermination of a resolution path for a multiuser conflict should default unless user intervention is allowed based on a data-processing exception.

When you're using bound objects in a form, automatic locking is enforced from the underlying tables. Only one user is allowed update privileges, whereas all other users are afforded read-only status. In update queries, locks may be set to determine which fields are controlled in the update process.

A fine degree of locking control is afforded by the use of lock codes in Visual Basic. Assessing the critical point at which locking is essential to ensure the integrity of the data processing, the Visual Basic programmer must determine a minimum lock interval and location. The Visual Basic locking can also be extend the default lock provided by the bound object to a period determined by externally imposed rules.

In a production multiuser environment, you should restrict access to the workgroup information file and the Options dialog box you reach through the Tools menu. You should withhold security information and settings that are specified here from view and modification.

A user opens a database table or query in *shared mode*. A file is created by the Jet Database Engine to lock records. Additional users may add to the file records reflecting locks on other records in the database or encounter the same lock and be denied update privileges. As users complete transactions and close database files, the entries in the lock records are deleted. As the last user closes the database, the lock file is deleted. The following code sample specifies the number and interval of update attempts to be made when a locking conflict is encountered:

```
Application.SetOption "Number of Update Retries", 5
Application.SetOption "Update Retry Interval (msec)", 500
```

You use the *exclusive mode* to lock an entire database. For "brute force" editing and updates to the database, it is possible to open the database in exclusive mode, which will prevent any other user from opening the database in exclusive mode or from locking any records. To enable this feature, use the File menu to open the database. The Open database dialog box contains a checkbox that enables exclusive mode.

> **CAUTION**
>
> It is recommended that users be prevented from opening database files manually to enable or disable exclusive mode operation. In a shared database environment, record locking should only be applied when necessary by developer specification.

Batch updating for purposes such as month-end data processing is an example where exclusive mode should be enabled.

To open an Access source in exclusive mode, you can use the following `OpenDatabase` method:

```
OpenDatabase(DBname, Exclusive, Read/Write, Source)
```

This method identifies the Access database source, the rights, and the type/connection string. Exclusive mode may also be enabled programmatically. A subroutine can be called whenever an update to the `Company` database is warranted. This could include the following call:

```
Call OpenExdb("c:\data\company)
```

The `Employees` table is located in the `Company` database. The Visual Basic code could be written as follows:

```
Sub OpenExdb(Name As String)
Dim db As DATABASE
Set db = DBEngine.Workspaces(0).OpenDatabase(Name, False, _False, "")
Dim errCurrent As Error
' Disable Error Messaging and trap errors '
On Error Resume Next
' Attempt to lock the page'
Set dbs = OpenDatabase("Company.mdb", True)
' Handle the error manually'
If Err <> 0 Then
    ' If errors occur, display them.
    For Each errCurrent In DBEngine.Errors
        Debug.Print errCurrent.Description
    Next
Else
    ' Exclusive access enabled.
    Debug.Print "Exclusive mode enabled."
End If
dbs.Close
End Sub
```

The system will resume error handling as the subroutine ends. The developer can handle the error manually in the following ways:

- By timing out and trying again
- By aborting and recording the information in an error table
- Through user intervention

You use *recordset locking* to control user access to one or more tables in a database. Recordset locking applies to table- and dynaset-type `Recordset` objects only. Snapshot- and forward-only-type `Recordset` objects are read-only objects.

The default recordset lock is a write lock, which prevents other users from editing data in the locked records. You can prevent users from reading the data by setting a read lock while making bulk changes to a `Recordset` object to prevent users from reading the data until you have completed your update. To set a read lock, specify the `dbDenyRead` constant in the `options` argument of the `OpenRecordset` method.

If you want to implement recordset locking, you must open your database in shared mode. When a database is opened in shared mode, multiple users can simultaneously access the database, and Jet handles conflicts between users. To open an Access source in exclusive mode, use the following `OpenDatabase` method:

```
OpenDatabase(DBname, Shared, Read/Write, Source)
```

This method identifies the Access database source, the rights, and the type/connection string. You can use code to open a database in shared mode. Use the `OpenDatabase` method on the current Workspace object, and specify `False` for the `options` argument. This routine is called with the following code:

```
Call OpenShdb("c:\data\company)
```

The `Employees` table is located in the company database. The Visual Basic code could be written as follows:

```
Sub OpenShdb(Name As String)
Dim db As DATABASE
Set db = DBEngine.Workspaces(0).OpenDatabase(Name, False, _False, "")
Dim errCurrent As Error
' Disable Error Messaging and trap errors '
On Error Resume Next
' Attempt to lock the page'
Set dbs = OpenDatabase("Company.mdb", False)
' Handle the error manually'
If Err <> 0 Then
   ' If errors occur, display them.
   For Each errCurrent In DBEngine.Errors
      Debug.Print errCurrent.Description
   Next
Else
   ' Exclusive access enabled.
   Debug.Print "Exclusive mode enabled."
End If
dbs.Close
End Sub
```

After you open the database in shared mode, you can implement recordset locking by specifying various constants in the `options` argument of the `OpenRecordset` method. If you open a `Recordset` object without specifying any value for the `options` argument, Jet uses page locking by default. It opens the `Recordset` object in shared mode and locks only the data that's being edited in the current page.

You can use a combination of the available constants to more precisely specify the type of locking you want to implement. This routine calls the following code:

```
Call OpenExTable("Employees)
```

For example, the following code locks a table by opening it with the dbDenyWrite and dbDenyRead constants specified in the options argument of the OpenRecordset method:

```
Function OpenExTable(Table As String) As Integer
Dim db As Database
Set db = CurrentDb()
Dim rs As Recordset
On Error Resume Next
Set rs = db.OpenRecordset(Table, dbOpenTable, dbDenyRead + dbDenyWrite)
If (Err = 0) Then Msgbox = "Record Updated"
If (Err <> 0) Then Msgbox = "Record Access Denied"
End Function
```

As with opening databases in exclusive mode, setting locks on Recordset objects can cause errors if the lock fails. You use a routine to turn off error handling, attempt the operation, check for errors and handle any that occur, and turn on error handling.

> **TIP**
>
> The most common error in recordset locking is error number 3262, `Couldn't lock table <name>; currently in use by user <name> on machine <name>`. This error occurs when the OpenRecordset method is used on an object that can't be locked. There is usually another user who has the same table or tables locked in a way that prevents locking. To respond to the error, implement a timing loop in the routine.

While exclusive mode locks the entire database, and recordset locking locks one or more individual tables, *page locking* locks only the page containing the record that is currently being edited. This is the least restrictive level of locking. When page locking is in effect, other users can read data from the locked page, but they cannot change it. Page locking is the default locking level for Recordset objects.

In the parts of an application that lock a page of data, specify which type of page locking you want to use. Two types of page locking are available: pessimistic locking and optimistic locking.

Pessimistic locking locks a page when you start editing a record with the Edit method. The process locks the page until the changes are saved by the Update method or canceled with the CancelUpdate method or by moving from the record. The default type of locking for Recordset objects is pessimistic.

You specify the type of page locking for a Recordset object by using either the dbPessimistic or the dbOptimistic constant in the LockEdits argument of the OpenRecordset method. The LockEdits property can also be used to set the type of page locking after you open a Recordset object. Set the LockEdits property to True for pessimistic locking. Setting the LockEdits property to False causes optimistic locking when the record is edited.

After successfully locking a record with the pessimistic approach, conflicts will not be encountered. Pessimistic locking ensures that the version on the screen is a current copy of the data in storage because no other user can change the record being edited.

> **CAUTION**
>
> Pessimistic locking prevents an entire page from being changed while you're editing any record on the page. Multiple records can be locked because they may reside on the page with the one being edited. The developer may take steps such as building records that occupy an entire page (2048 bytes), ensuring that only one record is locked when a page is locked. This is not recommended when disk space is at a premium.

In the following example, employee records are being entered without an area code. For consistency, an area code is added programmatically to an employee's record. To implement pessimistic locking, use the following code, in which the subroutine is first called to pass the table name and an area code to the subroutine:

```
Call EditPsRec("Employees","714")
```

Then the subroutine executes a transaction against the current database to add the area code to a phone number in the Employees table:

```
Sub EditPsRec(Table as String,AreaCode as String)
Dim db As Database
Set db = CurrentDb()
Dim rs As Recordset
Set rs = db.OpenRecordSet(Table, dbOpenDynaset)
' Set Pessimisstic Locking
rs.Lockedits = True
rs.Edit
rs!PhoneNumber = AreaCode & rs!PhoneNumber
rs.Update
' End Transaction and release lock
End Sub
```

Optimistic locking locks the page when the user saves the changes to the record with the Update method. The process is called *optimistic* because of the view that another user will probably not retrieve and lock a record within the time frame of your edit. Retrieval of the record by another user will "dirty" the page and nullify your lock attempt. A lock is applied for a shorter interval, minimizing conflicts.

To implement optimistic locking, use the following code, in which the subroutine is first called to pass the table name and an area code to the subroutine:

```
Sub EditPsRec(Table as String,AreaCode as String)
Dim db As Database
Set db = CurrentDb()
```

```
Dim rs As Recordset
Set rs = db.OpenRecordSet(Table, dbOpenDynaset)
' Set Optimistic Locking
rs.Lockedits = False
rs.Edit
rs!PhoneNumber = AreaCode & rs!PhoneNumber
' lock is attempted
rs.Update
' End Transaction and release lock
End Sub
```

The same routine is used to call and execute the Update method, with the exception of the LockEdits property being set to False. The Jet Database Engine provides automatic transaction management. The BeginTrans and CommitTrans methods are not required when Jet is used. However, when working with non-Jet data sources, these methods are useful. Pessimistic locking is always used for transaction processing. Transactions prevent modification of data until the transaction is committed. The following subroutine illustrates a transaction variation of the code to modify a phone number:

```
Sub EditPsRec(Table as String,AreaCode as String)
Dim db As Database
Set db = CurrentDb()
Dim rs As Recordset
Set rs = db.OpenRecordSet(Table, dbOpenDynaset)
' Setup transaction workspace
Dim ws as Workspace
ws = DbEngine(0)
ws.BeginTrans
rs.Lockedits = False
rs.Edit
rs!PhoneNumber = AreaCode & rs!PhoneNumber
' lock is attempted
rs.Update
ws.CommitTrans
' End Transaction and release lock
End Sub
```

Usually transaction processing is used in situations such as multiple file updates, where an entire set of files is affected during a single transaction. Even though the LockEdits property may have been set to False, a pessimistic lock is set.

Several performance enhancements have been built into Jet version 3.5. New Registry settings determine a number of locks that will force transactions to commit. The Registry setting MaxLocksPerFile enables efficient completion of large queries against NetWare– and Windows NT–based servers by forcing partial commit transactions. The DAO SetOption method specifies the value for this setting.

Avoiding Data-Locking Conflicts

Application of locking strategies is determined by the interrelationship and extent of updates across the database. Minimal locking is intended for updates to individual records, although a number of adjacent records may be affected. An entire 2KB page of records is locked in the process, which may make users wonder why records that are not in conflict are withheld from their update. The alternative broader, locking schemes support sweeping updates and queries that depend on table images underlying bound objects associated and locked as a record set. Periodic processing of an entire database where the developer wants to preserve the database image for an entire session will be facilitated by exclusive mode. The first exclusive-mode user to enter the database locks out any others. That user remains in control of the entire database until he exits. The recordset locking level will only be activated when an object is processed. Any tables related to that object will be locked while the control is active. The least amount of multiuser conflict will be generated by the page locking level. Records can be padded to a 2KB size to ensure that only one record at a time is locked; however, this may result in large amounts of space allocated to prevent a small number of potential conflicts in use between users.

Background population control is an important server process that permits efficient data search and retrieval and helps to eliminate idle time. It can run into problems, however, when multiple users are accessing the server simultaneously because it will assign priority to certain disk processes while ignoring others. The developer can modify the rate at which Access reads records from the server during idle time by creating a table named `MSysConf` on the server and setting the number of rows of data that are retrieved at one time and the number of seconds of delay between each retrieval. For a large amount of interactive use with the server, set the number of rows retrieved to a lower number and increase the delay. If there is an inordinate amount of idle time, you can increase the number of rows retrieved while decreasing the delay between each retrieval. To favor a particular process and favor the amount of processing time for that process, increase the number of rows while increasing the idle time between retrievals.

> **CAUTION**
>
> `Recordset` objects created in Visual Basic code are not populated during idle time. If your server places read locks on records as they are retrieved, you should not remain on a record or page for an extended period of time.

Page locking may fail when you're generating error codes. When an error is encountered, you should trap it and use `case` routines to determine the appropriate action.

Some common error messages and strategies for error handling are listed in Table 23.3.

Table 23.3. Locking error handling.

Error Number	Description	Recommended Handling
3186	`Couldn't save; currently locked by user <name> on machine <name>.`	Send a message to the users, use a timing loop to try again, or quit at the user option.

Error Number	Description	Recommended Handling
3197	The database engine stopped the process because you and another user are attempting to change the same data at the same time.	Requery the data and give the user another chance to edit.
3260	Couldn't update; currently locked by user \<name> on machine \<name>.	Send a message to the users, use a timing loop to try again, or quit, as the user wishes.

> **CAUTION**
>
> When message 3260 is generated, the page is locked, which might not mean that two users are writing to the same record. The record key can be compared and provides a basis for action. In the case that the users are editing different records, you can handle the error with a simple timing routine on the process that fails to lock.

A subroutine may be developed to handle locking conflicts. The following code calls a subroutine, detecting a lock set on the Employees file:

```
Call CheckLock("Employees")
```

The subroutine uses the IsItLocked function to detect another user's lock on the recordset:

```
Sub CheckLock(Table as string)
Dim db As Database
Set db = CurrentDb()
Dim rs As Recordset
Set rs = db.OpenRecordSet(Table, dbOpenDynaset)
Dim Locked As Boolean
Locked = IsItLocked(rs)
MsgBox Locked
End Sub
```

Using this code as a skeleton routine, you can incorporate a set of case statements to determine action based on the type of error generated. Indexed columns display better multiuser concurrency, meaning that more users can read and update indexed columns without getting locking conflict messages.

Jet 3.5 allows more users to retrieve and update indexed table columns, avoiding locking conflicts.

Creating a Client/Server Application

The rapid pace of advances in database technology has caused some confusion among developers. Some of the concepts and terminology used in this area are vital for developers to communicate effectively. Table 23.4 addresses frequently asked questions (FAQs) about client/server development.

Table 23.4. Client/server frequently asked questions.

Question	Answer
What is client/server architecture?	Client/server architecture separates software into modules executed from different workspaces. Client software modules process data that has been requested from a server. The server portion processes data that is provided to the client(s). The objectives in this methodology are rapid development, better performance in a multiuser (networked) environment, and reduced maintenance. Each component developed in client/server programming is a "black box" model, meaning that each component can be developed and maintained independently, adhering to standards when data is exchanged. Client and server processes communicate through a well-defined set of standard application program interfaces (APIs) and RPCs. Due to these standard interfaces, component sets are scalable both in number and type of client workstation and number and variety of servers. Data is mostly manipulated, stored, and queried as a shared resource from modules developed for the server.
What is a client process?	Client programs contain functions dedicated to the user interface, data entry/display, and, to a minor degree, the local manipulation of data. The client is a program that messages a server program requesting it to perform a task. A user or agent program interacts with a client software module. The client executes

Question	*Answer*
	logic specific to local processing needs and manages local resources such as peripherals. In this architecture, the program detects user actions and generates messages to other client modules or the server for processing.
What is a server process?	The server program responds to messages sent by the client(s) and generates messages that encapsulate data. Access uses SQL/ODBC, statements, formatted data, and simple messages between clients and servers. These processes perform database retrieval, perform rule-based updates to the database, and maintain data integrity. More than one server program can reside on a computer and run concurrently. Both Access and FoxBASE may be running on the same machine. At the other extreme, the server program may not reside on the computer on which it executes instructions. Access can run on a workstation linked to tables on a separate computer with only the database file resident. Expanding this model, a single client may make requests from database servers, transaction servers, and application servers within the client/server framework. Users could execute Access forms and reports from one server, trigger transaction processing on a second server, and request database services from a third server program. All these programs may reside on the same physical computer; however, usually at least two computers are typically used, connected by a network.
What is a transaction server?	Applications use transaction servers to execute mission-critical tasks with control over security and database integrity. Transaction servers are components of online transaction processing (OLTP). The performance characteristics of a transaction

continues

23

Table 23.4. continued

Question	Answer
	server should provide a response within 3 seconds. This is achieved by sending and receiving only simple messages to and from the transaction server. In actual practice, completion of a transaction request may be more than 10 seconds because of the number of requests being serviced and network traffic. Users typically have a "patience threshold" just over 10 seconds, so the developer might want to send a message such as "please wait" before 10 seconds to prevent spurious keyboard interruptions in the process.
What is distributed processing?	The use of multiple processors to complete a task is the objective in distributed processing. Usually this involves more than one physical machine connected by a network. A simple example would be in a shipping application that must update sales data and inventory. The packing slip would contain ship-to data retrieved from the sales order processing system in the accounting department, while the availability of the parts being shipped would be retrieved from the warehousing database server. The application is executed in stages assigned to each processor. In complex processes, a high degree of coordination and checkpoint programming ensures that each process performs its part of an application. The ability to reassign incomplete stages achieves a degree of software application fault tolerance.
What is remote data management?	In its simplest form, remote data management is one application sending SQL requests to a server. The server responds to the requested task, sending a message or formatted data. When the database splitter is

Question	Answer
	implemented and the back-end tables of the database are placed on another computer, remote data management can be performed over the network. Relational database management software such as the Jet database engine is used to connect the application layer to the database layer. Distributed data management is a complex form of remote data management. Linking tables from multiple remote servers to a client program is the basis of this architecture. The user is unaware of the data origin and destination. These parameters are defined in the connection string of the `Dataset` property connecting Jet to the remote data.
What is data warehousing?	Data warehousing is the appropriate actions of the information systems staff and database administrators to provide users with secure access to data required in their jobs. This process has been made more complex by the array of technologies available to the users, the type of data, and where the date is located. The first stage in this process may be to create a backbone of servers that can be accessed by client workstations with password protection. Next, gather the data into the server environment either by converting and rehosting or by linking to the external data source if it cannot be imported. The interface to the server must be consistent with the client/server strategy. Finally, promote the use of client applications that will give the users the appropriate technology to serve their job function. One user may need to run queries and use sophisticated planning tools. Another may require only a dedicated Access application fixed to a view of certain databases.

23

MULTIUSER DEVELOPMENT

continues

Table 23.4. continued

Question	Answer
What is data mining?	Data mining is the extraction of data from a distributed data processing environment pertaining to a particular question or problem. The difference between this process and routine queries and reports is that the data must be gathered in researching possible solutions that have not been investigated previously or currently have no established programs and pathways to the data that can be effectively utilized. Access is a superior tool for data mining. The ability of Access to link to many disparate data sources across a network and treat them in a homogeneous manner is a quality required for this practice. Further, the toolset is robust (especially compared to standard Visual Basic) and has wizards and menu-driven capabilities, which are appealing to a wide range of users. Although specialized data-mining tools with heuristic logic and decision management built into the database engines are more useful in dedicated data mining, the majority of studies that have been cited in this area can be accomplished with the Access toolset.

There are two types of queries available in Access client/server environments: normal queries on remote tables and Pass-though queries. Access compiles and runs normal queries through the Jet Database Engine to the server. With a Pass-through query, the SQL statement is sent to the server uncompiled.

Normal queries to a server can be updated as a dynaset, which only passes the record key back to the client from the server. Query-by-example tools, user-supplied parameters, and user functions can be used to construct normal queries with a consistent format, regardless of the target database on the server.

Pass-through queries have an advantage over normal queries in that they create less network traffic. SQL procedures and security supported by a particular server must be closely followed. Error messages should be trapped and handled by the client as a part of post-query processing.

Batch updates and reports are ideal candidates for Pass-through queries. You should limit the number of records per query to fewer than 500 for better performance.

> **TIP**
>
> To work around the fact that Pass-through queries do not create dynasets, use a pass-through snapshot to retrieve the data, and then populate an array with the locally updated record. Finally, use the update method to write changes to the server.

An example of a Pass-through query to a server retrieving employee records follows:

```
SELECT * FROM employees WHERE hire_date BETWEEN '1/1/1997' AND '2/31/1997'
```

You must be careful to manage the network traffic and connections required for this query. Specify a limit of 100 records per query to use only one connection for the query. Visual Basic code may also be an alternative to the user interface so that connections can be opened and closed more quickly.

> **TIP**
>
> Establish a local database subset for development, where Access tools can be used to write the SQL statements. After verifying the query, copy the SQL statement to create a Pass-through query. Be sure the server database will execute the Access-generated procedure.

To develop an Access client/server application, store data in remote tables on a database server instead of in a local database. Queries and updates would be sent to the server to retrieve data as needed from the remote tables. The client/server environment offers many advantages over a local database in the development of multiuser applications. Considerations must be given to Access performance issues as you establish a client/server strategy.

The client/server environment separates processing tasks between an application on a client computer system and a database on a server. The Access client makes requests for services provided by the server, such as querying a database, printing a document, and backing up data. The client performs operations on the data that is returned by the server and interacts with the user.

Access client/server environments have the following benefits:

- Multiple users can concurrently update a database.
- In most cases, the data retrieved across the network from the server is a small subset of the entire table.

- Users can utilize ODBC Direct to enhance performance in database transactions.

- Flexible security measures can be implemented from a central location.

ODBC Direct is an integration of ODBC into the architecture of Windows 95. The process, when enabled, loads the Jet Database Engine directly into memory. You use the ODBC Manager to set up an ODBC data source for each remote database to which you want to connect. The ODBC Manager can be started from the 32-bit ODBC in the Windows 95 Control Panel.

Normally an Access table is created and used to develop an application within a single database. This is convenient for the developer and is easy to maintain. After testing the finished application and prior to deployment in the user environment is the best time to move the table outside the workstation to the database server. Linking the external tables back to the local database before finalizing the design can cause some complications you'll want to avoid:

- Exporting and then linking a table may require modification of the modules containing code that use the table. The Index property or the Seek method will be ineffective on remote tables. Also, local data-definition methods and properties are not an influence on remote tables.

- Internal table indexes will not be exported. Before linking the exported table, use a Pass-through query or a separate server-based tool to create a unique index to update the table's data. You can improve query performance by defining the other indexes as well.

- Default field values are not exported with a table, so create them after exporting the table. The defaults will automatically display after the record is saved.

- Access exports AutoNumber fields as Long fields. To create an artificial AutoNumber, you can create an insert trigger on the server that provides the next counter, or you can write an event procedure to provide this functionality.

- A database operation that violates referential integrity on the server will elicit an error message from the ODBC driver. Use server-based triggers or local form-level event procedures to simulate or trap errors for referential integrity and cascading relationships.

- The server is not affected by security established in the Access database, nor is the client program aware of security violations established in the server. The developer must trap errors and anticipate solutions that can be applied programmatically. For example, if you're editing a remote table for which you don't have permission to insert data, Access does not restrict you from typing a new record. However, when you try to save the record, the server returns an error message and the record is not inserted. When possible, synchronize local and remote user permissions and passwords. This means you only log on once because Access automatically attempts to log on to the server by using your local user permission and password and prompts you only if the attempt to log on fails.

A communication link across the network to the server must be established by your application. First, establish link tables and SQL views from the server. Then convert SQL statements to Pass-through queries. Finally, execute all Visual Basic code directly on the server.

There may be a set of stored procedures defined to retrieve data and one to update data. Pass-through queries must be used exclusively where procedures are called to access the remote table. Use the `AfterUpdate` and `AfterInsert` event procedures from forms updating the remote table or update in one event associated with an unbound form. In both, a Visual Basic subroutine uses a Pass-through query with the name of the procedure and the data from the form.

A connection must be established to pass messages and data between the client and server. The developer's objective in this endeavor is to minimize the time to connect and to reduce the overall number of connections. Connection strategies include preconnecting and reducing connection use.

Preconnecting allows caching of the authentication information and reuse. A user establishes a connection through these parameters, and their availability will speed connectivity and reconnect faster if the connection is lost. The delay in connecting through the Jet Engine will be minimized.

> **TIP**
>
> Instead of establishing an identity for each user, establish security in the back end or front end of the application so that the connections are identical. This will permit more than one user to share the same connection.

Strategies in reducing connection use, thereby enhancing performance for an individual user, are dependent on the task and the server database engine. Using some database engines that allow multiple connections to be shared by different users such as Jet may facilitate higher performance. Other engines—such as SQL Server, which allows one user one connection—are most efficient at a certain level of resource use despite the strategy. It is recommended that the size of a dynaset query be kept to a minimum. Ranges are good guides for expectation of performance. Consider the following connection ranges to be about the same level of performance:

    1 to 5

    6 to 10

    10 to 25

    25 to 100

In all ranges of connectivity, the greatest impact on performance will be gained by keeping the number of connections to a minimum and limiting the amount of data moving across the network. The former can be accomplished by sharing connections and using Visual Basic to connect and disconnect programmatically. The latter must be considered during application development: How much data is absolutely necessary to accomplish the task for the user? Allowing the user to scroll through pages of data that meet some vague query criteria certainly does not facilitate performance across the network. It is better to ascertain more specifics within the characteristics of the data to derive a minimal set of records or values meeting the users' exacting requirements.

You can improve performance in the lower ranges through connection strategies implemented in software; this is a lower-cost solution. The first consideration should be to tune the database engine for the standards recommended for a level of use by the manufacturer. Next is to establish groups of users into the same authentication so that connection use can be shared and can overlap. Finally, modify applications to limit the nature and amount of connect time.

In the upper range of connections, a greater cost and effort result in smaller perceived gains in performance. These strategies may include redistributing the client/server components from a two-tiered implementation of an application layer and a server layer to a three-tiered structure that includes a transaction layer.

Although tuning may result in some low-cost, albeit incremental, improvement in performance, radical measures may be required to significantly affect large numbers of connections being handled efficiently. Conversion to a database engine with proven performance in the range of connections, users, or transactions may be warranted.

The developer may also recommend "throwing hardware at the problem" by increasing and splitting the database server onto a number of computers. The network should be checked for bottlenecks, especially if large amounts of data are being moved in one transaction. The cost of a high-speed network must be weighed against the benefit of the performance gained.

Performance Considerations in a Multiuser Environment

This section discusses techniques you can use to improve the performance of Access in multiuser client/server applications, particularly how to design queries that maximize the use of the server and thereby improve query performance.

Access limits the amount of information available over the network by interpreting portions of the queries locally and only passing to the server expressions that are supported by that server. The following is a list of commonly supported expressions:

- Heterogeneous joins between local tables and remote tables
- Heterogeneous joins between remote tables in different ODBC data sources
- SQL extensions for Access, including financial and domain aggregate functions
- Functions in Visual Basic that evaluate remote fields
- Expressions or Union queries mixing Text and Numeric data types

- Multiple SQL statements
- Numeric, string, and date/time functions
- Conversion functions

Position is everything in SQL. By using evaluation tools provided with the database engine or following procedures outlined in SQL programming textbooks, you can obtain a high degree of efficiency. Depending on the expression and the location in the statement, the query can be evaluated locally or will be passed to the server. Expressions in the SELECT clause that occur in a Totals query, a Union query, or a query that uses the DISTINCT predicate are evaluated locally. Other expressions such as WHERE, ORDER BY, and GROUP BY cause at least part of the query to be evaluated locally.

> **TIP**
>
> Limit the data Access requests from the server. When it is necessary to use a WHERE clause, index the fields on the server for maximum efficiency. Be sure to check the functionality and standard level of SQL supported on the server; otherwise, the processing may have to be performed by the client.

This statement

```
SELECT * FROM Employees WHERE Status - IIf([What Status?]-'Rehired',1,2)
```

allows the user to limit the search to rehired employees and sends the following statement to the server:

```
SELECT * FROM Employees WHERE Status -?
```

This technique will reduce network traffic and improve efficiency.

Access performs heterogeneous joins between local and remote tables by requesting all the records in the remote table or tables and performing the join locally. Performing a remote index join for each key in the local table requests only the records with a matching key value.

You can enhance performance in remote table queries by keeping the local table small and using a remote field index. Limit the amount of data requested for the join by supplying additional restrictions on remote fields, which will improve the performance of queries that use a heterogeneous join.

> **TIP**
>
> A minimalist approach to application development is reflected in improved multiuser performance. Only retrieve fields from the server that you must display. Design your forms with only essential data required for the task at hand.

23

MULTIUSER DEVELOPMENT

Store data for tables that do not change in a local database. If the table is joined in queries with remote tables, also keep a copy of it on the server to avoid heterogeneous joins. Store data that changes infrequently both locally and remotely; however, remember to provide a way to download the current data when it changes and remember to query to see if the tables are out of sync.

Although dynasets might give you more options in updating a recordset, setting the query type to Snapshot is more efficient for the application, resulting in faster retrieval times for a recordset. Dynasets are more efficient when using large recordsets or recordsets containing `Memo` or `OLE Object` fields because `Memo` and `OLE Object` fields are retrieved only if they are displayed on the screen or directly referenced in your code.

> **TIP**
>
> Visual Basic functions are inherently more focused in functionality contributing to a conservation of resources in a multiuser environment. The Snapshot data view is made more efficient by using `dbForwardOnly` in the `OpenRecordset` method.

Using a version field (or timestamp) maintained by the server that automatically changes its value each time the record is updated is an easy way to prevent unnecessary update processing and improve performance. Transactions improve performance when multiple updates are batched and written as a single batch. Batch operations ensure that all users are working with mirrored data as batched transactions succeed or fail as a group, thus shielding other users from partially completed updates. You can use Visual Basic to control transactions by using the `BeginTrans`, `CommitTrans`, and `Rollback` methods. But using these methods instead of sending server-specific transaction commands in pass-through queries might confuse the internal tracking of server transactions performed by Jet.

You can also save new records for data-entry forms or multiple records of data in a local holding table and then transfer batches of records from the holding table to the server in a single transaction to improve performance.

Each `Workspace` object represents an isolated transaction when you're working with local data, whereas the reverse is true for remote data used within the `Workspace` object. You can, however, force a `Workspace` object to have a distinct remote transaction space by setting the `IsolateODBCTrans` property of the `Workspace` object to `True`. This prevents the `Workspace` object from sharing connections with other workspaces and guarantees transaction isolation.

> **TIP**
>
> It's a good idea to keep transactions as short as possible and to not write code sequences that require user input because most servers lock out the user's ability to change or read transactions until they are committed or rolled back.

Linking to the Web

The Internet is a complex web of networks joined by a common communication standard (TCP/IP), a server standard (HTTP), and a presentation language (HTML). Intranet technologies have recently evolved from those created for the Internet. Programs developed under Internet standards can be successfully implemented in a LAN environment. The same programs now move from the intranet through the Internet.

Standards have recently evolved for database server functionality over the Internet. Access 97 incorporates these standards of operation. The developer has Access as a candidate Internet database server and can also use HTML code and HTTP references for intranet applications. One of the major benefits of using HTML for client application development is maintenance. All clients use a standard browser, which provides a standard user interface while specific functionality is derived from HTML code on an HTTP server.

Justification for the use of these technologies in a comprehensive information systems strategy is a recent issue. Certainly a compelling reason for using this approach lies in the consistency that can be gained across platforms and network topologies. Also, the attraction of limited licensing requirements for these technologies will lower the cost per client seat. Other considerations come from the way client software is developed.

Applications are combinations of HTML token-based text and references to graphics and multimedia links, as well as application modules (applets) such as can be accomplished with Java. Changes made to the HTML code on the HTTP server will automatically be updated in the next session of the client workstation.

End-user computing and rapid application prototyping are manifesting themselves through HTML. The new programming languages such as Java give the developer a finer control of functionality within the HTML environment. These applets complement the HTML to push the functionality desired by users out to the client workstations. A drawback to this approach is the large amount of memory required in the workstation to run the operating environment for the applet.

The use of database technology in Internet/intranet development has only begun. Access 97 contains an interface to HTML tables, which will be the subject of further discussion. One potential that has only recently been explored is using the database server to populate the HTML code as it is requested by the client. This concept would involve text and references being stored in one table, which would be projected through an HTML template from another table. This approach lends itself to easier development once the database is established, as well as considerably easier maintenance and version control.

Access can interpret and import data from tables from HTML documents. An HTML table is a series of tags that describe the component parts of the table. Linking to an HTML table,

Access parses the string that contains the table. The following describes the table format in HTML pseudocode:

```
<TABLE>This marks where the table begins
<CAPTION...>This space contains the caption for the table</CAPTION>
 <TH...>This space contains a heading for the table</TH>
<TR...>This marks the beginning of a row
<TD...>This space contains a data cell</TD>
<TD...>This space contains a data cell</TD>
<TD...>This space contains a data cell</TD>
.
.
.
This marks the end of a row</TR>
This marks the location where the table ends</TABLE>
```

A table following this simple format without embedded lists or tables can be imported as file type HTML.

Output from an Access application may be converted to HTML via the Publish to the Web Wizard. Static or dynamic HTML documents can be generated from data sheets, forms, or reports. A hyperlink object data type can contain references to addresses using universal naming convention or uniform resource locator syntax. These capabilities enable a rudimentary Web server capability. A company's Access database can be utilized by customers and business partners to perform service functions such as checking inventory availability and pricing.

Summary

A multiuser environment typically consists of independent workstations connected through a network. Development and performance considerations may include, but are not limited to, the following:

- Platform compatibility
- Networking (Internet, intranet)
- Number of connections
- Transaction volume
- Order and sequence of processing
- Workstation throughput
- Server throughput
- Network throughput

An initial cost/benefit analysis model will establish a baseline performance range of expectations. If your existing system experiences an increase in volume, you can make performance improvements by adjusting this model through modifications to the database software and hardware. Your goal is to distribute database components that reflect the demands of the system to accomplish a desired level of response.

Tables can be assigned to one physical file. This file can be shared by multiple users on a network. This is typically the initial stage of development and is most useful for a series of transactions where users do not require simultaneous access to the same records. The shared information is updated and available from one source. You should consider the following areas:

- Availability—There will be a threshold above which data will not be available to a significant number of users at one time.
- Data integrity—The reliability of the data will be superior to any distributed system security. A single file in one location is much easier to secure.

You can only ensure that these areas are under control if a backup process is scheduled and files are adequately maintained.

IN THIS PART

Performance, Optimization, and Troubleshooting

CHAPTER 24

Improving Performance with Access 97 Database Utilities

by Jude Mullaney

IN THIS CHAPTER

This chapter covers the performance and optimization of Access 97. It shows you how to enhance the execution of your databases and increase the transactions that are carried out by that database.

Many different ways exist to increase the performance of Access. These ways can be divided into two groups. The first group deals with the interface of the database itself—for example, how fast a form opens. The second group deals with data retrieval, such as how long it takes to display data. While learning about these performance issues, you also will learn about the right hardware, the Registry, and Access improvements that are tangible items that can be modified to increase the performance of Access. Another subject covered in this chapter is how to handle existing databases from previous versions of Access. Finally, you will learn about repairing and compacting databases.

Improving the Performance of Your Database

Improving the performance of your database is tricky because there are so many different variables to look at. Making this task even harder is the fact that each database is different; a performance enhancement may work on one database while other factors in another database would negate the performance enhancement. Some improvements may be only minimal, whereas others will increase performance as the number of records in your database increases. Even Microsoft has taken measures to make Access perform more quickly. This section shows you some items that usually improve performance in the reaction time of the database and its ability to bring in records, along with the improvements in Access 97 that make it run faster.

Hardware

When speaking about the performance of Access (or any other software product), it is important to look at the hardware on which it is running. Access should run on a Pentium 100MHz-class machine or better. It should have at least 16MB RAM and a 1GB hard disk. Will Access run on a machine that is below that standard? The answer is yes, but you will not be happy with its performance. The higher the megahertz and the more RAM you have, the faster your machine and Access will perform.

Registry Modifications

There are other things that you can do to the computer system that can increase the performance of Access itself. For example, Access uses settings in the Windows Registry, which is a database that Microsoft Windows uses to set up and configure the hardware and software. By tweaking the Access settings in the Registry, it is possible to increase the program's performance. Access's initialization information is also stored in the Registry.

It is *not* usually recommended that you change settings in the Registry. However, if you must make changes to the Registry and you're using Windows 95, choose Run from the Start button's pop-up menu and type REGEDIT in the dialog box that appears. If you are working with NT Workstation, choose the Run command from the File menu of either the Program Manager or the File Manager, and type REGEDT32 in the box that appears.

There are two keys that contain the Access Registry information:

```
\HKEY_LOCAL_MACHINE\SOFTWARE\Microsoft\Office\8.0\Access
\HKEY_LOCAL_MACHINE\SOFTWARE\Microsoft\Jet\3.5
```

These keys are different for different versions of Access. You need to open them and make your edits in Notepad. It is highly recommended that you back up your Registry before you make any changes to it. Any changes made to the keys will take effect the next time Access is run. If you make changes to the Microsoft Jet Engine, it may affect Access and any other program that uses the Jet Database Engine, such as Excel 97.

> **WARNING**
>
> Any changes to the Windows Registry may affect not only Access but other programs running in Windows as well. Changes can (and have) produced unexpected results, causing the user to need to reinstall Access. Please make sure that you back up the Windows Registry before you make any changes.

Access 97 Improvements

There are several features Microsoft has instituted that make your databases run faster because Microsoft has enhanced Access itself. Access 97 is a much faster development tool than any of the previous versions. The following list enumerates some of the features new to Access 97 that offer some performance improvements:

- Some of the contents of Access that are not required for some databases are not loaded. VBA and DAO are examples of items that are not loaded until they are needed. This lessens the amount of time it takes to load your database.

- Forms and reports that do not have any code associated with them open faster because event procedures do not execute any form or report modules. Transitional forms and reports are objects that have code behind them.

- The FailOnError property allows you to send bulk update queries to the server so that many records are processed at one time, as opposed to one at a time.

- Modules are not loaded until the VB code in a module is executed.

- The performance of ActiveX controls has been improved.

- The compiled state of a database is sustained even if it is changed. Only the modified code will be decompiled.

- Combo boxes are faster.
- Printing and previewing actions are faster.
- Find, delete, insert, and update actions performed on recordsets are faster when explicit transactions are not used.
- Finding information on tables in Datasheet View is faster.

Database Design

It is also important to mention database design when speaking about performance. Good database design is paramount to its speed. No matter what machine you run your database on, it will perform better if the program has been designed well. Things to consider when you are trying to come up with a good database design are

- Why is the database being created? Usually, it is to track information and produce reports.
- What tables are needed? This is extracted from the information tracked and the reports needed.
- What fields are being tracked by this database?
- Are there any fields that should have unique values? A good example for this is Social Security numbers.
- How do the tables relate to each other? This can be done either through the relationships window or on an object-by-object basis.
- Are the other objects that you create, like forms and reports, tracking the right data?
- Can the Analyzer help improve the structure of your database?

When you are designing a database, you have to consider how many people will be simultaneously using the application. *Standalone* systems are applications that are stored and performed on one machine. *Multiuser* systems are applications that are used by two or more simultaneous users. There are two types of multiuser systems: two-tier and three-tier implementations. Many books are written about these implementations; I will try to give you a condensed version here.

Single-user systems are designed with the data stored in the database. Multiuser systems usually implement a two-tier format, with the database containing the data on one machine and the database containing the code on another machine. The old school of thought was to store *all* the data on the server and have the individual PCs on the network perform the analysis. Depending on the size of the database, the number of records, and the number of users, this may not be the most efficient method. This should *not* be considered a hard-and-fast rule when designing multiuser database systems for high-speed performance. Another style for a multiuser system is to implement the three-tier format, where the PC works with the user interface, another machine has a database that stores the data, and still another database contains the information pertaining to the business rules. One of the machines in this type of system will probably be a SQL Server machine. An example of the different tier-system formats is shown in Figure 24.1.

FIGURE 24.1.

The different tier implementations of a database.

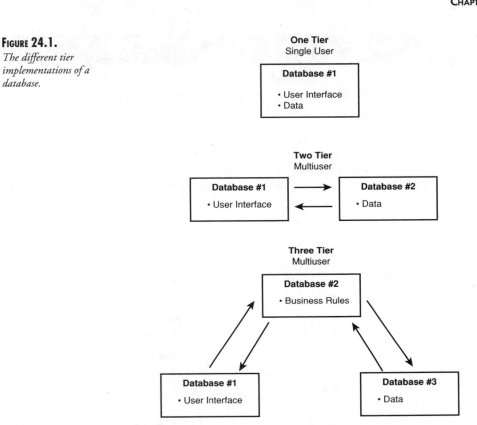

In a single-tier implementation of a database, the data as well as the user interface (forms) are stored in the same database. In a two-tier system, most of the data usually is stored in one database, whereas the other database deals with the user interface. If a user tries to access a report he does not have permission to see, the report may still be generated in the Data database, and, after the report is finished, the system may then determine that the user does not have permission to access the report. If there are a lot of users on the network, the database is tied up generating a transaction that it later will have to cancel because the user did not have permission to access the report. This can increase the traffic on the network and decrease the response time to the other users on the network.

A three-tier format system has a User Interface database and a Data database, just like the two-tier format. As you can see in Figure 24.1, the third database is the Business Rules database. The system works like this: The user requests information from the Business Rules database. The Business Rules database determines whether he is allowed to have that information and, if he is allowed, requests the information from the Data database and passes it back to the user. Some data may even be stored in local tables for the end user so that he can perform analysis on the data locally. This can increase performance by having multiple databases perform the work of one database.

> **TIP**
>
> The best way to increase the performance of a multiuser system is to minimize the traffic on the network and process any data on the fastest computer on the network.

When you build your application, it is important to pay attention to several aspects of the database. The design of the database is most important; however, the design of its tables, queries, forms, and reports, along with any VBA coding, can also affect the performance of the database. The next few pages cover the different techniques used to optimize queries, forms, and reports.

Tables

One of the key trademarks of a good database design is the reduction of redundant data. A database, in its truest sense, never has duplicate data. This is very hard to achieve, but it is possible to get close.

If you have duplicate data in two or more tables, it may be possible to split that data into yet another table. Reducing redundant data makes for smaller and faster databases.

When working with linked tables, it is important to remember that each time you view the data in a linked table, Access has to retrieve the records from another database. If the other database is on a network, you have just increased the traffic and reduced the performance of not only your database, but that of others who are also on the network. Once Access has gotten the data from the linked database, the Jet Engine closes the linked database. You can increase the performance by creating a linked table that forces the Microsoft Jet Engine to keep the linked database open, as opposed to opening and closing it for every data-transaction request and creating and deleting the associated .ldb file. You can do this by creating a dummy table in the linked database and linking the table to the main database. Use the OpenRecordSet method to open the linked table. This will keep it open and increase the performance of the main database.

Another way to keep traffic down is to view only the data you need. The more you page up and down, the more traffic you create. If you need to add a new record, select the Data Entry item from the Records pull-down menu. You may even want to look at creating queries to limit the number of records to be viewed in the datasheet. By reducing the number of records being processed by the linked database, you decrease the traffic on the network and increase the performance of your database. You can even increase the performance by setting the DataEntry property to Yes. When a form based on a linked table is executed, it automatically opens in Data Entry mode. Time is saved because Access does not have to get all the records *before* opening the form.

If you do decide to use queries on linked tables, try to stay away from using aggregate functions on the linked tables. What do you do if you need to perform aggregate functions on data in linked tables? If the data you require does not change too quickly, you may want to consider using a Make-table query on the linked table data and perform your calculations from the newly created table. After you are finished with the calculations, you then delete the table created by the Make-table query.

When working with linked tables, it is important to understand the difference between snapshots and dynasets. Snapshots are static views of data that are not updatable, and dynasets are objects that store the keys of tables and update the tables only when the data has been changed. It depends on the amount of data being retrieved. If the amount of data being retrieved is relatively small, you will want to look at using snapshots of the data for recordsets, especially if you are just viewing the data and not updating it. If you are retrieving large amounts of data or need to update the data in a linked table, you will want to use dynasets as recordsets for forms and reports.

One more aspect that has to be considered when working with linked tables is record locking. Make sure you choose the appropriate record locks and avoid holding those records in a locked state. There may be other people trying to use the same data.

Queries

Query optimization is easier now than it was in Access 2.0, mostly due to the advances made in the Microsoft Jet and Rushmore technologies. Gone are the days when you had to decide which column should appear first. The advantages in Jet have made that technique obsolete. Today, you need to be concerned with indexing fields used to set criteria for the query. The Jet Database Engine will create an index on a foreign key if there is not an index already.

> **NOTE**
>
> If there are two tables in a query, one table is local and the other an ODBC server table, and both fields in the join are indexed, the Jet database optimizes the join automatically. The key is that both fields in the join are indexed. The improvement in performance comes because Access requests only the necessary records from the server.

24

IMPROVING
PERFORMANCE
WITH UTILITIES

Remember to choose the smallest data type that is suitable for the data that will be stored in a field. This actually takes place in the Table module of the database; however, the performance can be seen in the Query module when that table with its fields and their data types is used. You will also need to use compatible data types for joined fields. For example, if you have one joined field that is an Autonumber, you should use a Number or Long Integer as opposed to a Text.

Keep the number of fields that appear in the query to a minimum. Uncheck the Show box for fields that you need to create the query but do not need to see in the datasheet. This reduces the number of fields that need to be displayed and can increase the performance of the query.

You also want to stay away from calculated fields in subqueries if possible. It is better to have the expression in the top-level query if you need to have calculated fields. It is important to know that there are two types of expressions: simple and complex. All the simple expressions are optimizable through Rushmore technology. *Simple expressions* include the use of comparison operators or expressions performed on single fields in the grid (for example, [City] = "Charlotte" or [Grade]>80).

More complex expressions may be entirely optimizable, partially optimizable, or not optimizable at all through Rushmore technology. These expressions combine two simple expressions with the And or Or operator. The expressions can even be one complex expression that may not be optimizable. An example of a complex expression is [City]= "Charlotte" Or [FirstName] = "Jude". This is a complex expression not because the operator is an Or, but because it is likely that the field [FirstName] is not an indexed field.

Another way to increase the performance of a query is to use the Group By option on the joined field in the same table as the one that is performing the aggregate function. When you use this option, Access first joins all the records and then performs the aggregate function. Note that when working with the Group By option, you should keep the number of fields being returned to a minimum. Also, if you are working with groups in a query where two or more tables are joined, you might want to create a query on the joined tables and then create another query based on the first to perform the aggregate function. This has been known to increase the speed of the query.

Certain action queries that deal with ODBC data sources can be optimized. When working with Update or Delete queries, you want to set the FailOnError property for the query to Yes. This lets you know when an error has occurred during the update or delete to the ODBC data source by terminating the execution of the query.

If it is possible, avoid using restrictive query criteria on non-indexed fields as well as calculated fields. Also, try not to sort records of multi-table queries. This has been known to slow down the performance.

Forms and Reports

Form and report optimization is also important when you are trying to increase the performance of your database. There are several measures that you can take that may increase the reaction time of your Form and Report objects. Change any SQL statements in the RecordSource property for forms and reports to queries, and then name the queries in the RecordSource property. You can do this from within the object by bringing up the SQL window for the RecordSource property of the object and selecting File | Save As. You can then name the query and store it in the current database. The new query will appear in the drop-down list associated with the RecordSource property for the object.

Sometimes it is necessary to have expressions in the output of a form or report. Place any expressions that need to appear in forms and reports in controls.

Also, try to stay away from using bitmaps or other graphics objects, because they tend to slow down the opening of forms and reports. If you do use unbound object frames to display graphics, change them to image controls. When working with bitmaps and reports, use black-and-white bitmaps rather than color bitmaps, especially if you are printing to a non-color printer.

Forms can have their open response time increased if you set the `Data Entry` property to `Yes`. This is especially helpful if you just need to perform data entry and do not need to view the other records. You can use another form to view all the existing records instead of using the data entry form.

What about forms that are not being used? Should you close them or open them? If you need the form itself to open quickly every time it is evoked, you will want to leave it open; however, having many open forms actually can decrease the overall speed of the database itself. The answer to the question is simple, really. Do you want your forms to open quickly, or do you want the database itself to perform quickly? If the answer is to have the database perform quickly, close all the forms that are not being used.

When working with subforms, try to minimize the number of fields that appear in the subform. You may need to create a query based on the table containing the data that is to appear in the subform. This will allow you to specify which fields are to appear in the record source of the subform. Extra fields that are not needed in the subform can decrease the performance of the form overall. You will also want to index all the fields that appear in the subform and are linked to the main form. If there are any fields used for criteria, you will want to index those, too. If the subform is just for reference purposes or to view data, you will want to set the subform's `AllowEdits`, `AllowAddtions`, and `AllowDeletions` properties to `No` or set the `RecordSetType` property to `SnapShot`. These methods have been known to increase the performance of the subform.

Earlier in this chapter, you learned that one of the new Access 97 performance features is that non-transitional forms and reports objects open faster because event procedures are not included in the form or report module. This tip is activated by the `HasModule` property found on the form or report. When you set this property to `No`, the form or report will open more quickly and take up less space. You can still use code with the form or report in objects such as command buttons, but you will be using macros or hyperlinks. Even though the default of the `HasModule` property is set to `No`, in order for you to take full advantage of the performance, you must physically set it to `No` (`0`).

Even the `Filter By Form` object can have its performance increased. To modify the factors that affect the performance of such an object, select Options from the Tools pull-down menu. Clicking on the Edit/Find tab will bring up the information that is shown in Figure 24.2.

The bottom half of the tab contains information that can be modified to increase the performance of the `Filter By Form` objects. The Show List of Values In Local Indexed Fields option allows users to display lists of data only for fields that are indexed in the local tables. When the Local Nonindexed Fields box is checked, the user can view the data for local table fields that are not indexed. The ODBC Fields box allows the user to access data from fields that are not local to the database. If you use the `Filter By Form` object only to return records based on indexed fields, you might want to uncheck the Local Nonindexed Fields option. If you use the `Filter By Form` object to return records on certain nonindexed fields all the time, you might want to consider indexing those fields to increase the performance.

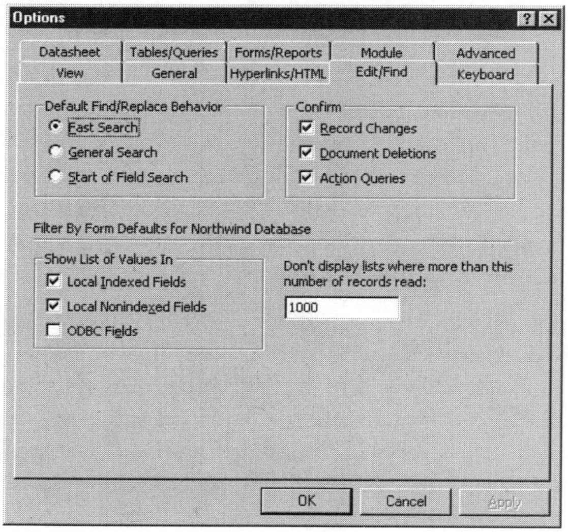

FIGURE 24.2.

You can alter the performance of the `Filter By Form` *object in the Edit/Find tab.*

The more items that are checked in this tab, the slower the performance of `Filter By Form` will appear. The final piece of data that can be modified for the `Filter By Form` object is the maximum number of records that will be displayed when that object is executed. In Figure 24.2, the maximum number is 1,000.

> **NOTE**
>
> There are two points to consider when working with this field. The first is that if the number of records being returned by the `Filter By Form` object is greater than 1,000, a datasheet containing *no* records will be displayed. The second is that all the records displayed contain unique values, even on nonindexed fields.

Another way to increase the performance of a database that is linked to an ODBC database is to work with transactions. If you have a data entry form that is used to enter multiple changes to the database, you should consider using a *holding table*. A holding table is a location where the data entries are entered, and then you execute a single batch update. Not only does this reduce the amount of traffic on the network, but it increases the response time of the database.

When trying to maximize the performance of reports, you have several options. Some of the same things that increase the performance of forms can be applied to reports: Do not let controls overlap; limit the use of bitmaps; when using bitmaps, make them black and white instead of color; and place graphics in image controls. The other tips you can try are described in this section.

If you are sorting data or grouping data for a report, use only the indexed fields. If the fields you need are not indexed, you might want to consider indexing them. More indexes in a database slow down the writing of a record in a database and make the database itself bigger. You must determine whether additional indexes are worth the reduction of speed in writing a record or the increase in the size of the database. Any field that is linked to the main report needs to be indexed. Sometimes it is necessary to have expressions appear in the subreport. When they do have to appear, try to stay away from sorting or grouping on expression fields; that has been known to reduce the overall performance of a report.

Subreports that are based on queries instead of on tables tend to perform better because the number of fields that are displayed can be limited to a number that is less than the number of fields in the table. Reducing the number of fields being displayed increases the performance of the report, especially if the number of records is large.

You can optimize the `RecordSource` for the report by basing it on an optimized query. This means that you avoid using both complex expressions and domain aggregate functions. Single comparison operators and limited use of the `And` operator in combining two single comparison operators allow the Jet engine to optimize a query. When you use complex expressions that include multiple comparison operators or the `Or` operator, you cause a drag on the Jet engine that fuels the muscle used to return the records.

Another trick to increasing the performance of a report is to use the `HasData` property or the `NoData` event to determine whether a report is going to generate an empty recordset. A subreport within a report may or may not contain data, depending on the actions of the user. You can set the `HasData` property to `No (0)` if the user has neglected to perform an operation before generating the report. This is determined when you do a print or a print preview and can increase the response of the report.

The `NoData` event occurs only when a report is being printed and will cancel a print if the report or subreport is bound to an empty recordset.

Most reports use criteria to restrict the values in certain fields. If the report is based on a query and the criteria is set on one of the join fields, you need to test to see which is faster. Is the report faster when the criteria is set on the join field on the one side or on the many side? It differs from database to database due to the many extenuating circumstances that can appear and are different for each database.

Overall, reports based on tables are faster than reports based on queries (unless a subreport is involved). When the data being used in the report does not change often but you need a query to generate the data for a report, you may want to consider using a Make-table query to generate the data, and base the report on the newly created table. If the report still seems slow, check to make sure your indexes are on target.

One last tip concerning the increase of performance on a report is to avoid using domain aggregate functions to access data from a table. A *domain* is a record returned by a table, query, or SQL statement, and its functions are prefixed with the letter D (for example, DSum or DLookup). You can get the same data from the table if you use it in a query and place your criteria on the desired field. Domain aggregate functions cannot be optimized by the Microsoft Jet Engine.

The Performance Analyzer

All the information stated so far has pertained to the individual tips and tricks used by professional developers to increase the performance of a database on the object level. The next section of this chapter deals with a tool provided by Access 97 to help end users as well as developers increase the performance of their databases. This tool is called the Performance Analyzer.

The Performance Analyzer evolved from usability labs instituted by the Microsoft Access team. Microsoft noticed that even though Access was an easy development tool for Windows-based products, developers were not taking advantage of the full range of options available to them. Access allowed programmers so many different ways to create databases that certain features were not being used to their fullest extent.

To make things easier, Microsoft created the Performance Analyzer to provide you with tips and tricks about common programming situations to allow you to increase the performance of your databases. These tips were generated by Microsoft Access team members who have a thorough knowledge of Access and the Jet database engine and can help you increase your databases' performance by as much as 20 percent. The Performance Analyzer makes a list of suggestions that can be used; if you decide to implement those suggestions, Access will do it for you automatically. You launch the Performance Analyzer by selecting Analyze | Performance from the Tools pull-down menu, as shown in Figure 24.3.

Once the Performance Analyzer has been launched, you are presented with a list of different options that can be analyzed by Access. In Figure 24.4, you can see there are eight tabs to select from. You can choose to analyze only certain objects within a database, such as only the objects that pertain to Customer information—the Customer table, Customer queries, and Customer forms and reports. You can also choose to select entire objects within the database to be analyzed, such as all the tables or all the queries. Finally, you can choose the All tab and view or select all the objects in the database and have them analyzed.

To select an object, click on its checkbox to place a checkmark in the corresponding box. You can select entire groups by clicking the Select All button on the right side. To deselect an object that you do not want analyzed, click the item again—it's like a toggle switch that turns on and off with each click. You can also uncheck a large number of objects by clicking the Deselect button.

FIGURE 24.3.

The Performance Analyzer is located in the Tools menu.

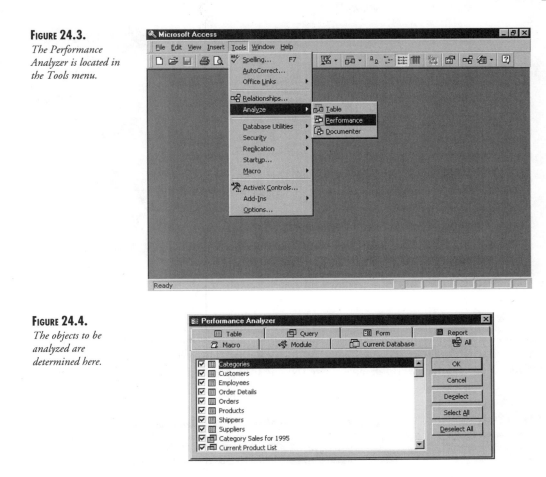

FIGURE 24.4.

The objects to be analyzed are determined here.

When all the objects that you want to analyze have been checked, click the OK button to execute the Performance Analyzer. Access will analyze all the checked objects, as shown in Figure 24.5. It usually takes only a minute or two, but the time can differ, depending on the size of the database and the number of objects selected.

FIGURE 24.5.

The Performance Analyzer in action.

The Analysis Results and Notes of the Performance Analyzer for the Northwind database are shown in Figure 24.6.

24

IMPROVING
PERFORMANCE
WITH UTILITIES

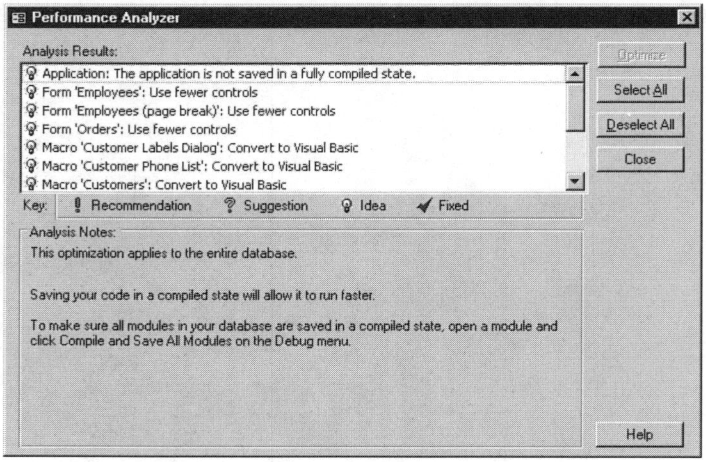

FIGURE 24.6.

*The Performance
Analyzer's Analysis
Results and Notes.*

FIGURE 24.6.

*The Performance
Analyzer's Analysis
Results and Notes.*

The advice given by Access is grouped into three categories: recommendations, suggestions, and ideas. Each piece of advice has a small icon associated with it that lets you know what kind of advice it is.

When the Performance Analyzer is run on a fictitious database that was designed by Microsoft, the results returned are slanted toward the Idea category. However, if the Performance Analyzer is run on a real-world database, like the one in Figure 24.7, some real, helpful tips and tricks can be learned.

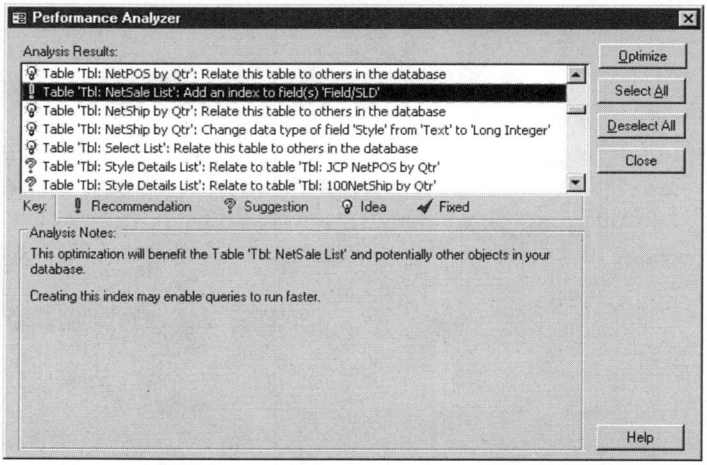

FIGURE 24.7.

*The Analysis Results
and Notes for a real-
world database.*

The categories of advice that can be the most helpful to programmers are the Recommendation and Suggestion categories. These items are illustrated with an exclamation point and a question mark, respectively, as shown in Figure 24.7. The recommended course of action on each line item can be seen in the Analysis Notes box toward the bottom of the form. To optimize a single item, highlight the item and click the Optimize button. If you click the Select All button and then click Optimize, Access will perform optimization on only the Recommendation and the Suggestion line items. The Idea line items are just that—ideas. If you would like to incorporate an idea, you must read the Analysis Notes section for that Idea line item.

> **NOTE**
>
> Once an optimization has been performed, it cannot be undone. Please make sure you read the Analysis Notes before you optimize.

Before the Performance section of this chapter can be concluded, it is important to touch on the subject of encryption. *Encryption* is the process of creating a second database and changing it so that it is indecipherable by other utility programs or word processors. Encrypted databases perform more slowly than non-encrypted or decrypted databases. If the database that is being encrypted works with data from another ODBC database, the performance can be even slower. Be prepared to lose anywhere from 10 to 15 percent of your performance if you encrypt your database.

Compacting the Database

When a database is *compacted*, it is condensed to a smaller size. One of the net results is that the database's performance is increased. Why would you want to compact a database? As you build a database and work with it, you probably will go through a number of object additions and deletions. When you start to delete tables from a database, the data becomes *fragmented*, which means that the data is stored on the hard disk inefficiently. Compacting the database rearranges the database file and how it is stored on the hard drive.

In the old days of Access programming, to compact a database, you had to close it. With Access 97, you can compact a database that is open. Figure 24.8 illustrates what happens while you are compacting the database. Basically, the only thing that you can see is found in the status bar.

If you need to compact a database that is not already open, you must close the database that is currently open (if you have one running). From the Tools menu, select Database Utilities and click Compact Database. You will be presented with a dialog box like the one in Figure 24.9. Select the desired database and click Compact.

FIGURE 24.8.

You can compact an open database.

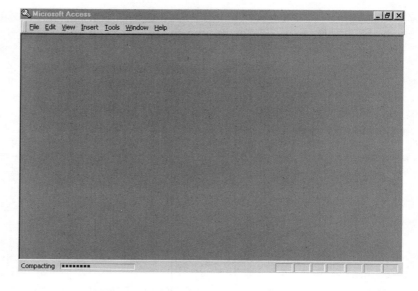

FIGURE 24.9.

The dialog box for compacting a database.

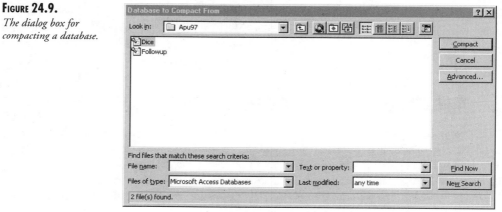

Once you have selected a database to compact, you will be prompted for a new location and name for the compacted database. In Figure 24.10, you can see that the compacted database will be renamed but stored in the same location.

If you compact an open database, Access will save the compacted database with the same name. However, if you compact a closed database, you can rename the compacted database and retain a version of the database before it was compacted.

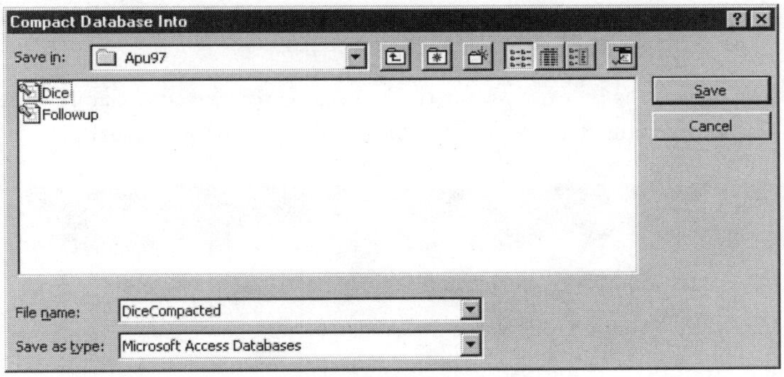

FIGURE 24.10.

A compacted database must be named and given a location where it will be stored.

> **TIP**
>
> If you compact a closed database, you may be able to get a smaller, tighter compaction than if you compact an open database.

Compacting has been known to speed up queries. This is because the data is reorganized in the table so that it can be found in the same place on the hard disk. Another good feature of compacting a database is that it allows the reset of the AutoNumber field for tables that have had deleted records. The AutoNumber value will reset to the largest AutoNumber in the table, plus one. That means that if you have deleted records in the middle of a table and have added new records with new AutoNumber fields, compacting the database will not let you go in and renumber records with the deleted AutoNumbers from the middle of the table. For example, if the last three records were AutoNumbered with 10, 11, and 12 and you deleted records 10, 11, and 12 and compacted the database before another record (AutoNumber 13) could be added, the compacting will allow you to use AutoNumbers 10, 11, and 12 again because the largest AutoNumber field is now 9. This is the syntax for the code used in the CompactDatabase method:

```
DBEngine.CompactDatabase olddb, newdb, local, options, password
```

- ■ *olddb* is the name of an existing database that is closed. The path of the database is entered here, and you can access a database over the network.

- ■ *newdb* is the name of the new, compacted database. Again, the path of the database is entered here, and you can work over the network. However, you are not allowed to use the same filename and location as the old database.

- ■ local is an optional piece and specifies the collating order for the new database. The default for this argument is the same as for the old database.

24

IMPROVING
PERFORMANCE
WITH UTILITIES

■ *options* is an optional piece and allows you to combine constants that indicate multiple options as specified in Settings.

■ *password* is where you set the password for the new database is set. Make sure that you concatenate the password string with `;pwd=NewPassword`.

TIP

This switch can be added to the `CompactDatabase` module:

`/Compact <target database name>`

It compacts the database and closes Access.

When the `CompactDatabase` option is executed, Access creates a temporary database and then exports all the objects from the first database to the temporary database. Then, it either re-names the temporary database to the original database name (if none is specified in the `CompactDatabase` method or if you execute from the opened database) or names the temporary database to the new database name as specified in the `CompactDatabase` method. If you rename the database, you still retain the original database.

If your database will not compact, it can be for a few reasons. First, there may not be enough hard-disk space left to compact a database *and* retain the original database. Second, you might not have the exclusive rights turned on for the database, and someone else may be using it.

NOTE

If you compact a database created with a previous version of Access, the database will not convert to an Access 97 format. The `CompactDatabase` method should not be used to convert 1.x versions of a database to a higher version. The fact that the database was compacted with an older version of the Microsoft Jet engine means that only other applications using the same version of Jet will be able open that converted/compacted database. To convert a database, select Database Utilities from the Tools pull-down menu and click the Convert Database item.

Earlier, you learned that compacting a database resets the `AutoNumber` field to the highest `AutoNumber` and adds one. When you are working with a `RecordCount` property, the value should equal the number of records accessed. So, if you are working with a dynaset and have viewed only one record, the `RecordCount` property is equal to 1. To view or visit all the records, use the `MoveLast` method after the recordset is open. There may be a time when multiple users can interfere with the `RecordCount` or when you have to abort the `MoveFirst`/`MoveLast` method. Either of these situations can give you an inaccurate `RecordCount` value. When a database is compacted, the `RecordCount` number is restored to its correct value.

I have one last comment about compacting databases, and it has to do with replicable databases. Every change made to the design of a replicable database is stored by the Microsoft Jet engine. This information is stowed in the MSysSchemaChg system table, and each time the database is changed, the newest version is stored there until it is synchronized. The MSysSchemaChg system table is comparable to the Windows Clipboard, except that the newest copy is saved to the Clipboard in preparation for a paste. When you compact the replicable database, you clear out the MSysSchemaChg system table and reduce the overhead for storing changes. This makes your database more efficient; it is recommended that a replica database be compacted frequently and just before synchronization.

Repairing the Database

One of the new features with Access 97 is the capability to perform database utilities on open databases. Repair Database is one of those database utilities. The Repair Database utility applies to databases that you have open and to which you have exclusive access. The database cannot be opened by another user at the same time that you are trying to repair it.

Why would you ever want to repair a database? An event may have taken place that caused Access to close down abruptly—perhaps in the middle of a write operation. Power outages, computer hardware/software failures, or anything that causes Access to close in an abnormal manner might cause corruption that you will need to repair. If Access closes the regular way, by the user choosing File | Close, corruption problems do not happen.

Usually, Access can detect a problem with a database when it is first opened or compacted and will then recommend that you repair the database. However, there are times when Access will not detect a problem, but problems still arise with a database that has worked fine in the past and has not had any changes to its structure. These problems may be reproducible, or they may be intermittent; in any case, you may need to repair your database to see if the problems cease.

To repair a database, select Database Utilities | Repair Database from the Tools pull-down menu, as shown in Figure 24.11.

When a database has been repaired successfully, you will get a dialog box like the one in Figure 24.12.

There may be times when you want to repair a database, but you cannot open it. Closed databases can be repaired by closing any opened database but not closing Access. Select Database Utilities | Repair Database from the Tools pull-down menu. If no databases are open, you will be presented with a dialog box like the one in Figure 24.13.

Depending on the size and number of problems with the database, the repairs can take anywhere from a few seconds to a few minutes.

You can write code that will perform the same repair function as the one found in the Database Utilities under the Tools menu. The syntax is

```
DBEngine.RepairDatabase.dbname
```

24

IMPROVING
PERFORMANCE
WITH UTILITIES

Figure 24.11.

Selecting Repair Database from the Tools menu.

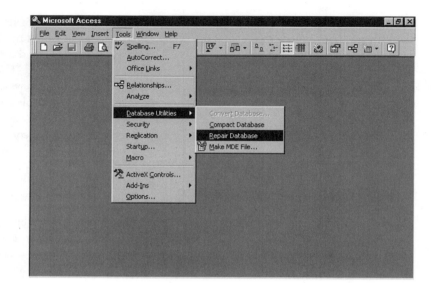

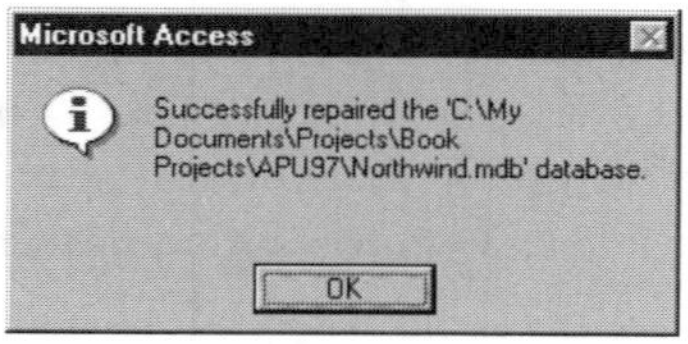

Figure 24.12.

Access notifies you when it has successfully repaired a database.

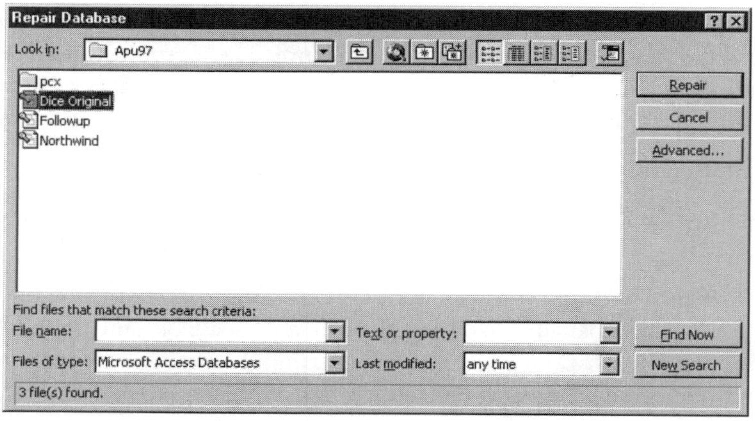

Figure 24.13.

You can perform a repair on a closed database.

dbname should contain the path and filename of the database that is to be repaired. If you just type in a filename, Access will search the current directory. You can also specify a network path if your system supports UNC, the Uniform Naming Convention.

24

> **TIP**
>
> You can use a switch in the RepairDatabase module. By adding
>
> /Repair
>
> to the syntax, you can repair the desired database and then close Access.

Table, Query, Index, and Data Object Corruption

When you evoke the RepairDatabase method, Access tries to validate all the system tables and their indexes, as well as all the pages. Data is stored on pages—and a page is about 2KB in size. Depending on the size of the record, multiple records can reside on one page. Repairs to a database require that Access look at the data in a database, too.

When a repair is executed, the RepairDatabase method checks the tables, the indexes, and the pages of data. The RepairDatabase method works primarily on Table and Query objects. Any corrupt data is usually discarded by Access.

If a RepairDatabase method is executed and the database cannot be repaired, you will get a dialog box like the one in Figure 24.14. There are two reasons that a database cannot be repaired. The first is that the data, tables, or indexes are so corrupted that RepairDatabase cannot repair the damage. The second is that Form, Report, Macro, and Module objects are corrupted. The repair utility does not even attempt to repair damaged objects other than those of the Table and Query types; it only copies them to the new database.

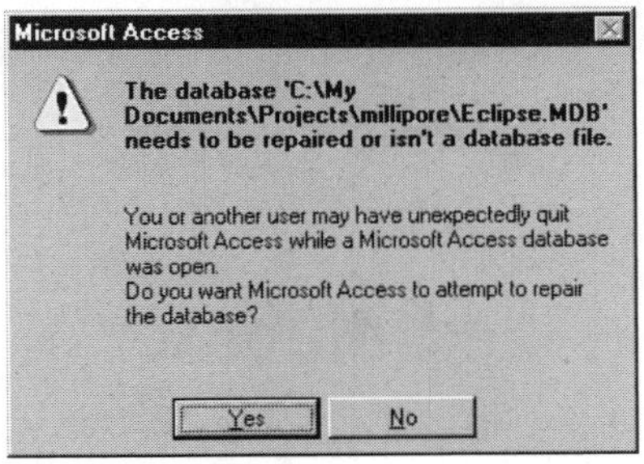

FIGURE 24.14.
This database had a problem with the RepairDatabase *method.*

Form or Report Object Corruption

In the event that you do have corruption in other objects, there is corrective action that you can take. You need to determine if the damage is *in* a form or report or *on* the form or report.

If the damage is in a form or report, try creating a new form or report. Copy all the objects from the old, corrupt form or report and place them in the new form or report. If the damage is to the form or report directly, the newly created form or report should work.

If the damage is to an object on the form or report, you will have a little more work to do. Create a new form or report. Bring the objects on the corrupted form or report over to the new form or report, piece by piece. Each time you bring over an object, close the form or report and test it. This process of elimination is called "starting from a known condition." You know the new form or report is not corrupted, so bringing over each individual object from the corrupt form or report allows you to test which object is corrupt. When you identify the corrupt object, simply create a new object that performs the desired tasks and delete the old, corrupt object.

Macro or Module Corruption

The types of corruption that can happen to a `Macro` or `Module` object can be grouped into two categories. The first is to the object itself; the second is to the contents of the macro or module. When you have damage to the macro or module, try creating a new macro or module and copying the contents from the old to the new. This should solve the problem. When the damage is to the contents of a macro or module, you still have to create a new macro or module. However, instead of copying the contents from the old to the new, you will need to re-create the contents from scratch.

> **NOTE**
>
> The Repair Database option tries to repair corrupted Microsoft Jet databases only. If the preceding tactics do not work in helping you recover your database, it might be damaged beyond repair. However, if you are a good programmer, you probably have been making daily and weekly backups of your system. Even though backups are inconvenient, good programmers make the time to close the file and perform the backup. This practice of backing up databases can make you a hero in your company. Restore an older version of the database. If you don't have an older version, you may need to re-create the entire database.

Converting the Database

As your computer hardware and software progress, your database applications built with that hardware and software must progress also. Only a few years ago, a 16-bit machine was fine for development because Access databases were not only created with a 16-bit version (Access 2.0), but they ran on 16-bit machines (486-class machines were predominant) and on 16-bit platforms (Windows 3.*x*). Now that software platforms have advanced, as well as the machines that they run on, you will need to upgrade your older databases.

Converting with Database Utilities

There are several ways that you can convert an existing database. If Access is already open and there is not a database open, too, you can select the Convert Database option from the Database Utilities item on the Tools pull-down menu, as shown in Figure 24.15.

FIGURE 24.15.

Databases can be converted through Database Utilities.

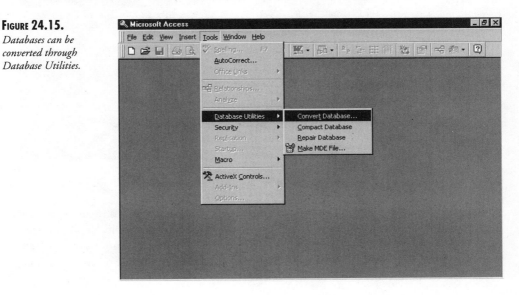

Because no database is open, Access prompts you with a search dialog box so that you can navigate to the location of the database that is to be converted. This dialog box is shown in Figure 24.16.

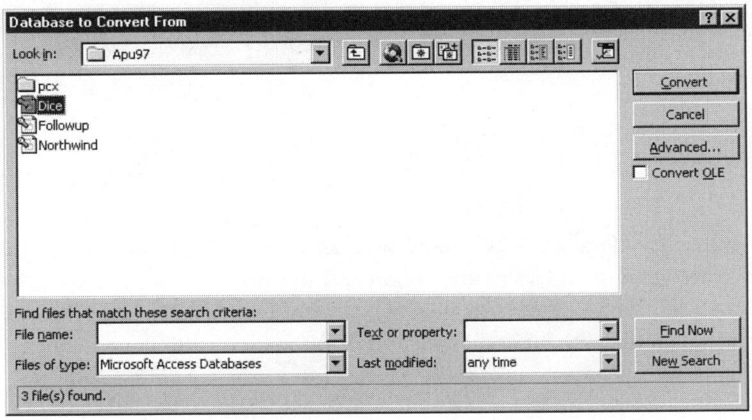

FIGURE 24.16.

Navigating to the location of the database to be converted.

Access will let you change the name of the converted database. You can also choose a different location for the converted database to be stored. (See Figure 24.17.) When Access has finished converting the database, it will appear in the location to which you saved it.

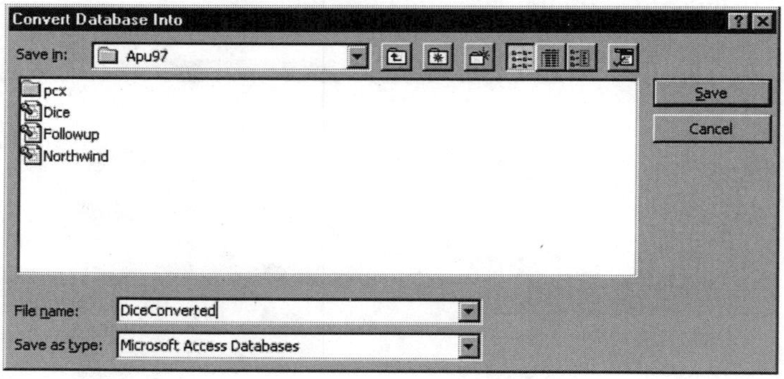

FIGURE 24.17.

FIGURE 24.17.

Choosing the new name and location of the converted database.

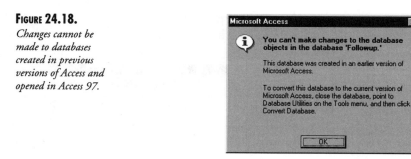

Opening Previous Versions of Databases

If you tried to go through the Explorer to open a database created with a previous version of Access, you would be prompted with a dialog box. The dialog box would let you know that because the database was created in an earlier version of Access, you cannot make any structural changes to the database. (See Figure 24.18.) You can add and delete records, but you will not be able to modify any of the existing objects.

FIGURE 24.18.

Changes cannot be made to databases created in previous versions of Access and opened in Access 97.

Because the database was created with an earlier version of Access, it uses older development technology and strategies and might not perform as well as if it were converted or rebuilt in Access 97. As it opens, bugs may appear. In Figure 24.19, you can see that opening a database that was built with an earlier version of Access has caused a few bugs.

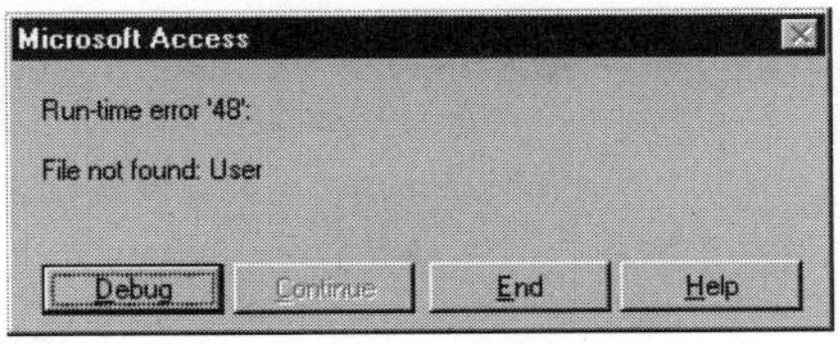

24

IMPROVING
PERFORMANCE
WITH UTILITIES

FIGURE 24.19.
*You might have some
problems opening an
older database in
Access 97.*

TIP

You can prevent Startup code from executing when a database is launched by holding
down the Shift key when you open the database. This can help reduce the number of bugs
that will appear when opening an older database in Access 97.

Database Conversion with the File Menu

You cannot convert an open database. If you want to convert it, you must close it and then
select Database Utilities | Convert Database from the Tools menu or select File | Open from
the Access menu and choose to convert the database. The dialog box that appears is shown in
Figure 24.20. You can elect to open the database or convert it.

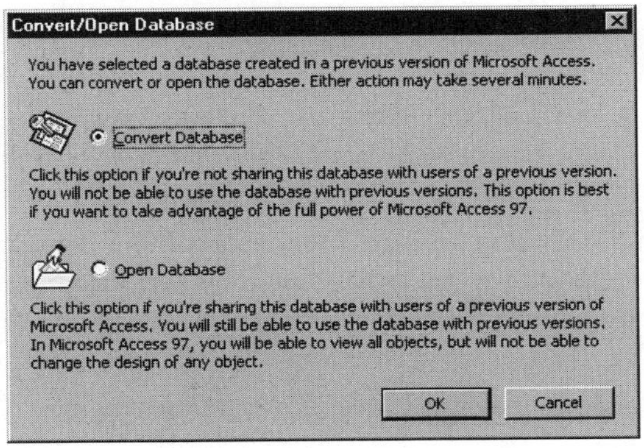

FIGURE 24.20.
*Access 97 will know if
the database being
opened was created
with an older version.*

Once you convert a database created in an older version of Access, you cannot open it in that
version of Access again. Access performs a binary conversion on the database so that you can
use all the Access 97 tools such as 32-bit architecture, the Jet database engine version 3.0, an
enhanced DAO model, and VBA.

WARNING

Back up before converting. If any problems occur in the conversion, you can revert to the
backup. Once a conversion has been done, you cannot go back to the old version.

NOTE

The more objects you have in a database, the slower the conversion process will be. Each object must be converted to Access 97.

TIP

The conversion process can be made more efficient by compiling your old database and compacting it *before* you convert it. You can compile your database by selecting Run | Compile All Modules from a module in Design View.

There will be a number of features from your old database that may or may not be converted. Following is a list of some of the things you might need to correct for Access 97, depending on how you constructed your original database:

- Any 16-bit calls that you made in the database will have to be changed to 32-bit API calls.

- Some code may not get compiled because it is moving from Access Basic Code (ABC) to Visual Basic for Applications (VBA). You can go line-by-line to convert the syntax by selecting Compile All Modules from the Debug menu found under the module Design View.

- Your custom controls might not convert because they were created with 16-bit OLE technology. There might be controls that existed in the 16-bit world but do not have a 32-bit equivalent that is registered on your system.

- Tables that had more than 32 indexes will not convert because the Jet database has a limit of 32 indexes per table. Referential integrity creates an index on the foreign key side, so you may have many more indexes than you thought. You can fix this by opening the database in the version it was created in and modifying the design.

- Some macros may not convert, but you can fix that by saving the object as a VBA module.

- An object name can stop a conversion if the name is the same as an Access 97 reserved word. You can open the database in the version it was created in and rename it and then proceed with the conversion.

- If you used a continuation character (_) in your Access 95 VBA code, it may not convert to Access 97. Open any Access 97 module in Design View and choose Debug | Compile And Save All Modules. As errors are encountered, correct them.

- You could run into error-trapping problems during conversions because you may not be trapping on the right error numbers anymore.

- Dating problems with literal dates may have appeared. If your query criterion specifies years from 1900 to 1929, you might get different results in Access 97. Access 97 interprets year-ending digits of 00 to 29 as the year 2000. For any year typed in from `00` to `29`, Access assumes that the user meant 2000 to 2029. If the user types in `30` to `99`, Access assumes that the user meant 1930 to 1999. This is to work with the "year 2000" problem that seems to be plaguing older databases. You can work around this problem by changing the date to `cdate("date as string")` in the criteria to force Access to accept the correct date.

- OLE Automation code will require modification on your part if you used code that referenced a specific product version.

- If you used Access wizards to generate code, that code may or may not convert to Access 97. In part, this is due to the change from 16-bit architecture to 32-bit architecture. `DoCmd` (space) statements are now `DoCmd` (dot) objects. This does not seem to apply to many of the macro actions such as `DoMenuItem`.

- `SendKeys` that were used in previous versions may not work correctly in Access 97 because menu trees have changed slightly.

- ActiveX controls that were created in a 16-bit architecture will not convert to the Access 97 32-bit equivalents. You will have to re-create them manually. However, 32-bit ActiveX controls created in Access 95 should convert to Access 97 without any problems.

- Any library database or add-in created with previous versions of Access will have to be manually converted.

- Report margins that were set to `0` in older versions will change to the new defaults when converted. Also, if the computer that the conversion is being created on does not have a default printer, an error will occur. Create a default printer and the error should go away.

Conversion Through Import

Some databases are large and can take a long time to convert. It may even appear as if your computer has stopped responding. There is another way to convert your old database without actually "converting" it. Create a new Access 97 blank database. Select File | Get External Data | Import, and import the objects of the old database into the new database.

This conversion-through-import method can be repetitive, especially if you have a large number of objects. Import 20 or so objects at a time until you have imported the entire database. This method will increase the footprint of your database. After you have finished importing, compact the database. (For safety, compact it into a new filename.)

Converting Replicas

Replicas created in Access 95 cannot be opened by Access 97 unless you convert the design master and associated replicas to Access 97. However, you can enable 95 replicas to run using 97 if you open an enabled, synchronized 95 replica in 97. By converting the 95 design master, you trigger the conversion of the other databases in the replica set. When you synchronize a replica with the converted design master, the replica is automatically converted to 97. Make sure that all your users upgrade to 97 before you synchronize the Design Master.

Conversion and Memory Problems

The 32-bit versions of Access have a limit of 1,024 total for VBA modules. If the database you are in the process of converting has a large number of Form, Report, and Module objects, you may get an error. Try dividing the objects from the old database into two or more databases. You could also store the code in libraries.

Custom Menu Conversion

Custom menus created with macros in older versions probably will continue to work in Access 97. However, menus in 97 are actually CommandBar object modules. To convert a macro-based custom menu, highlight the macro in the database window, and choose Tools | Macros | Create Menu From Macro. You can use the same process to create toolbars and shortcut menus. If you have a problem with the images for the toolbars, you may need to re-create the old button image.

Converting 16-bit ODBC Data Sources

You will get an error when you convert a link to an ODBC Data Source. You can fix it by creating an identically named datasource using the 32-bit version of the ODBC driver. After creating the 32-bit version, delete the 16-bit object.

Converting Passworded Databases

There is no real tip or trick that coincides with converting a secured database. When you convert the database, you will be required to type the password of the database twice. After the conversion, it works exactly as it did before the conversion.

Converted Action Queries and Restrictions

Action queries such as Make-table, Update, Append, and Delete queries now can be restricted by a new Windows Registry setting. This setting is called the `MaxLocksPerFile` and limits the number of page locks allowed in a transaction. When the transaction number exceeds the `MaxLocksPerFile` setting, the action is split into two or more transactions. The query is executed in several transactions until completed. This functionality was added to prevent Novell NetWare 3.1 server crashes and to improve performance. The default setting is `9500`. Any errors that occur during the execution of an Action query that exceeds the `MaxLocksPerFile` setting will allow you to continue with the Action query, but you will not be able to undo the data changes made by the Action query.

Summary

This chapter covers the different situations that can arise when you convert databases conceived in older versions of Access. It explains what will convert automatically and what will probably need manual attention after the conversion. It also covers the various ways a database can be compacted and repaired. The crux of this chapter deals with the performance issues of Access: How you can increase the execution of your database, as well as Access itself.

Optimizing Code

by Teresa Bergman

This chapter contains information on ways to optimize code and to increase the performance and speed of the code in an application. When code is optimized, the performance and speed of the application will increase, the size of the application may decrease, and the user can complete his job efficiently. This means that not only has the application's code been optimized, but now you, as the designer, can maintain the application more efficiently.

Simplifying Code

There are many reasons for simplifying code when optimizing applications:

- Maintenance of the code and application is made easier. When the code has been simplified and optimized, all unnecessary code has been removed. This involves the cleanup of unused variables and code. Most of all, it means removing *spaghetti code* (code that has no meaning and is left over from debugging or unused or repetitive code within the same module) and grouping procedures into modules that perform a specific function.

- Simplifying and optimizing code also increases the readability of the code. The true mark of optimized code is the ability for any developer, including the original developer, to be able to understand the logic and flow of the code. If there is no continuity or sound reasoning in the code, it becomes hard to read and understand. If you are not the original developer, it is even harder to fix and understand code that has not been simplified into a logical order.

- When code has been optimized, its performance and speed are increased. As you know, nothing can frustrate a user more than working with a slow application. Not only does it cost the user valuable work time, but if the code has not been optimized, the developer may lose time trying to fix the problems.

When code has *not* been optimized, it becomes a no-win situation for both the user and the developer.

How Code Issues Affect Performance and Speed

An application's poor performance and speed can be attributed to several different code issues. In some cases it can be poor code planning or straying from the planned course of action. It can be due to how the information is referenced, how the data is manipulated, how much unnecessary code is included, error trapping, or the code not being compiled.

Planning the Code

Writing efficient code is the key to increasing the speed and performance of an application. The design of the code is just as important as the design of the application's tables, relationships, forms, reports, and so on. Many times, code is just slapped into the application with no thought of how it relates to the overall picture—that is, with no thought of how it interacts with the other objects in the application.

Organizing Code into Cohesive Modules

When planning the code, start with writing an algorithm of what it is supposed to do. It's a good programming practice to write the algorithm before coding a module, as it will form the outline of the code that you want to write. Once the outline is written, the code will seem to flow more smoothly; this will reduce the chances of redundant code being entered, because you will be able to see where the duplication of code can take place. Listing 25.1 shows a simple algorithm for importing or exporting information from or to Excel.

Listing 25.1. Sample algorithm to import/export an Excel 8.0 spreadsheet.

```
 1: Public Sub Transfer()
 2:    '* 1. Check the type of transaction _
➡to perform
 3:    '*    A) If import
 4:    '*       I) Check if all the required _
➡data has been entered
 5:    '*       II) Check if importing specific _
➡sheet and cells
 6:    '*           a) Yes - set the range variable _
➡to the entered range
 7:    '*           b) No - set the range variable _
➡to nothing
 8:    '*    B) If export
 9:    '*       I) Check if all the required data _
➡has been entered
10:    '*       II) Set the range variable to nothing
11:    '* 2. Perform the transferspreadsheet method
12:    '* 3. Create an error trap area
13:    '*    A) If an error occurs, use a case _
➡statement to handle it
14:    '*       I) Check if the spread sheet is _
➡closed and exists (use error trap)
15:    '*       II) Check if the specified sheet is active
16:    '*       III) Check for other errors.
17:    '*    B) Exit Sub
18: End Sub
```

If there is no organization to the code, there is a greater chance that the code will affect the speed and performance of the application.

Another way to plan your code is to create a flow chart showing how the data flows. This method works with the algorithm as a pictorial view of the algorithm. It's more up to you as the developer to decide whether an algorithm, a flow chart, or both will be used when creating the application. For those complex modules, you will find that having a flow chart or algorithm will improve the efficiency of the application.

Organizing Parent/Child Procedures into One Module

A *child procedure* is a procedure that is called by another procedure (the *parent*). In some cases, including the child's code within the parent's code will improve the performance; however, it may not increase the readability of the code. The main drawback is the repetitiveness of the code (if the child is called in more than one place within the parent). This will add to the complexity of the procedure. If the readability of the code is more important, or the parent procedure becomes too complex, keep the child as a procedure of its own within the module.

Keeping related procedures in one module is not only a good programming practice, but it makes maintaining the code much easier and helps optimize the usage of the code. If the parent procedure was in one module and a child procedure in another module, Access would have to search through the modules to find the child procedure. Once it found the module that contains the child, the module in its entirety would be loaded into memory. At this rate, if the code is not organized, all the modules that you've written for the application could be loaded into memory. This is where the code's performance can be affected. In large applications where there are a lot of code modules, this type of loading of modules can slow down the application. By organizing all procedures related to a specific function in one module, the amount of code loaded into memory and the amount of time needed to find and load the code are decreased.

> **NOTE**
>
> Remember, each time a procedure within a module is called, the entire module is loaded into memory. If two procedures are needed, each in different modules, it would mean that both modules had to be loaded. This would decrease the amount of available memory as well as the performance of the application.

Code Behind Forms

Access 97 has a new feature added to the forms and reports: the `Has Module` event. This event is used to show whether there is code included in the form or report. Having code included in the form can decrease the performance of the form, but not necessarily the performance of the code. In many cases the performance of the code will be increased, because all the procedures are loaded with the form or report and then unloaded when the form or report is closed. Referencing objects in the form or report's event procedure becomes easier using the `Me!` method.

Portability of the form or report has increased as well since the procedures used are included now. When planning code, try to use Code Behind Forms (CBF) if the code is specific to a form or report and won't be used elsewhere.

Referencing and Using Variables and Objects

Access 97 introduces some new ways of referencing objects, fields, controls, properties, and variables. The ! has more uses than in previous versions of Access. There are also new methods that make the writing of more efficient code easier when referencing objects, fields, controls and properties (see the `With...End With` statement).

Dimensioning Variables

The way that variables are dimensioned can have a big impact on the performance of the application. One type to stay away from is dimensioning a variable as type Variant. This is the slowest type and must be converted before being used.

For example, if you are adding two variables together, such as 1 and 9 for example, assigning each variable as a Variant type would not be a logical choice. Because these are integer values, they should be dimensioned as type Integer.

When dimensioning a variable, keep in mind the type of variable it is. If it is a number, assign it a type of Integer, Long, Double, or Currency. If it is a Boolean variable, assign it as Boolean. Even dates can be assigned as type Date. In previous versions of Access, date values were usually assigned as type Variant.

NOTE

The smaller the type of variable, the faster any processing with the variable will be. You always want to assign the smallest type that is appropriate for the variable. For example, if the value of the variable is an integer, don't assign the variable as Double; use Integer instead.

Containers, documents, objects, and controls can all be dimensioned as exactly what they are (see Listing 25.2).

Listing 25.2. Dimensioning formats.

```
Dim ctrTables As Container
Dim docTables As Document
Dim ctlTextBox As TextBox
Dim objForm As Object
Dim ctlControl As Control
Dim intA As Integer
dim bolTF As Boolean
Dim ctlButton As CommandButton
```

By dimensioning a variable as exactly what it is, performance can be enhanced, and the code has become optimized.

Using constants to replace variables that have values "written in stone" can also optimize the way the code is written. A constant does not need to be evaluated while the code is being run, because like its name, it remains a constant value throughout the code. A variable, on the other hand, is evaluated each time the code is run to find the current value and can change throughout the code.

Using dynamic arrays instead of fixed arrays can also increase performance by reducing the amount of memory being used. In some cases, you may want to keep the array as a fixed array, which is fine, but remember that even though the Erase command may have been issued for the array, the memory used by the fixed array is not reclaimed. The only memory reclaimed would be from the actual values stored in the array, not the array itself. If using a dynamic array, the Erase statement would completely eliminate the array from memory and release the memory stored by the array, instead of just releasing the values that are stored in the array:

```
Erase lngDateArray
```

If some of the values in the array are to be kept, or the size of the array is to be made smaller, use the ReDim statement with the Preserve keyword to reclaim the memory used by data that is no longer needed:

```
ReDim Preserve lngDateArray(2)
```

If using Declare statements to reference the Windows API, DLL calls, and so on, remove any statements that are no longer used. Use the Find command in the Edit menu to do this.

Using Me and ! for Referencing

Referencing objects can be optimized by using the Me! reference when working with controls and their properties within an event procedure on a form or report. The Me! reference restricts the searching for the control to the form or report from which the code is currently running. Instead of using the full reference to a control (Forms!frmTab!txtDate) within the event procedure, use Me!txtDate to reference the same control. To access that control's properties, try using the With...End With statement to increase the efficiency (see Listing 25.3).

Listing 25.3. Referencing control properties using Me!.

```
Public Sub cmdUpdate_Click()
  With Me![txtQD]
    .Enabled = False
    .Locked = True
    .TabStop = False
    .ControlSource = "=DateDiff(""s"", [txtQS], [txtQE])"
  End With
End Sub
```

The !, or bang operator, can also be used to make code more efficient and increase the performance of the code. Consider Listing 25.4. Using the `With...End With` statement to update the value in the `invoice_paid` field is made easier and more readable by using the ! operator.

Listing 25.4. Using the ! to reference a table's field.

```
Public Sub UpdatePaid()
  Dim dbCurrent As Database, recInvoice As Recordset
  Set dbCurrent = CurrentDb()
  Set recInvoice = dbCurrent.OpenRecordset("invoice", dbOpenTable)
  With recInvoice
   .Edit
   !invoice_paid = True
   .Update
  End With
End Sub
```

Not only is the code more readable, but there is less referencing of variables, which optimizes the code.

If using variables of type `Object`, consider setting the value of the object to `Nothing` when you are finished using it. Each time an object variable is used, it takes up memory and other associated resources. By using this method to set the object to nothing, the memory and resources are freed:

```
Set objTable = Nothing
```

Using With...End With

Using `With...End With` is a new function with Access 97. Using this statement not only reduces the amount of code that needs to be written, but also increases the performance of the code. No longer do you need to type in the long references to a control, such as `Forms!frmTab!txtDate.Visible = True`. This code can now be replaced with

```
With Forms!frmTab!txtDate
    .Visible = True
    .Enabled = True
    .Locked = False
End With
```

The name of the control is referenced at the beginning of the `With...End With` statement. Once the reference to the control is made, all the properties can be referenced, evaluated, and modified easily by only entering `.<property>`, where `<property>` is the name of the property.

The `With...End With` statement is not only for use with controls. It can also be used to reference collections, documents, objects, and so on. The following code sample can be used to reference the collections, and in each collection, reference all the documents within. Listing 25.5 uses the `With...End With` statement, while Listing 25.6 uses the more traditional method.

Listing 25.5. Documents referenced using With...End With.

```
Sub ContainerObjectX()
  Dim dbCurrent As Database
  Dim ctrLoop As Container
  Dim docLoop As Document
  Set dbCurrent = CurrentDb()
  With dbCurrent
    For Each ctrLoop In .Containers
      Debug.Print "Documents in " & ctrLoop.Name & " container"
      For Each docLoop In ctrLoop.Documents
        Debug.Print "  " & docLoop.Name
      Next docLoop
    Next ctrLoop
    .Close
  End With
End Sub
```

Listing 25.6. The traditional approach to referencing documents.

```
Public Sub ContainerObjectTraditional()
  Dim dbCurrent As Database
  Dim ctrLoop As Container
  Dim docLoop As Document
  Dim intC As Integer
  Dim intD As Integer
  Set dbCurrent = CurrentDb()
  For intC = 0 To dbCurrent.Containers.Count - 1
    Set ctrLoop = dbCurrent.Containers(intC)
    For intD = 0 To ctrLoop.Documents.Count - 1
      Set docLoop = ctrLoop.Documents(intD)
      Debug.Print docLoop.Name
    Next
  Next
End Sub
```

Listings 25.5 and 25.6 both return the same information: a list of documents in each container. When comparing the two modules, on a large application the code in Listing 25.5 will run faster because it is directly referencing the containers and documents.

Using the String ($) Versions of Statements

Using variables set to the variant type tends to decrease the performance of the application. When using statements such as the Left, Right, and Trim statements, consider using the string ($) versions (Left$, Right$, Trim$). A String type variable can be evaluated faster than a Variant type variable, because VBA does not have to convert the variable when it is not a Variant type variable.

Working with True/False Booleans

Writing code where Boolean functions have to be evaluated has become easier. When optimizing the performance where results of Boolean variables are used and evaluated, consider using the Not reserved word to reduce and clarify the code.

> **TIP**
>
> A Boolean variable defaults to True unless set to False before evaluation.

Using NOT to Check or Change State

When checking for or changing to a False state, use the Not keyword to do the work.

The following code displays the most common way of checking for True and False and then assigning a variable to True or False:

```
If A = True Then
    B = False
Else
    B = True
End If
```

As you can see, this can be inefficient in that the code is not optimized and before B can be assigned True or False, the If statement will have to be evaluated to see whether the value is True or False. The following code is a more efficient way to evaluate the same expression:

```
B = Not(A)
```

A one-line piece of code replaces the five lines that were previously used to give the results shown in Table 25.1.

Table 25.1. Not (A) evaluation results.

Value A	Value B (Not(A))
True	False
False	True

Use the keywords True and False to replace <>0 (True), -1 (True), and 0 (False). Combine this with the reserved word Not, and working with Boolean values will be much easier.

Working with Data

Most procedures are designed to work with the data in the application. There are some general rules to follow concerning when or when not to use a procedure to work with data. There has also been some improvement in processing batch transactions within the Jet Engine.

General Rules

There are three general rules that, as a developer, I tend to follow. These rules can improve the performance of your application and in the long run, make it easier to maintain:

- If an Action query can be used, use it!
- If an Action query won't work, look for alternative methods for updating or adding the data.
- Last resort: Use code to update or add the data.

If an Action query can replace the code you are writing, use the Action query. (An *Action query* is an Append, Update, Make-table, or Delete query.) This increases the efficiency of the application. In some cases where there is very little data in the table, an Action query, such as an Update query, may take a few seconds more. However, as the table grows in size, the query will become the faster option. Not only does it increase the performance of the application, but the code is optimized as well. If you are updating information on an SQL server, try using an Action Pass-through query to update or add the data to the SQL server instead of code.

If you are using an Action query, create and save the query first, and then call the query using `DoCmd.OpenQuery("<query name>")`. Using the `Docmd.RunSQL` statement should be avoided at all costs when writing code. Although this may be a valid SQL statement, it is not a compiled query. When the code is run, the SQL statement has to be compiled. Even though the code may have been compiled, the SQL statement hasn't. Like decompiled code, the SQL statement will slow the performance of the application. This statement should be used as a last resort.

If an Action query can't be used, try to find an alternative way of updating or adding the data to the table. This may mean redesigning a form, which may be time-consuming when designing, but may improve the processing of the data in production.

As a last resort, if neither of the first two rules can be applied, update or add the data by using code. This will affect the performance of the application by decreasing the efficiency and speed of the application. The effect may not be noticed much when there are only a few records, but when there are thousands of records, it will be.

If using code is the only way to update or add information, keep the indexes of the table in mind, and use those indexes to seek the information that you need to update.

For example, if there are 20,000 invoice records and you need to update the invoice paid for one invoice, the invoice table is indexed with the invoice number as the key to the table. Use the `Seek` method to find the records that you want to update (see Listing 25.7).

Listing 25.7. Using the Seek method.

```
Public Sub UpdatePaid()
Dim dbCurrent As Database
  Dim recInvoice As Recordset, lngInvoice As Long, varBookMark As Variant
  Set dbCurrent = CurrentDb()
```

```
    Set recInvoice = dbCurrent.OpenRecordset("invoice", dbOpenTable)
    With recInvoice
      .Index = "invoice_id"
      .MoveFirst
      lngInvoice = 2
      Do Until .EOF
        varBookMark = .Bookmark
        .Seek "=", Val(lngInvoice)
        If .NoMatch Then
          MsgBox "Invoice not found."
          .Bookmark = varBookMark
        Else
          .Edit
          !invoice_paid = True
          .Update
          Exit Do
        End If
      Loop
      .Close
    End With
End Sub
```

Listing 25.7 opens the invoice table and then sets the index to `invoice_id`. By using the index to begin the `Seek` function on the table, the performance has been improved. If the index wasn't used, or the incorrect index was used, this will slow the processing down. The next step is to set a bookmark. Adding bookmarks can increase the speed as well. This is the quickest way to access the record. In this example, a variable has been set to the value of the bookmark. This means that if an error occurs during the processing of the record, the record can be accessed again by setting the bookmark to the value of the variable. It's a quick and efficient way to move back to where you were last in the recordset. The `!invoice_paid` is a direct reference to the field to be updated in the invoice table. Formerly, the field may have been referenced by `recInvoice("invoice_paid")`. The first method is a more efficient way to access the table's field by referencing it directly.

Transaction Methods

With earlier versions of Access, the transaction methods (`BeginTrans`, `CommitTrans`, and so on) were recommended when batch-processing data. This placed all the transactions in a buffer when the `BeginTrans` statement was issued and saved the transactions when the batch was completed with the `CommitTrans` statement. With Access 97, improvements have been made to the Jet Engine that have improved the performance of the Jet Engine's own transaction handling. Depending on the situation, the only way to find out which is more efficient in processing your data is to test using the transaction methods and using only the Jet Engine to see which one is more efficient.

25

OPTIMIZING CODE

Cleaning Up Code

A final step before sending the application out to the user is to clean up the code modules. This involves removing any *white space* (unnecessary, empty lines of code) and removing unused variables and modules. You may also want to consider stripping any comments from the code.

Removing White Space and Comments

Why remove white space from code? White space includes the blank or empty lines that have been inserted into your code. Sometimes these empty lines have been included for readability. When compiled, these empty lines are treated like a line of code and therefore take up memory when the module is loaded.

Comments also can take up memory when the module is loaded and add to the size of the application as well. While these comments are useful when developing and maintaining the code, they become a burden when the application is in production.

Before removing the white space and comments, copy the code to a text file. It will become a hard copy of the actual code, complete with comments. This text file can then be used as a reference for maintaining the code in the user's application. Once the code has been copied to a new text file, the comments and white space can be removed from the application's code.

> **TIP**
>
> Keep the text file copy of the code with the application's documentation. This way it will always be accessible, and future developers will have a reference as to how the code is to work.
>
> Each time the code is changed, update the text file as well.

Before the white space and comments have been removed, compile and save all the modules. Run the application and test the performance. Remove all the white space and comments, compile and save all the modules, and then test the performance. If there were a lot of comments or white space in the original code, there will be an increase in the speed and performance of the application. If there weren't a lot of comments or white space, there might be a slight increase of performance. You might even notice that suddenly the database has become smaller in size because there are now fewer code lines.

Unused Variables

Keeping unused variables in your code can also slow down the performance of the application. Not only is the code not optimized, but it contains useless information. Before removing any unused variables, make sure that the module's Declarations section has the following line of code:

```
Option Explicit
```

This option acts as a check to make sure that all referenced or used variables are dimensioned or declared within the module. When cleaning up unused variables, comment out the variable's dimension (Dim) statement and compile the code. If an error occurs (Variable Not Set), this means the variable is used. Uncomment the Dim statement and continue to the next variable. Checking for unused variables this way is a time-consuming method. There are third-party add-ins created that will check for unused variables within your code. Use one of these if it's available. The other option is to use the Find function to find all instances of that variable being used within the code. This is a much faster way to find out whether or not the variable is used.

Unused Code

When code has been optimized, all unused code has been removed. Unused code can consist of statements, such as Stop or Debug.Print, that are used during the debugging stage of the design. This code is often left in as either uncommented or commented code lines. Like unused variables, this code is unused and takes up memory and space in the application. This unused code can be identified and removed by choosing the Find command from the Edit menu. Again, there are third-party add-ins that can be used as well to find the instances of unused code.

Unused Modules

Unused modules can take the form of unused procedures within a module as well as the entire module itself. The modules may have been used at one point in the development of the application, but in the final version, they are no longer used. This happens quite often as the development of the code evolves in the application. Using the Find command under the Edit menu can identify the code to be removed or kept.

> **CAUTION**
>
> Make sure you back up your database before removing any code. If code is accidentally removed, there will still be a complete copy of the application available from where the removed code can be copied.

Error-Trapping Code

Error-trapping code is an important feature of optimizing your code. Code that is well-thought-out will contain an error routine that will handle all errors that occur within the procedure. Placing error handling on every procedure in each code module is not always the correct way to optimize. In some cases, if the parent as well as the child procedure has error trapping, when the child is exited, the child procedure will return the error, but the error handling on the parent's procedure will display the error to the user. Chapter 26, "Errors," contains more information on error handling within an application (see Listing 25.8).

Listing 25.8. Child and parent—parent with error handling.

```
Public Function Parent()
On Error GoTo ErrParent
  Dim intChild As Integer
  Call Child
  Exit Function
ErrParent:
  Err.Raise (Err.Number)
  MsgBox Err.Description
  Exit Function
End Function
Public Sub Child()
On Error GoTo ErrChild
  Dim intAns As Integer
  intAns = 1 / 0
  Exit Sub
ErrChild:
  Err.Raise (Err.Number)
  Exit Sub
End Sub
```

In Listing 25.8, the procedure `Parent` uses the `Err.Raise(Err.Number)` method to get the returned error's information and display the error message in the message box statement. Include an `Err.Raise` statement on the `Child` procedure to raise the error so the parent procedure can handle the error and then exit the child procedure. Not only is the code optimized (unused code lines have been removed), but the error handling has been optimized with only the parent handling the error and the child raising the error.

Compile All Code Before Sending It to the User

Before sending the application to the user, all modules must be saved in a compiled state. When the code modules have not been saved in a compiled state, Access has to recompile the code when it's called. This can decrease the performance of the application. Not only will it cause the code to run more slowly, but forms and reports will load slowly as well.

The following are some reasons for compiling all code before sending it to the user:

- It increases the performance and speed when loading forms and reports.
- It reduces the amount of memory the application uses.
- The code does not have to be recompiled when used on the user's machine.
- It preserves the compiled state of all code, including code behind forms.

The `Compile` and `Save Module` function is found in the Debug menu. (Open a code module to find this menu option.) This function takes some time to complete because all code within the application is being compiled. Once all the code has been compiled and saved, the performance of the application can be checked, or the application can be sent to the user.

> **TIP**
>
> The performance should be tested before sending the application out to the user.

> **NOTE**
>
> Only use the `Compile and Save Module` function when the application is complete and ready to be sent to the user or when the performance of the application is to be tested.

Use the `Make MDE` Function

The `Make MDE` function is new to Access 97.

The following are some reasons to make an application into an `.mde` file (code viewpoint):

■ Code can't be modified (in modules, forms, or reports).

■ Memory usage can be decreased.

■ Size of application has decreased.

Code can take up space in an application as well. The MDE application will not store the editable Visual Basic source code. The code's compiled state is stored instead. This alone will increase the performance because the code can't be in a decompiled state at any given time.

Summary

Optimizing code can be done in various ways, from the way the data is dimensioned or declared to making the code into an MDE file. A combination of one or more of the optimizing tips described in this chapter can improve the performance of the application. The key thing to remember when writing code is that the user does not want an application that is slow and clunky. Optimizing the way the code is written is one way to give the users what they expect— a fast and efficient application.

Errors

by Teresa Bergman

IN THIS CHAPTER

26

CHAPTER

Trapping and handling errors is one of the most important parts of writing code. The way errors are handled is a mark of professionalism. If the application goes into production with little or no error trapping within the code or on the forms and reports, the users tend to do one of the following:

- Ignore errors that may be serious.
- Become frustrated with the amount of errors and downtime.
- Not use the application due to all the errors occurring.
- Lose faith in the application and any future software designed by the software company or department.

 The examples used in this chapter can be found on this book's CD-ROM in the `Chap26.mdb` database.

What Errors Are, and What to Expect

Errors can happen when a condition in code fails. Logic that does not work the way it was expected to work, or a mistake such as referencing an object with the incorrect name, can also cause an error.

This section discusses the differences between fatal and non-fatal runtime errors, why error trapping is used, and when to implement error trapping in your code.

Fatal Runtime Errors

Fatal runtime errors (or non-recoverable errors) can cause an application to halt and in some cases can cause the database to become corrupted. These errors usually can't be corrected in the code and most times are unexpected. These errors include

- incorrect calls to Windows API
- incorrect declaration to Windows API
- incorrect DLL calling conventions

The most severe runtime errors can cause a general protection fault (GPF). In each case, there is no escape from the error that is returned, and the application is terminated (or should be). Many times, these errors can't be trapped, as in the case of the general protection fault.

One such error that can produce a general protection fault is changing printers for a report through code. In order to make a generic multiprinting report engine, the idea is to give the user a list of all printers available on their computer and network. The user can then select the printer from the list. Some offices have new printers as well as old printers, while other offices can only access the old printers. When the user selects one of the new printers, a general protection fault would occur. However, when an old printer is selected, there is no general protection fault. The problem is that the newer printers' driver has a longer driver name than that of the older printers driver, and the printer driver installed was not the OEM printer driver. This becomes a potentially dangerous error, because it can corrupt the database as well as being a fatal error that can't be solved by the user or through error handling in code.

Non-Fatal Runtime Errors

Non-fatal runtime errors (or recoverable errors) are errors that can be trapped by code. These errors can be resolved by either the user being involved (such as entering the value of a missing field) or without the user's involvement (using a `GoTo` statement to send the processing somewhere else). These errors, unlike fatal runtime errors, can be trapped by and handled through code and usually are not dangerous. Many times they can be ignored, as when making a calculation on a field that can be null. If the value is `null`, an error will occur. Adding a `Resume Next` to the error handling will ignore the error and continue with the rest of the code. This error isn't fatal to the running of the application.

Another such non-fatal error happens when a parameter for a query is missing. If the query is expecting a parameter that hasn't been entered, the error shown in Figure 26.1 will be displayed.

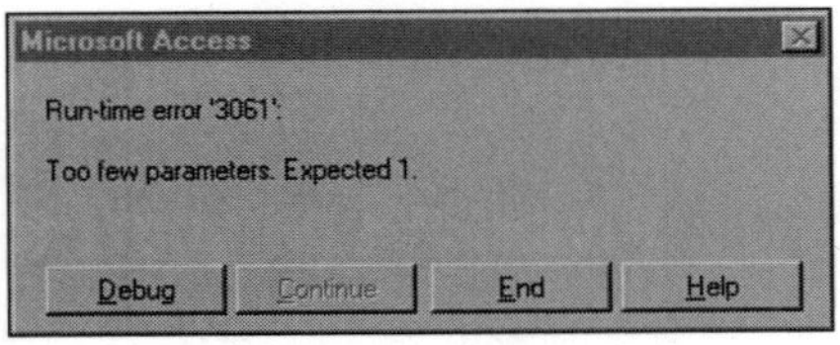

FIGURE 26.1.

A non-fatal parameter error.

Later in this chapter, I will discuss how to recover from this error. (See the "Recovering From Recoverable or Non-Fatal Errors" section for more explanation on how to recover from this error.)

Why Use Error Trapping?

Why should you place error trapping and handling in your application? A better question is, why would you *not* put error trapping in your application? Some of the reasons for placing error trapping in your application are listed here:

- It creates a more professional-looking application.
- As the developer, it increases your efficiency in responding and resolving errors.
- It creates a user-friendly error message when the error occurs.

By placing the error trapping within your application, the user is less likely to

- Ignore errors that may be serious.
- Become frustrated with the amount of errors and downtime.

- Not use the application due to all the errors occurring.
- Lose faith in the application and any future software designed by the software company or department.

Creating User-Friendly Error Messages

Access error messages are usually cryptic and hard to understand; such is the case of the error message in Figure 26.2.

FIGURE 26.2.

An Access-generated error message.

By using error trapping in your application, this error can be replaced by the message in Figure 26.3.

FIGURE 26.3.

An error-trapping–generated error message.

A message that is user-friendly, easy to understand, precise, and to-the-point will give your application a professional look. By explaining the error and giving a possible solution to the error, users will gain more confidence in the application and be able to do some of the basic troubleshooting themselves. This decreases the amount of time you, as the developer, will take when resolving an error.

Recovering from Recoverable or Non-Fatal Errors

When error trapping has been implemented in your application, recovering from errors becomes easier.

For example, a table made by a Make-table query forms the base of a report. The query is run and seems to have completed successfully (no error messages), but when the report is opened, an error message is displayed saying that Access can't find the input table. Tracing this problem without having error trapping implemented in the database makes solving this problem more complicated. No reasonable explanation is available, because there seemed to be no problem. The only way the error can be solved is by placing error trapping on the code that ran the query. The next time the code is run, the error-trapping routine will return an error that says `Insufficient memory to run operation`.

This example happens more often than you think. This error even happens in Windows 95.

Recovery from an error like the one in the previous example is a simple matter, if you know what you are doing. Shut down Windows and clean up any `.tmp` files in the TEMP directory. The average user, however, doesn't know this and would end up becoming frustrated because she cannot print her report. She would then contact you, the developer, or her M.I.S. (Technical Support) department to help resolve the error.

The response shown in Figure 26.4 would be a better response to the insufficient memory error.

FIGURE 26.4.
The new insufficient memory error message.

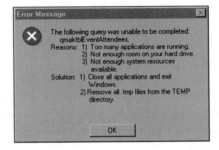

Providing a solution along with the reason why the error happened makes it easier for you to fix and easier for the user to recover from.

Other recoverable errors can also be trapped and handled in a specific way. If the error has no effect on the process that is being done, such as in Listing 26.1, resume to the next statement and continue the execution of the code.

Listing 26.1. A division by 0 error.

```
Public Sub DivBy0()
On Error Resume Next
    Dim intA As Integer
    intA = 1/0
End Sub
```

When to Use Error Trapping

Some form of error trapping should appear within any code that is written, whether it is simply placing an `On Error Resume Next` or using the `On Error GoTo` statement in the code. Either statement will evaluate the error and perform the necessary process (see Listings 26.2 and 26.3).

Listing 26.2. Error handling with On Error Resume Next.

```
Public Sub cmdClose_Click()
    On Error Resume Next
    DoCmd.Close
End Sub
```

Listing 26.3. Error handling with On Error GoTo.

```
Public Sub cmdClose_Click()
    On Error GoTo ErrCloseClick
    DoCmd.Close
    Exit Sub
ErrCloseClick:
    Msgbox "An unexpected error occurred." _
        & Err.Number & "  " & Err.Description
    Exit Sub
End Sub
```

The code in Listing 26.2 demonstrates how to use the On Error Resume Next statement to ignore any errors that may occur while closing the form. If an error occurs during the closing of the form, no error message will be displayed. Listing 26.3, however, uses an error-handling area to handle any unexpected errors that may occur when the form is closed. The On Error GoTo ErrCloseClick statement directs the code to the ErrCloseClick line label if an error occurs during the closing of the form. The code in Listing 26.3 should be used instead of the code in Listing 26.2. If an error occurs while closing the form, the code in Listing 26.2 will ignore it, while the code in Listing 26.3 will return the error message that occurred. The second method is therefore a more desirable way to trap for errors in any place in your code.

Trappable Microsoft Jet and DAO Errors

The next few sections discuss how to access the error object, collection, and common errors, the differences between Access errors and Visual Basic errors, and how to handle specific errors. Writing error-trapping procedures and the format of the error-trapping codes are discussed in detail in the next section.

How to Access the Errors Collection and Err Object

WARNING

The Errors collection is different in Access 97 than in previous versions of Access. The 97 version introduces the use of Visual Basic error objects to display information on an error. The Err object will be discussed in more detail later in the chapter.

Listing 26.4 is a sample of how the `Errors` collection and object can be accessed.

Listing 26.4. Using the Err object's properties.

```
Option Compare Database
Option Explicit
Dim strMsg As String
Dim strCont As String
Public Function Unexpected_Error(lngErr As Long, strWhere As String) As Variant
    '* This function is used to return the value of the unexpected
    '* error that occurred in the program.
    strMsg = "An unexpected error has occured in your application."
    strCont = "Please contact M.I.S.."
    Err.Raise(lngErr)
    MsgBox strMsg & Chr(13) & Chr(10) & "Error#:   " & Err.Number  & _
            Chr(13) & Chr(10) & "Error:   " & _
            Err.Description & Chr(13) & Chr(10) & _
            "In:   " & strWhere & Chr(13) & Chr(10) & _
            strCont, vbCritical + vbOKOnly, "Unexpected Error"
End Function
```

This procedure is an easy way to include a global error-trapping area in your code. By including a reference in a module to this procedure, it can be accessed by all of your procedures and present a uniform format for how an error is displayed. When an error occurs, this procedure can be called. The calling procedure passes in the error number and where the error occurred. When the error occurs, the user can tell you, the developer, which error occurred, what the message said, and where the error happened. In the `Chap26.mdb` database, when the `ParentProc()` procedure is run, it makes a call to the error code in the Listing 26.4. Listing 26.5. shows how to call this procedure.

Listing 26.5. How to call the Unexpected_Error procedure.

```
Public Function ParentProc() As Variant
On Error GoTo ErrParent
    Dim varMsg As Variant
    Call ChildProc
    Exit Function
ErrParent:
    varMsg = Unexpected_Error(Err.Number, "basErrorTrap(ParentProc)")
    Err.Clear
    Resume Next
End Function
```

This code returns the error message shown in Figure 26.5.

FIGURE 26.5.

*The unexpected error
message.*

Common Errors

There are many errors that should be trapped for that usually occur during the normal running of an application. My personal favorites are

- `Duplicate Records` (Trap for the error on the `Form_Error` event.)
- `Type Mismatch` (Usually found when trying to compare an alpha character within a numeric field.)
- `Not In List` (Occurs when the `Limit To List` event is set to `Yes`.)
- `Insufficient Memory` (Usually occurs when the available GUI memory is below 20 percent or there is very little space available on the hard drive—under 20MB.)
- `Resume Without Error` (No error occurred, but a `Resume Next` statement was accessed—could happen when there is no `Exit Sub` before the error-handling area.)
- `Division By Zero` (You can't divide by zero—it's just not mathematically possible.)
- `File Not Found` (Found most often when accessing a network drive. For some reason the drive is no longer available, so the file can't be found.)
- `Permission Denied` (Usually occurs when trying to run a Make-table query in a secured database and the user running the query doesn't have permission to modify the design of the table.)
- `Invalid Use Of Null` (An example would be performing a calculation on two values where one or both may be null—has no effect—might want to set the value to `0` if `Null` is found.)

These are just a sample of commonly occurring errors.

How to Display Error-Trapping Functions and the Differences Between Them

With this version of Access, there are now two different areas that an error can occur in, along with two different ways to access these errors.

Access Errors

Access errors are errors that are local to the interface, DAO, and Jet Engine. These errors can be trapped and displayed using the `Error` event on forms and reports.

Visual Basic Errors

Visual Basic errors are local to the code that is written. Trapping for these errors should be done within any code that is written using the `On Error` statement.

The format for using the `On Error` statement within code is shown in Listing 26.6.

Listing 26.6. The format of using the `On Error` statement.

```
Public Sub Example()
On Error GoTo ErrExample
     < your code goes here >
     Exit Sub
ErrExample:
     < your error handling code goes here >
End Sub
```

The statement `On Error GoTo ErrExample` tells the code to go to the line with the label `ErrExample`. This is where the error will be handled. Notice that the last line before the error handling starts is the `Exit Sub` statement. This statement tells the code that when all processing has been run, exit the procedure without running the error-handling code. The reason why including this line in your code is important and is discussed in more detail in the "How to Write a Simple Error-Trapping Procedure" section later in this chapter.

Error Handling

Incorporating the error-handling code in your application is a simple process that should be added when designing the code, not when the code has been completed. This way, when testing the code, any errors can be trapped for and handled.

How to Write a Simple Error-Trapping Procedure

Writing an error-trapping procedure is easy. One suggestion is to write a global error-trapping procedure where the error number, object name, control name, or procedure name is passed in. When errors occur, the same format for an error message will be displayed. Including the object name, control name, or procedure name gives you a way to evaluate and resolve the error more quickly by explaining where the error occurred.

When the error-trapping code is activated, the code must determine which error occurred and then determine how to address the error. Visual Basic and Access each have different ways to retrieve the information on the error that has occurred. Generally, trapping for an Access interface, for a Jet Engine, or for DAO errors are done on the form or report `Error` event. Any Visual Basic code written should use the `Err` object to reference the error information (see Table 26.1).

Table 26.1. The error-trapping format that should be used.

Where	Error-handling format
Access interface, Jet Engine, or DAO	`Form Error, Report Error` events
Visual Basic error	`On Error GoTo` statement

WARNING

The most important part of writing the error-trapping procedure is to use the correct format of error handling. Previous versions of Access used the `Err` and `Error$` statements to display errors. Access 97, however, has two areas to perform error trapping, as shown in Table 26.1: the interface, which is DAO and Jet Engine combined, and Visual Basic. The correct format of error handling should be used at all times.

TIP

If the error is caused by the form or report itself (duplicate value in index, and so on), use the `AccessError` method in the form or report's Error event. If the error is caused by the Visual Basic code you've written, use the `Err` object and an error message box (customized, preferably).

When displaying an error message, use the `MsgBox` statement to display a user-friendly message. The `MsgBox` statement uses the following icon constants that can help the user identify whether the error is critical, not as critical (warning), or informational. Never display an error message box without an icon. As they say, "A picture is worth a thousand words," and if the user can associate an icon to the severity of the error, they will begin to understand that a critical icon means that the error could mean that a function has ended unexpectedly (see Table 26.2).

Table 26.2. Message box icon constants.

Type	Constant
Informational	`vbInformation`
Question	`vbQuestion`
Serious	`vbExclamation`
Critical	`vbCritical On Error GoTo` statement

Depending on the type of error, you may want to give the user a chance to respond to the error in order to fix it. The message can tell the user that a value was missing or null and give the user the option to exit the routine, fix the problem and re-run the routine, or just continue on with the routine as is. Table 26.3 lists the different types of response buttons that the message box can display.

Table 26.3. Message box buttons.

Button(s)	Constant
OK only	vbOKOnly
OK and Cancel	vbOKCancel
Yes and No	vbYesNo
Yes, No, and Cancel	vbYesNoCancel
Retry and Cancel	vbRetryCancel
Abort, Retry, and Ignore	vbAbortRetryIgnore

The values for each button are shown in Table 26.4.

Table 26.4. Button values.

Button	Constant	Value
OK	vbOK	1
Cancel	vbCancel	2
Abort	vbAbort	3
Retry	vbRetry	4
Ignore	vbIgnore	5
Yes	vbYes	6
No	vbNo	7

The syntax for the error message is

```
MsgBox strMsg, vbOkOnly + vbInformation, strTitle

intRetValue = MsgBox (strMsg, vbYesNo + vbInformation, strTitle)
```

Listing 26.7 displays a sample of using both formats of the MsgBox statement within your error-trapping code.

Listing 26.7. Samples of MsgBox Statements.

```
strMsg = "An error has occurred."
strTitle = "Error"
MsgBox strMsg, vbCritical, strTitle
intRetVal = MsgBox (strMsg, vbYesNo + vbQuestion, strTitle)
Select Case intRetVal
    Case 6 '* Yes
    case 7 '* No
End Select
```

In Listing 26.7, the statement `MsgBox strMsg, vbCritical, strTitle` displays a simple message box with only the OK button, message (`strMsg`), and the critical icon (`vbCritical`). The second example, `intRetVal = MsgBox (strMsg, vbYesNo + vbQuestion, strTitle)`, is used to evaluate the user's response (`intRetVal`) to the error message (`strMsg`). The response can be either Yes or No (`vbYesNo`). This response is then evaluated by the `Select Case intRetVal` statement. Depending on which button the user clicked, an action is triggered to handle the error. The actions can include exiting the procedure, closing the form, continuing from where the error happened, or exiting the application. This version of error trapping can be used where the user can make a choice to either make changes to the data to correct the error or continue processing the information even though an error occurred.

Err, Error$, and AccessError

If an error is related to Access itself, such as a DAO error, the `Err` object won't be able to return the error (or may return an incorrect error). The correct method to determine the error description would be the `AccessError` method.

> **NOTE**
>
> For compatibility, the `Error$` statement has only been included for backward compatibility. Use the `AccessError` method to retrieve the error description.

The syntax for the `AccessError` method is

```
[application name].AccessError([error number])
```

where `[application name]` is the name of the application that is running (optional entry) and `[error number]` is the error number that occurred. See Listing 26.8 for an example of how to use this method.

Listing 26.8. An AccessError example.

```
Private Sub Form_Error (DataErr As Integer, Response As Integer)
    MsgBox "The following error has occurred:" _
           & DataErr & "        " & AccessError(DataErr), _
           vbExclamation,"Unexpected Error"
```

```
        Response = acDataErrContinue
End Sub
```

If a form or report error is generated by the Access interface, DAO, or Jet Engine, the error will be trapped by the Error event on the active form or report. The procedure in Listing 26.8, passes the error to the DataErr variable (global variable). Then, based on the error that was passed in, the AccessError method will return the description of the error.

> ## WARNING
>
> The Error event of the form or report can only be used through code. Because the error number has to be passed in to the code (DataErr), a macro can't be used to display the error.

If you are testing for multiple errors (duplicate records, null values, type mismatch, not in list, and so on), use constants that are assigned to the error values that are to be trapped for specifically. Then use a Select Case DataErr statement to determine which error occurred and what the error message box should say. (You can either use Access's description or a customized description.) See Listing 26.9 for an example.

Listing 26.9. Multiple error trapping using AccessError.

```
Private Sub Form_Error (DataErr As Integer, Response As Integer)
      Const DupKey = 3022
      Const IndxNull = 3058
      Const NoSave = 2169
Response = acDataErrContinue
Select Case DataErr
        Case DupKey '* duplicate record
            MsgBox "Event ID " & Me![EventID] & " has already been " _
                "assigned to a previously entered event. Please enter a " _
                "new Event Id." & Chr(13) & Chr(10) & "Solution:  Press " _
                "the ESC Key to remove the entered data,or enter a new " _
                "Event Id number.", vbOKOnly + vbCritical, "Duplicate " _
                "Event ID"
             Exit Sub
        Case NoSave '* can't save a duplicate record
            MsgBox "The current record could not be saved because " _
                    "it is a duplicate record.",vbCritical,"Can Not Save"
            Exit Sub
        Case IndxNull '* index or primary key can't contain a null value
            MsgBox "An Event ID must be entered before continuing.", _
                    _ vbOKOnly + vbCritical, "Duplicate Event ID"
             Exit Sub
        Case Else
            MsgBox "Err = " & DataErr & "   " & AccessError(DataErr), _
➥_ vbExclamation, "Unexpected Error"
             Exit Sub
    End Select
End Sub
```

Listing 26.9 is used to trap for multiple errors that can occur on a form. Because
e most common errors that may occur, each error number has been assigned to a
lue (DupKey, IndxNull, and NoSave). The first step is to set the Response value. To
stomized error message, set the value of Response to acDataErrContinue. This means
fault error message will not be displayed when it occurs, and a custom message can
stead. The next step is to use a Select Case statement to evaluate the value of DataErr.
the error that has occurred in the form.) If the DataErr value is one of the predefined
ants, the Select Case statement will display the correct format of the error statement for
e error that occurred. The last statement in the Select Case statement is the Case Else statement. This will handle any unexpected errors that occur while the form is being used.

Err.Raise, Err.Number, and Err.Description

If the error is generated by the code itself, the Visual Basic error method should be used. To
trap and handle these errors, include the On Error statement combined with either the GoTo or
Resume Next statement to direct which line label in the code is the error handler's location.

When writing your error-handling code, the GoTo line label specifies which line of your code
contains the error-handling code. As soon as an error occurs, the On Error GoTo statement directs the control to the appropriate line of code and continues the execution of the code from
there. Once the procedure becomes inactive (has been completed), the error trapping is terminated. The procedure is still considered active if

- no Exit Sub, Exit Function statement is executed.
- no End Sub, End Function statement is executed.

To turn off error handling, there are two different statements that can be used. On Error GoTo
0 turns off error handling. On Error Resume Next moves to the next line of code after the error
has occurred—ignoring the error and not reporting it. The second way is slightly dangerous,
because a potentially serious error may be ignored. Along with the Resume Next statement is
the Resume statement. This statement is used when the user must make a correction (such as
entering a parameter, or value, for example). Once the user has made the correction, the code
will resume from the place where the error occurred. Another format of the Resume statement
is the Resume line label. This sends the control to a specific line of code. It's especially helpful
when the user must input data before an action can happen (see Listing 26.10).

Listing 26.10. Use of the Resume statement.

```
Public Function TestResumeLine()
On Error GoTo ErrTestResumeLine
    Dim varDate As Date, strMsg as string
    strMsg = "Please Enter A Date."
GetDateValue:
    varDate = InputBox(strMsg,"Enter Date",Date())
```

```
        If varDate>=DateAdd("d",-1,Date()) Then
            Resume GetDateValue
        Else
            Exit Function
        End If
ErrTestResumeLine:
    MsgBox Err.Description
    Exit Function
End Function
```

Listing 26.10 is used to validate the date, which could cause an error later in the code if the date entered is not what is expected. The first step is to evaluate the date entered by the user. If the date is evaluated as yesterday's date, the `Resume` line of code sends the control back to the `GetDateValue` line label. This continues until the user enters a date that is less than yesterday's date. While this isn't an error, it is a format of error trapping for data entry and data validation errors. Most errors occur in data entry.

The code in Listing 26.11 displays a simple error-trapping procedure. If an error occurs while opening the form, the code is directed to the `cmdOpenFormClick` line label. Here the error is displayed, and then the procedure is exited. If there is no error during the opening of the form, the next step would be to exit the procedure—never running the error-handling code.

Listing 26.11. Using the On Error Statement.

```
Private Sub cmdOpenForm_Click()
On Error GoTo cmdOpenFormClick
    DoCmd.OpenForm "Events"
    Exit Sub
cmdOpenFormClick:
    MsgBox Err.Description
    Exit Sub
End Sub
```

WARNING

Before any error-handling line labels appear in code, the line before should contain an `Exit Sub` or `Exit Function` statement. This will prevent a null error from appearing (meaning there was no error).

Listing 26.11 used a new method of displaying an error description. While the `Err.Description` statement may not be new to those who are familiar with Visual Basic, this *is* new to those who have never used Visual Basic. Along with the `Err.Description` statement, there is a difference in the way errors are referenced, displayed, and handled. The `Err` object now contains the following options:

■ Number—The actual error number that occurred in the code.

■ Source—Usually the name of the database—specifically, the name of the Visual Basic project.

■ Description—This is the actual description of what the error is (replaces the `Error$` statement).

> **NOTE**
>
> If the error description is nonexistent, the description returned by the `Err.Description` statement would be an `Application-defined` or `Object-Defined` error.

■ HelpFile—The location of the Visual Basic help file (drive, path, and filename).

■ HelpContextID—The help context ID that corresponds to the current error number (`Err.Number`).

■ LastDLLError—If a system error occurred in a DLL, the last DLL error that occurred would have its information here. This is a read-only property and can't be changed through code.

Syntax for the `Err` object would be

```
Err(Number,Source,Description,HelpFile,HelpContextID,LastDLLError)
Err.Number
Err.Source
Err.Description
Err.HelpFile
Err.HelpContextID
Err.LastDLLError
```

The properties of the `Err` object are set whenever an error occurs in your code and the properties are cleared or reset by

■ `Resume Next`

■ `Exit Sub`

■ `Exit Function`

■ `End Sub`

■ `End Function`

■ `Exit Property`

■ `Err.Clear`

To manually generate an error in your code, use the `Err.Raise Number := (number)` or `Err.Raise(number)` statement.

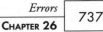

> **NOTE**
>
> The `Err.Raise Number:= (number)` statement will generate the last error number that occurred.

Either the `Err.Raise Number := (number)` or `Err.Raise(number)` statement will raise an error for the entered number value. This too, is new to Access users (see Listing 26.12).

Listing 26.12. Samples of the `Err.Raise` statement.

```
Public Sub TestErrRaise()
On Error GoTo ErrTest
    Err.Raise (10)
    Exit Sub
ErrTest:
    MsgBox Err.Description
    Err.Clear
    Exit Sub
End Sub
```

Listing 26.12 introduces how to use the `Err.Clear` method. This method is used to clear the `Err` object after the error has been handled. While the `Err.Clear` statement has been added to this code example, it is not necessary to always include the `Err.Clear` statement in your error-handling routine. Why? Because when the following statements are executed, the `Clear` method is automatically run to clear the error:

- Any format of the `Resume` statement
- `Exit Sub`, `Exit Function`, or `Exit Property`
- `End Sub` or `End Function`
- `On Error` statement

Where to Use Error Handling in Code

When using parent and child procedures, error handling should be implemented on either or both the parent and child procedures. With these types of procedures, there is no need to add error-handling code to the child process (just raise the error in the error-handling error). When the error occurs, the error-handling code on the parent procedure traps and handles the error. Why? Because the `Err` object's value is global, and therefore, the `Err` object can be passed back to the parent procedure where it can be handled. When the error is handled, a `Resume` statement should theoretically send the code back to the child procedure, `Resume Next` should go to the next statement in the parent procedure, and `Exit Sub`, `Exit Function`, or `Exit Property` should end the procedures (see Listing 26.13).

Listing 26.13. Parent and child error handling.

```
Public Function Parent()
On Error GoTo ErrParent
    Call Child
    Exit Function
ErrParent:
    MsgBox Err.Description
    Exit Function
End Function
Public Sub ChildProc()
On Error GoTo ErrChild
    Dim intAns As Integer
    intAns = 1 / 0
    Exit Sub
ErrChild:
    Err.Raise (Err.Number)
    Exit Sub
End Sub
```

WARNING

When the error occurs in the child procedure, control may not be sent back to the child after the parent procedure has handled the code.

WARNING

Using the Resume statement can cause endless looping through code, if not implemented correctly.

This is only one place where error handling should be implemented. If there is no error handling and an error occurs, the user may be surprised and confused as to why the error has occurred.

Error trapping becomes even more important if the application is being compiled into a runtime version using the Developers Edition of MS Office 97. When an unexpected error occurs in a runtime version of the application, the result is usually an application runtime error, and the actual error message may not be displayed. If there is no error trapping on the code that generated the error, there will definitely be no error message displayed. This can also happen when using an add-in. All add-ins, wizards, and builders that you create should have error trapping built-in. Remember, if the application is being sold or distributed as shareware, a professional look can make a sale, while errors can break a sale.

The more complex the application, the more complex the error handling becomes. Because there may be many modules, you will want to make sure that all the errors are caught and that no unexpected errors will fall through the cracks.

There are two ways to ensure that any unexpected errors will appear:

1. Use the `Raise` method to raise any errors that have not been addressed in the error-handling code.

2. Create a global error-trapping procedure that can be called from anywhere and that passes in the error number and as well as where the error occurred.

Mission Critical Functions

All functions that are critical to a process being completed should have error handling on it, whether it is a child or parent procedure. If it is a child procedure, have the error handling procedure in the parent procedure. This is called *nesting error handling* and should be used frequently. In most cases, the parent relies on the child procedure's being completed correctly and without errors. This kind of reliance on one procedure being completed before another can finish is considered a *mission critical function* of the application.

Mission critical functions can take many forms—parent/child procedures (nested procedures), update and add data, or transaction processing. These types of functions or procedures should have error trapping implemented. For example, if using the `Begin Trans` or `Commit Trans` statements always include the `Rollback` statement in the error-handling code. Ask the user whether they wish to commit the transactions already completed or not. If the user doesn't want to commit the transactions, the `Rollback` statement can be executed. Listing 26.14 displays how to set up an error handler by using transaction processing.

Listing 26.14. Error handling for transaction processing.

```
Public Sub TransTest()
On Error GoTo ErrTrans
    Dim wrkSpace as WorkSpace
    Dim recEvent as Recordset
    < set wrkSpace and recEvent code>
    wrkSpace.BeginTrans
    With recEvent
        Do Until .EOF
            If !EventType = 2 Then
                .Edit
                !EventType = 5
                .Update
            End If
            .MoveNext
        Loop
    End With
    wrkSpace.CommitTrans
    Exit Sub
```

continues

Listing 26.14. continued

```
ErrTrans:
    strMsg = "The following Error occurred:   "  _
            & Err.Number & "   " & Err.Description & _
            Chr(13) & Chr(10) & "Save changes?"
    intRetVal = MsgBox(strMsg, vbYesNo + vbCritical, "Error") Then
    Select Case intRetVal
        Case 6 '* Yes
            wrkSpace.CommitTrans
        Case 7 '* No
            wrkSpace.Rollback
    End Select
End Sub
```

Listing 26.14 shows how to implement the RollBack statement when an error occurs. If there is an error during the transaction processing, the user will be given the option to commit the transaction (save) by using the CommitTrans statement, or return the changed values to their original value (RollBack statement). This option is done by using a simple message box that returns the value (intRetVal) of the button the user pressed.

The user can accept lost, missing, or incorrect if there is an error message stating that an error occurred during the procedure that updated or added data to the application and halted the processing of said procedure. This reassurance associated with an informative error message will help to offset the fact that what took time to enter may have to be redone. The error message helps foster that "warm fuzzy" feeling. An error that occurs with no error message, however, means not only the loss of the data or changes, but the "warm fuzzy" feeling and the user's confidence in the application may not be as high as when an error message is displayed. Always place error trapping on procedures where the updating or adding of data is being done. In the end, you'll have saved yourself, your help desk, and the user valuable time.

Parameter and Referencing

During the design of your application, field, control, and object names can be changed or deleted. If the names are referenced in your code in the old format, this will cause an error. Trapping for invalid references will help you make sure all references to information are correct during the design and testing stages.

Referencing a control on a form or report that isn't there or is named differently also creates an error that can be trapped for (see Figure 26.6).

FIGURE 26.6.

An incorrectly referenced or missing control will cause this error message to appear.

Parameter entry is also another area where error trapping is important. If a control on a form contains a parameter in a query or SQL statement, or a variable on a form or report, the value should always be checked before the query, SQL statement, or variable is used. The last thing you want the user to see as an error message is the error in Figure 26.7.

FIGURE 26.7.

The missing parameter error dialog box.

If you are using a RunSQL statement in your code, make sure that the parameters are entered and referenced correctly. See Listing 26.15 for an example of a DoCmd.RunSQL statement that has an incorrect referencing to a parameter on a form.

Listing 26.15. A parameter error.

```
DoCmd.RunSQL "Select * Into TempA From TableA Where FieldA = " _
             "Forms!Form!ControlA;"
```

This error should be caught and handled during testing and replaced with the code in Listing 26.16.

Listing 26.16. The revised parameter entry.

```
DoCmd.RunSQL "Select * Into TempA From TableA Where FieldA = " _
             & Forms!Form!ControlA & ";"
```

Checking for Null or Empty values in code variables, controls, or fields should also be done along with the error handling code. This may not be an error, but when you think about it, it becomes a snowball effect. If the query or code isn't expecting a Null or Empty value, it returns an error. For the sake of simplicity, check to see whether the value is Null or Empty, returns an error message that tells the user that some input is required, or that the value can't be Null or Empty, before you need to use the value. In some cases it doesn't make a difference, but because this section is dealing with mission critical processing, this may become a factor. Tables 26.5 and 26.6 and Listing 26.17 display some of the results that may occur when the code in Listing 26.17 is run without error trapping.

Table 26.5. Wicket data—before update.

Product	Price	Qty on hand	Value
Wicket A	$10.00	3	?
Wicket B	NULL	4	?
Wicket C	3.00	Null	?

Listing 26.17. With...End With to update on hand value (no error trapping).

```
Public Sub UpdateValue()
    Dim dbCurrent As Database
    Dim recWicket As Recordset
    Set dbCurrent = DBEngine (0) (0)
    Set recWicket = dbCurrent.OpenRecordset("WicketData")
    recWicket.MoveFirst
    With recWicket
        .Edit
        !OnHandValue = (!Price * !Qty)
        .Update
        recWicket.MoveNext
    End With
End Sub
```

Table 26.6. Wicket Data—after update.

Product	Price	Qty on hand	On Hand Value
Wicket A	$10.00	3	$30.00
Wicket B	NULL	4	NULL
Wicket C	3.00	Null	NULL

Wickets B and C both have a null value in the On Hand Value column. In a real-life situation, this would not be acceptable. Since this is a mission critical error (the data is not up-to-date and therefore any reports are going to be incorrect), error handling must be placed on the code (see Listing 26.18).

Listing 26.18. With...End With to update on hand value (error trapping).

```
Public Sub UpdateValue()
On Error GoTo ErrUpdateValue
    Dim dbCurrent As Database
    Dim recWicket As Recordset
    Set dbCurrent = DBEngine (0) (0)
    Set recWicket = dbCurrent.OpenRecordset("WicketData")
    recWicket.MoveFirst
    With recWicket
        .Edit
        !OnHandValue = (!Price * !Qty)
        .Update
        recWicket.MoveNext
    End With
    Exit Sub
ErrUpdateValue:
    MsgBox "Null or Empty information has been found " _
           "while calculating the On Hand Value.  The "_
           "procedure will terminate and allow any Null " _
           "or Empty values to be checked.", vbCritical, _
           "Updating On Hand Value Error"
    Exit Sub
End Sub
```

Anticipate the Worst-Case Scenario

One rule to follow when adding error trapping and handling to your code is to expect the worst. By anticipating the worst-case scenario, your application will become user-friendly and will not be prone to errors. If the worst-case scenario is ignored, the chances of an unexpected error happening as a result of this missing error check can prove to be catastrophic. Just because you know that certain steps have to be completed and in order, that does not necessarily mean that the user will follow those steps. As the creator of the program, developers sometimes think that everyone else will never be less than perfect when using an application they, the developers, have designed. This is far from true. The average user will not follow the same steps that you followed to get the expected results. This is the worst-case scenario. Many unexpected errors can occur if these little "bugs" aren't trapped for. Many programmers call them features. An application that has been thoroughly error trapped should have very few of these unexpected features—most of which should be trapped for and handled either through data validation or error trapping.

Here is an example of trapping for a potential error:

Before the update of a record can happen, the user must enter a valid P.O., date, amount, and payment method. If the user just enters the P.O., date, and amount, there should be some sort of data validation or error trapping that traps for this potential problem.

Although data validation isn't really considered part of error trapping and handling, it can cause an unexpected error to occur. Always be aware of where data validation should be, and make sure that it is either handled by checking to see the value of each variable or that the error message returned is explicit enough to tell the user that they should have entered value *X* in control *A*.

Always anticipate these kinds of scenarios. Many times they are ignored and the user *will* always find them. It is Murphy's Law—what you don't think will happen, will!

Form and Report Properties

Previously, the `Error` event on forms and reports was mentioned as one place that error handling should be implemented. There are other events that should also have error trapping implemented. Many of these events are used to trap for empty or null values and to make sure that parameters are entered, and that there is data in the record source (reports only). The properties discussed are only some of the properties that should have error trapping incorporated.

Most of the time, the errors that occur are a result of a combination of the data entered by the user and the events that occur outside the user's and the developer's control.

Most developers do not think of checking for data validation when designing, but by using the properties on forms and reports to validate the data, fewer errors will occur in your applications.

Properties

Any time that code is included on a property, error trapping should be included—whether it is to trap an actual Visual Basic error or just to trap a data validation error.

■ `Before Update`

Before any information is entered into the database, use the `Before Update` property to check to see whether the data entered is valid.

■ `After Update`

`After Update` can also be used to validate the data that has been entered.

■ `Before Insert`

`Before Insert` is another area that should have some format of data validation and error checking. Duplicate errors can be easily caught here before the form's `Error` event is activated.

■ Not In List

This property is used with combo and list boxes. This in itself is a type of error trapping built into the properties of the form. Its purpose is to warn the user that the value entered into the combo box is not in the list provided. This property, however, is only activated when the Limit To List property must be set to true.

Listing 26.19. The Not In List event procedure.

```
Private Sub EventTypeID_NotInList(NewData As String, Response As Integer)
    MsgBox "The Event Type entered was not in the list."
    Response = acDataErrContinue
End Sub
```

TIP

Set the Limit To List property to Yes when you want to limit the user to entering a value that is in the list. This is part of referential integrity in your database.

On_No_Data

The On_No_Data event, which is used only with reports, was introduced in the previous version of Access. This event should always be used when printing reports. If there is no data for the report, the report can, and usually does, hang the application. The only way to end the report is to use the Ctrl+Alt+Del keys (soft boot) and select the End Task button.

Trapping for no data in the report can save the user from corrupting their application or becoming frustrated with the report not running. The code in Listing 26.20 shows how to trap for no data in the report.

Listing 26.20. A no-data error.

```
Private Sub Report_NoData(Cancel As Integer)
    MsgBox "There is no data to display in the report.", _
➡ vbExclamation, "No Data"
    Cancel = 7
End Sub
```

Display a custom message to tell the user that there was no information to display in the report, and then cancel the request to print the report. The resulting error message is shown in Figure 26.8.

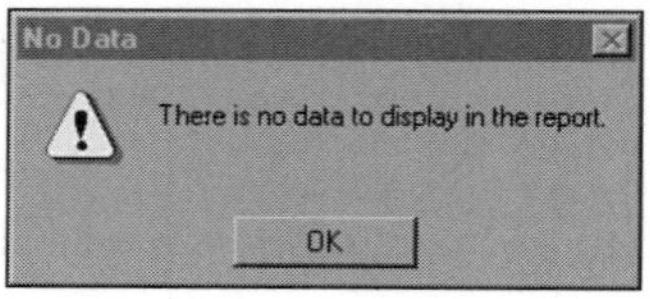

FIGURE 26.8.

Ending a report that has no data.

On_Error of a Form or Report

Previous topics in this chapter have discussed how to address errors that occur on forms and reports, such as duplicate keys, value isn't in the list provided, and so on. The code in Listing 26.21 revisits how to set up the error trapping on the Error event for a report.

Listing 26.21. Report Error event.

```
Private Sub Report_Error(DataErr As Integer, Response As Integer)
    DataErr = acDataErrContinue
    MsgBox AccessError(DataErr)
    Exit Sub
End Sub
```

DataErr is the error number that occurred, while Response is used to display whether the default error message is displayed or not. Table 26.7 lists the Response constants and the actions they perform.

Table 26.7. Response Constants.

Constant	Action
acDataErrContinue	Allows a custom error message to be displayed.
AcDataErrDisplay	Displays the default error message.

Summary

Error handling and trapping play an important part in creating your application. When ignored, serious problems may occur, and users may ignore errors that could have serious repercussions within the application. Functionality as well as presenting a professional look to your application should be your key goals, and both are enhanced by including error handling and trapping in your applications.

PART

X

Programming for Internet and Intranet Use

Access 97 and the Internet

CHAPTER 27

IN THIS CHAPTER

Access 97 provides many ways to create applications to display, run, and publish content on the Internet or on an intranet. For example, you can use Access to publish information from data sheets and reports as Web pages. You can also use Access to create files that query a database on a Web server, and then return a Web page to display the results of the query. In addition, you can save an Access form as a Web page that emulates many of the features of the form so that users can view, enter, and update information in your database.

You can also use Access 97 to create applications that display HTML documents in forms, and create hyperlinks that you click to move between database objects and other Office documents located on a hard disk or on a local area network (LAN).

The following list summarizes the features available in Access 97 that you can use to work with content on the Internet or an intranet.

Access 97 Web Development Features

- Store hyperlinks in fields with the Hyperlink data type and follow the hyperlinks to display Internet content.

- Browse the folders of FTP sites in the Link To File dialog box when you insert or edit hyperlinks (for example, by choosing Insert Hyperlink from the Insert menu).

- Bind a text box control on a form to a field with the Hyperlink data type to enter, display, or follow a hyperlink.

- Bind a text box control on a report to a field with the Hyperlink data type to create a hyperlink when you save the report as an HTML document or to print the hyperlink address.

- Reference a hyperlink from a label, an image control, or a command button on a form or report.

- Use Visual Basic for Applications (VBA) methods and properties to work with hyperlinks. For example, you can use the `Follow` method to go to the address referenced in a hyperlink, and use the `AddToFavorites` method to add a hyperlink to the Favorites folder.

- Connect to other Office documents and files on an intranet.

- Go to Access objects in the current database or other databases by using hyperlinks from the current Access database or from another Office application.

- Go to documents from other Office applications by using hyperlinks from Access databases.

- Use the Back and Forward buttons on the Web toolbar to move between followed hyperlinks to database objects and other Office documents.

- Locate Access databases with Web Find Fast. Microsoft Office 97 has a search page you can use to find files or information on a subject on your organization's intranet, even if you do not know where the files or information are located.

- Publish and share data in a database on the Web.

- Save the data from table, query, and form data sheets or from reports as static HTML documents.

- Create Internet Database Connector/HTML extension (IDC/HTX) files to query data from a table, query, or form data sheet in a database on an Internet or intranet server and display it in a Web page.

- Save an Access form as an Active Server Page (ASP) that emulates many of the features of the form so that users can view, enter, and update information in a database on an Internet or intranet server.

- Create an ASP (Active Server Page) to query data from a table, query, or form data sheet in a database on an Internet or intranet server and display it in a Web page.

- Use the Publish to the Web Wizard to automate the process of publishing and sharing data, store settings from previous publications, and call the Web Publishing Wizard to copy Web files to your Internet or intranet server.

- Export HTML documents, IDC/HTX files, or ASPs using the `OutputTo` method or action of the application object.

- Attach HTML documents, IDC/HTX files, or ASPs to e-mail messages using the `SendObject` method or action of the application object.

- Export tables as HTML tables by using the `TransferText` method or action.

- Replicate databases over the Internet. Synchronize a database replica with a replica or Design Master on an Internet or intranet server.

- Import, link, and export data located on the Internet or on an intranet. Import and link HTML tables and lists by using the Import HTML Wizard and the Link HTML Wizard. (When you link HTML tables, the data is read-only.)

- Import and link any data on an Internet or intranet server that is supported by a built-in Access driver. (When you link data on an Internet server, the data is read-only.)

- Use the Import and Link dialog boxes to browse FTP sites when you import or link data (for example, by choosing Get External Data from the File menu and then clicking Import or Link table). You can also use the Import and Link dialog boxes to enter an HTTP address when you are importing or linking data.

- Import or link HTML tables by using the `TransferText` method of the application object. (When you link HTML tables, the data is read-only.)

27

ACCESS 97 AND THE INTERNET

- Import or link data by using HTTP and FTP addresses, and export data by using FTP addresses in the following Visual Basic for Applications properties, methods, and actions:

    The `Connect` property

    The `CreateTableDef` method

    The `OutputTo` method

    The `TransferDatabase` method

    The `TransferText` method

    The `TransferSpreadsheet` method

- Display Web pages and other documents in Microsoft Access forms.
- Use the WebBrowser control on your application's forms to browse Web sites, view Web pages and other documents, and download data located on the Internet or an intranet. (You can also use the WebBrowser control to browse folders on your hard disk or on a network.)

Using Hyperlinks in Microsoft Access 97 Applications

With Access 97, you can create two kinds of hyperlinks in tables, forms, and reports:

- Hyperlinks to display and run standard Internet content, such as HTML documents.
- Hyperlinks that allow you to move between Microsoft Word documents, Microsoft Excel worksheets, Microsoft PowerPoint slides, and Microsoft Access database objects that are stored on a hard disk or on a LAN.

You do not need Internet connections or intranet servers to use Office hyperlinks to move between Office documents or files. You can use both kinds of hyperlinks in the same database application.

There are two ways you can use hyperlinks in Access 97 applications:

- Create a field with the Hyperlink data type to store hyperlink addresses in a table and then bind that field to a text box on a form. Like other bound fields, as the user moves from record to record, the value in the text box changes to display the current record's hyperlink value. For example, you can use hyperlinks in this way to create an application in which users can go to Web pages, or to other content on the Internet or an intranet, from a predefined list of addresses. You can also create an application that displays and manages Office documents.
- Create a label, image control, or command button on a form that references a specified hyperlink address. In this case, the hyperlink does not change as you move from

record to record. For example, you can use hyperlinks in this way to go to other database objects within the same database, or to open a Web page on an intranet that contains updated information about how to use your application.

Regardless of how a hyperlink is defined in your application, if the hyperlink goes to a database object or opens another Office document, you can use the Web toolbar to move between the hyperlinks that you have previously followed. Once you have clicked the hyperlink, you can use the Web toolbar to move between other objects you have opened with hyperlinks.

Similarly, if you follow a hyperlink from a Microsoft Access form to a Word document, you can click the Back button on the Web toolbar in Word to return to the Microsoft Access form.

> **NOTE**
>
> By default, after a user clicks a hyperlink on a form, Access continues to display the Web toolbar when the user closes the form. If you want to prevent this, you can use Visual Basic for Applications code in the `OnClose` event of the form to hide the toolbar. To see an example of this code, open the `Products` form in the `Northwind` sample application in Design View, and then display the event procedure in the `OnClose` event of the form.

Storing Hyperlinks in Tables

In Access 97, a field in a table can store hyperlinks as data. To create a hyperlink field, add a field in the table in Design View, and set its `DataType` property to `Hyperlink`. You can also create a hyperlink field in a table when in Datasheet View with the Hyperlink Column command (accessed through the Insert menu).

You can follow a hyperlink that is stored in a table by clicking the field within the table, but the field is more typically bound to a text box control on a form. This should be the easiest means of accessing the hyperlink.

To see an example of how to use a hyperlink field, open the `Suppliers` form in the `Northwind` sample database application. Go to Record 2, `New Orleans Cajun Delights`. The Home Page text box on the form is bound to the `HomePage` field in the `Suppliers` table. Clicking the hyperlink in the text box starts your Web browser and displays the supplier's home page. (See Figure 27.1.)

You can also use hyperlinks in Access to go to database objects and other Office documents. For example, you could create a document-management application that uses a hyperlink field to store paths to Word documents on a network. Users of such an application could add records to track new documents or click the hyperlink in a previously added record to open the specified document.

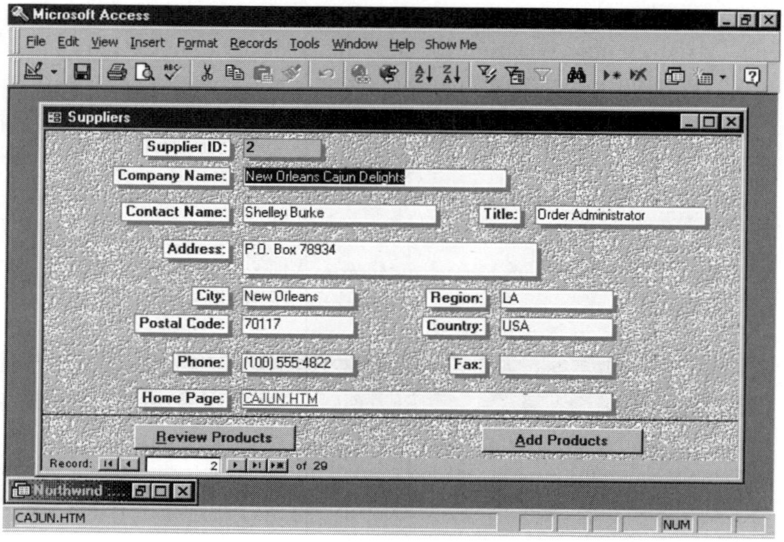

FIGURE 27.1
A hyperlink to a supplier's home page on the World Wide Web. Notice the Internet Web address in the Home Page text box.

Editing the Hyperlink Field

A hyperlink field stores up to three pieces of information: the text to display in the field, the address, and the subaddress. Each piece is separated by the pound sign (#), in the following format:

displaytext#address#subaddress

The following list describes each piece of the hyperlink field's storage format:

- *displaytext*: Not required. This is the text the user sees in the hyperlink field in a table or in a text box bound to the hyperlink field. You can set the display text to any text string. For example, you might want the display text to be a descriptive name for the Web site or object specified by the address and subaddress. If you do not specify the display text, Access displays the value of address instead.

- *address*: Required (unless the subaddress points to an object in the current database file). This is either a valid URL that points to a page or file on the Internet or an intranet, or the path to a file on a hard disk or LAN. If you enter a path on a LAN, you can omit a mapped drive letter and use the UNC (universal naming convention) format: *server\share\path\filename*. This prevents the path from becoming invalid if the database is later copied to another hard disk or shared network folder.

- *subaddress*: Not required. A specific location within a file or document (for example, a database object, such as a form or report). When referring to a database object, the name of the object should be preceded by its type: Table, Query, Form, Report, Macro, or Module. Other possible values for subaddress include a bookmark in a Word document, an anchor in an HTML document, a PowerPoint slide, or a cell in a Microsoft Excel worksheet.

Each piece of the hyperlink field storage format can be up to 2,000 characters. The maximum length of the entire hyperlink field value is 6,000 characters. To display the stored hyperlink format move the insertion point into a hyperlink field using the cursor keys on your keyboard and then press F2. You can edit the stored hyperlink in this form as long as you enter the pound signs in the appropriate locations. To add or edit the `displaytext` part of a hyperlink field right-click a hyperlink in a table, choose Hyperlink from the shortcut menu, and then type the display text in the Display Text box.

For more information about the Hyperlink field storage format, see the Microsoft Access online help.

Entering a URL as a Hyperlink Address

To create a hyperlink that goes to a Web page or other Internet content, you must enter a valid uniform resource locator (URL) as the hyperlink address. You can enter a URL that points to any Internet file type or resource supported by the browser or to an ActiveX control, such as the WebBrowser control, that is used to display or run it. You enter most URLs in the following format:

`protocol://serveraddress/path`

- `protocol` specifies the Internet protocol used to establish the connection to the server, and is generally followed by a colon and two slash marks.
- `serveraddress` specifies what is usually called the *domain name* of the Internet server.
- `path` specifies the location and name of the page or file on the Internet server.

For example, the URL to the home page of the Microsoft Access Developer Forum is

`http://www.microsoft.com/accessdev/`

If you create a field by importing a column of data, and all records in the imported data begin with an Internet protocol, Access automatically sets the data type of the imported field to Hyperlink. Similarly, if you create a new table in Datasheet View, and every entry you make in a field begins with one of these protocols, Access sets the data type of the new field to Hyperlink when you save the table.

Creating Labels, Image Controls, or Command Buttons That Reference a Hyperlink Address

To create a label, image control, or command button on a form that references a specified hyperlink address, set the `HyperlinkAddress` and `HyperlinkSubAddress` properties of the control to point to the content on the Internet or on an intranet, or to the Office document or Access database object to which you want to go.

Additionally, to create the hyperlink display text for a label or command button control, you must set the `Caption` property. Because no text displays for an image control, there is no corresponding display text setting.

You can also create a label that references a hyperlink address by opening the form in Design View and then choosing the Hyperlink command from the Insert menu. This method does not, however, define the display text. To define the display text, you must set the `Caption` property of the label.

Using Visual Basic Methods and Properties to Work with Hyperlinks

Access 97 provides several methods and properties you can use to work with hyperlinks in Visual Basic for Applications code. Table 27.1 summarizes these methods and properties.

Table 27.1. VBA methods and properties used for hyperlinks.

Method or Property Name	Description
`Follow` method	Has the same effect as clicking a hyperlink. When you use the `Follow` method, you do not need to know the address specified by a `HyperlinkAddress` or `HyperlinkSubAddress` property, or by the hyperlink field that is bound to a text box control. You only need to know the name of the control that contains the hyperlink.
`FollowHyperlink` method	Goes to a hyperlink specified in code or passed to the method from an unbound text box. For example, you can prompt a user to type a hyperlink address in a dialog box, and then use the `FollowHyperlink` method to go to that address. You can also use the `FollowHyperlink` method to specify a hyperlink for controls other than labels, image controls, and command buttons, or text boxes bound to hyperlink fields.

Method or Property Name	Description
`AddToFavorites` method	Adds the hyperlink address specified in the referenced control to the Favorites folder.
`Hyperlink` property	Returns a reference to a hyperlink object in code. You can use the `Hyperlink` property to gain access to the hyperlink-specific properties and methods of any control that contains a hyperlink.
`HyperlinkAddress` property	Specifies or determines the address of a hyperlink for a label, image control, or command button.
`HyperlinkSubAddress` property	Specifies or determines the location within the Office document or object specified by the `HyperlinkAddress` property.
`HyperlinkPart` function	Parses the information stored in a hyperlink field.

Making Access Data Available on the Internet

With Access, you can make your data available on the Internet or an intranet by

- Saving data as HTML documents.
- Synchronizing a database replica with a replica or Design Master on an HTTP or FTP server.

Saving Data as HTML Documents

Microsoft Access provides four ways to save data from your database as an HTML document:

- Save data as static HTML documents.
- Create static HTML documents from table, query, and form data sheets and from reports. When you save data as static HTML documents, the resulting pages reflect the state of the data at the time it was saved. If your data changes, you must save the pages again to share the new data.
- Save table, query, and form data sheets as IDC/HTX files.

Saving Forms and Data Sheets as ASPs

You can save your forms as ASPs that emulate most of the functionality of your forms and display data from a database located on a Web server. You can also save table, query, and form data sheets as ASPs that display current data from a copy of your database located on a Web server.

Automating the Publishing of Dynamic and Static HTML Documents

You can use the Publish to the Web Wizard to automate the process of saving multiple objects to any combination of all three file types. In the Publish to the Web Wizard, IDC/HTX files and ASP files are referred to as dynamic Web pages because these file types display current data to users.

Saving Data as Static HTML Documents

With Access 97, you can save table, query, and form data sheets and reports as static HTML documents. (See Figure 27.2.)

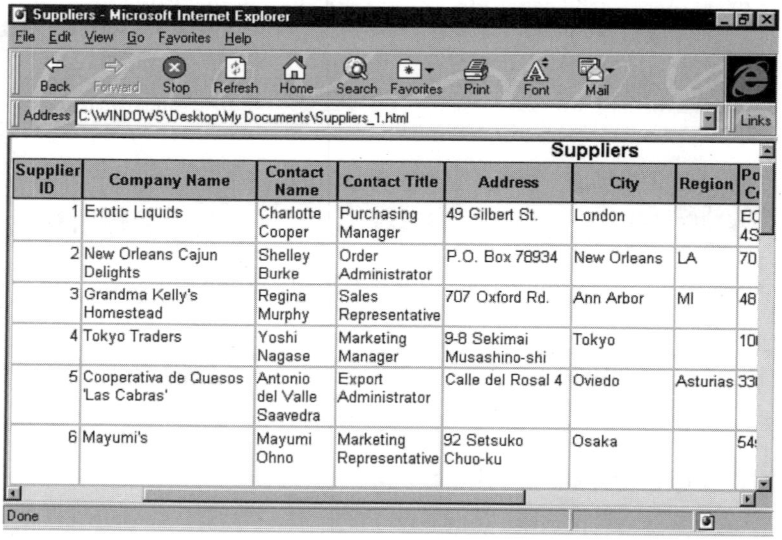

FIGURE 27.2.

A static HTML page generated from the Northwind *sample database's* Suppliers *table and displayed in Microsoft Internet Explorer version 3.x.*

To save a table, query, or form data sheet or a report as a static HTML document, follow these steps:

1. In the Database window, click the table, query, form, or report you want to save.

2. From the File menu, choose Save As/Export.

3. In the Save As dialog box that appears, click To an External File or Database, and then click OK.

4. In the Save as type list, click HTML Documents.

5. To open the resulting HTML document in your Web browser automatically, select the Autostart checkbox.

6. Specify a filename and location for the HTML file, and then click Export.

7. In the HTML Output Options dialog box, specify whether you want Microsoft Access to merge an HTML template with the resulting HTML document, and then click OK.

You can also save data as static HTML documents by using the Publish to the Web Wizard (available through the Save As HTML command on the File menu), the `OutputTo` method in code, or the `OutputTo` action in macros.

When saving table, query, and form data sheets, Access saves each data sheet to a single HTML file. Access saves reports as multiple HTML documents, with one HTML file per printed page. To name each page, Access uses the name of the object and appends `_Page#` to the end of each filename after the first page: for example, `ProductList.htm`, `ProductList_Page2.htm`, `ProductList_Page3.htm`, and so on.

Saving Table, Query, and Form Data Sheets as Static HTML Documents

When you save a table, query, or form data sheet as an HTML document, the HTML document generated is based on the table or query associated with the data sheet, including the current setting of the `OrderBy` or `Filter` property of the table or query, which determines how the table, query, or form is sorted or filtered.

The HTML document contains an HTML table that reflects as closely as possible the appearance of the data sheet by using the appropriate HTML tags to specify color, font, and alignment. The HTML document follows as closely as possible the page orientation and margins of the data sheet. Whenever you want to use settings that are different from the default orientation and margins for a data sheet, you must first open the data sheet and then choose Page Setup from the File menu to change settings before you save the data sheet as an HTML document.

If a field has a `Format` or `InputMask` property setting, that setting is reflected in the data in the HTML document. For example, if the `Format` property of the field is set to `Currency`, the data in the HTML document is formatted with a dollar sign, a comma as the thousand separator, and two decimal places: for example, $7,000.00.

Saving Reports as Static HTML Documents

When you save a report as a series of HTML documents, the HTML documents generated are based on the report's underlying table or query, including either the current `OrderBy` or `Filter` property setting of the table or query.

The HTML documents closely approximate the proportions and layout of the actual report and follow as closely as possible the page orientation and margins set for the report. To change the page orientation and margins, open the report in Print Preview and then choose Page Setup from the File menu to change the settings before you save the report as HTML documents. These settings are saved from session to session for reports, so if you change them once, they will be used the next time you save the form or report as HTML documents.

If you specify an HTML template that contains placeholders for navigation controls when you save a report as multiple HTML documents, Access creates hyperlinks the user can use to go to the first, previous, next, and last pages in the publication. Where Access places the hyperlinks depends on where you locate the placeholders in the HTML template.

How Microsoft Access Saves Data Types in HTML

When you save data as static HTML documents, Access saves values from most data types as strings and then formats them as closely as possible to their appearance in the data sheet or report. There are two exceptions:

- OLE object fields are not saved.
- Hyperlink field values are saved as hyperlinks in the HTML document. The hyperlinks use HTML anchor tags with an HREF attribute, as follows:
  - If the hyperlink does not include a subaddress:

    `<A HREF="address">displaytext</A>`

  - If the hyperlink includes a subaddress:

    `<A HREF="address#subaddress">displaytext</A>`

  - If the display text is not specified:

    `<A HREF="address">address</A>`

Access determines the *displaytext*, *address*, and *subaddress* values in the anchor tags by parsing the value stored in the hyperlink field.

Saving Table, Query, and Form Data Sheets as IDC/HTX Files

With Access, you can save a table, query, or form data sheet as an IDC/HTX file that generates HTML documents by querying a copy of your database located on a Web server. (See Figure 27.3.) In contrast to static HTML documents, IDC/HTX files display current data from your database; therefore, the HTML documents they generate are dynamic.

Microsoft Internet Information Server uses IDC and HTX files to get data from an ODBC data source and format it as an HTML document. HTX files are HTML text files that contain keywords that control how data is formatted and placeholders specifying where that data is inserted in the HTML document. The HTX files act as templates specifying how to format data as an HTML document when data is returned from SQL statements specified in IDC files. IDC files are text files that specify how to connect to an ODBC (Open Database Connectivity) data source, and they contain SQL statements to execute.

The following list details the procedure for saving your table, query, or form data sheet as HTX/IDC files. You can save a table, query, or form data sheet as an IDC:

1. In the Database window, click the table, query, or form you want to save.
2. From the File menu, click Save As/Export.

3. In the Save As dialog box that appears, click To an External File or Database, and then click OK.

4. In the Save as type list, click Microsoft IIS 1–2.

5. Specify a filename and location for the IDC/HTX files, and then click Export.

6. In the HTX/IDC Output Options dialog box, specify:

  ■ The data source name to use for a copy of the current database.

  ■ A username and password, if required to open the database.

  ■ An HTML template, if you want Access to merge one with the HTML extension (HTX) file.

FIGURE 27.3.

Saving a table, query, or form data sheet as an HTX/IDC file.

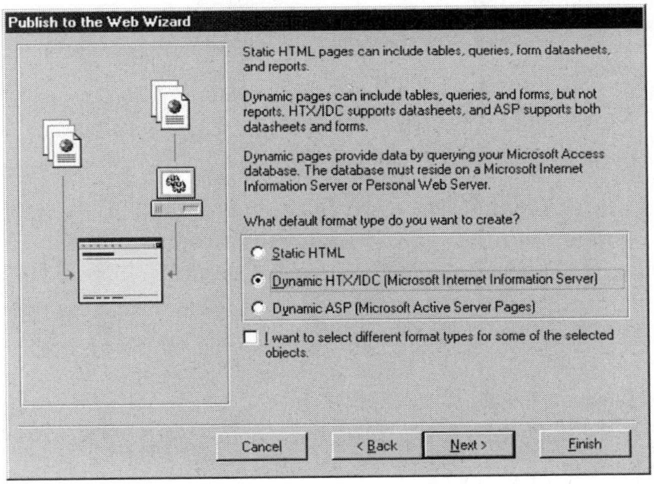

Publish to the Web Wizard

Static HTML pages can include tables, queries, form datasheets, and reports.

Dynamic pages can include tables, queries, and forms, but not reports. HTX/IDC supports datasheets, and ASP supports both datasheets and forms.

Dynamic pages provide data by querying your Microsoft Access database. The database must reside on a Microsoft Internet Information Server or Personal Web Server.

What default format type do you want to create?

○ Static HTML

● Dynamic HTX/IDC (Microsoft Internet Information Server)

○ Dynamic ASP (Microsoft Active Server Pages)

☐ I want to select different format types for some of the selected objects.

Cancel   < Back   Next >   Finish

NOTE

You can specify any of these items later, except the HTML template, by editing the resulting IDC file in a text editor, such as Notepad.

You can also save a table, query, or form data sheet as an IDC/HTX file by using the Publish to the Web Wizard (available through the Save As HTML command on the File menu), the OutputTo method in code, or the OutputTo action in macros.

How the Internet Database Connector Works

When you save a table, form, or query data sheet as an Internet Connector file, Access creates two files: an Internet Database Connector (IDC) file and HTML extension (HTX) file. These files are used to generate a Web page that displays current data from your database.

An IDC file contains the necessary information to connect to a specified ODBC data source and to run an SQL statement that queries the database. The information needed to connect to the database includes the data source name and, if user-level security is established for the database, the username and password required to open the database. For example, if you save the Current Product List query data sheet from the Northwind sample database application as an IDC/HTX file, Access creates the following IDC file:

```
Datasource:Northwind
Template:Current Product List.htx
SQLStatement:SELECT [Product List].ProductID, [Product List].ProductName
+FROM Products AS [Product List]
+WHERE ((([Product List].Discontinued)=No))
+ORDER BY [Product List].ProductName;
Password:
Username:
```

An IDC file also contains the name and location of an HTML extension (HTX) file. The HTX file is a template for the HTML document; it contains field merge codes that indicate where the values returned by the SQL statement should be inserted. For example, if you save the Current Product List query data sheet from the Northwind sample database application as an IDC/HTX file, Microsoft Access creates the following HTX file:

```
<HTML>
<TITLE>Current Product List</TITLE>
<BODY>
<Table Border=1 BGCOLOR="#ffffff"><FONT FACE="ARIAL" COLOR="#000000">
<CAPTION><B>Current Product List</B></CAPTION>
<THEAD>
<TR>
<TD><FONT SIZE=2 FACE="ARIAL" COLOR="#000000">Product ID</FONT></TD>
<TD><FONT SIZE=2 FACE="ARIAL" COLOR="#000000">Product Name</FONT></TD>
</TR>
</THEAD>
<TBODY>
<%BeginDetail%>
<TR VALIGN=TOP>
<TD ALIGN=RIGHT><FONT SIZE=2 FACE="ARIAL" COLOR="#000000"><%ProductID%><BR>
➥</FONT></TD>
<TD><FONT SIZE=2 FACE="ARIAL" COLOR="#000000"><%ProductName%><BR></FONT></TD>
```

```
</TR>
<%EndDetail%>
</TBODY>
<TFOOT></TFOOT>
</BODY>
</HTML>
```

Microsoft Access saves the HTX file to be used with an IDC file with the same name as the IDC file, but with an `.htx` extension rather than an `.idc` extension. After the database information has been merged into the HTML document, the HTML document is returned to the Web browser.

> **NOTE**
>
> You can also reference an HTML template when you create IDC and HTX files. An HTML template contains additional HTML code to enhance the appearance of the resulting pages. If you specify an HTML template, it is merged with the HTX file.

Requirements for Using IDC/HTX Files

To display and use IDC/HTX files, a copy of your database and the IDC/HTX files must reside on a computer running one of the following operating systems and Internet server environments:

- Windows NT Server version 3.51 or later running Microsoft Internet Information Server (IIS) version 1.0, 2.0, or 3.0.
- Windows NT Workstation version 4.0 with Peer Web Services installed.
- Windows 95 with Personal Web Server installed.

If no more than 10 users use your server simultaneously, Peer Web Services or Personal Web Server should be used to test IDC/HTX files. Microsoft IIS, Peer Web Services, and Personal Web Server use a component called the Internet Database Connector (`Httpodbc.dll`) to generate Web pages from IDC/HTX files.

The Internet Database Connector component requires ODBC drivers to gain access to a database. To gain access to an Access database, the Microsoft Access Desktop driver (`Odbcjt32.dll`) must be installed on your Web server. This driver is installed when you select the ODBC Drivers And Administration checkbox during IIS setup.

But the Microsoft Access Desktop driver is not installed with Peer Web Services or Personal Web Server. If Access is installed on the computer you are using to run Personal Web Server, and if you selected the driver when you installed Access, the driver is already available. If you do not have Access installed on the computer you are using to run Personal Web Server, you must install the Microsoft Access Desktop driver (see Figure 27.4).

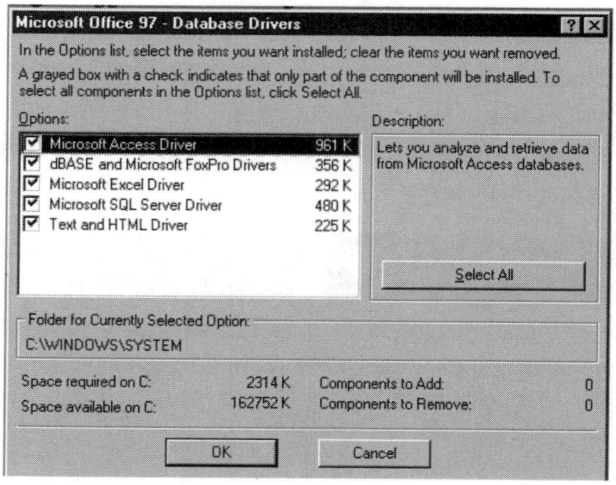

FIGURE 27.4.

Installing the Access 97
Desktop driver.

To install the Microsoft Access Desktop driver, follow these steps:

1. Start the Office or Microsoft Access Setup program. If you are running Setup for the first time, click Custom; if you are rerunning Setup, click Add/Remove.

2. Select the Data Access option, and then click Change Option.

> **WARNING**
>
> The Microsoft Access option must also be selected or the driver will not be installed.

3. Under the Database Drivers option, select the Microsoft Access Driver checkbox, and then click the OK button.

After the Microsoft Access Desktop driver is installed, you must create either a system DSN or a file DSN that specifies the name and connection information for each database you want to use on the server. You then specify that DSN when you generate the IDC/HTX files.

Saving Forms and Data Sheets as Active Server Pages

With Access, you can save a form as an active server page (ASP) that emulates much of the functionality of your form. When saving a form as an ASP, Access saves most, but not all controls on the form as ActiveX controls that perform the same or similar functions.

Access does not save or run Visual Basic code behind the form or controls. To copy the layout of your form as closely as possible, Access uses the Microsoft HTML Layout control to position the controls on an ASP. The resulting page uses a feature of the ASP component of Microsoft Internet Information Server 3.0, called *server-side scripting*, to connect to a copy of your database on an Internet server.

Users who open a form saved as an ASP can browse records, update or delete existing records, and add new records.

You can also save table, query, and form data sheets as ASPs. When you open a data sheet saved as an ASP, Access displays current data from a copy of your database located on an Internet server, much like IDC/HTX files do. However, unlike IDC/HTX files, ASPs require only one file per data sheet. The ASP file uses scripting to establish a connection to the database on the server and contains information that it uses to format the data sheet. Unlike a form saved as an ASP, users cannot update existing records in or add new records to a data sheet saved as an IDC/HTX file (see Figure 27.5).

FIGURE 27.5.

Saving forms or data sheets as ASPs.

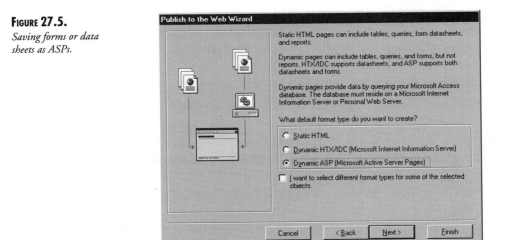

The following list details the procedure for saving your forms or data sheets as ASPs:

1. In the Database window, click on the form or data sheet you want to save.
2. From the File menu, click Save As/Export.
3. In the Save As dialog box that appears, click To an External File or Database, and then click OK.
4. In the Save as type list, click Microsoft Active Server Page.
5. Specify a filename and location for the ASP file, and then click Export.
6. In the Microsoft Active Server Page Output Options dialog box, specify the following:

■ The data source name to use for a copy of the current database.

■ A username and password, if required to open the database.

■ An HTML template, if you want Access to merge one with the ASP.

■ The URL for the server where the ASP will reside.

■ The session time-out setting, which determines how long a connection to the server is maintained after the user stops working with the ASP.

As illustrated in Figure 27.5, you can save forms and data sheets as ASPs by using the Publish to the Web Wizard (available through the Save As HTML command on the File menu), the `OutputTo` method in code, or the `OutputTo` action in macros.

Form Views Supported for ASPs

If the form you save as an ASP has its `DefaultView` property set to `Single Form` or `Continuous Forms`, the ASP is displayed as a single form, unless it is opened in Datasheet View with the Save As/Export command from the File menu. If the form has its `DefaultView` property set to `Datasheet`, the ASP is displayed as a data sheet. Subforms are always displayed as data sheets, regardless of their `DefaultView` property setting. All field data types are saved unformatted; that is, the `Format` and `InputMask` property settings are not saved.

Control Types Supported for ASPs

When Microsoft Access saves a form as an ASP, it replaces Access controls with ActiveX controls, as described in Table 27.2.

Table 27.2. Access controls replaced with ActiveX controls when a form is saved as an ASP.

Access Control	*Replacement ActiveX Control*
Text box	Text box. A text box control bound to a Hyperlink field that displays the hyperlink text, but the hyperlink cannot be followed.
List box	List box (single column only).
Combo box	Combo box.
Label	Label. If the label has the `HyperlinkAddress` or `HyperlinkSubAddress` property set, a hyperlink is created for the label.
Command button	Command button, but any code associated with the button is lost. If the command button has the `HyperlinkAddress` or `HyperlinkSubAddress` property set, a hyperlink is created for the button.
Option group	Option group, but without a group frame.
Option button	Option button.

Access Control	*Replacement ActiveX Control*
Check box	Checkbox.
Toggle button	Toggle button.
ActiveX control	ActiveX control, but any code associated with the control is lost.

Microsoft Access does not support the following when saving a form as an ASP:

- Tab controls
- Rectangles
- Lines
- Page breaks
- Unbound object frames
- Bound object frames
- Image controls
- Background of a form set with the `Picture` property

Requirements for Using ASPs

To display and use an ASP, a copy of your database and ASP components must reside on a computer running one of the following operating systems and Internet server platforms:

- Microsoft Windows NT Server 3.51 or later running IIS 3.0.
- Microsoft Windows NT Workstation 4.0 and Peer Web Services with the ASP components installed.
- Microsoft Windows 95 and Personal Web Server with the ASP components installed.

The Microsoft HTML Layout control must be installed on the computer opening the ASP. If the computer opening an ASP produced by Access 97 does not have the HTML Layout control installed, a message is displayed, prompting the user to download the control. To display the ASP, the user must click Yes to download the control.

> **TIP**
>
> Microsoft HTML Layout control is not included on the Office CD-ROM, but you can download it directly from the Web. To download the Microsoft HTML Layout control, connect to
>
> `http://www.microsoft.com/ie/download/ieadd.htm`

If no more than 10 users use your server simultaneously, use Personal Web Server or Peer Web Services to test ASPs. ASPs also require the Microsoft Access Desktop driver and a valid DSN to gain access to a database.

Using the Publish to the Web Wizard

With the Publish to the Web Wizard, you can publish a set of Microsoft Access database objects to any combination of static HTML documents, IDC/HTX files, or ASPs. Using the wizard, you can

- Pick any combination of tables, queries, forms, or reports to save.
- Specify an HTML template to use for the selected objects.
- Select any combination of static HTML documents, IDC/HTX files, or ASPs.
- Create a home page to tie together the Web pages you create.
- Specify the folder where you save your files.
- Use the Web Publishing Wizard to move the files created by the Publish to the Web Wizard to a Web server.
- Save the answers you provide to the wizard as a Web publication profile and then select that profile the next time you use the wizard. This saves you from having to answer all the questions again.

> **NOTE**
>
> The Publish to the Web Wizard and Web Publishing Wizard cannot copy the database itself or create a DSN on your server when publishing IDC/HTX or ASP. You must perform these operations yourself.

Using an HTML Template When You Save Data as HTML Documents

When you save data as HTML documents, you can use an HTML template to give a consistent look to the HTML documents you create. For example, you can include your company logo, name, and address in the page header; use the background that is used throughout your company; or include standard text in the header or footer of the HTML document.

> **NOTE**
>
> You can use an HTML template when you save data as static HTML documents, when you save data sheets as IDC/HTX files, when you save a form or data sheet as an ASP, and when you use the Publish to the Web Wizard.

The HTML template can be any HTML document; that is, a text file that includes HTML tags and user-specified text and references. In addition, the HTML template can include placeholders that tell Access where to insert certain pieces of data in the HTML documents. When data is saved as HTML documents, the placeholders are replaced with data. Table 27.3 describes each of the placeholders you can use in an HTML template.

Table 27.3. Access 97–specific HTML template placeholders.

Placeholder	Description	Location
`<!--AccessTemplate_Title-->`	The name of the object being saved	Between `<TITLE>` and `</TITLE>`
`<!--AccessTemplate_Body-->`	The data or object being saved	Between `<BODY>` and `</BODY>`
`<!--AccessTemplate_FirstPage-->`	An anchor tag to the first page	Between `<BODY>` and `</BODY>` or after `</BODY>`
`<!--AccessTemplate_PreviousPage-->`	An anchor tag to the previous page	Between `<BODY>` and `</BODY>` or after `</BODY>`
`<!--AccessTemplate_NextPage-->`	An anchor tag to the next page	Between `<BODY>` and `</BODY>` or after `</BODY>`
`<!--AccessTemplate_LastPage-->`	An anchor tag to the last page	Between `<BODY>` and `</BODY>` or after `</BODY>`
`<!--AccessTemplate_PageNumber-->`	The current page number	Between `<BODY>` and `</BODY>` or after `</BODY>`

27

ACCESS 97 AND THE INTERNET

When you install Microsoft Access, sample HTML template files and graphics files are installed in the `Program Files\Microsoft Office\Templates\Access` folder.

Synchronizing Database Replicas over the Internet

With Access 97, you can synchronize replicas over the Internet. Before you can synchronize over the Internet, however, you must configure your Internet server for replication. To configure your Internet server, you need Replication Manager, which includes a wizard that guides you through the configuration process. Microsoft includes Replication Manager with the Office 97 Developer's Edition on the ODE Tools CD-ROM. Replication Manager is installed when the user installs the ODE tools.

Importing, Linking, and Exporting Data to the Internet

With Access, you can import or link data from HTML tables or other data sources on an Internet server. You can also export data in your database to an Internet server. The following sections explain these procedures.

Importing and Linking Data from HTML Tables

You can import or link data formatted as an HTML table to an Access database. Before Access imports or links the data, it copies the data into the local cache. Whenever you open a linked table, Access makes a local copy from the original on the Internet or an intranet before opening it. For this reason, the data in the table is read-only. Similarly, if you export the linked HTML table to an HTML file, Access exports from the local copy of the file, not from the original file on the Internet (see Figure 27.6).

FIGURE 27.6.

Importing or linking data from HTML tables.

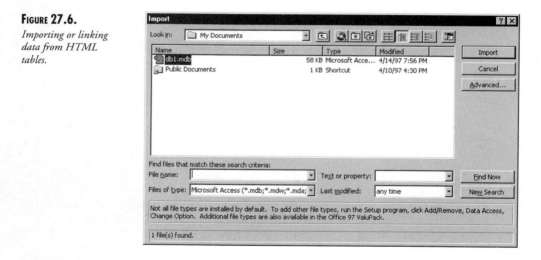

The following list details the procedure for importing or linking data from HTML tables:

1. From the File menu, choose Get External Data, and then click either Import or Link tables.

2. In the Files of type list, click HTML Documents.

3. To specify the file from which to import or link, use the Look in box to browse through the file system on your hard disk or LAN. In the File name box, type a valid HTTP or FTP URL; in the Look in box, click Internet Locations (FTP) and select a previously defined FTP site.

4. Next, in the Look in box, click Add/Modify FTP Locations, and then specify a new FTP site and browse its files.

5. Click Import or Link.

When you import or link data from an HTML table, Microsoft Access parses the information contained within the HTML tags. The primary HTML tags that define tables are described in the Table 27.4.

Table 27.4. Primary HTML tags for defining tables.

HTML Tag Pair	Description
`<TABLE>...</TABLE>`	Specifies the beginning and end of the table
`<TH...>...</TH>`	Specifies table header cells
`<TR...>...</TR>`	Specifies a row in a table
`<TD...>...</TD>`	Specifies table data cells
`<CAPTION...>...</CAPTION>`	Specifies the table caption, usually at the beginning or end of the table

Access applies the following rules when it interprets the progression of tags and tag pairs within the HTML table it imports or links:

- The `<TD>` tag pair may be closed with either a `</TD>` tag or a `</TH>` tag.
- The `<TH>` tag pair may be closed with either a `</TH>` tag or a `</TD>` tag.
- The `<TR>` tag is not required to start a new row. If a `<TD>` tag follows a `</TR>` tag, Access assumes this is the beginning of a new row.
- If a `</TABLE>` tag is not preceded by a `</TR>` tag, Access assumes this is the end of the row.

In many cases, a table cell can display something other than text. If a table cell contains an embedded graphic file, there is a `<IMG SRC...>` tag associated with it. This tag may have additional text that would be displayed. If additional text is present, Access imports it, but does not import the embedded graphic or the tag that defines it. However, Access imports anchor tags as hyperlink fields.

HTML tables can contain lists that are embedded within a table cell. Lists in an HTML table cell are formatted with the `<LI>` and `</LI>` tags. Access inserts a carriage return and line feed (`<CR><LF>`) after each list item and imports each item in the list as a separate field for that record.

HTML tables can also contain tables that are embedded within a table cell. You can import these as separate tables. To achieve the most predictable results, however, import simple HTML tables with a fixed number of fields per record, without embedded lists or tables.

27

ACCESS 97 AND
THE INTERNET

Exporting, Importing, and Linking Data from Other Data Sources on Internet Servers

You can export any Access-compatible external data file to an FTP server (see Figure 27.7). You cannot export files to HTTP servers through the Internet, however, because you cannot write to them using the HTTP protocol.

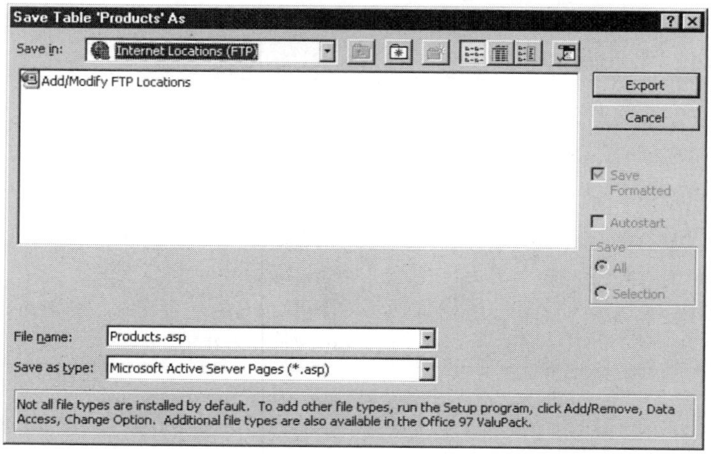

FIGURE 27.7.

Exporting data from external data sources on Internet servers.

The following list details the procedure for exporting, importing, and linking data from other data sources on Internet servers:

1. From the File menu, choose Save As/Export.

2. In the Save As dialog box that appears, click To an External File or Database, and then click OK.

3. In the Save as type list, select the type of file you want to export.

4. To export files on an FTP server, enter a valid FTP URL in the File name box; then, in the Save in box, click Internet Locations (FTP) and select a previously defined FTP site.

5. Next, in the Save in box, click Add/Modify FTP Locations, and then specify a new FTP site and browse its files.

6. Click Export.

You can also import and link any Access-compatible external data file, except Access databases and ODBC data sources, by using an FTP or HTTP connection. An FTP or HTTP connection is only maintained long enough to perform a single transaction; therefore, when you import or link a file located on an FTP or HTTP server, Access copies the data file to the user's local cache. Access then imports or links to the data file in the local cache. For this reason, files linked with an FTP or HTTP connection are read-only.

To export or link data from external data sources on Internet servers, follow these steps:

1. From the File menu, choose Get External Data, and then click either Import or Link Tables.

2. In the Files of type list, click on the type of file you want to import or link.

3a. To import or link files on an FTP server, enter a valid FTP URL in the File name box; in the Look in box, click Internet Locations (FTP) and select a previously defined FTP site. Next, in the Look in box, click Add/Modify FTP Locations, and then specify a new FTP site and browse its files.

3b. To import or link files on an HTTP server, enter a valid HTTP URL in the File name box.

4. Click Import or Link.

Displaying Web Pages and Other Documents in Microsoft Access Forms

The Microsoft WebBrowser control is an ActiveX control that you can use on your Access database application forms to browse Web sites, view Web pages and other documents, and download data located on the Internet. The WebBrowser control is useful in situations where you do not want to disrupt the work flow in a database application by switching from Access to a Web browser or another document-viewing program.

The WebBrowser control can display any Web page that Microsoft Internet Explorer version 3.0 can display. For example, the WebBrowser control can display pages that include any of the following features:

- Standard HTML and most HTML enhancements, such as floating frames and cascading style sheets
- Other ActiveX controls
- Most Netscape plug-ins
- Scripting, such as Microsoft Visual Basic, Scripting Edition (VBScript), JScript, and most JavaScript
- Java applets
- Multimedia content, such as video and audio playback
- Three-dimensional virtual worlds created with Virtual Reality Modeling Language (VRML)

In addition to opening Web pages, the WebBrowser control can open any ActiveX document, including most Office documents. For example, if Office is installed on a computer, an application that uses the WebBrowser control can open and edit Excel spreadsheets, Word documents, and PowerPoint presentations from within the control. Similarly, if Microsoft Excel Viewer, Word Viewer, or PowerPoint Viewer is installed, users can view those documents within the WebBrowser control.

With the WebBrowser control, users of Microsoft database applications can browse sites on the Web, as well as folders on a hard disk or on a LAN. Users can follow hyperlinks by clicking them or by typing a URL into a text box. Also, the WebBrowser control maintains a history list that users can browse to view previously browsed sites, folders, and documents.

> **TIP**
>
> Additional ActiveX controls that you can use to work with content on the Internet or an intranet are available in the Microsoft Office 97 Developer's Edition.

Developing Access Applications for the Internet or an Intranet

This section shows you how to use Microsoft Access to develop applications that retrieve, publish, and share information on the Internet or on a local area network (LAN). For example, you can create applications that display HTML documents in forms, or you can publish or share information from a database located on a Web server. You can also create hyperlinks that you click to navigate to database objects and other Microsoft Office documents located on a local hard disk or a local area network.

HTML was originally a simple system for publishing documents on the Web, but it's rapidly evolving to include features you can use to create sophisticated, interactive applications.

If you install Internet server software on servers connected by a local area network (LAN), you can use these same Internet technologies to share data within an organization. As mentioned previously in this chapter, such a system is called an *intranet* or *internal Web*. For example, your organization could post human resources information for all employees on a Web page, or a project team could post information about its members and provide hyperlinks to important documentation about the project. All the features of Microsoft Access and Microsoft Office that are designed for the Internet can also be used on an intranet.

Microsoft Office and Microsoft Access Internet Features

In all Office 97 applications except Outlook, you can create hyperlinks in documents or files to display and run standard Internet content. These applications also extend hyperlink technology so that you can create hyperlinks to navigate between Word documents, Excel worksheets, PowerPoint slides, and Access database objects that are stored on a local hard disk or on a LAN. This can be done without Internet connections or servers. You can use both internal Office 97 hyperlinks and universal Web-based hyperlinks in the same application.

The following sections summarize the capabilities available in Office 97 and Access 97 that you can use to work with content on the Internet or an intranet.

Internet High-Level Protocols

The Internet system architecture supports certain high-level protocols that are used to define the type of information resource connected to the Internet, or the type of service needed to access the resource. Table 27.5 lists these protocols.

Table 27.5. High-level Internet protocols.

Protocol	Protocol Definition	Description
http	Hypertext Transfer Protocol	Jumps to Web pages that contain text, graphics, sound, and other digital information from a Web server on the World Wide Web.
ftp	File Transfer Protocol	Transfers files between computers on the Internet.
Gopher	Gopher protocol	Displays information on a Gopher server.
wais	WAIS protocol	Accesses a wide area information server database.
File	File protocol	Opens a file on a local hard drive or LAN.
https	Hypertext Transfer Protocol with privacy	Establishes an HTTP connection that uses Secure Sockets Layer (SSL) encryption.
mailto	MailTo protocol	Opens your electronic mail program to send a message to the specified Internet e-mail address. A URL that uses the MailTo protocol has a different format: `mailto:username@domain`.
msn	Microsoft Network protocol	Jumps to a location on the Microsoft Network.

continues

Table 27.5. continued

Protocol	Protocol Definition	Description
News	News protocol	Starts a newsreader and opens the specified Usenet newsgroup. A URL that uses the News protocol has a different format: `news:newsgroupname`.
nntp	Network News Transfer protocol	Performs the same function as the News protocol, except two slashes follow the colon (`nntp:/newsgroupname`).
mid	Musical Instrument Digital Interface (MIDI) protocol	Plays MIDI sequencer files if the user's computer has a sound card.
cid	CompuServe Dialer (CID) protocol	Establishes a Point-to-Point Protocol (PPP) connection with the Internet through CompuServe's network.
prospero	Prospero protocol	Opens files on the Prospero distributed file system.
telnet	Telnet protocol	Starts a telnet terminal-emulation program. (A terminal-emulation program is a command-line interface that you can use to issue commands on a remote computer. For example, by using telnet to connect to a UNIX server, you can issue UNIX commands to perform operations on that server.)
rlogin	Rlogin protocol	Starts an Rlogin terminal-emulation program.
tn3270	TN3270 protocol	Starts a TN3270 terminal-emulation program.

Protocol	Protocol Definition	Description
pnm	RealAudio protocol	Plays RealAudio streaming audio from a RealAudio server. Streaming audio and other streaming media formats establish a connection to the server and start playing immediately without downloading an entire file.
mms	Microsoft Media Server (MMS) protocol	Plays media such as ActiveMovie streaming format files (.asf) from an MMS server.

If you create a field by importing a column of data, and all records in the imported data begin with one of these protocols, Access automatically sets the data type of the imported field to Hyperlink. Similarly, if you create a new table in Datasheet View, and every entry you make in a field begins with one of these protocols, Access sets the data type of the new field to Hyperlink when you save the table.

Using the VB Follow Method

This example uses the Follow method to automatically open the Web page specified in a text box bound to a hyperlink field on a form. Add the following code to the OnCurrent event of a form (note that you must use the Hyperlink property to return a reference to the object that contains the hyperlink):

```
Private Sub Form_Current()
Dim txt As TextBox
On Error GoTo Error_Form1
Set txt = txtAddress
txt.Hyperlink.Follow
Exit_Form1:
Exit Sub
Error_Form1:
MsgBox Err & ": " & Err.Description
Resume Exit_Form1
End Sub
```

Using the FollowHyperlink Method

This example uses the FollowHyperlink method to add a hyperlink to a control that doesn't support the HyperlinkAddress or HyperlinkSubAddress properties. Add the following code to the Click event of an unbound object frame named OLEUnbound1 to start a Web browser and open the specified hyperlink address when you click the image:

```
Private Sub OLEUnbound1_Click()
Dim strAddress As String
On Error GoTo Error_OLEUnbound1
strAddress = "http://www.microsoft.com"
Application.FollowHyperlink strAddress, , True
Exit_OLEUnbound1:
Exit Sub
Error_OLEUnbound1:
MsgBox Err & ": " & Err.Description
Resume Exit_OLEUnbound1
End Sub
```

> **TIP**
>
> Controls that don't support the `HyperlinkAddress` or `HyperlinkSubAddress` properties don't provide any feedback to the user to indicate that they contain a hyperlink. One way to inform a user that the control contains a hyperlink is to set the control's `ControlTipText` property so that a text message appears when users rest the pointer on the control.

Summary

The Internet is an exciting and vast resource for sharing and acquiring data. Combined with Access 97, it provides a flexible solution-development environment capable of meeting almost any desktop or small workgroup Internet database need.

This chapter covers many of the development issues you will deal with to make your applications Web-ready. However, because this is such a dynamic technology, I encourage you to research the Microsoft Web site periodically at `http://www.microsoft.com` to stay abreast of the changes.

Of particular interest to you should be the emerging Active HTML technology and similar innovations that will change the way users work on the Internet.

> **NOTE**
>
> Replication over the Internet is a simple, inexpensive, yet functional way to automate small businesses with multiple locations.

We hope that you enjoy working with Access 97 to develop exciting Web-ready applications. A quality Web-integrated database application can revolutionize most organizations' business models.

XI
PART

Access 97 and Office 97

Office 97 Integration

CHAPTER 28

Jude Mullaney

IN THIS CHAPTER

Most computers that are bought and sold today come with software pre-installed. On more than 80% of those PCs, the Microsoft Windows software is the operating environment of choice. Most of these computers with the Windows operating system installed also have the Microsoft Office productivity tools: Word, Excel, PowerPoint, Exchange, and Access (available in the Office Professional line).

Databases are the central information hub for most businesses, and Access allows you to take advantage of the data found in other applications such as Word and Excel. When you complete this chapter, you will have learned how to maximize Access's ability to work with the other Microsoft Office products and increase the productivity of the users working with your applications. These applications, which can include links to Word, Excel, and PowerPoint, can even be used on your intranet without investing a lot of time in trying to become a Webmaster.

Moving Access 97 Data to and from Other Office Products

Users can create applications in Access at its most basic level through the use of templates and wizards. Developers take Access applications to a more sophisticated level that allows them to integrate the other Office products: Word, Excel, PowerPoint, and Outlook. Once you learn how to share data between other Office products, you can create high-powered applications that utilize all the Office line.

As long as computer software has existed, data has been saved in different formats. Word processing data is usually stored in Word, while spreadsheet and graph data is usually stored in Excel. Customer data, such as name, address, and phone information, whether it be a flat file or relational, is usually stored in a database program such as Access. The act of making the different Office products integrate seamlessly to the user is the job of the programmer. Earlier versions of Access and Office allowed programmers to cut and paste data between programs, and before that method was available, there was not a standard method of sharing data among multiple programs. With Access 97, this process of functionality has been made easier than it has ever been. The next few pages describe how you can pass data to and from the different Office products.

Automation (OLE) Versus DDE

With Office 97, it is easy to integrate all the Office products; it is just as easy to put data from Access into Word or Excel as it is to put data from Word or Excel into Access. This is accomplished through *Automation*. In earlier versions of Office, Automation was referred to as *object linking and embedding* (OLE). There is a difference between OLE and Automation: Automation is an enhanced version of OLE, and it is a way to work with the objects of one application through a development tool or another application. Automation is a feature of the Component Object Model (COM) and is considered an industry standard.

When you determine that you want to automate your Access database with other Office products, there are two ways to do it: The first way is to link; the second way is to embed. The difference between the two has to do with the updating of a source file. When data is *linked* into another application, as the source of the link is changed, the changes made in the source are also updated in the destination file. When data is *embedded* into another file, as the source data is changed, those changes are not reflected in the destination file. However, when data is embedded into another file, you can double-click the data in the destination file; the application used to create the data will automatically execute, and you can make modifications to the embedded data in its native application. When an object is embedded or linked into Access, Access is called the *client* or *controller*, and the other application that is being driven by Access is called the *server*.

Another form of integration is performed through the user interface: An object can be embedded or linked to a table; a picture of an employee, for example. A form can be bound to that table, and it would be possible for a user to double-click the picture object and get to the server application.

> **NOTE**
>
> Non-Microsoft products can be used in the Automation process if they can use Dynamic Data Exchange (DDE).

To Word from Access

Microsoft Word can track data, as you can see in Figure 28.1. Not only can it track data, but it can perform queries on that data. This is not, however, Word's forté. Similarly, Access can produce a word processing document, but its forté is not word processing—it is relational database management.

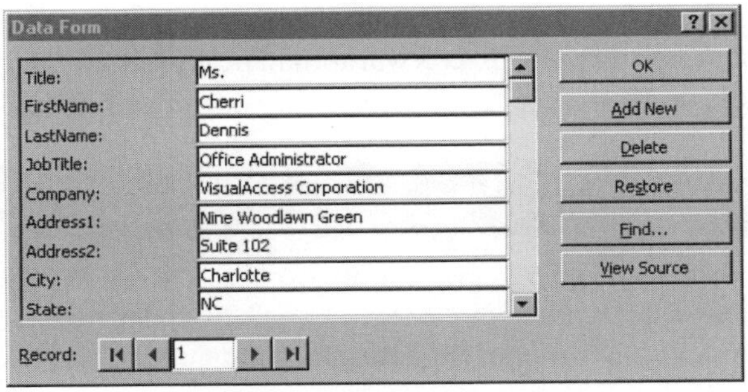

FIGURE 28.1.
Word can track data.

Even though Word can track data like Access, it is not the right tool for the job. With this in mind, you can see how the integration of Access and Word is a valuable asset to your program. There are several ways to integrate these two programs. The most common way is to use the Merge It with MS Word option from the Office Links button on the Access toolbar, as shown in Figure 28.2.

FIGURE 28.2.

The Office Links button is a common way to integrate Word with Access.

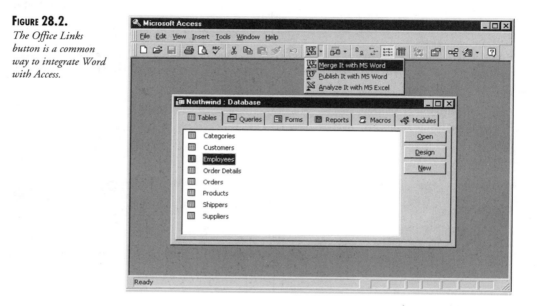

Access takes the highlighted object, in this case the Employees table from the Northwind database, and links it to a Word document. A wizard is executed to guide you through the merge process. Here, Access is the client, and Word is the controller. By placing fields onto the document from the Field list, as shown in Figure 28.3, you actually create the link.

Each time the link is executed from Access, the data that is current at the time of execution will appear in the linked Word document. Conversely, if you open the Word document with the link to the Access database, Access will automatically execute, and the link will retrieve the records in the table or query that are current at the time of execution.

> **TIP**
>
> If you try to highlight a form or report object, the Merge It Office Links button will not be available. Data is not stored in forms or reports, so the Merge It option is not available. However, you can still get the data into Word through the Publish It Office Links button.

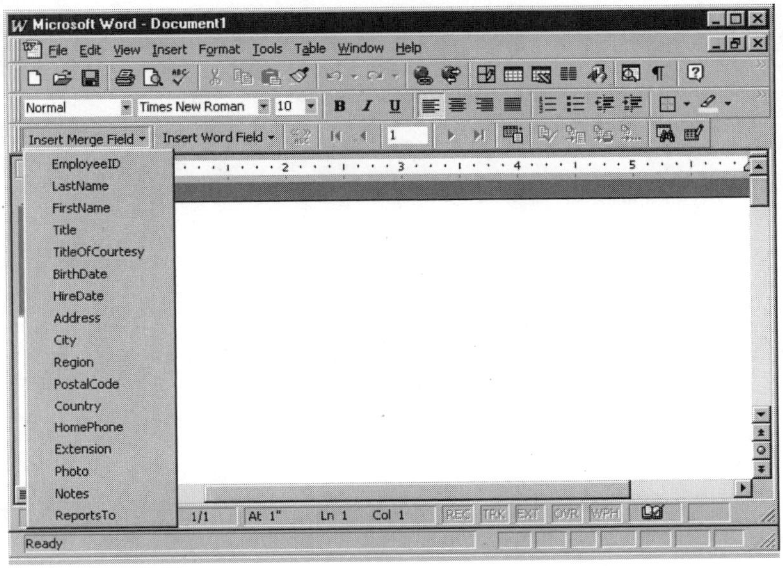

FIGURE 28.3.

The link is established as soon as the first field from the Insert Merge Field list is placed on the document.

Tables and queries are usually used to merge with documents for the purpose of mailing information. In Word, you can use tables and queries, as well as forms and reports, through the Publish It Office Link button. The Publish It button takes the data from the highlighted report and exports it to a new Word document. The difference between Merge It and Publish It is that Publish It works with tables, queries, forms, and reports, while Merge It only works with tables and queries. In Merge It, the data is presented in its Datasheet View, and you can make your manipulations to its appearance from within Word.

Information from Access can be shared with Word in other ways as well. You can export table, query, form, and report objects from Access by highlighting the desired data and selecting Save As | Export from the File pull-down menu. In some cases, the formatting that was used in Access can be preserved when you export the data. By saving the file as a Rich Text Format file (RTF), you can save the fonts and colors used in creating the object. In Figure 28.4, you can see that most of the formatting for the Customer Labels report from Northwind (on the right) is visible in the RTF export of the object (in the Word document on the left).

TIP

You can extract some of the records instead of exporting the entire Access object. To do this, open the object in datasheet view and highlight the desired records. Then select Save As | Export from the File menu.

FIGURE 28.4.

Saving an export as an RTF file will try to maintain all the fonts, colors, and styles as they appear in the source object from Access.

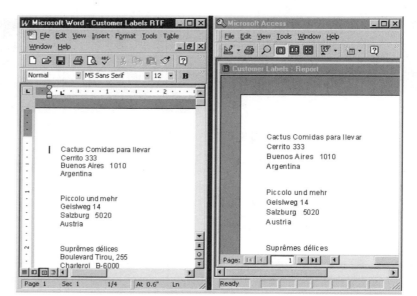

FIGURE 28.4.

Saving an export as an RTF file will try to maintain all the fonts, colors, and styles as they appear in the source object from Access.

In the case of some forms, some objects may not be exported exactly as they appear in the original source. Take the Employees form, for example. In Northwind, the Employees form contains a photo, but when this object is exported and saved as an RTF file, the picture object is not available as it is in Access. In Figure 28.5, you can see how the file looks when it is exported as opposed to how it looks in the table's Datasheet View.

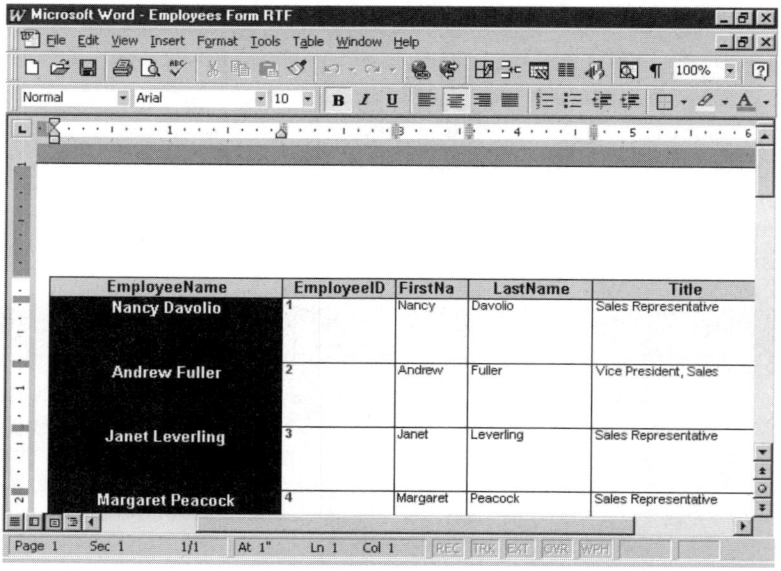

FIGURE 28.5.

RTF files do not export picture objects.

NOTE

When you export data from a form or report object and save the exported file as an `.RTF` file, the data displayed in the Word document might not have the formatting preserved exactly as it appeared in Access. In some cases, the data may be displayed in Datasheet View and not in Form View or Print Preview.

There is yet another way to get objects from Access into Word. Open both Access and Word. Resize the windows so they are similar to Figure 28.6. Click on an object in Access and drag it to the Word document. The Datasheet View of the object will appear in the Word document. The important thing to remember is that the dragging and dropping of objects from Access to Word only works with objects that store data: tables and queries. Form, report, macro, and module objects will not drag and drop into Word.

FIGURE 28.6.

Some objects can be dragged from Access into Word.

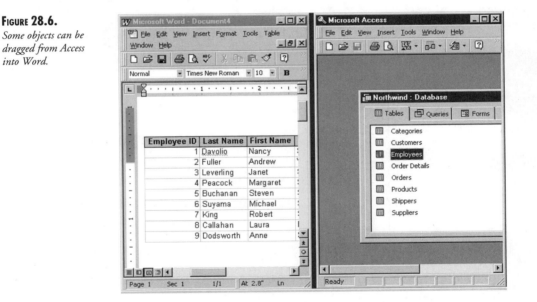

TIP

If you use ODBC to get information from Access into Word, the Queries tab may not be available. The reason for this is that ODBC reads data files directly without opening Access. Data is stored in tables and manipulated through queries. Because Access is not running, the query is not available because there is no data stored in it. Use DDE instead of ODBC when you want the data source to be a query. DDE automatically opens Access. You can also generate a Make-table query and use the new table as the source.

To Access from Word

So far, I have discussed some of the different ways to get data out of Access and into Word. You can get data out of Word and into Access just as easily. When would you ever want to move data from Word to Access? There are some situations when data already exists in Word documents that you want to use in Access forms. You could just move that information into Access; however, if the document changes on a regular basis, you might want to just link the data from Word into Access every time the data in Word changes.

In Figure 28.7, you can see a Word document. In this example, you want to have the text New suppliers applying between 1-1-97 and 3-31-97 have a start date of 1-1-97 appear on your Access form. This can be done by highlighting the desired text and selecting Copy from the Edit menu in Word.

FIGURE 28.7.

The selected text will be linked to an Access form.

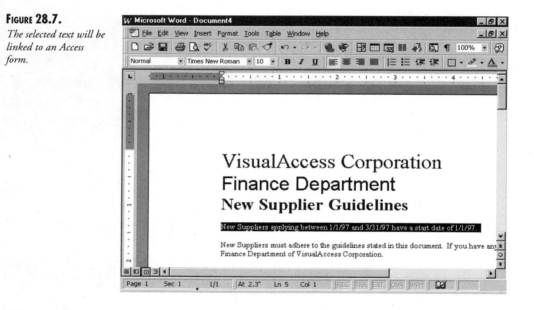

Open your Northwind database. Make a copy of the Suppliers form and save it as New Suppliers. In Design View of the New Suppliers form, select Paste Special from the Edit menu. In the dialog box that appears, click the Paste Link option (see Figure 28.8).

Every New Suppliers form will now have the data from the Word document displayed on it. As the data in the Word document changes, so will the data on the New Suppliers form. This is shown in Figure 28.9.

Another way that data from Word can be passed to Access is, ironically, passed from the data source in the mail merge feature. Word allows you to store basic mail merge information in a Word table. By selecting Mail Merge from the Tools menu, you can navigate to the Data Source step of the Mail Merge Helper, as shown in Figure 28.10.

FIGURE 28.8.
Click the Paste Link option to move the Word data.

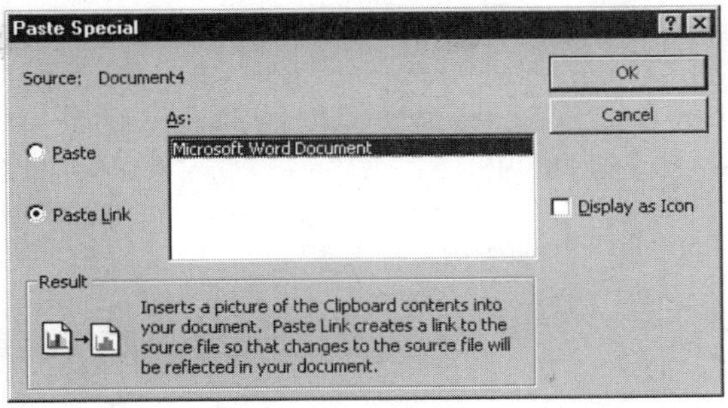

Paste Special

Source: Document4

As:
Microsoft Word Document

○ Paste
● Paste Link

☐ Display as Icon

OK
Cancel

Result
Inserts a picture of the Clipboard contents into your document. Paste Link creates a link to the source file so that changes to the source file will be reflected in your document.

FIGURE 28.9.
As the data in the Word document changes, so does the data on the Access form.

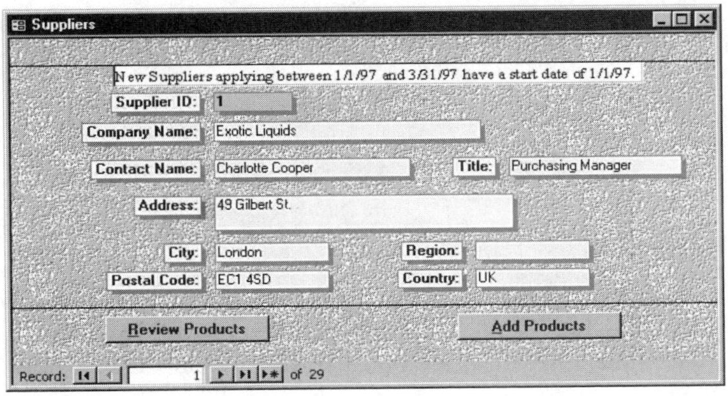

Suppliers

New Suppliers applying between 1/1/97 and 3/31/97 have a start date of 1/1/97.

Supplier ID: 1

Company Name: Exotic Liquids

Contact Name: Charlotte Cooper   Title: Purchasing Manager

Address: 49 Gilbert St.

City: London   Region:

Postal Code: EC1 4SD   Country: UK

Review Products   Add Products

Record: 14 ◄ 1 ► ►I ►＊ of 29

28

OFFICE 97
INTEGRATION

FIGURE 28.10.
Word allows you to track a limited database.

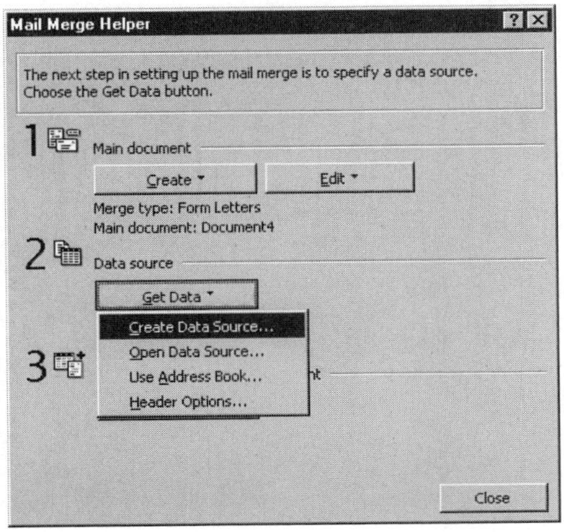

Mail Merge Helper

The next step in setting up the mail merge is to specify a data source. Choose the Get Data button.

1 Main document

Create ▼   Edit ▼

Merge type: Form Letters
Main document: Document4

2 Data source

Get Data ▼

Create Data Source...
Open Data Source...
Use Address Book...
Header Options...

3

Close

When you create a data source for a Word document, Word stores fields that are most commonly used in mail merges. In Figure 28.11, you can see the standard list of fields that will be tracked. There are 13 commonly used fields already in the list. You can choose to remove fields from the list by highlighting the desired field and clicking the Remove Field Name button. You can add fields to the list by typing in the field name and clicking the Add Field Name button. When all the fields you need are present, you can click the OK button.

FIGURE 28.11.

You can add or delete field names for your Word database.

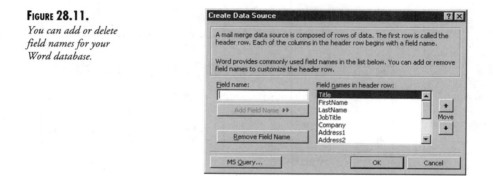

You will be prompted to save your Word database. You can choose from several file formats in which to save your Word database. If you choose Word Document, your data will appear in a Word document like the one on the left side of Figure 28.12. If you choose to save it as Text Only With Line Breaks or Text Only, the file will be saved as a Notepad file, as shown on the right side of the figure.

FIGURE 28.12.

The file can be saved in different formats.

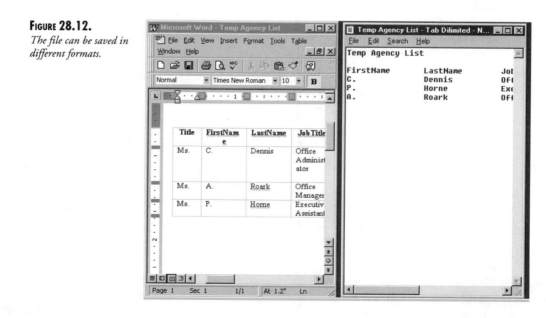

In Access, the data entry for a table is through the datasheet. In Word, you get a small form showing all the fields you selected in the Mail Merge Helper step. (See Figure 28.13.) You even have limited data-modification capabilities in Word: You can find a record in the database, or add or delete records from the database.

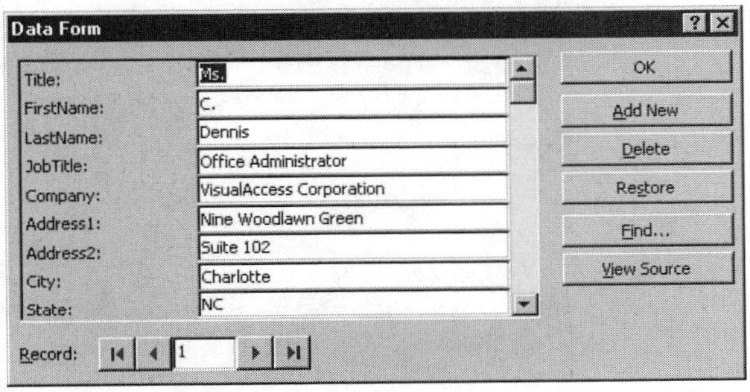

FIGURE 28.13.

Data for the Word database is entered here.

Once the data has been inputted into the Word database, it can be imported back into an Access database. Make sure that any Word data sources are saved as a text file. This will allow the file to be imported into Access.

> **NOTE**
>
> When you want to import a Word data source, make sure that you save it as some kind of text file—either as a Text File or a Text File With Line Breaks. The Access import files will look for other database files or text files, not for Word documents.

Another way to move between Word and Access is through *hyperlinks*. Hyperlinks are one of the hot, new features of Office 97. You have probably come across a situation when you were in your Access database and needed to view some Word documents pertaining to a specific client. In the old days, you would have to open Word or Explorer and hunt down the desired document file. However, if you had end users working with your Access database, they might or might not know how to navigate through the local and server hard drives to find the desired document, which would cause a problem. With hyperlinks, that has all changed.

Simply go to the table that stores the client information and add a new field. This field's data type needs to be Hyperlink. When you run the table, you can store the path for the document that relates to the client. In Figure 28.14, the contracts for the ABC Company can be displayed by clicking on the hyperlink field.

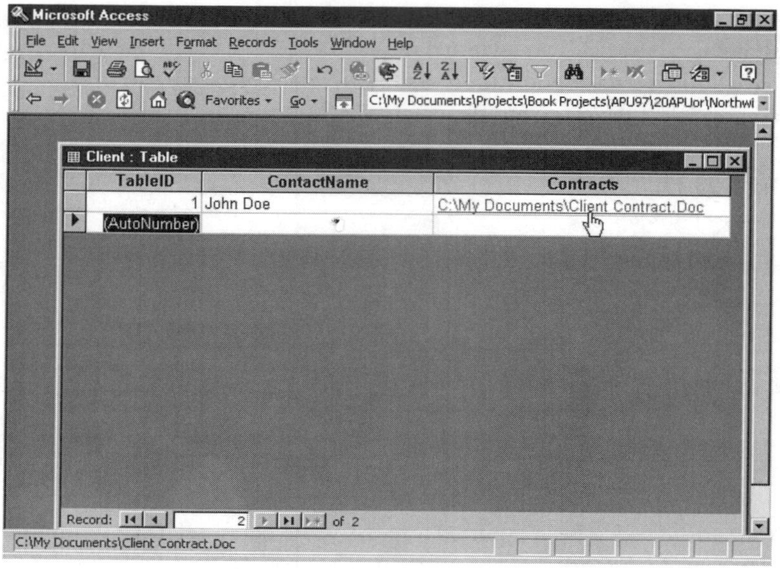

FIGURE 28.14.

Different documents can be linked to a particular client or customer through the hyperlink field, which is denoted by the underlined text.

Notice that the pointer changes to a pointing finger as it moves over the hyperlink address, which functions just like any other hyperlink field. The hyperlink field is colored blue before it is accessed, and changes to purple when it has been accessed. When clicked, it opens Word and brings up the document.

> **NOTE**
>
> You can change the colors of the hyperlink text by selecting Options from the Tools menu in Access. Click on the Hyperlinks/HTML tab to make the changes.

In Figure 28.15, you can see that there is an additional toolbar to the Word document. This is the Web toolbar; it allows you to perform functions on this object (the Word document) just like any other Web object. To return to the Access database, click the Go button on the Web toolbar and you can move backward and forward.

You can hyperlink to just about anything:

- A word processing document
- A bookmark in Word
- A spreadsheet
- A cell in an Excel spreadsheet
- An object in the current database
- An object in another database

- A field in an object in a database
- A presentation application
- A slide in a PowerPoint application
- A WWW address

FIGURE 28.15.

When a hyperlink is executed, the Web toolbar is automatically displayed.

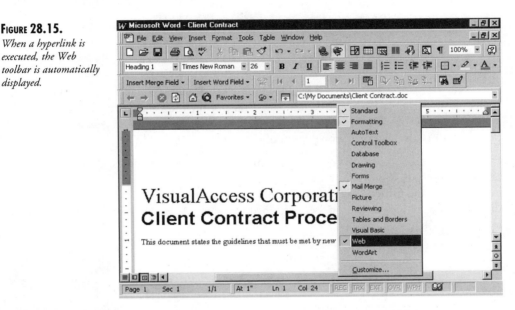

The syntax for the hyperlink address can be obtained by browsing the computer files, as shown in Figure 28.16, or by entering it in by hand. The correct syntax is divided into three parts, separated by the pound sign (#):

```
displaytext#address#subaddress
```

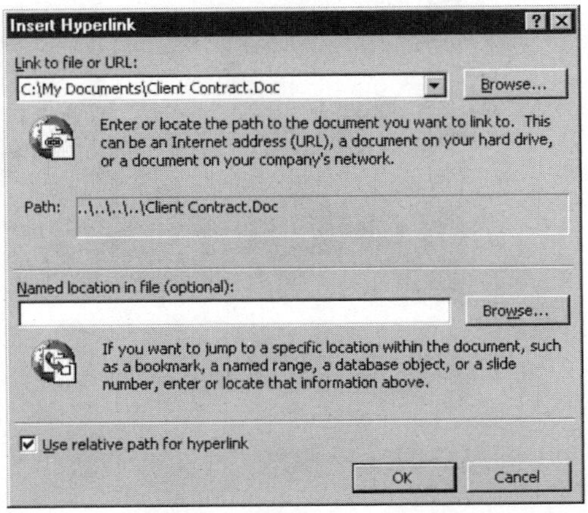

FIGURE 28.16.

You can use the Access browser shown in the Insert Hyperlink dialog box to locate the object you want to link.

The address can change for each record or remain the same for a recordset. If you want to store different hyperlinks for each contact, you will need to have a field in the table for each contact. If you want one jump to another location for a recordset, you can just have a field on a form that stores the hyperlink address.

A more detailed look at using code to access data between Word and Access is covered more thoroughly in the "VBA Automation and Understanding DAO" section of this chapter.

To Excel from Access

Access's strong suit is referential database manipulation, whereas Excel's strength lies in the analysis and manipulation of numerical data. Many of the tools that are available in Excel are not available in Access. There will be times when you want to move data between the two applications; this can be done through a number of different methods.

One of the most common ways to get data from Access to Excel is to use the Office Links button on the Access toolbar. In Figure 28.17, you can see the result of using the Analyze It button (found under the Office Links button in Access) to export data from Access into Excel. Although complex calculations can be performed in Access, Access may not always be the right tool for the job.

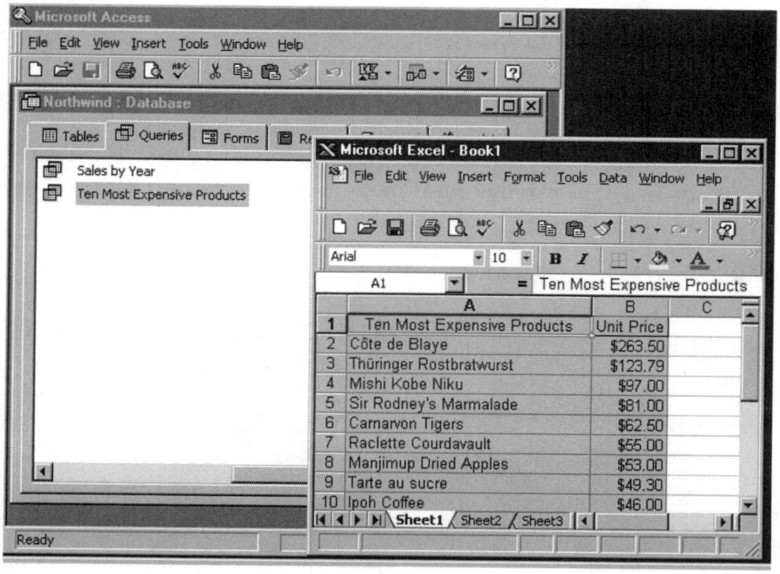

FIGURE 28.17.

Access data can be analyzed in Excel.

NOTE

When you are analyzing forms and reports, remember that any form or report that has a subform or subreport will not be saved to the Excel worksheet. Only the main form and main report data will be available in Excel.

There are a number of different reasons that you, as a developer, would want to integrate Excel and Word into your applications. Excel is an excellent "what if" tool; data can be exported into Excel and manipulated by the end user for what-if scenarios. Another reason that you would want to get the data into Excel is for secure reporting purposes. If you give the end user direct access to the data tables, he can change it. By you getting the data into an Excel spreadsheet, the end user can change the information to his heart's content, but the integrity of the data is still retained.

There is still another good reason that you would want to get your data into Excel—charting. *Charts* provide a graphical representation of data. They are usually found on forms or reports; in older versions of Access, they were referred to as *graphs*. Access uses the MS Graph engine. This is a good graphing engine, but it is not as powerful as the graphing engine in Excel. The Access Chart Wizard gives you 20 different types of charts to choose from, but Excel will offer you more than 90 charts. In Figure 28.18, you can see the 20 chart types offered through Access on the left. On the right is the Chart Wizard for Excel. There are more than 70 standard types of charts, and Excel allows you to create custom charts as well.

FIGURE 28.18.

Excel offers more types of charts than does Access.

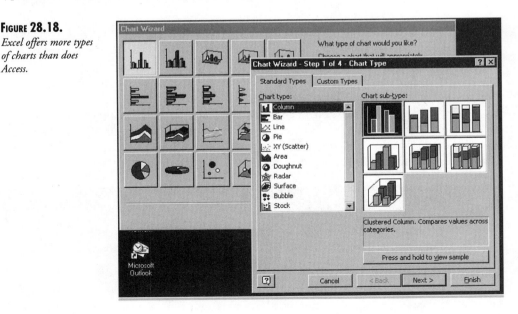

Another common way to move data from Access to Excel is through the drag-and-drop method. In Figure 28.19, you can see that the Ten Most Expensive Products query from the `Northwind` database is being dragged from Access to Excel. The pointer indicates that the information is being copied—not moved—to Excel.

FIGURE 28.19.

Data can be dragged from Access to Excel.

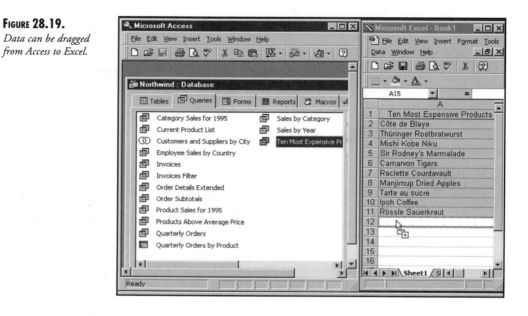

You can use other methods to move data from Access to Excel. Instead of using the Analyze It Office Links button, you could highlight the desired object and select Save As | Export from the File menu. You can choose to send the data to another database or save it in another file format. Data in Access can also be saved as an RTF file and then imported into an Excel spreadsheet or another spreadsheet. To save an object as a text file, highlight the desired object and select Save As | Export from the File menu. Save the object to an external file, and in the Save As Type box, select the Rich Text Format option. If you export data to another database, you must make sure that the data structure is compatible. For example, you cannot export a Text data type into an AutoNumber data type field.

> **NOTE**
>
> You can only save table, query, form, and report objects as RTF files. You can save a module object as a text file, but macro objects can only be exported to other Access databases.

There is also the reliable copy-and-paste method. This option allows you to determine whether the object highlighted in Access will be pasted into Excel as a linked object or an embedded object. In Figure 28.20, you can see that when the Paste Special option is selected from the Edit menu, you have the option to link the object that is on the Windows Clipboard.

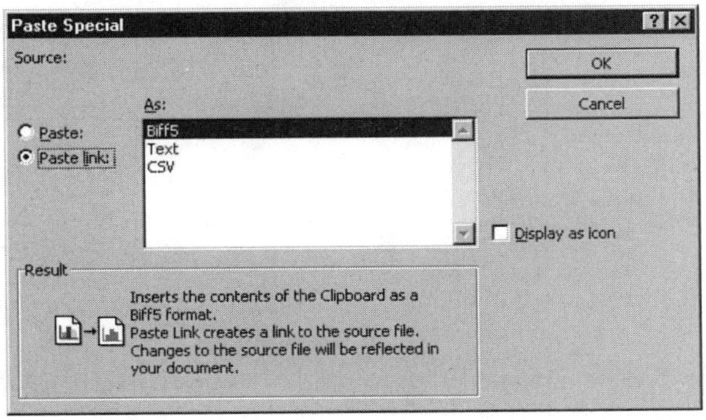

Figure 28.20.

The Paste Special option allows you to choose between embedding an object and linking the object.

> **NOTE**
>
> You can copy segments of a table or query to a spreadsheet. In Access, open your table or query in datasheet view and highlight the row and column cells that you want to appear in Excel. From the Edit menu, select Copy. Open the Excel spreadsheet and select Paste from the Edit menu.

These are all user-friendly tools that can be utilized to integrate Access with other Office applications. In the Macro tab of a database, you can still launch data to an Excel spreadsheet through the RunApp action. The Command Line argument holds the path of the program along with any switches to execute the application in a specific mode, such as minimized.

> **TIP**
>
> You can use the SendKeys action to get the same effect, but the RunApp is more efficient.

The TransferSpreadsheet action can also be used to import and export data between Access and Excel. In Figure 28.21, you can see the different arguments for the TransferSpreadsheet action. Through this action, you can choose to link or embed the data.

For more control, programmers usually prefer to use code. The code used is called *Visual Basic for Applications* (VBA), and it uses procedures to modify data and objects in applications that adhere to the VBA standard. The Sub and Function procedures can be found in the forms, reports, and modules of an Access database. The RunApp action cannot be used in VBA. You need to use the Shell function. The correct syntax for this function is

```
Shell(pathname[,windowstyle])
```

windowstyle is an optional argument that can have six different values. The default value will run the application in minimized mode with focus. Table 28.1 lists the different values for windowstyle.

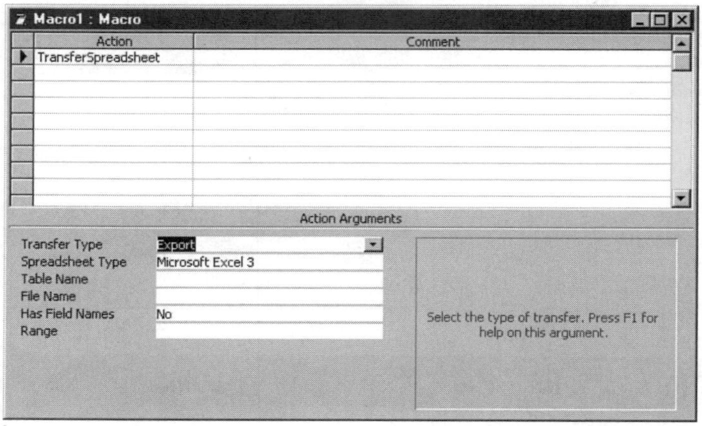

FIGURE 28.21.

The
TransferSpreadsheet *action is a quick way to move data between Access and Excel.*

Table 28.1. The windowstyle values.

Constant	Value	Description
VbHide	0	Focus is passed to the hidden window.
vbNormalFocus	1	Window is restored to its original size and position.
vbMinimizedFocus	2	Window is an icon with focus.
vbMaximizedFocus	3	Window is maximized with focus.
vbNormalNoFocus	4	Window is restored to its most recent size and position. The currently active window remains active.
vbMinimizedNoFocus	6	Window is displayed as an icon. The currently active window remains active.

You can also use the CreateObject and GetObject functions to move data between the two applications. The correct syntax for the CreateObject function is

CreateObject(class)

The class is made up of the appname and the objecttype. You would need to Dim an object and then Set that object, as follows:

```
Dim App As Object

Set App = CreateObject("excel.application")
```

The `CreateObject` function has two parts: the `appname` and the `objecttype`. In this example, Excel is the `appname` and the `objecttype` is application, as opposed to sheet or workbook.

The `GetObject` function is like the `CreateObject` function, but its syntax looks like this:

```
GetObject([pathname] [, class])
```

If the pathname is `""` (zero-length string), the `GetObject` creates a new object instance.

The difference between the `CreateObject` and `GetObject` functions is that you use the `GetObject` function when there is a current instance of the object you want to create. You can also use the `GetObject` function if you want to create the object with a file already loaded. If you don't, use the `CreateObject` function.

If an object has registered itself as a single-instance object, only one instance of the object is created, no matter how many times `CreateObject` is executed. With a single-instance object, `GetObject` always returns the same instance when called with the zero-length string (`""`) syntax, and it causes an error if the `pathname` argument is omitted. You can't use `GetObject` to obtain a reference to a class created with Visual Basic.

You can even add a new worksheet within an existing workbook in Excel through the `Set` statement in Access. The `Set` statement gives an object reference to a variable; its syntax is as follows:

```
Set objectvar = {[New] objectexpression ¦ Nothing}
```

`objectvar` is the name of the variable or property and is required. `New` is one of the latest reserved key words in Access and implies the creation of an object. In this case, it is an optional keyword. `objectexpression` is a required expression that contains the name of an object, a function, a method, or another declared variable. Finally, `Nothing` is an optional word that releases any and all the memory resources used with the referenced object when no variable is referring to it.

To Access from Excel

There will be times when you want to move data from Excel to Access. One of the most common methods of doing that is to select Save As from the File menu in Excel. Choose Text (Tab Delimited) from the Save As Type combo box, and it will save the current worksheet to a text format. This format can then be read in Access by choosing Get External Data from the File menu.

> **TIP**
>
> If there are multiple sheets in a workbook, you can only save the active worksheet to a text file for import back into Access. Any other sheets should be saved individually if you need to get them back into Access.

28

OFFICE 97
INTEGRATION

There are three additional ways to move data to and from Excel. They can be found under the Data menu, as shown in Figure 28.22. The MS Access Form selection allows you to create an Access form and enter and save data directly to the Microsoft Excel List. The Form Wizard launches and allows you to create a quick form for Excel data entry.

FIGURE 28.22.

From the Data menu, you can select three different Access-specific options.

You can create a form in an existing database or in a new database. The dialog box in Figure 28.23 shows you where the Excel List data entry form will be located.

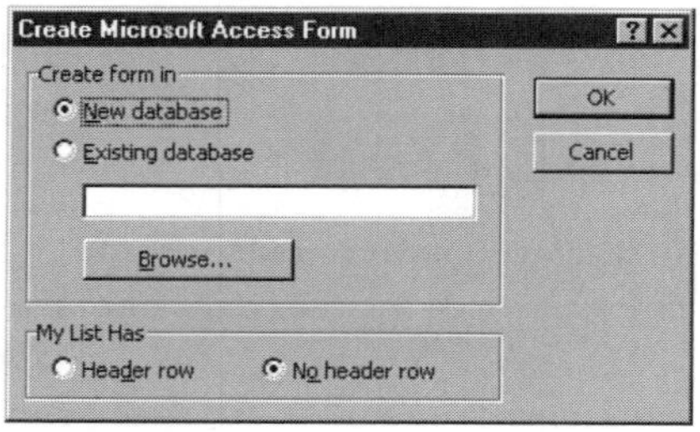

FIGURE 28.23.

You can choose where your Excel List data entry form will be located.

The MS Access Report option launches an Access Report Wizard to help you create a quick Access report with an Excel List. The report is updated based on the information in the list and by clicking on the View MS Access Report button that is placed directly on the worksheet.

Another option in the Data menu is Convert to MS Access. This option takes the Excel List and converts it to an Access database. If you make changes to the data through Access, those changes are not reflected in the Excel List.

Using the Template Wizard, also found under the Data menu in Excel, is another way to move data from Excel to Access. This differs from the Convert to MS Access option in that a link is established, and every time that information is changed in Excel, it is reflected in the Access database. In Figure 28.24, you can see the Template Wizard option being selected. Once you have completed the five-step wizard, your database will be completed.

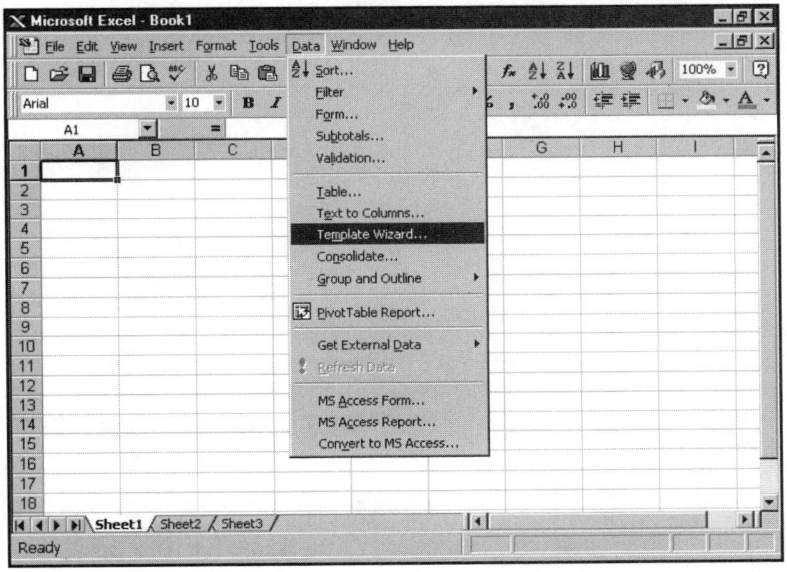

FIGURE 28.24.

The Template Wizard helps you link data from Excel to Access.

You can also use the Microsoft Query or a VB macro to get access to an Access database. From the Data menu, select the Create New Query from the Get External Data option, as shown in Figure 28.25.

The next step allows you to choose the database that contains the data or to create a new database. In Figure 28.26, the Northwind database has been selected.

You can choose the data from the existing tables in Northwind, as shown in Figure 28.27. As you move information into the Columns in your query list box, you create the query for Excel.

The next step in the Query Wizard allows you to choose your criteria for the query. In Figure 28.28, you can see that a pretty sophisticated Select query can be created by clicking fields and selecting a filter. This step also allows you to specify sort orders.

28

OFFICE 97
INTEGRATION

FIGURE 28.25.
New queries can get data into Excel from Access.

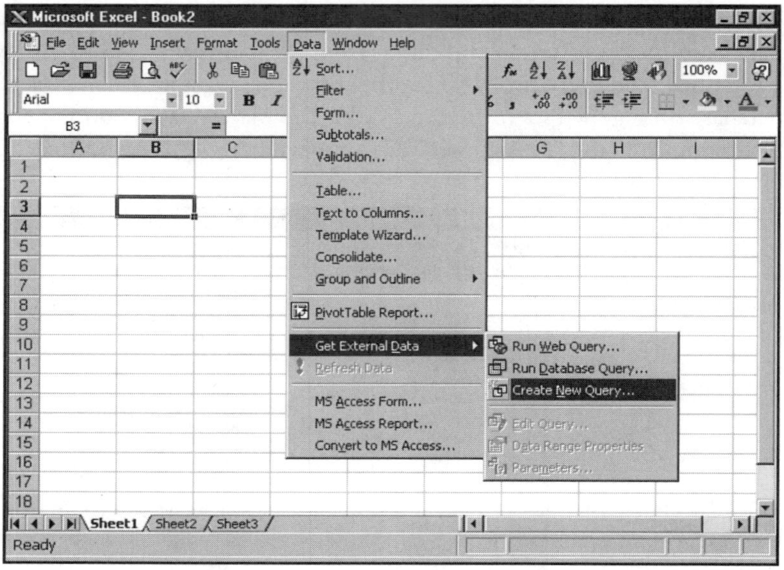

FIGURE 28.26.
Select the database or create a new one.

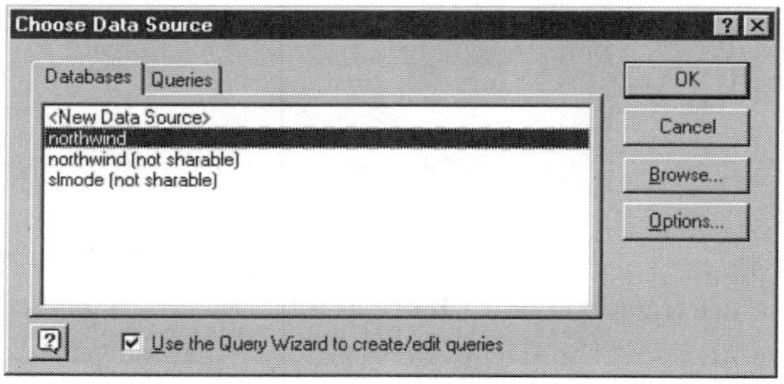

FIGURE 28.27.
You can choose the tables and/or fields for your query.

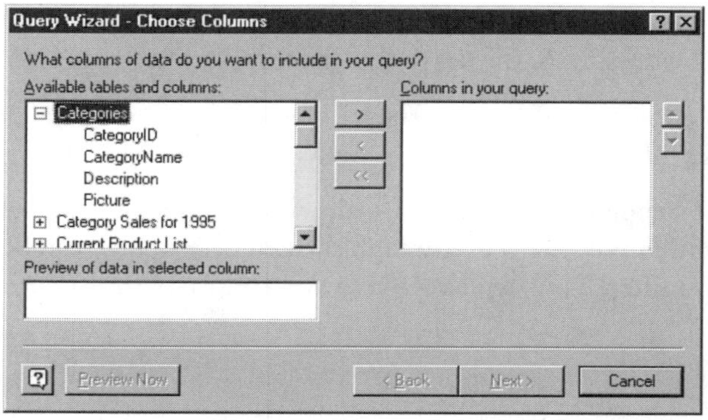

FIGURE 28.28.

Filters are entered here.

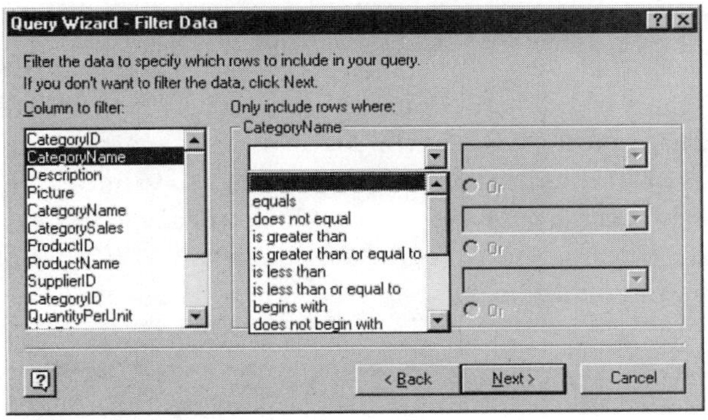

You can save the query so you can use it again later, or you can just have the data returned to Excel. In Figure 28.29, you can see how the data is available in Excel.

FIGURE 28.29.

The query returns the data to Excel.

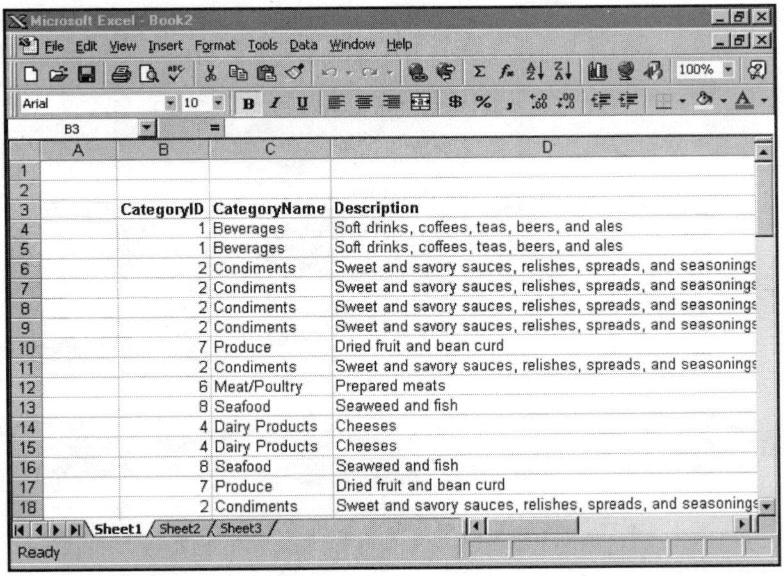

There are more sophisticated ways of accessing data as well. A more detailed look at using code to access data between Word and Access is covered in the "VBA Automation and Understanding DAO" section of this chapter.

To PowerPoint from Access

PowerPoint is a Microsoft Office application that is primarily used for presentation purposes. There are several situations when you may want to get data from Access into a PowerPoint slide. You can use the usual copy-and-paste method to move data from Access into PowerPoint. You can also use the drag-and-drop method, where you resize the window of each application so that they are both visible at the same time and then move objects into PowerPoint. Both methods will produce useful results, as shown in Figure 28.30.

FIGURE 28.30.

Data from Access can be dragged or copied into PowerPoint.

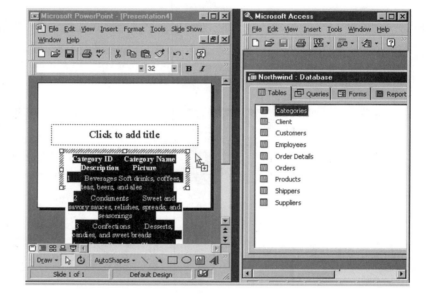

TIP

Only table and query objects from Access can be dragged or copied and pasted into PowerPoint. The Datasheet View of the table or query object is pasted into PowerPoint. Form, report, macro, and module objects cannot be copied into PowerPoint. This includes form objects that have the `Views Allow` property set to `Datasheet`.

There are a number of different ways to get data from Access into PowerPoint other than using the Clipboard. It is possible to send data from Access into a Word document and then, from the Word document, send it to PowerPoint. You can also do it by sending data to an Excel spreadsheet and then sending it to PowerPoint. With so many different options, it can be confusing when deciding which method to use. Table 28.2 can help you select the right data-routing method for your situation.

Table 28.2. Selecting a data-routing method.

Use	When
Word	You want a table/query that can be easily included in a PowerPoint presentation
Word	Your table/query includes complex graphics formatting
Excel	Your table/query includes complex calculations, statistical analysis, and/or charts
Excel/Access	Your table/query has sorting and searching capabilities
Access	Your table/query has relational database capabilities

TIP

When you need to move data between Office applications, you must make sure that the data in contained in a table or query. Data from forms or reports usually is not used between applications because data does not actually *reside* in a form or report; those objects just pull data from a table or query.

PowerPoint can also be invoked from Access through a macro. Figure 28.31 shows the RunApp macro action. The RunApp action works hand-in-hand with the Command Line arguments. This macro's Command Line argument actually executes PowerPoint.

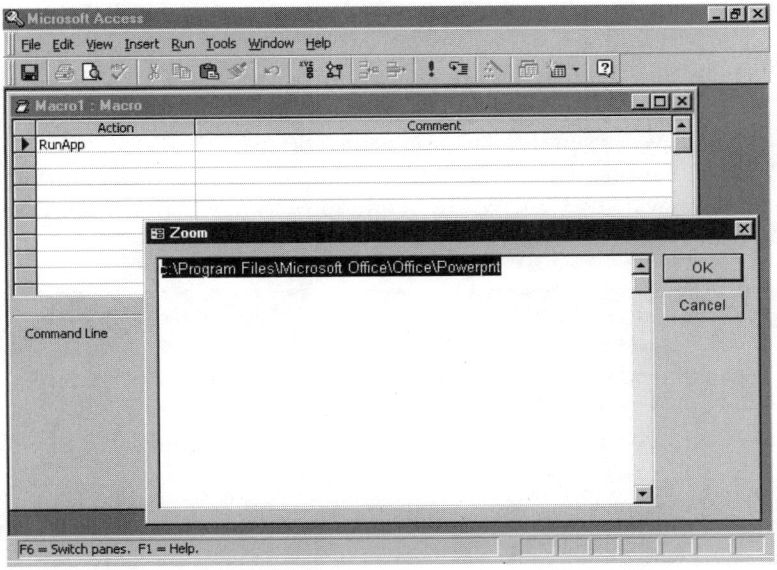

FIGURE 28.31.

PowerPoint can be called from a macro.

To Access from PowerPoint

It is as easy to get data from PowerPoint to Access as it is to get data from Access to PowerPoint. You can use the same methods of copy-and-paste and drag-and-drop to move data from PowerPoint to Access just as you would to move it from Access to PowerPoint. There are other ways of working with PowerPoint through Access; one way is via a hyperlink. This feature is new to the 32-bit platform and is simple to implement. You can either store individual references to PowerPoint for each record in a table or store one reference to PowerPoint. If you are storing individual references for each record, you need to add a new field to the table. In Figure 28.32, the hyperlink field has been added to the Suppliers table. This links an individual record to the home page of the supplier.

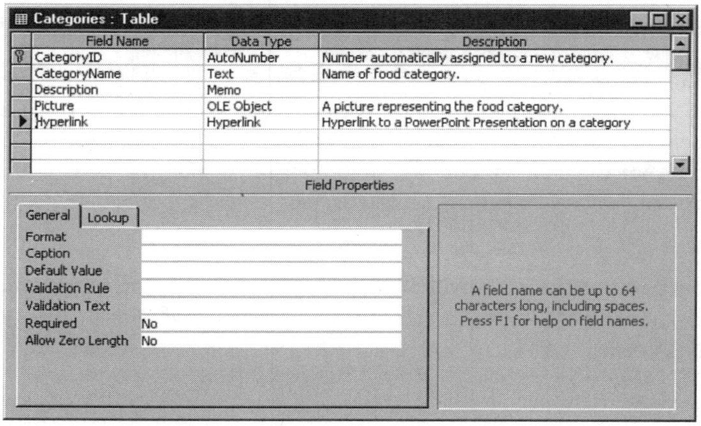

FIGURE 28.32.

Hyperlink is now a data type.

You can store an individual PowerPoint presentation for each individual category. In Figure 28.33, you can see that the Beverages category has a hyperlink to a Beverage PowerPoint presentation. When you click on the hyperlink field, the associated PowerPoint presentation runs. You get the same Web toolbar throughout the process so you can perform simple operations such as moving back a screen (to return to Access), selecting it as a Favorite, or changing the address to view a different Web address.

> **TIP**
>
> An entire presentation can be saved in HTML format. Once it is saved in this format, it can be called from any Microsoft Office application.

Something new to PowerPoint 97 is the Macro Recorder. This is the same type of recorder that is found in Excel (see Figure 28.34). With the Macro Recorder, you can simplify mundane, repetitive routines via commands and functions. These commands and functions are stored in a Visual Basic module that can be executed on command.

FIGURE 28.33.
A hyperlink field in Access is the same as a hyperlink in any other Office application.

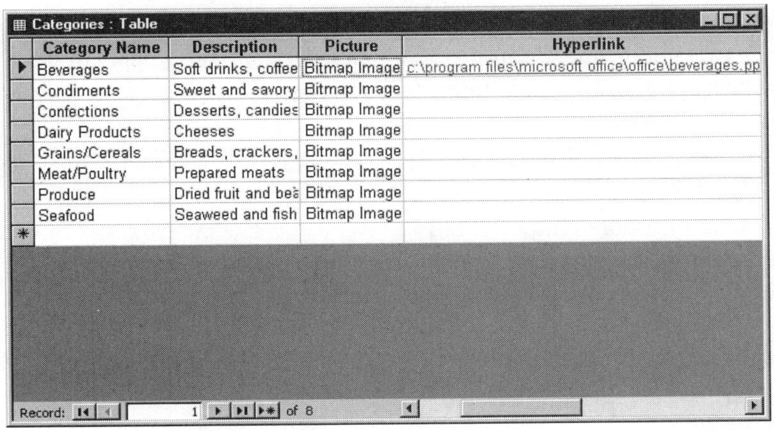

Categories : Table
Category Name
Description
Picture
Hyperlink
Beverages
Soft drinks, coffee
Bitmap Image
c:\program files\microsoft office\office\beverages.pp
Condiments
Sweet and savory
Bitmap Image
Confections
Desserts, candies
Bitmap Image
Dairy Products
Cheeses
Bitmap Image
Grains/Cereals
Breads, crackers,
Bitmap Image
Meat/Poultry
Prepared meats
Bitmap Image
Produce
Dried fruit and bea
Bitmap Image
Seafood
Seaweed and fish
Bitmap Image
Record:
1
of 8

NOTE

If you invoke the Macro Recorder while you are working with a template, the Visual Basic module is stored with the template. It will not be available to other presentations created with that template. You will need to store the Visual Basic module with each presentation.

FIGURE 28.34.
The Macro Recorder in PowerPoint is the same as the Macro Recorder in Excel.

Microsoft PowerPoint - [Presentation1]
File Edit View Insert Format Tools Slide Show Window Help
Times New Roman
40%
Spelling... F7
Style Checker...
Language...
AutoCorrect...
Look Up Reference...
AutoClipArt...
PowerPoint Central
Presentation Conference...
Meeting Minder...
Expand Slide
Macro
Add-Ins...
Customize...
Options...
Macros... Alt+F8
Record New Macro...
Visual Basic Editor Alt+F11
Draw
AutoShapes
Slide 1 of 1
Default Design

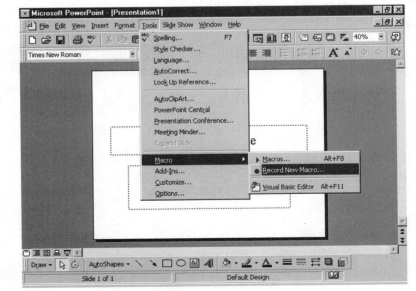

Access and PowerPoint can work hand-in-hand seamlessly by using code to access data between the two applications. This method is covered more thoroughly in the "VBA Automation and Understanding DAO" section of this chapter.

To Outlook from Access

Communication is important to a corporation. The information communicated throughout a corporation may include Human Resources policies, client relations information, and product/service information. Outlook is the tool that can make it easy for employees to communicate information. It can be used internally through local area networks (LANs) and intranets, or externally through the Internet.

Outlook is a sophisticated electronic messaging system that manages your appointments, contacts, tasks, and activities as well as shares information. E-mail messages that contain Uniform Resource Locators (URLs) work in conjunction with Hypertext Transfer Protocol (HTTP) to make hyperlinks active. (*Hyperlinks* are colored and underlined text or graphics that users can click to take them to a file, a location on the intranet, or a location on the World Wide Web.)

Outlook is one of the few products that does not include VBA 5.0. You may be wondering how it can be used in the Automation process of the Office products if it does not contain VBA. It works because it does support VBScript and a complete type library. That means that applications other than Outlook can program Outlook objects through VBA (provided that the other applications support VBA). Outlook can program other application objects through VBScript because VBScript is a subset of Visual Basic.

NOTE

A *type library* is a file or a part in a file that contains Automation standard descriptions of exposed objects, properties, and methods. Components in a type library are visible through the Object Browser.

You can use Outlook in conjunction with Access for the purpose of getting contact data from Access tables into the Contacts folder in Outlook. Outlook has an Import Wizard that can assist you through the importing process. To initiate the Import Wizard, select Import/Export from the File menu in Outlook. In Figures 28.35 and 28.36, you can see the crux of the Import Wizard.

TIP

You can import data from applications other than Access. The Import Wizard will accept data from dBASE, Lotus, Excel, FoxPro, Schedule+, as well as text files in the format of tab- and comma-seperated values.

Figure 28.35.
The Employees *table from the* Northwind *database is selected.*

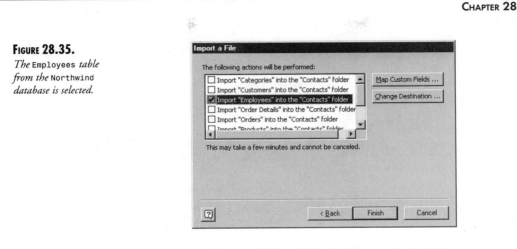

Figure 28.36.
The destination for the Employees *table from* Northwind *is the Contact folder in Outlook.*

Just because you select an import object and a destination, it does not assure that your data will actually be imported. You must map your fields from the source to the fields in the destination. In Figure 28.35, you can see the Map Custom Fields... button. Clicking this button takes you to the screen shown in Figure 28.37, where you click the fields in the table on the left and drag them to their corresponding fields on the right.

The time it takes to import the data from Access into Outlook is dependent on the number of records in the table. Once the import is complete, the data from the table is available in Outlook. This is shown in Figure 28.38.

NOTE

Only data in table objects is made available through the Import Wizard in Outlook. Queries are not made available in the wizard; however, if you need to get data from a query into Outlook through the wizard, you can change your query to a Make-table query and use the new table as the source for your import.

There are other ways to get data from Access into Outlook. For example, you can create a form in Access that allows you to enter data directly into Outlook. In Figure 28.39, you can see the form that will be used to enter in data. All the fields on the form are unbound text box objects.

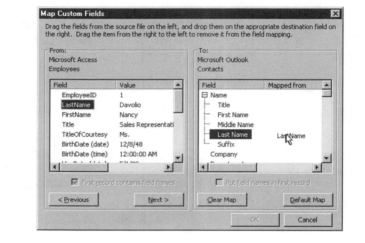

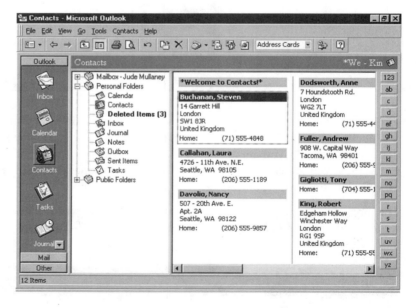

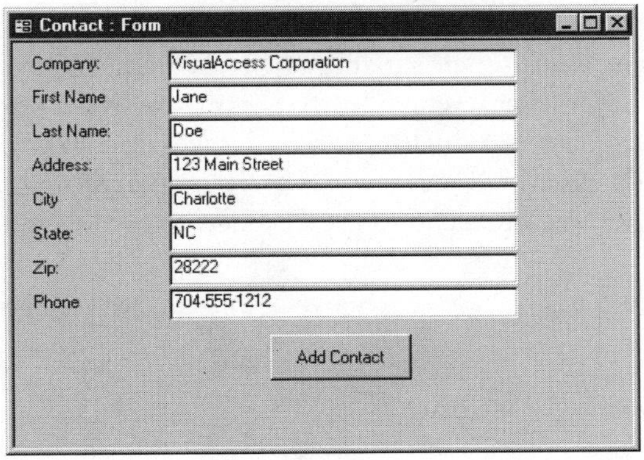

FIGURE 28.39.

A form in Access can get data into Outlook.

The real magic to integrating Access with Outlook is found on a button on the form. The following code was entered in the OnClick property of the button:

```
Private Sub Command1_Click()

    If OLApp Is Nothing Then
        StartOutlook
    End If


    Dim objFolder As MAPIFolder
    Dim NewContact As ContactItem

    Set objFolder = OLNameSpace.GetDefaultFolder(olFolderContacts)
    Set NewContact = objFolder.Items.Add

    With NewContact
        .CompanyName = Me!Company
        .FirstName = Me!FirstName
        .LastName = Me!LastName
        .BusinessAddress = Me!Address
        .BusinessAddressCity = Me!City
        .BusinessAddressState = Me!State
        .BusinessAddressPostalCode = Me!Zip
        .BusinessTelephoneNumber = Me!Phone
        .Save
    End With

End Sub
```

Notice that a piece of this code is bold. This part of this code refers to a function in a module that was created earlier. The function code for this module, called vaOutlook, is as follows:

```
Function StartOutlook() As Boolean

    Set OLApp = New Outlook.Application
    Set OLNameSpace = OLApp.GetNameSpace("MAPI")

End Function
```

28

OFFICE 97
INTEGRATION

The heart of the "magic" is found in the two Set statements in the code for the button on the form. The first is setting the variable objFolder to the Contacts folder in Outlook. The second is adding a new contact item. The With statement is new to Access 97. It allows you to set a series of statements on a single object. This saves time by reducing the number of keystrokes it would take to enter in NewContact for every property listed in the code. In Figure 28.40, you can see the new record added to the Contacts folder in Outlook.

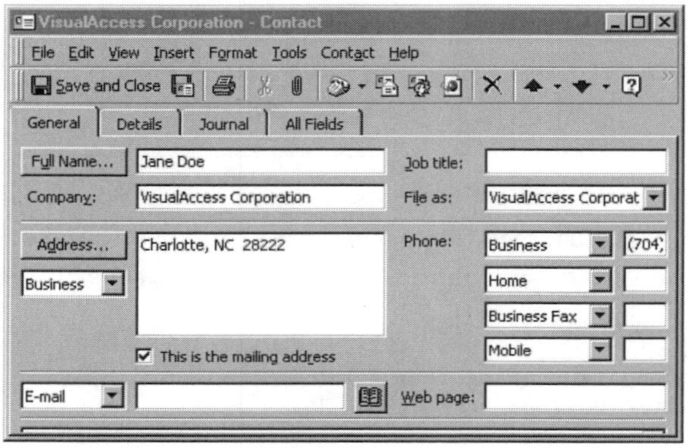

FIGURE 28.40.

Data entered in an Access form appears in the Contacts folder in Outlook.

There is an easier way to get data from Access to other employees in the company through Outlook, and that is through a macro action. In Figure 28.41, you can see the macro action called SendObject. This macro action enables you to send objects in the database to another colleague through the e-mail service (Outlook).

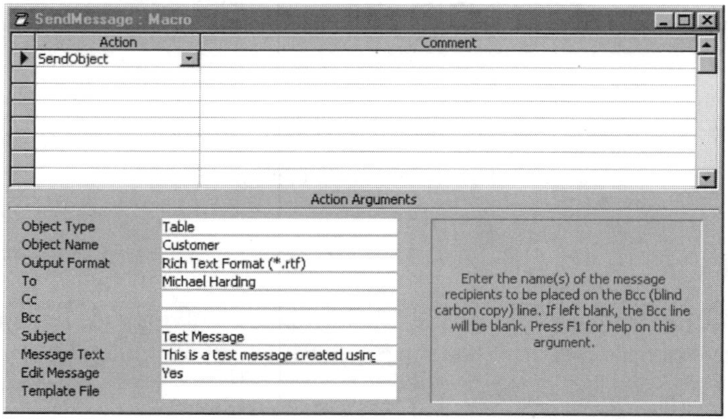

FIGURE 28.41.

A macro action can also help you utilize Outlook.

The Action Arguments section lets you specify what object is sent, what format it is sent in, and to whom it is sent. You can even specify a certain message to be sent each time the macro is executed. When the macro is run, a mail message appears with To, CC, Subject, and the Object being sent, and the message already in place. (See Figure 28.42.) This option can be helpful if you need to send sales figures or customer information to an employee who does not have access to the database.

Through Automation, you can create a form that looks similar to an Outlook e-mail message and use that form in your database to send information and objects from Access to Outlook. Figure 28.43 shows the form. It looks very similar to a regular e-mail message, but it is an Access form.

FIGURE 28.42.

A macro can send objects from Access to an employee through Outlook.

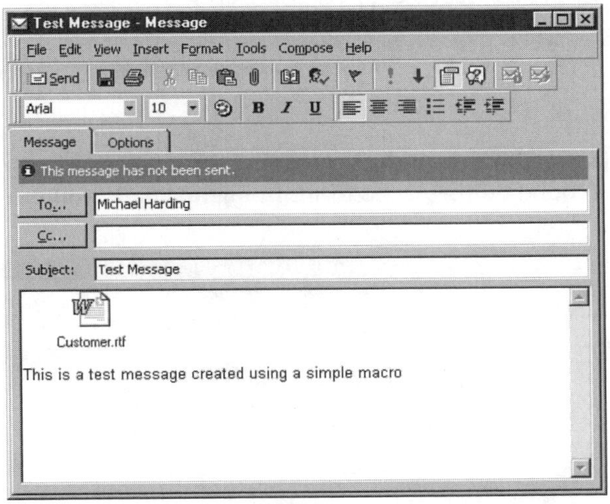

FIGURE 28.43.

You can create e-mail messages through Access forms.

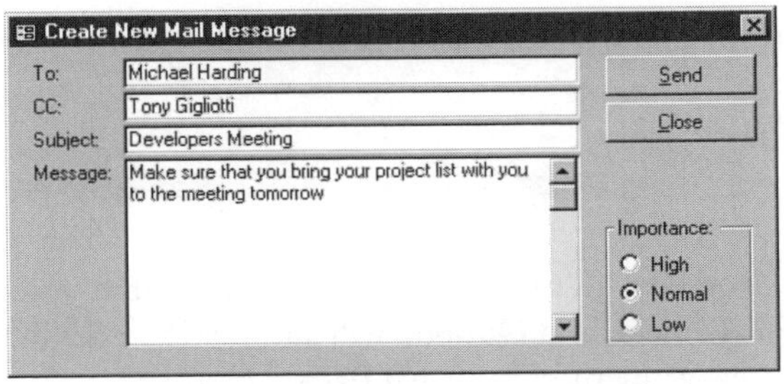

The code that makes this form work is found behind the Send button. It is as follows:

```
Private Sub cmdSend_Click()

    Dim OLApp As Outlook.Application, objNewMail As MailItem
    Set OLApp = New Outlook.Application
    Set objNewMail = OLApp.CreateItem(olMailItem)
    With objNewMail
        .Recipients.Add Me!To
        .Recipients.ResolveAll
        .CC = Me!CarbonCopy
        .Subject = Me!Subject
```

```
        .Body = Me!Message
        .Importance = Me!Importance
        .Display
    End With

End Sub
```

This piece of code works hand-in-hand with the following code, which initializes Outlook (this function is a global function):

```
Function InitializeOutlook() As Boolean

    Set gOLApp = New Outlook.Application
    Set gOLNameSpace = gOLApp.GetNamespace("MAPI")

End Function
```

When the Send button on the form is executed, the mail message is created, based on the information found on the Access form. In Figure 28.44, you can see that mail message.

If you have worked with Outlook for any length of time, you know that you can just type a few letters in the To field, and Outlook will automatically fill in the rest of the field for you. This is called a Resolve method in Visual Basic, and it tries to resolve a Recipient object. It works with the Address Book in Outlook to make sure that a recipient for an e-mail message is filled out before the message is sent. In the code for the Send button of the form, you can see the Resolve method:

```
.Recipients.ResolveAll
```

It follows the To part of the code to make sure that the recipient is available in the Address Book in Outlook. The only line really needed in an Outlook message is the To line; all the other lines can be blank, and the message will still be delivered to the recipient. If you checked the High Importance option on the delivery of the e-mail, it will be reflected in the Properties section of the Outlook mail message itself, as shown in Figure 28.45.

FIGURE 28.45.

Different options in the e-mail message can be controlled from Access.

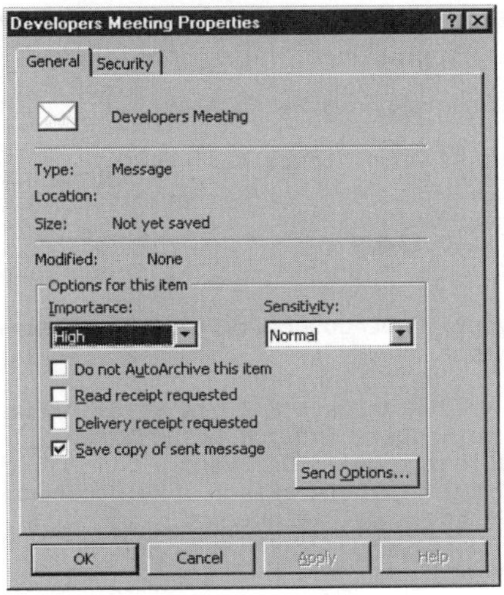

> **TIP**
>
> When you use the code to create an e-mail form in Access, be careful with the CC field. If your user does not always state a name in the CC field, the code will not work. You can either remark out the statement by placing an apostrophe in front of it, or you can write additional code to check for zero-length strings.

There are several different folders that you can work with when moving data from Access to Outlook. In Figure 28.46, you can see a form that is used to enter data into an Outlook Appointment folder.

FIGURE 28.46.

An Access form gets data into an Outlook Appointment folder.

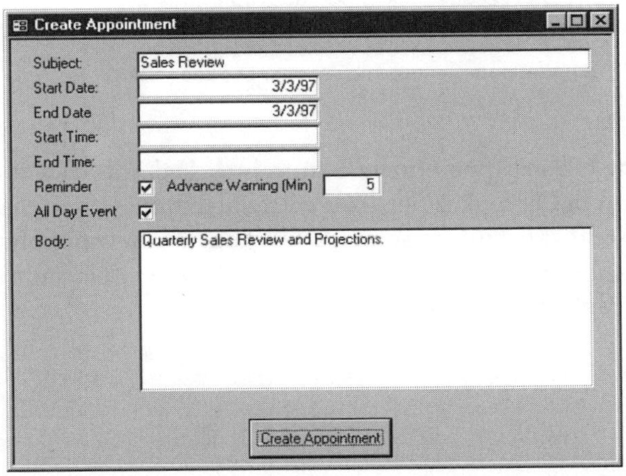

Like the other forms created in Access, this one also contains unbound text boxes. The code behind the Create Appointment button is as follows:

```
Private Sub cmdCreateAppointment_Click()

  Dim objNewAppt As AppointmentItem

    If gOLApp Is Nothing Then
        InitializeOutlook
    End If

    Set objNewAppt = gOLApp.CreateItem(olAppointmentItem)
    With objNewAppt
        .Subject = Me!Subject
        .Start = Me!StartDate & " " & Me!StartTime
        .End = Me!EndDate & " " & Me!EndTime
        .AllDayEvent = Me!AllDayEvent
        .ReminderMinutesBeforeStart = Me!ReminderBefore
        .ReminderSet = Me!ReminderSet
        .Body = Me!Body
        .Display
    End With

End Sub

Private Sub ReminderSet_Click()

    If Me!ReminderSet = True Then
        Me!ReminderBefore.Visible = True
    Else
        Me!ReminderBefore.Visible = False
    End If

End Sub
```

This code works with the code in a module object to move data from Access to Outlook.

The InitializeOutlook procedure initializes Outlook:

```
Function InitializeOutlook() As Boolean

    Set gOLApp = New Outlook.Application
    Set gOLNameSpace = gOLApp.GetNamespace("MAPI")

End Function
```

When the Create Appointment button is clicked, this code is executed and a New Appointment form in Outlook is filled out with the information in the Access form. In Figure 28.47, you can see that the information has filled out the New Appointment form in Outlook. When you click the Save and Close button on the Outlook form, the appointment is entered into your schedule.

FIGURE 28.47.

Data in Access is used in an Outlook appointment.

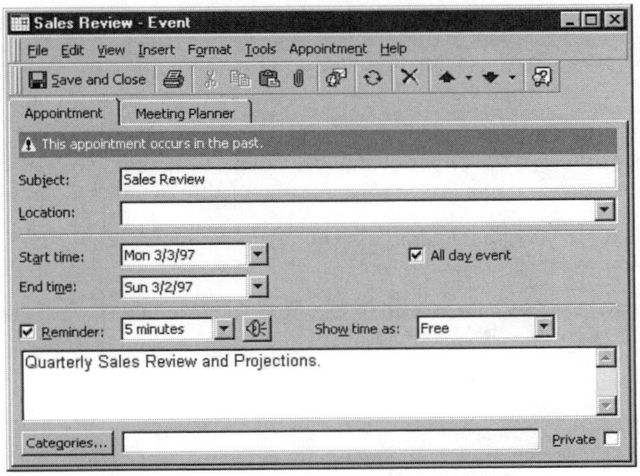

To Access from Outlook

It is just as easy to move data from Outlook to Access as it is to move it from Access to Outlook. You can move a listing of the Contacts in Outlook to a form in Access. In Figure 28.48, the form contains an unbound list box. When the List Items button is clicked, items found in different folders in Outlook are displayed in the unbound list box. In this case, all the items found in the Contacts folder in Outlook are displayed in an Access form.

FIGURE 28.48.

Access uses VBA to show items from Outlook.

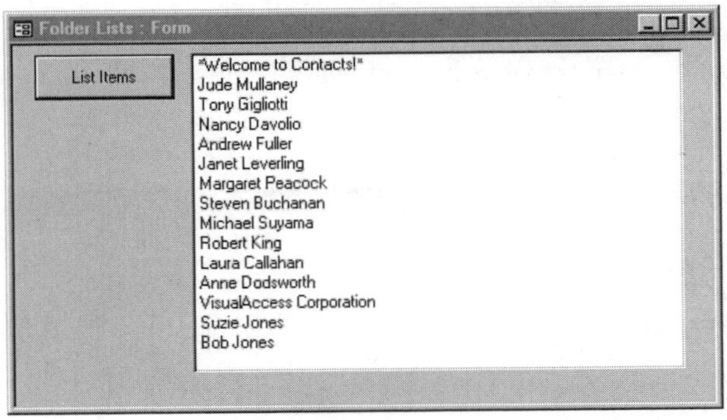

The VBA code used to make this happen can be found on the OnClick property of the List Items button. The following code makes the unbound list box display the items in the Contacts folder in Outlook:

```
Private Sub Command1_Click()
    Dim oleApp As Object
    Dim CurrentFolder As Object
    Dim Addr As String
```

```
    Dim NumItem As Integer
    Dim ReadItem As Integer
    Dim LoopNumber As Integer

    Me!ResultList.RowSourceType = "Value List"

    Set oleApp = GetObject("", "Outlook.Application").GetNameSpace("MAPI")
    Set CurrentFolder = oleApp.Folders("Personal Folders").Folders("Contacts")

    NumItem = CurrentFolder.Items.Count
    ReadItem = 1

    Me!ResultList.RowSource = CurrentFolder.Items(NumItem)
    Me!ResultList.Requery

    LoopNumber = 1

    Do Until LoopNumber > NumItem
        If LoopNumber = 1 Then
            Me!ResultList.RowSource = CurrentFolder.Items(ReadItem)
            Me!ResultList.Requery
        Else
            Me!ResultList.RowSource = Me!ResultList.RowSource & ";" & _
_CurrentFolder.Items(ReadItem)
            Me!ResultList.Requery
        End If
        LoopNumber = LoopNumber + 1
        ReadItem = LoopNumber
    Loop

End Sub
```

This code reads the items in the Contacts folder in Outlook. Notice that the word `Contacts` is bold. You can change this to another folder name in Outlook to retrieve another list set. In Figure 28.49, `Contacts` has been changed to `Tasks`. The item list returned is the same as the items that appear in the Tasks folder in Outlook.

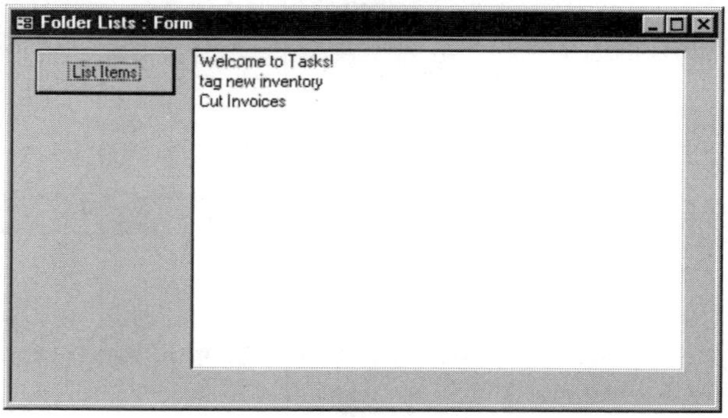

FIGURE 28.49.

When the folder changes to Tasks, the items in the Tasks folder are displayed.

Data from any of the folders in Outlook can be displayed in Access by changing the folder name in the VBA code. The name of the folder is shown in bold type in the previous code; you must type it in exactly as it appears here (as the code appears in Outlook). If you wanted to list all the items in the Sent Items folder in Access, you would remove the word Contacts from the code and put Sent Items in its place.

> **NOTE**
>
> When you request information from Outlook, it is not the same as creating a linked object. When new information is added to Outlook, you will need to requery the action used to bring the data into Access. This can be done by closing and reopening the object that triggered the data from Outlook to appear in Access or by writing a routine in VBA to include a Requery method.

Access and Outlook can work hand-in-hand seamlessly by using code to access data between the two applications. This method is covered more thoroughly in the next section of this chapter.

VBA Automation and Understanding DAO

So far, the discussion has dealt with moving data between Access and the other Office applications through the user interfaces. That is a quick-and-dirty way to move data, however. If you want more control over the process of automating Word, Excel, PowerPoint, and Outlook with Access, you will want to do it through code. One of the great new features of Office 97 is that the applications use Visual Basic for Applications (VBA) code. In previous versions, some of the applications used VBA; others, such as Word, used Word Basic. Now that almost all the applications adhere to the VBA standard, integrating all the applications is easier than ever.

> **NOTE**
>
> Outlook does not use VBA, but it does use VBScript, which is a subset of Visual Basic. Other applications can use VBA to manipulate Outlook, but Outlook uses VBScript to manipulate other applications.

There are two components to understand about Automation: Automation Server and Automation Controller. Automation Servers allow their functionality to be exposed through their object models; Automation Controllers control Automation Servers through programming code and can get access to the functionality of Automation Servers through the exposed object models. Word, Excel, Access, and PowerPoint are examples of Automation Servers because they "serve" the Automation Controllers through their exposed object models. Visual Basic and C++ are examples of Automation Controllers because they can "control" the Automation Servers through programming code.

To understand the Office Automation process thoroughly, you have to understand the concept of data access objects (DAO), objects, and collections. In this section, I will try to make some sense of the DAO hierarchy and how it pertains to the different applications in the Microsoft Office Professional Suite.

Each application in the Office 97 suite has its own DAO Object Model. Microsoft's DAO Object Model hierarchy for Access is shown in Figure 28.50. At first, it looks pretty confusing, but if you think of it as an outline tree it will make more sense. This hierarchy is made up of objects and collections. One or more items (members) make up a *collection*, and one or more collections make up an *object*.

FIGURE 28.50.

The Microsoft Access DAO Object Model.

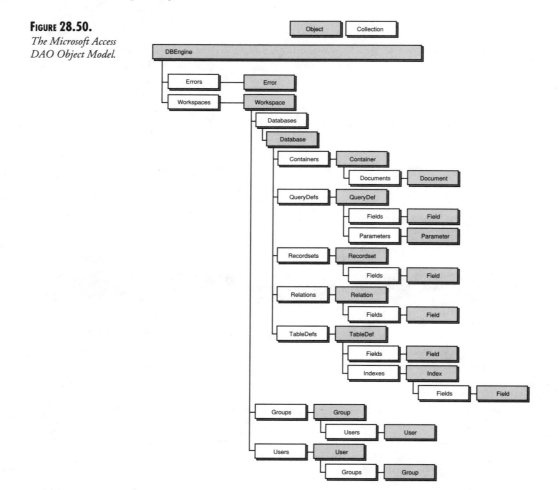

All applications share two qualities: they have content and functionality. The *content* of an application is its words, numbers and graphs, fonts, sizes, and colors. The *functionality* of an application is the way it works with the contents, such as opening, closing, and editing. All applications are compartmentalized into objects. These objects are then arranged into a hierarchy. The structure of this hierarchy is called the *Object Model*.

At the top of the Object Model, you will find the Application object. As you drill down to different levels of objects, each lower-level object is the child of the object above it, and each object that has object(s) beneath it becomes a parent object. Just like in the real world, children can have children. A person can be a child and a parent at the same time. Each object can be a child object and a parent object at the same time. Each object in the Object Model can have multiple objects that are related to it. An object with multiple relatives is called a *collection object*. The Microsoft Access, Excel, Word, and PowerPoint applications all have their own Object Models. Just as the application is devised of content and functionality, so is each object found in the Object Models.

There are many objects in an Access database. Some are content objects and store data, some display data, and some are forms and reports.

If you are used to working with Code Behind Forms (CBF) in Access, that level of object is not found near the top of Access's Object Model, but toward the bottom. The content and functionality of an object is manipulated through its properties and methods. You will find that as you become more proficient with VBA, most of the properties and methods have the same names as the properties and methods used in the user interface of the application.

There will come a time when you need assistance in determining how to reference an object. The Object Browser can help you navigate to the right object. In Figure 28.51, you can see the different objects that pertain to a Button class object. The properties, methods, and events associated with the Button class object are shown on the right side.

28

OFFICE 97 INTEGRATION

FIGURE 28.51.

The Object Browser can help you navigate to the correct object.

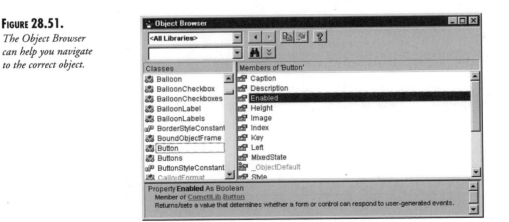

> **TIP**
>
> If the application type library is not available in the Object Browser, make sure that it is selected as an object that can be referenced. You do this through the References item in the Tools menu.

The lower section of the Object Browser is the Details section. This area shows you the correct syntax and a little more information about the highlighted object. You can copy the syntax or drag and drop the syntax to a module. This will help you with the required and optional arguments by keeping them in their correct order.

Once you have an understanding of the DAO hierarchy for an application, whether it be Word, Excel, Access, PowerPoint, or Outlook, you can automate tasks in Office. How, you ask? By referencing the object that contains the functionality and content that you need (Word, Excel, Access, PowerPoint, or Outlook) and then applying properties and methods to that object (sub procedures and functions). Table 28.3 specifies the different applications and their objects and classes. These objects and classes all point to instances of the application; for example, `Access.Application` points to an instance of Microsoft Access.

Table 28.3. Overview of Office objects and classes.

Application	Object	Class
Access 8.0	Application	Access.Application
Word 8.0	Application	Word.Application
	Document	Word.Document
Excel 8.0	Application	Excel.Application
	Chart	Excel.Chart
	Worksheet	Excel.Worksheet
Graph 8.0	Application	Graph.Application
	Chart	Graph.Chart
Outlook	Application	Outlook.Application*
Project 4.1	Application	MSProject.Project

*Outlook does not use VBA but uses VBScript—a stripped-down version of Visual Basic.

The first step in automating a task in Office is to return a reference to the desired object. The next step is to apply properties and methods to that object. To integrate it with other `Application` objects, you need to make sure that you can reference them. From a module window, select References from the Tools menu to bring up the dialog box shown in Figure 28.52.

The object libraries or database items that have checks will be available. You can also set the priority of the object libraries or databases to determine which references are resolved first.

FIGURE 28.52.

The Application *objects that are allowed to be referenced are listed here.*

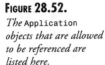

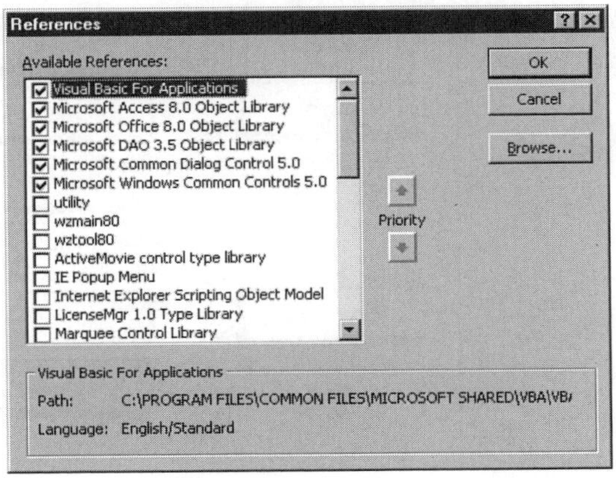

The Access 97 object library itself has its own hierarchy. It looks similar to the Access Data Objects hierarchy, but it is different. The library is what is referenced by other applications in the Microsoft Office suite and other applications that support Automation. Figure 28.53 gives a pictorial view of the Microsoft Access Object Library hierarchy.

How does this apply to Access? Access is made up of objects and collections (which are objects of the same type that are grouped together). Earlier in this chapter, you saw the References list that shows all the Object Libraries that are referenced in Access. When an Object Library is referenced, the objects and collections for the library are available for you to reference. You can manipulate these objects to respond to the end user's actions. The objects that come with Access 97 are listed and described on the following pages in their hierarchical order.

The Application Object

The Application object references the Access application itself. Because it is at the top of the Access object hierarchy, it contains objects and collections. Because it is the top of the Access structure, it is a default object, which means that you do not have to explicitly reference it when you are working with methods, properties, and other objects in Access. It does have to be referenced when you are working with other Microsoft Office applications for the purpose of Automation.

When you are working in other Office applications and need to automate Access, there are four simple steps that you have to keep in mind. First, to work with Access from Excel, Word, or PowerPoint, you have to reference Access from within Excel, Word, or PowerPoint. Remember that every application in Office has its own object hierarchy. When you reference an Application object, each Office object has its own Application object. You saw this in Table 28.3.

FIGURE 28.53.
*The Microsoft Access
Object Library
hierarchy.*

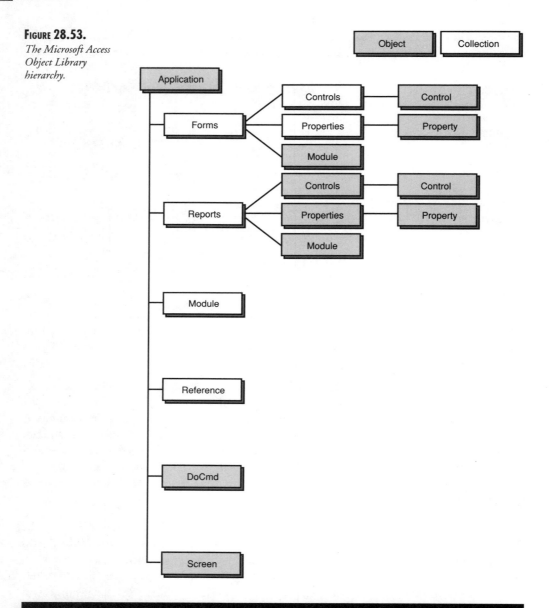

Make sure that the Access 97 (Access 8.0) reference is set up by opening up a module in
Design View and selecting References from the Tools menu.

The second step is to represent the Access Application object by declaring an object variable. This variable will represent the Access Application object, just as if you wanted to represent another Office program, like Excel or Word, you would use a variable to represent the Excel Application object or the Word Application object. The variable can be any word that you would like it to be. You could even use a word like OpenForm to reference an Application object, but that might be confusing to other programmers who may be working with your applications. It is better programming to use a variable that describes the Application object that is being represented. The following statement shows that the reference to the Access Application object is AccessApp:

```
Dim AccessApp as Access.Application
```

> **TIP**
>
> It is considered poor programming to use a vague variable to name a variable because it may get confusing to other programmers who need to work with your code. Make sure that you keep the variable you use to reference objects simple and relative to the object, collection, or action you are working with.

The third step is to return a reference to the Application object. The two most common ways to return a reference are through the GetObject and CreateObject functions. If Access is already running, you will need to use the GetObject function. If it is not running, you will want to use the CreateObject function.

The third step of returning a reference works hand-in-hand with the fourth and final step, which is to assign the reference to the object variable. One of the most common ways to assign the reference is through the Set statement. The following is the code that allows Access to be automated from other Office applications:

```
Dim AccessApp as Access.Application

Set AccessApp = GetObject("Access.Application.8")
```

You can view all the members of the Application object through the Object Viewer. In Figure 28.54, you can see the Application object on the left side of the browser; all the members of the Application object are visible on the right side for the Northwind database.

Once the gate to the Access Application object is opened, you can use any of the objects that fall under the Access Object Model hierarchy. This means that you can run Access forms and reports from other applications, such as Word and Excel.

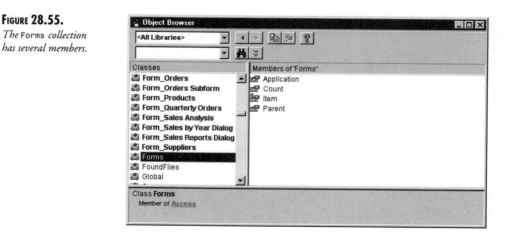

The Forms Object/Collection

The Access Object Library has its own object hierarchy that is made up of objects and collections. The top level of this hierarchy is the Application object. The second level contains several objects, and these objects are the child objects of the parent object: the Application object. Because there is a third level of objects, the objects on the second level are also parent objects; each second-level object has child objects under it. The Forms object is not just an object but a collection. There are multiple Form objects that make up the Form Object/Collection. To refer to a Form object, you have to go through the Forms collection. The Forms collection for the Northwind database is shown in Figure 28.55. The members of the Forms collection are visible on the right side of the browser.

The Form Object

The reason you are using Automation from one Office application to another is to access objects. If you are in Word or Excel, you may need to use a Form object in Access. To get to a Form object in Access, you have to drill down through the Forms collection in the Access Object Library hierarchy. To use an Access form from another application, that form must be opened. The view does not matter; it can be in Design View, Form View, or Datasheet View. In Figure 28.56, you can see the object browser with the Form object highlighted on the left. The items in the right window of the browser are all members of the Form object.

FIGURE 28.56.

The Form object has methods, events, and properties shown on the right.

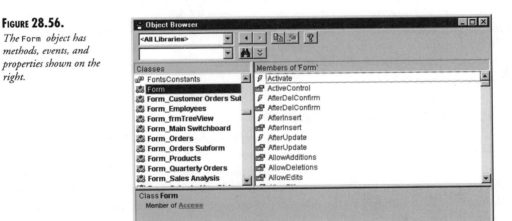

28

OFFICE 97
INTEGRATION

Each Form object has its own set of properties that can be manipulated from applications outside Access. Not only can you run forms from other Office applications, but you can change them. Because there are multiple properties for a Form object, Properties becomes a collection. The individual properties are like objects within the Properties collection. An individual property, such as the form's BackColor property, is the child of the Properties collection. The RecordSource property can be or is already set to a table, query, or SQL statement. You can see and change the data from the table, query, or SQL statement that the Access form is based on from an application other than Access.

> **NOTE**
>
> The collections and objects are listed on the left side of the Object Browser. The right side of the browser contains all the associated objects, methods, properties, and events of the highlighted object or collection.

Controls

Controls can be found in the third level of the Access Object Library hierarchy. It is a collection as well as an object. The objects that it contains are called Control objects. Control objects are considered to be a fourth-level object in the hierarchy.

Modules in Forms

The Module property references a module object that is associated with a form. In older versions of Access, every time a form was created, it automatically had a module associated with it even if there was no code within that module. In Access 97, Microsoft increased the speed and reduced the size of forms by setting making sure that when a form is created, it does not have a module associated with it. The only time that a module is associated with a form is when you create it. Form modules are found on event procedures of that form and are usually form specific.

The Reports Object/Collection

A Report object represents a single, open report. The Reports collection represents all the open Access reports. The Reports object of the Access Object Library is also a collection because it contains multiple Report objects. To refer to an individual Report object, you have to go through the Reports collection. You can view the objects in the Reports collection through the Object Browser. In Figure 28.57, all the members of the Reports collection are visible on the right side of the browser.

FIGURE 28.57.
The Reports collection has several members.

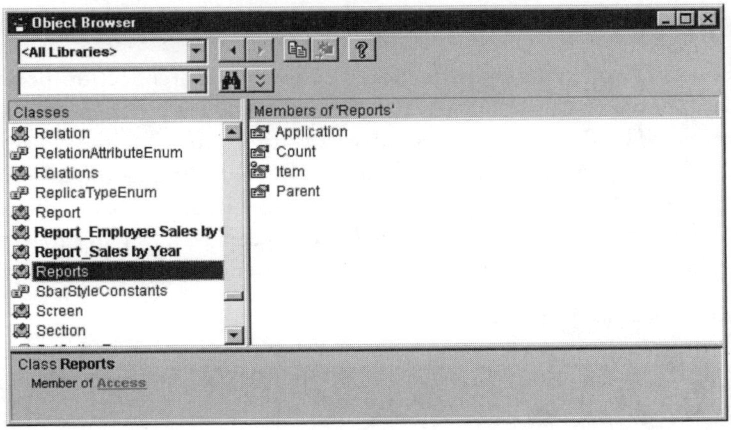

The Report Object

To work with an individual `Report` object, you have to drill down through the `Reports` collection. If you need to reference a `Report` object in Access, it must be open. It does not matter whether the report is open in design view or print preview, but it must be open. It can be opened through the `OpenReport` method of the `DoCmd` object. (The `DoCmd` object is discussed in greater detail later in this chapter.) In Figure 28.58, you can see all the events, properties, and methods of the `Report` object through the Object Browser.

FIGURE 28.58.
The events, properties, and methods of the `Report` *object are visible through the Object Browser.*

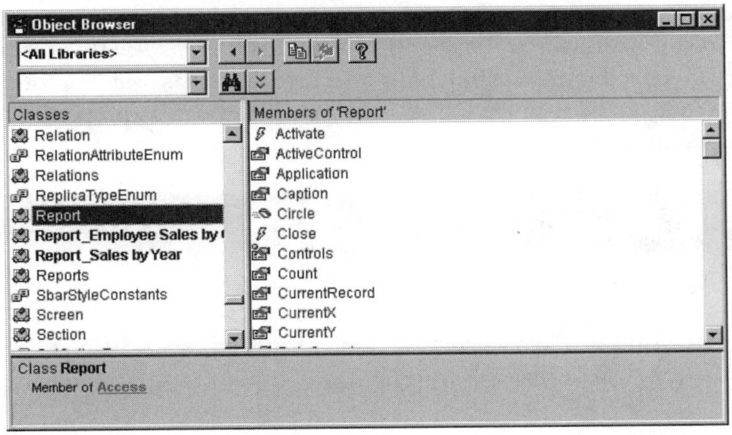

Controls

Like other collections, the `Controls` collection is a collection because it contain multiple `Control` objects. `Control` collections are also contained by `Forms` objects. There are two types of controls. The first group is called Access controls; these are the controls found in the toolbox. The second group of controls is called ActiveX controls; these are custom controls or (in the older versions) OLE controls. The `Control` objects in a `Controls` collection contain properties and hyperlinks. When you need to refer to a specific control on a form or report, you will utilize the bang (!) operator. The following code references the checkbox on the `Product List` form:

```
Forms![Product List]!Discontinued
```

> **NOTE**
>
> There are a few controls in the `Control` object that have control collections of their own; the tab control and the option group control, for example. As long as there is at least one object associated with a control, that control is also a collection.

Modules in Reports

The `Module` property references a `Module` object that is associated with a report. Access 97 increased the speed and reduced the size of reports by making sure that when a report was created, it did not have a module associated with it. The only time that a module is associated with a report is when you create it. Report modules are found on event procedures of that report and are usually report specific. Notice that the `Has Module` property of a report defaults to `No`. If you enter in code for events on a report, the `Has Module` property changes to `Yes`. After the code has been entered, if you change the `Has Module` property back to `No`, all the code for the events will no longer be available.

> **TIP**
>
> If you set the `HasModule` property for a form or report back to `No`, that means there was some code on an object in the form or report. Any code will be deleted, but macros that are associated with the form or report will not be affected. Code from separate modules will also not be affected.

Module Objects

Three boxes in the Access Object Library hierarchy refer to modules. The first is an object contained in the `Application` object. The second and third are contained by the `Forms` and

`Reports` collections, respectively. A single, open module object is called a `Module` object. All the open `Module` objects can be found in the `Modules` collection. A set of all the modules in an Access database (opened or not) is called a Visual Basic project, and each database can have its own project.

You cannot really discuss modules without covering Standard and Class modules. In this section, I will try to cover the distinctions between the two. There are two types of modules in Access: Standard and Class. Code that is to be used throughout the application is usually of the Standard type. A Standard module is a public module that can be called from a procedure within the current database or referenced from another database. Conversely, Class modules are private and usually pertain to a form or report. They cannot be called by other procedures or referenced by other Access applications. Both are found in the Visual Basic project of a database. Class modules really only have two events associated with them: `initialize` and `terminate`. They occur when you create and delete a custom object in memory.

Reference

A `Reference` object makes a reference from Access to another project or to another object library. There are `Reference` objects as well as `Reference` collections, and each `Reference` object matches a reference set in the References dialog box through the Tools menu or an object library (`.olb` file).

> **NOTE**
>
> A project is a collection of all the modules in an Access application—whether they are opened or not.

A `Reference` object has properties; a `References` collection has methods and events as well as properties. With `Reference` objects, you can add, remove, or check on existing references through VBA. There are three syntax forms you can use when referencing a `Reference` object:

```
References!reference name
References: ("referencename")
References: (index)
```

> **NOTE**
>
> When using the `index` argument in a reference, the index is the `Reference` object's numerical position inside the `References` collection.

DoCmd

The DoCmd object allows you to use methods to run macro actions from Visual Basic. This object allows you to run macros that perform actions that are not supported from other objects. You can open and close just about any table, query, form, report, macro, or module through the DoCmd object. In Figure 28.59, you can see the list of the members of the DoCmd object in the right side of the Object Browser. There are over 40 different members; their correct syntax is shown in the Details section at the bottom of the Object Browser when the desired object is highlighted.

FIGURE 28.59.

The DoCmd *object and its members can be seen in the Object Browser.*

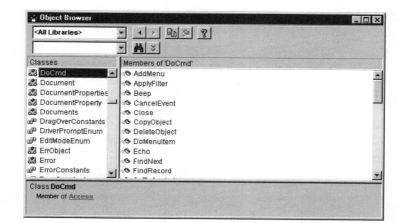

Screen

The Screen object lets you reference a control, form, or report that has the current focus. This can let you reference a form or report without knowing the name of the form or report. This is similar to the ActiveForm property and the Me property, but ActiveForm returns a reference to the form that is active on the screen, and Me returns a reference to the code that is currently being run. A form can be active, but other code can be in the process of running. To make sure you get the object that has focus, you will want to use the Screen object.

> **TIP**
>
> If you use the Screen object to reference an active form or report, and the object that has focus is a module window, the Screen object will return an error. This can be handled by using the SetFocus method, the SetObject method, or the DoCmd object.

When you are working with other Office applications, you can maneuver through their objects both through code and by using their Object Model hierarchies. Each Office product has its own Object Model hierarchy.

Summary

Through Automation, there are several ways that data can move to and from Access to the other Office products. This chapter covered the most common ways, such as cut and paste, cut and paste special, drag and drop, import/export, link and embed, Save As Text or RTF, using the Office Links button in Access, and instituting macro actions. More advanced methods of moving data between the Office products include using code. When you use code, you must be familiar with the object hierarchy. Each product in the Office line has an Object Model hierarchy; this chapter depicts each of the hierarchies and describes the difference between objects and collections.

28

OFFICE 97 INTEGRATION

I
INDEX

MACMILLAN COMPUTER PUBLISHING USA

A VIACOM COMPANY

Technical ----┐
               └---- ## Support:

If you need assistance with the information in this book or with a CD/Disk accompanying the book, please access the Knowledge Base on our Web site at **http://www.superlibrary.com/general/support**. Our most Frequently Asked Questions are answered there. If you do not find the answer to your questions on our Web site, you may contact Macmillan Technical Support **(317) 581-3833** or e-mail us at **support@mcp.com**.

Alison Balter's Mastering Access 97 Development, Second Premier Edition

Alison Balter

One of the premier corporate database applications, Access is a powerful application that can be programmed and customized. This book shows users how to develop simple and complex applications for Access 97. This title also demonstrates how to create tables, forms, queries, reports, and objects, and teaches readers how to program Access applications for a client/server environment. The CD-ROM includes source code, reusable functions, forms, and reports.

$49.99 USA $70.95 CDN

1,100 pp.

0-672-30999-8

Accomplished—Expert

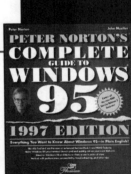

Access 97 Unleashed, Second Edition

Dwayne Gifford, et al.

Access has become one of the most accepted standards of database management for personal computers. The *Unleashed* format of this book allows current and new users to quickly and easily find information on the new features of Access 97. The book also serves as a complete reference for database programmers who are new to Access. Readers will learn advanced techniques for working with tables, queries, forms, and data, and they are shown how to program Access and how to integrate the database with the Internet. The CD-ROM includes Access utilities and applications and an electronic Access reference library.

$49.99 USA $70.95 CDN

1,100 pp.

0-672-30983-1

Accomplished—Expert

Peter Norton's Complete Guide to Windows 95, Second Premier Edition

Peter Norton & John Mueller

Following the success of the best-selling *Peter Norton Premier* series, this complete reference provides users with in-depth, detailed insights into this powerful operating system. Users will master all the tricks of the trade as well as learn how to create a Web page. This title covers the new Internet Explorer interface, DSD, OEM Service Pack 2.1 enhancements, and provides advanced tips, optimization techniques, and detailed architectural information. There is also extensive coverage of the Microsoft Plus! Pack. The Peter's Principles and quick reference sections, along with the tear-out survival guide, make learning easy.

$35.00 USA $49.95 CDN

1,224 pp.

0-672-31040-6

Accomplished—Expert

Teach Yourself Active Web Database Programming with Visual Basic in 21 Days

Dina Fleet, et al.

Based on the best-selling *Teach Yourself* series, this must-have tutorial uses a day-by-day approach and real-world examples to teach readers the ins and outs of Visual Basic programming with databases for the Web. Readers will explore data-aware controls, database connectivity with Visual Basic, and HTML scripting, and also learn how to use Visual Basic to create powerful content on the Web.

$39.99 USA $56.95 CAN

700 pp.

1-57521-139-4

New—Casual

Teach Yourself Database Programming with Visual Basic 5 in 21 Days, Second Edition

Michael Amundsen & Curtis Smith

Visual Basic is used by programmers to create Windows and Windows 95 applications. It can also be used to program applications for the Web. This book shows programmers how to design, develop, and deploy Visual Basic applications for the World Wide Web. The material, which was written by a Microsoft Certified Visual Basic Professional, is presented in a daily format with each week focusing on a different area of database development. The CD-ROM includes sample code and third-party utilities.

$45.00 USA $63.95 CAN
1,000 pp

0-672-31018-X
New—Casual—Accomplished

Teach Yourself Database Programming with JDBC in 21 Days

Ashton Hobbs

Linking both corporate and home databases to the Web is critical for a Web site to be successful, and Sun's JDBC API allows users to do just that! Using a step-by-step, conversational approach, users will learn how to develop JDBC components to create complete database applications for Web connection. This title explores database basics, JDBC interfaces, database connectivity and transactions, and more! The CD-ROM is packed with all the source code from the book, two complete real-world database examples, and a Web page linking to several useful JDBC resources.

$39.99 USA $56.95 CDN
600 pp.

1-57521-123-8
New—Casual—Accomplished

Teach Yourself Database Programming with Visual J++ in 21 Days

John Fronckowiak and Gordon McMillan, et al.

Using a step-by-step, easy-to-follow format, this complete resource takes users beyond the basic product information and guides them through database integration and interface development. This title highlights new technologies, including JavaBeans, JDBC, DAO Object Library, RDO Object Library, ActiveX, and COM. The CD-ROM is loaded with scripting and author source code.

$39.99 USA $56.95 CAN
750 pp.

1-57521-262-5
New—Casual—Accomplished

World Wide Web Database Developer's Guide with Visual Basic 5

Mark Swank, Drew Kittel, & Mark Spenik

Written by developers for developers, this advanced guide shows users how to use the latest version of Microsoft Visual Basic to design, develop, and deploy secure client/server databases on Internet and intranet Web sites. This book includes real-world examples and applications throughout the book for users to implement on their sites. The CD-ROM is loaded with the author's source code and a collection of Web and database tools.

$59.99 USA $84.95 CAN
900 pp.

1-57521-276-5
Accomplished—Expert

Add to Your Sams Library Today with the Best Books for Programming, Operating Systems, and New Technologies

The easiest way to order is to pick up the phone and call

1-800-428-5331

between 9:00 a.m. and 5:00 p.m. EST.
For faster service please have your credit card available.

ISBN	Quantity	Description of Item	Unit Cost	Total Cost
0-672-30999-8		Alison Balter's Mastering Access 97 Development, Second Premier Edition (Book/CD-ROM)	$49.99	
0-672-30983-1		Access 97 Unleashed, Second Edition (Book/CD-ROM)	$49.99	
0-672-31040-6		Peter Norton's Complete Guide to Windows 95, Second Premier Edition	$35.00	
1-57521-139-4		Teach Yourself Active Web Database Programming with Visual Basic in 21 Days (Book/CD-ROM)	$39.99	
0-672-31018-X		Teach Yourself Database Programming with Visual Basic 5 in 21 Days, Second Edition (Book/CD-ROM)	$45.00	
1-57521-123-8		Teach Yourself Database Programming with JDBC in 21 Days (Book/CD-ROM)	$39.99	
1-57521-262-5		Teach Yourself Database Programming with Visual J++ in 21 Days (Book/CD-ROM)	$39.99	
1-57521-276-5		World Wide Web Database Developer's Guide with Visual Basic 5 (Book/CD-ROM)	$59.99	
		Shipping and Handling: See information below.		
		TOTAL		

Shipping and Handling: $4.00 for the first book, and $1.75 for each additional book. If you need to have it NOW, we can ship product to you in 24 hours for an additional charge of approximately $18.00, and you will receive your item overnight or in two days. Overseas shipping and handling adds $2.00 per book. Prices subject to change. Call for availability and pricing information on latest editions.

201 W. 103rd Street, Indianapolis, Indiana 46290

1-800-428-5331 — Orders   1-800-835-3202 — FAX   1-800-858-7674 — Customer Service

Book ISBN 0-672-31049-X

What's on the CD-ROM

The companion CD-ROM contains all of the author source code, samples from the book, and many third-party software products.

Windows NT Installation Instructions

1. Insert the CD-ROM into your CD-ROM drive.

2. From File Manager or Program Manager, choose Run from the File menu.

3. Type `<drive>\SETUP.EXE` and press Enter, where `<drive>` corresponds to the drive letter of your CD-ROM drive. For example, if your CD-ROM drive is D:, type `D:\SETUP.EXE` and press Enter.

4. Installation creates a program group named "Access 97 Prog Unleashed." The icons in this group will be used to browse the CD-ROM.

Windows 95 Installation Instructions

1. Insert the CD-ROM into your CD-ROM drive.
2. From the Windows 95 Desktop, double-click on the My Computer icon.
3. Double-click on the icon representing your CD-ROM drive.
4. To run the installation program, double-click on the icon titled SETUP.EXE.
5. Installation creates a program group named "Access 97 Prog Unleashed." The icons in this group will be used to browse the CD-ROM.

NOTE

If Windows 95 is installed on your computer and the AutoPlay feature is enabled, the SETUP.EXE program starts automatically whenever you insert the disc into your CD-ROM drive.